118074

INTRODUCTION TO
THE NEW TESTAMENT

INTRODUCTION TO
THE NEW TESTAMENT

Raymond F. Collins

DOUBLEDAY & COMPANY, INC.
Garden City, New York
1983

Nihil Obstat: Reverend Msgr. Emil A. Wcela, S.S.L.
                   Censor Librorum
                   February 4, 1983

Imprimatur: ✠Most Rev. John R. McGann, D.D.
                   Bishop of Rockville Centre
                   February 8, 1983

The Nihil Obstat and Imprimatur are official declarations that this material
is free of doctrinal or moral error. They do not imply any endorsement of
the opinions and statements contained in the work.

Library of Congress Cataloging in Publication Data
Collins, Raymond F., 1935–
  Introduction to the New Testament.
  Includes bibliographies and indexes.
  1. Bible. N.T.—Hermeneutics. I. Title.
BS2331.C64   1983   225.6'01
ISBN: 0-385-18126-4
Library of Congress Catalog Card Number: 82–45070

CONTENTS

v

CONTENTS

vi

CONTENTS

LIST OF ABBREVIATIONS

Adv Haer	*Adversus Haereses*
Adv Marc	*Adversus Marcionem*
Apoc Abr	Apocalypse of Abraham
Apoc Mos	Apocalypse of Moses
Apoc Pet	Apocalypse of Peter
Apol	*Apologia*
AV	The Authorized Version
BT	Babylonian Talmud
CDC	Cairo Damascus Covenant
1 Clem	1 Clement
Dial	*Dialogue with the Jew Tryphon*
Did	*Didache*
DS	*Enchiridion Symbolorum,* a collection of official Roman Catholic Church statements edited by H. Denziger and C. Bannwart, revised by A. Schönmetzer. 32nd ed., Freiburg: Herder, 1963.
En	1 Enoch
Ep	Epistula
Ep Barn	Epistle of Barnabas
Ep Phil	Epistle to the Philippians
Esd	Esdras
ET	English Translation
FRLANT	*Forschungen zur Religion und Literatur des Alten und Neuen Testaments*
G Pet	The Gospel of Peter
G Thom	The Gospel of Thomas
JB	The Jerusalem Bible
Jub	Jubilees
KEK	*Kritisch-exegetischer Kommentar*
N^{26}	*Novum Testament Graece,* ed. by Kurt Aland et al. 26th ed., Stuttgart: Deutsche Bibelstiftung, 1979.
NAB	New American Bible
NEB	New English Bible

NT	New Testament
NTA	*New Testament Abstracts*
OT	Old Testament
OTA	*Old Testament Abstracts*
par.	Parallel
Par.	Paragraph
PBC	Pontifical Biblical Commission
PBI	Pontifical Biblical Institute
PG	*Patrologia Graeca* [*Patrologiae cursus completus. Series Graeca*], edited by Jacques-Paul Migne. 161 vols. Paris: Migne, 1857–66.
PL	*Patrologia Latina* [*Patrologiae cursus completus. Series Latina*], edited by Jacques-Paul Migne. 221 vols. Paris: Migne, 1844–64.
Q	*Quelle,* the German word for "source," specifically used in reference to the hypothetical Sayings Source used by Matthew and Luke.
1QpHab	Pesher on Habakkuk from Qumran Cave 1.
1QS	Manual of Disciple [Serek] from Qumran Cave 1.
4QFl	Florilegium of Eschatological Midrashim from Qumran Cave 4.
RSV	Revised Standard Version
RV	The Revised Version
San	The tractate Sanhedrin
SB	*Kommentar zum Neuen Testament aus Talmud und Midrasch,* edited by H. L. Strack and Paul Billerbeck. 6 vols. Munich: Beck, 1922–61.
SBL	The Society of Biblical Literature
ST	*Summa Theologica*
T Job	Testament of Job

ABBREVIATIONS OF THE NAMES OF BIBLICAL BOOKS (WITH THE APOCRYPHA)

(These abbreviations are consistent with the standards set by the Society of Biblical Literature.)

Gen	Nah	Add Esth	Acts
Exod	Hab	Bar	Rom
Lev	Zeph	Bel	1,2 Cor
Num	Hag	1,2 Esdr	Gal
Deut	Zech	4 Ezra	Eph
Josh	Mal	Jdt	Phil
Judg	Ps (*pl.:* Pss)	Ep Jer	Col
1,2 Sam	Job	1,2,3,4 Mac	1,2 Thes
1,2 Kgs	Prov	Pr Azar	1,2 Tim
Isa	Ruth	Pr Man	Tit
Jer	Cant	Sir	Phlm
Ezek	Eccl (*or* Qoh)	Sus	Heb
Hos	Lam	Tob	Jas
Joel	Esth	Wis	1,2 Pet
Amos	Dan	Matt	1,2,3 John
Obad	Ezra	Mark	Jude
Jonah	Neh	Luke	Rev
Mic	1,2 Chr	John	

INTRODUCTION

Why a Catholic Introduction?

Fr. Collins' *Introduction to the New Testament* is one of the most important contributions to American Catholic biblical studies in the last few decades. I make this statement with full awareness that various scholars will take issue with it on a number of grounds.

First of all, some will object that their shelves are already amply supplied with Catholic introductions to the New Testament. To take the grand example, there is Alfred Wikenhauser's *New Testament Introduction,* first translated from the German in 1956 and updated in recent years. Many other works could be mentioned as well; but even as the titles come to mind, one reason for the Collins volume becomes apparent. These works largely represent Catholic scholarship of the forties, fifties, and early sixties. This is not said to denigrate in any way the brave, pioneering work of revered Catholic exegetes. If Catholic biblicists today are able to pursue their studies in complete freedom and integrity, it is due largely to the sometimes unknown, often persecuted scholars who preceded them. Scholarship, however, stands still in no field, least of all in biblical studies. What was new or even shocking to Catholics in the fifties is now taken for granted or, in some cases, rightly discarded in the face of further investigation and a sharpening of the critical sense.

In particular, it must be admitted that the Catholic biblical scholars of the fifties still worked under the cloud of possible reprisals. Let us not forget that such threats became realities for a short period toward the end of the reign of Pope Pius XII (died 1958) and during the tenure of Pope John XXIII (1958–63). For all his many fine qualities, John XXIII was not overly fond of critical biblical research. It was only the accession of Pope Paul VI (1963) and the acceptance of the revised schema of the Dogmatic Constitution on Divine Revelation (1965) which truly set Catholic biblicists free. Considering the insecure position of the pioneers, we need not be surprised that the Catholic introductions of the fifties now strike us as apologetic or even polemical in tone. There is a great desire to defend traditional attributions of authorship, and a somewhat uncritical appeal to the opinions of the early Fathers of the Church. Granted, some of these tomes from the fifties have since been revised. Still, perhaps what Catholic biblical scholarship needs is the fresh start Fr. Collins offers in this present volume. The Fathers of the Church are by no means dismissed by him. But their testimony is sifted critically, as is the biblical witness. It makes no sense to allow historical criticism its place in Scripture studies, only to demand naïve acceptance when one moves into the realm of patristics.

Another value of this new introduction is that it is written by an American for Americans. Up until now, most of our Catholic introductions have been translated from German or French. For the first time, one American Catholic scholar, comfortable with critical methods, has produced a sizable volume ranging over the whole spectrum of the New Testament canon. Thanks to his years at Louvain, Fr. Collins is quite conversant with Continental scholarship. Yet, at the same time, he is consciously speaking as an American scholar to an American audience. In a sense, then, this volume joins the company of the *Jerome Biblical Commentary* and a number of other post-Vatican II works that have sealed and certified the coming of age of American Catholic biblical scholarship.

My harping on American *Catholic* scholarship will probably give rise to a second objection. Isn't the very concept of a Catholic introduction to the New Testament outdated and unecumenical? With such fine works as Werner G. Kümmel's revised *Introduction to the New Testament* at hand, who needs a new Catholic introduction? Haven't we outgrown the ghetto period of Catholic scholarship when Catholics had to have their own biblical encyclopedias, dictionaries, introductions, and even Greek texts of the New Testament?

A couple of observations are in order. First, no one denies the superb quality of Kümmel's introduction. It is a standard work used by Protestants and Catholics alike. But a quick glance will show that Collins has conceived his introduction along different lines. He does not devote separate chapters to each book of the New Testament. Rather, he takes a "methodological approach." His work moves through a step-by-step explanation of the main methods of contemporary biblical research and then applies these methods to the various books of the New Testament. As a result, Collins' volume is not simply a reference work but also a "workbook," where the reader is invited to work through a number of examples to appreciate the particular method described. This "work-along-with-me" approach distinguishes Collins' offering from the Introductions of Kümmel, Perrin, Kee-Young-Froehlich, and others. It also prevents the present volume from becoming simply a biblical telephone directory, with chapter and verse instead of area code and exchange. Collins' book can speak to a much wider audience than merely the professional scholar or seminary student.

But still, why a specifically *Catholic* introduction? Isn't such a confessional approach outdated? The fact is, everything written is written from some point of view. And that holds doubly true for any theological or scriptural work. All theologians and Scripture scholars write within or out of a particular philosophical and/or theological context, acknowledged or unacknowledged. Indeed, the real danger to honest Scripture scholarship is the claim to total objectivity and neutrality. Such a claim usually hides a secret agenda, be it confessional or agnostic. Joachim Jeremias, for instance, sought to reconstruct the historical Jesus, with all the objective tools of modern critical inquiry. But, as Norman Perrin pointed out, Jeremias' categories often betray the thought-world of German Lutheran pietism. One does not have to read a great deal of Rudolf Bultmann and his disciples to realize what a heavy dose of Luther-Heidegger vaccine has been injected into a main artery of German exegesis. James D. G. Dunn is one of the most brilliant writers in the field of New Testament studies today; he is also unmistakably low-church British. Robert Gundry has a vast knowledge of the Old Testament textual traditions used in the Gospel of Matthew; the results of his exegesis are especially acceptable to conservative American Evangelical Protestants. Norman Perrin was quite open about how his personal spiritual pilgrimage affected his shifting exegetical views. The later Perrin was obviously influenced by the atmosphere around the Divinity School of the University of Chicago. None of this is meant in a disparaging way. It simply underlines the truism that everyone comes to a text with his or her own presuppositions. The important thing is to admit and examine one's presuppositions, realize their potential strengths and dangers, and allow them to be addressed and challenged by the text.

Collins has done this to an admirable degree. He makes no apology for being a Catholic and approaching the Scriptures out of a particular history: the explosive Catholic encounter with the Bible in this century. His review of the problems involved in canon, inspiration, the interplay between church authorities and scholars, and the roller-coaster ride of Roman pronouncements over the span of sixty years makes clear that any other approach on the part of a Catholic would be a scholarly parody of the three wise monkeys. All too many Catholics and Protestants are ignorant of why Catholic biblical scholarship is at the point it is at and how it got there. Collins' presentation informs us both of the state of the art and of the bumpy road by which the art arrived at its present state. His historical criticism is therefore truly critical because it is self-conscious and self-critical. Unlike many historical critics who think that they are magically exempt from the limitations studied by their own discipline, Collins knows, evaluates, and communicates to us the history that has produced him and his work. Would that all "critical" exegetes were so critical! Many are unconsciously confessional precisely because they do not "confess" their confessional background.

Does this honest statement of his Catholic context restrict the relevance and usefulness of Collins' book to the Catholic community? I think not. As a glance at his up-to-date bibliographies will quickly reveal, Collins' knowledge is wide-ranging, international, and ecumenical. He is well aware of the impact Protestant scholars have had on Catholic biblical studies, an impact that has now become reciprocal. Any Christian—indeed, a well-disposed inquirer of any background—will find here a mine of information and not a few challenging, thought-provoking insights.

I venture to suggest that conservative Evangelical Protestants especially would profit from thoughtful study of this volume. Many Evangelical scholars are going through the throes of the same faith-versus-reason or dogma-versus-history debate which upset Catholic Scripture scholarship from 1905 down to 1965. I think the Evangelicals can learn a great deal from the pain and conflict, the dead ends and new breakthroughs, which their Catholic cousins have experienced. Needless to say, the theological contexts are different, especially as regards ecclesiology. I am convinced, however, that a critical and open debate over the questions of canon and inspiration, history and faith, will push all of us to a renewed appreciation of how Scripture and Church are necessarily intertwined. An honest encounter between Catholic and Evangelical approaches to the problems raised by historical criticism could be one of the most fruitful developments on the contemporary ecumenical scene. Collins' work could prove a welcome stimulus to such cross-fertilization.

The same holds true for the dialogue between Catholic and liberal Protestant scholars. So close is their agreement on some issues that Evangelicals often suspect Catholic biblicists of being crypto-liberal Protestants. It is true that Catholic and liberal Protestant exegetes share a certain amount of common presuppositions. On the other hand, the liberal Protestants are puzzled by the Catholics' ability to reconcile critical scholarship with acceptance of an authoritative magisterium. The refusal of most Catholic exegetes to reject *a priori* the possibility of special divine activity in this world likewise leaves some liberal Protestants bewildered. Perhaps this is the particular mission of Catholic exegetes to their liberal confreres: to act as a question mark, raising some doubts about whether historical-critical scholarship necessarily entails all the philosophical and theological positions espoused by liberal Protestantism. In itself, the historical-critical method is—or should be—open to use by any theological or confessional tradition. Catholic scholarship bears valuable witness to the truth that this method is the monopoly of no one group. Indeed, some Catholic scholars might feel they have the best of both worlds today. They are free to pursue scholarly questions with total rigor and integrity, and yet they do so firmly within traditional Christianity. From Justin to Augustine, from Aquinas to Descartes, from Cardinal Newman to Bernard J. Lonergan and Karl Rahner, there has always been a strong drive within the Catholic tradition to correlate faith and reason, dogma and history, divine revelation and human experience. The balance struck by contemporary Catholic exegetes is simply the latest example of the Catholic thrust toward synthesis. This is not said in any self-congratulatory or smug, triumphalistic tone. The history of the Catholic Church shows that balance and synthesis can be fragile commodities, easily lost if not constantly refurbished. Here too, Collins' volume performs a service. By retelling our bloody past and summing up our happy present, he implicitly points the way to a better future. Protestants and Catholics alike can benefit from the tale, the summation, and the prophecy.

A Tourist's Guide

In this massive work, Fr. Collins has given us the distillation of years of study, teaching, and writing. Faced with this rich banquet, the reader may wonder how to proceed through the various courses. As with any meal, this depends to a great degree on how hungry the consumer is at any given moment.

At any banquet, some of us are nibblers, others light eaters, and others bottomless pits. The nibblers among us may prefer to scan the table of contents and dip here or there into a section which promises to be of special interest. I must admit, this was the way I initially approached this volume, before I started to devour it whole and entire. It is an especially useful approach for those whose background is limited and who need to get their feet wet before they can work up the courage to take the plunge.

The light eaters may decide to consume a chapter here and a chapter there, not necessarily in the order presented but according to their own designs. Each chapter can be approached as a relatively independent essay, complete with select bibliography and, in some cases, detailed examples to be worked through.

It is, however, the exegetical gourmand, who proceeds through the whole banquet in the order in which it is served, who will enjoy and benefit most from the feast. Fr. Collins has carefully structured his book so that one chapter leads logically to the next. Only those who follow his lead can appreciate the full cogency of his presentation. In what follows, I shall try to assist the committed zealot by laying out something of a road map as an aid to keeping one's sense of direction. Naturally, space does not allow even an adequate summary of each chapter's contents. I shall simply highlight a few points which I judge to be of relative importance.

Some introductions to the New Testament throw their treatments of the canon of the New Testament to the end of the volume; others give the canon no separate consideration at all. Fr. Collins purposefully begins his volume with a chapter on the formation of the New Testament. In his treatment, Collins avoids two extremes. Conservatives would like to think the formation of the New Testament canon was a simple, rapid process orchestrated directly by God and by no one else. On the conservative Protestant side, one hears talk of the canon's imposing itself upon the Church. On the conservative Catholic side, there is a hazy idea that some council and/or Pope issued a dogmatic definition early on that settled the whole matter. The real history of the canon is, of course, far more complex, bewildering, and meandering. Fr. Collins' treatment does justice to the many avenues of development and the persistent disagreements that attended some books. His reminder that as late as the ninth century some Western manuscripts of the New Testament omitted the Epistle to the Hebrews should put an end to any pious ideas about an easy and very early consensus on all the books now in the canon.

The opposite extreme in studies on the canon is to declare that there was no norm for distinguishing "orthodoxy" and "heresy" in primitive Christianity and that the canon we now have is the totally fortuitous result of one Christian group's triumph over another Christian group. Collins skillfully undermines this approach. He begins his treatment by pointing out the various elements of authority and norms for discernment that already existed in first-century Christianity. From the beginning, the Church was endowed with authoritative leaders, with the Jewish Scriptures, and with set traditions about Jesus of Nazareth, all of which prevented Christianity from becoming whatever the latest enthusiast thought it should become. Long before there was a canon of twenty-seven books there was a "canon of truth," a measuring rod of basic faith to which Paul and other preachers could appeal as universally known and universally binding (cf., e.g., 1 Cor 15:1–11). In a sense, the canon of New Testament books was the ultimate, centuries-long working out of what was implicit in the various "canons" or normative structures and traditions already present in first-century Christianity.

Fr. Collins' treatment of canon is especially welcome at a time when there is much talk of "canon criticism" or, on the other hand, "the canon within the canon." The problem is, a facile approach to the complex reality of canon can soon lead either to a neo-fundamentalism (in the case of canon criticism) or to a Marcion-like truncation of the canon (in the case of the canon within the canon). To avoid superstitious idolatry of the canon, both approaches need a critical awareness of the pivotal role the Church played in developing and fixing the canon. To hear some scholars talk in hushed tones about the canon, one would swear that it fell from heaven one starry night. The more one studies the history of the canon, the more one appreciates that the problem of canonicity is a problem of ecclesiology. It is strange that some Protestants play off the canon against the Church, as though the possession of the first dispenses from the necessity of the second. While it is true that the preached word and the preaching Church are mutually dependent, each one in a sense calling forth the other, it is equally and indisputably true that the Church fixed the canon, and not vice versa. The higher one's esteem for the canon, the higher logically should be one's esteem for the Church, which fixed the canon. Collins does well to underscore this indispensable role of the Church. At the same time, he does not deny the ongoing problems posed by a canon in which some books are obviously more weighty than others. It is indeed proper to give more attention to certain voices within the canon, provided the other voices are not effectively silenced.

In Chapter Two, Collins explains the basic principle of the historical-critical method(s): the New Testament must be studied in its historical context. In a sense, Chapter Two is programmatic for the rest of the book. Collins sketches here the historical origins and development of the various methods which will be examined in greater detail in the later chapters. Naturally, special consideration is given at the beginning of Chapter Two to Ferdinand

Christian Baur, the great pioneer of historical-critical research. But it is typical of Collins' sensitivity to his American audience that he gives us information about two early disciples of historical criticism here in the United States: Philip Schaff and Benjamin Wisner Bacon. Since Collins is tracing the chronological course of various methods, and history is never as neat as we would like, he has to weave back and forth among developments in general Synoptic studies, the quest for the historical Jesus, Markan priority, studies in New Testament environment (the various languages, cultures, and writings of the time, with special emphasis on Judaism), form criticism, and redaction criticism. Collins the teacher is careful to conclude this account of scholarly give-and-take, spread over a number of centuries, with a short statement of the scholarly consensus today. Intent on informing the reader about the latest developments in New Testament research, Collins includes a short treatment of structuralism, psychoanalytic readings, and Marxist or materialistic readings. He will explain structuralism at greater length in Chapter Seven.

In Chapter Three, Collins tackles text criticism, a topic sure to unnerve the novice. Again, Collins shows he is a superb pedagogue by initiating the newcomer step by step into the mysteries of text criticism. After pointing out to the fearful that the Fathers of the Church were aware of the problem of variant readings in New Testament manuscripts, Collins switches to some examples of textual problems taken from modern life, to prepare the reader for what is to come. Explaining the various kinds of New Testament Greek manuscripts, Collins gives the usual classifications: papyri, majuscules, minuscules, and lectionaries. Ancient translations (versions)—especially Syriac, Latin, and Coptic—and citations from the Fathers of the Church provide secondary and tertiary witnesses to the original Greek text. Collins then proceeds to explain how scholars draw up "genealogical trees" of manuscripts. These genealogies depict the dependence of one manuscript on another and indicate how whole groups of manuscripts form "families" and "types." Various rules for and examples of choosing the best among a number of possible readings are given. There follows a short history of printed editions of the New Testament from the sixteenth century to the present. Collins concludes with a couple of examples of New Testament text criticism in practice. The reader should note that the two texts chosen, the Message of the Baptist and the Stilling of the Storm, will return in subsequent chapters to serve as models for other types of criticism.

In Chapter Four, Collins explains that he is now focusing upon "literary criticism" in the most traditional sense of that phrase—namely, source criticism. Again, he uses some contemporary examples to help the reader understand the main point of source criticism. He then examines four criteria for discerning sources (redundancy, context, vocabulary and style, and ideology). Collins next zeroes in on the "Synoptic fact" and the "Synoptic Problem," which make the relationships among Matthew, Mark, and Luke a source of endless fascination. Collins quickly reviews the theories of Augustine and Griesbach-Farmer, but he himself prefers the Two-Source theory

(Matthew and Luke are both dependent on Mark and a Sayings Source called Q, but do not know each other). I think Collins is correct in espousing and emphasizing the Two-Source theory, despite attacks on it from many quarters today. It enjoys not absolute certitude but practical viability. In other words, it works. It has proved itself over the long haul of many detailed commentaries and monographs. The same cannot be said for most of its competitors.

With regard to the Acts of the Apostles, Collins draws the prudent conclusion that Luke did make use of sources, but that it is nigh impossible for the modern critic to isolate them. Collins then considers hymns as a source used in Paul's letters. Much more problematic are the suggested interpolations some critics see in the letters. Collins wisely shows himself dubious, especially with regard to Walter Schmithals' wild theories. After consideration of the relationships between Colossians and Ephesians and between 2 Peter and Jude, Collins turns to the Johannine corpus, where Bultmann's theory on sources naturally receives detailed study. As regards Revelation, Collins rightly emphasizes the unitary character of Revelation's language and symbol system, a point that makes many theories of sources questionable. The concluding examples of source criticism, the Message of the Baptist and the Stilling of the Storm, give the reader a chance to work with both Q and Markan material.

In Chapter Five, "Form Criticism," Collins takes great care to make sure the reader understands what form criticism is: a study and classification of the different types, categories, or set patterns of oral and written expression. Modern examples from jokes, letters, and newspapers make clear that all of us constantly use set patterns of communication, each with its own particular goals and rules. Different literary forms can reflect different social situations or "settings in life" (*Sitze-im-Leben*). Form criticism must thus be concerned with sociological analysis as well as literary analysis. In a given city, for example, different newspapers evincing different styles and content probably reflect diverse audiences with distinctive sociological backgrounds. Granted this social link, it is not surprising that changes in the social situation may cause changes in the forms of written or oral communications as they are passed along from one communicator to another, or from one generation to the next. With sufficient material, one can trace the development of such changes and draw up a "tradition history" of the material. Moreover, just as the form tells us something about the needs of the audience, it also tells us something about the purpose of the author.

Having explained these key insights of form criticism, Collins then reviews the history of twentieth-century form criticism. In the Synoptics, the great names are, of course, Karl Ludwig Schmidt, Martin Dibelius, and Rudolf Bultmann. Vincent Taylor "domesticated" their findings for a more conservative British audience. The insights of form criticism naturally fostered a new approach to the old question of the historical Jesus. Collins goes beyond many surveys of form criticism by including consideration of John's gospel. The book of Revelation has also drawn much attention lately, for it invites research into the larger form of the apocalyptic and the smaller component forms, such as letters, visions, prophecies, prayers, and hymns. A similar distinction between the larger form of letter and the smaller component forms (apocalyptic, hymns, blessings, sentences of holy law, apostolic parousia, peristatic catalogues, catalogues of virtues and vices, household codes, creedal formulas) is made in the treatment of epistles. Similar component forms (creedal formulas, self-revelation formulas, speeches) can be isolated in Acts. At the end of the chapter Collins returns to his two favorite pericopes, the Message of the Baptist and the Stilling of the Storm, to show how form criticism sheds light on each one's message.

If source criticism dominated New Testament scholarship before World War I and form criticism reigned supreme between the two World Wars, redaction criticism has been dominant, especially in Synoptic studies, from World War II until the present day. In Chapter Six, "Redaction Criticism," Collins the pedagogue returns to his newspaper to illustrate how the same story from the same news service can be edited very differently in two different papers because of different viewpoints on the part of the two editors involved. Redaction criticism highlights this final editorial work. The evangelists (or other New Testament authors) creatively forged disparate units of tradition into a coherent literary whole, each gospel reflecting the special theology of the individual redactor. Redaction criticism aims at understanding the purpose of the final author and the needs of his particular community.

Collins then reviews the major contributors to this type of criticism: William Wrede, Ernst Lohmeyer, and Willi Marxsen on Mark's Gospel; Hans Conzelmann on Luke's; and Günther Bornkamm, Gerhard Barth, and H. J. Held on Matthew's. Typically, Collins also mentions the various recent attempts at updating and correcting these pioneer works. In the Acts of the Apostles, Ernst Haenchen and Ulrich Wilckens have done the basic redaction criticism; again, the questionable elements in their otherwise fine work do not go unnoticed. In the epistles, redaction criticism must be understood rather as composition criticism—i.e., a study of how Paul in particular adapted and developed the general Hellenistic letter form into his striking apostolic letter form. The study of letter forms has also influenced recent research on the redaction of Revelation by Krister Stendahl and Elisabeth Schüssler Fiorenza. As for redaction criticism in John's Gospel, J. Louis Martyn has emphasized the ejection of Jewish Christians from the synagogue as the key life situation which moves the evangelist to retell the story of Jesus in terms of the conflicts of his own day. At the end of the chapter, the Message of the Baptist and the Stilling of the Storm return, like the Flying Dutchman, to illustrate redaction criticism in practice. By applying the different types of criticism to the same pericopes, Collins highlights both the specific nature of each kind of criticism and the many levels of meaning present in one pericope.

It has been Collins' desire to write a contemporary Introduction which will survey all the major approaches to New Testament criticism used today. Hence, he feels obliged to include a chapter on structural analysis, which has been developed especially by the French (Chapter Seven). He begins by admitting quite honestly that biblical scholars debate the very legitimacy of structural analysis as a form of biblical research. I must confess I am one of the doubting Thomases. My own jaundiced view is that structural analysis is a sterile academic exercise which only makes biblical studies more esoteric and inaccessible than they need be. The usable results, often meager at best, sometimes proceed from the fertile imagination of the expositor rather than from anything in the text. If the reader thinks I am being too harsh, I suggest he or she read Chapter Seven right now and then reconsider my remarks. Personally, I would have preferred to substitute a chapter on Hans-Georg Gadamer and Paul Ricoeur, who have had more impact on Catholic Scripture scholars here in the United States. Here I commit the original sin of the critic: trying to rewrite an author's book instead of commenting on it. Collins' decision may yet be vindicated by the future course of biblical studies. At least one must admire his pedagogical skill in bringing back the Stilling of the Storm for yet another critical analysis—this time, structural.

After having studied the various kinds of criticism (text, form, redaction, structure) in detail, Collins steps back in Chapter Eight ("Exegesis and the Church") and asks some larger philosophical and theological questions. Here Collins moves beyond the question of exegesis proper (what *did* the text say to its first audience) to the broader question of hermeneutics (what *does* the text say to us today). Harking back to the ecclesiological note he struck in his study of the canon, Collins stresses the need to situate this hermeneutical question within the life, worship, faith, and theology of the Church. Far from being an enemy of the Church's faith, the historical-critical method can serve the believing and theologizing Church of today. With regard to systematic theology in particular, Collins holds that exegesis has a fivefold task. It is *constitutive* of theology in that it reveals the normative common thread of early Christian experience. It has a *critical* function in that it calls into question theological tendencies that do not do justice to the full range of the New Testament witness—e.g., on such matters as morality. Exegesis has an *indicative* function in that it points out the direction which various events, institutions, and teachings in the New Testament took as they developed historically. This has relevance for such present-day questions as the teaching office in the Church and divorce. Exegesis has a *provocative* function in that it suggests areas which dogmatic theology has largely overlooked—e.g., the role of women in the Church and the importance of Spirit-induced phenomena. Finally, exegesis has a *validating* function in that it confirms various practices and Christian experiences that have arisen in the course of the Church's history. Collins then proceeds to consider the practical relation of exegesis to the magisterium, to preaching, to catechesis, and to prayer. The great merit of this chapter is that in it Collins, unlike many scholars who simply affirm the relevance and usefulness of scientific exegesis, shows concretely how exegesis can serve the various dimensions of the life of the Church.

In taking up the question of inspiration (Chapter Nine), Collins knows that he is entering a difficult area. As he points out, the problems raised by historical-critical research have tended to make the traditional treatments of inspiration in main-line churches look outmoded. Unfortunately, instead of new thinking and a new synthesis, silence has reigned, except among the Evangelicals. Collins attempts to correct this post-Vatican II lapse. Starting with a detailed exegesis of the two key New Testament texts, 2 Timothy 3:16 and 2 Peter 1:20–21, he proceeds to examine the concept of inspiration in Judaism and in the Fathers of the Church. The idea of God as the author of the Scriptures is then traced through the Fathers and Church councils. Collins next outlines the history of the theological discussion on inspiration, from the medieval Scholastics, through the Reformers and the post-Reformation Scholastics, down to Catholic thinkers of the nineteenth century (notably Cardinal Newman, J. B. Franzelin, Leo XIII, and M.-J. Lagrange). Unfortunately, progress was checked in the early twentieth century when the Modernist crisis provoked a spate of archconservative statements from the magisterium. These effectively put an end to all meaningful development until the "second spring" inaugurated in *Divino Afflante Spiritu* of Pius XII (1943) and culminating in *Dei Verbum* of Vatican II (1965). Collins rightly notes that Vatican II purposely avoided speaking of inerrancy (a rather late term in these discussions anyway) and chose rather to speak in a positive and traditional way of the truth of Scripture. Collins indicates that the way of the future is the way which situates inspiration in a context of salvation history, of the Incarnation, and of the function of charisms within the Church. Again, a favorite theme of Collins is struck: the social, ecclesial, and historical dimensions of Scripture. Only in this light can one understand the various nuanced ways in which Christians must speak of the truth of Scripture as a truth that is preserved from error. In a sense, the first eight chapters of Collins' book must be properly digested before one can fully grasp the complex question of the inspiration and truth of Scripture. Collins chose well when he opened his volume with the canon and kept the chapter on inspiration close to the end.

Since the question of inspiration led us into a number of recent Roman documents, it is only natural that Collins conclude his work with an epilogue on Rome and the critical study of the New Testament (Chapter Ten). The bumpy road I have already mentioned is now mapped out with all its sad detours clearly marked. The value of Collins' survey is that for the first time the infighting among Roman officials and scholars is detailed for the general American audience. Vatican documents cease to be faceless decrees in a timeless vacuum and become what they usually are: the record of one party in the Roman Curia battling another party in the Curia. With special fondness and respect, Collins recalls martyrs like Maximilian Zerwick and Stanislas Lyonnet. Their Christian endurance under unjust persecution contributed greatly to the triumph of scientific scholarship over the obscurantists, a triumph consecrated in Vatican II's Dogmatic Constitution on Divine Revelation (*Dei Verbum*). It is fitting that Collins conclude his treatment with the words of Pope John Paul II to the newly reorganized Biblical

Commission. For all the talk of John Paul's conservatism, his speeches and documents have usually been marked by great critical care in the use of Scripture. His Wednesday talks on the first chapters of Genesis are especially worth reading; they give no comfort to fundamentalists or creation scientists.

In sum, Fr. Collins' monumental survey of the scientific study of the New Testament is breathtaking in the range of material it takes in, the judicious care with which the material is sifted, and the clarity with which the material is presented. All of us who will use and recommend this sure guide to contemporary Catholic biblical studies owe Fr. Collins an unpayable debt of thanks. *Ad multos annos.*

John P. Meier
St. Joseph's Seminary, Dunwoodie
Yonkers, NY

Pentecost Sunday, May 30, 1982

PREFACE

As the formative era of the New Testament was drawing to a close, the author of the second letter to Timothy wrote: "All Scripture is inspired by God and profitable for teaching, for reproof, for correction, and for training in righteousness, that the man of God may be complete, equipped for every good work" (2 Tim 3:16–17).

This book was born of the conviction that the words of the ancient author apply to the men and women of God in the twentieth century just as much as they did to the Church leader of almost twenty centuries ago. The question which now confronts the reader of the Scriptures is that of the meaningful understanding of the Sacred Text. The Old and the New Testaments are the principal pieces of a religious literature that has shaped the Christian tradition and formed the Christian personality for almost two thousand years. How can they be understood in an age that is marked by a profound historical consciousness and a deep awareness of historical relativity? Were the Old and the New Testaments considered only as religious documents coming from the past, one would have to ask how to approach them in order to understand them. When one belongs to a community of believers which proclaims the abiding relevance of these texts, the question of their meaning becomes even more urgent.

My response to the question of meaning is that the New Testament exists among us as a singularly important collection of *religious* literature, but that it is *literature* nonetheless. Therefore, in order to understand this collection, one must approach it with that same concern and discernment with which one approaches all other literature, ancient and modern, secular and religious. Accordingly, the central section of this book is an exposition of a method of interpretation of literature that the reader of the New Testament will undoubtedly find helpful, because it is the fashion in which the reader approaches every text which falls under the eyes.

Chapters Three to Seven thus form the core of the present work. Each of the chapters begins with a brief reflection on some aspect of how we humans understand that which we read. Then I offer some reflections as to how this approach has been applied to the books of the New Testament in the unending endeavor to articulate their meaning. The final section of each of these central chapters reflects on the gospel stories of the preaching of John the Baptist and Jesus' Stilling of the Storm, in order that the reader can come to an appreciation of how the five methods I have exposited complement one another.

In New Testament studies, this method has traditionally been called the historical-critical method. I have chosen to complement the classical use of the method with some reflections drawn from the newer method of structural analysis. In this respect the present book is a product of its age, just as the New Testament itself was a product of its own times. Therefore the first part of this book reflects on the history of the New Testament and the history of New Testament scholarship. Its two chapters seek to respond to a twofold question. Where did the New Testament come from? How did our manner of reading the New Testament come into being? Both our method of studying the New Testament and the New Testament itself are products of a unique set of historical circumstances. It is to an exposition of these circumstances that I have devoted the first chapters of this book.

While an exposition of a method of understanding the New Testament is undoubtedly sufficient for the academician who wishes to interpret the text, the method itself is a necessary condition, but not the sufficient condition, for the men and women of God who believe that the New Testament contains the Word of God and therefore has abiding meaning for the believer. Chapter Eight reflects on the usefulness of the New Testament as the Church's Scriptures. The question to which it responds is: how does the New Testament, interpreted according to the normal canons of intelligent reading, enter into the religious life of the believing community and its members? My final chapter explains why the Church holds the New Testament in such esteem. It presents the New Testament as an inspired work. It is theology—*theou logos,* the word of God and the word about God.

In short, this book is an extended hermeneutical reflection on 2 Timothy 3:16–17, applied to the New Testament and the age in which we live. It has arisen as a response to the words addressed to Timothy by one who has lived and taught the New Testament from within the Roman Catholic tradition. I hope that there is little confessional bias reflected in these pages and that reading them will be useful to students of the New Testament from other religious traditions. Nonetheless I must acknowledge my own tradition— hence the epilogue—and respond to the particular problematics that have arisen within it in the search to respond obediently to the Word of God.

This book is directed to students of the New Testament who, like Timothy, have been exhorted to find profit in the ancient and sacred text. To help them in their search for understanding, I have added a twenty-five-item bibliography at the conclusion of each chapter. The choice of bibliographical materials is somewhat arbitrary. The need for conciseness that prompted the elimination of the many footnotes I would like to have included has also led to very short bibliographies. Insofar as is possible, the articles and books cited in these bibliographies are those which have been published in English. My chief concern in the bibliographical listings is, however, to offer a selection that more or less covers the range of material treated in the chapter.

Since the book is directed to students of the New Testament, I have added two appendices for their benefit: one for those who want to go further, and one for those who are just starting out. For those who want to pursue their study of the New Testament, an annotated bibliography of the principal texts and tools has been provided. For those to whom the language of the New Testament scholarship is "so much Greek," a brief glossary of terms has been added.

Had this book contained footnotes that one normally finds in scholarly works, the names of many scholars would have appeared. Surely, some of those who read this book will recognize within these pages much of their own thought. In fact this book is a product of my personal dialogue with New Testament scholars of many languages, cultures, and religious traditions. In a corporate fashion I must acknowledge my dependence on them, and offer them my thanks. Without them, this book would never have seen the light of day. For the light provided by my colleagues, scattered far and wide, I am profoundly grateful. To my own students I am no less grateful. It has been their enthusiasm and their challenge which have moved me to write this book. To all my students, I extend a note of thanks. It was dialogue with them that provided the vision and the strength.

Only with some hesitation do I dare cite some by name. I am most grateful to Ms. Florence Morgan, a doctoral student at the Catholic University of Louvain, who read the manuscript in first draft and made many helpful suggestions. I am thankful, too, to Mr. Frank Clinch who assumed responsibility for typing the initial manuscript, and to those who worked with him in the time-consuming process, especially Steven Tinkle, George Darling, and Terence Grant. Likewise I am grateful to Ms. Donna Barrett, who prepared the typescript. Finally, I must thank a special group of people, those endowed with the gift of a particular patience as they labored long in proofreading the manuscript, the Rev. Brian Henneberry, Anne Stevenson, Sheila Judge, and most especially Chaucy Bennetts, my copy editor, without whose invaluable assistance and suggestions this book would not have been what it is today. To all of these and to so many others as well, I owe a debt of gratitude.

This book is directed to students of the New Testament. It is dedicated to those who have studied the New Testament with me. Ours has been a common quest, but the quest is not yet ended for the Word of God has not yet been fully heard, nor are the children of God yet complete.

CHAPTER ONE

THE FORMATION OF THE NEW TESTAMENT

When believers, church leaders, and students of ancient literature speak of the "New Testament," they are convinced that they are speaking about a clearly defined reality. The New Testament is surely a collection of some twenty-seven writings, written by various authors in a relatively short period of time after the death on the cross of Jesus of Nazareth. Throughout the centuries this group of writings has enjoyed a pride of place within Christian churches to such a degree that acceptance of the New Testament would seem to be of the very essence of the Christian Church.

If prodded, those who speak of the New Testament would probably agree with the Council of Trent (1st Decree, 4th Session; February 4, 1546) which cited the books of the New Testament as follows: "The four Gospels according to Matthew, Mark, Luke and John; the Acts of the Apostles written by Luke the Evangelist; fourteen epistles of the apostle Paul, i.e., to the Romans, two to the Corinthians, to the Galatians, Ephesians, Philippians, Colossians, two to the Thessalonians, two to Timothy, to Titus, Philemon, and the Hebrews; two epistles of the apostle Peter, three of the apostle John, one of the apostle James, one of the apostle Jude, and the Revelation of the apostle John" (DS 1503). Perhaps a contemporary student of the New Testament would disagree with the Council of Trent's unqualified designation of the authors of the different books of the New Testament, but he or she would hardly disagree with the contention that the Tridentine list adequately indicates the contents of the well-defined entity known as the New Testament.

Actually, the listing of the books of the New Testament at the Council of Trent was no mere exercise in pedantry. The listing of the books was

1

proclaimed in the midst of a heated controversy. It came as a response to Luther's decision to relegate the Epistle to the Hebrews, the Epistles of James and Jude, and the book of Revelation to a lesser status than that enjoyed by the other twenty-three books of the New Testament. Luther included Hebrews, James, Jude, and Revelation only as an appendix to his German-language New Testament. With respect to this situation, the Council of Trent underscored its listing of the twenty-seven books of the New Testament (as well as forty-five books of the Old Testament) with the solemn warning that "If anyone does not accept all these books in their entirety, with all their parts, as they are being read in the Catholic Church and are contained in the ancient Latin Vulgate edition, as sacred and canonical and knowingly and deliberately rejects the aforesaid traditions, *anathema sit.*"

From the words of the conciliar decree one might almost get the impression that the identification of the contents of the New Testament is a fruit of controversy. The history of the Christian churches shows that this is precisely the fact of the matter. The identification of the books of the New Testament represents a decision of the Church made in the heat of controversy, and resulting from a rather complex historical process whose details are even now somewhat difficult to distinguish. What is in any case patently clear is that the reality which we so readily identify as the New Testament is the result of a complex historical process.

In point of fact, the earliest listing of twenty-seven books which alone are to be regarded as canonical has been preserved for us by Athanasius, bishop of Alexandria, in his Easter letter of 367. He wrote: "Again it is not tedious to speak of the books of the New Testament. These are the four Gospels, according to Matthew, Mark, Luke, and John. Afterwards, the Acts of the Apostles and Epistles (called Catholic), seven, viz., of James, one; of Peter, two; of John, three; after these, one of Jude. In addition, there are the fourteen Epistles of Paul, written in this order. The first, to the Romans; then two to the Corinthians; after these, to the Galatians; next, to the Ephesians; then to the Philippians; then to the Colossians; after these, two to the Thessalonians, and that to the Hebrews; and again, two to Timothy; one to Titus; and lastly, that to Philemon. And besides, the Revelation of John." Athanasius introduced this listing of the New Testament books (along with those in the Old Testament) with a paraphrase of the introduction to Luke's Gospel: "Forasmuch as some have taken in hand, to reduce into order for themselves the books termed apocryphal, and to mix them up with the divinely inspired Scriptures . . . it seemed good to me also . . . to set before you the books included in the Canon, and handed down, and accredited as Divine. . . ." These introductory remarks clearly indicate that for Athanasius, the New Testament canon was a polemical matter.

Athanasius' Easter letter expresses the view of one influential bishop writing for the benefit of his local church. His letter, therefore, does not represent an official position to be espoused by the universal Church. It is, however, significant in that it verbalized a point of view which was apparently shared by other local churches. Thus, some fifteen years after Athanasius' letter a Roman synod was convened during the reign of Pope Damasus (366–84), the pontiff of the Roman Primacy. Damasus, who was engaged in a struggle with several different schisms during his pontificate, introduced Jerome (342–420) into the papal chancery. Under the influence of Jerome, the Roman synod of 382 promoted a canon of the New Testament which contained the same twenty-seven books cited in Athanasius' listing, albeit in somewhat different order:

> Likewise the order of the writings of the New and eternal Testament, which the holy and Catholic Church supports. Of the Gospels, according to Matthew one book, according to Mark one book, according to Luke one book, according to John one book.
> The Epistles of Paul [the apostle] in number fourteen; To the Romans one, to the Corinthians two, to the Ephesians one, to the Thessalonians two, to the Galatians one, to the Philippians one, to the Colossians one, to Timothy two, to Titus one, to Philemon one, to the Hebrews one.
> Likewise the Apocalypse of John, one book. And the Acts of the Apostles, one book.
> Likewise the canonical epistles in number seven. Of Peter the Apostle two epistles, of James the Apostle one epistle, of John the Apostle one epistle, of another John, the presbyter, two epistles, of Jude the Zealot, the Apostle one epistle.
> The canon of the New Testament ends here (DS 180).

This excerpt from the so-called "Decree of Damasus" (382) was preceded by a listing of the books of the Old Testament and an introduction which clearly indicates that the canon of both testaments results from the decision of the Church. The introduction states that "we must treat of the divine Scriptures, what the universal Catholic Church accepts and what she ought to shun." In effect, a study of the formation of the New Testament is a study of a decision made by the churches. By the end of the fourth century, the various Christian churches were coming to a point at which each recognized that twenty-seven books constituted the canon of the New Testament—that is, a collection accepted as the authoritative norm and criterion of Christian faith and practice.

This canonization of Matthew, Mark, Luke, John, Acts, Romans, 1,2 Corinthians, Galatians, Ephesians, Philippians, Colossians, 1,2 Thessalonians, 1,2 Timothy, Titus, Philemon, Hebrews, James, 1,2 Peter, 1,2,3 John, Jude, Revelation represents, then, a point of arrival rather than a point of departure when we speak of the New Testament. Accordingly, it may prove useful to divide the history of the formation of the New Testament into four periods. The first period is that of the first Christian writings, the era to which the books presently collected into the New Testament give witness along with a limited number of other early writings which were not canonized by the later judgment of the churches. The second period is that

3

of the recognition of some of the early Christian writings as Scripture, so that these writings were accorded definite authority in one or another local church. The third period is the conscious formation of closed collections of Christian writings, and the exclusion of other writings from these collections —a process tempered by the fires of controversy. The fourth period is that of canonization, properly so called, when the concern was not with the acceptability of one or another book as such, but with the formation of the entire list of New Testament books.

I. THE FIRST CHRISTIAN WRITINGS

The assumption that the twenty-seven writings which we have become accustomed to identifying as the New Testament are, as a whole, the earliest Christian writings is one that flies in the face of contemporary scholarship. Luke's prologue (Luke 1:1–4) suggests that there was Christian documentation prior to his own writing of the Gospel. Much of that early documented witness to the words and ministry of Jesus has been lost except in the measure that it has been recorded in one of our "canonical" Gospels. It is also clear that Paul wrote some letters that are apparently no longer extant (cf. 1 Cor 5:9–11; 2 Cor 2:4; Col 4:16). On the other hand, we have some early Christian documents that were written at the same time as, or perhaps even before, some of the books which were included in the New Testament by the decision of the Church of a later era. Thus it is commonly acknowledged that the letter of Clement of Rome was written before 2 Peter. Clement has not been included in the New Testament, whereas 2 Peter has been included even though contemporary scholarship holds that the epistle was not written by the apostle Peter himself.

Authority

The twenty-seven books of the New Testament, written over the space of several decades, give but limited witness to the activities and concerns of the Church during its formative years. Nevertheless, they do witness to a Church whose activities and concerns were not unlike those which would result in the formulation of a New Testament canon in the fourth century. Foremost among those concerns was the issue of authority. Paul's first letter to the Corinthians, surely our best entry into the life, activity, and concerns of an early Christian community, tells us something about the issue of authority in the mid-first century of the Christian era. In his response to questions on marriage and virginity (1 Cor 7), Paul relies on the authority of the Lord as well as on his own authority, which he carefully distinguishes from that of the Lord (1 Cor 7:10, 12, 25). Even in the absence of a traditional saying of Jesus, Paul does not hesitate to respond to practical concerns as the need arises, because he is convinced that he possesses the Spirit (1 Cor 7:40).

The Scriptures

In fact, there were several authorities to which the Christians of the earliest generations could appeal in order to resolve practical problems and clarify doctrinal issues. The Scriptures (*hai graphai*) are unique among the authorities cited in the New Testament. Thus, Paul could appeal to Deuteronomy 25:4, "You shall not muzzle an ox when it is treading out the grain," in developing his arguments in favor of the evangelist's right to be supported by the community to which he preached (1 Cor 9:9). Each of the evangelists portrays Jesus as one who takes the Scriptures seriously and interprets them for his followers. Mark, whose "Gospel" is certainly the most ancient of the four canonical gospels, portrays Jesus engaged in rabbinical-type discussions about the meaning of the Scriptures (Mark 12:18–37). Matthew shows Jesus to be a scribe who is capable of interpreting the law "with authority" (Matt 5:21–41; 7:30). Luke begins his Gospel with a programmatic scene in which Jesus interprets Isaiah (Luke 4:16–22a, 30). In John's Gospel, Jesus offers a midrashic treatment of Exodus 16:4 in the discourse on the Bread of Life (John 6:25–59). Undoubtedly we must inquire as to the extent to which these portrayals of Jesus correspond to the interests and needs of the early Church and the extent to which they represent a tradition about the historical Jesus. In either case, each of the evangelists is pointing to the authority the Scriptures enjoyed within the churches of New Testament times.

The Scriptures that enjoyed such authority within the emerging Church are what Christians call the Old Testament. However, the Old Testament had not yet been canonized during the times in which the books of the New Testament were written. While a distinction must be made between that which was written—the Scriptures—and the oral tradition which served as a "fence around the law," the various factions within Judaism disagreed among themselves as to what was normative and what was (legitimate) interpretation. All agreed that the Torah—the five books of Moses—constituted an authority within Judaism. Beyond that general point of agreement there was a wide variety of opinion. Eventually the Scriptures received some form of "canonization" about A.D. 90, at Jabne [Jamnia] but that decision represents the judgment of one branch of Pharisaic Judaism within Palestine. The decision, moreover, seems not to have been made final prior to the end of the first century. Nevertheless, Jesus and the Christians of the first generations could appeal to the Scriptures. For them, the Scriptures represented a qualitative reality, but they did not yet constitute a closed and well-defined collection of authoritative works.

The Word of the Lord

In addition to the Scriptures, the word of the Lord represented a decisive authority for the early churches. Having appealed to the Scriptures in the

5

presentation of his argument that those who proclaim the gospel should get their living by the gospel (1 Cor 9:8), Paul also appealed to the command of the Lord (v. 14; cf. 1 Cor 14:37). As early as 1 Thessalonians, written barely a generation after the death and resurrection of Jesus, Paul appealed to the word of the Lord (*ho logos tou kuriou*) (1 Thes 4:15) in his reflections on the expectation of the Parousia. In neither of these cases does Paul clearly point to an otherwise known saying of Jesus. There can be little doubt, however, that the word of the Lord to which the apostle refers in 1 Corinthians 7:10–11 is the traditional dominical logion on divorce which has been reproduced in one form or another by each of the Synoptics (Matt 5:31–32; 19:9; Mark 10:11–12; Luke 16:18). It is hardly necessary to examine each of the possible Pauline uses of traditional Jesuanic sayings in order to reach the conclusion that believers of the second Christian generation appealed to the word of the Lord as to a definitive authority. Paul's practice in both 1 Thessalonians and 1 Corinthians clearly attests to the custom.

No less indicative of the use made of dominical logia by first-century Christian churches is Luke's citation of the words of the Lord Jesus in Acts 20:35. The fact that, at a very early stage of the Church's existence, the sayings of Jesus were collected together in a documentary source that had been translated into Greek is a phenomenon perhaps even more significant than the occasional references to an isolated word of the Lord scattered throughout the New Testament. The preservation of Jesus' words in this Sayings Source (the *Q* source or *Quelle*), their translation from Aramaic into Greek, their later incorporation into Matthew and Luke, and the possible use of *Q* sayings by Mark point to the significant authority enjoyed by Jesus' words in the Church of the second and third generations. Not only were Jesus' sayings preserved as tradition deriving from a revered rabbi, they were also valued insofar as they could resolve practical issues in dispute within the churches. An actualizing exegesis of Jesus' words helped to sustain their abiding and normative significance. The addition of "in that day"—apparently a reference to the practice of a commemorative fast among Christians—in Mark 2:20, and the ecclesiastical explanation (Mark 4:10–20) appended to the parable of the sower are but two cases in point.

The Twelve, and Paul

After the death and resurrection of Jesus, those who served as official witnesses to his resurrection enjoyed considerable authority within the Christian community. Their authority is the subject of considerable theological reflection in Luke's Acts of the Apostles. His understanding of the Twelve is that they should have been with Jesus during his ministry and that they should likewise have been witnesses to his resurrection (Acts 1:21–22). The Spirit, given as the eschatological gift of God, descends upon the Twelve (Acts 2). Their preaching and ministry is constitutive of the mother Church of Jerusalem. From thence the gospel is carried to the corners of the earth. The Lucan account of the Council of Jerusalem (Acts 15), manifestly a composite account, confirms the authority of the Twelve, since it is to the apostles and elders that Paul and Barnabas have recourse in order that the dispute on circumcision be resolved.

Among the Twelve, a certain primacy of place is accorded to Peter, whose experience of the resurrected Jesus is attested to in Luke 24:34. It is Peter who serves as the spokesperson among the Twelve in proclaiming the significance of the Pentecost event to Jerusalem and Judea (Acts 2:14; cf. 1:8). Peter's vision and his reception of Cornelius (Acts 10) anticipate the decision of the Jerusalem Council and prepare for Peter's intervention there (Acts 15). No wonder, then, that Luke presents Peter as the fisher of men (Luke 5:1–11).

Although the presentation of the Twelve, the apostles, and Peter in Acts represents Luke's own theological interpretation and is not without need of extensive investigation by exegetes and theologians, Paul's letters, written fully a generation before Acts, attest to the authoritative position enjoyed by Peter and the apostles within the Church of his times. Even in the epistle to the Galatians, in which he sets out to maintain his independence from Jerusalem, Paul has to explain that he went to visit Cephas (1:18), and that he laid his gospel before the apostles (Gal 2:2). As a matter of fact, Paul calls Peter and others of the apostles "pillars" of the Church (Gal 2:9; cf. 1 Tim 3:15). Paul mentions Cephas and the Twelve as first among the official witnesses to the Resurrection (1 Cor 15:5). Indeed, in his *apologia pro vita sua* (1 Cor 9), Paul cites the rights of the other apostles as justification for his own rights as an apostle.

If Paul mentions these other apostles, it is in support of his own apostolic rights. Paul considers himself as an authority within the Church, with responsibility and rights similar to those of Peter and the others from the Jerusalem community (Gal 2:1–10). Even as they, he has had an experience of the risen Jesus (1 Cor 15:8). No less than they is Paul the bearer of the Spirit (1 Cor 7:40). Paul's understanding of the functional similarity between himself and Peter is given a different expression by Luke in the Acts of the Apostles. Luke's triple account of Paul's conversion (Acts 9; 22; 26) is intended to portray Paul's Easter experience and qualify him for his mission to the Gentiles. If Peter serves as chief spokesman of the gospel in Jerusalem and Judea (Acts 1:8), it is Paul who carries the gospel to the ends of the earth. The legitimacy of his Gentile mission is accordingly recognized by Peter and the apostles of Jerusalem, as the narrative of the Council of Jerusalem dramatically testifies. The authority enjoyed by Paul and Peter within the Church of New Testament times is effectively confirmed by the New Testament documents which have been patronymically ascribed to them (probably 1,2 Tim, Tit, 2 Pet; and possibly Eph, Col, 2 Thes, 1 Pet).

The Holy Spirit

In sum, the basic bearers of authority within the Church of New Testament times were the Scriptures, the words of Jesus, and the apostles (the

Twelve, especially Cephas, and Paul). However, the authority *par excellence* and the ground of all other authority is the Spirit. Paul's assertion "I have the Spirit of God" (1 Cor 7:40) serves as the expression of his conviction that it is from the Spirit that all authority flows. In a statement that would become classic, the author of 2 Timothy wrote that "All scripture is inspired by God and profitable for teaching, for reproof, for correction, and for training in righteousness . . ." (2 Tim 3:16). Although the author's language is borrowed from the philosophic-religious vocabulary of ancient Hellenism, his conviction that the words of the prophets, set down in writing, come from the spirit of God is at one with Jewish and Christian tradition. Thus Mark 12:36 indicates that David was "inspired by the Holy Spirit" when he declared the words of Psalm 110:1. Several years later, the author of 2 Peter forcefully reminded his audience that all Scripture is inspired by the Spirit: "First of all you must understand this, that no prophecy of scripture is a matter of one's own interpretation, because no prophecy ever came by the impulse of man, but men moved by the Holy Spirit spoke from God" (2 Pet 1:20–21).

Each of the evangelists offers a portrayal of the Spirit's descent upon Jesus at the outset of the public ministry. Although the theological interests of each writer are apparent in his description of the baptismal scene (Matt 3:13–17; Mark 1:9–11; Luke 3:21–22; John 1:29–34), the four accounts are at one in focusing upon the coming of the Spirit of God to Jesus. Luke reflects still further upon the significance of the event by linking the baptismal account to his programmatic account of Jesus' preaching in the synagogue of Nazareth (Luke 4:16–22). In parallel fashion, the Lucan narrative of the Pentecost event identifies the Twelve apostles as men filled with the Holy Spirit (Acts 2). As he had used a passage from Isaiah (Isa 61:1–2) to underscore and interpret the descent of the Spirit on Jesus, so Luke has used a passage from Joel (Joel 2:28–32) to underscore and interpret the descent of the Spirit on the Twelve. The phenomenon of glossolalia indicates the purpose of this Spirit gift, whose authority among the Twelve is pointedly emphasized in the apostolic letter to the Christians of Antioch, Syria, and Cilicia: "For it has seemed good to the Holy Spirit and to us to lay upon you no greater burden than these necessary things" (Acts 15:28).

The Lucan Paul is no less a bearer of the Spirit. To highlight the gift of the Spirit to Paul, Luke concludes his first account of the conversion narrative with a description of Paul's recovery from blindness, a sign that he has been filled with the Holy Spirit (Acts 9:17–18). It is clear that, for Luke, the Spirit thus given is the eschatological Spirit of prophecy. It is no less clear that the Spirit is one of the gifts by which the Church is constituted, according to the understanding of the author of the Fourth Gospel. The role of the Church-constituting Spirit is indicated in John's account of the Farewell Discourse. In this account the departing Jesus speaks of the coming gift as follows: "He will teach you all things, and bring to your remembrance all that I have said to you" (John 14:26). In short, although the pages of the New Testament point to several bearers of authority within the Church, there is but one source of authority, namely the very Spirit of God.

The Scriptures

Among the bearers of authority especially valued by the Church of New Testament times, the Scriptures merit particular consideration insofar as they were *written* texts of which the early churches made abundant use. The utility of the Scriptures was underscored by the author of the second letter to Timothy who wrote that: "All scripture is inspired by God and profitable for teaching, for reproof, for correction, and for training in righteousness, that the man of God may be complete, equipped for every good work" (2 Tim 3:16–17). The author of these words would have his audience know that it is not simply the Scriptures in general which are useful, but that every passage of the Scriptures is useful. Redundant emphasis as well as the apposite purpose clause shows that the author of the letter has a halakic use of the Scriptures in mind. He is not so much interested in stressing that the Scriptures are inspired by God as he is in suggesting that the Scriptures are a useful guide to Christian conduct because they are "inspired by God."

That some of the early Christian churches used the Scriptures, almost in catechetical fashion, in order to provide guidelines for conduct is further suggested by Matthew's Sermon on the Mount (Matt 5 – 7) and the discussion as to the greatest commandment in the Law, of which some version is found in each of the Synoptics (Matt 22:34–40; Mark 12:28–34; Luke 10:25–28). Yet it is not only insofar as they provided a basis for some limited Christian halakah, during the Church's formative years, that the Scriptures were found useful in early Christianity.

Evidence that the reading of the Scriptures was a feature of early Christian liturgical assemblies is not particularly evident in the New Testament, but there are traces of the practice nonetheless. Revelation 1:3 is a sure indication of the author's awareness that the prophets were read publicly among the Christians. Otto Michel has suggested that 1 Timothy 4:13–15 offers evidence that a homily followed upon the reading of the Scriptures in the early Church. Admittedly this sparse evidence attests to a practice within the Church at a relatively advanced stage of its early development. However, the respect paid to the Scriptures by Christians and the general similarity between the earliest gatherings of the Christian assembly and the Jewish synagogal services make it quite likely that the reading of the Scriptures was one of the focal points of early Christian "liturgical gatherings." Indeed, the very first generation of Palestinian Christians were Christian Jews, for whom the reading of the Scriptures would have constituted the normal religious service. These facts serve as the basic ground of argumentation for those authors who hold that three among the Gospels, namely Matthew, Mark, and John were developed by way of commentary on the Jewish lectionary.

If the evidence for the early Church's use of the Scriptures in its own liturgy—that is, apart from the Jewish synagogal services in which the Christians of the first generation(s) participated—is sparse indeed, there is more than enough New Testament evidence to justify the inference that the Scriptures served as a norm for theologizing and a source for teaching within the churches of the earliest Christian generations. Paul's citation of a creedal formula with the expression "according to the Scriptures" (*kata tas graphas*) in each of its two parts (1 Cor 15:3–4) shows the influence of the Scriptures in the articulation of the Christian faith. In this creedal formula the Scriptures are indicated as a hermeneutical device for interpreting the death and resurrection of Jesus. The fulfillment formulas of Matthew and John—for example, Matthew 8:17 and Isaiah 53:4 with respect to Jesus' miracles; John 19:37 and Exodus 12:46 with respect to Jesus' death—patently reflect a pattern of systematic theological reflection upon the Scriptures in an attempt to interpret the life and death of Jesus of Nazareth. The pattern of fulfillment formulas found in each of these Gospels may well point to the existence of a Matthean and/or a Johannine school, well versed in the study of the Scriptures. Yet even apart from the existence of these hypothetical schools, the abundance of scriptural citations, references, and allusions in the pages of the New Testament is so evident as to establish beyond any reasonable doubt that the Scriptures were authoritative for the early Christians.

To make mention of the early churches' estimation of the Scriptures as authoritative almost seems to imply that "the Scriptures" constitute a rather well-defined entity. Such is far from the reality of the matter. True, Luke 11:51 seems to indicate that its author was familiar with the Jewish tradition (cf. 4 Esd 14:41–46) which would eventually accept a twenty-four-book canon from Genesis (which narrates the death of Abel) to 2 Chronicles (which narrates the death of Zechariah). The twenty-four books would include: the Torah (Genesis, Exodus, Leviticus, Numbers, Deuteronomy), the Prophets (Joshua, Jude, 1,2 Samuel, 1,2 Kings, Isaiah, Jeremiah, Ezekiel, 12 Prophets), and the Writings (Psalms, Proverbs, Job, Scrolls—Canticles, Ruth, Lamentations, Ecclesiastes, Esther—Daniel, Ezekiel, Nehemiah, 1,2 Chronicles). Nevertheless the small letter of Jude cites both the Apocalypse of Moses (Jude 8–9) and 1 Enoch (Jude 14–15) in a reverential manner even though neither of these writings would eventually enter into the canon of the Scriptures. "The Scriptures," therefore, represents connotative rather than denotative language. It represents the written and authoritative word of God rather than any specific material content.

Liturgical Readings

If it is likely that the Scriptures were read to assembled bodies of Christian believers during the formative years of the Church, it is quite apparent that at least some of the churches had also acquired the practice of reading Christian documents in very early times. Paul's first letter to the Thessalonians, the oldest book among those that constitute our New Testament, concludes with the exhortation that the "letter be read to all the brethren" (1 Thes 5:27). Before adding a personal signature, the author of the letter to the Colossians exhorts his audience as follows: "And when this letter has been read among you, have it read also in the church of the Laodiceans; and see that you read also the letter from Laodicea" (Col 4:16). While the authorship of Colossians is a matter of scholarly dispute, and whereas neither of these passages can be taken as a sure indication that the celebration of the Eucharistic synaxis immediately followed upon the reading of the letters, these two exhortations clearly show that during the second Christian generation at least three of the Pauline churches knew the practice of the public reading of Paul's epistles, namely, the churches of Thessalonica, Colossae, and Laodicea.

Other epistles in the Pauline corpus are less explicit in this respect, but some of them do serve to support the contention that the reading of the letters was not limited to the three churches that have been mentioned. Thus, despite an English translation (Revised Standard Version, New American Bible) that is more precise than the Greek text necessarily calls for (the Greek anagnōsis literally means "reading," not necessarily the "reading of the Scriptures"), 1 Timothy 4:13 suggests that Christian writings were read in the liturgical gatherings of the Christian churches. The use of the second person plural in 1 Timothy 6:21 (cf. 2 Tim 4:22; Tit 3:15) suggests that the document is intended for a larger audience than the beloved co-worker of Paul to whom it is apparently addressed. The presence of liturgical greetings at the close of 1 Thessalonians (5:28) as well as at the end of so many other letters in the New Testament suggests that these letters were destined for public reading before an assembled body of the brethren.

Thus it is difficult to take issue with the claim that Paul's letters, whether authentic or not, were intended by their author for public reading. The Gospels were written much later than the authentic Pauline letters and are much too long for a single-session public reading. However, history-of-tradition criticism suggests that many of the gospel traditions were shaped by liturgical narration (oral tradition in a liturgical context), if not by a liturgical reading of a text. Nevertheless an exhortative rubric in Mark 13:14 (par. Matt 24:15) shows that Jesus' eschatological discourse, if not the entire Gospel of Mark, was read before the Christian assembly. The redactor's aside shows that the reader should be attentive to his speech, since it is he who is responsible for the interpretation of the passage by reason of his reading of the text. Perhaps the parenthetical charge may be a warning to the reader lest he apply the eschatological logia too easily to the Romans, among whom Mark is supposed by some to have lived when he wrote his gospel. At any rate, the directive, not embodied within the text itself, reminds us of one of the significant activities of the early Christian churches.

Tradition

From the very outset, the Christian churches were concerned with the faithful transmission of tradition—that is, the passing along of teaching and practices. Nowhere is this concern more evident than in the writings of Paul, the former rabbi. In 1 Corinthians 11:23 and again in 1 Corinthians 15:1–3, Paul's language reflects the technical language of tradition. His "received" (*parelabon*) corresponds to the Hebrew *qibbel;* his "delivered" (*paredōka*) to the Hebrew *masar*. The Hebrew terms were used in rabbinic circles to denote the process whereby a rabbi faithfully handed on the tradition he had received from his rabbinic master to his own disciples. The Mishnaic tractate *Pirke Aboth* ("Sayings of the Fathers") is the result of the use of such procedures in rabbinical circles.

To suggest that Christians, even those in the Matthean and Johannine schools, made use of the full gamut of procedures developed by the Jewish rabbis in order to assure the accurate transmission of tradition is to go beyond the evidence that is available to us. Nevertheless Paul's use of the technical rabbinic language shows that both he and the churches to which he addressed himself were concerned with the faithful transmission of the traditions about Jesus. To affirm this early church concern for the accurate transmission of its tradition is, of course, not to suggest that the tradition enjoyed a degree of accuracy that would be required of modern historians. At most it consisted of stereotyped and easily retained formulas that were easily and accurately passed along from one generation of Christian preachers to the next.

In a later period the deutero-Pauline epistles, born of a need to direct the ordering of the Church, showed a similar concern for the faithful transmission of Christian tradition. Much has been written about the formula "The saying is sure" (*ho pistos ho logos*). The expression, which occurs with some frequency in the Pastoral epistles (1 Tim 1:15; 3:1; 4:9; 2 Tim 2:11; Tit 3:8; cf. Tit 1:13), is used in connection with short summaries of traditional material. The formula has been appended to this material, either by way of introduction or by way of conclusion, to proclaim that the traditional material has been faithfully handed down and ought to be retained. The author's use of the stereotyped expression bespeaks his claim that his teaching is faithful to the tradition which he has received.

The technical language of Paul's epistles and the stereotyped expressions of the Pastoral epistles provides us with a clear indication of the New Testament authors' concern for the faithful transmission of tradition as well as with a clue to the esteem with which the churches of New Testament times valued the traditions that had been faithfully transmitted. This insight is supported by Paul's use of the word "tradition" (*paradōsis*) in reference to Christian tradition in 1 Corinthians 11:23 and 2 Thessalonians 2:15; 3:6, in a way that recalls the use of the same terminology for Jewish traditions in Galatians 1:14 and Mark 7:3.

In addition to the use of technical formulas, there are other more subtle indications which show that the authors of the early Christian churches were aware that a Christian tradition was in the process of formation and that they were responsible for passing on these traditions in an accurate manner. One need only mention Paul's citation of a primitive creedal fragment in 1 Thessalonians 1:9–10 and Matthew's retention of an archaic *Q* formula in 12:28. One could also refer to the prologue to Luke's Gospel (Luke 1:1–4). The relatively late exhortations to be wary of false teachers could also be cited as an indication of a pervasive concern for the faithful transmission of traditional teaching among the churches of New Testament times. In this respect the farewell discourse which Luke attributes to Paul offers a remarkable case in point (Acts 20:17–35, esp. vv. 29–30).

The Collection of Writings

If the Christian churches of the first three Christian generations were concerned with the faithful transmission of traditional teaching, they were also well aware that it was possible for those Christian writings which were read in public assembly to be misinterpreted. Indeed, it would appear that the interpretation of Paul's writings, our oldest extant Christian documents, was always somewhat problematic. The apostle was fully aware that his positions could be misconstrued (cf. Rom 6:1, 15, etc.). The author of the epistle of James took issue with a Pauline contention pushed to a somewhat awkward conclusion (Jas 2:18–26). Indeed, it would appear that the most recent words presently contained in the New Testament are a warning against the misinterpretation of Paul's letters. As he brings his "letter" to a close, the author of 2 Peter writes: "So also our beloved brother Paul wrote to you according to the wisdom given him, speaking of this as he does in all his letters. There are some things in them hard to understand, which the ignorant and unstable twist to their own destruction, as they do the other scriptures" (2 Pet 3:15–16).

Some commentators have cited this passage as still another indication that Paul's letters were publicly read in the churches. While there is no serious reason to take issue with this conclusion, the passage is interesting from other points of view as well. First of all, it compares Paul's letters to "the other scriptures." Paul surely would have avoided such a description of his occasional letters to the churches, but it is clear that within a relatively short period of time after Paul's death his letters had a function within the Christian churches similar to that of the Scriptures. Secondly, the author's manner of speaking of "all his letters" presupposes that Paul's letters had been collected together. There is no way of telling whether the author of 2 Peter was cognizant of fewer or of more Pauline letters than are presently contained in the Pauline corpus, but his words do seem to acknowledge the existence of some sort of a collection of Paul's letters.

It cannot be maintained that any of the authors, not even the author of 2 Peter, who wrote the documents presently collated in the New Testament, had any idea that they were contributing to a fixed collection which would enjoy a normative function in the Church of later times. Nevertheless the author of 2 Peter has demonstrated an awareness that would eventually contribute to the fixation of a New Testament canon. Some Christian writings were accorded a status similar to that which the Scriptures had enjoyed from the first formative years of the Christian churches. Then, for a variety of reasons, these Christian writings were gathered together into collections whose contents were determined by the Church. These processes contributed to the formation of the canon of the New Testament during the first centuries of the Christian Church.

II. CHRISTIAN SCRIPTURES

It has sometimes been suggested that the fixation of the Jewish canon of the Scriptures at Jabne was at least partially in reaction to the appearance of esteemed writings within various Christian communities. Within Judaism the emergence of Christianity was a sectarian phenomenon. Gradually, however, the dominant streams of Judaism dissociated from themselves those Christian Jews who had accepted Jesus as Messiah. Both Luke (6:22) and John (9:22) allude to the late-first-century exclusion of Jesus-confessing Jews from the synagogue. This "excommunication" was associated with a change in the formulation of the Great Benedictions. In each worship service of the Pharisaic synagogue, the formal prayer known as the Great or Eighteen Benedictions played an important role. At Jabne, the wording of the twelfth benediction was reformulated so as to constitute a curse upon the Minim (Christian heretics). A Christian invited to pronounce the benedictions would be unable to proclaim the twelfth. Thus identified, he would be excluded from the synagogue.

Even earlier, congregations of Christians had developed which were quite independent of the Jewish synagogue (1 Thes 1:1). Undoubtedly this phenomenon first occurred outside Palestine, but it was parallel to the formation of identifiable groups of Jewish Christians within Palestine. Within Palestine the double movement of Christian consciousness of its proper identity and the Jewish exclusion from the synagogue of Jesus-confessing Jews led to the recognition of Christianity as a phenomenon distinct from Judaism, certainly from the type of Pharisaic Judaism, heir to the legacy of Hillel, which would dominate at Jabne. Jabne's fixation of a canon of Scriptures developed partially as a response to the Christian movement. It was imperative for a Judaism that wanted to build a fence around the Law to exclude from its ambiance Christian "prophetic" and "apocalyptic" writings.

Within Christianity, almost as variegated in form as was Judaism of the first century, there developed an ever-increasing esteem for the letters that had been written by Paul, the writings that gave testimony to Jesus, and texts that emanated from Christian prophets. We ought not arrive too quickly at the conclusion that the Christian communities of the late first century and the beginning of the second century were eager to qualify the documents produced by Christian writings as Scripture. In fact, the opposite would seem to be the case. There was a reluctance to equate Christian writings with the Scriptures. This reluctance is due, first of all, to the fact that the Christian churches of the first several generations already possessed "the Scriptures." These scriptures (*hai graphai*) were those writings traditionally identified as the Scriptures. Roughly equivalent with what Christians today identify as the Old Testament, the Scriptures continued to be valued by the Christian churches as the inspired word of God. Among these churches there was a decided disinclination to have a competing set of scriptures. Nevertheless, the fact that the Scriptures (of the "Old Testament") did not become a quantitatively limited entity within Judaism until after the effective separation between Judaism and Christianity left the door somewhat ajar so that Christian communities might consider the writings of their own inspired authors as Scripture.

There was, however, another factor which impeded the recognition of Christian documents as Scripture. This was the value the churches ascribed to the living voice of Spirit-inspired prophecy. For example, Papias (ca. 60–130), an early bishop of Hierapolis in Asia Minor, is quoted as esteeming the living word above the written word. Papias' important five-volume work, *Interpretation of the Oracles of the Lord,* has been preserved for us only insofar as it has been quoted by Irenaeus (ca. 130–ca. 200) and Eusebius (ca. 260–ca. 340), the great Church historian. Eusebius quotes Papias as having said: "For I did not suppose that information from books would help me so much as the word of a living and surviving voice" (*Ecclesiastical History* III, 39, 4). Although we have only a secondhand witness to this testimony, Papias' words epitomize the high value accorded to the Spirit-inspired spoken word during the first century of the Church's existence. Subsequent developments would ensure that the esteem in which the spoken word was held would be transferred to those Christian writings in which that spoken word was preserved. Thus even Christian writings would come to be called "the Scriptures."

In fact, this tendency is seen even in some of the more recent writings included in our New Testament. For example, 2 Peter 3:16, which some authors would date as late as 150 or even 180, compares Paul's letters with "the other scriptures" (*hai loipai graphai*). In the deutero-Pauline first letter to Timothy we read: "For the scripture says (*legei gar hē graphē*): 'You shall not muzzle an ox when it is treading out the grain,' and 'The laborer deserves his wages'" (1 Tim 5:18). This first citation is of Deuteronomy 25:4, clearly a passage of Scripture. The second citation is a logion of Jesus, otherwise preserved at Luke 10:7. While it may be that the author of 1 Timothy was citing from memory and thus confused an element of the Jesus tradition with the Scriptures, his text nevertheless qualifies a logion of Jesus as Scripture. The tendency to qualify in this fashion the logia of the Jesus tradition would continue to develop during the time of the Apostolic Fathers.

At the Turn of the First Century

In a letter written about A.D. 96 in the name of the church of Rome to Corinth, where a struggle was ensuing because of the deposition of some presbyters, Clement of Rome wrote: "Let us do what is written . . . especially remembering the words of the Lord Jesus, which he spoke when he was teaching gentleness and patience. . . . Be merciful, so that you may obtain mercy; forgive, so that it may be forgiven you; as you do, thus it will be done to you; as you give, thus it will be given to you; as you judge, thus you will be judged; as you are kind, thus kindness will be shown you; with the measure you measure, by it will be measured to you" (1 Clem 13). Clement's exhortation echoes the words of Jesus attested by both the Matthean and the Lucan versions of the Sermon on the Mount (Matt 5:7; 6:14–15; 7:1–2, 12; Luke 6:31, 36–38). The passage is introduced by significant formulas, "what is written," and "the words of the Lord Jesus," but its words are not unequivocally identified as Scripture or Gospel.

The only time that Clement explicitly mentions the Gospel as such is by way of allusion to Philippians 4:15. He wrote: "Take up the epistle of the blessed Paul the apostle. What did he first write you at 'the beginning of the gospel'? With true spiritual insight he wrote you about himself and Cephas and Apollos, because even though you had made yourselves partisans . . ." (1 Clem 47:1–3). In this passage Clement not only makes use of the borrowed expression "the beginning of the gospel" (cf. Phil 4:15), he also apparently refers to 1 Corinthians 1:12; 3:22. In fact, this is but one of several allusions made by Clement to Paul's first letter to the Corinthians. Such allusions are naturally quite appropriate in a letter written to the same church approximately forty years after the apostle's correspondence. In his own letter Clement also shows some awareness of Galatians, Philippians, Ephesians, Hebrews (esp. in 1 Clem 36) and Paul's letter to the Romans. After paraphrasing Romans 1:29–32 in 1 Clement 35:5–6, Clement continued with "For the scripture says . . ." Thus it appears that even though Clement highly valued the authority of the apostle Paul, he was wont to distinguish Paul's letters from the Scriptures.

Likewise associated with the name of Clement is the so-called Second Epistle of Clement. In fact, the origin of this document is unknown, but it may well be the earliest surviving Christian sermon, apart from those contained in the New Testament itself. In its description of the Christian life and the necessity of repentance, the sermon makes frequent allusion to the words of the Lord. The author writes, "The Lord said, 'If then the wolves rend the lambs?' Jesus said to Peter, 'Let the lambs not fear the wolves after they die; and you, fear not those who kill you and cannot do more to you, but fear him who, after you die, has power over soul and body to cast them into the Gehenna of fire' " (2 Clem 4:5). Here we recognize a tradition of the words of the Lord to which Luke 10:3 and 12:4–5 also bear witness. Some passages in the homily have a Matthean ring. Still others seem to be a pastiche of Pauline material. For example, "I do not suppose that you are ignorant that the living 'Church is the body of Christ.' For the scripture says, 'God made man male and female': the male is Christ, the female the Church. And furthermore the books and the apostles declared that the Church is not merely present but was from the beginning. . . ." (2 Clem 14). In this passage, which strongly echoes Ephesians, the unknown author cites Genesis

1:27 with the stereotyped lemma, "For the scripture says." This classical introductory formula is similar to one found in 2 Clement 2:4, where we read: "Another scripture also says (*kai hetera de graphē legei*) 'I come not to call the righteous but sinners.'" The quotation is most likely of that logion of Jesus preserved in Matthew 9:13. Citing a logion of Jesus in this fashion immediately after a passage from Isaiah, 2 Clement gives evidence of the tendency we have already identified in 1 Timothy 5:18, the tendency to qualify the words of Jesus as "Scripture."

The so-called Epistle of Barnabas, written anonymously sometime between A.D. 70 and 100, probably in Alexandria toward the latter date, finds an esoteric sense in the Scriptures which is then used as a testimony for Christianity and against Judaism. Among Christian writings the author shows some knowledge of the traditions contained in Matthew and John, as well as the Pastoral epistles. His references to the Passion of Jesus are Matthean in tone (cf. Ep Barn 5:9; 7:3). At one point he uses the lemma "it is written" (Ep Barn 4:14) to introduce a tradition found in Matthew 20:16 or 22:14. Elsewhere (Ep Barn 16:5) the lemma is used to introduce a quotation from 1 Enoch, a lengthy Jewish pseudepigraphical writing. Hence the use of the lemma is not of particular importance as an indication of the status of the Matthean tradition in the eyes of the one who composed the Epistle of Barnabas.

The *Didache,* or *Teaching of the Twelve Apostles,* is another early anonymous writing whose origins are clouded in uncertainty. The weight of evidence seems to suggest that it is a late first century or early second century Syrian document. Containing but sixteen chapters, it is a relatively short treatise on Christian morals and Church tradition. In a fashion similar to that of Clement, the Didachist uses the words of Jesus contained in the Sermon on the Mount in his moral exhortation. He writes, for example: "Bless those who persecute you, and pray for your enemies; fast for those who persecute you. For what credit is it if you love those who love you? Do not the gentiles do the same? But as for you, love those who hate you, and you will have no enemy" (*Did* 1:3). The words recall those found in Matthew 5:44, 46, 47; 7:12; Luke 6:31–33. Toward the end of his work, the Didachist writes: "Do not reprove one another in wrath, but in peace, as you have it in the gospel, and let no one speak to anyone who wrongs his neighbor, nor let that one be heard among you until he repents. But perform your prayers and alms and all your actions as you have it in the gospel of the Lord" (*Did* 15:3–4). Since these words echo those found in Matthew 5:22–26; 18:15–35, it is highly probable that when the Didachist refers to what Christians have "in the gospel of our Lord" (*en tō euaggeliō tou kuriou hēmōn*), he is referring to Matthew. On first impression, it would appear that the Didachist has made use of the written text of Matthew. That may well be the case, but J. P. Audet, who published a critical edition of the text in 1958, is inclined to the view that the Didachist has made use of a written Gospel text only for chapters 11–16, the earlier chapters of his work being reliant upon an oral gospel tradition. In any event, it is clear that it is the word of the

17

Lord, rather than a written document, which constitutes the primary authority for the author of the *Didache*. His catechesis suggests familiarity with the words of Jesus presently contained in Matthew, Luke, and John. The Fourth Gospel's traditions must be cited as lying within the purview of the Didachist, insofar as his version of the eucharistic prayers (*Did* 9–10) seemingly alludes to the Johannine discourse on the Bread of Life (John 6) and Jesus' high priestly prayer (John 17).

The Didachist's contemporary, Ignatius of Antioch (ca. 35–ca. 107), is best known for his seven letters, written to the churches of Ephesus, Magnesia, Tralles, Rome, Philadelphia, Smyrna, and to his brother bishop St. Polycarp. These were penned while Ignatius was enroute from Antioch to Rome, where he would suffer martyrdom. The letters are inspired by those of Paul. Among those of the apostle most cited were 1 Corinthians and Ephesians, two letters in which the unity of the Church is most strongly emphasized. The letters of Ignatius also contain passages which seem to indicate that their author was conversant with the Gospels, especially John and Matthew, perhaps Luke. Thus Ephesians 5:1 speaks of the Eucharist as the "bread of God" (cf. John 6:51–58) and Smyrna 1:1 notes that Jesus was baptized by John so that all righteousness might be fulfilled by him (cf. Matt 3:15). Among scholars a dispute exists as to whether Ignatius knew our present written Gospels, or whether he was merely acquainted with the traditions upon which the Gospels are based. In any event it is clear that Ignatius particularly appreciated those words of the Lord which could be used in pastoral exhortation. Indeed, he cites the authority of the Lord as superior to that "which stands written in the records." Although Ignatius thus relegates the Scriptures (the Old Testament) to an inferior status, he nowhere identifies any of our New Testament writings as Scripture.

Papias and Polycarp

The fourth-century historian Eusebius of Caesarea refers to both Clement and Ignatius, as well as to Papias, bishop of Hierapolis. In his *Ecclesiastical History* (A.D. 312) Eusebius cites Papias as follows:

> This also the Presbyter used to say, "When Mark became Peter's interpreter, he wrote down accurately, although not in order, all that he remembers of what was said or done by the Lord. For he had not heard the Lord nor followed Him, but later, as I have said, he did Peter, who made his teaching fit his needs without, as it were, making any arrangement of the Lord's oracles, so that Mark made no mistake in thus writing some things down as he remembered them. For to one thing he gave careful attention, to omit nothing of what he heard and to falsify nothing in this." Now, this has been related by Papias regarding Mark, and regarding Matthew he has spoken as follows: "Now Matthew collected the oracles in the Hebrew language, and each one interpreted them as he was able" (*Ecclesiastical History* III, 39, 15–16).

From what we know, Papias' exposition seems not to have cited Luke, but Papias may have been familiar with the Johannine tradition. The bishop of Hierapolis speaks of Christ as "The Truth" (John 14:6). Moreover, his criticism of Mark's lack of order may well result from an unfavorable comparison between the Second and Fourth Gospels, even though other authors allege that the critical remark made apropos of Mark results from a comparison between Mark and Matthew. In any event Papias' testimony is among our oldest surviving accounts of the composition of Mark and Matthew. It is clear that Papias intended to confirm, on the basis of a tradition which predated him ("The presbyter used to say"), that Mark's Gospel contains Peter's catechesis.

It is, however, much more difficult to ascertain with precision the point Papias is making apropos Matthew. While his remarks on the composition of Matthew "in the Hebrew dialect" (*hebraidi dialektō*) are generally taken as an indication of a Matthean composition in Aramaic, the popular language in Palestine at the time of Jesus, there are some authors who claim that the phrase refers to the style rather than to the language of the Matthean composition. Moreover, there is some dispute among scholars as to the precise meaning of "the oracles" (*ta logia*). Until recently, most scholars have taken "the oracles" to mean the First Gospel, which contains extensive discourse material and which is structured along the lines of five major sermons (Matt 5–7; 10; 13; 18; 23–25). More recently some scholars have suggested that Papias was making reference either to a collection of Jesus' sayings (therefore, a document somewhat akin to the reconstructed Q source) or a collection of messianic oracles similar to one that existed at Qumran (4QF1). If either of the latter two opinions is to be accepted, then the oracles which Papias ascribes to Matthew lie at the origin of either the discourses or the fulfillment citations presently found in the First Gospel.

Polycarp of Smyrna (ca. 69–ca. 155) is also cited in Eusebius' *Ecclesiastical History*. Fortunately his Epistle to the Philippians has survived. It contains important testimony on the books of the New Testament. In his letter Polycarp cites, for example, 1 John 4:3. An exact citation of Matthew 13:14–15 in Ep Phil 6:2 seems to suggest that Polycarp had a written copy of the Lord's words, perhaps Matthew itself, at his disposition. The use of the introductory lemma, "The Lord said," to introduce Matthew 26:41 in Ep Phil 7:2 confirms the impression. Along with "the Lord himself," Polycarp cites "the apostles, who brought us the gospel," and "the prophets, who foretold the coming of the Lord," as his authorities.

In Polycarp's letter, the times of the apostles are sharply distinguished from the author's own era. Indeed, Polycarp does not ascribe the epistles of the venerable Ignatius to the apostles even though he considers that these letters "contain faith, endurance and all the edification which pertains to our Lord" (Ep Phil 13:2). On the other hand, Polycarp seems definitely to include Paul among the apostles. Certainly Polycarp knew of the writings of Paul. He clearly alluded to Romans, 1 Corinthians, Galatians, Ephesians,

Philippians, 2 Thessalonians, and 1,2 Timothy. In a commentary upon the Pauline letters, Polycarp notes that, "When Paul was among you in the presence of the men of that time, he accurately and steadfastly taught the word of truth, and when he was absent he wrote you letters; by studying them you will be able to build yourselves up into the faith given you" (Ep Phil 3:2). The passage, with its reference to Paul's "letters" in the plural, seems to suggest that Polycarp knows of a collection of Paul's letters.

Later in his letter, Polycarp writes: "As it is said in these scriptures, 'Be angry and sin not' and 'Let not the sun go down on your wrath.'" The maxims are to be found in Ephesians 4:26. Thus, on face value, Polycarp's comment suggests that he considers Ephesians as Scripture. However, the first of the maxims is a citation of Psalm 4:4. It is, therefore, not impossible that Polycarp mistakenly believed that he was citing the traditional Scripture (the Old Testament) when he offered the double maxim in Ep Phil 12.

During the lifetime of Polycarp, Christianity was making inroads among some of the educated classes within the Roman Empire. At the same time the Church came into conflict with the state over its very right to exist. Among the Apologists who arose during these times to defend the Church by dispelling slander and explaining its doctrines by applying the Scriptures to Christianity, the most famous was undoubtedly Justin Martyr (ca. 100–ca. 165). Justin was the first orthodox Christian theologian to possess what may be called a doctrine of Holy Scripture. Justin's *Dialogue with the Jew Tryphon*, written just a few years before his death, was inspired by a dispute with Tryphon that had taken place about twenty-five years earlier. In this work Justin explains that his Christian faith is built on the Scriptures (that is, the Old Testament). He also makes reference to the memoirs (*apomnemoneumata*) composed "by the apostles or those who followed them" (*Dial* 103:8). From the quotations offered (in *Dial* 103:3 and 104:1), it is clear that Justin understands the memoirs to be what we call the Synoptic Gospels. In an earlier writing, the *Apology* (ca. 155), Justin had noted that the memoirs of the apostles or the writings of the prophets are read liturgically during Sunday worship (*Apol* 67:3). Apparently Justin did not include the Fourth Gospel among the memoirs of the apostles, even though he occasionally cites a passage seemingly from John with one or another distinctive introductory lemma—"Christ said" (*ho christos eipen*), or "it is written in the gospel" (*en tō euaggeliō gegraptai*). While the passages thus introduced (*Apol* 61:4; *Dial* 100:1) are most easily explained as reminiscences of the Fourth Gospel, it is not totally certain that Justin is dependent upon John. His fashion of citing the words of the Lord, however, seems to indicate that he puts them on a par with the Scriptures of the Old Testament.

In summarizing the development of the prehistory of the New Testament during the time of the Apostolic Fathers and the first Apologists, one would have to note the authority enjoyed by Paul, whose letters are cited and alluded to with some frequency. The words of Jesus are likewise cited, particularly in a context of hortatory or consolatory paraenesis, or to assist the Church to decide practical and moral issues in its life. The normative significance of the Lord's words is directly dependent upon the Lord himself. By and large this normative quality is not transferred to the documents which have preserved the words. Nevertheless the Christian churches were aware that the words of the Lord had been written down. Consequently, some of them are cited as Scripture. This designation provides a theological qualification and a type of authority for the tradition of the Lord's words. Given the significance of the words of the Lord, it is particularly the Gospel of Matthew which enjoyed authority, much more so than either Mark or Luke. Indeed, in the Syrian church Matthew continued to enjoy the reputation of being *the* Gospel until the fifth century. The Gospel of John made but limited impact on the Greater Church (Ignatius' *hē katholikē ekklēsia*). In the middle of the second century Justin Martyr did not even include it among "the memoirs of the apostles." These memoirs, along with the writings of the prophets, were used in the Sunday liturgical services of the Christian churches.

III. CLOSED COLLECTIONS

It is in reaction to Marcion (died ca. 160) that the Greater Church first began to develop closed collections of the Scriptures. Marcion's writings, the most important of which is the *Antitheses,* have all been lost. Yet it is possible to describe his fundamental positions on the basis of descriptions provided by the ecclesiastical writers who took issue with him. From these sources it would appear that Marcion's central idea is the radical incompatibility between Christianity and Judaism. The Christian God of love has nothing to do with the God of law and wrath, to which the Scriptures of the Old Testament attest. Criticism of the God of the Old Testament had already begun before Marcion—for example, with the Valentinians—but Marcion brought matters to a head by developing a collection of writings designed to provide a substitute for the Scriptures of the Old Testament. As a matter of fact, Marcion was so opposed to the Old Testament that he even rejected the allegorical type of exegesis by means of which many of his Christian contemporaries were able to find Christian significance in the traditional Scriptures.

Marcion's version of the gospel stands in a double opposition to the world. It is opposed both to the Law and its legalistic righteousness, and to those earthly desires which keep humanity in servitude to the world. To the extent that Marcion's gospel reflects a freedom from the Law, it is akin to Paul; to the extent that it represents redemption from a state of being lost, his gospel is somewhat akin to the message of Jesus himself. From the writings of Tertullian, we know that Marcion's Bible consisted of two parts, a single gospel and a collection of the writings of Paul, known as the *Apostolicon.* The *Apostolicon* included ten Pauline letters—Galatians, 1,2

Corinthians, Romans, 1,2 Thessalonians, Laodiceans (our canonical Ephesians), Colossians, Philemon, Philippians—that is, all but the Pastorals and Hebrews.

In fact, it was Marcion's Paulinism which led him to include within his Bible a gospel as well as the Pauline letters. These letters frequently make mention of "the gospel" or "my gospel." Marcion interpreted those references as references to a book. He was, in fact, the first author to take "gospel" in the sense of a book. Marcion was, however, convinced that the evangelists were largely blinded by remnants of Jewish influence. Thus he chose to include only a highly bowdlerized version of Luke in his Bible. In regard to this, Tertullian has written that "Marcion expressly and openly used the knife, not the pen, since he made such an excision of the Scriptures as suited his own subject matter" (*On Prescription of Heretics,* 38). On the basis of citations of Marcion by various ecclesiastical authors, it is apparent that Marcion modified his text of Luke and somewhat shortened it in an attempt to restore its "original" meaning. Marcion systematically deleted from his text the biblical citations and the infancy narratives, and effectively altered it so as to produce a text with stronger anti-Jewish highlights. By so doing, he influenced not only the development of a New Testament canon, but also the transmission of the text. Many of the so-called Western readings of Luke represent the shortened version of the text that circulated among the Marcionites. For the benefit of these disciples, Marcion composed brief introductions to the Pauline letters, the "Prologues," which eventually made their way into some Latin biblical manuscripts and provoked the composition of a series of anti-Marcionite prologues.

Two Tendencies and a Two-Part Canon

Although Adolf von Harnack (*Marcion: Das Evangelium vom fremden Gott. Eine Monographie zur Geschichte der Grundlegung der katholischen Kirche;* 2nd ed., 1924) believed that the four-Gospel canon was already in the process of development before Marcion, the studies of John Knox and Hans von Campenhausen prompt us to consider it more likely that the four-Gospel canon emerged as a reaction of the Greater Church to Marcion's Bible, a bible which had been produced for dogmatic reasons of his own choice. But which four?

Tatian (died ca. 160), Justin's pupil, produced the *Diatesseron* at approximately the same time that Marcion developed his eleven-book Bible, perhaps even in opposition to Marcion's work. The *Diatesseron* was essentially a harmony of the four Gospels which Tatian had developed by omitting the parallels and reconciling the discrepancies. Tatian's text was used in the Syrian churches until the fifth century, when it was replaced by the four separate Gospels. According to Jerome (342–420) (Ep 121:6), no less a person than Theophilus of Antioch (late second century) likewise combined the words of the four evangelists in a single work. The initiatives taken by Tatian and Theophilus serve both to underscore the particular authority of the four Gospels and to highlight the fact that the text of these Gospels was not yet considered inviolable at an early stage in the history of the Church.

There is also a story told about Serapion (died 211), who became bishop of Antioch in 199. During a visit to the church of Rhossus, Serapion was asked for and gave permission for the Gospel of Peter to be read in church. Having obtained a copy of this gospel, Serapion read through it and concluded that it denied the humanity of Jesus. Consequently he wrote a letter to Rhossus, preserved for us by Eusebius (*Ecclesiastical History* VI, 12, 4–6), withdrawing the permission he had given and promising to visit the church again in order to set its teaching right. Nevertheless the *Didascalia Apostolorum,* a third-century Syriac document, continued to make use of the Gospel of Peter, whose public reading had been rejected by Serapion. In Rome, the Valentinian Gnostics seemed to have relied not only on the Gospels of Matthew, Mark, Luke, and John, but also upon traditions which are contained in the so-called Gospel of the Egyptians and the Gospel of Thomas.

There were, then, two somewhat conflicting tendencies in the churches of the second century. On the one hand, there was an attempt to overcome the multiplicity of the gospels with a new, composite Gospel. On the other hand, there were frequent attempts to create new gospels, and to reject or modify the existing Gospels on dogmatic grounds. The restriction of acceptability to the "canonical" Matthew, Mark, Luke, and John is the result of a gradual development which sought to counter both of these tendencies, particularly insofar as they derived from Marcionite or other heretical inspiration. It is during this late-second-century time span that there apparently developed the practice of citing the "Gospel according to" (Matthew, Mark, Luke, or John), a system of nomenclature that respected both the oneness of the Gospel and the multiplicity of gospels. Although Mileto of Sardis had mentioned an Old Testament (*palaia diathēkē*) in 180, the earliest surviving mention of a New Testament (*kainē diathēkē,* as the name of a book) did not occur until 192. By that time it would appear that dogmatic conflicts were gradually pushing the churches toward the recognition of a two-part canon of the Scriptures, which would include the fourfold Gospel as a significant element.

Irenaeus of Lyons

Irenaeus of Lyons (ca. 130–ca. 200) was the first Catholic theologian to know and acknowledge the New Testament both in theory and in practice. His *Adversus Haereses* (*Against Heresies,* ca. 180) represents a first attempt to give the original teaching of Jesus and the apostles so significant a status that not even the heretics, particularly the Gnostics and Marcionites, would be able to counter it. Irenaeus did not yet know of "the New Testament" as an umbrella designation for the books about which he was writing, but he often grouped various Christian works under the rubric of "the Scriptures," an epithet which he also used in reference to the Old Testament. Irenaeus included the Shepherd of Hermas, an early-second-century Christian writing, among the Scriptures, but he painstakingly and systematically refused to apply this designation to the much esteemed First Epistle of Clement.

For Irenaeus, the four Gospels stand out as worthy of his immediate consideration. According to Irenaeus, historical circumstances indicate that these four Gospels contain the direct record of the apostolic proclamation. These four are the only true and reliable Gospels. Indeed, Irenaeus writes, "These Gospels possess such a degree of certainty, that even the heretics themselves testify to them, and every apostate strives to maintain his own teaching with their assistance" (*Adv Haer* III, 11, 7). To support his position that there are only four Gospels that contain the reliable record of apostolic proclamation, Irenaeus appeals to a symbolic argument:

> Since there are four regions of the world we live in, and four universal winds, and the Church has been thickly sown all over the earth, and pillar and prop of the Church is the Gospel and spirit of life; it is only reasonable that she has four pillars, from every quarter breathing incorruption and giving fresh life to men. From which it is clear that the Logos, Artificer of all things, he who is seated upon the cherubim and holds all things together, when he has been manifested to men, gave us the Gospel in four forms but united by one spirit.

The fourfold face of the cherubim (Ezek 1, Rev 4:6 ff.) shows the appropriateness of the fourfold Gospel—the lion, bull, man, and eagle representing John, Luke, Matthew, and Mark respectively (Jerome would later use the eagle for John and the lion for Mark).

On analysis, Irenaeus' presentation presupposes rather than establishes the fourfold Gospel. For the rest, it is in Irenaeus' work that Acts and the Pastorals are first clearly indicated as having a useful purpose within the Church. He cites 1 Peter and seems to know at least two of the Johannine letters, but does not incorporate these writings within his great Scriptural proof. Revelation, which seems to stand on its own in Irenaeus' estimation, is likewise not included. Acts, on the other hand, is almost an appendix to the fourfold Gospel collection. Irenaeus established the authority of Acts on the basis of the authority of the Gospel of Luke: "For perhaps God so arranged it that a great many things in the Gospel which all need to use should be recorded by Luke, in order that all men, following his subsequent testimony about the deeds and teaching of the apostles, and possessing therein an uncorrupted norm of truth, might be saved" (*Adv Haer* III, 15, 1).

Here Irenaeus writes of the "norm of truth" (*kanōn tēs alētheias*) as a description of the essential basic content of the Christian faith. Irenaeus, as is well known, has an ordered and unitary view of reality. There is one God, one faith, one Christ, one Church, and one basic content of the faith. Consistent with this view is his notion that from the Acts one can gather the same orthodox teaching as is found in the other apostles. Thus, there can be found a definite coherence between the epistolary literature of the New Testament and Acts. Nevertheless, while Irenaeus has a well-defined understanding of the norm of truth as the standard of the Christian faith—that is, orthodox teaching—his notion of "norm of truth" is not that of a standard list of writings. Yet with his strong plea for the fourfold Gospel, and Acts, Irenaeus gave an impetus to the eventual formation of a "canon" within the Greater Church.

Irenaeus' special pleading for Luke-Acts suggests that Marcionism continued to be an abiding concern in his times. For Irenaeus, it was no more permissible for the disciples of Marcion to accept but one Gospel, Luke, than it was for the Ebionites to accept only Matthew, some Docetists only Mark, and some Valentinians only John. On the other hand, an acceptance of the Gospel should mean the acceptance of the Acts and other apostolic writings consistent with Acts. Despite Irenaeus' pleas in Lyons, there was some hesitancy within the Greater Church to accept fully the Gospel that Marcion had been able to employ to his own advantage. Thus in the African church, Tertullian (ca. 160–ca. 225) was inclined to relegate Luke to a lesser status: "Luke is not even an apostle, but the disciple of an apostle, not a teacher but a pupil, and so decidedly a lesser figure than the teacher" (*Adv Marc* IV, 2, 4). Nevertheless, Tertullian accepted Luke among the four Gospels, which he calls Scripture, because it was commissioned by an apostle (Paul) and contains nothing except what he had learned from that source, just as Mark was commissioned by Peter and contains the Petrine teaching.

Clement of Alexandria (150–220) had read Tertullian. He knows "the four Gospels delivered up to us" (*Stromateis* III, 13, 93). Like Tertullian, he writes of these Gospels (which, as in Irenaeus, are simply called "the Gospel") as Scripture, but rarely uses this expression to speak of other Christian writings. Within the Gospels, Clement paid particular attention to the words of Jesus, especially the parables, which he subjected to an allegorical exegesis. Clement often wrote about the two covenants. Normally this was in order to contrast the old and new dispensation of salvation. Nevertheless, we can discern in his writings a tendency to use the term *diathēkē* (covenant or testament) in the sense of a body of literature.

Among the Gospels, it was not only Luke which was received with some hesitancy within the Greater Church by reason of its appropriation by a less than orthodox group; the Gospel of John suffered much the same treatment. Irenaeus speaks of some orthodox Christians who rejected this Gospel (*Adv Haer* III, 11, 9). Most probably this excessive caution is in opposition to the exaltation of John among the Montanists who capitalized on the Fourth Gospel because of its announcement of the gift of the Paraclete. The Montanists profited even more from Revelation, whose apocalyptic utterances were not dissimilar to the prophetic pronouncements emanating from Montanist circles.

Indeed, the reaction of the Greater Church was a manifest hesitancy and great caution with respect to Revelation, John, and the Johannine epistles. Gaius, an early-third-century Roman presbyter, went so far as to ascribe both John and Revelation to the Gnostic Cerinthus, suggesting, in fact, that the use of these writings was not acceptable in orthodox circles. That John was so different from the Synoptics and that Revelation contained so many unfulfilled oracles only served to strengthen his judgment that these works were unacceptable. Epiphanius (315–403) even reports that there existed a whole sect of Christians who did not accept the Johannine literature. Epiphanius dubbed these anti-Johannists the Alogoi (those who reject the gospel of the Word, the *a/logos*. This is a Greek pun since *alogos* also means irrational), but it cannot be proven that the Alogoi actually existed as a formal sect. At any rate the reluctance of the Western Church to accept Hebrews is also linked with the Montanist crisis and the consequent anti-Montanist *apologia*.

In sum, the late second-century and early third-century stress upon the fourfold Gospel—to which Irenaeus, Tertullian, and Clement attest—is a reaction both to excessive caution within orthodox circles and to the arbitrary use of the Scriptures by Marcionite and Montanist groups. Lest the accepted gospels be any fewer in number than four, these Fathers of the Church reaffirmed the traditional fourfold Gospel. The reaffirmation of this tradition was, nonetheless, also directed against the veritable spate of sectarian Christian literature which made its appearance in the second, third, and fourth centuries.

The Apocryphal Literature

Much of this literature is known to us only through the writings of the Fathers of the Church. Until recently it was thought that only a limited amount of this literature had survived, and that in fragmentary form. However, a whole body of literature produced in Gnostic circles was discovered at Nag Hammadi (the ancient Chenoboskion) in upper Egypt in 1946. The Nag Hammadi finds included a few apocryphal "gospels" and a veritable library of other Gnostic literature. Study of these documents has contributed a great deal to our understanding of Gnosticism and the history of thought patterns within the Church. Among the "gospels" discovered at Nag Hammadi are the Gospel of Thomas, the Gospel of Truth, and the Gospel of Philip. Apparently these three were not cited very frequently by Church Fathers, yet they deserve immediate attention because they are textually extant and are important for contemporary scholarship.

The Gospel of Thomas (second century) was found at Nag Hammadi in the form of a fourth-century Coptic document with clearly discernible Gnostic tendencies. This "gospel" derives its name from its opening words, "These are the secret words which the living Jesus spoke, and Didymus Judas Thomas wrote them down," to which reference is made again at the conclusion of the work. Among the Gnostics, Thomas is one of the most highly revered disciples of Jesus (along with Matthew and Philip); hence the patronymic ascription. In fact, the Gospel of Thomas is a collection of some 114 logia (secret sayings) directed to an elite group. Within the collection, some small groups of logia can be identified, but there does not seem to be any general ordering of the material. Thus, this gospel is a disparate collection of discourse material—parables, maxims, proverbs, etc.—juxtaposed one after another without benefit of any narrative framework. While many of the logia seem to depend on the Synoptics, some of them apparently derive from a very ancient Jewish-Christian oral tradition. In effect, because of its significance for the history of the transmission of the Jesuanic logia, the discovery of the Gospel of Thomas has generated considerable interest among New Testament scholars.

The Gospel of Truth (mid-second century) is actually an extended meditation on the divine name. Its Gnostic tendencies are so similar to those of Valentinian Gnosticism that some scholars believe it to have been composed by Valentinus himself shortly before the middle of the century. However, the speculations contained in the Gospel of Truth have nothing at all to do with the life of Jesus and so other scholars have come to the conclusion that its contents are, in fact, pre-Christian.

The Gospel of Philip (second century) is much more related to the Jesus tradition than is the Gospel of Truth, relying as it does on our canonical John. Its principal value lies in the insights it offers on the understanding of the sacraments among the Gnostics.

A Gospel of Peter (mid-second century) had been used for some time in the church at Rhossus. Serapion was sure that the gospel had not been written by Peter. Nevertheless, as has been noted, he permitted its use until such time as a reading of the text convinced him that it fostered a Docetist point of view. In 1886–87 a fragment of the gospel was discovered in a Christian tomb at Akhmîm in Egypt. The fragment contains a portion of the Passion-Resurrection narrative. It is clearly dependent upon the four traditional Gospels, but is not so clearly docetic. Its tendentiousness is rather to be discerned in the apologetic tone and anti-Jewish shaping of the narrative.

The Gospel of the Egyptians (first half of the second century) was widely circulated in the early Church, indeed to such an extent that it is cited by Clement of Alexandria, Theodotus, and Origen. It is characterized by an excessively ascetic or encratite point of view. It portrays, for example, Christ as one who condemns marriage. From this gospel only a few quotations survive today.

The Gospel of the Ebionites (mid- or late second century) is one of several Jewish-Christian gospels known to the Fathers. Since none of them survives—they are known to us only in the references and quotations of the Fathers—it is difficult to determine just how many of these documents existed. There is, moreover, some confusion in terminology. Modern scholars have chosen the rubric the Gospel of the Ebionites, but the document they have identified in this fashion might well be the one mentioned in Origen under the title the Gospel of the Twelve Apostles or cited by other Fathers under the reference of the Gospel of the Hebrews.

Through the Fathers we know of the sometime existence of the Gospel of the Hebrews (second century), which was heavily reliant upon Matthew. Apparently the document contained an interesting variant upon the parable of the talents (Matt 25:14–30), as well as the Johannine story of the woman taken in adultery (John 7:53 – 8:11). The Gospel of the Hebrews may well be related to the Gospel of Thomas, since it contained at least one logion now attested in it: "he who seeks will find . . . it will be opened to him" (G Thom 94). Most probably the Gospel of the Ebionites, known to us only from the writings of Epiphanius, is to be distinguished from this Gospel of the Hebrews. It, too, is drawn from Matthew, and claims Matthew as its author. The fragments cited by Epiphanius concern the beginning of Jesus' public ministry. They demonstrate a blatantly adoptionist Christology. The Ebionite affinities of the work are further reflected in its vegetarian sympathies. For example, the Baptist eats honey, but not locusts (cf. Matt 3:4).

The Protogospel of James

The Protogospel of James (second century) is so called because it deals with events which culminate in the birth of Jesus, rather than with his public ministry. The document is a unified literary work dependent upon Matthew and Luke. The book has been written in order to glorify Mary, whose Davidic ancestry, life, and virginity are particularly highlighted. It abounds in legendary details which have had a not inconsiderable influence upon the development of Christian piety. For example, the liturgical feast of Sts. Joachim and Ann (July 26) is based on the tradition that these were the parents of Mary, a detail supplied by the protogospel. There is some possibility that the work was known to Justin. If so, this protogospel must be ascribed to a Gentile Christian author who lived during the first half of the second century.

The Infancy Gospel of Thomas (mid-second century)—to be distinguished from the Gospel of Thomas discovered at Nag Hammadi—is known to us through the writings of Irenaeus and several extant manuscripts (including ancient Latin, Slavonic, and Syriac translations). Like the Protogospel of James, the Infancy Gospel is an attempt to complement the traditional four Gospels by filling in the details of Jesus' life absent from the texts which the Greater Church would eventually canonize. The text abounds in fantastic stories about an almost capricious prodigy. For example, it tells the tale of Joseph the carpenter who one day cut a board too short. Jesus, the young wonder worker, responded by miraculously stretching the board to its proper length.

Among the apocryphal gospels it is clearly the Protogospel of James that has had the strongest influence on the Greater Church, yet it is the Gospel of Thomas, one of whose sayings was already known to Hippolytus (ca. 170–ca. 236), that is of the greatest importance for understanding the New Testament as it exists today. By and large, the apocryphal gospels are secondary compositions, manifestly dependent upon the four traditional Gospels, but otherwise abounding in legendary details and anachronisms. For example, the tale of Mary's miraculous conception told in the Protogospel of James is quite obviously based on the biblical narrative of the barrenness of Hannah, the mother of Samuel (1 Sam 1–2), but is devoid of historical value as far as Mary, the mother of Jesus, is concerned. The doctrinal and apologetic interests of the apocryphal gospels are painfully apparent. For example, the Gospel of Peter describes the Easter morning vision of the soldiers posted at the tomb (cf. Matt 27:62–66; 28:5, 11–15) in this fashion: "They saw three men come out from the sepulcher, with two of them sustaining the third, and a cross following them. The heads of the two reached to heaven, but that of him whom they led by the hands overpassed the heavens" (G Pet 10:39–40). The account is a graphic description of the resurrection of Jesus, the divine man. It should be noted that although these apocryphal gospels have traditionally been called "gospels," many of them cannot be considered as gospels in our sense of the term. Since they do not offer the life of Jesus, the Gospel of Thomas, the Gospel of Truth, and the Protogospel of James hardly merit the classification of "Gospel."

Within the Christian literature of the first two centuries there have been other writings which, for one reason or another, were not later canonized by the Greater Church. Nevertheless such very early Christian texts as the First Epistle of Clement, the *Didache,* and the Epistle of Barnabas were so highly valued in the churches of the second, third, and fourth centuries that some of these texts have been preserved within various manuscripts of the New Testament. Clement of Alexandria considered as apostolic and inspired not only the three aforementioned, but also the Apocalypse of Peter, the Preaching of Peter (early second century), and the Shepherd of Hermas.

Apocryphal Apocalypses

The latter is a particularly interesting second-century work that is often classified within Christian apocalyptic literature even though it is a didactic tract on Christian morals. Of its author we know nothing except what he tells us. His story is that of a slave sold to a Roman matron named Rhoda, by whom he is later freed. The matron appears to him in a vision so that he is able to recognize her as a symbol of the Church. Hermas, a shepherd (pastor), interprets the vision for him. In all there are five visions, twelve mandates or commandments, and ten similitudes or parables. The work appears within the fourth-century Codex Sinaiticus, but its chief value lies in its exposition of the moral values held by second-century Roman Christians.

The Apocalypse of Peter (second century) is the most important of the apocryphal apocalypses. Even Clement of Alexandria was convinced that Peter had written it. During the fifth century it was still being read in some Palestinian churches on Good Friday. Part of the work was discovered in the Akhmîm Fragment and an Ethiopic version was discovered in 1910. Many of the classical features of apocalyptic literature are missing from the Apocalypse of Peter, but it is still classed among the apocalypses because it offers a vision of heaven and hell. Its vivid description concentrates more on the fate of sinners than on that of the righteous. In the vision an appropriate and particularly dehumanizing punishment corresponds to each type of sin. Because of its description of the localities of heaven and hell, the Apocalypse of Peter has had a lasting influence on the Church.

The apocalypses were valuable didactic works. Harnack—and in this opinion he was followed by many others—thought that a unit of Christian prophetic writing, similar to the fourfold Gospel and the corpus of apostolic letters, would eventually have made its way into the New Testament had it not been for the anti-Montanist reaction within the Greater Church. The reaction caused some Christians to hesitate in their acceptance of the Fourth Gospel. It led to the practical exclusion of Hebrews from acceptance in the West, a situation that was not definitively reversed until several centuries later. The "New Prophecy" so highly touted in Montanist circles revealed the need for a closed collection of Christian Scriptures and contributed to ·the creation of a set of circumstances which would not be conducive to the normative acceptance of apocalyptic writings like Hermas and the Apocalypse of Peter by the Greater Church.

Pauline Apocrypha

That the letters of Paul were saved from a similar fate during the anti-Marcionite reaction is largely due to Polycarp and Irenaeus. Polycarp vigorously promoted Paul as one who accurately and steadfastly taught the word of truth. Just as vigorously he rejected Marcion and anyone else who would twist the Lord's words in accordance with his own desires. Irenaeus legitimated Paul by means of Luke's Acts, and Luke's Acts by means of Paul. Thus it was not only within Marcionite and Gnostic circles that Paul was extolled as *ho apostolos;* he was considered "the apostle" even within the Greater Church. The value which the Pauline letters were given can be illustrated by means of a story told about the trial of the Scillium Martyrs, seven men and five women, under the proconsul Saturninus (ca. 180). When the magistrate inquired as to the contents of their *capsa* (book box), the martyrs responded with "the books and letters of Paul, the just man." The story illustrates the value attached to the letters of the apostle by these Christians who were soon to be put to death because they would not renounce their faith. The epistles were esteemed, just as were their "books"—probably a designation of the Gospels, even though it might be taken as a reference to the books of the Old Testament.

Given Paul's significance in the Church of the patristic era, it would have been remarkable indeed had an apocryphal literature not developed around his patronym. In fact, the second half of the second century saw the writing of the Acts of St. Paul, an apocryphal document probably written by an orthodox Christian of Asia Minor. In an attempt to glorify the apostle, the author made use of the Pauline letters, Luke's Acts, and the apocryphal Acts of Peter, itself dependent on the Acts of John. The Acts of Paul include the Martyrdom of St. Paul, the Third Epistle of Paul to the Corinthians, and the Acts of Paul and Thecla. The latter, which scholars had long treated as a separate document, enjoyed considerable popularity in the patristic churches. It tells of Paul's preaching chastity at Iconium. Having won Thecla away from her fiancé, Thamyris, Paul was civilly charged and condemned to a beating. Thecla was condemned to a death, from which she miraculously escaped. Although this contribution to early Christian hagiography enjoyed some success within the Church, Tertullian tells us that the Asian presbyter who had composed the Acts "from love of Paul" was deposed from his office (*De baptismo*, 17).

In the third and fourth centuries, other literature would be written and ascribed to the apostle. Once again, the apocryphal Pauline literature is demonstrably secondary with respect to those epistles presently contained in the New Testament. Thus a fourth-century Apocalypse of St. Paul describes in detail what Paul saw when he was taken up into the third heaven (2 Cor 12:2). An apocryphal Epistle to the Laodiceans, of uncertain date, is a patchwork of Pauline phrases, largely drawn from Philippians and occasioned by Colossians 4:16. A third-century Correspondence between Seneca and Paul, consisting of eight letters attributed to the philosopher and six to the apostle, demonstrates the acceptability of the Pauline message among the Italian masses.

Besides the Two-Stage Movement

During the second century the Greater Church was definitely on its way to accepting the four Gospels (with Acts) and the Pauline collection as normative. While the process was underway, certain groups within the Church were adapting some of this literature for their own ends, and were even producing a rash of (apocryphal) material ascribed to various apostles and designed to fill in the gaps left by the more traditional writings. In any event, until the fifth century there was some fluidity in the Church's use and evaluation of New Testament writings.

Apart from the Western hesitancy on the subject of Hebrews, there was considerable discussion about the Johannine literature as well as some difference of opinion about the "letters" which would later be called the Catholic epistles (Jas, 1,2 Pet, 1,2,3 John, Jude).

Among the four Gospels, John was the last to receive general acceptance within the Church. This tardiness was due to its use by the Montanists. Moreover, as has been previously mentioned, the anti-Montanist stance urged within the Greater Church had an inhibiting effect upon the acceptance of a prophetic and apocalyptic book like Revelation. In the middle of the second century Justin had classified it among "our writings" (*hēmetera suggrammata*) (*Apol* 28:1; cf. *Dial* 81). In Rome, however, during the early third century, Gaius rejected Revelation as the work of Cerinthus, the Gnostic heretic. In mid-century, Dionysius the Great (died ca. 264), bishop of Alexandria, argued from the language, style, and content of Revelation that it could not have come from the hand of the author of John and 1 John. Dionysius did not reject Revelation outright, since he was aware that "many brethren prize it highly," but he did cast sufficient doubts on the Johannine authenticity of the writing to postpone its full acceptance in the East until virtually the end of the millennium. In the interim, Eusebius would appear to entertain doubts about its suitability. A late-fourth-century bishop of

Iconium, Amphilochius (340–95), noted that most declared Revelation to be spurious. The great Cappadocian Fathers of the fourth century, Gregory of Nazianzus, Gregory of Nyssa, and Basil, would not accept Revelation. Thus it continued to remain on the fringes even though the Greater Church was rapidly moving toward the canonization of its normative Scriptures.

The Johannine epistles did not generate as much discussion as did the Gospel and the book of Revelation, which was also attributed to John. Nevertheless there was some reluctance to ascribe any particular authority to 2 and 3 John. That these letters were relatively short and that there was a clear tendency to distinguish the presbyter (meaning elder; cf. 2 John 1; 3 John 1) from the John whom tradition recognized as the author of John and 1 John, and probably Revelation as well, kept the discussion of these texts well removed from center stage. Neither Irenaeus nor Tertullian seems to have a specific estimation for 3 John. Tertullian does not even hold 2 John in as high repute as Irenaeus does. Despite this ambiguity, it would nonetheless appear that the Johannines were in the process of becoming a distinct part of the Catholic collection during the third and fourth centuries.

Much the same could be said for the Petrines. Both Irenaeus and Tertullian have a positive appreciation of 1 Peter, but are disinclined to ascribe a similar value to 2 Peter. Luther's later rejection of James as "a letter of straw" had a less vehement predecessor in the attitudes of both of these Fathers toward James. On the other hand, Tertullian was favorably disposed toward the acceptability of Jude, whereas Irenaeus was not. At this point in the history of the Greater Church, the discussion over the Catholic collection was not yet a matter of exclusion from or inclusion in the canon of the New Testament. The closed, comprehensive list of normative Scriptures had yet to be established within the Greater Church. Thus the differences between Tertullian and Irenaeus as to the acceptability of 1,2 Peter, James, and Jude were merely differences of opinion as to the acceptability or nonacceptability of these books. Some decades later, all four letters would be judged acceptable by Clement of Alexandria. Still later, they would be accepted into the canon of the New Testament by the Greater Church.

IV. CANONIZATION

Oftentimes it is considered that a final turning point in the long history of the formation of the canon of the New Testament came with the so-called Canon Muratori. The document contains a list of New Testament books found in Milan's Ambrosian Library in 1740 by Lodovico Antonio Muratori (1672–1750). Written in a poor Latin which is obviously a translation from the Greek, it is preserved in a mutilated codex of the seventh or eighth century. The beginning of the text is lost. That it ends quite abruptly has led scholars to the conclusion that it is a copy of a more ancient and mutilated text. This so-called Muratorian Fragment is as follows:

. . . but at some he was present, and so he set them down.

The third book of the Gospel, that according to Luke, was compiled in his own name on Paul's authority by Luke the physician, when after Christ's ascension Paul had taken him to be with him like a legal expert. Yet neither did he see the Lord in the flesh; and he too, as he was able to ascertain events, begins his story from the birth of John.

The fourth of the Gospels was written by John, one of the disciples. When exhorted by his fellow-disciples and bishops, he said, "Fast with me this day for three days; and what may be revealed to any of us, let us relate it to one another." The same night it was revealed to Andrew, one of the apostles, that John was to write all things in his own name, and they were all to certify.

And therefore, though various ideas are taught in the several books of the Gospels, yet it makes no difference to the faith of believers, since by one sovereign Spirit all things are declared in all of them concerning the Nativity, the Passion, the Resurrection, the conversation with his disciples and his two comings, the first in lowliness and contempt, which has come to pass, the second glorious with royal power, which is to come.

What marvel therefore if John so firmly sets forth each statement in his Epistles too, saying of himself, "What we have seen with our eyes and heard with our ears and our hands have handled, these things we have written to you"? For so he declares himself not an eyewitness and a hearer only, but a writer of all the marvels of the Lord in order.

The Acts, however, of all the Apostles are written in one book. Luke, to the most excellent Theophilus, includes events because they were done in his own presence, as he also plainly shows by leaving out the passion of Peter, and also the departure of Paul from the City on his journey to Spain.

The Epistles, however, of Paul themselves make plain to those who wish to understand it, what epistles were sent by him, and from what place or for what cause. He wrote at some length first of all to the Corinthians, forbidding the schisms of heresy; next to the Galatians, forbidding circumcision; then he wrote to the Romans at greater length, impressing on them the rule of the Scriptures, and also that Christ is the first principle of them, concerning which severally it is not necessary for us to discuss. For the blessed Apostle Paul himself, following the rule of his predecessor John, writes only by name to seven churches in the following order—to the Corinthians a first, to the Ephesians a second, to the Philippians a third, to the Colossians a fourth, to the Galatians a fifth, to the Thessalonians a sixth, to the Romans a seventh; although for the sake of admonition there is a second to the Corinthians and to the Thessalonians, yet one Church is recognized as being spread over the entire world. For John too in the Apocalypse, though he writes to seven churches, yet speaks to all. Howbeit to Philemon one, to Titus one, and to Timothy two were put in writing from personal inclination and attachment, to be in honor however with the Catholic Church for the ordering of ecclesiastical discipline. There is in circulation also one to the Laodicenes, another to the Alexandrians, both forged in Paul's name to suit the heresy of Marcion, and several others, which cannot be received into the Catholic Church [*in catholicam ecclesiam recipi non potest*]; for it is not fitting that gall be mixed with honey.

The Epistle of Jude no doubt, and the couple bearing the name of John, are accepted in the Catholic Church; and the Wisdom written by the friends of Solomon in his honor. The Apocalypse also of John and of Peter only we receive, which some of our friends will not have read in the Church [*quam quidam ex nostris legi in ecclesia nolunt*]. But the Shepherd was written quite lately in our times in the city of Rome by Hermas, while his brother Pius, the bishop, was sitting in the chair of the church of the city of Rome; and therefore it ought indeed to be read, but it cannot to the end of time be publicly read in the Church to the people [*se publicare in ecclesia populo*], either among the prophets, who are complete in number, or among the apostles.

But of Arsinous, called also Valentinus, or of Miltiades we receive nothing at all; those who have also composed a new book of Psalms for Marcion, together with Basilides and the Asian founder of the Cataphrygians are rejected.

This extended fragment offers a list presented in such a fashion that it verifies the notion of a canon—a closed list of the normative writings accepted in the Church. It is clear that the number of prophets and primitive Christianity belong to the past and therefore cannot be extended. The listing specifically excludes writings from Gnostic, Marcionite, and Montanist (Cataphrygian) circles. The acceptable books are those from the normative period which are to be read publicly in the church to the people. While some rejected works are deprecated because of their content, at least one, the Shepherd, is judged to be useful for piety's sake even if it does not enjoy normative status.

The Muratorian Fragment lists but twenty-two books. It is not the entire New Testament but the individual sections which are enumerated. This is particularly clear in the author's listing of the Pauline literature. The primary listing of seven letters symbolizes the totality of the Church and shows that the Pauline letters are intended for the entire Church. The list of twenty-two books does not include Matthew and Mark, but they were undoubtedly cited in the portion of the text that has been lost. The list omits Hebrews from the Pauline collection, and James, 1,2 Peter, 3 John from the Catholic collection, without further discussion. In contrast, the Fragment includes the Wisdom of Solomon and the Apocalypse of Peter. The author of the canon is quite obviously aware of the division among the churches with respect to the acceptability of both the Apocalypse of Peter and Revelation, which he is ready to include within his list even though the number of prophets and apostles is complete.

Despite its lack of elegance with respect to its use of the Latin language, the text of the Muratorian Fragment clearly attests to the existence of what we today would readily call a canon of the New Testament, obviously tempered in the fires of the Greater Church's polemic with various heretical

34

groups. Of vital importance for an adequate understanding of the history of the New Testament canon is the dating of the Canon Muratori. The dating of this canon is also important for dating the apocryphal Pauline letter to the Laodiceans (Laodicenes), to which reference has previously been made.

The extant Latin translation of Canon Muratori is much too late to serve as any sure indication of the date of the original Greek text. Scholars are left to rely on the internal evidence of the text itself in their attempt to date the canon. Generally they have judged the text to be a Western, catholic and ecclesiastical text formulated toward the end of the second century (180–200). Recently, some scholars such as Frederick F. Bruce and Albert C. Sundberg have taken issue with this judgment. In a number of significant studies Sundberg has shown that the existence within the Greater Church of a fixed, normative collection of writings with authority equal or superior to that of the Old Testament was unknown prior to the fourth century. Sundberg has subjected each of the arguments advanced in favor of a second-century dating of the Canon to a careful analysis. Not only has he found these arguments wanting, but he has also shown that Canon Muratori reflects an Eastern orientation. On the basis of his studies, Canon Muratori represents a fourth-century Eastern list rather than the second-century Roman product which it is commonly thought to be.

One of the key elements in Sundberg's new appreciation of Canon Muratori is a reassessment of Eusebius' remarks apropos Origen (185–254). In Book VI (25:3–11) of his *Ecclesiastical History,* Eusebius has gathered together the passages in which Origen discusses the books of the New Testament. Apparently Origen has distinguished three categories of ecclesiastical writings: the undisputed books (*anatirrēta* or *homologoumena*), the disputed books (*amphilballomena*) and the false books (*pseudē*). To the first category belong the four Gospels, 13 Pauline letters, 1 Peter, 1 John, Acts and Revelation. To the second belong 2 Peter, 2,3 John, Hebrews, James, and Jude. The third category would include the so-called gospels of the Egyptians, Thomas, Basilides, and Matthias. This classification is clear and useful, but it seems to be Eusebius' own reconstruction. Sundberg concurs with R. P. C. Hanson's 1954 study, which showed both that Origen did not have a list of New Testament books and that he did not reflect the notion of a New Testament canon.

Interest in a New Testament canon, as such, first appears in Eusebius (260–340) among the Eastern Fathers of the Church, and in Jerome (342–420) among the Western Fathers. Eusebius offers a threefold classification of Christian writings: the recognized books (*homologoumena*), the disputed books (*antilegomena*), and the altogether absurd and impious books (*atopa pantē kai dussebē*). Eusebius' first category—those books accepted by all the churches—includes the four Gospels, Acts, fourteen letters of Paul (including Hebrews), 1 Peter, 1 John and, "if it seems correct" (*ei ge phanein*), Revelation. Eusebius' second category is subdivided between a group of writings that are approved in many of the churches (James, Jude, 2 Peter and 2,3 John), and a group that is generally not accepted (Acts of

Paul, Apoc Pet, Shepherd of Hermas, Ep Barn, and *Did*). To his reflections on the acceptability of the various books in the New Testament, Eusebius devotes chapter twenty-five of the third book of his *Ecclesiastical History:*

> It seems reasonable, having arrived at this point, to summarize the writings of the New Testament which have been mentioned. First, we must put the holy quaternion of the Gospels, and the writing of the Acts of the Apostles follows these. After this we must reckon the Epistles of Paul. Next to these in order we must recognize the Epistle of John called the first and similarly the Epistle of Peter. After these, if it seems well [*ei ge phanein*], we must place the Apocalypse of John, the arguments concerning which we will set forth at the proper time. These are among the recognized books. Among the disputed works, but yet known to most, are extant the so-called Epistle of James, that of Jude, the second Epistle of Peter, and the so-called second and third Epistle of John whether they really belong to the Evangelist or even to another of the same name. Among the spurious works must be placed the work of the Acts of Paul and the so-called Shepherd, and the Apocalypse of Peter, and in addition to these the extant letter of Barnabas and the so-called Teachings of the Apostles, and again, as I have said the Apocalypse of John, if it should so appear. Some, as I have said, reject it, but others classify it among the accepted books. Now, among these some have also placed the Gospel according to the Hebrews, in which the Hebrews who have accepted Christ especially delight. All these might be among the disputed books, but we have nevertheless, of necessity, made a list of them, distinguishing those writings which according to the tradition of the Church are true, genuine, and recognized from those which are different from these in that they are not canonical but disputed, although known by most of the writers of the Church, in order that we might be able to know these works themselves and the writings which are published by the heretics under the name of the Apostles, including Gospels such as those of Peter and Thomas and Matthias, and some others besides these, or Acts, such as those of Andrew and John and the other Apostles. To none of these has anyone belonging to the succession of the writers of the Church considered it right to refer in his writings. Furthermore, the character of the phraseology is at variance with apostolic style, and both the thought and the purpose of what is related in them is especially in discord with true orthodoxy and clearly proves that they really are forgeries by heretics. They ought, therefore, to be placed not even among spurious works, but should be shunned as altogether absurd and impious.

The Consensus

After Eusebius, interest in the formulation of a definite list of New Testament books, with the concomitant exclusion of books that were not acceptable, continued throughout the fourth century. During these years canonical lists of the New Testament books appear in many parts of the Church. From Syria and Palestine came not only Eusebius' list but also those of Cyril of

Jerusalem (315–86) (*The Catecheses,* 4, 33, A.D. 348); Epiphanius (315–403) *Panarion* (or *Haereses* 8, 6); John Chrysostom (347–407) (*Synopsis Sacrae Scripturae,* ca. A.D. 407); the list found in the Codex Claromontanus; and a Syrian canon of about A.D. 400. From Africa came a canon of about A.D. 360, the Carthaginian Catalogue of 397, and Athanasius' Easter letter in 367. From Asia Minor (present-day Turkey) came the list of Gregory of Nazianzus (329–89) (*Carmen de Vita Sua* 12, 31) and that of Amphilochius of Iconium (340–95) (*Iambi ad Seleucum*). From Italy came the list contained in the Decree of Damasus (382).

The Roman list influenced that endorsed by the Council of Hippo (393). Later it was incorporated into the *Decretum Gelasianum.* The decisions of some local councils—Laodicea (363) in the East, Hippo (393) and Carthage (397) in the West—showed that by the end of the fourth century there was at last substantial agreement among the churches as to the constitution of the New Testament. In one sense the process of formation of the canon of New Testament books, to which Vatican Council II's *Constitution on Divine Revelation* (Par. 8) refers, had taken three hundred years to run its course. Yet, in another sense, the process had not yet been completed by the fifth century. If the fourth-century Codex Sinaiticus contained Epistle of Barnabas and Shepherd of Hermas after Revelation, the fifth-century Codex Alexandrinus included both 1 Clement and the so-called Second Letter of Clement. The acceptability of Hebrews for the New Testament would remain problematic for centuries to come. Eventually the authority of Hilary (died 367) and Jerome (died 420), whose thoughts were enriched by contact with the East, would prove to be such that Hebrews would be accepted in the West. Nevertheless as late as the ninth century some Western manuscripts of the New Testament omit Hebrews. In the East, the acceptability of Revelation continued to remain something of a dilemma. Eusebius reflected the sharp diversity of opinion with respect to Revelation at his time. The complex history of the transmission of the text of Revelation confirms the fact that the dilemma continued for a long time thereafter.

In any event, the formation of a closed New Testament canon is unequivocally the decision of the churches. It results from a historical process in which many factors can be discerned, of which no single one can be identified as the final determinant of the New Testament. Certainly the Church's self-understanding had a vital role to play in the historical process. On the one hand, the Greater Church's awareness that the Gnostics, Marcionites, and Montanists proposed tenets in opposition to those recognized within the Church, and that these movements found these tenets expressed in a sacred literature, led the Greater Church gradually to identify its own sacred literature. On the other hand, the Church's awareness that it was in continuity with a Judaism from which it was also distinct led to a doctrine of Scripture among some of the most influential ecclesiastical writers—men like Justin, Irenaeus, Tertullian, and especially Origen. Among the Scriptures there were some texts written prior to the time of Jesus and some written by his disciples, whose chief concern was to bear witness to their Christian faith.

Certainly orthodoxy is among the criteria to which churchmen appealed in making their judgments as to the acceptability of certain books and their eventual inclusion in the official lists. Serapion, Tertullian, Eusebius, and the Canon Muratori attend to the concern that the Church make use of only those writings that are in accordance with the "norm of truth." It is not, however, quite so certain that a judgment as to the apostolic origins of the writings in question was as significant a factor. Both Eusebius and the Decree of Damasus include 2,3 John among their books of the New Testament, even though they were not written by one of the Twelve. It is true that Papias and others linked Mark and Luke with Peter and Paul, respectively. Yet on balance it seems better to distance canonization from a historical judgment as to the apostles, apostolic men, and the hearers of apostolic men, in order to affirm that canonization results from a judgment based on a dogmatic principle of salvation history. The acceptable works derive from the primitive Christianity which is of the past, a primitive Christianity whose formative writings were constitutive of the Greater Church of later times.

In sum, the New Testament canon reflects a historical judgment as to what essentially constitutes the Church. Luther could take issue with the Roman church and relegate Hebrews, James, Jude, and Revelation to something of a subcanonical status and practically adhere otherwise to a "canon within the canon." In response, the Council of Trent reaffirmed the twenty-seven-book canon of the New Testament. Ecclesial self-consciousness continues to bear upon the significance of the canon of the New Testament even in our own day. There are those Christians who look to the formulation of a New Testament canon as an episode in the history of the Church. As such, the canon has historical significance, and only that. By preference, one ought to study early Christian literature rather than those twenty-seven books which the accidents of history served to highlight during the second, third, and fourth centuries. This is the opinion of such serious scholars as the turn-of-the-century William Wrede and our contemporary, Helmut Koester. On the other hand, there are those Christians who look to the formulation of a New Testament canon as something more than just one episode among many in the history of the Church. They look to the New Testament canon as an authoritative decision as to what constitutes the Church, a decision that has normative value for those churches in which tradition has a particularly important function in the Church's self-understanding. Thus Roman Catholic scholars generally consider the New Testament canon as a normative dogmatic fact which they must take into serious consideration.

How one views the canon of the New Testament depends, in a word, on one's ecclesiology. No matter what his or her ecclesiology, the historian must admit the existence of the New Testament canon as a fact, or rather as an event in process. The historian and believer alike must admit that the twenty-seven books have had a greater influence on the formulation of Christian faith down through the centuries than have other works of early

Christian literature. Nevertheless, a concern for the truth of history calls for the admission that some books within the canon have had a more influential function in shaping the expression of the Church's faith than have others within the canon, and that some books outside of the canon have had a more striking impact on the formulation of the Church's faith than have some individual books among the canonical twenty-seven. In effect, the canon of the New Testament must be considered with the utmost seriousness, yet it can be no more simply equated with the canon of truth in our day than it was at the time of Irenaeus.

SELECT BIBLIOGRAPHY

Aletti, Jean-Noël. "Le canon des Écritures. Le Nouveau Testament." *Études,* 349 (1978), 109–24.

Best, Ernest. "Scripture, Tradition and the Canon of the New Testament." *Bulletin of the John Rylands Library Manchester,* 61 (1979), 258–89.

Collins, Raymond F. "The Matrix of the New Testament Canon." *Biblical Theology Bulletin,* 7 (1977), 51–59.

Dahl, Nils A. "The Particularity of the Pauline Epistles as a Problem in the Ancient Church." In *Neotestamentica et Patristica. Supplements to Novum Testamentum,* 6. Leiden: Brill, 1962. 261–71.

Dillon, Richard J. "The Unity of the Gospel in the Variety of the Canon." *Proceedings of the Twenty-Seventh Annual Convention, The Catholic Theological Society of America.* Bronx, N.Y.: Catholic Theological Society of America, 1973. 85–115.

Dungan, David L. "The New Testament Canon in Recent Study." *Interpretation,* 29 (1975), 339–51.

Freedman, David Noel. "Canon of the OT." In *The Interpreter's Dictionary of the Bible,* Supplementary Volume. Nashville: Abingdon, 1976. 130–36.

Gamble, Harry. "The Redaction of the Pauline Letters and the Formation of the Pauline Corpus." *Journal of Biblical Literature,* 94 (1975), 403–18.

Grant, Robert M. *The Formation of the New Testament.* Hutchinson University Library. New York: Harper & Row, 1965.

Hahn, Ferdinand. "Die Heilige Schrift als älteste christliche Tradition und als Kanon." *Evangelische Theologie,* 40 (1980), 456–66.

Käsemann, Ernst. "The Canon of the New Testament and the Unity of the Church." In *Essays on New Testament Themes. Studies in Biblical Theology,* 41. London: SCM, 1964. 95–107.

Moule, Charles F. D. *The Birth of the New Testament. Harper's New Testament Commentaries.* 3rd ed. rev., San Francisco: Harper & Row, 1981.

Pederson, Sigfred. "Die Kanonfrage als historisches und theologisches Problem." *Studia Theologica,* 31 (1977), 83–136.

Sand, Alexander. *Kanon. Von den Anfangen bis zum Fragmentum Muratorianum. Handbuch der Dogmengeschichte.* I, 36. Freiburg: Herder, 1974.

Sanders, James A. "Biblical Criticism and the Bible as Canon." *Union Seminary Quarterly Review,* 32 (1977), 157–65.

Sundberg, Albert C., Jr. "The Biblical Canon and the Christian Doctrine of Inspiration." *Interpretation,* 29 (1975), 352–71.

———. "Canon Muratori: A Fourth Century List." *Harvard Theological Review,* 66 (1973), 1–41.

———. "Canon of the NT." In *The Interpreter's Dictionary of the Bible,* Supplementary Volume. Nashville: Abingdon, 1976. 136–40.

———. "The Making of the New Testament Canon." *The Interpreter's One Volume Commentary.* ed. by C. M. Laymon. Nashville: Abingdon, 1971. 1216–24.

———. "Towards a Revised History of the New Testament Canon." *Studia Evangelica,* 4 (1968), 452–68.

Tyson, Joseph B. *A Study of Early Christianity.* New York: Macmillan, 1973.

Vielhauer, Philipp. *Geschichte der urchristlichen Literatur. Einleitung in das Neue Testament, die Apokryphen und die Apostolischen Vater.* Berlin-NY: DeGruyter, 1975.

Von Campenhausen, Hans. *The Formation of the Christian Bible.* London: A & C Black, 1972.

Wainwright, Geoffrey. "The New Testament as Canon." *The Scottish Journal of Theology,* 28 (1975), 551–71.

Ziegenaus, Anton. "Die Bildung des Schriftkanons als Formprinzip der Theologie." *Munchener Theologische Zeitschrift,* 29 (1978), 264–83.

CHAPTER TWO

HISTORICAL-CRITICAL METHODOLOGY

To have the New Testament as a collection of twenty-seven books is one thing; to interpret it is yet another. Differences of approach to the interpretation of the New Testament have marked the long history of Christianity. While the New Testament was still in the process of being formed as a canonical collection of normative books, theologians at Alexandria and at Antioch differed among themselves as to the interpretation of its several books; the school of Alexandria adopted an allegorical method of interpretation, while the school of Antioch opted for a more realistic method of interpretation.

Christianity's second millennium saw the development of a systematized approach to the theological endeavor. The schoolmen looked to the Scriptures as their principal source for theological reflection. The Scriptures were their *sacra pagina,* their "holy text." In the interpretation of the Scriptures, they identified a variety of senses: the literal, the allegorical (doctrinal), the tropological (moral), and the analogical (mystical). What the patristic and medieval interpreters of the New Testament had in common was that they approached the Scriptures in order to understand God and his will for humankind. They studied the Scriptures of the New Testament with a decided bias—that is, for theology's sake.

With the Renaissance and its attention to things ancient and classical came a renewed interest in the New Testament text itself. This interest would lead to the development of a critical approach to the text of the New Testament, one of whose earliest proponents was the sixteenth-century French Oratorian priest Richard Simon. With the coming of age of the science of textual criticism in the nineteenth century, a major step was reached in the Church's understanding of the historicity of the New Testament text itself. Nonetheless the content of the text was regarded almost as if it were characterized by a timelessness similar to the eternity which was predicated of God as one of his principal attributes.

In the eighteenth century, the emergence of the Enlightenment, with its spirit of rationalism, skepticism, and empiricism, marked a critical point for the interpretation of the New Testament. When some nineteenth-century scholars proposed that not only the extant manuscripts but also the New Testament itself—that is, its content—must be understood within its historical context, thoroughly examined, and critically scrutinized, no small trauma was experienced among the churches. In the eyes of some believers, the examination of the New Testament by means of a historical and critical methodology was tantamount to a denial of the faith itself. More than one interpreter who opted for the use of the new methodology was sanctioned by ecclesiastical authority. Nonetheless a scientific age was determined to use a scientific methodology in an attempt to understand the New Testament scriptures. The science which appeared most capable of shedding light upon the New Testament was history.

I. THE NEW TESTAMENT IN A HISTORICAL CONTEXT

A professor of Church History and Dogmatics at the University of Tübingen in Bavaria (Germany), Ferdinand Christian Baur (1792–1860), was the first to attempt a consistently historical study of the New Testament. His ability to see things as a whole led him to consider that the New Testament must be seen as part of the history of the Church. Thus the starting point for the critical study of the New Testament had to be the Pauline epistles, since these are the most ancient of the New Testament texts. Baur appreciated the development of ideas within the New Testament and consequently recognized the difference in character between John and the other three Gospels. In 1833 Baur came under the influence of the ideas of Georg Wilhelm Friedrich Hegel, the philosopher and pedagogue to the German world. The second law of Hegelian logic provided Baur with a model for understanding the process of early Church history: the confrontation between Jewish Christianity (the thesis) and Gentile Christianity (the antithesis) gave rise to "Early Catholicism" (*Frühkatholicismus*) (the synthesis). Against the background of this understanding of the history of the early Church, "tendency criticism" (*Tendenzkritik*) came into being. It sought to interpret the various books of the New Testament by identifying their "tendency" (Jewish Christian, Gentile Christian, or early Catholic) and thus determine their situation within the history of the early Church.

Baur's influence was widespread, extending beyond Europe even to the United States. One of the leading Protestant thinkers in the United States during the nineteenth century was Philip Schaff (1819–93) who had studied at Tübingen, Halle, and Berlin, where he was named lecturer in 1842. Two years later Schaff was called to be professor of Church history and biblical literature at the Theological Seminary of the German Reformed Church at Mercersburg, Pennsylvania. In 1865 he left Mercersburg and went to New York, where in 1870 he became professor at the Union Theological Seminary.

Schaff's importance in the history of American biblical scholarship can be seen in the fact that it was in his office that the germinal meeting of the Society of Biblical Literature and Exegesis took place on January 2, 1880. Subsequently Schaff became one of the thirty-five original members of the Society. Toward the end of the century he chaired the American Committee on the Revision of the Authorized Version of the Bible, from whose efforts the American Standard Version emerged in 1901.

Schaff's fundamental understanding of the apostolic church and the interpretation of the New Testament was clearly dependent upon that of Baur. According to Schaff, three stages can be discerned within the development of apostolic theology: the Petrine (Jewish Christian), the Pauline (Gentile Christian), and the "Johannean," which "adjusts the differences of the Jewish and Gentile Christianity, and merges the systems of Peter and of Paul in its sublime and profound conception of the mysterious theanthropic person of the Savior" (Schaff: 1857). According to Schaff, each New Testament book represents one or another of these theological tendencies: the Petrine tendency is reflected by Matthew, Mark, James, Jude, and 1,2 Peter; the Pauline by the fourteen letters in the Pauline corpus, Luke, and Acts; and the "Johannean" tendency by John, 1,2,3 John, and Revelation. A clearer enunciation of Baur's views than that made by Schaff is almost unimaginable.

No less influenced by Baur than Schaff was Benjamin Wisner Bacon (1860–1932), the "founder and pioneer" of American biblical criticism. The Yale professor was convinced that Baur's theory was of lasting validity since (1) it was concerned with the history of Christian ideas as embodied in the literature of early Christianity and (2) it looked to Paul as providing the starting point for the examination of the issues within early Christianity. In Bacon's own understanding of early Christianity the Baurian antithesis between the Petrine and Pauline Gospels was of paramount importance. Nonetheless Bacon was inclined to locate the beginning of the resolution of the tension, the synthesis, in the times of Paul himself. This viewpoint was abetted by Bacon's contention—modified in his posthumously published work on John, *The Gospel of the Hellenists*—that the Fourth Gospel, the major witness to the "Ephesian synthesis," is historically and theologically dependent upon Paul.

From Baur, Bacon also gleaned an appreciation of Hegel, whose influence is noticeable in the more than two hundred and fifty studies penned by this prolific American scholar. Were it not for the Lutheran bias that "German theology is best of all" (Martin Luther) and the fact that the First World War all but discontinued scholarly cooperation between the United States and Germany, Bacon would surely be remembered as one of the major contributors to the development of the historical-critical method. A patron of the method he certainly was, yet he was also one of its principal pathfinders. Just two years after his initial appointment to Yale, Bacon visited Germany where he met such scholars as Bernhard and Johannes Weiss and Heinrich Julius Holtzmann. Nonetheless Bacon's methodology was particularly his own. In his study of the New Testament documents he paid particular attention to the "appreciation of differences," and developed what he called the "etiological" method in order to account for extant practices and beliefs. The goal of writing a Life of Jesus eluded Bacon, but he had laid the groundwork for such a project, carefully distinguishing the Gospel of Jesus from the Gospel about Jesus and developing along the way a method of New Testament criticism that was an isolated precursor of Synoptic source criticism, form criticism, and even redaction criticism.

Nonetheless it is to German scholarship that the current form of these methods of New Testament study owes its distinctive character. Thus we must return to Baur, who sensitized the German world to the importance of studying the New Testament within its historical context. Baur's influence was, in fact, so great that since 1850 historical criticism has been the methodology used in the study of the New Testament. New Testament scholars can no longer dispense with a serious and critical consideration of the history of New Testament times, nor may they overlook the historicity of the New Testament itself.

Nevertheless Baur's work, like the New Testament itself, was also the product of its times. The scientific positivism of his age was integral to Baur's own world view and led to the adoption of a scientific methodology as the means for attaining truth, almost as if it were the only means. Moreover, Baur's provincialism, his rationalism, and his Hegelian idealism led him to the use of methods that were sometimes neither critical, nor scientific, nor historical. The use of a single principle for interpretation led to a narrowness of view which, for example, failed to appreciate the real diversity within Gentile Christianity itself.

Baur's efforts did not take place within a vacuum. Although his teaching and writings mark a definitive orientation toward history as the vantage point from which the New Testament writings must be examined if they are to be understood at all, his work followed upon the works of earlier scholars who sought to approach the New Testament in a consistently historical manner.

Johann Georg Hamann (1730–88) had attacked the rationalism of the Enlightenment but saw more clearly than any of his contemporaries the significance of history as the medium of revelation. Johann Salomo Semler (1725–91) of Halle prepared the way for the "free investigation" of the New Testament by making an important distinction between the "Word of God" and the "Holy Scriptures." The Word of God has abiding authority and is always useful "unto salvation," whereas the Holy Scriptures contain books which were important only for the times in which they were written. Since, moreover, the determination of the canon was made by the Church at a given moment in history, it is necessary to investigate the circumstances in which each of the books was written in order to determine its religious value. Each of these ideas constituted a new thrust in Semler's time and made him a pioneer in the historical study of the New Testament.

In Semler's personalized view of the Church, the supporters of Peter had an aversion to the disciples of Paul. Given this division between Palestinian Christians and Gentile Christians, Semler believed that he was able to ascribe the individual books of the New Testament to one or the other faction within the Church.

The Synoptics

Semler's Göttingen contemporary, Johann David Michaelis (1717–91), sought to interpret the New Testament without any dogmatic presuppositions. He attacked the unity and integrity of the canon by accepting as inspired only those books which were written by apostles. Thus it was not the ecclesiastical doctrine of canonicity but the historical fact of apostolic authorship which was for him the determining factor in the judgment on inspiration. Accordingly, Michaelis held that Matthew and John were inspired, but denied the inspiration of Mark and Luke. In similar fashion, although he was open to considering Hebrews and Revelation as inspired, Michaelis denied the inspiration of James, Jude, and Acts.

Thus free from traditional presuppositions, Michaelis was willing to entertain the possibility of contradictions within the New Testament and wrote in opposition to the traditional view which maintained that some literary dependence existed among the Synoptics. Michaelis opted for a common use of the "other apocryphal gospels" as the principal factor which explained the sources of the gospels and preferred the suggestion of the existence of a *Urevangelium* to the traditional position of mutual interdependence. As for John, Michaelis was among the first to explain the Fourth Gospel against the background of a Gnostic world view and suggested that it had been directed against the disciples of John the Baptist. In effect, Michaelis stressed the singularity of each of the books of the New Testament and suggested that historical questions must first be answered if the individual books of the New Testament are ever to be correctly interpreted. Michaelis' innovative ideas were introduced into the English-speaking world by his pupil and translator, Herbert Marsh (1757–1839), the Bishop of Petersborough, England. Marsh made the British aware that it was possible to doubt the verbal inerrancy of the Scriptures and still remain Christian.

In Germany, the study of the literary relationship among the Synoptics was continued by Johann Jakob Griesbach (1745–1812), Gotthold Ephraim Lessing (1729–81), and Johann Gottfried Eichhorn (1752–1827), one of Michaelis' former students. Griesbach's *A Synopsis of the Gospels of*

Matthew, Mark, and Luke (*Libri historici Novi Testamenti Graece. Pars prior, sistens synopsis Evangeliorum Matthaei, Marci et Lucae*), originally published in 1774, avowedly separated John from the Synoptics and refused to attempt a harmonization of the Synoptics. This refusal was based on Griesbach's conviction that even the Synoptics did not offer a reliable chronological account of the life of Jesus. Griesbach also went counter to then current scholarship in proposing that Mark was the last of the Synoptics to be composed. He claimed that Mark is essentially a digest of the other Synoptics. According to Griesbach, the author of Mark customarily borrowed the material for his shorter account from Matthew, occasionally supplementing it with material taken from Luke. In this same study Griesbach first advanced the opinion that the original ending of Mark had been lost.

Shortly after the publication of Griesbach's *Synopsis*, several essays written by Lessing were published posthumously by his brother. In these writings, Lessing maintained that each of the Synoptics, independently of one another, depended on an Aramaic *Gospel of the Nazarenes*. In his view a shorter version of this *Urevangelium* served as the principal source for Mark, the shortest of the Synoptics. Eichhorn, a Göttingen scholar, concurred with the opinion that each of the evangelists had made use of a *Urevangelium*. He gave the thesis a defensible form by arguing that each of the evangelists had used a different form of this primary document, which was originally composed in Hebrew or Aramaic. Since Matthew and Luke have some common material in addition to that which both share with Mark, Eichhorn concluded that an additional literary source had been available to Matthew and Luke.

A different approach to the Synoptic problem was advocated by Gottlob Christian Storr (1746–1805), who argued convincingly for the hypothesis of Markan priority. Only thus, Storr reasoned, could the absence of so much Synoptic material from Mark be logically explained. The study of the basic source of the Gospel material was advanced one step further by Johann Gottfried von Herder (1744–1803). Herder made note of the fact that the very first Gospel was the proclamation of Jesus himself. After the death of Jesus, the oral Gospel was transmitted in such a fashion that the words of Jesus were passed on more faithfully than was biographical material about Jesus. This primitive oral Gospel was best preserved by Mark, among our present Gospels. In Herder's estimation, John, the last of the Gospels to be written, showed some familiarity with Gnostic vocabulary and ideology. The Fourth Gospel was clearly written to proclaim that Jesus is the Savior of the world and thus serves as a clear proof that the Gospels were not intended to be biographies in the modern sense of the term. Herder's thesis on the oral proclamation of the Gospel was more moderate than that of Johann Karl Ludwig Gieseler (1792–1854), who pursued the oral-tradition hypothesis to such a point that he ultimately postulated three oral sources behind the Synoptics. This extreme form of the oral-tradition hypothesis, taken at full value, renders any literary connection among the Gospels extremely tenuous. Herder's thesis, on the contrary, with its stress on oral tradition and the aims of the evangelists, was the unwitting precursor of the twentieth-century form-critical approach to the Gospels.

The Historical Jesus

As the historical-critical methodology began to develop during the early nineteenth century, another area for research into the Gospels emerged in addition to the study of their literary origins. By the publication of seven sections of the anonymous *Wolfenbüttel Fragments** (*Fragmente eines Ungenannten*) in 1774–78, Lessing set off the Quest of the Historical Jesus whose tale would be chronicled by Albert Schweitzer more than a century later. In 1813 Lessing's son revealed that the fragments were in fact the work of Hermann Samuel Reimarus (1694–1768).

Before Reimarus, no one had attempted to form a historical conception of the life of Jesus. His attempt, principally set forth in the last of the seven fragments, was strongly influenced by the English Deists. Reimarus made an absolute distinction between what Jesus taught and what the Apostles taught about him. To bring the Synoptic and Johannine accounts into harmony, he virtually neglected John. According to Reimarus, Jesus preached a political kingdom of God. The apostles overcame their frustration at the death of Jesus by falling back upon a second Jewish eschatological schema. Then, gathering followers who shared their expectation of a second coming of Jesus the Messiah, they created a different Jesus from the fabric of various historical assumptions. In effect, the apostles perpetrated a deception for their own materialistic reasons.

Heinrich Eberhard Gottlob Paulus (1761–1851) carried this type of theorizing one step further. In both his three-volume *Philological, Critical and Historical Commentary on the First Three Gospels* (*Philologisch-kritischer und historischer Kommentar über die drey ersten Evangelien*), 1800–2, and his two-volume *The Life of Jesus as the Basis of a Purely Historical Account of Early Christianity* (*Leben Jesu als Grundlage einer reinen Geschichte des Urchristenums*), 1828, Paulus showed that he was a thoroughgoing rationalist with an innate distrust of anything that went beyond the boundaries of logical thought. Using neither source criticism nor historical criticism, Paulus constructed a pragmatic account of the history of Jesus. He considered the miracles as merely natural events mistakenly construed by the ancients. In presenting this reconstruction of the life of Jesus, Paulus was prevented by his own rationalistic presuppositions from seeing that the faith of the disciples played a decisive role with respect to the historical Jesus.

In 1810, between the publications of Paulus' monumental works, Friedrich Ernst Daniel Schleiermacher (1768–1834) had become dean of the Theological Faculty of the newly formed University of Berlin. In 1819 he began to lecture on the life of Jesus, presenting Christ in terms that corre-

---

* The asterisk here and subsequently indicates that the work has been published in English translation.

47

sponded to his Christian faith. Schleiermacher had a clear preference for John and a relative distrust of the Synoptics (with the exception of Luke, which Schleiermacher considered to be the only Synoptic Gospel with some semblance of historical order). Schleiermacher viewed the Synoptics as compilations of various narratives, which had arisen independently, and of discourses that are composite structures. Schleiermacher's lectures were printed after his death, but his ideas had already traveled to England by 1825 when Connop Thirlwall (1797–1875)—later to become bishop of St. David's, but at this time not yet a priest—translated into English Schleiermacher's 1821 lecture on Luke.

Schleiermacher's notion that the Gospel material circulated in the form of memorabilia was to become a linchpin in the development of the form-critical approach to the Gospels. It was not possible to write a life of Jesus based on his premises; accordingly, Schleiermacher wrote not of Jesus, but of Christ. Nevertheless, his suggestion that a collection of sayings of Jesus had been incorporated into Matthew touched upon a real problem. In another domain, Schleiermacher's study of the language of 1 Timothy and his inability to fit it into a schema of Paul's life led him to deny its Pauline authenticity. Schleiermacher avoided a pitfall by not denying thereby the canonicity of 1 Timothy as Michaelis would have done. Nevertheless, Schleiermacher did not go far enough in his language study. Just a few years later, Eichhorn clearly demonstrated that the language of all three Pastorals is remarkably similar but remarkably different at the same time from that of Paul.

Life of Jesus Research

The greatest of Baur's ideological predecessors was his own pupil David Friedrich Strauss (1808–74), who shook the theological world with the publication of *The Life of Jesus Critically Examined** (*Das Leben Jesu, Kritisch bearbeitet*) (2 vols., 1835–36). Because of the appearance of this single work, the year 1835 has been called "the great revolutionary year of modern theology" (Theobald Ziegler). On a visit to Berlin in 1831–32, Strauss had become acquainted with Schleiermacher's lectures on the life of Jesus. Along with Schleiermacher, Strauss concluded that it was impossible to write a life of Jesus. Since the Gospel material consists of isolated fragments, the attempt to write a life of Jesus is to impose a subjective order on material whose true order and connection will forever escape us.

On the other hand, Schleiermacher's predilection for John did not fare so well in Strauss's evaluation. The young teacher at Maulbronn clearly demonstrated that the evangelist had imposed his own language on Jesus as well as on the Baptist. Strauss also showed, with particular reference to the tension between the Agony in the Garden scene and the Farewell Discourses, that some form of myth formation was clearly involved in the composition of the Fourth Gospel. From this position, New Testament scholars would find the John/Synoptics dilemma unavoidable.

The young Strauss, moreover, clearly influenced by Hegel's distinction between the "form" and the "idea" of religon, raised a question as to whether the historical elements of the New Testament belong to the "form" or to the "idea" of religion, and whether they are thus negligible for or essential to Christianity. In response to his own question, Strauss offered a "mythical" presentation of Jesus to replace "the antiquated systems of supernaturalism and naturalism." Thus he turned his attention away from the explanation of events to the narrative account that portrayed them. Strauss made it quite clear that it is impossible to write a Life of Jesus, since that would represent an attempt to fit Jesus into our ordinary human categories, something the evangelists steadfastly refused to do.

Strauss never clearly defined what he meant by mythical. In his exposition on the Transfiguration account, for example, he rejected both the rationalist and the supernatural interpretations, holding to the view that two more primitive narratives have been combined in the present account, one containing the conversation dating from a time when the Baptist was considered to fulfill the Elijah expectation, the other a later account dating from the messianic time of Jesus. The result is a "myth":

> . . . the tendency of which is twofold: first, to exhibit in the life of Jesus an enhanced repetition of the glorification of Moses and secondly, to bring Jesus as the Messiah into contact with his two forerunners—by this appearance of the lawgiver and the prophet, of the founder and the reformer of the theocracy, to represent Jesus as the perfecter of the kingdom of God, and as the fulfillment of the law and the prophets; and besides this, to show a confirmation of his messianic dignity by a heavenly voice (*The Life of Jesus Critically Examined*, p. 545).

For Strauss the myth was essentially "the clothing in historical form of religious ideas, shaped by the unconsciously inventive power of legend and embodied in an historical person" (John F. O'Grady). Nonetheless, in his presentation of Jesus, Strauss steadfastly maintained as indisputably reliable that Jesus knew himself to be the Messiah. Strauss assumed that Jesus arrived at this idea only gradually; yet he had no doubt about the reality of this aspect of Jesus' self-consciousness.

Despite his views on the self-consciousness of Jesus, Strauss's mythical presentation of Jesus produced such shock waves within the Church that he was forced to abandon his tutorial post in Tübingen. A close examination of his work reveals that Strauss almost completely overlooked the role of the Christian Church in forming the Gospel materials. In another sense, his work, like that of Baur, suffered from a serious methodological defect in that he had not subjected the Gospels, which served as his sources, to an exacting literary and historical criticism. Nevertheless, in Strauss and Baur were expressed the two great alternatives which were to dominate Life of Jesus research during most of the nineteenth century: either historical or supernatural, either Synoptic or Johannine. From a consideration of these two dilemmas there could be no turning back.

During the second half of the nineteenth century, the literary hypothesis advanced by the Tübingen school for the explication of the Gospels—

Matthew representing Jewish Christianity, Luke Gentile Christianity, and Mark Early Catholicism—was gradually dropped. It was to be replaced by the hypothesis of Markan priority and the Two-Source theory with respect to the composition of Matthew and Luke. Nevertheless, the Tübingen theory on the history of the primitive Church, for which the conflict between Jewish and Gentile Christianity served as the touchstone, continued to dominate New Testament research. Even this theory, however, was quickly subjected to some modification. Although he still considered himself to be a disciple of Baur, Albrecht Benjamin Ritschl (1822–89), professor at Bonn and the future father-in-law of Albert Schweitzer, took issue early on with Baur's contention that the conflict between Jewish and Pauline Christianity lasted until the end of the second century, as well as with his radical rejection of the authenticity of all letters in the Pauline corpus apart from the so-called major epistles. Later, severing himself from Baur and his disciples, Ritschl recognized that a distinction was to be made between the apostles and Jewish Christians. Thereby Ritschl was able to challenge the very underpinnings of Baur's understanding of the history of the early Church.

Ritschl's work was carried further along by Karl von Weizsäcker (1822–99) who not only recognized the difference between the original apostles and the extreme Judaizers, but who also showed that the tension between these Judaizers and Paul was due to the recognition of Paul's ministry by Peter and the original apostles. For the rest, Weizsäcker is noted for his early acceptance of the two-source theory (1864) and his espousal of many of Baur's ideas, including a generally skeptical attitude toward both John and Acts. In his *magnum opus, The Apostolic Age of the Christian Church* (*Das Apostolische Zeitalter der Christlicher Kirche*), 1886, Weizsäcker opted for a late dating of many New Testament books.

Markan Priority

With respect to the literary relationship among the Synoptics, such late-eighteenth-century figures as J. B. Koppe and G. C. Storr had advanced a theory of Markan priority. Then, in 1830, Karl Lachmann (1793–1851), who was in the process of preparing his edition of the Greek New Testament, mentioned that he had not been able to convince himself that Mark had used Matthew and Luke. In an article which appeared some five years later, Lachmann demonstrated that agreement between the narrative material in Matthew and Luke exists only to the extent that these Gospels mutually agree with Mark. Thus Lachmann inferred the literary priority of Mark and made the suggestion that Matthew had inserted a collection of Jesus' sayings into the Markan schema.

In 1838, Christian Gottlob Wilke (1786–1854), showing a remarkable sense for the study of detail, argued convincingly for the literary priority of Mark. Although he held to the independence and originality of each of the Gospels and claimed that Mark was no more an eyewitness of the Jesus events than were Luke, Matthew, and John, Wilke argued that Mark's pictorial vividness was such that it represented the most primitive tradition. In 1838 as well, a two-volume work entitled *Critical and Philosophical Study of the Gospel History (Die evangelische Geschichte kritisch und philosophisch bearbeitet)*, strongly influenced by Strauss, appeared under the authorship of Christian Hermann Weisse (1801–66). Like Wilke, Weisse was impressed by the graphic detail of the Markan narrative. For him, the simplicity of the Markan outline was a telling argument in favor of its priority. The clinching argument in his exposition was the consideration that the order of the Matthean narrative agrees with that of Luke only when it also agrees with that of Mark, through which it was mediated—a point previously made by Lachmann. As for the discourse material in Matthew and Luke, Weisse cited an agreement in wording, if not in order, between the two Gospels but noted that the Evangelists were more faithful in their use of Mark than they were in their use of the *Logoi* document.

Finally, Bruno Bauer (1809–82), a Hegelian and disciple of Strauss who went so far beyond the positions of his master as to write the first skeptical Life of Jesus, offered an exegesis of the confession at Caesarea Philippi (Mark 8:27–33), for Bauer the central fact of Gospel history, which points to the priority of Mark. Nevertheless, Bauer's radical skepticism and his assignment of Mark to the reign of Hadrian (A.D. 117–38) vitiate the significance of his contribution to the study of the literary relationship among the Synoptics.

The Two-Source Theory

The study of the literary relationship among the Synoptics required not only that reflection on the narrative order common to all three which resulted in the theory of Markan priority, but also some consideration of the discourse material that is common to Matthew and Luke. In 1832 Schleiermacher turned his attention to the words of Papias, preserved in Eusebius' *Ecclesiastical History:* "Matthew collected the oracles in the Hebrew language, and each one interpreted them as he was able." Schleiermacher proposed that Papias had ascribed to Matthew not the Gospel of Matthew as we know it, but a collection of Jesus' sayings. He did not, however, formulate a theory on the literary relationship among the Synoptics. In 1835 Lachmann's *On the Order of the Narratives (De Ordine Narrationum)* suggested that Matthew had inserted material from a sayings source into a Markan schema. In 1838 Wilke spoke of a logia document utilized by Matthew and Luke.

Responsibility for developing a comprehensive theory on the literary relationship among the three Synoptics eventually fell to Heinrich Julius Holtzmann (1832–1910), a young professor at Strasbourg. In an 1863 volume, *The Synoptic Gospels (Die synoptischen Evangelien)*, Holtzmann proposed that the Markan order derived from an Apostolic document, in effect a *Urevangelium,* which he denotes by the letter A and which also served as a source of Matthew and Luke. These two evangelists also depended on a second source, a collection of the sayings of Jesus (logia), represented by the siglum Λ. Twenty years later, under the influence of Edward von Simons,

51

Holtzmann modified his theory somewhat by postulating the direct dependence of Matthew and Luke on Mark, thereby eliminating the hypothetical A. In this fashion the classic version of the Two-Source theory of the Synoptic Gospels came into being.

In the meantime, during the same second half of the nineteenth century the historical point of view adopted by the Tübingen school was still considered to be valid in large measure. A key point in this theory was the radical opposition between Pauline (Gentile) and Jewish Christianity. Since the Pauline literature was considerably older than the Gospels, a certain preponderance was afforded to it for the study of early Christianity. Indeed, by the end of the century there were those who considered that Paul was the real founder of "Christianity." What then of Jesus?

Following upon the work of Strauss, the Quest of the Historical Jesus continued. Perforce it was a quest based on the study of the Gospels, a study dominated by the two great alternatives, historical or supernatural, Synoptic or Johannine. Increasingly, however, the Life of Jesus that resulted from this research was one which had little to do with the historical Jesus of Nazareth. Skepticism impeded sound historical reconstruction. Thus, in an 1840 study, Bruno Bauer concluded that no part of John's Gospel could be attributed to a factor other than subjective creativity of the evangelist himself. Bauer was no less severe in his judgment on the work of Mark and the other Synoptists, producing a variety of works which offer "the first skeptical Life of Jesus."

In 1882 Gustav Volkmar presented a Life of Jesus which used only Mark as its source. He reasoned that as Jesus could not have accepted the current political understanding of messiahship, he must not have made any claims to messiahship whatsoever. Jesus was just a religious reformer who intended to extend the reign of God throughout the earth and who enlisted a band of disciples to follow his cause.

The Latin world remained relatively free of influence coming from Life of Jesus research until 1863. At that time the French philosopher-theologian, Joseph Ernest Renan (1823–92), published his *Life of Jesus* (*La Vie de Jésus*) which he had begun during a stay in the Near East some three years previously. One year later, Renan was removed from his professorship at the College de France. Nonetheless his work, although written in a tone which lacked sincerity, met with instant success. In three months eight editions of it were published in France; within the year some five German translations were made. What the book offered was a romantic portrait of a genial Galilean preacher. Renan's portrait of Jesus was devoid of supernatural elements and the message of Jesus' prophetic call to conversion.

The influence of Teutonic scholarship beyond the borders of Germany was, however, quite pronounced in the Divinity School of the newly established University of Chicago (1891). Its founding president, William Rainey Harper (1856–1906) had taught at the Baptist Union Theological Seminary in Chicago and at Yale University in New Haven. His vision for the new university was that, within its halls, the study of the Scriptures would stand as a scientifically respectable discipline alongside the other disciplines. In order that this might take place, Harper saw to it that the biblical department was the largest in the university and that it was staffed by men who shared the critical and historical approach to the Scriptures that had been developed in Germany. His program of courses placed greater emphasis on the study of Greek, textual criticism, and the history of the New Testament than was found in such older institutions as Harvard and Yale. Harper believed that scholarship conceived along these lines would win the victory for Scripture "in the spirit but not the letter of orthodoxy, and in accordance with the norms of historical science" (Robert W. Funk).

As chairman of the New Testament department, Harper brought to his university Ernest DeWitt Burton (1856–1925), who had been at Leipzig and Berlin even though most of his formal education had taken place in the United States. During his thirty-one-year tenure as chairman of the New Testament department, Burton wrote a number of books that interpreted the New Testament within its historical setting and according to a proper understanding of its language and grammar. In such works as *Constructive Studies in the Life of Christ* (1901) and *A Harmony of the Gospels* (co-authored by William A. Stevens, 1909), Burton demonstrated a Schleiermachian predilection for the Fourth Gospel which "perhaps . . . aims to correct and supplement the other accounts," but showed manifest skepticism in dealing with the Synoptics. Although he maintained that he was in sympathy with those who held conservative positions and steadfastly maintained the reality of the resurrection, for which the experience of the believer is "the real force of the evidence," Burton held that probably none of the sources behind the Gospels had full command of the facts and that it is impossible to determine the historical situation to which each of the parallel sayings of Jesus belongs.

Two years after he had become chairman at Chicago, Burton co-opted as Associate Professor of New Testament Shailer Mathews (1863–1941), who had been teaching sociology in Colby College in Maine. At the time of his appointment to Chicago, Mathews had spent only three years in Colby after a year's study of history and political economy at the University of Berlin. There he had acquired some mastery of the historical method that could be applied to the New Testament texts. In his study of the Gospels, Mathews carefully distinguished the teachings of Jesus from the editorial material— that is, the "introductions, transpositions, explanations, reflections, prophetic antitypes, and verbal changes" added by the evangelists. Because he distinguished tradition from redaction, Mathews should be cited as an unacknowledged forerunner of form and redaction criticism. However, he is best known for his role as the prototypical representative of the so-called Chicago School, of which Shirley Jackson Case was the foremost figure. Using carefully defined exegetical methods, Mathews sought to elucidate "the social philosophy and teachings of the historical person Jesus the Christ" (Mathews: 1897). He thus focused on early Christianity as a social reality and upon Jesus as a social reformer, and paved the way for the "Social Gospel" (Walter Rauschenbusch et al.) which would dominate much of American Protestant Christianity during the early part of the twentieth century.

It is surprising that during his Berlin stay Mathews did not attend a single lecture given by Adolf von Harnack (1851–1930). At that time Harnack, the leading patristic scholar in the German language world, was lecturing in Berlin. Harnack came to the study of the New Testament from his study of the early Church. With Harnack the attempt to write a popular Life of Jesus from the point of view of the liberal perspective resulted in a classical formulation of the results of Life of Jesus research. While a professor in Berlin in 1899–1900, Harnack delivered a series of lectures on Christianity which were published in 1900 under the title *What is Christianity?* * (*Das Wesen des Christentums*). This volume summed up the proclamation of Jesus in terms of the coming of the Kingdom of God, the brotherhood of man and the infinite value of the human soul, and the higher righteousness with its love commandment. For all his sound methodology, Harnack had made of Jesus a man of Harnack's time instead of allowing Jesus to live as a man of his own time.

Meanwhile, B. W. Bacon's Yale colleague Frank Chamberlain Porter (1859–1946) took issue with the liberals and the Ritschlians. In the face of opposition to attempts to recover the historical Jesus, including that of Martin Kähler whose *The So-called Historical Jesus and the Historic Biblical Christ* * (*Die sogenannte historische und der geschichtliche, biblische Christus*) had appeared in 1892, Porter vigorously defended the historical method but held that the Jesus to which historical science can return satisfies only the intellectual sense. For Porter the religious experience, in search of which the Scriptures usefully serve for guidance and inspiration, is more significant than the results of historical inquiry, to wit:

> Let us suppose that Jesus never lived or that the picture of him in the gospels is so far an idealization that the historical Jesus is hidden from us, would it follow that the ideal is untrue? This is really the crucial question. . . . To me it seems that our Christian experience justifies us only in saying that it comes to us as truth and works in us as a saving and renewing power, through that gospel picture of Jesus Christ; not that the truth of the picture depends upon his historical actuality.

The Demise of Life of Jesus Research

While Porter regarded the apocalyptic elements in the New Testament lightly, it was to the credit of Johannes Weiss (1863–1914) that he sought to interpret Jesus' proclamation of the Kingdom of God according to its original historical meaning without introducing ideas that were modern or foreign to Jesus' way of thinking. Weiss, son of the famous exegete and text critic Bernhard Weiss (1827–1918), was professor of New Testament exegesis at Göttingen. In a small but quite successful volume, *Jesus' Proclamation of the Kingdom of God* * (*Die Predigt Jesu vom Reiche Gottes*) (1892), the younger Weiss clearly showed that the late Jewish apocalyptic expectations of the Kingdom of God were the framework within which Jesus proclaimed the coming of the Kingdom. Jesus pronounced the imminence of the coming of the Kingdom, his ethical demands, and his own claim to be the Son of Man within this apocalyptic framework. With the work of Weiss, the third great alternative for Life of Jesus research had been established: eschatological or natural.

In 1906 Albert Schweitzer (1875–1965), then a lecturer at Strasbourg but later the Nobel Peace Prize-winning missionary of Lambaréné in French Equatorial Africa, the present-day Gabon, published *The Quest of the Historical Jesus** (*Von Reimarus zu Wrede*), a brilliant review of more than a century of Life of Jesus research. His volume was, in fact, a reaction to the 1901 publication of *The Messianic Secret in the Gospels** (*Das Messiasgeheimnis in den Evangelien*) by William Wrede (1856–1909) who was then professor at Breslau after having spent an earlier period of his life at Göttingen. Wrede showed that the psychologizing Life of Jesus produced by the liberals was a bit of historical guesswork, quite unscientific in its results. He demonstrated that it was impossible to read the psychological development of Jesus' messianic self-awareness back into the life of Jesus on the basis of Mark, since this Gospel presents a theological interpretation of Jesus. The idea of Jesus' secret messiahship could have arisen only after the Resurrection was thought of as the beginning of the messiahship. In effect the messiahship of Jesus was a statement of faith of the early Church; it was unknown to Jesus and was ignored by his disciples and their opponents during his historical ministry. For Wrede, the frequent recourse to the "messianic secret" in Mark's retelling of the tale of Jesus is a theological and literary device used to indicate the total ignorance of Jesus' messiahship that reigned prior to the Resurrection.

While Schweitzer could look to Wrede's work as an ally in showing the error in Life of Jesus research, he did not agree with Wrede's denial of the historicity of Jesus' claim to messiahship. Schweitzer's Jesus proclaimed the imminent coming of the Kingdom of God and saw himself as the coming Messiah. Jesus' ethical demand was an "interim ethic" whose urgency and radical character derived from the imminence of the Kingdom. This Jesus went to death for his convictions, convinced until the end that he was indeed the Messiah. Thus Schweitzer, a sometime student of H. J. Holtzmann, opted for a thoroughgoing eschatological perspective as the key to understanding the historical ministry of Jesus. In *The Quest,* Schweitzer surveyed the work of two hundred and fifty authors, but acknowledged the value of only that of Johannes Weiss, since it was Weiss who had shown that the message of Jesus was wholly eschatological. In any event, with the publications of Weiss, Wrede, and Schweitzer, the liberal Quest of the Life of Jesus was shown to be thoroughly unscientific and to have led to unhistorical conclusions.

II. MODERN CRITICAL METHODOLOGY

Thus, by the turn of the century the liberal Quest for the Historical Jesus had foundered on the shoals, Baur's literary theory on the Synoptics had been replaced by the two-source theory, and the key notion in his historical theorizing had been somewhat modified. The negative results of the Life of Jesus research did not mean, however, that the historical-critical approach to the study of the New Testament was to be abandoned. Heidelberg professor Ernst Troeltsch (1865–1923) worked out a theory on the historical-critical method in his essay *On the Historical Dogmatic Method in Theology* (*Über historische und dogmatische Methode*) (1898). According to Troeltsch, historical criticism operates with three indissolubly connected principles: criticism, analogy, and correlation. Criticism denotes the methodological skepticism with which the historian approaches all historical tradition. Such criticism is made possible by analogy—the intrinsic similarity in all historical realities. Thus the historian must assume that the experience of the past cannot have been fundamentally dissimilar to that of his own time. Correlation requires the critic to examine his findings within the total structure of historical events, thus examining the findings with a critical eye. Accordingly Troeltsch, who had been much influenced by Ritschl, opted for the use of the historical-critical methodology in theology, since it places religious experience within the total progress of history.

Criticism Outside of Germany

While German New Testament scholarship during the second half of the nineteenth century was largely concerned with Life of Jesus research, British scholarship also adopted a historical-critical methodology of New Testament study but did not come to the same conclusions as did Baur and his Tübingen disciples. From the time of his nomination to the post of tutor at Trinity College, Cambridge, Joseph Barber Lightfoot (1828–89), a private student of Brooke Foss Westcott (1825–1901), had made classical and biblical studies his main field of interest. As Hulsean professor of divinity, he continued to lecture on the New Testament in Cambridge. His recognition that Paul must be the starting point for historical study of the New Testament led him to the study of such Fathers as Ignatius and Clement. Lightfoot found that neither of these early Church authors showed any evidence of the conflict between the Pauline and Petrine factions in Christianity which had served as the cornerstone of the Tübingen view of history.

Lightfoot's Cambridge lectures served as the basis for his published studies on Galatians (1865), Philippians (1868), and Colossians and Philemon (1875). These commentaries, marked by a critical methodology and wide erudition, were quickly hailed throughout the world of scholarship. Together with two other Cambridge contemporaries—Westcott, his mentor, and F. J. A. Hort (1828–92), the text critic—Lightfoot planned to publish a complete philological, historical, exegetical, and doctrinal commentary on the entire New Testament. The work was to be divided among the three scholars, Lightfoot treating the Pauline Corpus, Westcott the Johannine, and Hort the rest of the New Testament. Although the work was never completed, enough of it appeared in print to achieve the lasting reputation of the Cambridge Three as the founders of a conservatively critical school of New Testament criticism. In retrospect the great failure of the Cambridge school seems to have been its neglect of the Synoptic problem and the Life of Jesus, the very topics which preoccupied contemporary German scholarship.

To some extent this neglect was remedied by a later Cambridge scholar, Sir Edwyn Clement Hoskyns (1884–1937), who had been a friend of Schweitzer and had listened to Harnack. In his essay "The Christ of the Synoptic Gospels" (1926), Hoskyns vigorously refuted each of the two pillars of the liberal lives of Jesus—namely, that the real founder of Christianity in its traditional historical form was not Jesus but Paul, and that the increasing complexity of the Church's beliefs about Jesus resulted from a later stage of the developing theological tradition. Hoskyns showed that the teaching behind the Synoptics was much more complex and much more Catholic than the liberals were willing to admit. In 1931 Hoskyns co-authored a volume on the principles underlying the critical and historical study of the New Testament. Under the influence of Karl Barth, Hoskyns became still more realistic and dogmatic in his approach. His posthumously published study on John (1940) shows—unfortunately, yet all too clearly—that Hoskyns also suffered from the Cambridge weakness: a failure to respond to the historical question: What really happened in the life of Jesus?

The Synoptic problem was, nevertheless, not neglected by British scholarship. In his 1911 contribution to the *Oxford Studies in the Synoptic Problem,* an Oxford don, Burnett Hillman Streeter (1874–1937), took a major step toward winning the assent of the English-speaking world to the two-source theory and the existence of a Sayings source. *The Four Gospels* (1924) offered a number of original ideas about the formation of the Synoptics. Specifically, Streeter reasoned that if Mark emanated from Rome it was likely that each of the other major centers of early Christianity would also have had its body of traditions about Jesus. Thus Streeter argued that *Q,* the Sayings Source, had its provenance in Antioch. From Jerusalem and Caesarea came two bodies of traditions about Jesus; these would have served as sources for Matthew and Luke respectively. In effect, Streeter had modified the classical two-source theory by suggesting that each of the later Synoptists had a proper source available to him, the Jerusalem M for Matthew and the Caesarean L for Luke. In fact, Streeter's theorizing about the literary relationship among the Synoptics included a theory of a proto-Luke—that is, a first draft of the Third Gospel resulting from the compilation of material from *Q* and from L. Later this draft was supplemented by material taken from Mark. In this way Streeter was able to explain the particularity of the Third Gospel as well as the Markan schema that is clearly discernible in the present version of Luke.

It was not, however, the Synoptic problem which occupied the attention of Charles Harold Dodd (1884–1973), who has been rightly called the leading British New Testament scholar of this century. Dodd's professorship spanned a thirty-five-year period (1915–49) during which he lectured successively at Oxford, Manchester, and Cambridge. His much debated theory on "realized eschatology" was put into significant literary expression in *The Parables of the Kingdom* (1935) and other writings of that era. Essentially Dodd maintained that the eschatological promises of the Bible and Jesus' message as well have been realized in the Incarnation and its consequences for mankind. In *The Apostolic Preaching and Its Developments* (1937), he analyzed the preaching of the early Church, carefully distinguishing between *kerygma* (proclamation) and *didache* (teaching). In two volumes on John (*The Interpretation of the Fourth Gospel,* 1953; *Historical Traditions in the Fourth Gospel,* 1963) Dodd argued that the Fourth Gospel has a much greater claim to historical value than most contemporary German scholarship would have attributed to it.

The turn-of-the-century world of Roman Catholic scholarship was also not untouched by the principle that the books of the New Testament must be understood within their proper historical context. In 1890 Alfred Firmin Loisy (1857–1940) was appointed professor of biblical exegesis at the Catholic Institute in Paris. By that time he had already adopted a critical attitude toward the Bible. The publication of his ideas in his own journal, *L'Enseignement biblique,* led to Loisy's removal from the professorship. Nevertheless, Loisy entered the lists against Harnack with a volume entitled *The Gospel and the Church** (*L'Évangile et l' Église*) (1902). Although taking issue with Harnack's liberal interpretation of the proclamation of Jesus by adopting an eschatological view of Jesus' message and messianic claims and offering a novel defense of the Church, Loisy noted that the Gospels were a product of and witness to the ancient faith, and suggested that John is a symbolic description of the truth of Jesus. His denial of the historical value of John, which he considered to be a late-first-century allegorical presentation of Christianity, was most clearly expressed in *The Fourth Gospel** (*Le Quatrième Évangile*) (1903). This work showed clearly that Loisy was walking along the path blazed by Strauss and Baur. Following that path led to Loisy's excommunication from the Roman Catholic Church in 1908. Nevertheless Loisy continued to publish significant commentaries on the New Testament as well as works on the philosophy of religion.

Manifest sympathies for the historical-critical position were expressed in a more moderate fashion by Marie-Joseph Lagrange, O.P. (1855–1938), in a significant memorandum presented to the International Congress of Catholics at Fribourg, Switzerland, in 1897. In 1890 Lagrange founded a Practical School of Biblical Studies in Jerusalem, the influential École Biblique. Two years later he established the *Revue biblique internationale.* Lagrange's conservatively critical position underlies the methodology which led to his publication of monumental works on each of the four Gospels between 1911 and 1925.

In Rome, the Pontifical Biblical Institute was established in 1909. In Belgium, the faculty of theology of the University of Louvain adopted a thoroughgoing historical-critical methodology which was soon reflected in the writings of Honoré Coppieters and Edouard Tobac. The latter was succeeded by Lucien Cerfaux (1883–1968) whose historical appreciation of the New Testament Scriptures is apparent in his trilogy on St. Paul as well as in his studies on the Hellenistic background of the New Testament, the main areas for his scholarly concern during the early part of his academic career.

The New Testament Environment

Indeed, it was a fuller historical appreciation of the world in which the New Testament developed that occupied the attention of many scholars during the first half of the twentieth century. *The Influence of Greek Ideas and Usages on the Christian Church* was the subject of Edwin Hatch's (1835–89) Hibbert Lectures in 1888. Posthumously published two years later, the lectures focused on the interaction between Christianity and its Hellenistic environment, carefully distinguishing the Semitic elements from the Hellenistic in the expression of Christian faith. William Mitchell Ramsay (1851–1939), once a student at Göttingen and later an eminent authority of the geography and history of Asia Minor, came to a moderately conservative position as a result of his archaeological and historical studies. At first skeptical about the historical value of Acts, he came to recognize the basic reliability of Luke as a contemporary historian. Another Oxford scholar, Robert Henry Charles (1855–1931), was the greatest authority of his time on the subject of Jewish eschatology and apocalyptic expression. In 1913 he published a two-volume corpus of late Jewish writings, *The Apocrypha and Pseudepigrapha of the Old Testament,* which students of the New Testament still find valuable. It was, moreover, interest in the eschatology of Jesus and the Gospels which led the American scholar Amos Niven Wilder (1895–   ) to conclude that "Jesus and the first Christians used Jewish-apocalyptic terms."

Interest in the Jewish background of the New Testament has, in fact, been expressed in a number of different ways. In 1866 August Hermann Cremer (1834–1903) published a *Biblico-Theological Lexicon of New Testament Greek** (*Biblisch-theologisches Wörterbuch der neutestamentlicher Gräcität*), surely a significant forerunner of Kittel's work, which noted that the words of the Greek New Testament do not have the same sense as they did in classical Greek. Although Cremer's thesis was that New Testament Greek was the organ of the Holy Spirit, his methodology pointed to a kinship between the sense of the words in the New Testament and the vocabulary of rabbinic Judaism. In Britain the Cambridge Three, especially Lightfoot, had similarly noted the influence of the Bible, via the Septuagint, on the Greek of the New Testament. In 1898 Gustaf Hermann Dalman (1855–1941), tutor of Old Testament at Leipzig, published *The Words of Jesus** (*Die Worte Jesu*). The study argues from the fact that Jesus spoke Aramaic to "the duty of biblical scholarship to investigate the form which the sayings of Jesus must have taken in the original and the sense which in this form they must have conveyed to Jewish hearers." Accordingly, Dalman worked out a retroversion or back translation of Jesus' words in order to get a "fresh apprehension of his message in the light of the primary language and the contemporary modes of thought."

A number of Anglo-Saxon scholars also focused upon the Aramaic question as one to be dealt with seriously if the full import of Jesus' teaching was to be exploited. Oxford's Charles Fox Burney (1868–1925) emphasized the importance of the Aramaic background of the Gospels for their proper understanding in *The Aramaic Origin of the Fourth Gospel* (1922), which claimed that John is a translation from an Aramaic original. In 1925 St. Andrews' Matthew Black (1908–   ) published *An Aramaic Approach to the Gospels and Acts*. Having noted that the concentration of Gospel Semitisms is to be found in the sayings of Jesus, Black argued for the existence of an Aramaic sayings source, either oral or written, underlying the Synoptic Gospels. In the thirties, Yale's Charles Cutler Torrey (1863–1956) wrote two books in which he advanced the view that each of the Gospels is a translation from an Aramaic original. Interest in the Aramaic background of the New Testament continues to be an abiding concern of the American Jesuit Joseph Fitzmyer (1920–   ) who has devoted a number of studies to various aspects of the issue.

In post-World War I Germany, two authors had graphically argued that if Jesus was a Jew, the study of late Palestinian Judaism is necessary for a proper understanding of the Gospels. Paul Billerbeck (1853–1932), a Brandenburg pastor, began the publication of a four-volume *Commentary on the New Testament from the Midrash and Talmud* (*Kommentar zun Neuen Testament aus Talmud und Midrasch*) (1922–61). In this work, in cooperation with H. L. A. Strack, Billerbeck made available an enormous amount of rabbinic and other late Jewish material which would be useful for the interpretation of the New Testament. Tübingen's Gerhard Kittel (1888–1948) published a number of works on the relationship between later Judaism and early Christianity. *The Problems of Later Judaism and Primitive Christianity* (*Die Probleme des palästinischen Spätjudentums und das Urchristentum*), 1926, is surely the most significant of his works on this specific topic, but Kittel's interest in the subject is also reflected in the monumental *Theological Dictionary of the New Testament** (*Theologisches Wörterbuch zum Neuen Testament*) (1933–79) whose first volume appeared under his editorship in 1933.

More recently Joachim Jeremias (1900–79), a former student of Dalman and longtime professor at Göttingen, has perhaps proven to be the "principal custodian in our time of the heritage of detailed and exacting, philological, environmental research about Jesus" (James M. Robinson). Before the publication of a final synthesis in 1971, *New Testament Theology I: The Proclamation of Jesus** (*Die Verkündigung Jesu*), Jeremias had published major monographs on Jesus' eucharistic words and on the parables. In his various publications, Jeremias has forcefully argued that the meaning of the *ipsissima verba Jesu* can be significantly elucidated against the background of the Palestinian and Aramaic-language environment in which Jesus lived and taught. Jeremias' studies may yet prove to be the permanent legacy of the Quest of the Life of Jesus. They were surely motivated by his conviction that only the Son of Man and his word can invest the message with full authority.

Knowledge of the Jewish background of the New Testament has been considerably advanced in the years since the Second World War by the manuscript finds at Nag Hammadi in Egypt (1945) and Qumran and the nearby Wadi Murabba'at in Palestine (1947–56). The manuscripts taken from the Egyptian cemetery and the Palestinian caves have clearly shown that it is not legitimate to make a sharp distinction between normative Judaism (George Foot Moore's designation for a largely pharisaic and Palestinian form of Judaism) and Hellenism as if they were two unrelated worlds of thought. The Qumran finds have shown that dualism is not an exclusively Hellenistic phenomenon. Accordingly, the Dead Sea Scrolls have raised significant questions with respect to a possibly Palestinian background for the Fourth Gospel. Moreover, studies which compare these manuscripts with the New Testament have shown that the manner of interpreting the Bible [OT] attested by the Qumran *pesharim* (biblical commentaries) is rather similar to that employed by Paul, John, and Matthew. On the other hand, the Nag Hammadi Codices are largely Gnostic in inspiration. Yet their study has made it clear that Gnosticism is not simply a heterodox form of Hellenistic Christianity. Rather, Gnosticism is a broader historical phenomenon, not unrelated to Judaism. From Nag Hammadi comes the third-century Coptic Gospel of Thomas whose 114 sayings, patently Gnostic in their present expression, are comparable to and sometimes parallel with the logia of Jesus preserved in the Synoptics. In effect these discoveries have not only clarified the Judaic and Gnostic thought worlds which are the proper environment of the New Testament, but they also shed significant light on particular New Testament texts and the problems of New Testament interpretation.

In Germany prior to World War II and notwithstanding the linguistic studies of Dalman and Jeremias, the principal research on the environment in which the New Testament originated was conducted chiefly by members of the History of Religions school, a movement that looked to Near Eastern religious syncretism as providing the essential context for the development of New Testament traditions. The growth of the school owed much to Wilhelm Bousset (1865–1920), whose *Religion of Judaism in the New Testament Age* (*Religion des Judentums im neutestamentlicher Zeitalter*), 1903, showed that late Palestinian Judaism was influenced by the religions of a Hellenistic culture. Thus the matrix from which the Gospel emerged by a "creative miracle" was a form of syncretistic Judaism. In *Kyrios Christos* (1913), a work whose English translation bears the same title as the original German text,

Bousset advanced the thesis that in the cult of Hellenistic Christianity the "Kyrios Christos" replaced the eschatological Son of Man of the earlier Jewish expression of Christianity. Effectively Bousset raised two significant issues: that of the relationship between eschatology and cult, and that of the influence of Hellenistic Oriental piety on Paul and his disciples.

Bousset's contemporary, Richard Reitzenstein (1861–1931), studied the influence of the religious and philosophical movements in Hellenism on early Christianity. In 1910 his *The Hellenistic Mystery Religions* (*Die hellenistischen Mysterienreligionen*) specifically identified Paul as a Hellenistic mystic and Gnostic whose ecstatic experience is comparable with that of the Hellenistic mystics. Reitzenstein claimed that Paul's presentation of the Christ myth is borrowed from the pre-Christian Gnostic redeemer myth. Indeed, Reitzenstein viewed Paul not as the first, but as the greatest, Gnostic.

Form and Redaction Criticism

Two other proponents of the History of Religions approach to the study of the New Testament are better known for their contributions in developing form criticism as a useful methodology for the interpretation of the New Testament. Martin Dibelius (1883–1947) succeeded Johannes Weiss as professor of New Testament Exegesis and Criticism at Heidelberg in 1915. In 1919 he published the first edition of *From Tradition to Gospel** (*Die Formgeschichte des Evangeliums*), a work whose German title contributed its name to the new methodology. Working on the foundations laid by Weiss, Dibelius placed great emphasis on preaching as the medium of transmission of Jesus' words. He developed the view that the Gospel material was shaped by the liturgical, catechetical, paraenetic, and missionary needs of the early Church as part of the oral transmission process. The individual units of tradition, thus shaped, were collated into Gospel form by the evangelists. Accordingly the Gospels cannot be considered literary works in the proper sense of the term; at best they represent a form of popular literature (*Kleinliteratur*). Dibelius' general approach to the Synoptics was similar to that of Karl Ludwig Schmidt (1891–1956), whose *The Framework of the Story of Jesus* (*Der Rahmen der Geschichte Jesu*) (1919) effectively demonstrated that the orally transmitted individual Gospel stories had their life situation in the worship of the early Christian community, and that Mark, followed by the other Synoptists, had created the literary framework in which these Gospel traditions were preserved. Thus Schmidt showed not only that the New Testament tradition about Jesus owes its preservation to the faith interests, rather than the historical interests, of the early Church, but also that the study of the written Gospels is clarified when a distinction is made between tradition and redaction.

Rudolf Bultmann (1884–1976), who had been a pupil of Johannes Weiss and who was also strongly influenced by Bousset and Reitzenstein, carried form-critical methodology to a point of radical skepticism in his 1921 publication *The History of the Synoptic Tradition** (*Die Geschichte der Synop-*

tischen Tradition). In a much more radical fashion than either Dibelius or Schmidt, Bultmann questioned the historicity of the Gospel material. A comparison of the discourse and narrative material in the Synoptics with similar material found in rabbinic tradition and the stories associated with the cult of Asclepios enabled Bultmann to categorize significantly the various units of Gospel material, but it also allowed him to regard the Gospel as the product of the creative imagination of the early Church. In his monumental studies on Paul and John, especially his two-volume *Theology of the New Testament** (*Theologie des Neuen Testament*) (1951–53) and his commentary on *The Gospel of John** (*Das Evangelium des Johannes*) (1941), Bultmann showed how much he remained a member of the History of Religions school. He forcefully argued that Pauline Christology was radically shaped by the Gnostic redeemer myth and that the major discourses of the Fourth Gospel derived from a Revelation discourse source whose origins are to be found in early Oriental Gnosticism.

If Bultmann had only written works on the Synoptics, Paul, and John, he would have been a major figure in the history of this century's study of the New Testament. However, he also made significant contributions to the development of the "New Hermeneutic." For thirty years Bultmann was professor of New Testament studies at Marburg. There he came under the influence of a colleague, Martin Heidegger, the existentialist philosopher (1889–1976). Heidegger's ideas on time, existence, and language shaped Bultmann's existential interpretation of the New Testament and his idea of the *kerygma*. For Heidegger the goal of selfhood is the giving up of the self in death. For Bultmann, existential existence—to live free from the past and open to the future—is made possible by the acceptance of the *kerygma* in faith. The proclamation of the *kerygma,* which requires only the mere fact of Christ's death on the Cross as its content, allows for a new self-understanding. Since it is but the fact of Christ crucified which is necessary for the proclamation, the rest of the proclamation preserved in the New Testament can be considered outmoded mythology. In effect the New Testament must be demythologized if the *kerygma* is to become meaningful address for modern man.

Although Bultmann's notion of the *kerygma* is a singular quality, born of the union between the characteristic Lutheran doctrine of justification by faith alone and the philosophical ideas of the young Heidegger, it has proved to be the final nail in the coffin of the Quest of the Historical Jesus. Since World War II, Bultmann has been the dominant figure on the German exegetical scene. His disciples, the "old Marburgers," have worked within his shadow; nevertheless, they have been sufficiently independent to create a new trend of exegesis in which concern for the language event is all important. Among the post-Bultmannians we can cite Günther Bornkamm in Heidelberg, Hans Conzelmann at Göttingen, Ernst Fuchs at Marburg, Ernst Käsemann at Tübingen, Helmut Koester at Harvard, and James M. Robinson at Claremont, California.

One of the most characteristic trends to be discerned in the writings of the post-Bultmannians is an interest in the historical Jesus. A programmatic statement of this concern was voiced by Käsemann in a 1953 address to Bultmann's former students on the subject of "The Problem of the Historical Jesus." The crucial interest in this "New Quest of the Historical Jesus" (*Das Problem des historischen Jesus*) is "the question as to the continuity of the gospel in the discontinuity of the times and the variations of the *kerygma.*" This new quest has a different view of the sources and a different understanding of history from those had by the nineteenth-century questers. In effect it is an attempt to show that the Christ of the *kerygma* is a faithful representation of the historical Jesus. In this respect, Günther Bornkamm's *Jesus of Nazareth** (*Jesus von Nazareth*) (1956) was one of the first expressions of the post-Bultmannian movement. The new quest seeks not so much after the historical Jesus as after the historic Jesus. It finds in the word and work of Jesus an indication of the eschatological understanding of his person. What can be said about Jesus yields the basis for what Conzelmann has called an implicit Christology. Thus the new quest marks a significant step in a renewed theological understanding of the Scriptures. This understanding would be still richer were the post-Bultmannians to take John as seriously as they take the Synoptics.

From the standpoint of the development of the historical-critical methodology rather than that of hermeneutics, Conzelmann was one of the first German authors to use the method of redaction criticism. His *Theology of St. Luke** (*Die Mite der Zeit*) (1954) ranks alongside Willi Marxsen's *Mark the Evangelist** (*Der Evangelist Markus*) (1956) and *Tradition and Interpretation in Matthew** (*Überlieferung und Auslegung im Matthaeusevangelium*) (1960), to which Günther Bornkamm and two of his disciples, G. Barth and H. J. Held, have made contributions, as the major signposts which have indicated the emergence of the new methodology. Use of this methodology focuses on the work of creative editing accomplished by each of the Synoptists. With the presupposition that both Matthew and Luke have edited their Markan material, redaction criticism generally accepts the Two-Source theory of Synoptic composition as a working hypothesis. The use of the methodology cannot, however, be limited to the study of the later Synoptics. Use of the methodology rehabilitates each of the evangelists as editor/author and as theologian. Thus it has also contributed to a fuller understanding of the New Testament Scriptures.

The Reaction

The development of the historical-critical methodology has followed a course like that of the Meander itself. With the ebb and flow of its tides, significant deposits of silt have been left on its shores. Among the results of the historical-critical method there is surely a common consensus that the New Testament, it its entirety and in its several parts, must be examined within its proper historical context. The writings of Paul (A.D. 50–58) are clearly appreciated as the oldest of the New Testament documents. The

Gospels (A.D. 70–96) are later literary compositions, but to a large extent they are based upon earlier oral traditions and documentary sources, each with its own history. Since the Gospels are literary works, they express the vision of their respective authors. Moreover, since each book of the New Testament has its place within the categories of literature, it is useful to compare the writings of the New Testament with other literary works. On comparison, it is apparent that the New Testament books are not works of history; rather they are attestations of faith. In sum, it is impossible to write a biography of Jesus in the modern sense of the term even if analysis of the New Testament texts allows us to attain, in some measure, to the historic Jesus as well as to the early Christian communities and those who have given literary expression to their faith.

Since the results of the historical-critical method are not insignificant in themselves and because they make a certain degree of comprehension of the New Testament texts possible for men and women of a rational and scientific age, the methodology has, in principle, won increasing acceptance since the Second World War. Not only the scholars, but also the churches have been turning to the historical-critical methodology as a means of presenting the legacy of their Scriptures to contemporary men and women. In an epilogue, we trace the reaction of one ecclesiastical body, the Roman Catholic Church, to the historical-critical method. Roman Catholicism's authoritative point of view has been articulated in a variety of documents published since the late nineteenth century. The history of the Roman reaction is not atypical. Writ large, this history is that of a movement from caution through curiosity and criticism to acceptance. The movement is hardly uniform and the acceptance is not unqualified. At best one can say that the method itself has been accepted in principle, but that not each and every result coming from the pen of someone who has adopted the method is acceptable.

Reactions to the use of the historical-critical method have come from other quarters as well. There are some who continue to shun it as if the use of the method would contaminate the "eternal verities." This is the position, often unstated, of many fundamentalists. Others would accept the historical-critical method as one valid approach to the texts of the New Testament but would question whether it is the only valid approach to the understanding of the New Testament. Objections along these lines have been voiced by proponents of the method of structural analysis (see Chapter Seven).

The structuralists contend that many of the practitioners of the historical-critical method of New Testament exegesis have separated the meaning of the text from the text itself. From their vantage point the structuralists see the historical-critical method as locating meaning in the process through which the text has been produced rather than in the text itself. Structuralists criticize the "exegetes" on the grounds that the latter are more concerned with history than they are with meaning. In contrast, the structuralists methodically avoid historical issues in order to concentrate on the text at hand. Since the text at hand is normally a text of the New Testament in one of the modern translations, the structuralists rarely examine the Greek text of the

New Testament (the focus of interest for the "exegetes"); rather they are concerned with the meaning of one of the modern versions of the text. In an attempt to elicit the meaning of this text, the structuralists employ a method of literary analysis largely dependent upon contemporary linguistics. Various attempts at structural analysis of the New Testament have appeared in France, Germany, and the United States with increasing frequency since the early 1960s.

During the 1970s a psychoanalytic reading of the New Testament began to be spoken of in certain French-language circles in Northern Europe. The names of Louis Beirnaert and Antoon Vergote are in the forefront of this movement. The psychoanalytic reading of the New Testament texts requires that the reader methodically abandon everything previously learned about the text, in order that the text reveal a meaning which is not stated explicitly within the text itself. Practitioners of this art must be well versed in the concepts of psychoanalysis, and so most of the psychoanalytic reading of the New Testament thus far has been done by psychoanalysts rather than by exegetes trained in the historical-critical methodology.

Many of these psychoanalysts see an analogy between the Gospel narratives (parables and miracle stories) and dreams and visions. To some extent each is the product of pre- and un- conscious factors. Since the dramas constitutive of the human psyche, and part of the vital experience of virtually every human, are reflected in the New Testament texts, one can approach the New Testament with an attitude similar to that proposed by Freud in *The Interpretation of Dreams*. Consequently the language of classical psychoanalysis, especially in regard to the Oedipus myth, is reflected in the writings of those engaged in the psychoanalytic reading of the New Testament. Nonetheless, most of those who have approached the New Testament psychoanalytically operate within the universe of discourse of the structuralist psychoanalysis of Jacques Lacan. Thus we find that notions of need and demand, desire and frustration, lack and its function, the Subject and the Other, abound in the various published psychoanalytic readings of the New Testament.

The fundamental principle of the psychoanalytic reading of any text, including the texts of the New Testament, is that nothing in discourse results from chance. Even if much of the motivation lies at pre- and un- conscious levels, everything in a written text is motivated. With this presupposition, the analyst who reads the New Testament is particularly attentive to significant elements within the text that will enable him or her to bring to light something of its hidden message. The analyst is generally attentive to the gaps, the discordances, the slips, the omission of material available in the author's sources, and so forth. These factors can be as significant for an understanding of the text as what the author has stated. Another particularly significant element within the text that has drawn the attention of the analysts is the symbolic language employed by an author. Such symbols sometimes recall the unconscious symbolic representations that emerge in dreams and fantasies.

In effect, the psychoanalytic reading of the New Testament text has en-
larged the concept of authorship, just as form criticism and structural analysis have done from their respective points of view. Obviously, then, a primary
area of interest in the psychoanalytic reading of the New Testament text is
the author himself. What is his personality structure? What is his emotional
development? How do these contribute to the work which has been produced? One can ask these questions of a Luke or of a Paul whose sixth and
seventh chapters of the Letter to the Romans are fertile territory for a psychoanalytic reading.

A psychoanalytic reading can be attentive to the psychoanalysis of the
characters portrayed in the New Testament, as well as to the author who has
portrayed them. The parable of the Prodigal Son (Luke 15:11–32) is an
ideal passage for psychoanalytic reading. The parable speaks of sibling rivalry
in conflict with paternity. Georges Crespy has seen in the prodigal son's
conduct a living-out of the Oedipal conflict, while Beirnaert speaks of desire
in regard to both the prodigal and his father. From a psychoanalytic point of
view, the conduct of the elder son is a story of aggression. From the individual characters whose tale is at least partially told in the New Testament,
one can turn to Jesus himself. A psychoanalytic reading of the New Testament offers the possibility of a psychoanalysis of "Jesus"—not as he was in
reality, but as he was portrayed by the evangelists.

Beyond the author and his characters, a psychoanalytic reading of the
New Testament must be attentive to the work itself. In this regard, Beirnaert
wrote, in a 1977 article on the psychoanalytic reading of the miracle narratives: "The work of analysis consists not in disengaging the hidden
significance of a manifest content but in disclosing in history what is being
said there about the relationship to meaning, of the place of death and
effacement of the speaking subject, and of the mechanism of distortion. . . .
We have to wait for the accounts of the passion and resurrection in order to
have it said that the death and effacement concern the speaking subject himself and in order to have what sustains Scripture and its meaning presented
in a content."

His comments bring us to the fourth and final concern of those who practice the psychoanalytic reading of the New Testament, namely its readers.
How does the reader identify with the text? To what sort of unconscious
desires does the text respond? These are but two of the questions the analyst
asks as he or she approaches the New Testament. The analyst's reading of
the text is, therefore, not an exercise in history, nor is it a theological study.
Rather it is a psychoanalytic endeavor, which, departing from an anthropology different from, but complementary to, the anthropologies of history
and theology, allows the New Testament to be "understood" in a new light.

The psychoanalytic reading of the New Testament is properly called
"reading" rather than exegesis since it presupposes a theory of the text,
namely that the text is the product of pre- and un- conscious factors as well
as those conscious factors of which the author is quite cognizant. A materialistic reading of the New Testament text also presupposes a theory of the

text. The operative theory is that a text, and therefore the New Testament text as well, is the product of an economic-political-ideological process. The materialistic—usually Marxist—reading of the New Testament text shares with those who are engaged in the psychoanalytic reading of the text a dependence on structural analysis. All three of these approaches to the New Testament look upon the New Testament as a narrative, rather than as a source for historical investigation or a basis for theological reflection.

Whereas the psychoanalytic reading of the New Testament is particularly attentive to the gaps and discordances in the text and its use of symbolic language, the materialistic or Marxist reading of the text requires that attention be drawn to the various linguistic codes (topographical, effective, strategic, analytic, etc.) used by the author in the exposition of his narrative. Identification of the codes running throughout the narrative and analysis of their interaction are all-important for the materialistic understanding of the text. The identification of the codes makes it possible to take account of the effect of the social, political, and economic formation process in the very detail of the text itself. The significance of the codes has been highlighted by Fernando Belo (1933–   ), the Portuguese Marxist Christian. In *A Materialist Reading of the Gospel of Mark** (*Lecture matérialiste de l'évangile de Marc: Récit-Pratique-Idéologie*) (1974), Belo exploits two uses of the social code in Mark 1, to wit, the "fishermen" of Mark 1:16 and the "scribes" of Mark 1:20. Belo has noted that the use of "fishermen" identifies the four disciples as belonging to a dominated class. Apropos of Mark 1:20, he wrote that "A *new* practice stands over against a habitual, repetitive ideological practice: there is a difference between the practice of SOC [Society] and the practice of J [Jesus]." From these examples one can get a taste of the importance of the codes as well as of the orientation of Belo's reading of Mark.

Since Belo's work has been called "the most sensational and startling production of this genre" (Robin Scroggs)—that is, of the materialistic reading of the New Testament—it might be well to identify some of the principal themes present in his reading of Mark. The notion of Jesus' messiahship is of major importance. For Belo, Mark reveals a Jesus who is a teacher and actor of a messianic practice. The doing of his messiahship is more important than his teaching about it. Praxis is more important than ideology. In Belo's materialistic understanding of Mark, the resurrection of the body is an important symbol. The Gospel is oriented toward the Resurrection. By reading Mark, the reader is pointed toward the future, which is life in the body. In Belo's reading of Mark, this feature is construed as anti-idealist and anti-bourgeois. It can be attained only by following the messianic practice of Jesus.

It has been objected that Belo's reading of Mark is highly subjective and that its methodological approach represents a demythologization which is even more radical than that of Rudolf Bultmann. From it results a "Jesus" who is a communist, and a Christian charity which is no more than a Marxist sharing of what one has. Although the objection may well be justified, Belo's efforts at least point to the fact that the understanding of a text depends not only on the text itself, but also on the reader of the text. Moreover, Belo has raised the question, and posed it in very sharp fashion, as to whether the Gospel has something to say to men and women of the twentieth century who are suffering from political oppression, economic domination, and other forms of human and social ill. In posing the question in this radical fashion, Belo has joined other radical thinkers, notably José Miranda (*Marx and the Bible;* *Marx y la biblia,* 1971) and the Czech author Milan Machoveč (*A Marxist Looks at Jesus;* *Jesus für Atheisten,* 1972).

The Marxist reading of the text conveyed by their provocative essays is not to be dissociated from a broader current in New Testament interpretation. During the past few years a fair amount of research into the social history of the early Church has been done by Gerd Theissen in Germany, as well as by such Americans as the Yale scholars Wayne Meeks and Abraham Malherbe. Theissen has, moreover, used the sociological model of role analysis to characterize the "wandering charismatics" of Palestinian Christianity and Paul, the "community organizer." In this respect, Theissen is a pioneer in the sociological analysis of early Christianity.

In short, the history of the development of a methodology for understanding the New Testament is a history whose final page has not yet been written. The search for an adequate methodology is still in process. The process has nonetheless yielded some significant results. To these we can now turn in a systematic exposition of some aspects of the historical-critical methodology.

SELECT BIBLIOGRAPHY

A. GENERAL WORKS

Bovon, François, and Rouiller, Grégoire, eds. *Exegesis. Problèmes de méthode et exercices de lecture.* (*Genèse 22 et Luc 15*). Neuchatel-Paris: *Bibliothèque théologique,* 1975.

Brown, Raymond E., and Cahill, P. Joseph. *Biblical Tendencies Today. An Introduction to the Post-Bultmannians. Corpus Papers.* Washington: Corpus, 1969.

Davidson, Robert, and Leaney, A. R. C. *The Pelican Guide to Modern Theology.* Vol. III: *Biblical Criticism.* Harmondsworth: Pelican, 1970.

Ellis, E. Earle. *Paul and His Recent Interpreters.* Grand Rapids: Eerdmans, 1961.

Genthe, Hans Jochen. *Kleine Geschichte der neutestamentlichen Wissenschaft.* Göttingen: Vandenhoeck & Ruprecht, 1977.

Harris, Horton. *The Tübingen School.* Oxford: Clarendon, 1975.

Hein, S. "The Crisis in Biblical Authority: A Historical Analysis." *Concordia Theological Quarterly,* 41 (1977), 61–77.

Krentz, Edgar. *The Historical-Critical Method. Guides to Biblical Scholarship.* Philadelphia: Fortress, 1975.

Kümmel, Werner Georg. *Das Neue Testament im 20. Jahrhundert. Ein Forschungsbericht. Stuttgarter Bibelstudien,* 50. Stuttgart: KBW, 1970.

————. *The New Testament. The History of the Investigation of Its Problems.* London: SCM, 1973.

Küng, Hans, and Moltmann, Jürgen, eds. *Conflicting Ways of Interpreting the Bible. Concilium,* 138. New York: Seabury, 1980.

Lewis, Jack P. "The New Testament in the Twentieth Century." *Restoration Quarterly,* 18 (1975), 193–215.

Meier, Gerhard. *The End of the Historical-Critical Method.* St. Louis: Concordia, 1977.

Meyer, Ben F. *The Aims of Jesus.* London: SCM, 1979.

Mussner, Franz. *Geschichte der Hermeneutik. Von Schleiermacher bis zum Gegenwart. Handbuch der Dogmengeschichte,* vol. I, 3c, part 2. Freiburg: Herder, 1970.

Neill, Stephen. *The Interpretation of the New Testament: 1861–1961.* London: Oxford, 1964.

Nineham, David E. *New Testament Interpretation in an Historical Age.* London: Athlone, 1976.

Olbricht, Thomas H. "New Testament Studies at the University of Chicago: The First Decade, 1892–1902." *Restoration Quarterly,* 22 (1979), 84–99.

Les Quatres fleuves 7 (1977) *Lectures actuelles de la Bible.*

Ridderbos, Hermann. *Paul.* London: SPCK, 1977.

Robinson, James M. *A New Quest of the Historical Jesus. Studies in Biblical Theology,* 25. London: SCM, 1959.

Rogers, Jack Bartlett, and McKim, Donald H. *The Authority and Interpretation of the Bible. An Historical Approach.* New York: Harper & Row, 1979.

Scroggs, Robin. "The Sociological Interpretation of the New Testament: The Present State of Research." *New Testament Studies,* 26 (1980), 164–79.

Stancil, B. "Structuralism and New Testament Studies," *Southwestern Journal of Theology,* 22 (1980), 41–59.

Vergote, Antoon. "Jesus de Nazareth sous le regard de la psychologie religieuse." Ch. 3 in *Jesus Christ, Fils de Dieu. Publications des facultés universitaires Saint-Louis,* 18, by Albert Dondeyne et al. Brussels: Facultés universitaires Saint-Louis, 1981, pp. 115–46.

B. A FEW MONOGRAPHS

Bacon, B. W. *Benjamin Wisner Bacon. Pioneer in American Biblical Scholarship,* 2. *Schools and Scholars,* 2. by R. A. Harrisville. Missoula: Scholars Press, 1976.

Bauer, Walter. "That Dictionary Man Walter Bauer," by J. A. Flora. *Ashland Theological Bulletin,* 6 (1973), 3–11.

————. "Walter Bauer—Exeget, Philologe und Historiker. Zum 100 Geburtstag am 8.8. 1977," by Georg Strecker. *Novum Testamentum*, 20 (1978), 75–80.

Bonnard, Pierre. "Pierre Bonnard, exégète du Nouveau Testament," by J. Zumstein. *Bulletin du Centre Protestant d'Études*, 30 (1978), 5–12.

Bultmann, Rudolf. *Bultmann et l'interprétation du Nouveau Testament. Théologie*, 33, by René Marlé. Paris: Aubier, 1956.

———. *Gedenken an Rudolf Bultmann*, ed. by O. Kaiser. Tübingen: Mohr-Siebeck, 1977.

———. *Index to Literature on Barth, Bonhoeffer and Bultmann. Sonderband zur Theologische Zeitschrift*, 7, by M. Kwiran. Basel: Friedrich Reinhardt, 1977.

———. *The Origins of Demythologizing. Philosophy and Historiography in the Theology of Rudolf Bultmann. Studies in the History of Religions*, 28, by R. A. Johnson. Leiden: Brill, 1974.

———. "A Salute to Bultmann," by D. Nineham. *Epworth Review*, 4 (1977), 7–12.

———. *The Theology of Rudolf Bultmann*, ed. by C. W. Kegley. New York: Harper & Row, 1966.

———. *The Thought of Rudolf Bultmann*, by A. Malet. Shannon: Irish University Press, 1970.

Case, Shirley Jackson. *Shirley Jackson Case and the Chicago School. The Socio-Historical Method*, by William Hynes. Chico, Calif.: Scholars Press, 1981.

Cerfaux, Lucien. "Msgr. Lucien Cerfaux (1883–1968)," by R. F. Collins. *Louvain Studies*, 5 (1974–75), 298–305.

Daniélou, Jean. *Jean Daniélou. 1905–1974*, by M. J. Rondeau et al. Paris: Cerf, 1975.

Dodd, C. H. *Charles Harold Dodd, 1884–1973. A Bibliography of His Published Writings. Lexington Theological Seminary Library Occasional Studies*, by R. W. Graham. Lexington: Theological Seminary, 1974.

———. "C. H. Dodd. His Work and His Interpreters," by R. W. Graham. *Lexington Theological Quarterly*, 8 (1973), 1–10.

———. *C. H. Dodd. Interpreter of the New Testament*, by F. W. Dillistone. London: Hodder & Stoughton, 1977.

Ebeling, Gerhard. "La teoria del linguaggio teologica in Gerhard Ebeling," by V. Pasquetto. *Ephemerides Carmeliticae*, 26 (1975), 3–45.

Goodspeed, E. J. *Edward Johnson Goodspeed: Articulate Scholar*, by James I. Cook. Chico, Calif.: Scholars Press, 1980.

Griesbach, Johann Jakob. *J. J. Griesbach: Synoptic and Text-critical Studies 1776–1976*, ed. by Bernard Orchard and Thomas R. W. Longstaff. *Society for New Testament Studies Monograph Series*, 34. Cambridge: University Press, 1978.

Harnack, Adolf von. "Adolf Harnack und Theodor Zahn. Geschichte und Bedeutung einer gelehrten Freundschaft," by F. W. Katzenbach. *Zeitschrift für Kirchengeschichte*, 83 (1972), 226–44.

Hodge, Charles. "Charles Hodge as an American New Testament Interpreter," by T. H. Olbricht. *Journal of Presbyterian History,* 57 (1979), 117–33.

Holtzmann, H. J. "Holtzmann, von Hugel and Modernism," by H. Rollman. *Downside Review,* 97 (1979), 128–43, 221–44.

Hort, F. J. A. "F. J. A. Hort, 1828–1893. A Neglected Theologian," G. A. Patrick. *Expository Times,* 90 (1978), 77–81.

Jeremias, Joachim. "Joachim Jeremias," by M. Hengel. *Zeitschrift des Deutschen Palästina-Vereins,* 94 (1978), 89–92.

Lagrange, M.-J. *Memorial Lagrange. Cinquantenaire de l'École biblique et archéologique française de Jerusalem, 15 Nov 1890–15 Nov 1940,* ed. by L. H. Vincent. Paris: Gabalda, 1940.

————. *The Work of Père Lagrange,* by F. M. Braun. Milwaukee: Bruce, 1963.

————. "Père Lagrange and the Modernist Crisis," by H. Wansbrough. *Clergy Review,* 62 (1977), 446–52.

Lightfoot, R. H. "The Place of R. H. Lightfoot in British New Testament Scholarship," by B. G. Powley. *Expository Times,* 93 (1981), 72–75.

Loisy, Alfred. *Alfred Loisy als Historiker der Urchristentums (Grundzuge seiner neutestamentlichen Arbeit),* by P. Klein. Bonn: Rheinische Friedrich-Wilhelmsuniversität, 1977.

————. "Great Interpreters—VII. Alfred Loisy (1857–1940)," by A. H. Jones. *Scripture Bulletin,* 8 (1977), 15–16.

————. "Problema del cristianesimo e critica storica in Alfred Loisy," by M. Ivaldo, *Rassegna di Teologia,* 18 (1977), 360–75.

Machen, J. Gresham. "J. Gresham Machen: Apologist and Exegete," by C. Story. *Princeton Seminary Bulletin,* 2 (1979), 91–103.

Porter, F. C. *Frank Chamberlain Porter. Pioneer in American Biblical Criticism. Studies in American Biblical Scholarship,* 1. *Schools and Scholars,* 1, by R. A. Harrisville. Missoula: Scholars Press, 1976.

————. "Porter of Yale—Teacher of the Niebuhrs: A Tiny Page in the History of American Biblical Scholarship," by R. A. Harrisville. *Dialog,* 14 (1975), 283–88.

Reimarus, H. S. *Hermann Samuel Reimarus (1694–1768). Ein "bekannter Unbekannter" der Aufklarung in Hamburg.* Göttingen: Vandenhoeck & Ruprecht, 1977.

Renan, Ernest. "Ernest Renan as a historian of religions," by R. Williamson. *Religion,* 9 (1979), 59–72.

Schaff, Philip. "Blazing the Frontiers of American Ecumenism," by J. C. Meyer. *Louvain Studies,* 6 (1966–67), 3–10.

Schlatter, Adolf. "Great Interpreters—III. Adolf Schlatter (1852–1938)," by R. Morgan. *Scripture Bulletin,* 4 (1972), 3–4.

Schweitzer, Albert. *Albert Schweitzer. A Comprehensive Biography,* by J. Brabazon. New York: G. P. Putnam's Sons, 1975.

————. *Albert Schweitzer. Grüsse und Grenzen. Eine kritische Wurdigung des Forschers und Denkers,* by H. Groos. Munich: Reinhardt, 1974.

————. "Albert Schweitzer: escatologia y hermeneutica," by A. Bentue. *Teologia y Vida,* 16 (1975), 152–64.

————. "Il metodo esegetico di Albert Schweitzer," by C. Ognibene. *Ricerche Bibliche e Religiose,* 12 (1977), 7–34.

————. "Albert Schweitzer and the New Testament," by C. K. Barrett. *Expository Times,* 87 (1975), 4–10.

Strauss, D. F. *David Friedrich Strauss and His Place in Modern Thought,* by R. S. Cromwell. Fairlawn, N.J.: Burdick, 1974.

————. *David Friedrich Strauss and His Theology. Monograph Supplements to the Scottish Journal of Theology,* by H. Harris. New York: Cambridge University Press, 1974.

Tischendorf, Constantin von. *Constantin von Tischendorf and the Greek New Testament,* by M. Black and R. Davidson. Glasgow University of Glasgow, 1981.

Wilder, Amos Niven. "Amos Niven Wilder: Bibliography and Vita," by A. J. Dewey. *Semeia,* 13 (1978), 263–86.

————. "Amos Niven Wilder: Poet and Scholar," by W. A. Beardslee. *Semeia,* 12 (1978), 1–14.

————. *A Fragile Craft: The Work of Amos Niven Wilder* by John Dominic Crossan. Chico, Calif.: Scholars Press, 1981.

C. A FEW CLASSICS

TRANSLATIONS INTO ENGLISH OF SOME OF THE MAJOR MILESTONES IN THE HISTORY OF NEW TESTAMENT CRITICISM.

Baur, F. C. *Paul the Apostle of Jesus Christ: His Life and Work, His Epistles and His Doctrine.* 2 vols. 2nd ed., London: Williams-Norgate, 1875–76. cf. "Biblical Classics: II. F. C. Baur: Paul," by R. Morgan. *Expository Times,* 90 (1978), 4–10.

Bousset, Wilhelm. *Kyrios Christos.* Nashville: Abingdon, 1970.

Bultmann, Rudolf. *Jesus and the Word.* New York: Scribner's, 1934. cf. "Biblical Classics: XII. Rudolf Bultmann: Jesus and the Word," by G. Stanton. *Expository Times,* 90 (1979), 324–28.

————. *The History of the Synoptic Tradition.* New York: Harper & Row, 1963.

————. *Theology of the New Testament.* 2 vols. New York: Scribner's, 1951, 1955.

Cremer, Hermann. *Biblico-Theological Lexicon of New Testament Greek.* 4th Eng. ed., New York: Scribner's, n.d.

Dalman, Gustaf. *Jesus-Jeshua. Studies in the Gospels.* New York: KTAV, 1971.

————. *The Words of Jesus,* Edinburgh: T & T Clark, 1902.

Dibelius, Martin. *From Tradition to Gospel.* New York: Scribner's, n.d.

Harnack, Adolf von. *The Sayings of Jesus. The Second Source of St. Matthew and St. Luke. New Testament Studies,* 2. New York: G. P. Putnam's Sons, 1908.

————. *What is Christianity?* New York: G. P. Putnam's Sons, 1901.

Jeremias, Joachim. *The Parables of Jesus.* New York: Scribner's, 1963.

Kähler, Martin. *The So-called Historical Jesus and the Historic Biblical Christ.* Philadelphia: Fortress, 1966.

Loisy, Alfred. *The Gospel and the Church.* Philadelphia: Fortress, 1976.

————. *The Origins of the New Testament.* New York: Macmillan, 1950.

Reimarus, H. S. *Reimarus: Fragments.* Philadelphia: Fortress, 1970.

Schweitzer, Albert. *The Mysticism of Paul the Apostle.* New York: Holt, 1931.

————. *Paul and His Interpreters. A Critical History.* London: A & C Black, 1912. New York: Macmillan, n.d.

————. *The Quest of the Historical Jesus.* New York: Macmillan, 1961.

Strauss, D. F. *The Christ of Faith and the Jesus of History. A Critique of Schleiermacher's The Life of Jesus.* Philadelphia: Fortress, 1977.

————. *The Life of Jesus Christ Critically Examined.* Philadelphia: Fortress, 1972.

Weiss, Johannes. *Jesus' Proclamation of the Kingdom of God.* Philadelphia: Fortress, 1971.

Wrede, William. *The Messianic Secret of the Gospels.* Cambridge: Clarke, 1971.

CHAPTER THREE

TEXTUAL CRITICISM

I. AN INTRODUCTION TO THE METHOD

The study of the history of the New Testament canon (see Chapter One) indicated that it is only toward the end of the fourth century that a consensus was reached as to which of the works of early Christian literature should be included in an authoritative canon. This fact makes it quite likely that our oldest manuscripts of the complete New Testament would date from approximately the same time. In point of fact, the Codex Sinaiticus and the Codex Vaticanus, our oldest extant complete manuscripts of the New Testament, are fourth-century documents. The oldest more or less complete manuscript of any one of the twenty-seven books in the New Testament is a copy of the Gospel of John, the Bodmer Papyrus II, $\mathfrak{p}^{66}$, dating from around A.D. 200 and presently preserved in the Bodmer Library near Geneva, Switzerland.

Thus we do not possess the autograph copy of any single New Testament book, nor do we have an autograph copy of even a single verse of the book. That we don't have at hand the original copy of any New Testament book is not at all surprising. The circumstances of the Church at the time when the New Testament writings were composed were not conducive to the preservation of these texts. For us a problem then arises when we compare the ancient New Testament manuscripts among themselves. No two ancient manuscripts of the New Testament agree in every respect. When any two of these manuscripts are compared, it is found that they differ in several respects and in several places. Indeed, uniformity of text had to await the invention of the printing press in the fifteenth century. Prior to that time, manuscripts were hand-copied and were subject to the inevitability of human error as well as to the occasional caprice of a scribe's whim or erudition. Thus all the manuscripts produced in the ancient scriptoria show marked variation one from another.

Some of the Fathers of the Church were well aware of this situation. In the early third century, Origen (ca. 185–254) complained that:

> the differences among the manuscripts have become great, either through the negligence of some copyists or through the perversity of others; they either neglect to check over what they have transcribed, or, in the process of checking, they lengthen or shorten as they please (*Comm. in Mt* 15:14).

Among the variant readings of which Origen was aware were two readings of Matthew 18:1: "At that time the disciples came to Jesus, saying, 'Who is the greatest in the kingdom of heaven?'" Origen noted that some manuscripts read "on that day" (*en ekeinē tē hēmera*) whereas others read "at that hour" (*en ekeinē tē hōra*). The Alexandrian Father also noted that some manuscripts of Hebrews 2:9 read, "But we see Jesus, who for a little while was made lower than the angels, crowned with glory and honor because of the suffering of death, so that by the grace of God (*chariti theou*) he might taste death for everyone," whereas other ancient witnesses read "without God" (*chōris theou*) instead of "by the grace of God."

The awareness that there did indeed exist variant readings for several passages of the New Testament was not limited to the East. Almost two hundred years after the death of Origen, Augustine of Hippo (354–430) voiced his perplexity on discovering that not all the manuscripts of Matthew ascribed the saying "And they took the thirty pieces of silver, the price of him of whom a price had been set by some of the sons of Israel, and they gave them for the potter's field, as the Lord directed me" (Matt 27:9–10) to the prophet Jeremiah. Some manuscripts simply ascribed the prophetic utterance to "the prophet." Augustine commented:

> A majority of manuscripts contain the name of Jeremiah, and those who have studied the Gospel with more than usual care in the Greek copies report that they have found it to stand so in the more ancient Greek exemplars (*De consensu Evangeliorum*, III, 7, 29).

Augustine himself believed that the reading of Matthew with the reference to Jeremiah was more correct. Indeed, Augustine proved to be somewhat of a forerunner of the science of textual criticism when he noted this further consideration:

> . . . there was no reason why this name should have been added and a corruption thus created; whereas there was certainly an intelligible reason for erasing the name from so many of the manuscripts.

The phenomenon of variant readings already known to Origen and Augustine is even more fully appreciated at the present time. Not only do we know that no two ancient manuscripts fully agree with one another, we also have come to discover that some of the ancient manuscripts were themselves corrected, so that we must distinguish between the work of the original copyist —the so-called *prima manus* (first hand)—and the work of "correctors." In the seventeenth century, John Mill (1645–1707) was able to identify some 30,000 variant readings in the manuscripts known by him. Today, with over 10,000 entries in our catalogue of New Testament manuscripts, the number of variant readings numbers about 200,000. Some of these variants are merely the mechanical and clerical blunders of scribes who have misspelled words and transposed letters. Other variants are far more significant.

Immediately there arises the question: what is the text of the New Testament? This question must be posed in very precise terms. The Greek text of the New Testament found in the *Novum Testamentum Graece* edited by Kurt Aland et al. (26th ed., 1979), the most popular handbook edition of the Greek New Testament, contains approximately 2,500 variants from the reading offered by any one of the typical ancient manuscripts. Modern editors have apparently come to the conclusion that no one of the ancient manuscripts offers a "correct" reading of the New Testament text in all its details. Accordingly it falls to the science of textual criticism to judge the ancient manuscripts and thus ascertain the "correct" reading of the text of the New Testament.

Some Modern Examples

Some elements of the science of textual criticism are well known to many of us, especially to office workers and editors. Some months ago, for example, I wrote to the registrar of our university about a student who did not have sufficient credits in philosophy and thus had not fulfilled the prerequisite for admission to our graduate program in theology. An excerpt from the draft of my letter was as follows:

> ". . . background in philosophy. At the University of Washington he followed a course in philosophical analysis (logic) and a course of introduction to social ethics. At the Catholic University of America, he followed an additional course in ethics, Approaches to Morality . . ."

The secretary typed up the letter from my draft and presented me with a copy which read as follows:

> ". . . background in philosophy. At the University of Washington he followed an additional course in ethics, Approaches to Morality . . ."

The letter which the secretary placed before me for my signature was incorrect because she had omitted two lines from my draft text. It was easy to explain the omission. The secretary's eye had jumped from "followed" in the second line of my draft to "followed" in the fourth line. Somewhat unfamiliar with the particularities of the case about which I was writing, she did not catch her own mistake. I caught the error because I knew how the finished letter should have read. The correction of the letter resulted from the fact that I had practiced one of the very simple techniques of textual criticism. The correction was easy because both the original draft and the copy were made within a relatively short period, and I (the author of the draft) was in personal contact with the copyist (the secretary).

It sometimes happens that I dictate letters, either directly to a secretary or to her with the help of a dictating machine. In these instances homonyms are particularly vexing. More than once I have begun a paragraph, "To cite your reference . . ." or "to cite . . ." (with the name of a particular author), but the typed text I would receive would read, "To sight your reference" or "to sight Smith" as if I were a landscape engineer or an actor looking out upon his audience. Once again the advantages of being in close proximity to the circumstances have allowed for an accommodation of the mistaken version to the "correct text."

Oftentimes, moreover, I have found that I have had to perform a simple exercise in text criticism when reading a book or correcting a printer's galley proofs. In the latter case, even though I might not have been the author of the text I was correcting, I usually have had before me the author's manuscript. So if the reading "In the remaining letters of the Pauline Corpus, an exception being made for Heb with has its own particular understanding of faith . . ." doesn't ring true, I can check the galleys against the manuscript copy. Yet even if I don't have the original manuscript, I can surmise that the original text must surely have read ". . . an exception being made for Heb which has its own . . ." Otherwise the text doesn't make any real sense.

When reading a printed text, I frequently come upon obvious mistakes which I spontaneously correct, attributing the error to a typist or typesetter. When reading an article on John 2:1–11, I recently read that ". . . Spicq is perhaps pressing the point tto far. The Christology of the story of water-become-wine would seem to be more functional than ontolofical." There was no difficulty in considering that the passage contained a pair of typographical errors. I read "too" in the first sentence, and "ontological" in the second and my text made full sense. Earlier on in the same article, however, I read ". . . the Fourth Gospel tells the tale of but seven of eight miracles performed by Jesus . . ." At that point my judgment as to what the original text ought to have been was not so well defined. Did the author mean to imply that there were eight miracles narrated in the Signs Source and that the evangelist chose seven of them for his Gospel? This would be the case were I to take the second "of" at its face value. Or did the author mean to imply that the evangelist chose for his Gospel seven or eight miracles from among the many narrated in the Signs Source? To suppose that the second "of" was mistakenly inserted into the text in place of "or" by a careless typesetter is to suppose that the printer veiled the author's doubt either as to whether the Signs Source contained the narrative of the miraculous catch of fish (John

21) or whether the Walking on Water (John 6:16–21) should really be classified as the tale of a miracle.

Although some aspect of the work of textual criticism had to be employed in "correcting the text" in all the examples cited above, the task was relatively simple. In each instance I was dealing with one copy and one original text. Both the copy and the text were produced in an environment which was familiar to me, the language was my own, and I was relatively familiar with the type of thought being expressed. Indeed, in many of the cited instances it was my own thought that was misexpressed. When we are dealing with the New Testament manuscripts, however, we are dealing with a time span of several centuries. This space of time obviously implies that there was no possibility of personal contact between the original author (Paul, for example) and the copyist responsible for the text of Romans in the fourth-century *Codex Sinaiticus*. Between Paul and his copyist there was a wide idiomatic, ideological, and cultural gap.

Moreover when we are dealing with the textual criticism of New Testament manuscripts, it is not a matter of comparing a single copy with the original or autograph text, but of trying to reconstitute an "original text" on the basis of many widely divergent copies. In this situation the fact that the original author is not available to assist in the determination of the "correct reading" certainly means that the science of New Testament text criticism is rather a bit more complicated than my own correction of a letter which I had personally composed in draft form.

In any event, the critical and popular editions of the Greek New Testament are based on judgments made by text critics on the basis of the several manuscripts available to them. Increasingly, New Testament text critics are working in collaboration with one another. Modern technology (microfilm, infrared rays, etc.) has made it possible for text critics to have an increasingly large quantity of manuscript material available for comparison's sake.

Given the multiplicity of the evidence and the complexity of the issues, it might be better to think that text criticism is a task that would be more correctly styled the "art" of text criticism than the "science" of text criticism. In that case the strictly "scientific" role of text criticism can be restricted to the work of dating and localizing the available New Testament manuscripts. Beyond that specifically technical endeavor, a fair amount of judicious judgment on the part of the text critic enters into the work of text criticism. Indeed, if one were to assess the text-critical studies of New Testament manuscripts with full honesty, one would have to admit that they yield neither the "original text" nor the "correct text" of the New Testament. The best result that can be obtained from the text-critical study of the New Testament is the reconstitution of a text which is relatively original—that is, a text which was in use in the churches of relatively ancient times. It is to the reconstitution of that text, today printed as "The Greek New Testament," that we must now turn our attention.

II. THE USE OF TEXTUAL CRITICISM IN NEW TESTAMENT STUDIES

The Material

Almost a century ago, the Cambridge scholar Fenton John Anthony Hort (1828–92) stressed the idea that knowledge of the documents should precede a final judgment of readings. The principal documents used by textual critics in their attempts to establish a relatively original text of the New Testament are some 5,000 Greek New Testament manuscripts. These manuscripts are generally divided into several different categories according to the material of the manuscripts (papyrus and parchment), the script utilized in the manuscript (majuscules and minuscules), and the use to which these texts are put (lectionaries).

The Papyri

The *papyri* constitute our most ancient extant manuscripts of the New Testament. Thus far some eighty-eight fragmentary manuscripts have been identified and catalogued. The papyri manuscripts are designated by a Gothic or Old English "P" ($\mathfrak{p}$) with a numerical exponent, from 1 to 88, indicating a specific New Testament papyrus. As their name indicates, the papyri are made of the stalks of the papyrus plant. The plant grows in abundance along the banks of the Nile and several other East African rivers. The cut leaves of the papyrus plant are placed side by side in sheet form upon another sheet of papyrus leaves. Pressed together and dried out, papyrus leaves provided an early form of paper. Up to twenty sections of pressed papyri could be pasted together to form a roll (*volumen*); alternatively papyrus sheets could be bound together in the form of a book (*codex*).

The principal New Testament papyri date from the third and fourth centuries, but some date from as late as the seventh century, and one comes from the early second century. This fragment, the oldest copy of any portion of the New Testament known to be in existence, is preserved in the John Rylands Library, Manchester, England. The 2½-by-3½-inch manuscript is designated $\mathfrak{p}^{52}$. Although the papyrus contains but a few verses of John's Gospel (John 18:31–33 recto and John 18:37–38 verso), it is a singularly important witness to the antiquity of the Fourth Gospel. $\mathfrak{p}^{1}$ is a third-century papyrus presently preserved in the museum of the University of Pennsylvania in Philadelphia. It contains some considerable parts of the first chapter of Matthew (Matt 1:1–9, 12, 14–20).

The most important papyri for the study of the New Testament are those that belong to the Chester Beatty and Bodmer collections. Three third-century papyri were acquired by A. Chester Beatty in 1930–31. They have been edited by F. G. Kenyon and are presently preserved in the Beatty Museum outside of Dublin, Ireland. $\mathfrak{p}^{45}$ is the designation given to a 220-leaf codex of which some thirty leaves are preserved in the Dublin museum. There are six leaves of Mark, seven of Luke, and thirteen of Acts but only two each of Matthew and John. Thus the Beatty text of John contains but John 10:7–25; 10:30–11:10, 18–36, 42–57. Another leaf containing some fragments of Matthew has turned up in a collection of papyri at Vienna. $\mathfrak{p}^{46}$ is the oldest of the three biblical papyri in the Beatty collection. Some 86 mutilated leaves of the codex's 104 original leaves have been preserved. These leaves contain fragments of nine Pauline letters according to the following order: Romans, Hebrews, 1,2 Corinthians, Ephesians, Galatians, Philippians, Colossians, 1 Thessalonians. $\mathfrak{p}^{47}$ represents the ten middle leaves of a thirty-two-page codex. The text contains Revelation 9:10–17:2.

The Bodmer collection is housed in the Bodmer Library of World Literature at Cologny, near Geneva, Switzerland. The biblical papyri $\mathfrak{p}^{66}$, $\mathfrak{p}^{72}$, $\mathfrak{p}^{73}$, $\mathfrak{p}^{74}$, and $\mathfrak{p}^{75}$ were acquired by Martin Bodmer in 1955–56. Among these five papyri, $\mathfrak{p}^{66}$, $\mathfrak{p}^{72}$, and $\mathfrak{p}^{75}$ are considerably older than the other two. $\mathfrak{p}^{66}$ (Bodmer II) dates from about A.D. 200 and represents one of the oldest longer fragments of the Greek New Testament. It contains John 1:1–6:11; 6:35–14:26, 29–30; 15:2–26; 16:2–4, 6–7; 16:10–20:20, 22–23; 20:25–21:9. One fragment of this codex, that containing John 19:25–28, 31–32, is presently preserved with the Beatty papyri in Dublin. The text of $\mathfrak{p}^{66}$ offers some 370 variants from the "neutral" text identified by Westcott and Hort. $\mathfrak{p}^{72}$ (Bodmer VII–VIII) contains a variety of ancient texts, including one of the Odes of Solomon and the apocryphal correspondence of Paul with the Corinthians. Within this assortment of disparate material is to be found the earliest known copy of the Epistle of Jude as well as a copy of 1,2 Peter. $\mathfrak{p}^{75}$ (Bodmer XIV–XV) contains some considerable portions of the Gospels of Luke and John on 102 leaves. Thus the papyrus represents the oldest extant text of the Gospel of Luke and one of the earliest of John.

At the turn of the century (1897–1907), at Oxyrhynchus, near Behnesa in Upper Egypt, B. P. Grenfell and A. S. Hunt discovered a veritable treasure trove of papyri manuscripts. These manuscripts date from the second century B.C. until the seventh century A.D. They contain a wide assortment of texts, including fragmentary manuscripts of both the Old and New Testament and apocryphal collections of Jesus' sayings as well. Among the Oxyrhynchus papyri, $\mathfrak{p}^{77}$ (P. Oxy. 2683), containing a codex fragment of Matthew 23:30–39, deserves particular attention. This text, written in the late second century, is one of the oldest New Testament texts available to us. $\mathfrak{p}^{70}$ (P. Oxy. 2384) and $\mathfrak{p}^{71}$ (P. Oxy. 2385), dating from the third and fourth centuries respectively, also contain fragments of Matthew, while $\mathfrak{p}^{69}$ (P. Oxy. 2383) is a third-century fragment with nine verses of Luke

(22:41, 45–48, 58–61). 𝔭⁷⁸ (P. Oxy. 2684) is a double leaf from a small codex. It is a third- or fourth-century manuscript containing Jude 4–5, 7–8.

The Majuscules

Parchment manuscripts are written on processed animal hides. New Testament parchment manuscripts are normally classified in two principal categories according to the script employed by the scribe. The uncial or majuscule style was in use from the fourth to the tenth centuries A.D. This style of writing is so called by reason of the size of the letters, *uncia* being the twelfth part of something, thus an inch. The letters were rounded capitals and were written on the parchment without any space between them. The New Testament uncial manuscripts make frequent use of abbreviations, particularly for the *nomina sacra* (sacred names) and other proper names. Occasionally the abbreviation consists of the first and the last letters of the Greek word (θΣ = *theos,* God; ΚΣ = *kurios,* Lord; ΙΣ = *Iēsous,* Jesus). At other times the abbreviation consists of the first two and the last letters of the Greek word (ΠΝΑ = *pneuma,* Spirit; ΔΑΔ = *Dauid,* David; ΜΑΡ = *matēr,* mother); the first letter and the final two letters (ΠΗΡ = *patēr,* father; ΣΗΡ = *sōtēr,* Savior; ΙΕΛ = *Israēl,* Israel); or the first letter and the final syllable (ΑΠΟΣ = *anthrōpos,* man; ΟΝΟΣ = *ouranos,* heaven; ΙΛΗΜ = *Iērousalēm,* Jerusalem).

Each of the parchment manuscripts, like each of the papyri, was transcribed at a given moment in time in a specific place. Normally a specific purpose, if only that of replacing a worn-out copy of the text or of providing a fresh copy for a new community, lies behind the transcription of each manuscript. These circumstances of time, place, and purpose are often reflected in the manuscripts themselves. The information they provide is of value to the Church historian as well as to the New Testament scholar (see below, "The Genealogical Method"). The Codex Sinaiticus, for example, commonly held to be the oldest complete manuscript of the New Testament, was transcribed in Egypt during the middle of the fourth century. It represents the work of four scribes, two of whom worked on the New Testament text. From the fourth to the twelfth centuries, the manuscript was emended by nine different correctors.

A system of sigla was devised for the identification of the uncial manuscripts by Johann Jacob Wettstein (1693–1754). He designated the then known uncials by capital letters, using first Latin letters and then Greek. Wettstein's system of classification is of limited use today because of the abundance of uncial manuscripts, of which 274 have thus far been catalogued. So, in addition to the traditional letter designation of New Testament uncial manuscripts, there is also in use a system of manuscript designation devised by Caspar René Gregory (1846–1917), a professor at the University of Leipzig. Gregory designated each of the uncials by an Arabic numeral preceded by a zero. Gregory's system of classification of the uncial manuscripts is in wide use, even though most authors still prefer to refer to the most frequently cited uncials according to the letter system devised by Wett-stein.

Among the principal New Testament uncials are the following:

ℵ   (01)   The Codex Sinaiticus, a fourth-century manuscript containing the entire Bible. It was discovered by Constantin Tischendorf (1815–74) in the monastery of St. Catherine on Mount Sinai in 1844. Presently it is preserved in the British Museum in London.

A   (02)   The Codex Alexandrinus, a fifth-century New Testament manu-script whose first leaves are missing. The manuscript lacks the leaves containing Matthew 1:1 – 25:6, John 6:50 – 8:52 and 2 Corinthians 4:13 – 12:6. The manuscript is housed in the British Museum.

B   (03)   The Codex Vaticanus, a fourth-century manuscript of the entire Bible from which the final leaves are missing. Thus Hebrews 9:14 – 13:25, 1,2 Timothy, Titus, Philemon, and Revelation are not found in the manuscript. The manuscript is presently pre-served in the Vatican Library where it has been since at least 1475.

C   (04)   The Codex Ephraemi Rescriptus, a fifth-century palimpsest of the Greek Bible. In the twelfth century several leaves of biblical text were erased and the parchment was reused for thirty-eight ascetical sermons of St. Ephraem (306–73), a Syrian biblical exegete and ecclesiastical writer. The manuscript, presently preserved in Paris at the Bibliothèque Nationale, contains 145 leaves of the New Testament.

D   (05)   The Codex Bezae Cantabrigiensis, a fifth-century manuscript of the Gospels and Acts, from which several leaves containing portions of Matthew (1:1–20; 6:20 – 9:2; 27:2–12) and John (1:16 – 3:26) are missing. The manuscript is preserved at Cam-bridge, England, in the University Library. It was presented to the university in 1581 by Théodore de Bèze (1519–1605), a Calvinist churchman and biblical scholar.

D   (06)   The Codex Claromontanus, a sixth-century manuscript which contains only the Pauline epistles (including Hebrews). Like D (05), it is a bilingual Greek and Latin manuscript with the Greek written on the left-hand page and the Latin on the right. Along with C, it is preserved in the Bibliothèque Nationale in Paris.

E   (07)   The Codex Basileensis, an eighth-century manuscript which con-tains the four Gospels on 318 leaves. The leaves containing

Luke 3:4–15 and 24:47–53 are missing. The manuscript is preserved at the University Library in Basel, Switzerland.

E   (08)   The Codex Laudianus, a sixth-century manuscript which contains the text of Acts in Latin and in Greek. It was formerly in the possession of Archbishop William Laud (1573–1645) who donated it and several other ancient manuscripts to the Bodleian Library at Oxford, where it is still preserved.

L   (019) The Codex Regius, an eighth-century manuscript from which several leaves (Matt 4:22–5:14; 28:17–20; Mark 10:16–30; 15:2–20; John 21:15–25) are missing. The most notable feature of this badly written manuscript is the presence of two endings for Mark, the traditional Mark 16:9–20 and a so-called "shorter ending." The codex is also to be found in the Bibliothèque Nationale in Paris.

W   (032) The Codex Washingtoniensis (Codex Freerianus), an early-fifth-century manuscript which contains the Gospels according to the following order: Matthew, John, Luke, Mark—the so-called western order. The codex lacks Mark 15:12–38, and John 14:26–16:7. It contains the "canonical ending" of Mark (Mark 16:9–20), with a lengthy insertion, the so-called Freer logion, at the end of Mark 16:14. It was acquired by Charles L. Freer of Detroit in 1905 and is presently located in the Freer Gallery of Art at the Smithsonian Institution, Washington, D.C.

Δ   (037) The Codex Sangallensis, a ninth-century Graeco-Latin interlinear manuscript. It contains the four Gospels with the exception of John 19:17–35. It is housed in the Stiftsbibliothek, St. Gall, Switzerland.

θ   (038) The Codex Koridethi, a ninth-century manuscript discovered in the Church of Sts. Kerykos and Julitta at Koridethi in the Caucasian Mountains. The manuscript contains the four Gospels with the exception of Matthew 1:1–9; 1:21–4:4; 4:17–5:4. It is presently preserved at Tiflis, in Soviet Russia.

The Minuscules

The *minuscule* style of writing, probably introduced in the beginning of the ninth century, predominated from the eleventh century. The letters of the minuscule manuscripts are written in a cursive hand, much smaller than the letters of the uncials. Frequently the letters are written sequentially, not lifting the pen from the page. Since the minuscule style of writing continued in use as long as books continued to be copied by hand, the vast majority of the Greek New Testament manuscripts are minuscules. New Testament minuscules are generally written on parchment, but several of these are fragmentary. The oldest New Testament minuscule (Ms. 461) dates from A.D. 835.

Following along the lines initially suggested by Gregory, the New Testament minuscules are generally identified by an Arabic numeral. The minuscules are too numerous to reference in detail, but the following minuscules can be cited as among the more important:

1   A twelfth-century Gospel manuscript, identified as a member of the so-called Lake family. It is to be found in the University Library in Basel, Switzerland.

13   A thirteenth-century manuscript of the Gospels, whose literary similarities with Mss. 69, 124, and 346 were identified by William Hugh Farrar in 1868. Ms. 13 is located in the Bibliothèque Nationale, Paris.

33   A ninth-century manuscript containing the entire New Testament with the exception of Acts. Frequently called the "queen of the cursives," it is housed in the Bibliothèque Nationale, Paris.

61   A sixteenth-century manuscript of the entire New Testament. It is preserved at Trinity College, Dublin, Ireland. Its significance lies in the fact that it is the oldest Greek manuscript known to contain the so-called Johannine Comma (1 John 5:7–8).

565   A ninth-century Gospel manuscript, written in gold letters on purple parchment. At the end of Mark it contains the so-called Jerusalem colophon, which states that it was copied and corrected "from the ancient manuscripts at Jerusalem."

1424   A ninth- or tenth-century manuscript of the entire New Testament. The books are presented in a rather strange order, viz., Gospels, Acts, Catholic epistles, Revelation, the Pauline epistles. With the exception of Revelation, all of the New Testament books are supplied with a commentary. The manuscript is preserved in the Lutheran Theological Seminary at Maywood, Illinois.

1739   A tenth-century manuscript of the Acts and the Epistles discovered at Mount Athos in 1879 by E. von der Goltz. It is important in that it presents a relatively pure form of the Alexandrian type of text of the Pauline epistles.

The Lectionaries

In addition to the types of manuscript material that have been briefly described, the lectionaries must also be cited as preserving the Greek New Testament text in a continuous reading. In some of the later uncials and in many of the minuscules (e.g., Ms. 1345) the readings appointed for specified liturgical services were indicated. A marginal rubric might indicate the day on which a given portion of text was to be read. The reading itself was often indicated by the abbreviations αρχ (= *archē,* beginning) and τελ (= *telos,* end). In time the readings were copied in separate volumes, called lectionaries. The lectionaries are classified by a small *"l"* followed by an Arabic numeral. To date, more than 2,000 lectionaries have been classified. Fragments of lectionaries date from the sixth century, with the oldest complete lectionary coming from the eighth century. A Gospel lectionary is called an Evangelion. The Apostolos contains liturgical readings from the Acts and Epistles, and the Apostoloevangelion contains readings taken from the entire New Testament.

The lectionaries have been studied by Ernest C. Colwell (*Studies in Methodology in Textual Criticism of the New Testament*). Colwell has come to the conclusion that enough evidence has been advanced to show that the lectionaries contain a distinct type of text, "the lectionary text." A particularly characteristic feature of the lectionaries is that readings from the Gospels are generally introduced by a stereotyped introductory phrase, the incipit ("It begins"). Among the most common incipits are: "At that time" (*tō kairō ekeinō*); "The Lord said" (*eipen ho kurios*); "The Lord said to his disciples" (*eipen ho kurios tois heautou mathētais*); "The Lord spoke this parable" (*eipen ho kurios tēn parabolēn tautēn*); "The Lord said to the Jews who had come to him" (*eipen ho kurios pros tous elēlutotas pros auton Ioudaious*); and "The Lord said to the Jews who had believed in him" (*eipen ho kurios pros tous pepisteukotas autō Ioudaious*).

The Versions

Besides having available some 5,000 Greek manuscripts of the New Testament, the textual critic can make use of the ancient versions. The principal ancient versions were prepared by the missionaries to assist them in the propagation of the faith among peoples whose native tongues were Latin, Syriac, Coptic, Gothic, Armenian, Ethiopic, and Georgian. Although the versions are only translations of the Greek text, many of them were made during the second and third centuries and thus bear witness to a state of the Greek text prior to that contained in our principal complete Greek New Testament manuscripts. Caution must nevertheless be exercised when the versions are used in order to establish the Greek text. All translations labor under the difficulty that some idioms of one language are not translatable into another, that the syntax of one language cannot be conveyed in that of another, and that adequacy of translation is proportionate to the care and competency of the translator. The study of the text of the New Testament on the basis of the ancient versions is further complicated by the fact that various translations made from one Greek text were sometimes corrected according to a different Greek text. Despite these difficulties, the ancient versions often prove to be a valuable aid in understanding the New Testament text. For this purpose the most important are undoubtedly the Syriac, Latin, and Coptic versions.

The Syriac Versions

Syria was extremely important in the history of the early Church. It was in Antioch that the disciples of Jesus were first called Christians (Acts 11:26). The Christian mission toward non-Jews took shape in Antioch so that Antioch can be considered a bridge between Jewish and Gentile Christianity. It is quite likely that *Q,* the Sayings Source used by Matthew and Luke, was written in Antioch of Syria toward the middle of the first century A.D. Matthew and Luke were probably composed in Syria later on during the century (A.D. 80–90). Ignatius (died 107), the letter-writing bishop of Antioch, was of Syrian origin. Since, moreover, the Syrian language is really a branch of Aramaic, the language spoken by Jesus and his disciples in first-century Palestine, the use of the Syriac versions is highly esteemed by New Testament textual critics.

Generally the critics distinguish five different Syriac versions (*syr*) of all or part of the New Testament: the Old Syriac, the Peshitta, and three later Syriac versions, the Palestinian, the Philoxenian, and the Harclean. These several Syriac versions date from the second to the seventh centuries. There are two known, but severely fragmented, manuscripts of the Old Syriac version. The manuscripts represent a text type which dates to ca. A.D. 200. The Syriac Sinaiticus (syr^s) is a fourth-century palimpsest manuscript discovered in the monastery of St. Catherine on Mount Sinai by Agnes Smith Lewis in 1892. The Syriac Curetonian (syr^c) is a fifth-century manuscript edited by William Cureton in 1858 and presently preserved in the British Museum.

The Syriac Peshitta (syr^p) is the Syriac Vulgate, or common text, prepared in the fifth century to replace the different Old Syriac texts then in circulation. Some 350 manuscripts of this text, some dating from the fifth and sixth centuries, are still extant. The Peshitta does not contain 2 Peter, 2,3 John, Jude, or Revelation. The Palestinian Syriac version (syr^{pal}) is quite independent of the other Syriac versions. This version, a translation into Aramaic (Christian Palestinian Syriac), was probably made during the fifth century. The version is known to us from several scattered fragments and three Gospel lectionaries of the eleventh and twelfth centuries. The relationship between the two remaining, and later, Syriac versions, the Philoxenian (syr^{ph}) and the Harclean (syr^h) is a mystery that is difficult to unravel. The former is generally attributed to a certain Polycarp who prepared the version for Philoxenus, bishop of Maboug, in 508. Some scholars consider the Harclean Syriac version to be but an edition of the Philoxenian text, whereas others consider it to be an entirely separate Syriac version. In any event the version derives from Thomas Harkel, bishop of Maboug in 616.

The Latin Versions

The earliest of the Latin versions of the New Testament was probably made in North Africa during the late second century. For the next two hundred years the New Testament was translated into Latin in other localities, particularly Italy and Gaul. Thus scholars are wont to identify two families of Old Latin versions, the African and the European. Further specification leads to the identification of sub-groups within the European cluster, these sub-groups being identified as the Italian, Gallic, and Spanish versions of the Old Latin. No codex of the Old Latin version is complete. Besides a number of isolated fragments, some thirty-two mutilated manuscripts of the Gospels, twelve of the Acts, four of the Pauline epistles, and one of Revelation have been identified. On comparison, these manuscripts yield a wide variety of readings. For example, the several Old Latin manuscripts offer some twenty-seven variant readings in Luke 24:4–5: "While they were perplexed about this, behold, two men stood by them in dazzling apparel, and as they were frightened and bowed their faces to the ground, the men said to them, 'Why do you seek the living among the dead?'"

The extant Old Latin manuscripts date from the third to the thirteenth centuries. As a group they are designated by the sigla OL (for Old Latin), VL (for Vetus Latina) or it (for itala) with a small letter of the Latin alphabet in exponent. It^a is the designation for the Codex Vercellensis, the oldest known manuscript belonging to the European family of the Old Latin version. It is ascribed, perhaps erroneously, to St. Eusebius (died 371), the bishop of Vercelli. It^k is the designation for the Codex Bobbiensis, the most important witness to the African family of the Old Latin versions. It was copied in North Africa about A.D. 400, but unfortunately only the leaves containing about half of the Gospels of Matthew and Mark are still preserved.

The Latin Vulgate

Great differences existed in the text of the Old Latin manuscripts circulating in the latter part of the fourth century. Accordingly Pope Damasus (304–84) asked Jerome (342–420), the most capable biblical scholar of his day, to prepare a revision of the Latin text of the Bible in order to eliminate these differences of translation. The request was made in 382. In 384 Jerome presented to the Pope the first fruits of his labor, a revision of the text of the four Gospels. The reviser explained to the Pontiff that he had made use of a relatively fine Latin text as the basis for his work. He claimed to have changed the text at hand only when its meaning had been distorted, a judgment at which he arrived by comparing his Latin manuscript with some old Greek manuscripts. Today it appears most likely that Jerome had at hand a text belonging to the European family of the Old Latin versions and at least one Greek manuscript with a text closely akin to that found in the Codex Sinaiticus (ℵ).

Whether Jerome personally revised the remaining books of the New Testament remains a moot question until this day. What is certain is that a revision of these books was made in a much more cursory manner than the revision of the Gospels. It is likewise certain that the earliest known reference to the revision of these other books is to be found in the writings of the early Pelagians. In any event, conservative reverence for the long and sacred traditions contained in the older text meant that Jerome's revision was accepted only with reluctance. For some time it coexisted with the Old Latin texts. Such coexistence led to a considerable amount of textual mixture: the translations which came to form the Vulgate (the *editio vulgata,* the "common edition") were mixed with reminiscences of the Old Latin text, and some manuscripts of the Old Latin text were "corrected" according to the Vulgate revision. Accordingly, several medieval scholars, most notably Alcuin (735–804) and Theodulf (750–821), attempted to produce a revised and purified edition of the Vulgate. These attempts only served to increase the mixture. Thus the 8,000 extant manuscripts of the Vulgate evidence considerable portions of textual mixture (cross-pollination).

The Fourth Session of the Council of Trent (April 8, 1546) pronounced the Vulgate to be the only authoritative Latin text of the Scriptures and decided upon the publication of an authoritative edition of the text. Pope Sixtus V (1521–90) authorized the publication of this authoritative edition in 1590 and commanded that variant readings not be printed in later editions. Nevertheless, a later pontiff, Pope Clement VIII (1536–1605), recalled the copies in circulation and issued a new authentic edition (1592) called the *Biblia Sacra Vulgatae Editionis Sixti Quinti Pont. Max. jussu recognita atque edita* even though it contains some 4,900 readings variant from the 1590 edition issued by Sixtus V. In works of textual criticism and in the critical apparatus of Greek editions of the New Testament, the Vulgate is cited under the rubric vg. The Clementine edition is cited as vg^{cl}. For the rest, the principal manuscripts of the Vulgate are indicated by capital letters of the first syllable of their names. Ms. A of the Vulgate is the Codex Amiatinus, the oldest extant manuscript of the Vulgate and one of the best witnesses to its text. The manuscript, presently preserved in the Laurentian Library in Florence, Italy, was written between A.D. 690 and 700 at either Wearmouth or Jarrow under the direction of the Abbot Ceolfrith, who sent it as a gift to Pope Gregory II (669–731) in 716.

The Coptic Versions

During the first centuries of the Christian era, the Coptic language, the latest form of the Egyptian language, was spoken in at least a half-dozen dialectical forms. New Testament manuscripts written in two of these dialects, the Sahidic and the Bohairic, are frequently cited by textual critics.

The manuscripts are written in Greek characters, supplemented where necessary by characters taken from demotic, the ancient Egyptian script. The translation into Sahidic took place in Upper Egypt, the southern part of the country, in the early third century. The Sahidic texts (cop^{sa}) differ widely from one another but generally agree with the so-called Alexandrian text type. The Chester Beatty collection presently contains three Sahidic New Testament manuscripts dating from the sixth or seventh century. Translation of the New Testament into the Bohairic dialect most probably took place in the fourth or fifth century. With the exception of one badly mutilated fourth-century manuscript of John, the extant Bohairic manuscripts (cop^{bo}) were written relatively recently. Thus, for example, the oldest complete Gospel codex in the Bohairic dialect dates from 1174. In addition to these principal witnesses to the Coptic translation, we also have Coptic translations made in the Fayyumic (cop^{fay}), Akhmimic (cop^{ac}) and Sub-Akhmimic (cop^{ac2}) dialects.

Other ancient versions of the New Testament are of more limited use in textual criticism. This situation is due to many factors, not the least of which is the generally later date of translation of these versions. Nonetheless, the Gothic version of the New Testament (goth) is generally dated to the middle of the fourth century. The half-dozen extant manuscripts of the version are fragmentary and date from the fifth and sixth centuries. The Gothic version of the New Testament is generally ascribed to Ulfilas, who is reputed to have created the Gothic alphabet for this purpose.

A new alphabet was also created for the translation of the New Testament into Armenian. The task was accomplished during the first half of the fifth century, but scholars do not agree among themselves as to the identity of the translator. In any case there are between 1,500 and 2,000 known manuscripts of the Armenian version (arm) of the New Testament—a total second only to that of the Vulgate among the ancient versions. Among the oldest of the Georgian versions (geo) are three manuscripts representing the two major Georgian traditions, the Adysh manuscript which represents geo^1 and the Opiza and Tbet' manuscripts which represent geo^2. The origins of the version are obscure but it is likely that the work of translation dates to the fourth or fifth century. This is the era in which some scholars ascribe the Ethiopic (eth) version, whereas other scholars would place it as late as the sixth or seventh century. Scholarly opinion is likewise divided as to the text from which the translation was made, some opting for a translation from the Greek while others hold that the Ethiopic version was made from a Syriac version.

The Fathers

A third category of witness to the ancient text of the New Testament are the patristic citations, the quotations of the New Testament to be found in the writings of the Fathers of the Church. These citations are so numerous that it has sometimes been thought they could serve as a basis for the reconstruction of the New Testament, should this prove to be necessary. Fortunately it has not been necessary to use the citations for this purpose. Indeed, the principal use made of the citations by textual critics is in dating the texts and versions of the New Testament. Accordingly, textual critics make frequent use of a number of Fathers of the second, third, and fourth centuries. The principal second-century authors to which reference is made are: Clement of Alexandria, the *Didache,* Irenaeus, Justin the Martyr, Marcion, Tatian, and Tertullian. From the third century, reference is made to Cyprian, Dionysius of Alexandria, Hippolytus, Methodius, Origen, and Porphyry. The principal fourth-century writers used by the textual critics include Adamantius, Alexander of Alexandria, Ambrose, the Ambrosiaster, Apollinaris, Athanasius, Augustine, Basil, Chrysostom, Cyril of Jerusalem, Ephraem, Epiphanius, Eusebius, Gregory of Nazianzus, Gregory of Nyssa, Hegemonius, Hilary, Lucifer of Cagliari, Nicetas, Priscillian, and Theodore of Mopsuestia.

Although patristic citations are of singular importance in bearing witness to the interpretation of the New Testament text at a given time and place in the Church's early history, special prudence must be used when patristic citations are employed in an attempt to make a judgment as to the reading of a specific New Testament text. At the very outset the critic must be aware that extant manuscripts of patristic writings were as subject to the vicissitudes of time and the whims of scribes as were the New Testament manuscripts themselves. Even when a reasonably accomplished critical edition of a patristic writing is available, the critic must make a judgment as to whether the ecclesiastical writer is citing a scriptural text verbatim, from memory, or by way of allusion. In the first instance, one has a chance of finding an exact rendering of the quotation in the patristic text. In the second, the critic must deal with the possibility of human error. In the third, the text at hand is at best an accommodated text. In effect, patristic citations are of limited, but occasionally very useful, value in determining the reading of the New Testament text. They nevertheless remain a valuable instrument in textual criticism since the dating of manuscripts and texts, for which the patristic citations are an important tool, is crucial to the development of the genealogical method of textual criticism.

The Genealogical Method

In his still valuable exposition of the procedures of textual criticism, Hort noted that every method of textual criticism corresponds to some one class of textual facts. The best textual criticism is that which takes into account every type of textual fact. The so-called genealogical method, used by Hort to demolish the authority of the *Textus Receptus* and frequently used by subsequent textual critics, takes into account the simple fact that readings do not exist independently of one another. This is so true that a few documents, merely on the basis of their relative rarity, cannot be presumed *a priori* to offer a less reliable text than many other documents simply on the basis of their numerical superiority.

Our extant manuscripts are only witnesses to the text of the New Testament. Of some ten witnesses who appear in a courtroom, four (A,B,C,D) might offer one body of testimony whereas six (E,F,G,H,I,J) might offer another body of testimony. If further examination then reveals that five (E,F,G,H,I) of the latter group of witnesses are merely echoing the testimony of the sixth (J), we do not have ten but only five presumably independent witnesses to the matter under judication. If, within the first group, the fourth witness (D) has been primed to repeat the testimony of the third (C) whereas the first (A) and second (B) witnesses are acting independently of each other, we really have three independent witnesses to the first body of testimony. Thus the weight of evidence is not six to four in favor of the second body of testimony, but three to one in favor of the first body of testimony.

Applied to the relationship among documents, the analogy implies that the textual critic must not consider each ancient manuscript as an independent witness to the text of the New Testament. Rather he must, in the words of Hort, consider each ancient manuscript as a fragment of a genealogical tree of transmission. Thus when the textual critic compares ten manuscripts he first seeks to determine the interrelationship among them so as to judge their relative authority. Thus, of some ten manuscripts a critic might judge that one is dependent on one of the others and that five manuscripts are dependent on still another. In effect he has four witnesses and not ten. To both the courtroom situation described above and the critic examining his ten manuscripts, the following schema is applicable:

It is witnesses A, B, C, and J whose testimony must be taken with the utmost seriousness.

In establishing such relationships among the New Testament texts, Hort adopted as a principle that the identity of reading implies an identity of origin. The working principle is valid but it must be considerably nuanced. Moreover, certain accidental occurrences inevitably do occur and must be relativized. Thus for example, "receive" is so often misspelled by modern users of the English language that one should not readily conclude that two texts were written by the same author because each of them contains "recieve." Implicitly this is to suggest that it is the identification of common errors which permits the textual critic to group manuscripts with one another. Having grouped the manuscripts he can proceed to the construction of the stemma or genealogical tree. Nevertheless, as the example has indicated, the argument from material similarity of text must be carefully weighed before judgment is made as to which manuscripts belong to a common group.

Reading the Manuscripts

In any event, the textual critic must begin with a *reading of the manuscripts* (Colwell, *Studies in Methodology*, 160–71). Frequently textual critics speak of variant readings. The terminology implies that there is a standard from which another text deviates. Since we do not have the standard for New Testament manuscripts (the autograph copies of the texts, and/or exact facsimiles thereof), it is better to adopt neutral terminology. Ernest Colwell appropriately speaks of "units of variation." The unit of variation is the length of text wherein manuscripts, when compared with one another, present at least two different forms. The unit of variation is normally something less than a verse, but not necessarily so, as, for example, when an entire verse of the text does not occur in one of the manuscripts. The unit of variation may be more than a single word as, for example, when the change in the number of a verb is inevitably accompanied by a change in the number of that verb's subject. Thus Colwell has identified some one hundred units of variation in the fifty-seven verses of John 11. Within this perspective a variant is simply one of the alternate readings found within a unit of variation.

Characteristics of the Manuscripts

The second task of the textual critic is to identify the characteristics of individual manuscripts and their scribes. It has been said that each scribe has his own pattern of errors. These errors are frequently identified as omission, addition, transposition, and substitution. Indeed, Alphonse Dain, whose work in textual criticism is not limited to biblical texts, has claimed that the most frequent scribal errors are parablepsis (an eye shift, similar to the one made by the secretary in the example cited at the beginning of the chapter), and the omission of short words. This is all very useful, but the textual critic must be more concerned with getting to know the manner of transcription of the scribe responsible for the manuscripts at hand than with classifying his work as characterized by so many errors. While the manuscript at hand may reveal a tendency of the scribe to repeat previously copied material because his eye has jumped from one word to the identical word previously appearing in his text, mention of a tendency to omit small words presupposes knowledge of the text which the scribe is transcribing. But it is the very purpose of the genealogical method to try to identify the genealogical stemma.

This caution aside, the fact that each scribe has a personal coefficient of the frequency of his errors may serve as a working hypothesis for the characterization of the amanuensis's pattern of scribal habits. Colwell's study of $\mathfrak{p}^{45}$, for example, has revealed that its scribe's tendency to misspell appears in one specific form of itacistic spelling, namely the replacement of the iota by an epsilon and an iota. Like many scribes, the scribe of $\mathfrak{p}^{45}$ frequently omits shorter words from his manuscript—adverbs, adjectives, nouns, participles, verbs, and pronouns. The result is a shorter, more concise text, which is nevertheless readable. Indeed, the scribe of $\mathfrak{p}^{45}$ occasionally makes a transposition of a word or phrase for the purpose of improvement of style or clarity of interpretation. His inclination to offer an intelligible text is also to be seen in the fact that when the scribe's manuscript offers a singular reading —that is, one not found in other manuscripts—that singular reading almost always makes sense. In effect the scribe who produced $\mathfrak{p}^{45}$ was a person concerned with the sense of his manuscript. He was, nevertheless, occasionally the victim of visual confusion as when he replaced the *heautous* of Acts 13:42 with *autous*.

While the presence of singular readings in a manuscript is important for characterizing and evaluating the quality of a scribe's work, the presence of singular readings in a critical apparatus would unduly clutter the apparatus. Mere nonsense readings, particularly those owing to clerical and mechanical blunder, are not to be taken much more seriously than would the typing error found on the pages of a modern manuscript or the transposition of letters on the printed page. Identification of these errors is valuable for determining the quality of the work of the scribe, typist, and lithographer, but not for identifying the text from which he might have been working. Citing them in the apparatus can only clog further stages of the work of creating a textual stemma. Similarly, dislocated readings, particularly those transcribed a second time through dittography, can be omitted from the apparatus. The presence of these types of errors in a manuscript tells us something about the care exercised by the scribe in his work of transcription, but they are of relatively little use in grouping the manuscripts, which is the next stage in the process of discovery of the textual stemma.

Text Types

The *grouping of manuscripts* can begin with consideration of their age and geographical distribution. Some manuscripts are found in archaeological contexts that permit a more or less precise determination of their dates, at least within a certain range of possibilities—the *terminus ante quem* and, to a lesser degree, the *terminus a quo*. Manuscripts are sometimes dated. Occasionally, however, dates are fraudulently indicated on manuscripts. Colwell, for example, has made a study of a Byzantine New Testament codex, Ms. 1505, which has the date 1084 *in fine*. The colophon that includes the notation of date was probably written during the late thirteenth century, when it was appended to the manuscript in order to predate it by two centuries. Thus paleography, the scientific study of handwriting styles, must always be used in order to date ancient New Testament manuscripts. For example, Colwell's study of more than one hundred minuscules has identified trends in the writing of epsilon, eta, lambda, and pi. A New Testament manuscript with uncial epsilons was written after 1166, more or less. A manuscript with the uncial eta and lambda was written after 1150, more or less. A manuscript with the uncial pi was written after 1066, more or less. In addition to consideration of these datable characteristics of scribal calligraphy, a study of the ornamentation that adorns the manuscripts can also be useful for dating them.

A second preliminary step is the creation of a context and a working hypothesis by means of so-called multiple readings. Since common ancestry is indicated by an agreement in reading, when a text is found in several different manuscripts there is a high probability that some of them are descended from a single, perhaps lost, archetypal manuscript. More precisely it is the agreement-in-error of manuscripts that provides for their tentative grouping. A list of readings can then be prepared which is characteristic of one or another form of text. Subsequently, a tentative analysis of a given manuscript can be made by determining the number of agreements it shows with each of the text types.

After locating a manuscript within the broad textual tradition, the textual critic should demonstrate the kinship between one manuscript and others by showing its agreement with them in a list of distinctive readings peculiar to the text type and not found in other text types. A striking example of the relationship of manuscripts to one another is the placement of the story of the woman taken in adultery (John 7:53 – 8:11) after Luke 21:38 in Ms. 13, as well as in all other manuscripts which have been identified as belonging to the so-called Farrar family. The specification of this characteristic trait is one of the factors that have allowed for the determination of kinship among the manuscripts of this group. In any event, the identification of kinship should be confirmed by means of a total comparison—that is, the members of a group must agree with one another in a large majority of the total amount of existing variants found within all Greek manuscripts of the New Testament. In the entire process it is the identification of shared peculiarities which permits the identification of groups of manuscripts.

The smallest identifiable group of manuscripts is the family. It has been defined as "that group of sources whose genealogy can be clearly established so that its text may be reconstructed solely with reference to the external evidence of documents" (Colwell). A type is "the largest group of sources which can be objectively identified." Intermediate-sized groups are the tribe or clan and the sub-text type, two or three of which may be identified as distinctive strains within a text type. The members of a family generally come from a relatively short span of time and a restricted geographic area. Thus far about twenty families have been identified. The most frequently cited among them are the Lake family, to which minuscules 1, 113, and 118 belong, and the Farrar family, to which minuscules 13, 69, 124, and 346 belong. In the literature and critical apparatus these are sometimes identified as Families 1 and 13 respectively; more frequently they are identified by the use of the sigla λ and ϕ.

Since the time of Johann Jakob Griesbach (1745–1812) it has been customary to distinguish three major text types: the Western, which includes

D (05) and the majority of the OL mss.; the Alexandrian, to which ℵ (01), A (02) except for the Gospels, and B (03) belong; and the Byzantine, to which most of the minuscules belong and whose oldest extant example is generally considered to be the Gospel text of the Codex Alexandrinus. Study of the ninth-century Codex Koridethi (θ) has led to the identification of a fourth major text type, the Caesarean. To this type of text belong—in addition to θ—λ,φ, and texts used by Origen in the third century, Eusebius in the fourth century, and the fifth-century translator of the Palestinian Syriac version. This nomenclature is predicated upon a judgment as to the origin of the text types. Accordingly, Frederic G. Kenyon proposed a neutral system of identification which simply adopts the letters of the Greek alphabet as its sigla. Thus alpha (α) indicates the Byzantine text type, beta (β) the Alexandrian text type, gamma (γ) the Caesarean text type, and delta (δ) the Western text type. He used epsilon (ϵ) for the Syriac text, which he distinguished from the delta type of text, and reserved vau ($\digamma$) (the sixth letter of the Greek alphabet in its earliest form) for readings not otherwise classified.

The Manuscript Tradition

The fourth step in the genealogical method is the reconstruction of the history of the manuscript tradition. This is, as Karl Lachmann (1793–1851) indicated, a "strictly historical task." However, Lachmann uttered a caution on his own work: "I have not established the true text, a text that no doubt is often preserved in a single source, though just as often wholly lost, but only the oldest among those that can be proved to have been in circulation." Indeed, one often attempts the reconstruction of the history of the manuscript tradition with the assumption that the purpose of the reconstruction is the restoration of the original wording of the text. In fact it is impossible to reconstruct the original text of the New Testament. Thus Lachmann sought to establish the text of the fourth century. With the aid of the relatively recent study of New Testament papyri, it has become possible for textual critics to push the parameters of their work back some two centuries. Hence the past fifty years have seen an important shift away from concern with the fourth-century text toward that of the second century.

At this juncture a caution voiced by Colwell is particularly apropos. Colwell urged that the effort to restore *the* text of a text type be abandoned because we must take into account the existence of a process within a text type. It is not as if there existed a prototypical text type from which variant readings have developed as deviations from a standard. Most variant readings were in existence before the beginning of the third century, but few, if any, of the text types were established at that time. Thus $\mathfrak{P}^{75}$ is closely related to B, and $\mathfrak{P}^{46}$, which appears to be proto-Alexandrian, also offers readings associated with the Byzantine text type. It is only toward the end of the third century that we can begin to speak of identifiable text types. The text types came into existence as a result of several historical developments, among which can be cited the triumph of Christianity over its rivals, the linguistic isolation of the Christian churches, the development of learning within the Church, and the strengthening of ecclesiastical authority. Indeed, the crucial factor in the establishment of text types would seem to be the achievement of control by ecclesiastical authority.

The critic must, moreover, be aware of the mixture phenomenon. As was the case with the manuscripts of the Vulgate which were "corrected" on the basis of OL manuscripts, so with the Greek manuscripts of the New Testament: significant mixture has resulted from the correction of the manuscripts of one family or type on the basis of manuscripts belonging to another type or family. The temporal and geographical juxtaposition of manuscripts belonging to various families not only gave rise to a Codex Vaticanus which contains texts belonging to both the Alexandrian and the Byzantine families, but also gave rise to a whole range of manuscripts which can best be characterized as belonging to a mixed type of text.

Once these cautions have been heard, some adjustment must be made in Hort's ambitious description of the genealogical method as:

> the more or less complete recovery of the texts of successive ancestors by analysis and comparison of the varying texts of their respective descendants, each ancestral text as recovered being in turn used in conjunction with other similar texts, for the recovery of the text of a yet earlier common ancestor (*The New Testament in the Original Greek*, 2, p. 57).

In light of the current study of texts, the quest for the hypothetical archetype of a text type must be abandoned. Likewise the often unstated presupposition that the use of the genealogical method will yield two parallel stemmata whose readings can then be compared must be exposed and abandoned.

Notwithstanding these several cautions and reservations, the genealogical method of textual criticism, so often abandoned because it admits of more than one interpretation or because of the difficulty in working with both external and internal canons of textual criticism, retains its validity as a methodology to be used. The proper task of textual criticism is to establish the form of the text of the New Testament in time and place. The genealogical method does just that by considering one set of facts: the interrelationship among the extant manuscripts.

Judging the Readings

The use of the internal canons of textual criticism for determining which of two or more readings is better has been variously described as the art of textual criticism (Bruce M. Metzger), rational criticism (M.-J. Lagrange) or the eclectic method (Colwell). In fact the choice of the most plausible among the different variant readings presupposes knowledge of the manuscripts and the various steps of analysis and classification we have described in reference to the genealogical method. Once the canons of that method have been applied, the scholar who wishes to publish an edition of the New Testament, as distinct from an edition of one of the manuscripts of the New Testament, is frequently faced with two or more alternative readings from among which he must make a choice for his edition.

For the past century scholars have made this choice principally on the basis of two principles, respectively called by Hort "intrinsic probability" and "transcriptional probability." The first principle is simply: That reading is to be preferred which best suits the context. Hence this principle is sometimes called "contextual probability." Application of the principle implies a judgment as to what the author was likely to have written. It supposes a knowledge of the sense and structure of the text as well as of the author's style. The critic must judge which of the two or more possible readings enjoys the favor of reasonable presumption—given, on the one hand, the author's vocabulary, language, style, manner of composition, way of quoting, etc., and, on the other, the natural meaning and structure of the passage.

Thus in editing 2 Thessalonians 3:8 the *nuktos kai hēmeras* reading of א, B, and G is to be preferred over the *nukta kai hēmeran* reading found in A, D, and most minuscules because of Paul's usage of the genitive in 1 Thessalonians 2:9 and 3:10. This is really a problem in linguistics since both of the Greek expressions are translated into English as "night and day." In John 1:3–4 the reading that punctuates *oude hen. ho gegonen* is preferable to the reading that punctuates *oude hen ho gegonen.*, since climactic or staircase parallelism seems to demand that the end of one line match the beginning of the next. Thus the expression "what was made" (*ho gegonen*) rightly should be translated as the beginning of verse 4 rather than the end of verse 3. This is, however, a judgment which only a modern editor has to make. The ancient manuscripts themselves lacked punctuation.

Deviational Probability

The second principle is this: That reading is to be preferred which best explains the origin of all the others. This principle is not immediately concerned with the relative excellence of the respective readings; rather it is concerned with the relative fitness of each reading for explaining the existence of the others. Conversely, the principle is concerned with explaining how all the readings deviated from a more original reading. Hence it is sometimes called the principle of deviational probability. Application of the principle supposes knowledge of the way in which ancient manuscripts were generally transcribed. The principle is applied with ever greater surety when knowledge is available about the specific circumstances in which a specific manuscript has been transcribed.

Sometimes a scribe transcribed on sight directly from a manuscript at hand. This created the possibility of simple visual error. For example, G reads *ama* in Romans 6:5 rather than the more widely attested *alla*. The confusion is due to the visual similarity between the way of writing ΑΜΑ and the way of writing ΑΛΛΑ in uncial manuscripts. One of the most common scribal errors of transcription is well known to all typists in our times. It results from a leap from the same to the same. This occurs when the eye of the scribe skips either backward or forward from one word to another with a similar ending and, in consequence, either omits or repeats a passage. This similarity is technically called *homoioteleuton* (same ending). The phenomenon of *homoioproton* is similiar to *homoioteleuton:* it causes the same result, but the troublesome similarity is found at the beginning rather than at the end of a word. When the result is an omission, the critics speak of haplography; when the result is repetition, they speak of dittography. That haplography occurs approximately three times as often as does dittography is undoubtedly because a scribe would more easily recognize that he had already transcribed a passage than he would catch a phrase which he had omitted. For example, the entire first part of Revelation 20:5 is missing from the Codex Sinaiticus. The sentence "The rest of the dead did not come to life until the thousand years were ended" has apparently been omitted because the Greek text of this sentence ends with "thousand years" (*chilia etē*), the very phrase found at the end of verse 4.

Sometimes texts were transcribed in scriptoria. In such cases a lector dictated the text to a group of scribes. Occasionally a scribe might miss a word because of inattention or a competing noise such as a dog's bark or a person's coughing. Occasionally, too, a scribe might be confused on hearing a word that sounds like another, so that he would write a homonym in his manuscript. Every modern businessman who dictates correspondence is aware of "their" which appears in the text as "there." In *koinē* Greek the tendency to confuse homonyms was all the more pronounced because of the phenomenon of itacism. The vowels eta, iota, and upsilon as well as the diphthongs epsilon iota, omicron iota, upsilon iota, and eta iota were pronounced in similar fashion. Thus "Death is swallowed up in victory" of 1 Corinthians 15:54 has become "Death is swallowed up in strife" in $\mathfrak{P}^{46}$ and B because of the confusion between *nikos* (victory) and *neikos* (strife). In somewhat similar fashion the *oligoi* (a few, masculine) of 1 Peter 3:20 has become *oligai* (a few, feminine) in C and in many minuscules. The tendency of $\mathfrak{P}^{45}$ to use an itacistic spelling with epsilon iota has already been noted. A similar phenomenon is to be found in $\mathfrak{P}^{66}$ whose scribe had the tendency to replace epsilon by alpha iota.

Textual critics sometimes speak of "errors of the mind" to describe another set of circumstances which might explain the difference between a transcribed manuscript and the original. Sometimes scribes transposed letters; at other times they changed the sequence of words. Thus the *elabon* (took) of Mark 14:65 has become *eballon* (threw) in some manuscripts. In Mark 1:5 the edited text usually reads *pantes kai ebaptizonto* but there are several variants: *kai ebaptizonto pantes* in the Byzantine manuscripts; *kai pantes ebaptizonto* in manuscripts of the Farrar family; *kai ebaptizonto* in θ; and *pantes ebaptizonto* in ℵ. Scribes occasionally omit particles and other small words. Indeed this is one of the two most common scribal errors. The

Codex Sinaiticus, for example, has omitted the *kai* from the text of Mark 1:5.

Akin to the scribal tendency to transpose and omit is the tendency to substitute synonyms. Thus in place of the usually accepted *praxas* (has practiced) in 1 Corinthians 5:2, $\mathfrak{p}^{46}$, $\mathfrak{p}^{68}$, D, and E read *poiēsas* (has done). Much more common is the tendency to interchange the particles, adverbs and conjunctions. Thus the *euthus* of Mark 5:2 has become *eutheōs* in D and θ. The *dioti* of 1 Peter 1:24 has become *hoti* in $\mathfrak{p}^{72}$. $\mathfrak{p}^{51}$, B, H, and many minuscules read *huper* at Galatians 1:4 whereas $\mathfrak{p}^{46}$, $\aleph$, A, D, and G read *peri*. A particular case of substitution of synonyms by New Testament scribes relates to the use of *nomina sacra,* the names for the Father and His Christ. The *ton kurion Iēsoun Christon* (the Lord Jesus Christ) of Romans 13:14 can be cited as but one example. The epithet otherwise appears as *ton Christon Iēsoun* (the Christ Jesus) in B, as *ton kurion Iēsoun* (the Lord Jesus) in 1739 and the Ambrosiaster, and as *Iēsoun Christon ton kurion hēmōn* (Jesus Christ our Lord) in $\mathfrak{p}^{46}$.

Another scribal tendency to be noted is a tendency to harmonize the text at hand with other familiar passages. Thus the text might be modified in accordance with the immediate context, general usage, or some specific remote parallel. The text might be harmonized with the immediate context by reason of the influence of a neighboring word, the scribe's desire to balance the clauses of the same sentence, or the familiar phraseology of the Gospel at hand. Thus at Matthew 19:24, in place of the generally accepted *basilean tou theou* (kingdom of God) a somewhat singular usage in Matthew, some manuscripts (33, and those of the Lake family) read the more familiar *basilean tōn ouranōn* (kingdom of heaven). On the other hand, the scribes who transcribed the text of 1 Timothy 1:17 in P, K, L, and 0142 were apparently influenced by Romans 16:27 as they wrote *monō sophō theō* (to the only wise God).

Although the scribal tendency to harmonize the text with other familiar passages is quite commonplace, some rather specific instances of the general phenomenon occur in particular reference to the text of the New Testament. First of all, there is the tendency of scribes to harmonize the text of one Gospel with a parallel passage in another Gospel. Thus the beatitude in Luke 6:20 has been "completed" by the addition of *tō pneumati* (in the spirit) from Matthew 5:3 in K and the manuscripts of the Lake and Farrar families. The text of Matthew 6:24 has been completed by the addition of *oiketēs* (from Luke 16:13) by the scribe responsible for L. Another specification of the universal tendency is to be found in the influence of liturgical usage upon transcription. The classical case is the addition of a doxology (L, W, ⊖, θ, and many minuscules) or a simple "Amen" (Ms. 17) to the text of the Lord's Prayer at Matthew 6:13. An "Amen" has also been added to the text of 1 Timothy 6:21 in P and many minuscules. Similarly the text of the Lord's Prayer in Luke 11:2–4 in C and D has been infiltrated by the more familiar version of the prayer found in Matthew 6:9–13 and widely used in the liturgy of the Church. Yet another particular form of harmonization encountered in New Testament manuscripts is the tendency to expand the Old Testament citations found in New Testament texts. Thus the familiar reading of Genesis 22:17 lies behind the expanded transcription of Romans 4:18 which we find in G: ". . . so shall your descendants be as the stars of heaven and as the sand which is on the seashore." G, along with D and many minuscules, adds "of his flesh and of his bones" to the text of Ephesians 5:30, apparently under the influence of Genesis 2:23.

"The Intelligent Scribe"

Although visual errors and those brought about by the confusion of sounds are clearly inadvertent, it is not very easy to determine whether a scribe harmonized his text to another Gospel passage unwittingly or whether he did so with the clear intention of modifying his text. In fact, for purposes of textual criticism it is not particularly important to determine whether a deviation is through design or inadvertence. What is important to the textual critic is that the deviation has taken place and is capable of a logical explanation. Nevertheless, the textual critic knows that he is sometimes dealing with the work of an "intelligent scribe." Such activity is most apparent in the case of the so-called dogmatic corrections. Augustine's awareness that some scribes had omitted an offending "Jeremiah" from the text of Matthew 27:9 has been noted. Among these "intelligent scribes" we can include those who produced Mss. 33, 157, and those of the Farrar family. The Codex Bezae Cantabrigiensis (D) as well as the Codex Washingtoniensis (W) omit from their text of Mark 2:26 the expression "when Abiathar was high priest." Most likely this was due to the scribe's awareness that Ahimelech was high priest at the time of the incident narrated in 1 Samuel 21:1–6. In each of these instances it was concern for historical accuracy that led to a scribe's modification of the New Testament text.

In other cases it is concern for doctrinal correctness which has led to a modification of the text. Luke 2:33, for example, and some other manuscripts insert "Joseph" in place of "his father" in the passage "and his father and mother marveled at what was said . . ." It was a similar concern for the tradition of the virgin birth which, according to Alfred Wikenhauser, led some scribes (C, D, and many minuscules) to drop from Matthew 1:25 "her firstborn" as a qualification of "son." In the second century Marcion dropped Luke 5:39 from his bowdlerized version of the Gospel. The reading "no one after drinking old wine desires new; for he says 'The old is good' " was apparently incompatible with Marcion's theory of a radical cleavage between the God of the Old Testament and the God of the New. Marcion's influence is felt in the absence of the verse from D and the writings of such Fathers as Irenaeus and Eusebius.

It was also for doctrinal reasons that the scribes of W and most of the later minuscules omitted the *oude ho huios* (nor the Son) from Matthew 24:36. The elimination of the offending text leaves as an untroublesome reading: "But of that day and hour no one knows, not even the angels of heaven, but the Father only."

In addition to modifying the text so as to accommodate it to historical fact or doctrinal criteria, ancient scribes occasionally modified the text in order to improve its style. It is for this reason that the sequence of words in a text was sometimes altered. At times a scribe replaced a colloquialism with a more literary expression. Thus the scribe of D has substituted *ptōma* (corpse) for *sōma* (body) in Mark 15:43. Not only did scribes attempt to improve the vocabulary and style of a text at hand, sometimes they attempted to improve its content by eliminating obscurities from the text or by offering an explanatory addition. Two examples from the Gospel of John illustrate the tendency. In the Revised Standard Version, John 7:39 reads: "Now this he said about the Spirit, which those who believed in him were to receive; for as yet the Spirit had not been given, because Jesus was not yet glorified." "For as yet the Spirit had not yet been given" corresponds to OL, syr, and the text used by Eusebius. Aland's *Novum Testamentum Graece* reads only *oupō gar ēn pneuma*—"the Spirit was not yet." This reading is obviously difficult to interpret. Accordingly, the scribes modified the texts to read: "The Holy Spirit was not yet" (by adding *hagion*, L, X, T, Δ, Λ); "The Holy Spirit was not yet upon them" (by adding *hagion ep autois,* D); "The Holy Spirit was not yet given" (by adding *hagion dedomenon,* B); or "For as yet the Spirit had not yet been given" (by adding *dedomenon* as in OL, etc.). In John 1:18 Nestle-Aland reads *monogenēs theos*—"the only God," as do 𝔭⁶⁶ and 𝔭⁷⁵. Since the interpretation of the text is difficult, the offending phrase has been replaced by a variety of alternative readings including *ho monogenēs huios*—"the only Son" (A and most of the Byzantine manuscripts), *ho monogenēs*—"the only [begotten]" (the text behind some manuscripts of the Vulgate and that used by several Fathers of the Church), and *monogenēs huios theou*—"the only Son of God" (some OL, Origen, Irenaeus).

Knowledge of the way in which scribes in general or even a single scribe tended to modify the text is the basis on which textual critics make their choices as to the preferred reading. They attempt to determine which reading among the several possible is the most likely to explain the others. Thus it is more likely that a scribe would have omitted the troublesome *oude ho huios* from Matthew 24:36 than that he would have added it by way of assimilation to Mark 13:32. Similarly, in the case of John 1:18 it is more likely that the later scribe would have replaced a troublesome reading and accommodated his text to John 3:16 (3:18 and 1 John 4:9) than that he would have substituted for a coherent and Johannine expression one which is difficult to interpret.

Some Difficult Cases

A particularly interesting passage for consideration is 1 Thessalonians 3:2 for which the manuscript tradition offers no fewer than eight readings. The abundance of readings seems to result from a difficulty experienced by some scribes trying to comprehend how Timothy could be called "God's co-worker." The textual critic who comes upon these different readings will envision his task as one in which he will try to determine which of the eight readings enjoys the greatest likelihood of being the source of the other seven. The one upon which his choice falls will then be considered as the reading most likely to have been written by Paul.

The eight readings are as follows:

1. *kai sunergon tou theou en tō euaggeliō tou christou*
   (and the co-worker of God in the Gospel of Christ), D, 33.

2. *kai sunergon en tō euaggeliō tou christou*
   (and co-worker in the Gospel of Christ), B, 1962.

3. *kai diakonon en tō euaggeliō tou christou*
   (and servant in the Gospel of Christ), some OL.

4. *kai diakonon tou theou en tō euaggeliō tou christou*
   (and God's servant in the Gospel of Christ), ℵ, A, ꬰ, 81.

5. *diakonon kai sunergon tou theou en tō euaggeliō tou christou*
   (the servant and co-worker of God in the Gospel of Christ), G, some OL.

6. *kai diakonon tou theou kai sunergon hēmōn en tō euaggeliō tou christou*
   (and the servant of God and our co-worker in the Gospel of Christ), K, 88, 104.

7. *kai sunergon hēmōn kai diakonon autou en tō euaggeliō tou theou kai sunergon tou christou*
   (and our co-worker and his servant in the Gospel of God and co-worker of Christ), syr[pal].

8. *kai sunergon tou euaggeliou tou theou kai patros tou christou*
   (and the co-worker in the Gospel of God and father of Christ), arm.

The RSV offers a translation based on the third reading in the list above, but Kurt Aland and his associates have chosen the first reading for incorporation into the text of *Novum Testamentum Graece*. The sixth reading is admittedly the most widely attested in the manuscript tradition but, in the judgment of the critics, it seems to represent a joining together (a conflation) of the second and fourth readings with the addition of "our." The fifth reading is like the sixth, but lacks the "our." Thus both the fifth and sixth readings seem to be dependent on the second and fourth readings. The second is an obvious attempt to correct the notion that Timothy is God's co-worker by eliminating "God," thereby implying that Timothy is but Paul's co-worker. The fourth reading achieves the same end by substituting "servant" for the offending "co-worker." The third reading is but a simplification of the fourth. Readings seven and eight are obvious conflates and little-attested readings. Thus the critic judges that the first reading is the best suited to explain all the others. In this case as in the two previously cited instances, the critic must make a judicious judgment with which other scholars might sometimes disagree. Knowledge of how ancient manuscripts were transcribed makes the choice more plausible, but it never totally removes the element of subjectivity from the judgment.

In making a judgment as to which of two or more readings is more likely to have been the "original," the critic makes reference both to the copyist and to the author. The principles of intrinsic probability and transcriptional probability are the core of the so-called eclectic method of textual criticism, and their application seems to be the predominant factor in the work of most textual critics. These two principles have virtually subsumed the older canons of criticism. Among these was the *lectio difficilior* rule of thumb popularized by Johann Albrecht Bengel (1687–1752). He reasoned that one should choose the harder reading as being the more primitive, since a scribe is not likely to have abandoned a better reading for a worse one. Some scholars held as working guidelines that one should opt for the *shorter* reading on the grounds that scribes tend to amplify their text, or that one should opt for the reading offered by the *older* witness. A canon still widely used, though often unavowed, holds that a reading in the *better manuscripts* is to be preferred. For Hort, it was in fact B which was the better manuscript. A too-facile application of the canon easily lends to abuse. Nevertheless, as F. W. Beare has shown, the choice of readings in 1 Peter made on the basis of B has been more or less confirmed since the discovery of $\mathfrak{p}^{72}$.

It sometimes happens that no one of the readings preserved in the extant manuscripts, carefully considered in the kinship relations, offers a likely reading for a given text. In such cases many editors offer a reading based on conjecture, the educated guess. At 1 Peter 3:18, the Revised Standard Version reads: "For Christ also died for sins once for all," rendering correctly the lection *hoti kai christos hapax peri hamartiōn apethanen* found in Nestle-Aland and other modern editions of the New Testament. However, there is no extant manuscript of 1 Peter 3:18 which reads the verse without two prepositional phrases "for sins" (*peri hamartiōn*) and "for you" (*huper humōn*). The RSV translation of the following verse, 1 Peter 3:19, reads: "in which he went and preached to the spirits in prison" (*en hō kai tois en phulakē*). Some scholars have proposed that ENΩK (*en hō k*) is remarkably similar, in sound and at sight, to ENΩX (Henoch). They conjecture that the name of the legendary figure was dropped from the text as a result of haplography (James Rendel Harris) or substitution (Bowyer). Obviously conjecture should only serve as a last resort. In principle, readings whose existence is documented are much more likely to have been found in the original documents than readings for which all documentary evidence has been lost.

Editing the New Testament

Our survey of materials related to the text of the New Testament has pointed to the existence of a variety of manuscripts and a very large number of variant readings. It has also indicated that some among the Fathers of the

Church were aware of the discrepancies among these readings and that Church authority occasionally intervened in the process of textual transmission in order to achieve some type of uniformity. Since the Renaissance, particularly during the nineteenth century, scholars have offered numerous editions of the New Testament in Greek.

Even before the publication of the *Textus Receptus,* it had been customary to divide the Bible into chapters and verses. Even some of the ancient uncials were divided into chapters, the *kephalaia.* The Codex Vaticanus divides Matthew into 170, Mark into 62, Luke into 152, and John into 80 sections. The Codex Alexandrinus offers a somewhat different division and also provides each chapter with a *titlos* or chapter heading. In A there are 68 *kephalaia* for Matthew, 48 in Mark, 83 in Luke, and 18 in John. The chapter division in use today derives from a thirteenth-century archbishop of Canterbury, Stephen Langton (died 1228). Our customary division of the New Testament into verses comes from a 1550 edition of the New Testament in Latin and Greek by Robert Estienne ("Stephanus") (1503–59).

Among the several Greek editions of the New Testament, Estienne's 1550 Greek edition was the first to contain a critical apparatus. Its text was virtually identical to that of the so-called "received text," the *Textus Receptus.* The *Textus Receptus* (TR) was ordinarily printed in editions of the Greek New Testament down to the latter part of the nineteenth century. It was the text used for the Authorized Version of the Bible and for Luther's translation of the Bible into German. Thus the *Textus Receptus* is singularly important, but its name is nothing more than an excerpt from an advertiser's copy. In 1633 the second Elzevir edition of the New Testament appeared. A casual phrase in the preface to the edition boasted *"Textum ergo habes, nunc ab omnibus receptum, in quo nihil immutatum aut corruptum damus"* (Therefore you have the text now received by all, in which we give nothing changed or corrupted). The boast contributed its name to a text of the New Testament which would, in fact, be "received by [nearly] all" for three centuries.

The first complete printed edition of the Greek New Testament was the fifth volume of the Complutensian Polyglot, printed in January 1514 under the patronage of Cardinal Francisco Jiménez de Cisneros, archbishop of Toledo and founder of the University of Alcalá. The New Testament translation was based on "the oldest and purest available" manuscripts, including some from the Vatican among which we can today recognize Mss. 140, 432, and 234. These minuscules are, in fact, of relatively recent origin. Nevertheless the edition was prepared with care. The New Testament volume was the first to appear in print, but the entire project did not receive papal approbation until 1520. Thus the Complutensian Bible did not enter into circulation until 1522.

In the meantime, the famous Basel printer Johann Froben ("Frobenius") had written to Desiderius Erasmus (1469–1536), the Rotterdam humanist, with the request that he go to Basel and prepare a Greek text of the New Testament. Erasmus accomplished his work on the basis of some minuscule manuscripts with a Byzantine type of text, principally Mss. 1 and 2. Since the Greek manuscripts at hand lacked the text of Revelation 22:16–21 Erasmus completed his edition by translating the final part of Revelation into Greek from the Vulgate. Erasmus' celebrated Greek edition of the New Testament and his translation of the text into classical Latin appeared in 1516. Thus it was in circulation six years prior to the appearance of the vastly superior Complutensian edition.

Five thousand copies of Erasmus' text were printed. It entered into several editions. The fourth and fifth editions were used by Estienne in his 1550 edition of the Greek New Testament. His critical apparatus included variants from the Complutensian Polyglot as well as from other Greek codices. In 1551 Estienne published a fourth edition of his Greek New Testament. The text was prepared by Théodore de Bèze, who subsequently published nine editions of the New Testament (between 1565 and 1604). A tenth edition was published posthumously in 1611. Bèze's edition of the New Testament is not very significant except insofar as it provides the conduit between Erasmus and the *Textus Receptus*. It was Bèze's 1565 edition of the Greek New Testament, substantially the work of Erasmus adopted by Estienne, that served as a basis for the 1633 Elzevir edition, the legendary *Textus Receptus*.

In the nineteenth century, three major editorial projects led to the abandonment of the *Textus Receptus*. Karl Lachmann's edition of the Greek and Latin New Testament first appeared in 1831 without detailed argumentation. Lachmann (1793–1851) was free of any dogmatic bias in favor of the TR and so based his work exclusively on the most ancient manuscripts available to him. A later edition of his work, including a substantial critical apparatus, appeared in 1842–50. Lachmann's 1831 edition inaugurated a new era in the history of the New Testament text. In 1831, for the first time, a text of the New Testament had been constructed directly from the ancient documents without the intervention of any printed edition. In 1831, a first systematic attempt to substitute scientific method for arbitrary choice in the discrimination of various readings was made.

Constantin von Tischendorf (1815–74), who had discovered the Codex Sinaiticus in 1844, edited more than seventy uncial manuscripts. In 1862 he finished an edition of the New Testament text. The eighth edition of that text, the *editio octava critica major* (2 vols., 1869, 1872) was furnished with an enormous critical apparatus and was the first edition of the New Testament to make use of the Codex Sinaiticus. Although subsequent discoveries have made more material available for critical editions of the New Testament, no edition of the New Testament yet made remains as complete and as practical as Tischendorf's *editio octava*.

In 1881 Brooke Foss Westcott (1825–1901) and Fenton John Anthony Hort (1828–92) published *The New Testament in the Original Greek*. Volume One was the text itself, published without a critical apparatus, while

Volume Two contained an explanation of the methodology adopted in the preparation of the text. Westcott and Hort had the best possible uncial texts, nineteen in all, available to them. They edited what they called a "Neutral Text" of the New Testament. It was principally reliant upon the Codex Vaticanus and the Codex Sinaiticus, with somewhat greater weight being accorded to B. Although scholars today question whether the so-called Neutral Text was really different from the Alexandrian text type, the text produced by Westcott and Hort still remains the basic text of the New Testament in Greek.

In 1893 Eberhard Nestle intended to edit a volume that would offer the result of nineteenth-century scientific scholarship instead of the then still widely used *Textus Receptus.* Unto this end he produced a volume, the *Novum Testamentum Graece,* based upon Tischendorf's *editio octava* and Westcott-Hort's 1881 edition. When the two critical editions did not agree on a particular reading, Nestle used *The Resultant Greek Testament* (1886), by R. F. Weymouth, as an arbiter. From the third edition on, Bernhard Weiss's *Das Neue Testament* (1894–1900) was used to solve the dilemma provoked by the different readings found in the two great nineteenth-century critical editions of the New Testament. Nestle's work was continued by his son, Erwin, and later by Kurt Aland. Today the *Novum Testamentum Graece,* now in a 26th edition (1979), still remains in use as the popular edition of the Greek New Testament.

Kurt Aland is associated with Münster's Institute for New Testament Textual Research. In cooperation with the Institute, the United Bible Societies have published *The Greek New Testament* (three editions–1966, 1968, 1975). The committee of editors includes Aland, Matthew Black, Bruce Metzger, Allen Wikgren and (since the second edition, in place of A. Vööbus) Carlo Martini, the present archbishop of Milan. The text is the same as that of the 26th Nestle-Aland edition, with but a few orthographical and punctuation differences. This UBS edition has been prepared with translators in view. Hence it offers a limited number of variant readings but provides an extensive amount of information about each of these variants. A companion volume, published in 1971 and edited by Metzger, a *Textual Commentary on the Greek New Testament,* provides the rationale for the choice made among the several available different readings. Accordingly, the companion volume interprets the A, B, C, or D grading attached to the reading chosen for insertion into the text by the editors. The letter A signifies that the text is virtually certain, while B indicates that there is some degree of doubt. The letter C means that there is considerable doubt whether the text or the apparatus contains the superior reading, while D shows that there is a very high degree of doubt concerning the reading selected for the text. Thus the student of the Greek New Testament is made aware that the reading of the New Testament is a matter of choice, and that not all judgments enjoy the same degree of scholarly support.

III. AN EXERCISE IN TEXTUAL CRITICISM

A. The Message of the Baptist: Mark 1:7–8

[7] And he preached, saying, "After me comes he who is mightier than I, the thong of whose sandals I am not worthy to stoop down and untie. [8] I have baptized you with water; but he will baptize you with the Holy Spirit."

To the Greek text of these two verses, published in the 26th edition of *Novum Testamentum Graece,* the editors have added four indications of variant readings. There are two units of variation in verse 7, and two in verse 8. In these verses each of the units of variation consists of only one word: After "me" (°*mou*); to "stoop down" (°¹*kupsas*); "with" water (*rhudati*); and "with" the (°*en*) Holy Spirit. In the critical apparatus at the bottom of the page appears a summary presentation of the data as follows:

> V.7 oB (Δ 1424 t ff²); Or
>
> o¹ p) D θ f¹³ 28*. 565 pc it
>
> V.8 ᵀ*en* A (D) L W (θ) f¹ ¹³ 𝔪 it: txt ℵ B Δ 33. 892* pc vg; Or
>
> o† B L b t vg; *txt* ℵA D W θ 0133 f¹ ¹³𝔪 it vgᵐˢˢ; Or

The first unit of variation concerns the pronoun *mou* ("me"). The critical apparatus indicates that the pronoun does not appear in the fourth-century Codex Vaticanus (B); Majuscule 037 (Δ), the Codex Sangallensis, a ninth-century ms. now located in St. Gall, Switzerland; Minuscule 1424, a ninth- or tenth-century manuscript, Gruber Ms. 152, presently located at the Theological Seminary, Maywood, Illinois; a fifth- or sixth-century Old Latin manuscript presently located at the University Library, Bern, Switzerland (t); a fifth-century Old Latin manuscript presently housed in the Bibliothèque Nationale, Paris (ff²); and Origen, a third-century Church Father (Or). Since the omission is restricted to a relatively few manuscripts, the editors have judged that the earlier text of Mark 1:7 most probably included the pronoun *mou.*

The second unit of variation consists of the participle *kupsas* (rendered as "stoop down and"). The critical apparatus indicates, first of all (pl), that in the judgment of the editors the omission has been influenced by parallel texts —that is, the participle does not appear in the saying such as it is found in Luke and John (Luke 3:16; John 1:27; comp Matt 3:11). Since the text of the major Gospels would have been more familiar to ancient scribes than the text of Mark, it is likely that some scribes inadvertently (or perhaps because they wanted to harmonize the texts) omitted the participle from Mark 1:7. After this initial suggestion, the apparatus indicates the texts from which the participle is missing. These are the fifth-century Codex Cantabrigiensis (D);

the ninth-century Codex Koridethi (θ); and the group of minuscules belonging to the Farrar family (f¹³). The original copyist (*prima manus*) of minuscule 28, an eleventh-century manuscript presently located in the Bibliothèque Nationale, Paris, did not have the participle, but a corrector has added *kupsas* to the manuscript. Finally the participle is lacking in minuscule 565 (a ninth-century ms. found in the public library of Leningrad) and in a few Old Latin texts (pc it).

In verse 8 the first unit of variation consists of the preposition *en* ("with") which the editors decided not to include in their edition of the Greek New Testament. The reader of the RSV will recognize that English language usage requires the appearance of the preposition "with" in the verse, whether it belonged to the Greek text or not. The critical apparatus indicates that the preposition *en* is present in the fifth-century Codex Alexandrinus (A); the fifth-century Codex Cantabrigiensis, although with some minor modifications ((D)); the eighth-century Codex Regius (L); the fourth- or fifth-century Codex Washingtoniensis (W); the ninth-century Codex Koridethi, with some minor modifications ((θ)); the Lake (f¹) and Farrar (f¹³) families of minuscules; the majority of other Greek texts (𝔪), and the Old Latin versions (it). The text as edited, in which the preposition *en* does not appear, corresponds to the reading found in the fourth-century Codex Sinaiticus (ℵ); the fourth-century Codex Vaticanus (B); the ninth-century Codex Sangallensis (Δ); and minuscule 33, a ninth-century codex. The preposition was not originally contained in a ninth-century minuscule (892*) presently located in the British Museum, London, but the text was amended by a later hand so as to include *en*. The preposition is even absent in a few manuscripts of the Vulgate (pc vg) and was not included by Origen. Bruce Metzger has explained the judgment of the editors as to the reading about which they entertain some degree of doubt (according to *The Greek New Testament,* the chosen reading is given only a B rating) as follows: "The tendency of scribes would have been to add *en* before *hudati* (compare the parallels in Mt 3:11 and Jn 1:26, which read *en hudati*)."

The second unit of variation in verse 8 consists of the preposition *en* ("with"), which this time the editors chose to incorporate in their text. The dagger (†) indicates that the 25th edition of Nestle-Aland did not include the preposition. The preposition was omitted from the Codex Vaticanus (B), the Codex Regius (L), the fifth-century Codex Veronensis with an Old Latin text (b), a fifth- or sixth-century Old Latin manuscript at the University Library in Bern (t), and the Vulgate (vg). The text in Aland's 26th edition corresponds to the reading in the Codex Sinaiticus (ℵ), the Codex Alexandrinus (A), the Codex Cantabrigiensis (D), the Codex Washingtoniensis (W), the Codex Koridethi (θ) (0133); the minuscules of the Lake and Farrar families (f¹⁻¹³); the majority of other Greek manuscripts (𝔪); the Old Latin (it); various codices of the Vulgate text (vgᵐˢˢ); and Origen. The editors have given an A rating, "virtually certain," to the inclusion of the preposition. Metzger comments: "The overwhelming weight of Greek manuscript evidence (the testimony of versions counts for little on a point such as this) supports the reading with *en*. The addition of *kai puri* in several witnesses reflects the influence of the parallels in Mt 3.11 and Lk 3.16."

In his commentary on verse 8, Metzger made mention of *kai puri* ("and fire"), which is not cited in the critical apparatus of the 26th edition of *Novum Testamentum Graece*. It was cited in the apparatus of the 25th edition, with the indication that it appears in some mss. under the attraction of parallel passages—those to which Metzger has made reference. In fact *kai puri* appears in a sixth-century ms. (024) presently in Wolfenbüttel, Germany, and in a few minuscules. The editors of N²⁶ have judged the textual attestation for this reading so weak as not even to warrant its inclusion in the critical apparatus. Were they to have included every possible unit of variation in their apparatus, the volume would have been unduly unwieldy.

B. The Stilling of the Storm: Mark 4:35–41

³⁵ On that day, when evening had come, he said to them, "Let us go across to the other side." ³⁶ And leaving the crowd, they took him with them, just as he was, in the boat. And other boats were with him. ³⁷ And a great storm of wind arose, and the waves beat into the boat, so that the boat was already filling. ³⁸ But he was in the stern, asleep on the cushion; and they woke him and said to him, "Teacher, do you not care if we perish?" ³⁹ And he awoke and rebuked the wind, and said to the sea, "Peace! Be still!" And the wind ceased, and there was a great calm. ⁴⁰ He said to them, "Why are you afraid? Have you no faith?" ⁴¹ And they were filled with awe, and said to one another, "Who then is this, that even wind and sea obey him?"

Aland's 26th edition of *Novum Testamentum Graece* indicates six units of variation in the Greek text of this miracle story, two in verses 36 and 38, and one each in verses 40 and 41. Of these, only one has been explained in *A Textual Commentary on the Greek New Testament*. Again it can be noted that the appropriate critical apparatus in N²⁶ does not give the complete list of possible units of variations. An additional three units of variation appeared in NA²⁵, but the editors dropped these from the later edition as being relatively insignificant.

The first unit of variation in verse 36 concerns the participial phrase *aphentes ton ochlon* ("leaving the crowd"). The apparatus cites two different readings. *Aphiousin ton ochlon* ("they left the crowd and") seems to be the reading found in the hardly visible text of the third century 𝔭⁴⁵. It is also found in three important majuscules, D, W, and θ; the Lake family minuscules, as well as 25, 565, and 700; and a few Old Latin texts. *Aphentes auton* ("leaving it") is the reading found in the Codex Alexandrinus. On assessment of the evidence, there cannot be any doubt that *aphentes ton ochlon* ("leaving the crowd") is by far the best attested reading.

The second unit of variation in verse 36 concerns the expression *alla ploia ēn met'autou* ("other boats were with him"), for which the apparatus indicates three alternative readings. A first alternative is the reading *alla de ploia ēn met'autou,* with the addition of the particle *de.* Hardly translatable into English, it serves at best to strengthen the adversative conjunction *alla* ("but"). The particle appears in A, D, L, and most of the Greek manuscripts, including the minuscules of the Farrar family. The particle was added to the Codex Ephraemi Rescriptus by a second corrector of the manuscript; it is reflected by the Syriac Harklian version. Within this same unit of variation other alternative readings can be indicated. The Codex Regius, the majuscule 0133, and many minuscules (including 1010) have a diminutive form, *ploiaria* ("little boats"). The majuscules D and 33 add the adjective *polla* before *ploia* (so, "many boats"). The Codex Cantabrigiensis has replaced the singular verb *ēn* (note that in Greek, a neuter plural subject can take a verb in the singular number) by the plural *ēsan* ("were"). These several varieties of change seem to represent a variety of stylistic modifications. No one of them is particularly well attested in the manuscript tradition.

A second alternative is the reading *ama polloi ēsan met'autou* ("many were together with him"). This reading, which anticipates the role of Jesus' companions (v. 38 ff.), is found in the Codex Washingtoniensis and a fifth-century Old Latin manuscript (e) found in the National Museum in Trent, Italy. The third alternative, *ta alla ta onta ploia met'autou* ("the other boats being with him"), is found in the Codex Koridethi (θ), minuscule 565, and, with some modifications, in the Lake family minuscules as well as minuscules 28 and 700. It is apparently a stylistic variant. The reading chosen by the editors is found in most of the Greek manuscripts, especially the Codex Sinaiticus (albeit with a verb in the plural) and the Codex Vaticanus, and a few manuscripts of the Vulgate. The chosen reading is, by and large, better attested. Considerations previously developed under the rubric "deviational probability" explain why the alternatives were substituted for the text chosen by the editors as the earlier reading.

In verse 38, a first unit of variation concerns the principal clause *autos ēn* ("he was"). This reading is found in such ancient mss. as ℵ, B, C, L, and Δ. In the majority of manuscripts, however, including A, D, W, θ, and the minuscules of the Lake and Farrar families, the sequence of the two words is inverted, the pronoun being placed after the verb without any significant change in meaning. An examination of Mark's style is not helpful here, since the expression does not occur elsewhere in the Gospel, except in a periphrastic construction in Mark 15:43. Apparently it was the value attributed to the Sinaiticus and the Vaticanus that prompted the choice of *autos ēn* by the editors of N[26]. Surprisingly, Tischendorf, who normally attributes great value to the readings of the Sinaiticus, chose an *ēn autos* reading for the *editio critica octava.*

The second unit of variation of verse 38 concerns the verb *egeirousin* ("they woke"). This reading is found in the Sinaiticus, the Vaticanus, the Ephraemi Rescriptus, and the Sangallensis. A compound form of the verb, *diegeirousin* ("they woke"), is found in the Alexandrinus. This compound form also appears as the work of a corrector's hand on B, and as the work of a second corrector on C. The correction would seem to be a stylistic one, since *diegeirō* represents a more precise usage for waking someone from sleep. Perhaps the emendation might have been suggested by theological considerations, insofar as the simple verb *egeirō* is a technical term in the resurrection kerygma. An alternative to this unit of variation is suggested by the aorist participial reading of the compound verb *diegeirantes* ("waking") found in D, W, θ, and a few minuscules. The minuscules of the Farrar family also have a participle, *egeirantes,* albeit a form of the simple verb *egeirō.* The use of the participle entails the omission of *kai* ("and") between the two verbs in the expression "they woke him and said to him." The use of either participial expression obviously represents a stylistic change.

In verse 40 the unit of variation focuses on *deiloi este; oupō* ("are you afraid? [Have you] no [faith?]"). The apparatus of N²⁶ indicates three alternatives, of which the first appeared in the text of NA²⁵. Attested by A, C, and the majority of Greek mss., as well as by two versions of the Syriac and an important Old Latin text, the first alternative is *deiloi este outōs; pōs ouk* ("are you afraid?" How is it possible that you don't [have faith?]). A second alternative reading is simply *deiloi este outōs* ("are you so afraid?" ["Do you have faith?"]), attested by the Codex Washingtoniensis and some mss. of the Old Latin version. The third alternative is basically the same, except that the negative particle is retained and the adverb is displaced. This reading, *outōs deiloi este; oupō* ("are you so afraid? [Have you] no [faith?]"), was apparently that of 𝔭⁴⁵ and the Lake, Farrar, and a few other minuscules. The reading adopted by Aland and his colleagues for incorporation in N²⁶ is attested by ℵ, B, D, L, Δ, θ, a few minuscules, as well as in the Old Latin and Coptic versions. Metzger has explained the choice, to which an A rating has been given, in this way: "The reading adopted as the text has by far the best external support. The reading . . . *pōs ouk* (A C K Π 33 *al*) seems to have arisen from a desire to soften somewhat Jesus' reproach spoken to the disciples."

The unit of variation of verse 41 also admits of three alternatives. It concerns the final words of the pericope *hupakouei autō* ("obey him"). This reading is attested by a second corrector of the Codex Sinaiticus, the Codex Vaticanus, the Codex Regius, and the ninth-century minuscule 892. A first alternative appears in the hand of the first corrector of the Vaticanus, the Codex Ephraemi Rescriptus, the Codex Sangallensis, a few minuscules including 28 and those of the Lake and Farrar families. The alternative consists simply of the inversion of the two words in the unit of variation, thus *autō hupakouei* ("obey him"). The Codex Cantabrigiensis (D) and a few Old Latin texts (ff², i, q) have a stylistic variant with the verb in the plural, thus *hupakouousin* ("obey") without any accompanying pronoun. The pronoun appears with a plural verb in A, W, θ, 0133, and the vast majority of Greek mss. This reading *hupakouousin autō* ("obey him") is also suggested by the Old Latin version. The *lectio difficilior* principle suggests the *hupakouei autō* ("obey him," in the singular number), the reading adopted by the editors of N^{26}. The other alternatives are then easily seen as scribal emendations in view of a stylistically improved text.

In these two examples just nine verses of the New Testament have been considered. The popular 26th edition of the *Novum Testamentum Graece* has cited ten units of variation within these few verses. The previous edition of *Novum Testamentum Graece* offered an additional four units of variation within the verses. Were the units of variation appearing in all the extant mss. of Mark 1:7–8 and 4:35–41 to have been cited, the critical apparatus would have become unwieldly. Fortunately the differences among the several readings of the texts are not such as to cause major problems for the interpreter of the passages under consideration. Nonetheless they are sufficient to show that the first task faced by the interpreter of the New Testament is the precise determination of the text itself. It is only when the Greek text has been established with reasonable accuracy that the interpreter can attempt to translate the text into one of our modern languages—a task which is already an interpretation—and proceed to a more extensive interpretation of the passage.

SELECT BIBLIOGRAPHY

Aland, Barbara. "Neutestamentliche Textkritik heute." *Verkündigung und Forschung,* 21 (1976), 3–22.

Aland, Kurt. *Kurzgefasste Liste der Griekischen Handschriften des Neuen Testaments.* Arbeiten zur neutestamentlichen Textforschung, 1. Berlin: Walter de Gruyter & Co., 1963.

———. *Materialen zur neutestamentlichen Handschriftkunde.* Arbeiten zur neutestamentlichen Textforschung, 3. Berlin: Walter de Gruyter & Co., 1969.

Amphoux, Christian-Bernard. "Éditions récentes du Nouveau Testament grec." *Études théologiques et religieuses,* 55 (1980), 427–33.

Bell, Albert A., Jr. "Jerome's Role in the Translation of the Vulgate New Testament." *New Testament Studies,* 23 (1977), 230–33.

Best, Ernest, and Wilson, R. McL., eds. *Text and Interpretation. Studies in the New Testament Presented to Matthew Black.* New York: Cambridge University Press, 1979.

Clark, Kenneth Willis. *The Gentile Bias and Other Essays. Supplements to Novum Testamentum,* 54 Leiden: Brill, 1980.

Colwell, Ernest C. "Biblical Criticism: Lower and Higher." *Journal of Biblical Literature,* 67 (1948), 1–12.

———. *Studies in Methodology in Textual Criticism of the New Testament.* New Testament Tools and Studies, 9. Leiden: Brill, 1969.

Elliott, J. K. "Plaidoyer pour un éclectisme intégral appliqué à la critique textuelle du Nouveau Testament." *Revue biblique* 84 (1977), 5–25.

———. "Textual Criticism, Assimilation and the Synoptic Gospels." *New Testament Studies,* 26 (1980), 231–42.

Epp, Eldon Jay. "The Eclectic Method in New Testament Textual Criticism: Solution or Symptom?" *Harvard Theological Review,* 69 (1976), 211–57.

———. "New Testament Textual Criticism in America: Requiem for a Discipline." *Journal of Biblical Literature,* 98 (1979), 94–98.

Fee, Gordon D. "Modern Textual Criticism and the Revival of the *Textus Receptus." Journal of the Evangelical Theological Society,* 21 (1978), 19–33.

Finegan, Jack. *Encountering New Testament Manuscripts: A Working Introduction to Textual Criticism.* Grand Rapids: Eerdmans, 1974.

Junack, Klaus. "The Reliability of the New Testament Text from the Perspective of Textual Criticism." *The Bible Translator,* 29 (1978), 128–40.

Metzger, Bruce M. *The Early Versions of the New Testament: Their Origin, Transmission, and Limitations.* Oxford: Clarendon, 1977.

———. *New Testament Studies: Philological, Versional, And Patristic.* New Testament Tools and Studies, 10. Leiden: Brill, 1980.

———. *The Text of the New Testament: Its Transmission, Corruption, and Restoration,* 2nd ed., Oxford: Clarendon, 1968.

———. *A Textual Commentary on the Greek New Testament. A Companion Volume to the United Bible Societies' Greek New Testament.* London: United Bible Societies, 1971.

Mohr, Ian A. "Tischendorf and the Codex Sinaiticus." *New Testament Studies,* 23 (1976), 108–15.

Parker, David C. "The Development of Textual Criticism since B. H. Streeter." *New Testament Studies,* 24 (1977), 149–62.

Pickering, Wilbur N. *The Identity of the New Testament Text.* Nashville-New York: Nelson, 1977.

Richards, W. L. "A Critique of a New Testament Text-Critical Methodology —the Claremont Profile Method." *Journal of Biblical Literature,* 96 (1977), 555–66.

Westcott, Brooke Foss, and Hort, F. J. A. *The New Testament in the Original Greek.* 2 vols. Cambridge-London: Macmillan, 1881.

CHAPTER FOUR

SOURCE CRITICISM

I. AN INTRODUCTION TO THE METHOD

Biblical criticism, of which New Testament criticism is a part, is the name given to that study of the Bible which employs rational rather than theological categories. Most commonly the categories used in the interpretation of the New Testament text are those of history and literature. Use of these categories by students of the New Testament involves them in an interpretative task whose methodology is not significantly different from the methodology used by interpreters of other ancient texts. What distinguishes New Testament criticism from the more general science of the interpretation of texts is the limited and well-determined amount of subject matter, not the methodology.

An examination of this common methodology reveals that it is really a cluster of somewhat distinct methodologies, the first of which is text criticism, whose general thrust and application to the New Testament has been studied in the previous chapter. Still closer examination of the cluster of methodologies which can be collected together under the single rubric of New Testament criticism reveals that, to a large extent, these methodologies were developed by students of the Bible from whom they were appropriated by interpreters of other ancient texts. Refined by these extrabiblical scholars, these methodologies have continued to be employed in the study of the New Testament. Together they attempt to tell us what the text meant at the time of its composition (the object of historical criticism) rather than what the text means today (the object of hermeneutics).

The history of the various methodologies constituent of New Testament criticism has been generally traced in Chapter Two. At that time it might have proved useful to make certain distinctions which I have retained until the present time, lest the introduction of too many distinctions interfere with the sense of the ebb and flow of historical tides.

One appropriate distinction, for example, is that between the so-called "lower criticism" and the so-called "higher criticism." Lower criticism is concerned with the establishment of the text that is to be studied. Figuratively speaking, lower criticism aims to unearth the terrain upon which subsequent criticism can be done. Lower criticism, attentive to the arrangement and presentation of the New Testament text, is now commonly referred to by New Testament critics under the rubric of text criticism. As such, lower criticism served as the principal focus of interest in the preceding chapter.

Literary Criticism

The remaining methodologies, which seek to establish the meaning of a New Testament text in its proper historical and literary environment, can be grouped together under the rubric of "higher criticism." Higher criticism encompasses a broad range of historical and literary methods that seek to interpret the New Testament text in the light of its own historical-literary context. Inevitably, higher criticism is involved with problems of authorship, authenticity, collaboration, revision, chronology, and a certain number of other related issues. To respond to the questions that arise in the consideration of these problems, various methods have been developed, some of which are appropriately gathered together under the umbrella of "literary criticism." Yet this terminology remains somewhat ambiguous.

For some scholars, literary criticism refers to that particular approach to the study of the New Testament which reached a recognizable point of systematic development during the nineteenth century. For these authors, literary criticism is virtually equivalent to source criticism, whose application to the New Testament reached its zenith a century ago in the formulation of the Two-Source theory as a solution to the problem of the literary relationship among the Synoptic Gospels. Since then the methodology has been subject to considerable refinement and has been applied to an ever larger portion of the New Testament.

Other students of the New Testament, however, understand "literary criticism" in a somewhat different fashion. For them, literary criticism is concerned with that study of a work which seeks to understand an author's intention and achievements by means of an analysis of the structure and component elements of his text. By analyzing John 1:1–18 with respect to its chiastic, spiral, or linear structuration, for example, the interpreter tries to understand the meaning of John's prologue in itself and to determine the reason why the evangelist appended these verses as a prologue to the Fourth Gospel.

Still other New Testament critics apply the category of literary criticism to those methods currently employed in the study of contemporary literature. They are concerned with the applicability of the laws of narrative to the Gospels and the individual parables within the Gospels. Cannot several of the New Testament texts be somewhat elucidated by means of the classical categories of comedy and tragedy? For authors who opt for this approach to the understanding of the New Testament, literary criticism is roughly synonymous with the methodology of "structural analysis," which will serve as the topic of Chapter Seven of the present work.

According to the most traditional usage, literary criticism principally consists of the application to the New Testament of the methodology of source criticism. During the nineteenth century the use of this methodology was clearly subservient to historical-critical purposes. Investigators concerned with Life of Jesus research were immediately confronted by the complexities of similarity and dissimilarity among the four canonical Gospels. These Gospels, which surely had to be counted among the earliest of historical documentation for the Life of Jesus, were generally considered to be literary documents, each of which was written by a single, though perhaps anonymous, author. For the researchers of the time, a critical issue which cried out for immediate resolution was the determination of which single Gospel offered the most reliable testimony to the historical Jesus. The reliability of the evangelists as witnesses to history was the principal issue at stake. The Gospel that was the oldest and might have served as the source for the others was presumably the most reliable. Thus there arose the question of the interdependence among the evangelists and their possible use of earlier documentary sources. Seen in this perspective, it is clear that it was the ensemble of issues relating to the so-called Synoptic Problem which prompted the Life of Jesus researchers to make use of source criticism in their study of the New Testament.

Life of Jesus research entered into a cul-de-sac at the turn of the century, at the same time the form-critical methodology emerged which emphasized the role of the oral tradition behind the written Gospels (see Chapter Five), leading to a considerable loss of popularity of the methodology among New Testament scholars during this century. It was true that the priority of Mark, along with the dependency of both Matthew and Luke, served as something of a given for New Testament critics during the early part of the twentieth century. It was also true that Rudolf Bultmann had developed (albeit never systematically) an extensive theory on the sources of the Fourth Gospel. Nevertheless, source criticism seemed to have foundered on the shoals of form criticism.

Form criticism, whose earliest manifestos appeared just after the First World War, considered the evangelists more as the compilers and conveyers of tradition than as literary authors in their own right. Thus it drew the interest of scholars away from a consideration of the documentary sources a New Testament "author" might have employed in the composition of his work to a consideration of the largely oral traditions that shaped the material incorporated into the several books of the New Testament. With this shift in emphasis came an eclipse which overshadowed the use of source criticism for almost two generations (1930–70).

This eclipse of the source-critical methodology was not only a result of the frustrations attendant on the Quest of the Historical Jesus and the growing popularity of the form-critical methodology. It was also due to the disparity of results obtained by the source critics themselves. Among students of the Synoptic Problem there was a consensus which generally acclaimed Mark as one of the sources employed by canonical Matthew and canonical Luke, but there was much less of a consensus as to the nature and extent of the Sayings Source, the so-called Q document. Scholars such as Bultmann suggested that even other parts of the New Testament, especially the Johannine corpus (John, 1,2,3 John, Rev), had also been composed by authors who used earlier documentation in their work, but the theories of these modern interpreters were often so sophisticated as to preclude general acceptance among New Testament scholars. As for Paul, whom Baur had raised to a pride of place with respect to the historical circumstances within which the New Testament was composed, there was little doubt that his epistles were, in fact, "letters" and that each of them was a single composition dictated as the circumstances of the early churches warranted.

A Renewal of Interest

With the development of redaction criticism and its widespread use by New Testament scholars, however, source criticism has once again come into its own. Redaction criticism (see Chapter Six) focuses upon the editorial use and modifications made by an author as he introduces his source material into his work. The degree of success with which this methodology is employed is related to the degree to which the interpreter has access to the source material with which the ancient author worked. Contemporary interest in the use of redaction criticism has occasioned a revival in source criticism, since it is the burden of source criticism to determine the sources used by New Testament authors.

Interest in the redaction of the Gospels of Matthew and Luke, and to some extent of Mark as well, has contributed to a renewed interest in the solutions advanced for the Synoptic Problem. At the same time, Johannine and Pauline scholars have become more aware of the fact that both the evangelist and the apostle have appropriated material which they themselves did not compose. Thus the methodology of source criticism cannot be limited to the study of the Synoptic Gospels, though the Synoptics were the prime area for the application of this methodology in the nineteenth century and remain even today an ideal area for the application of the methodology, in view of the widespread conviction that Mark is the source of Matthew and Luke.

In fact, one can say that the renewed interest in the use of source criticism as a method for the study of the New Testament derives from a concern which is at once literary, historical, and theological. The use of source criticism reflects a literary interest insofar as the student of the New Testament wants to know how each of the New Testament authors composed his work(s). As a matter of fact, the prologue to the Gospel of Luke (Luke 1:1-4) suggests that the author of the Third Gospel, who is the author of Acts as well, has collated and made use of source material in his account of the Good News. This avowal should prompt the student of the Gospels to analyze Luke's use of sources, not only for the composition of the Gospel, but for that of Acts as well. The critic who appreciates the New Testament books as works of ancient literature undoubtedly wants to know how the several authors composed their works.

From quite another vantage point, the renewed interest in the applicability of source-critical methodology to the New Testament stems from an interest in the history of the Early Christian Church. It is source criticism that affords the contemporary student of the New Testament some insight into the relative chronology of works that seem related, as, for example, Matthew, Mark, and Luke; Ephesians and Colossians; Jude and 2 Peter. Moreover, the students' historical interest is further whetted by the use of source criticism insofar as the determination of literary sources employed by the New Testament authors is concerned, and their reconstitution on the basis of the available documentation, when this is feasible, brings the student of the New Testament into contact with an earlier stage in the history of the Church than does an uncritical analysis of the work of this or that author. Among contemporary interpreters of the New Testament it is generally acknowledged that Paul's First Letter to the Thessalonians is the most ancient piece of Christian documentation. It is generally dated to A.D. 50 or 51. Yet many of those who share the common consensus as to the solution of the Synoptic Problem have reconstituted a Sayings Source (Q) which they commonly date to the time (but not the place) of Paul's first letter. The Sayings Source manifests an interest in eschatology that had largely passed from the scene by the time that the canonical Gospels were written some twenty or thirty years later.

Thus a judicious use of source criticism can open the thought world and even the sociology of various segments of the early Church to the contemporary student of the New Testament. Source criticism not only points to the sources used by the New Testament authors, but reveals the theology of this source material as well and even allows for some comparison between the theology of the sources and that of the extant documents. The interest in source criticism shown by the redaction critic not only allows him to focus upon modifications of style and wording, but also permits him to center on the theological interests of the final author or redactor of the text that lies behind him. Surely one should also attach some importance to the fact that the aretalogies (collections of miracle stories) which source critics claim to have discerned behind the Gospels of Mark and John, and which speak of a *theios anēr* (divine man) type of Christology, were not preserved in their naked form by the early Church. Similarly the Sayings Source employed by Matthew and Luke speaks of a wise man type of Christology, but the trace of this Christology has remained with us only because the Sayings Source, which affords a higher type of Christology than that of Jesus the sage, has apparently been taken over and preserved in a Gospel form. Similarly there is some major significance in the fact that the author of the Fourth Gospel has chosen to incorporate some prose segments which speak of John the Baptist (John 1:6–8, 15) into the hymn considered by most Johannine scholars to be the basis of the Prologue.

In effect, the quest for the sources of the New Testament writings is undertaken by interpreters of the New Testament with an interest and zeal which go beyond the satisfaction of mere historical curiosity. The issue of a New Testament author's use of sources is at bottom a literary question, but its resolution satisfies historical, sociological, and theological concerns as well.

The Method

In some respects the application of the method of source criticism is familiar to virtually every teacher. There is hardly a high school teacher or college professor in existence who has not had to employ the basic methodology of source criticism in the evaluation of homework assignments and term papers. The lot of the high school teacher is all too familiar to warrant a detailed description. Frequently he or she receives an essay purportedly written by a student whose known ability in English composition is limited. The first several paragraphs of the essay are written in a style and with a vocabulary with which the teacher is familiar because they reflect the linguistic ability of the student responsible for the work. Then, all of a sudden, a pattern of polysyllabic words replaces the monosyllables that characterized the initial paragraphs of the essay. The grammatical errors of those early paragraphs have yielded to a section marked by correct grammar and punctuation. The teacher rapidly comes to the conclusion that the student has "borrowed" material and incorporated it into the essay at hand. Perhaps the "borrowed" material has come from an encyclopedia; perhaps it has been written by a more qualified student; perhaps it has been copied from an essay written by another. The teacher may not be able to identify the source used by the student, but is quite correct in affirming that the student had made use of sources in the composition of the essay.

The lot of the college professor is not unlike that of the high school teacher. Frequently he or she will be called upon to correct term papers submitted for evaluation. To the evaluator, term papers often seem the product of a "cut and paste" operation effected upon pertinent source material, encyclopedia articles, and related texts. Even in the absence of quotation marks and the references which ought to be given in footnotes or end notes, the professor is able to tell that the student has not fully integrated the material about which he or she is writing. Rather than seeing an original work that results from a process of integration, the professor recognizes juxtaposed material from different sources. Since the professor is oftentimes well versed in the material on which the students are writing, it is frequently easy for him or her to identify the exact source employed by the student. Apart from his ability to identify the very sources used in the term paper, the professor can generally discern sufficient telltale signs to justify the conclusion that the student has made use of source material. Some typical telltale signs are the harsh connections that occur between one paragraph or section and another, the choice of vocabulary, and the meaning afforded to different terms. Quite frequently a professor recognizes that one of the student's sources has used terminology with one meaning, and that another of the sources attributes a slightly different connotation to that terminology.

In short the classroom teacher or college professor is quite familiar with the phenomenon of a student's use of unreferenced source material. Spontaneously he or she discerns that a student has incorporated borrowed material into an essay or term paper. A set of operative, though often unstated, criteria allow for the judgment to be made with all certainty even if the teacher or professor is unable to identify precisely the source material employed. The determination of that source material then becomes a second task to which the teacher or professor might set himself or herself should circumstances so warrant.

This rapid review of the teacher's evaluation process has isolated two of the main questions to which the methodology of source criticism seeks an answer. First of all, the source critic wants to know *whether* an author (in our example, the student; in our perspective, a New Testament author) has made use of one or more sources. If the answer to this first question is in the affirmative, then the source critic must ask another question: *What* are the sources used by the author? The answer to this second question is relatively easy for the classroom teacher and the professor who can often recognize the material and identify it as a selection, for example, from the Encyclopaedia Britannica, or, failing that, query the student who has submitted the essay or term paper. Indeed, the modern literary critic might be prompted to employ a computer in an attempt to identify the sources used by a modern author.

The answer to the question, What are the sources used by the author? is more difficult to obtain when we are dealing with ancient documents, whose authors are long since dead, whose autograph or prototype copy we do not have, composed in an era when it was considered acceptable for an author to incorporate borrowed material into his work (unlike our times, when such a process would be considered plagiarizing), and dating from a time when we have little, if any, parallel material with which to compare the documents at hand. In such cases a judicious use of criteria will nevertheless enable the critic not only to affirm that an ancient author has made use of sources, but also to reconstitute the sources used by the ancient New Testament author. A college professor might be able to confirm his judgment that a student has made use of borrowed material by confronting the student with the volume of the Encyclopaedia Britannica from which he or she had taken the material. Similarly the New Testament critic might find some confirmation of his judgment, based on an analysis of the texts themselves, that Matthew, Luke, Ephesians, and 2 Peter do not represent uniform literary compositions by comparing Matthew and Luke with Mark, Ephesians with Colossians, and 2

Peter with Jude. For the rest, however, the New Testament critic is left to the skill of his own art as he sets about the task of reconstituting the sources employed by New Testament authors. The critic's ability to determine criteria and verify their applicability is all-important to his task.

Thus, source criticism is the methodology employed by the interpreter of the New Testament who wants to know both whether a New Testament author has made use of sources and what are the sources used. The methodology is employed in the event that an author has neither indicated his use of sources nor identified them. Those which source criticism seeks to identify are literary (documentary) sources, not oral traditions upon which a New Testament author might have been reliant in the composition of his work. The methods of source criticism need not be applied to the interpretation of such passages as Matthew 13:14–15 and Acts 17:25, since the authors of these passages have specifically stated their reliance upon the prophet Isaiah (Isa 6:9–10) and the poets Epimenides and Aratus (if indeed the plural does not stand as a generic singular) respectively. Indeed, the application of source-critical methodology to the study of the New Testament has proved to be most beneficial not when the critic has identified some one or another snippet citation, but when he has identified a major source employed by one of the New Testament writers, or a significant body of material, such as a hymn, incorporated into one of these books.

In his attempt to answer the basic "whether?" and "what?" questions as he tries to discern the applicability of criteria, the New Testament critic must also be aware that many authors who have made use of sources have not simply been involved in a "cut and paste" operation in which material from one source is simply placed next to material from another source so that the end product represents the juxtaposition of material coming from several different sources. Were that the case, the task of the source critic would be relatively easy. In fact, however, an author who uses sources generally modifies the "borrowed" material somewhat. Conversely, the source material frequently influences an author's manner of composition, at least in respect to its immediate literary context. Given this dialogical relationship between an author and his sources, it is little wonder that source criticism represents an artistic endeavor rather than a strictly scientific discipline.

The practitioner of the art of source criticism must undoubtedly seek a response to the "whether?" and "what?" questions as his first order of priority. However, there are three additional questions which also must occupy his attention. In the first place, the interpreter must seek to determine just *how much* of the document he is studying is based upon the source whose existence he has discerned. Can one state with certainty, for example, that John has made use of the hypothetical Signs Source only for Chapters 2–12 of the Gospel? This question prompts the reverse question. How much of the source material has been incorporated into the document under examination? Did a New Testament author employ all of his source material in his work, or did he make a selection as the author of John seems to have done (cf. John 20:30–31)? Finally, the source critic should seek to know the fashion in which a New Testament author has made use of his source material. This "how?" question borders upon that aspect of New Testament criticism undertaken by the practitioner of redaction criticism, but it might legitimately be considered a pertinent part of the art of source criticism as well. Has the New Testament author cited his source material verbatim, or somewhat freely? In this respect, the student of the Synoptic Gospels might well conjecture that Matthew has made use of his *Q* material with a degree of freedom comparable to that with which he treated his Markan and Old Testament material. The New Testament critic must also ask subsidiary questions about the ordering of source material in the composite document, as well as questions about the New Testament author's preference for the incorporation of a block of source material into his own work in comparison with another type of procedure which would have scattered the borrowed material over a larger segment of the final document. Issues relative to the fashion in which the evangelists made use of their sources have certainly figured heavily in the consideration of the Synoptic and Johannine Problems. These issues require the delicate manipulation of criteria, and it is to these criteria that attention must now be turned.

The Criteria

The criteria utilized by the New Testament critic are not substantially different from those employed by Julius Wellhausen, generations ago, in his Pentateuchal analysis. Four such criteria seem to emerge as most germane to the interpretation of the New Testament. These are *redundancy, context, vocabulary* and *style,* and *ideology.*

In fact, redundancy or repetition is not all that common in the New Testament. There are parallel passages in different Gospels, and parallel passages among several of the Pauline epistles. Relatively rare, however, are the repetitions within a single New Testament work which would give the critic some indication that his author has made use of sources. One of the most glaring examples of redundancy within the New Testament is to be found within the "farewell discourses" of the Fourth Gospel (John 13 – 17). Chapters 15 and 16 are virtually a repeat performance of Chapters 13 and 14. Both passages, for example, make mention of the commandment "that you love one another" (John 13:34–35; 15:12). Each of them promises the coming of the Spirit (John 14:15–26; 16:5–15). A consideration of other factors confirms the impression of the composite nature of the farewell discourses, an impression initially made on the basis of redundancy.

Another example of redundancy in the New Testament is Jesus' saying on divorce, found in Matthew 5:32 and again, albeit with some slight modification, in Matthew 19:9. Further study of the repeated saying shows that Matthew 5:32 is based on the Sayings Source whereas Matthew 19:9 is based on Matthew's Markan source.

A second criterion for discerning the use of sources by an author is the context itself. The presence of aporias—the technical term used to designate the hard connections, disjunctions, inconsistencies, and even contradictions in a text—can indicate that an author has used various sources in the composition of his text. The aporias are a sign that the seam between the borrowed material and his own work has not been sufficiently welded by an author. In the Gospel of John, for example, a conclusion to the farewell discourse at 14:31b is a sure indication that the author has made use of sources in the composition of the discourse, just as the "conclusion" at 20:30–31 shows that the author's use of sources is not confined to the farewell discourses alone. Likewise the concluding phrase found in Romans 15:33 is one of the factors that have prompted many Pauline scholars to question whether Romans 16 was originally a part of Paul's letter to the Romans.

The Gospel of Mark is not often subject to extensive source-critical analysis, but there is some reason to believe that even Mark had written sources at his disposal, sources of which he made use in writing the first Gospel. Thus, in Mark's story of Jesus' healing a boy possessed by a spirit (Mark 9:14–29) there are aporias in sufficient number to convince the discerning critic that the narrative is a composite tale. To cite but a few of these inconsistencies, we can note that the crowd is twice introduced (vv. 14, 25), the boy is twice presented (vv. 17, 20), and the spirit is alternatively described as dumb (v. 17) and unclean (v. 25). Moreover, it has been held that the repetition of a catchword or phrase is oftentimes the clue to a later addition to a narrative. Such repetitions abound in Mark (e.g., 14:53, 66), which is characterized by the phenomenon known as the "sandwich technique," a literary device whereby one narrative is inserted within another (e.g., Mark 5:21–43).

A third criterion the critic will find useful for determining an author's use of sources is vocabulary and style. The presence of specific and general characteristics of style as well as the presence of distinctive terminology and vocabulary can assist in the identification of different strata in the composition of a literary work. A case in point would certainly be the Prologue of John's Gospel. The parallelism of verses 1–2, 3–4, and 10 stamp these verses as poetry and set them apart from the body of the Gospel, which is written in a prose style. Moreover, several expressions in the Prologue are found in John 1:1–18) but are not found in the body of the Gospel (John 1:19–21:25). Among the examples of such distinctive terminology within the Prologue we can cite "Word" (*Logos,* vv. 1, 2, 14), "grace" (*charis,* vv. 16, 17), and "fullness" (*plērōma,* v. 16).

The Prologue to Luke's Gospel (Luke 1:1–4) is a fine example of Hellenistic style. His Gospel contains some of the best Greek in the New Testament. Sandwiched between these elements of good Greek prose is Luke's Infancy Narrative (Luke 1:5 – 2:52). Characterized by Semitisms and "biblical language," it is set off sharply from both the Prologue that precedes it and the body of the Gospel that follows it. In this regard it is noteworthy that the Gospel proper is entirely lacking in those marvelously Semitic lyrical constructions which we have identified as the canticles of Mary (Luke 1:47–55), Zechariah (Luke 1:68–79) and Simeon (Luke 2:29–32). The distinctive style and vocabulary of the Infancy Narrative prompt us to ask whether its provenance is one with that of the rest of the Gospel.

Ideological characteristics serve as a fourth criterion for identifying an author's use of sources. Ideas, themes, theological tendencies, and points of view that are different from the ideas expressed elsewhere within a document can point to the possible use of sources. So too can distinctive vocabulary when it signifies a distinctive theological point of view rather than a merely stylistic phenomenon. Thus the discerning critic has no difficulty in pointing to the distinctive ideology of the Christological hymn in Philippians 2:6–11 and setting it off from the remainder of that epistle. Similarly the distinctive epithets applied to God in Romans 16:25–27 as well as the particular understanding of "mystery" in that passage have led many a critic to question whether the verses represent the authentic conclusion to Paul's letter to the Romans.

The working hypothesis behind the application of this criterion is that no matter how careful an author is, he is somehow bound to reproduce or reflect his source. Since no two authors share exactly the same point of view, it is inevitable that the disagreement between the source material, and material coming from other sources or from the author's own hand will occasionally rise to the surface. Such discrepancy of thought is a sure sign that a given author has employed sources in the composition of his work.

For source analysis, those criteria which are based on the text itself (i.e., redundancy and context) are the best. The duplication of given data and the relationship of conflicting data are more significant than the presence (or absence) of an absolute datum in determining that an author has made use of sources and in thus indicating a hypothesis for the composition of the work at hand. The hypothesis can be further refined as the linguistic, and stylistic characteristics as well as the ideological tendencies of the source material become identifiable. On the basis of this identification, further passages in the work under consideration can be identified as coming from the source(s).

As described thus far, the technique of source analysis is relatively simple to manipulate. In fact, the use of the technique is not a simple matter. First of all, apart from the criterion of redundancy, which is not at all common in the New Testament, the contextual criterion is the most objective and therefore the most effective for source analysis. However, a certain amount of imagination and experience are required for its effective use. Indeed, textual criticism might occasionally reveal a relatively large number of variant readings precisely at the juncture between one passage and another. Sometimes this multitude has been spawned by scribes who were trying to eliminate aporias in the text before them.

Occasionally knowledge of an author's style can help to determine which section of a work is an author's original composition. The residue can then be assumed to have come from his source. Conversely, certain features of style and vocabulary may appear only in the source, setting this off from the author's own composition as well as from material coming from other

125

sources. Yet the literary critic must always be aware of the possibility of literary osmosis, by means of which some characteristics of the source occasionally slip into the author's own work, and some of the author's own characteristics are embedded in the sources he employs.

Finally, we must be aware of the dangers of subjectivism and circularity in the working out of source analysis. Ideally, the more objective criteria should ground a working hypothesis as to an author's use of sources. The hypothesis can then be verified and confirmed by an application of the criteria of stylistic and linguistic characteristics and ideological tendencies. The use of these criteria can then warrant the assignment of other material to the hypothetical source. All too often, however, linguistic, stylistic, and ideological characteristics become the criteria for identifying the author's use of sources. In some cases, hypotheses are constructed on the basis of these criteria alone. Such a manner of proceeding might be the only feasible procedure in certain instances. It might even lead to results which are substantially correct. Yet it is fraught with the danger of subjectivism. To the extent that all four criteria are strictly applied, the danger of subjectivism is reduced and the use of a hypothetical source more readily ascertained.

II. THE USE OF SOURCE CRITICISM IN NEW TESTAMENT STUDIES

The Synoptics

The considerations advanced thus far have several times over made reference to the fact that the application of the source-critical method to the New Testament went hand in hand with Life of Jesus research. The Quest wanted to determine which of the Gospels offered the greatest possibility of being a reliable witness to the life of Jesus. The choice centered upon one of the first three Gospels, whose similarity had been noted by Griesbach (1774), who published the Gospels of Matthew, Mark, and Luke in three parallel columns. This arrangement, which highlighted the "synoptic fact," revealed that Matthew, Mark, and Luke are Gospels which look alike. Hence they are the Gospels which should be "seen together" (*sun hopsomai*), whence the name "Synoptics" as applied to the first three of our canonical Gospels.

The Synoptic Fact

The Synoptic fact of which scholars have been patently aware for the past two centuries actually bears upon three different but interrelated phenomena. The first is the selection of material. It is clear that the Gospels of Matthew and Luke are much longer than is Mark—that, in other words, they have much more material than does Mark. But it is also clear that virtually all of the material contained in Mark is contained in Matthew and/or Luke. Of the

661 verses in Mark, some 330 appear in both Matthew and Luke, while 310 appear in either Matthew or Luke. Thus less than 5 percent of the material contained in Mark is restricted to that Gospel. This material, the so-called Markan *Sondergut* (i.e., material proper to Mark), consists of two short miracle stories (7:32–37; 8:22–26), three short narratives (3:20–21; 4:26–29; 14:51–52) and a few isolated logia. Matthew contains some 1,068 verses, of which 622 appear in Mark and 235 appear in Luke. Thus the Matthean *Sondergut*, Matthew's special material, is limited to approximately 210 verses or some 20 percent of the Gospel. A good part of this material is to be found in forty-eight verses that comprise Matthew's version of the Infancy Narrative (Matt 1 – 2). Luke has 1,149 verses, of which 350 or so are to be found in Mark and 235 can be found in Matthew. Thus the Lucan *Sondergut* consists of 550 verses, or approximately 43 percent of the entire Gospel. Within the *Sondergut*, almost 40 percent (132 verses) is to be found in Luke 1 – 2.

(At this juncture it should be noted that the figures cited in this paragraph are approximate. Differences in text-critical judgments lead to slight differences among authors as to the number of verses in each of the Gospels. Then, in some instances, scholars differ among themselves as to whether the similarity between two verses is sufficient as to constitute a true parallel. Moreover a single verse in one Gospel may be represented by two parallel verses in another. Finally some scholars count as verses appearing in all three Gospels only those [approximately 330] that are found in the same sequence. I have counted all those for which there is similarity of content.)

A second constituent of the Synoptic fact is the similarity which exists with respect to particularities of vocabulary and style among the pericopes that are found in one or more of the Synoptic Gospels. In the pericope on the Question of Authority (Matt 21:23–27; Mark 11:27–33; Luke 20:1–8) there is substantial agreement of presentation, even as to the wording of the text. Indeed, the agreement among the Synoptics sometimes extends to relatively minor details. Thus the aside uttered by Jesus in the narrative of the healing of the paralytic, "but that you may know that the Son of man has authority on earth to forgive sins," is found in all three Synoptics (Matt 9:6; Mark 2:10; Luke 5:24). In their respective accounts of the question about fasting, each of these three evangelists employ an unusual expression, typically rendered in English as "wedding guests," but literally rendered "sons of the bridal chamber" (*hoi huoi tēs numphōnos*) (Matt 9:15; Mark 2:19; Luke 5:34).

A similar phenomenon can be noted when material appears in two of the Three Synoptics. Thus there is remarkable agreement between Matthew's version of the Call of the Disciples (Matt 4:18–22) and Mark's account of the same event (Mark 1:16–20), just as there is between Mark's account of the teaching and healing in the Synagogue of Capernaum (Mark 1:21–28) and Luke's version of the same incident (Luke 4:31–37). One can especially note the remarkable similarity, even of minute detail, in the presentation of the discourse material that is common to Matthew and Luke, for example, in the recounting of Jesus' Lament over Jerusalem (Matt 23:37–39; Luke 13:34–35). Finally one cannot overlook the fact that occasionally two of the Gospels agree among themselves, whereas the third is somewhat divergent. Thus in their consideration of the issue of Precedence among the Disciples, Matthew (20:24–28) and Mark (10:41–45) agree with each other, in comparison to Luke (22:24–27), who offers a somewhat different reflection on the matter.

The third component of the Synoptic fact—so significant that the visual presentation of it gave rise to "Synoptic" terminology—is the similarity in the arrangement of the Gospel pericopes. A quick look at any of the Synopses or Gospel Parallels shows that Matthew, Mark, and Luke coincide in their portrayal of the course of Jesus' ministry. After the description of John the Baptist's activity, there occurs a narrative account of Jesus' baptism and temptation. Subsequently each of the Synoptists describes Jesus' activity, both in word and in work, in Galilee. There follows the journey to Jerusalem, the account of the Jerusalem ministry, and the narrative of Jesus' arrest, trial, and death, followed by the discovery of the empty tomb.

Within this general development are to be found groups of material of similar content. The three Galilean controversies, the Healing of the Paralytic, the Call of Levi, and the Question about Fasting, appear grouped together in all three Gospels (Matt 9:1–17; Mark 2:1–22; Luke 5:17–39), as do the four "Jerusalem controversies," Tribute to Caesar, the Question about the Resurrection, the Great Commandment, and the Question about David's Son (Matt 22:15–46; Mark 12:13–37a; Luke 20:20–44). A similar sequence is often to be found within material found in only two of the Gospels. Thus Matthew's version of "By their fruits you will know them" (Matt 7:15–20) is immediately followed by his account of Jesus' saying about the House built upon the Rock (Matt 7:21–27). A similar order in the arrangement and presentation of Jesus' words is to be found in Luke 6:43–49.

In the face of such pervasive agreement among the first three Gospels, one must necessarily conclude that the Synoptics are literarily dependent upon one another. Any attempt to explain their similarities on the basis of a mutual dependence on historical reminiscence or a common oral tradition must cede in the face of verbal agreement which extends to minute detail. Hypothetically it could be suggested that all three Synoptics depend upon a common literary source. In that case, the common literary source must have been remarkably similar to our canonical Mark since such a large proportion of the Markan material appears in Matthew and/or Luke. Such indeed was the theory of Holtzmann, who suggested in 1863 the existence of an *Urmarkus*—a primitive version of the Gospel of Mark.

The Synoptic Problem

The evidence which arises from a comparative study of the three Synoptics thus points convincingly to a relationship of literary dependence among

Matthew, Mark, and Luke. The question which then arises is: To which of the Synoptics is to be attributed a literary priority? In *a priori* fashion one could envision eighteen relational possibilities:

A dependence of a second Gospel on a first, and of a third on the second—six possibilities:

A dependence of two Gospels on a first—three possibilities:

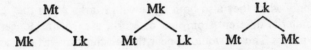

A dependence of one Gospel on both of the others—three possibilities:

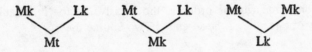

A dependence of a second Gospel on the first, with the third depending on both the second and the first—six possibilities:

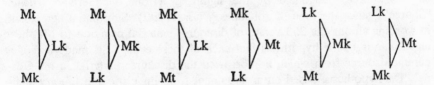

In the early fifth century, Augustine opted for the priority of Matthew, the dependence of Mark on Matthew (Mark is a summary of Matthew), and the dependence of Luke on Matthew and Mark (Luke represents an expansion of Matthew with some knowledge of Mark). The theory developed by Griesbach at the end of the eighteenth century is akin to that of Augustine, except that Griesbach held that Mark was written later than Luke and was dependent on both Matthew and Luke. Griesbach's solution to the Synoptic problem has been substantially supported in our times by William R. Farmer (1964) and Hans-Herbert Stoldt (1977). Farmer sees in the Griesbach hypothesis an explanation of the agreement among Matthew, Mark, and Luke, as well as an explanation of the extensive agreement between Matthew and Luke. For him and his disciples, there is substantial agreement between the

129

two longer Synoptics because of Luke's use of Matthew. In this view the similarity of order between Matthew and Mark would be due to Mark's following of the Matthean outline except where it diverged from Matthew in order to follow Luke.

The Griesbach-Farmer hypothesis is not without its difficulties, difficulties which most students of the Synoptic Problem consider sufficiently serious to warrant the abandonment of this two-hundred-year-old solution. Chief among the difficulties are Mark's omission of so much material from his documentary sources and the curious solution to the phenomenon of a similar ordering of the material on the part of Matthew and Mark. Indeed, if Griesbach and Farmer thought it highly unlikely that Mark was a simple résumé of Matthew, it is even more unlikely that Mark would be a summary of the composite Matthew-Luke. A far more serious difficulty is the similar ordering of the common material. A comparison of the sequence of material in Matthew, Mark, and Luke reveals an agreement in order between Matthew and Luke only when they also both agree with Mark. When they have an ordering of material different from that of Mark, each of the longer Synoptics goes its own way. Thus it would appear that Lachmann was correct in noting that, with respect to the sequence of material, Mark represents the common ground for Matthew and Luke. Hence most scholars are inclined to the view that Mark is one of the sources used by Matthew and Luke. For them the argument from similarity of order is the decisive factor in establishing the plausibility of one pole of the so-called Two-Source theory.

The Sayings Source

The second of the two sources to which the theory refers is the so-called Sayings Source, designated by the siglum Q (from the German Quelle, "Source") since the time of Johannes Weiss (1890). Substantial agreement in wording among the 253 verses of discourse material common to Matthew and Luke urges the hypothesis that each of these evangelists made use of a common source from which he borrowed the discourse material in his Gospel. The hypothesis, based on an argument from linguistic and literary similarity, is confirmed by the presence of doublets and double traditions in the discourse material found in Matthew and Luke. It has already been noted that the Jesuanic logion on divorce is found, in substantially the same form, in both Matthew 5:32 and Matthew 19:9. Matthew 5:32 is parallel to the saying of Jesus in Luke 16:18, whereas Matthew 19:9 is parallel to Mark 10:11 as an examination of the respective contexts (Matt 19:3–12; Mark 10:2–12) will clearly show. In Luke's Gospel, the mission of the disciples is twice reported, viz., in Chapters Nine and Ten. Upon examination, it would appear that Luke 9:1–6 substantially parallels the Markan narrative of the Commissioning of the Twelve (Mark 6:6b–13), whereas Luke 10:1–12, the Commissioning of the Seventy, is basically parallel with Matthew 10:7–16. For some authors it is the existence of doublets such as these which forms the principal argument for the existence of a Sayings Source.

The existence of a Sayings Source employed by Matthew and Luke had been suggested by Herbert Marsh (1757–1839), who added a hypothesis of his own on the subject of the mutual relationships among the Gospels to his translation of Michaelis' four-volume *Introduction to the New Testament*. Marsh considered that both Matthew and Luke were dependent upon a Sayings Source, designated by the siglum ב, and that all three Synoptics were dependent upon a primitive Gospel, denoted by א, the first letter of the Hebrew alphabet. A few decades later, in 1832, Friedrich Schleiermacher (1768–1834), who regarded the Griesbach hypothesis as the best solution to the Synoptic Problem, proposed that Papias, in his famous statement on the logia of Jesus, was actually making reference to a collection of sayings drawn up by Matthew. In 1863 Holtzmann not only criticized the proposition advanced by Griesbach and Schleiermacher, but also urged the existence of a Sayings Source which would have been utilized respectively by Matthew and Luke.

In fact, it is clear that both Matthew and Luke have inserted the discourse material taken from Q into their common Markan framework in a distinctive fashion. Matthew has collated much of this material into five major sermons or discourses: The Sermon on the Mount (Matt 5 – 7), the Mission Discourse (Matt 10), the Sermon in Parables (Matt 13), the Ecclesiastical Discourse (Matt 18), and the Eschatological Discourse (Matt 24 – 25). Each of these discourses concludes with the distinctive clause: "And when Jesus had finished . . ." For the rest, sayings of Jesus, appropriated by Matthew from the Q source, are scattered here and there throughout his Gospel. In contrast, Luke inserts the discourse material taken from Q into two significant sections of his Gospel, 6:20 – 8:3 and 9:51 – 18:14, the so-called minor and major (small and great) Lucan insertions. In view of their respective usages of discourse material, it might appear that no argument from similarity of order can be developed in favor of the existence of the Q source. Further examination proves quite the opposite to be true. If the discourse material in Matthew, presumed to have been taken over from Q, is arranged in six columns, one for each of the Matthean sermons and the sixth for the remaining material, it will be found that there is a basic similarity of order between each of these columns and the relative order of the parallel sayings in the Gospel of Luke. Thus the order of the Q material in Matthew and Luke proves to be a convincing argument for the existence of Q as a documentary source for both Matthew and Luke.

On the basis of his comparison of Matthew and Luke in 1832, Christian Hermann Weisse offered a reconstruction of Q. Later authors who have offered a reconstruction of Q have generally agreed with the views of Weisse, even though none of the sixteen reconstructions cited by James Moffatt in a 1918 study are exactly alike. In 1929 and again in 1932, however, Wilhelm Bussmann gave a new dimension to the matter by distinguishing two Sayings Sources, respectively designated T and R. T purportedly contained that material with respect to which Matthew and Luke show the greatest verbal similarity (including the narrative of the Centurion of Capernaum; Matt 8:5–13;

Luke 7:1–10), whereas R contained only discourse material, namely that with respect to which Matthew and Luke evidence a little divergence. Nowadays, since the Lucan wording seems demonstrably more primitive than that of Matthew, it is customary to reconstitute Q as a single document on the basis of Luke. Thus reconstructed—for example, by T. W. Manson in *The Sayings of Jesus*—Q seems to fall into four sections, as follows: (1) Jesus and John—Luke 3:7–9, 16–17, 21–22; 4:1–13; 5:20–49; 7:1–10, 18–19, 22–35; (2) Jesus and His Disciples—Luke 9:57–62; 10:2–16, 21–24; 11:9–13; (3) Jesus and His Opponents—Luke 11:14–52; 12:2–12, 22–34; (4) Jesus and the Future—Luke 12:35–59; 13:18–30, 34–35; 14:11, 15–27, 34–35; 16:13–18; 17:1–6, 22–37.

It is presumed that the history of Q is relatively complicated, but since the document shows a manifest interest in the lot of Gentiles and since several of its expressions are best understood as translations from the Aramaic, it is generally accepted that the Sayings Source was originally composed in Aramaic at Antioch around A.D. 50. The literary form of this document, already translated into Greek at the time of its use by the individual evangelists, is the same as that of the Mishnaic treatise *Pirke Aboth* (Sayings of the Fathers) or the *Gospel of Thomas*. Q did not contain a Passion narrative nor any significant narrative accounts, apart from the episode of the Centurion of Capernaum. Hence Q must be classified as *didache* or teaching. This teaching contains a variety of eschatological, prophetic, and wisdom motifs which represent distinct Christological and ecclesiological positions of a community of believers.

With the reconstruction of Q and the identification of Mark as a source of both Matthew and Luke, the majority of scholars have found a viable working hypothesis to explain the literary relationship among the Synoptics in a reasonable fashion. To be sure, the "minor agreements" between Matthew and Luke, where the two later evangelists agree with each other in their divergence from Mark, remain somewhat problematic, but the proposal of a hypothetical *Urmarkus* (primitive Mark) as a solution to this difficulty creates more problems than the minor ones it solves. While Farmer and others can continue to point out the difficulties inherent in the Two-Source theory, their alternative solutions are not without difficulty. Indeed, the very questions that the adversaries of the Two-Source theory can raise with respect to Markan priority must also be raised with respect to a hypothetical Matthean priority. Thus the Two-Source theory, whose main lines were sketched by Holtzmann a century ago, retains its value as the working theory for most contemporary students of the Synoptics.

The acceptance of the Two-Source theory has been a major element in the discernment of the relative chronology of the Synoptics. If Matthew and Luke depend on Mark, they are obviously to be dated after the composition of the Markan Gospel. It is commonly considered that Mark's Gospel was composed in a Roman setting around A.D. 70 by an author who intended to modify the Palestinian tradition about Jesus for a Gentile Christian community. Both Matthew and Luke were apparently written more than a decade later (between A.D. 80 and 90). The author of the first Gospel produced his work in Syria for a Greek-speaking community, many of whose members had a Jewish background. At about the same time, and perhaps in the same general area, Luke wrote his Gospel for the benefit of non-Palestinian Gentile Christians. The Gospel of John, which has but tenuous links with Mark, was written at a later date, probably during the last decade of the first century. Ephesian in origin, this distinct Gospel was intended to confirm the faith of the community of the Beloved Disciple, newly troubled by a variety of crises.

Additional Sources

In addition to the material taken over from Mark and *Q,* there remains a portion of Matthew, almost equal in quantity to the *Q* material and approximately 30 percent of Luke. This material is not found in either of the other Synoptic Gospels. B. H. Streeter's "Fundamental Solution," proposed in his classic work *The Four Gospels* (1924), suggests that there existed an earlier version of Luke, the so-called proto-Luke. The proto-Luke would have been composed at Caesarea on the basis of a compilation of material coming from *Q* and the Lucan *Sondergut* (L). Subsequently, Markan material would have been inserted into the Lucan framework. While Streeter's analysis had the logical advantage of associating a foundational document with each of the four major centers of primitive Christianity—M with Jerusalem (A.D. 60), Mark with Rome (A.D. 66), L with Caesarea (A.D. 60) and *Q* with Antioch (A.D. 50), his arguments lacked cogency except for the extent to which they pointed to a Lucan (L) *Sondergut.*

Similarly lacking an ability to convince was Pierson Parker's 1953 argumentation in favor of a proto-Matthew (his K). That Matthew enjoyed the advantages of traditions and material proper to himself (M) cannot, however, be denied by anyone who recognizes the distinct character of his Gospel. The existence of M was already affirmed by Streeter in 1924. Thus his "fundamental solution" is sometimes called the four-document (MK, *Q,* M, L) hypothesis. In fact, this hypothesis is but a useful refinement of the classic Two-Source theory.

In short, the most significant area for source analysis in the study of the Synoptic Gospels is the overarching network of issues relating to the Synoptic Problem. The associated issues with respect to a proto-Matthew, an *Urmarkus,* and a proto-Luke also require the use of the source-critical methodology. Yet with the practical rejection of these earlier-edition theories and the popular acceptance of the Two-Source theory, source analysis of Matthew, Mark, and Luke has not been completely exhausted.

With respect to Mark, presumed to be the oldest literary composition among the three extant canonical Gospels, there remains a variety of other questions. The two narratives of the Multiplication of Loaves (Mark 6:35–44; 8:1–10) are generally considered to be a doublet, taken from two different but parallel sources. The aporias present in the Markan version of the

Boy Possessed by the Spirit (Mark 9:14–29) and the Healing of the Blind Man (Mark 10:46–52) have led scholars to raise a question as to the possible use of an aretalogy, or collection of miracle stories, in the composition of Mark. Other scholars are convinced that the passion narrative in Mark represents an independent, coherent, and very early block of the gospel tradition, so that we ought to speak of a pre-Markan Passion narrative. Although this point of view has been argued by scholars with such divergent points of view as M. Dibelius, J. Jeremias, R. E. Brown and Rudolf Pesch, Vincent Taylor believed that he could find not one but two sources behind the Markan Passion narrative, the one a straightforward account written for the Roman community (Source A), the other based on the reminiscences of Peter (Source B). In the 1970s, however, scholars such as Eta Linnemann, Lugge Schenke, John Donahue, and Frans Neirynck have argued against the existence of an independent and coherent Passion narrative prior to Mark and for the literary and ideological homogeneity of the present text of Mark.

A case apart would have to be made for the canonical conclusion to Mark (Mark 16:9–20). The passage is full of aporias—for example, the "initial presentation" of Mary Magdalene in 16:9 even though she has already been cited by name in 15:40, 47, and 16:1. Questions raised by source analysis with respect to these verses are further highlighted by text-critical considerations. Thus Mss. B and ℵ do not contain the verses in question. Given the preponderance of the evidence, and despite the demurrer of a limited number of scholars, such as William R. Farmer, most scholars conclude that Mark 16:9–20 is a unified composition, appended to Mark by a later writer who consciously sought to imitate certain features of Mark's vocabulary and syntax, as well as develop his conceptual use of certain terms.

Different types of questions arise in regard to a consideration of the sources employed by Matthew and Luke respectively. Analysis of the material proper to each of these gospels leads to the assured conclusion that each of the evangelists was able to take advantage of source material which was apparently unknown to the other evangelists. In particular, source-critical analysis must be brought to bear upon the Infancy Narratives in Matthew and Luke. Questions must be raised as to whether either the Matthean or Lucan form of the Genealogy of Jesus (Matt 1:2–17; Luke 3:23–38) is dependent upon a documentary source that has been expanded and modified by the evangelist. In *The Birth of the Messiah,* Raymond E. Brown has argued that Matthew has written his Infancy Narrative on the basis of a pre-Matthean narrative which associated the birth of Jesus, son of Joseph, with the patriarch Joseph and birth of Moses. The pre-Matthean source, characterized by a typical pattern of angelic dream appearances, is reflected in the three narrative sequences of the Infancy tale: (1) Matthew 1:18b, 20–21, 24–25; 2:1a, 3–5a, 8a; (2) Matthew 2:13–15a, 16–17; (3) Matthew 2:19–21. Thus M, the Matthean *Sondergut,* should not be presumed to have existed prior to the composition of canonical Matthew as a single homogeneous document. M rather designates the totality of documentary sources and oral traditions available to the evangelist. Indeed even the hypothetical "Nazarene targum" (N) which B. W. Bacon postulated as Matthew's special source was considered by him to be a collection of "fungoid documents."

No less caution needs to be employed in reference to the material indiscriminately characterized as coming from L, the Lucan *Sondergut*. The material proper to Luke is demonstrably lacking in homogeneity. The assumption that the L material derives from Luke's own creativity is clearly unwarranted. Not only does the assumption fly in the face of the motley character of L, but it also is in contradiction with Luke's general fidelity to his sources as is seen in his use of Markan and *Q* material. To resolve the resultant dilemma, Heinz Schürmann and other scholars postulated that a large part of the L material actually derives from a portion of *Q* that has not been taken over by Matthew. Other scholars point to the notion that Luke might well have been dependent on one or two particular cycles of tradition. Finally, respect for the extensive research done on *Q* by the late Vincent Taylor (1887–1968) requires that we take note of his contention that Luke 22:14–24: 53 basically represents a pre-Markan documentary Passion narrative. In sum, Taylor's avowal of a pre-Lucan Passion narrative is part of a broad plea that one take seriously the possibility of a proto-Luke.

Acts

That Luke wrote not one, but two books in the canonical New Testament is a fact which those who would exercise source analysis must consider seriously in their studies of the Acts of the Apostles. The prologue to Luke (Luke 1:1–4) clearly implies a consultation of, if not necessarily the use of, such documentary sources as were available in the author's time and place. The first verse of Acts specifically recalls to Theophilus the existence of the Gospel as a "first book." That a single author composed Luke-Acts, that he explicitly linked the two books together, and that he noted his consultation of sources for the composition of the Gospel creates a strong *prima facie* impression that Luke most likely also used sources in the composition of the Acts of the Apostles.

This *a priori* assumption is confirmed by an analysis of the text itself. In the words of Jacques Dupont, who has made a now dated but still classic examination of the history of the source criticism of the Acts of the Apostles, "We find traces of rewriting, cases of juxtaposition, even of insertion of different materials one in the other. There are so many indications which set us on the track of pre-existing sources." Among the most significant clues to the fact that Luke did use sources in his composition of Acts, two phenomena emerge which deserve the most careful consideration: the presence in Acts of the so-called "we sections" and the abundance of aporias in the text.

In the second half of Acts there are four journey narratives written in the first person plural rather than in the third person like the rest of Acts. These so-called "we-sections" portray Paul's journey from Troas to Philippi (Acts 16:10–17), the journey from Philippi to Miletus (20:5–15), the journey from Miletus to Jerusalem (21:1–18), and the journey from Caesarea to Rome (27:1–28:16). Each of these narratives tells the tale of a journey at sea. They begin abruptly on land, and end just as abruptly with a return to land. Before the development of the historical-critical approach to the New Testament it was generally assumed that the we-sections were taken from the travelogue of Luke, commonly understood to have been Paul's travel companion. More recently it has been assumed that these four sections were taken over from a source used by Luke in the composition of his text. There remains, however, a broad area for discussion in this regard. It is clear that the passages under consideration are abruptly introduced into the text. It is just as clear that they differ in grammatical number (first person plural) from the surrounding narratives. However, the we-sections cannot be distinguished stylistically from the surrounding third-person narratives. Thus it is frequently argued that the use of the first person plural in the we-sections does not result from Luke's use of source, but that it represents an editorial device whereby the author of Acts wants to convey the impression that he has personally taken part in the events he is narrating—a trait typically found in accounts of journeys by sea.

Which Sources?

Notwithstanding the current trend to attribute the limited use of the first-person plural to the author's creativity, there remains the massive presence of aporias in Acts. To some extent the study of these aporias cannot be separated from the extensive text-critical issues that confront the student of Acts. Yet, once the text-critical problems have been resolved to the satisfaction of the scholar, there remains a vast number of aporias in the text of Acts. Two examples will suffice.

Among the many discourses in Acts, Stephen's speech (Acts 7:2–53) stands as a case apart. It does not seem to have been composed by Luke, as were the other speeches of Acts. Indeed, if Luke composed this speech, he ought to have fitted it more adequately to the accusation brought against Stephen (6:11–14). As a matter of fact, Stephen's speech seems to have been inserted in the account of the Martyrdom of Stephen (Acts 6:8–15; 7:55–8:2), which is broken off abruptly at 6:15. At that point the author presents a description of the transfiguration of Stephen to which he returns at 7:55.

That this speech derives from a source employed by Luke is confirmed by the application of two of the other criteria of source analysis. In terms of style and vocabulary, it has been noted that to a great degree the overview of salvation history conveyed by the speech agrees neither with the Masoretic (MT) nor the Septuagintal (LXX) text of the Old Testament. To the extent that one considers Luke to have been a Gentile Christian who was dependent on the LXX for his use of the Old Testament, the discrepancy between Stephen's speech and the rest of Acts can be considered a prime example of stylistic and vocabulary differences. In fact, one might consider dependence upon a different biblical tradition a matter of differing ideology. There is, in any case, considerable difference of ideology (i.e., theology) between the Stephen speech and the rest of Acts. One might first notice the absence of specifically Christian reference in the speech, apart from Acts 7, verses 42–43, 46, 49–51 and the Christian conclusion in verse 52. Furthermore, the Christology of the speech is not typically Lucan. Not only must we note the absence of some of Luke's favorite Christological titles (especially *kurios,* "Lord," and *christos,* "Messiah"), but the typological and Mosaic Christology present in the speech is quite distinctive. It can also be observed that the speech's radical rejection of Temple worship, although paired with the rejection of Law observance (Acts 15), is not consistent with Luke's overall views on worship and the Temple (e.g., Acts 3:1).

When attention is directed to Acts 15, the discerning critic once again encounters a number of aporias. Since our present purpose does not require a full examination of the pericope, but only the citation of some elements for consideration by way of example, the indication of aporias will be limited to those which bear upon the pericope on James's intervention in the so-called Council of Jerusalem (Acts 15:12–21). In some ways, the pericope is a doublet of the pericope on Peter's intervention (vv. 6–11). Thus the source analyst has to take the phenomenon of redundancy into account. Moreover the mention of the assembly listening to Barnabas and Paul (v. 12) seems to duplicate verse 4. Indeed there is a certain tension between the mention of Barnabas and Paul (in that order) in verse 12, and the mention, first of Paul, then of Barnabas in verses 2 and 22. A tension also exists between the Symeon of verse 14 and the Peter of verse 7. Although to the modern reader Symeon is presumably Peter, there is clearly a change in names—a phenomenon all the more significant in that Peter is nowhere in the entire New Testament called Symeon (a Greek name distinct from Simon; see 2 Pet 1:1). Furthermore James's intervention has to do with the matter of table fellowship, whereas the context indicates that the topic under discussion is the issue of circumcision (vv. 1, 5).

The discussion of Luke's possible use of sources in Acts 15 is further complicated by the fact that the burden of the point made by the citation of Amos 9:11–12 in Acts 15:16–18 is based on the Greek text of the Old Testament and not on the Hebrew text of the Bible, the one presumably used by James, a Palestinian Christian Jew. Use of the LXX would be consistent with Luke but not with James. Indeed, it is the manifest editorial work undertaken by Luke in the composition of the Acts which complicates the discussion of this second part of his two-volume work. Although Luke has clearly made use of sources in the composition of Acts, he has not simply transcribed the appropriated material. He has, rather, reworked his borrowed material so thoroughly that the imprint of his vocabulary, style, and ideology is apparent throughout the entire book of Acts.

Notwithstanding this rather thoroughgoing editorial activity by Luke, scholars have attempted to discern the sources that he might have used. A classic example of souce analysis of Acts was offered by A. von Harnack in

The Acts of the Apostles (Beiträge zur Einleitung in das NT. III: Die Apostelgeschichte, 1908). Harnack concluded that the Stephen story must have had a documentary source, to which he ascribed Acts 6:1 – 8:4; 11:19–30; and 12:25 (13:1) – 15:35. From this so-called "Antioch Source" must be distinguished a "Jerusalem-Caesarea Source," from which comes the material contained in Acts 3:1 – 5:16; 8:5–40; 9:31 – 11:18; 12:1–23. Harnack also considered that insofar as the beginning of Acts is concerned, the respectable Jerusalem-Caesarea Source had a worthless, legendary doublet (Jerusalem-Caesarea Source B) from which is derived the material in Acts 2:1–47 and 5:17–42.

During the decades that have passed since Harnack's work, much discussion has taken place with respect to the possible use of an Antioch source by Luke. Although the consideration of the possible use of this source by Luke receives a higher degree of verification among scholars than does the possible use of a Jerusalem-Caesarea Source, scholars agree among themselves neither as to its existence nor, if it did exist, as to the extent of its use by Luke. Dibelius, Bultmann, Jeremias, and Pierre Benoit have all entered into the debate without any resultant consensus. Indeed, there are those source analysts, such as Abram Spiro and C. H. H. Scobie, who are more comfortable with the idea that Luke made use of a more restricted "Samaritan Source" for his composition of Acts 7. The postulation of a Samaritan Source calls for a discussion of the extent of its use. Is its use, for example, also reflected in the composition of Acts 3? In any event, to the extent that the existence of an Antioch Source is accepted, it is considered to have been a largely apologetic document which would have focused upon issues concerning the relationship between Jewish and Hellenistic segments of early Christianity.

From the source analysts who have devoted their attention to Acts comes a more attractive hypothesis which holds that Luke made use of a source for the second half of his account in Acts. The discussion remains open, but there is substantial opinion to the effect that a documentary source lies behind Acts 9:1–30; 13:3 – 14:28; and 15:35 – 28:31. Styled a "Pauline" or "journey" source, to which the we-sections may or may not have belonged, this source would have contained material relating to Paul's visit to places where the Gospel was unknown and would have betrayed some interest in the legal status of the Christian mission in the Roman Empire. In the view of some of the proponents of the theory of a journey source, the presentation of the material would have followed a stereotyped schema, to wit, the arrival of Paul and his companions, their preaching in the synagogue, their rejection by the Jews, a turning to the Gentiles and expulsion by the Jews, with the resultant nucleus of Gentile Christians.

In sum, Luke has most probably made use of abundant source material in the composition of Acts. However, the hand of the historian-editor has been so skillfully exercised upon his material that he has covered his own tracks very well. This leaves the contemporary critic with a twofold conviction—namely, that Luke has indeed made use of sources, but that it is virtually impossible to decide with exactitude just what these sources are and where they lie.

The Letters

If Luke, the historian, evangelist, and chronicler, did make use of sources in his two-volume work, it would not seem immediately apparent that Paul, the letter writer, made use of sources as well. Paul's letters were written by him as occasion demanded. Even the longest of his letters, Romans and 1 Corinthians, are substantially shorter than either Luke or Acts. The letters clearly reflect the style, language, and thought of Paul. Thus we must approach the topic of the source analysis of the letters with the idea that a different type of consideration might arise. In fact, there are three or four different types of issues raised by a source-critical analysis of the letters in the New Testament.

Borrowed Material

A first question is whether Paul, or any of the other epistolary authors of New Testament works, have incorporated into their work material that has come from another source. Once again, this is not a matter of an author merely making use of an element of the liturgical tradition or making use of themes commonly employed in the missionary discourse of Hellenistic Judaism. Rather it is a matter of considering whether the author employed preexistent and coherent units of material which he incorporated into his letters.

To a large extent this issue centers upon the use of Christological hymns in the New Testament. Apart from the hymn generally considered to be the basic document (*Vorlage*) of the Prologue to John's Gospel, these hymns are found in Philippians 2:6–11; Colossians 1:15–20; Ephesians 2:14–16; 1 Timothy 3:16; 1 Peter 3:18–22; and Hebrews 1:3. Few passages in the New Testament have been the object of such intensive study as has the little hymn contained in Philippians 2:6–11. Not only has it been studied in depth by Jeremias, Cerfaux, Käsemann, et al., but significant monographs have also been devoted to it by Ernst Lohmeyer (1923) and Ralph P. Martin (1967). In the judgment of many scholars Philippians 2:6–11 is a pre-Pauline hymn, perhaps composed within the circles of Paul's own disciples, whose extraneous character is betrayed by the mention of the Cross in verse 8. The telltale phrase interrupts the rhythm of the hymn and bears the mark of Paul's concern to introduce a mention of the Crucifixion into a hymn in which the manner of Jesus' death seems not to have been a significant concern.

The arguments advanced in favor of the idea that the Christological hymn of Philippians 2 does not come from Paul's own hand fall principally into the categories of considerations of style and vocabulary on the one hand, and of ideology on the other. The hymnic style, characterized by rhythm and parallelism, set the seven verses apart from the rest of Philippians. The key words have no real parallel in Pauline usage. Expressions such as "form (*morphē*) of God" and "form of man" include the use of a term which is *hapax legomenon* in Paul. The designation of Jesus as servant (*doulos*) is not a typical Pauline characterization. Indeed, the Christology of the hymn contains several ideas seemingly foreign to Paul: the notion that Jesus has "equality with God," that he has received a gift from God, and that he has been exalted (Paul stressed the Resurrection of Jesus as Lord, rather than his Exaltation). Conversely several key elements of Paul's Christology and soteriology are absent from the hymn—for example, the doctrine of redemption through the Cross, the Resurrection, and the role of the Church. Finally, the fact that the relative clause with which the hymn begins contains a participle apparently modifying a relative pronoun (v. 6a) constitutes a serious aporia which sheds considerable doubt on the idea that Paul composed these verses for this letter. Some authors hold that Paul may have composed them himself, but for some other purpose. Most authors, however, find themselves convinced by arguments in favor of the non-Pauline provenance of the hymn.

Interpolations and Conflations

A second area for consideration with respect to source analysis of the canonical epistles is that of possible interpolations. The unity of several of the New Testament epistles has been called into question by various authors who have held that one or another passage represents a later addition to an earlier text. The passages frequently cited as having been interpolated certainly include 2 Corinthians 6:14 – 7:1 and 1 Thessalonians 2:13–16.

There are several arguments that have been evaluated by many different scholars as pointing to a non-Pauline origin of 2 Corinthians 6:14 – 7:1, a passage which clearly causes a marked interruption in the sequence of thought. Among the arguments is the fact that the passage contains nine Pauline *hapax legomena:* "mismated" (*heteroxugountes*), "partnership" (*metochē*), "accord" (*sumphōnēsis*), "Belial" (*Beliar*), "agreement" (*sugkatathesis*), "move among" (*emperipateō*), "welcome" (*eisdechomai*), "almighty" (*pantokratōr*), and "defilement" (*molusmos*). Ideologically, the use of "Belial" is significant in that Paul normally uses "Satan" (*Satanas*) to denote the hostile power. More significantly, the appeal for a rigorous separation of the Christian from the pagan seems inconsistent with Paul's own attitude toward pagans as expressed in 1 Corinthians 5:9–10 and elsewhere. Moreover, the affinities of vocabulary and ideology between 2 Corinthians 6:14 – 7:1 and those of Qumran have been frequently cited as arguments in favor of its non-Pauline provenance. In spite of the arguments along these lines advanced by Joseph Fitzmyer, Joachim Gnilka, et al., Jan Lambrecht has nonetheless forcefully argued for the Pauline provenance of the pericope on the basis of its Pauline style and the weight of the manuscript tradition.

To this day the discussion on 2 Corinthians 6 remains a moot question, but the evidence seems to fall more clearly on the side of Pauline authorship in regard to 1 Thessalonians 2:13–16. It has, however, been argued that 2:13–16 is repetitive of the earlier thanksgiving period (cf. 1 Thes 1:2) and that the apostolic parousia of 2:17–3:13 follows more naturally after 2:12 than it does after 2:16. Ideologically the disputed passage is somewhat problematic in that it contains an exhortation to follow the example of the churches, attributes the death of Jesus to the Jews, and projects an anti-Judaism which is seemingly inconsistent with Galatians 1 and 2, Romans 9–11, and Philippians 3:5–6. Ultimately the only real difficulty with the passage is the attitude it expresses toward the Jews. Yet this argument can hardly be conclusive, since Paul's attitude toward the Jews was certainly not unequivocal, as a careful examination of the well-thought-out letter to the Romans will clearly show.

A variant on the theme of interpolations into the letters of material coming from a hand other than that of the author is the possibility that material written by the author at another time has been interpolated into his own work by a later editor. Thus a third type of consideration in the source analysis of the New Testament letters is that advanced in respect to the various compilation theories. Source analysis must address itself to the suggestion that some of the New Testament epistles are, in fact, compilations of epistolary material. The most vocal spokesperson for the compilation theories has been Walter Schmithals, who addressed himself to the issue on several occasions during the 1960s. He claimed to have discovered six letters to the Corinthians, three letters to the Philippians, as well as four letters to the Thessalonians and two to the Romans. According to Schmithals' analysis, traces of all fifteen letters are to be found in canonical 1,2 Thessalonians, 1, 2 Corinthians, Philippians, and Romans. Possibilities of doublets and differences of vocabulary have served as weapons in Schmithals' arsenal, as has the fact that each of the canonical letters to the Corinthians mentions a letter which apparently has been lost (1 Cor 5:9; 2 Cor 2:3–4, 9). By means of his radical compilation theory, Schmithals believed that he had found a trace of the apparently lost items of correspondence. A major weakness in Schmithals' theorizing is that there is absolutely no evidence whatever that ancient authors or editors compiled single documents by juxtaposing earlier bits of correspondence.

Deserving more favorable consideration than Schmithals' thoroughgoing compilation theory are the suggestions that Philippians 3:2–21 and Romans 16 were not included by Paul as a part of the major document in which they are now found. There is certainly a poor articulation between Philippians 3:2–21 and the preceding chapters of the letter. Moreover this passage seems to suggest a set of dangerous circumstances, not a hint of which is given in the earlier portion of the letter. Although F. W. Beare has argued for the existence of "a fragment of another letter, undoubtedly a letter of Paul's, but written on a different occasion and for a different purpose," other scholars have concluded that the passage under discussion does belong to Philippians whose composition by Paul had been interrupted for some time.

141

Notwithstanding the recent studies of Harry Gamble, the status of Romans 16 remains quite a different issue. First of all, issues must be raised with respect to the pertinence of the final doxology (Rom 16:25–27) to Romans. Text-critical considerations already cast the authenticity of the passage into considerable doubt. The hymnic style of the verses sets them off from Romans, clearly written as a piece of epistolary prose. Ideologically, the epithets used of God ("wise," "eternal") are un-Pauline and, although the concept of "Mystery" (*mustērion*) is Pauline, the notion is absent from Romans. Hence a fair number of scholars have concluded that Romans 16:25–27 represents a post-Pauline addition to Romans. Then there is the matter of Romans 16:1–23. It articulates poorly with the body of the epistle, which is seemingly brought to a close with a farewell greeting at Romans 15:33. The content of the passage, a series of greetings and commendations, is not necessarily inconsistent with the content of Romans 1–15, but it does seem out of character for Paul to be addressing so many greetings to individuals who belong to a community that he has not yet visited. This quantity of greetings has suggested to many scholars the idea that Romans 16:1–23 was a letter of introduction of Phoebe addressed to the community of Ephesus, within which Paul had long labored and within which he must have had many friends.

Problems of Literary Dependence

A different type of problem is suggested by the manifest affinity between Ephesians and Colossians. In recent years, scholars have struggled with the issue of the authenticity of each of these letters. Authenticity is not our present concern. Our concern rather focuses upon the relationship between Colossians and Ephesians. Ephesians seems to show a special acquaintance with Colossians to the extent that one must inquire whether there is a relationship of literary dependence between the two letters. Thus the fourth type of consideration in the source analysis of the New Testament letters is really a minor Synoptic problem.

The issue of the relationship between Ephesians and Colossians deserves to be called a minor Synoptic Problem because an examination of the two documents shows that there are some elements which connect them and there are some elements which distinguish them. In favor of the notion that there is a literary dependence of Ephesians on Colossians is the fact that approximately one third of the 155 verses in Ephesians are parallel to Colossians, both in content and in sequence. Among the most striking parallels are those between Colossians 1:25–26 and Ephesians 3:2; Colossians 2:19 and Ephesians 4:15–16; Colossians 3:9–10 and Ephesians 4:22, 24; Colossians 3:18–4:1 and Ephesians 5:21–6:9; and Colossians 4:7–8 and Ephesians 6:21–22. A rapid comparison of the Christianized household codes found in Colossians 3:18–4:1 and Ephesians 5:21–6:9 respectively brings the issue into sharp focus. In these sections of the respective epistles, it would seem that Ephesians represents an expatiation of the outline provided by Colossians.

On the other side of the argument, however, are the differences between the letters. We will cite but one example. Although the ecclesiology of each of the letters has a universal perspective, the term church (*ekklēsia*) is used exclusively of the universal Church in Ephesians (e.g. 1:22) whereas it is used of both the universal Church and local congregations in Colossians. In any event, the question of the relationship between Ephesians and Colossians is intricately tied up with the issue of authorship. If neither of the epistles was written by Paul, one must at least admit that the author of Ephesians was acquainted with Colossians even if he did not use Colossians as an outline or first draft. If Colossians was written by Paul, and Ephesians was not, Ephesians most probably represents an accommodation of Paul's teaching, contained in Colossians, for the time and circumstances of the community at Ephesus. If the tradition that both letters were written by the apostle is to be upheld, it is difficult to determine why Paul would have written two letters that are so remarkably similar, especially in view of his exhortation to the community at Colossae that it exchange the letter addressed to it with another community (Col 4:16).

No less problematic than the relationship between Ephesians and Colossians is that between 2 Peter and Jude. The issue of the relationship between these two letters, one of which critical scholars consider to be the most recent of New Testament writings and the other which is certainly one of the shortest (like Philemon, Jude has but twenty-five verses), is another minor Synoptic problem to which the student of the New Testament must attend. Once again, he or she is confronted by similarities of content and sequence: Jude 2 and 2 Peter 1:2; Jude 3 and 2 Peter 1:5; Jude 5a and 2 Peter 1:12; most significantly Jude 5b–19 and 2 Peter 2:1 – 3:3; and Jude 24 and 2 Peter 3:14. Jude seems to have been written in a more elegant style than was 2 Peter, but its contents seem to reflect an environment that is more Judeo-Christian than that from which 2 Peter has come. In view of the similarities between the two documents, Luther proposed that Jude was dependent on 2 Peter. Some modern scholars, such as Bo Reicke, have proposed that both Jude and 2 Peter are dependent on a common source document. Nowadays, however, the more common opinion is that 2 Peter (especially Chapter 2) is dependent on Jude. This consensus is based not only on the generally accepted view that 2 Peter is the most recent of the New Testament writings, but also on the fact that the later authors tend to expand upon their source material rather than to epitomize it.

The Johannine Corpus

In this rapid overview of the application of source-critical methodology to the study of the New Testament, we have been able thus far to cite some of the major approaches to the source analysis of the various books of the New Testament, but have not yet touched upon the five books that constitute the so-called Johannine corpus. These five books, John, 1,2,3, John, Revelation, merit a separate review. Even a cursory reading of the books indicates that there are manifest affinities among them. They reflect a common, though somewhat amorphous, tradition and so may be seen as several different products of a Johannine school. For generations scholars have been raising questions about the origin and interrelationship of these several books. The network of these issues constitutes the Johannine Question, surely one of the most complex topics in New Testament study. Fortunately we can presently limit ourselves to the single issue of the use of sources in the composition of these works. We will continue to cite "John" as the author of these works, more because tradition designates this name as a convenient siglum for whoever the author of the individual works might have been, than because of any scholarly conviction that it was one and the same individual who wrote any two of the books.

The Gospel

Immediately upon opening John's Gospel, the reader is confronted by the issue of the author's use of sources. Its first few verses (vv. 1–5) are written in a poetic style, whose use of staircase parallelism is even more apparent in the Greek text than it is in most of the English translations of the Prologue. Very soon afterward, however, the reader comes upon a passage written in prose form (vv. 6–8) which begins abruptly with a classic opening line, "There was a man sent from God . . ." The formula is so stereotyped—almost akin to the words "Once upon a time . . ." with which so much narrative in the English language begins—that one has the impression that the Gospel really ought to have begun at 1:6. In Johannine study, the Prologue (John 1:1–18) has consistently merited special attention. It is clearly a topic unto itself. This is no less the case with respect to the source analysis of the Prologue than it is with respect to other exegetical reflections that can be brought to bear upon the interpretation of these eighteen verses. To a person, exegetes acknowledge the alternance of poetic and prose sections in the Prologue. Almost as readily do they unanimously assign verses 1–5, 10–11, 14, clearly written in a poetic style, to an original "hymn," of which the evangelist or later editor of the Gospel made use in composing the Prologue. Just as readily do the commentators assign the verses that concern the Baptist—verses 6–8, 15—to the hand of the evangelist and/or editor. The issue of the provenance of the remaining verses of the Prologue remains a moot question, there being almost as many solutions to the problem as there are authors who treat it. In any event, a reading of the Prologue introduces the student of the Fourth Gospel feet-first into the problem of John's use of sources.

A major proponent of the thesis that the evangelist did, in fact, employ sources in the composition of his work was the late Rudolf Bultmann, whose source analysis of the Fourth Gospel pervades his commentary on the text even though it has not been systematically presented in any of the editions of his epoch-making work (a cursory summary of Bultmann's theory written by Walter Schmithals has, however, been included as an introduction to the English translation of Bultmann's commentary). Bultmann exposited his commentary on the basis of a source analysis of John which postulated the existence of three major sources employed by the evangelist: the Signs Source, the Revelatory Discourse Source, and a Passion Source.

In Bultmann's analysis, the Signs Source, or *Semeia-Quelle,* would have furnished John with material for the main narrative sections of the first part of the Gospel. The source was supposed to have contained a series of miracle stories, from which John chose seven for his Gospel, and a group of other passages which are presently related to the miracle stories by reason of their similar vocabulary and style. The seven signs chosen by the evangelist were the Marriage at Cana (2:1–11), the Centurion at Capernaum (4:46b–54), the Healing at the Pool (5:1–15), the Feeding of the Five Thousand (6:1–15), the Walking on the Water (6:16–21), the Man Born Blind (9:1–41), and the Raising of Lazarus (11:1–44). The related passages would have included the Call of the First Disciples (1:35–51), the Discourse with the Woman of Samaria (4:4–42), Galilee and the Secret Journey to Jerusalem (7:1–13), and a double conclusion (12:37–38; 20:30–31). In isolating these several passages as deriving from a Signs Source, Bultmann apparently distinguished four criteria: (1) the Semitic character of the Greek text; (2) the enumeration of the signs (2:11; 4:54); (3) the "divine man" (*theios anēr*) Christology; and (4) the literary aporias.

The history of the post-Bultmannian discussion of the Signs Source has been competently chronicled by Gilbert Van Belle. From the discussion two significant issues seemed to have emerged, each of which requires still further study and discussion. One issue is that of the stylistic characteristics of the Fourth Gospel, to which Eduard Schweizer, Eugen Ruckstuhl, and W. Nicol have devoted considerable attention. From their combined efforts, some eighty-two characteristics of the evangelist's style have been identified. The other issue is that of the literary form of the Signs Source. For some, such as Bultmann, for all practical purposes, it is manifestly an aretalogy which contained a number of Synoptic-like miracle stories; for others, the Signs Source would have included a Passion narrative and thus would have been virtually a first draft of the Gospel itself (Robert T. Fortna). As a result of this lengthy discussion it would appear that contemporary Johannine scholarship has arrived at a consensus that John did make use of a Signs Source, even though the various authors do not exactly agree among themselves as to the content (did it contain the narrative of Jesus at the Sea of Tiberias, John 21:1–14, or not?) and the nature of the Source.

Much less agreement has been reached as to the Revelatory Discourse Source postulated by Bultmann. According to Bultmann, this source would have included the basic document of the Prologue and most of the discourse material in the Fourth Gospel. In this view, the discourses presently found in the Gospel represent a massive rearrangement and demythologization of the discourses found in the source whose dominant ideology would have been that of early Oriental Gnosticism. In 1956 a student of Bultmann, Heinz

Becker, studied the postulated source. He reconstituted it as a document with five parts: a Thanksgiving of the Community of Believers, the Introduction of the Body of Discourses, the Crisis Discourses, the Farewell Discourses, and a Farewell Prayer of the Believer.

For Bultmann, the Passion Source was a document distinct from the Synoptic Gospels. Written in an easy, Semitizing Greek, the Source would have provided not only the basis for John's Passion narrative (John 18–19) but also source material for the Johannine stories on the Appearance to Mary Magdalene (John 20:1–13), the Disciples without Thomas (20:20–23), and the Disciples with Thomas (20:24–29). A number of other authors who have studied John's use of sources in the Passion narrative have come to a somewhat different conclusion. Their conclusion is that the evangelist made use of the pre-Markan Passion tradition. Such a conclusion brings the critic to a head-on confrontation with the issue of John's relationship with the Synoptics. Since Percival Gardner-Smith's *St. John and the Synoptic Gospels* appeared in 1938 there has been a growing consensus on John's independence of the Synoptics. Demurrers to the consensus have been raised by Frans Neirynck and a number of North American scholars whose redactional studies on Mark have led them to conclude that John knew and used Mark, and point to the Passion narrative as a case in point.

The Epistles

Since Bultmann brought source criticism to bear so thoroughly upon his interpretation of the Fourth Gospel, one might expect that he would have approached 1 John, the second major work in the Johannine corpus, in much the same fashion. One's expectations in this regard have not been frustrated. In a number of articles and in his commentary on 1 John, Bultmann used criteria of style and content to distinguish a basic document used by John in the composition of the letter. Didactic in content and antithetical in style, the source document was distinct from the homiletic-paraenetic sections of the letter that come from the hand of the author. The source document, from which are supposed to have come 1 John 1:5–10; 2:4–5, 9–11, 29; 3:4, 6–10, 14–15, (24); 4:7, (8), 12, 16; 5:1, 4; 4:5, 6 (?); 2:23; 5:10, 12, is characterized by the use of twenty-six antithetical couplets whose presence gives the hypothetical document a poetic character and allowed Bultmann to postulate that the source document of 1 John came from the Gnostic source of Revelatory Discourses which he perceived behind John. The author of the letter would have used the source material in much the same piecemeal fashion as did the author of the Gospel in his composition of the great Johannine discourses. Nevertheless Bultmann claimed that the epistle gives the impression of having concluded at 2:27. This impression suggested to him that 1 John 1:5–2:27 was an originally independent writing, of which the remaining material in the letter is more or less repetitive. Thus Bultmann concluded that 1 John 1:5–2:27 basically represented a first draft of the epistle. Prior to Bultmann's source analysis of the letter, a 1907 study of 1 John by Ernst von Dobschütz also pointed toward the use of a source document by John. Since Bultmann's work, the main lines of his analysis have been supported by Hans Windisch, Herbert Preisker, Herbert Braun, and Wolfgang Nauck. Nevertheless the majority of scholars are not convinced that the stylistic differences between the didactic and paraenetic sections of 1 John are sufficient to warrant the conclusion that 1 John represents a reworking of documentary source material.

Revelation

In all studies of the New Testament, the Book of Revelation remains a somewhat isolated subject for study. This is no less true with respect to the study of its use of sources. The text is replete with repetitions, doublets, and artificial constructions. The logical flow of thought and the temporal sequence of the visions is often interrupted. These are the very stuff on which source analysis thrives. Accordingly many nineteenth-century authors, perceiving a lack of cohesion and logical development, as well as a number of passages which seem to be non- or pre-Christian in nature, proposed different source-critical solutions to the problem of understanding Revelation. Some of these scholars considered that the underlying source document (or documents) was a Jewish text, later reworked by a Christian author who added Chapters 1 – 3 and the epistolary framework to the material he had used. Indeed, a common conclusion drawn from a source analysis of Revelation is that the present text is a compilation of two earlier documents.

Among the more recent authors who have addressed themselves to the source analysis of Revelation is Marie-Émile Boismard, who claimed to have discerned two underlying documents, the one beginning at 10:2 and dating to the time of Nero, and the other beginning at 4:1 and dating to the reign of Domitian. For Boismard, material from these two documents was woven together by John who prefixed Revelation 1 – 3 to the compilation. In her Anchor Bible commentary, Jane Massyngberde Ford likewise assumes that Revelation is based on two earlier documents, but she has postulated that these were Jewish documents. A first document, deriving from the circle of John the Baptist, furnished source material for Revelation 4 – 11. A second document, from which comes the material for Revelation 12 – 22, was presumably written just prior to the fall of Jerusalem by a group of disciples who predicted the fall of the city and attributed the impending disaster to the unorthodox behavior of their contemporaries. In Ford's view, a Jewish Christian disciple of John the Baptist compiled the present text by combining the earlier documents and adding to them Revelation 1 – 3; 22:16a, 20b, 21. While consideration of the composition of Revelation is fraught with complexity, the unitary character of its language and symbol system must be acknowledged. Thus the plea for the interpretation of Revelation on the basis of John's use of different source documents (as distinct from his use of different apocalyptic traditions), now renewed in the twentieth century, has largely fallen on deaf ears.

III. AN EXERCISE IN SOURCE CRITICISM

A. The Message of the Baptist: Luke 3:7–18 (par. Matt 3:7–12; Mark 1:7–8)

Matthew 3:7–12	Mark 1:7–8	Luke 3:7–18
7 But when he saw many of the Pharisees and Sadducees coming for baptism, he said to them, "You brood of vipers! Who warned you to flee from the wrath to come? 8 Bear fruit that befits repentance, 9 and do not presume to say to yourselves, 'We have Abraham as our father'; for I tell you, God is able from these stones to raise up children to Abraham. 10 Even now the axe is laid to the root of the trees; every tree therefore that does not bear good fruit is cut down and thrown into the fire.		7 He said therefore to the multitudes that came out to be baptized by him, "You brood of vipers! Who warned you to flee from the wrath to come? 8 Bear fruits that befit repentance, and do not begin to say to yourselves, 'We have Abraham as our father'; for I tell you, God is able from these stones to raise up children to Abraham. 9 Even now the axe is laid to the root of the trees; every tree therefore that does not bear good fruit is cut down and thrown into the fire." 10 And the multitudes asked him, "What then shall we do?" 11 And he answered them, "He who has two coats, let him share with him who has none; and he who has food, let him do likewise." 12 Tax collectors also came to be baptized, and said to him, "Teacher, what shall we do?" 13 And he said to them, "Collect

11 "I baptize you with water for repentance, but he who is coming after me is mightier than I, whose sandals I am not worthy to carry; he will baptize you with the Holy Spirit and with fire. [12] His winnowing fork is in his hand, and he will clear his threshing floor and gather his wheat into the granary, but the chaff he will burn with unquenchable fire."

7 And he preached, saying, "After me comes he who is mightier than I, the thong of whose sandals I am not worthy to stoop down and untie. [8] I have baptized you with water; but he will baptize you with the Holy Spirit."

no more than is appointed you." [14] Soldiers also asked him, "And we, what shall we do?" And he said to them, "Rob no one by violence or by false accusation, and be content with your wages." [15] As the people were in expectation, and all men questioned in their hearts concerning John, whether perhaps he were the Christ, [16] John answered them all, "I baptize you with water; but he who is mightier than I is coming, the thong of whose sandals I am not worthy to untie; he will baptize you with the Holy Spirit and with fire. [17] His winnowing fork is in his hand, to clear his threshing floor, and to gather the wheat into his granary, but the chaff he will burn with unquenchable fire." [18] So, with many other exhortations, he preached good news to the people.

The student for whom the Two-Source theory is a methodological *a priori* will often look at these parallel passages and conclude that Mark 1:7–8 is the source used by Matthew at 3:11 and by Luke at 3:16. This impression easily finds support in a comparison among the three passages. Luke's verse 17 has the Markan image of "untying sandals" whereas Matthew's verse 11 has the image of "carrying the sandals." This could be readily interpreted as an example of Luke's following his sources more closely than does Matthew.

On the other hand it is easy to recognize that Matthew 3:7–10, 12 and Luke 3:7–9, 17 have been taken over from the *Q* source. In these verses we are dealing with discourse material. The discourse material is not found in Mark. There is remarkable similarity between the sayings in Luke and the sayings in Matthew, even down to the smallest verbal detail. This evidence is enough to convince those who admit the existence of a Sayings Source (*Q*) used by Matthew and Luke to admit that it is from *Q* that Matthew has taken verses 7–10 and Luke verses 7–9.

In Luke 3:10–14 we have additional discourse material that appears in neither Mark nor Matthew. Immediately one might conclude that this material has come from Luke's own source (L). This very conclusion has been reached by such scholars as A. M. Hunter, Harald Sahlin, and Walter Grundmann. Other scholars, however, are not so sure that the verses have come from Luke's own source material. One reason for their doubt is that Luke's special material contains no other traditions about John the Baptist (the ideological criterion). Some among these scholars therefore believe that these verses are Luke's own addition—a redactional addition—to the earlier traditions.

Doubts also can be raised with respect to the dependence of Luke 3:16 (= Matthew 3:11) on Mark 1:7–8. First of all both Luke and Matthew have an order which is different from that of Mark. The major Gospels speak of (1) water baptism, (2) the mighty one, (3) sandals and (4) Spirit baptism, whereas Mark speaks of (1) the mighty one, (2) sandals, (3) water baptism and (4) Spirit baptism. Both Luke and Matthew concur in the mention of "baptism with the Holy Spirit and with fire" over and against Mark's "baptism with the Holy Spirit." This suggests that Matthew and Luke have a common source which is other than Mark. Today scholars generally agree that this source is *Q* (upon which the Markan version of the Baptist's teaching may be dependent in some degree).

Now if Luke 3:7–9 comes from *Q* and 3:16–17 comes from *Q* as well, then it may be that 3:10–14 likewise comes from *Q*. 3:10–14 stands between two *Q* passages. Moreover, *Q* elsewhere attests to a difference of attitude toward the Baptist's baptism on the part of the leaders of the people and the masses (cf. Luke 7:29–30; comp Matt 21:31b–32). Hence a good number of modern scholars (Alfred Plummer, Heinz Schürmann, I. Howard Marshall) are convinced that Luke 3:10–14 also comes from *Q*, even though the passage in its present form has been strongly editorialized by Luke. In any event, Luke 3:15 represents something of an aporia. The people (*ho laos*) appear in contrast to "the multitudes" who appeared in verses 7, 10. Since "the people" is a Lucan theme, the aporia gives us reason to believe that verse 15 is a redactional link created by Luke.

Despite apparent editorial activity, the *Q* material cited by Matthew (3:7–12) and Luke (3:7–14, 16–17) seems to indicate that Luke was a bit more conservative in regard to the use of traditional material than was Matthew. Two examples will serve to make the point. First of all, Luke (v. 16) mentions the "untying of the strap of Jesus' sandals," whereas Matthew (v. 11) mentions the "carrying of Jesus' sandals." Mark 1:7 and John 1:27 show that "untying" is the more traditional image. Second, Luke 3:7, 10 talks about the multitudes. That must be the traditional language, because Luke would have preferred to talk about "the people" (cf. v. 15). Matthew (Matt 3:7) has replaced "the multitudes" of *Q* (= Luke 3:7) with "the Pharisees and scribes," who together form one of Matthew's major concerns.

What can be said about the hypothetical Q on the basis of this little exercise? First of all, we can draw attention to the evidence of an Aramaic stage in the development of the Q tradition. According to T. W. Manson, traces of an Aramaic original are to be seen in Luke 3:8. Luke's "Do not begin to say" represents a literal translation of a common Aramaic idiom. This contrasts with Matthew's "Do not presume to say to yourselves"— better Greek, but a less faithful rendition of the old tradition, and thus another example of Matthew's greater distance from Q than Luke's. In the same verse, there is probably a play on words in the saying about the raising up of children to Abraham (Luke 3:8; Matt 3:9). The Aramaic words for "children" and "stones" are almost identical.

Secondly, Q had a manifest eschatological interest. The imminence of the coming judgment is patent in the logia which the major evangelists have taken over from Q. A punitive judgment will soon fall upon those who do not repent. This realization prompts some further consideration on the meaning of baptism "with the Holy Spirit and with fire." It is quite likely that baptism "with the Holy Spirit" represents the interests of the Church, which contrasted Christian baptism with John's baptism of repentance. On the basis of a tradition history study (see Chapter Five), scholars are in general agreement that the original Q saying (Luke 3:6 = Mark 3:11) ran "baptize you with fire." Then the entire Q saying, in its original form, would have had a consistent outlook—that is, the coming judgment.

B. The Stilling of the Storm:
Matthew 8:23–27 (par. Mark 4:35–41; Luke 8:22–25)

Matthew 8:23–27	Mark 4:35–41	Luke 8:22–25
23 And when he got into the boat, his disciples followed him. 24 And behold, there arose a great storm on the sea, so that the boat was being swamped by the waves; but he was asleep.	35 On that day, when evening had come, he said to them, "Let us go across to the other side." 36 And leaving the crowd, they took him with them, just as he was, in the boat. And other boats were with him. 37 And a great storm of wind arose, and the waves beat into the boat, so that the boat was already filling.	22 One day he got into a boat with his disciples, and he said to them, "Let us go across to the other side of the lake." So they set out, 23 and as they sailed he fell asleep. And a storm of wind came down on the lake, and they were filling with water, and were in danger.
25 And they went and woke him, saying, "Save, Lord; we are perishing." 26 And he said to them, "Why are you afraid, O men of little faith?"	38 But he was in the stern, asleep on the cushion; and they woke him and said to him, "Teacher, do you not care if we perish?"	24 And they went and woke him, saying, "Master, Master, we are perishing!" And he awoke and rebuked the wind and the raging

151

Matthew 8:23–27	Mark 4:35–41	Luke 8:22–25
Then he rose and rebuked the winds and the sea; and there was a great calm. 27 And the men marveled, saying, "What sort of man is this, that even winds and sea obey him?"	39 And he awoke and rebuked the wind, and said to the sea, "Peace! Be still!" And the wind ceased, and there was a great calm. 40 He said to them, "Why are you afraid? Have you no faith?" 41 And they were filled with awe, and said to one another, "Who then is this, that even wind and sea obey him?"	waves; and they ceased, and there was a calm. 25 He said to them, "Where is your faith?" And they were afraid, and they marveled, saying to one another, "Who then is this, that he commands even wind and water, and they obey him?"

Even apart from the common acceptance of the Two-Source theory, it would be difficult to avoid the conclusion that these three pericopes are different versions of the same story. The similarities among them are so striking that one must conclude to some form of literary interdependence.

On the basis of a comparison of these three accounts, independent of a more general consideration of the Gospel material, it would be difficult to determine which of the three narratives served as the source of the other two. The general thrust of the narrative is common to all three Gospels. There are, however, relatively few places (in the Greek text) where there is literal agreement among all three stories. In fact, *kai egeneto galēnē* ("there was a calm") of Mark 4:39 is the only three-word expression to be found with the same sequence of words in all three Gospels. Matthew is faithful to the Markan source in preserving the use of "great" (*megalē*) to describe the calm, but for the rest he departs considerably from the Markan text—even to the point of having Jesus' discourse about faith prior to calming the storm. Luke shows greater agreement with the Markan text than does Matthew: " . . . day . . . Let us go across to the other side . . . storm of wind . . . And he awoke and rebuked the wind . . . He said to them . . . who then is this, that even . . ." Finally there are a number of "minor agreements" between Matthew and Luke: "into a boat . . . his disciples . . . and they went . . . saying . . . we are perishing . . ." One must have recourse to a general theory on Synoptic interdependence to conclude that both Matthew and Luke have made use of Mark. Within that framework, it is then easy to conclude that Luke has made use of his source more faithfully than did Matthew.

In the formulation of the Two-Source theory it is generally argued that the argument for order is the weightiest consideration in favor of Markan priority. In this respect it is noteworthy that in all three Gospels the story of the Stilling of the Storm is followed by the episode of the Gerasene Demoniac (Matt 8:28–34; Mark 5:1–20; Luke 8:26–39). In Luke's narrative, the Stilling of the Storm follows on the pericope about Jesus' True Kindred

(Luke 8:19–21), which follows several verses on the parables (Luke 8:4–18) beginning with the Parable of the Sower (Luke 8:4–8). In Mark, the Stilling of the Storm follows a lengthy section on parables (Mark 4:1–34), beginning with the Parable of the Sower (Mark 4:1–9). In Matthew, however, the Parable of the Sower is not narrated until 13:1–9.

If source analysis of the Synoptics with particular reference to Matthew 8:23–27 and Luke 8:22–25 leads to the conclusion that each of these narratives is dependent on Mark 4:35–51, a source analysis study of the texts is not yet complete. Many, but not all, contemporary students of Mark have concluded that the Markan narrative itself has been taken over from a source. Some authors point to the fact that the Stilling of the Storm is, in some senses, a doublet of another sea narrative, namely, the Walking on the Water (Matt 6:45–51). That there are aporias between Mark's version of the Stilling of the Sea and its present Markan context is only too apparent. In the Greek text, the narrative begins with the expression "he said to them," a variant of the typical Markan attachment formula. "On that day" seems to link the narrative to the day of the teaching in parables, which took place by the sea (Mark 4:1). Verse 35 seems to imply that Jesus is already in the boat, but then comes verse 36 with its puzzling "just as he was, in the boat." That is immediately followed by the mention of the other boats, which are introduced only to disappear from the narrative. It has also been noted that the story of Mark 4:35–41, as well as those contained in Mark 5, differ in style and motif from Mark's earlier miracle narratives. More specifically, in terms of a stylistic analysis, some authors—for example, Ernst Lohmeyer, Walter Grundmann, and Gottfried Schille—have thought it possible to discern a tale with a three-part rhythmic-strophic pattern behind verses 35–41. In the opinion of these authors the logia in direct address are the result of later additions to the earlier tale. Finally, in respect to ideology it has been noted that the underlying narrative projects a "divine man" Christology which is somewhat inconsistent with Mark's own Christology. In sum, some authors judge that each of the four typical indications of an author's use of sources is verified in regard to Mark's version of the Stilling of the Storm. Redundancy, the presence of aporias, difference of vocabulary and style, and ideological variation can be discerned in Mark 4:35–41.

Commentators generally agree that the story of the Stilling of the Storm is a pre-Markan tradition which Mark incorporated into its present context. The question then comes down to a consideration of whether the tradition came to Mark in written or oral form. Given the similarity of style and motif between Mark 4:35–41 and some of the miracle stories told later in the Gospel, some authors have come to the conclusion that Mark has made use of an aretalogy in the composition of his Gospel. An *a priori* argument in favor of the plausibility of this suggestion is to be found in John's use of a Signs Source. An example of this tendency in source analysis is to be found in the work of the American exegete Paul J. Achtemeier. From an analysis of the Markan miracle narratives, Achtemeier has concluded that Mark made use

of a pre-Markan cycle of miracles, which circulated in the form of two catenae as follows:

Catena I
4:35 – 5:43; 6:34–44, 53 (with 4:35, 5:21c, 5:43a, and 6:34bc as prob-
ably editorial, and 5:24 and 6:35b as clearly editorial):
The Stilling of the Storm (4:35–41)
The Gerasene Demoniac (5:1–20)
The Woman with a Hemorrhage (5:25–34)
Jairus' Daughter (5:21–23, 35–43)
Feeding of the 5,000 (6:34–44, 53)

Catena II
6:45–51; 8:22–26; 7:24b–30, 32–37; 8:1–10 (with 6:45c, 50c, 51b;
7:36; and 8:1a as editorial):
Jesus Walks on the Sea (6:45–51)
The Blind Man of Bethsaida (8:22–26)
The Syrophoenician Woman (7:24b–30)
The Deaf-Mute (7:32–37)
Feeding of the 4,000 (8:1–10)

The alternative suggestion, namely that Mark's narrative of the Stilling of
the Storm is immediately dependent on an oral tradition rather than a written document, raises a question as to the manner in which this tradition
came down to Mark, who was probably not an eyewitness to the events he
was narrating. If, on the other hand, Mark 4:35–41 is dependent upon a
written source, the exegete must inquire about the nature of the stories found
in the documentary source material and about the possibility that an oral
tradition lies behind the written stories. In short, no matter the nature of the
source material used by Mark in the composition of his Gospel, one must always ask questions about form and tradition. It is to questions of this kind
that the methodology known as form criticism addresses itself.

SELECT BIBLIOGRAPHY

Achtemeier, Paul J. "Toward the Isolation of Pre-Markan Miracle Catenae."
    Journal of Biblical Literature, 89 (1970), 265–91.

Beardslee, William A. *Literary Criticism of the New Testament. Guides to
    Biblical Scholarship.* Philadelphia: Fortress, 1970.

Best, Ernest. "An Early Sayings Collection." *Novum Testamentum,* 18
    (1976), 1–16.

Boismard, Marie-Émile. "The Two Source Theory at an Impasse." *New
    Testament Studies,* 26 (1979), 1–17.

Carson, D. A. "Current Source Criticism of the Fourth Gospel: Some
    Methodological Questions." *Journal of Biblical Literature* 97, (1978),
    411–29.

Collins, Raymond F. "A propos the integrity of 1 Thes." *Ephemerides Theologicae Lovanienses,* 65 (1979), 67–106.

Delobel, Joël, ed. *Logia. Les Paroles de Jésus—The Sayings of Jesus. Mémorial Joseph Coppens. Bibliotheca Ephemeridum Theologicarum Lovaniensium,* 59. Louvain: University Press, 1982.

Dupont, Jacques. *The Sources of Acts: The Present Position.* London: Darton, Longmann & Todd, 1964.

Edwards, Richard Alan. *A Theology of Q: Eschatology, Prophecy, and Wisdom.* Philadelphia: Fortress, 1976.

Farmer, William R. *The Synoptic Problem: A Critical Analysis.* New York: Macmillan, 1964.

Fortna, Robert T. *The Gospel of Signs: A Reconstruction of the Narrative Source Underlying the Fourth Gospel.* SNTS, MS, 11. Cambridge: University Press, 1970.

Gnilka, Joachim. "2 Cor 6:4 – 7:1 in the Light of the Qumran Texts and the Testaments of the Twelve Patriarchs." In *Paul and Qumran: Studies in New Testament Exegesis,* ed. by J. Murphy-O'Connor. London: Geoffrey Chapman, 1968. 48–68.

Hug, Joseph. *La finale de l'évangile de Marc, Mc 16, 9–20. Études bibliques.* Paris: Gabalda, 1978.

Lambrecht, Jan. "The Fragment 2 Cor VI 14 – VII 1. A Plea for Its Authenticity." In *Miscellanea Neotestamentica,* 1. Ed. by T. Baarda, A. F. J. Klijn, and W. C. van Unnik. Leiden: Brill, 1978. 143–61.

Manson, Thomas Walter. *The Sayings of Jesus.* London: SCM, 1949.

Martin, Ralph P. *Carmen Christi. Philippians ii. 5–11 in Recent Interpretation and in the Setting of Early Christian Worship.* SNTS, MS, 4. Cambridge: University Press, 1967.

Perkins Journal, 33:4 (1980).

Petersen, Norman R. *Literary Criticism for New Testament Critics. Guides to Biblical Scholarship.* Philadelphia: Fortress, 1978.

Schmithals, Walter. "On the Composition and Earliest Collection of the Major Epistles of Paul." In *Paul and the Gnostics.* Nashville: Abingdon, 1972. 239–74.

Schulz, Siegfried. *Q—Die Spruchquelle der Evangelisten.* Zurich: Theologischer Verlag, 1972.

Scobie, C. H. H. "The Use of Source Material in the Speeches of Acts III and IV." *New Testament Studies,* 25 (1979), 399–421.

Van Belle, Gilbert. *De Semeia-Bron in het Vierde Evangelie. Onstaan en groei van een hypothese.* Louvain: University Press, 1975.

Vassiliades, Petros. "The Nature and Extent of the Q-Document." *Novum Testamentum* 20 (1978), 49–73.

Zuntz, G. *The Text of the Epistles: A Disquisition upon the Corpus Paulinum.* London: Oxford, 1953.

CHAPTER FIVE

FORM CRITICISM

I. AN INTRODUCTION TO THE METHOD

In a general sort of way form criticism might be described as the analysis of the typical forms by means of which human experience is verbally expressed. The term "form criticism" is the common translation of the German *Formgeschichte* (literally, "history of form"). The German expression entered into usage among New Testament scholars after it first appeared in the title of Martin Dibelius' 1919 work *From Tradition to Gospel** (*Die Formgeschichte des Evangeliums,* literally, "the history of form of the gospel"). The nomenclature soon became the commonly accepted designation for a method of biblical study that had been in vogue among Old Testament scholars since the turn-of-the-century work of Hermann Gunkel (1862–1932) on the Pentateuch. Gunkel had called the method "research into literary types" (*Gattungsgeschichte*) or "history of literature" (*Literaturgeschichte*), but Dibelius' expression soon became the technical term for the method. Thus in biblical circles Gunkel is the father of the methodology to which Dibelius has given a name.

As the term employed by both of these German scholars indicated, the method has to do with the history of expression. Thus the methodology could more accurately be described as form analysis and the history of tradition. Whereas both text criticism and source analysis look to a book of the New Testament as a written document, of which several somewhat different versions exist and which may have been dependent, in whole or in part, on earlier documents, form criticism considers that each of the books of the New Testament is an expression of human experience with its own history.

156

Written in the language of human beings, the books of the New Testament are subject to the laws of the communication of human experience.

The presupposition of form criticism is that all forms of verbal communication among human beings, whether expressed orally or in writing, follow well-defined patterns. If verbal expression did not follow these patterns, it would be the making of so many words, rather than a form of communication among human beings. In reality this fact is so elementary that we humans are hardly aware of it when we communicate with one another. Nonetheless we still communicate according to certain patterns of expression. The telling of a joke is one form of communication among us. We need hardly be told that the successful telling of a joke requires an element of surprise and that consequently the "punch line" must come at the end of the tale. The letter is a written form of communication among us. In school we have been taught that the so-called "friendly letter" differs somewhat from the so-called "business letter." In the jargon of form criticism, this means that the form of the friendly letter is distinct from that of the business letter. During our school years we have been carefully taught how to compose a friendly letter and how to compose a business letter. In later years, however, we write a friendly letter or a business letter without giving a second thought to the form we will follow. The use of the appropriate form has simply become second nature to us. Indeed, were we to examine the letters that we write we would probably discover that our own use of the form of the friendly letter, like our use of the form of the business letter, has changed somewhat over the years—perhaps so much so that we have placed our own stamp upon the form we are using. Then too we might discover that the lines of distinction between the friendly letter and the business letter are not quite as clear as they were defined to be during our school years. Some of our business letters tend to convey personal greetings as well; some of our friendly letters have some business aspects that must be attended to. Despite the fluidity of the form of our letters, there are nonetheless some that we would characterize as friendly letters and others that we would describe as business letters. No matter how informal our business letters might have become, they are certainly different from our love letters. We who write them know the difference; so, too, do those who read them.

Experience tells us that it is the circumstances in which we write and the purpose which we hope to achieve by writing that dictate the form of our letter writing. In ordinary circumstances, a note hastily jotted on a postcard will hardly do as an application for a business position. In ordinary circumstances, too, a formal letter to one's wife or parent would hardly do as an expression of love and concern while one was absent from home during the course of a business trip. Circumstances dictate the appropriateness of the choice of form, thereby circumscribing our communication within more or less well-defined parameters. Indeed a writer who was to apply for a position within business by means of the hastily scribbled note would have to admit that he or she was sending an ambiguous signal to the prospective employer. Clarity of communication demands the choice of the appropriate form of communication, and one soon learns that the choice of this form determines both the choice of one's language and the content of one's communication. Some words are appropriate in a business letter and some are inappropriate, just as some words are appropriate in a friendly letter and some are inappropriate. As a matter of fact, some words change their meaning as they appear in different letter forms. While "dear" in the salutation of a business letter is nothing more than a customary expression of courtesy, it is the conveyer of affection in a love letter written to one's boyfriend or wife.

If a speaker or writer necessarily and spontaneously follows set patterns of verbal expression in his or her communication (oral or literary forms), it is necessary that the receiver of the communication (the listener or the reader) appreciate these patterns of communication if he or she is to understand the communication. Indeed, it is our familiarity with the patterns of communication normally used in our social circumstances which allows us to listen intelligently and to read with appreciation. If we need be told that a story is a joke, then it is not a joke for us. On the other hand, we need not be told explicitly that a poster tacked to a university bulletin board is a more or less important announcement. The fact that we recognize an official poster of the university conditions us to expect an announcement of some activity or other. Similarly we don't have to be told that an advertising circular is designed to persuade us to buy a given product. The imagery with which the product is portrayed, the glowing claims made in its behalf, and the price which is always "low" coalesce to inform us that the designer of the advertisement intends to convince us that his or her product serves our purpose.

Reading the Newspaper

Perhaps we can more fully appreciate the importance of the discernment of oral and literary forms in our lives if we reflect upon the reading of the daily newspaper. Since the newspaper consists of the written word rather than the spoken word, we are dealing with literary forms rather than oral forms. Our appreciation of the various patterns of communication contained in the newspaper conditions our response to each of them. As it were, we shift mental gears when we turn the pages of the newspaper. As a matter of fact, we even spontaneously ascribe different meanings to words according to our discernment of the pattern of communication in which they are found.

I can take as an example the copy of the *International Herald Tribune,* the English-language newspaper in Europe, which was delivered to my door this morning. On page one, I find a number of news items, headlines and bylines, pictorial captions, a weather report, and a price list. These represent five different forms of literary communication and I have not yet turned the page of this morning's newspaper. When I do turn the page, I discover advertisements, a movie review, editorials, an editorial cartoon, letters to the editor, the stock market report, financial news reports and analyses, a table of currency rates, a table of U.S. commodity prices, classified advertisements, a radio and TV guide, book reviews, comic strips, a crossword puzzle, the column on the game of bridge, articles on sports, major league standings, a few box scores, and a column called "People." In short, I have discovered twenty-four different patterns of communication in this morning's fourteen-page newspaper. Were I to have received one of the major U.S. dailies instead of my abridged and limited-circulation *IHT*, I would have discovered still other patterns of literary communication. They would have included political reports, obituaries, the necrology, a fashion report, movie advertisements, the society column, the gossip column, and columns offering various forms of advice (Ann Landers, medical, financial). In a major city Sunday newspaper we can discover still other forms of communication. As a matter of fact, we might even find it useful further to distinguish more specific forms of communication within some of these categories. Among the classified advertisements we might find it useful to distinguish the following: Real Estate—Sales, Rentals—For Sale, Help Wanted, Situations Desired, Lost and Found, Personal, etc.

It almost goes without saying that no one has ever really taught me how to read the newspaper. Yet I truly appreciate my newspaper when I can distinguish one form of communication from another. The discernment of the pattern of communication—i.e., the literary form—allows me to understand, really understand, what I am reading. In a word, the appreciation of the literary form of each of the items in my daily newspaper conditions my understanding of the newspaper. On the other hand, the extent to which I am not sensitive to the various forms of literary communication within the newspaper is the extent to which I have not understood the newspaper. Were I to spell this notion out in schematic fashion I would say that the identification of the literary form of a newspaper item determines (1) the reader's expectations as to content; (2) his or her attitude toward the content; and (3) his or her understanding of the words. A few examples will suffice.

The necrology, which appears in most newspapers, is a listing of the names of those who have died within the previous few days. The newspaper item covering each of the deceased is presented in stereotyped fashion. It typically gives the full name of the deceased, the date of death, the next of kin, the members of the immediate family, place of residence, an indication of the funeral parlor, an indication of the church service, and the calling hours—all of this, and no more than this. In contrast, the obituary appears in the newspaper only on the day after death. It contains all the information contained in the necrology and additional information as well. This additional information would include the deceased's life history—date and place of birth, place and length of employment, membership in church and social organizations, etc. Frequently it would also say something about the place of residence of the various members of the family of the deceased. It might also cite the various places of residence occupied by the deceased during the course of his or her life and particularly significant activities in which he or she had been engaged.

The realization that the reader can expect to find a somewhat different content in two different types of presentation of the death of an individual leads a discerning individual to a twofold conclusion. First, that the author who has opted for one literary form rather than another must write according to the often unstated canons of that literary form. There are some things that the writer must mention, and other things that he or she may not mention. There is an acceptable vocabulary and other terminology that is to be avoided. There is even a proper sequence of presentation to be followed. The sportswriter knows, for example, that the winner of an event must always be mentioned in the first sentence of the article. Secondly, there are different ways of presenting the same content material. For example, Ernest Lawrence Thayer's narrative poem *Casey at the Bat* might be formulated in box-score fashion in the following manner:

Mudville

	AB	H	R	E
Flynn	1	1	0	0
Blake	1	1	0	0
Casey	1	0	0	0

Strikeouts: J. Doe, 1.

The box score contains the essential information about Casey's striking out, but conveys none of the pathos that has made the poem a memorable item in American popular literature.

The reader's discernment of the literary form of the various items in the newspaper also colors the attitude with which he or she approaches the text. Front-page news items are presumed to give facts, and perhaps some analysis of these facts. Thus the reader approaches the front-page news items with an attitude of openness and acceptance. He or she may not be happy or inspired by what is read, but he or she accepts what is read because it is a presentation of "the facts" and there is no argument with the existence of reality. Editorials, however, are presumed to give opinions. Thus the reader approaches the editorial with the notion that he or she may agree or disagree with the ideas proposed in the editorial. The fact that the editorial has been written by a columnist whose political leanings are already known to the reader provides the latter with a prejudice as to whether he or she will accept the ideas presented in the editorial. The reader knows, moreover, that the editorial column is not the only form of editorial expression to be found in the daily newspaper. The editorial cartoon is certainly an expression of a political analyst's thought. So, too, at least on occasions are such comic strips as "Doonesbury."

To illustrate that the reader approaches different sections of the newspaper with different attitudes and expectations, we might also cite the different attitudes with which one approaches a movie review and a movie advertisement. It may well be that the review and the advertisement are addressing themselves to the same movie. The reader will take up the movie review with much the same attitude that he or she brings to the editorial. The review will give only one person's opinion, but the critic is deemed to have a certain amount of expertise and sensitivity. Thus the reader expects the critic's review to be a more or less accurate evaluation of the movie. What he or she expects to find in the advertisement, in addition to the movie's title, its cast, and its rating (G, PG, R, or X), is a highly selective encomium of the movie in hyperbolic language.

Thus a reader will often interpret words and expressions differently according to the literary form of the newspaper item in which they appear. If the newspaper reader finds "The Best Film of the Year" as part of an advertisement for a film, he or she might decide to go to it. But if the very same expression is found in the review by a critic whose judgment and taste are highly valued by the reader, he or she would most likely make the viewing of the film the goal of the next trip to a movie theater. Similarly the reader attaches a different connotation to the expression "An Exceptional Bank" found in an advertisement than when the same expression is found in a feature article on the financial page of the newspaper. Similarly the words "A Winner" have, for the average reader, a different meaning according to whether they appear in an advertisement for a car or as a headline on the sports page.

This extensive excursus on the reading of the daily newspaper can serve as a reminder that intelligent reading requires that the reader discern the literary form of the material being read. The reader must also shift attitude and expectations according to the different literary forms of the subject matter. When the same reader wants to communicate with some other person on the topics about which he or she has read, he or she chooses an oral or literary form that is appropriate to the time and circumstances. In short, all of us are well aware of the importance of oral and literary forms for effective communication and understanding. Most of us do not give them explicit attention because the forms commonly used in our culture at this time have really become part of our second nature. Yet the New Testament is also a piece of literature; as a composite of several documents it is a form of literary expression. What is contained in the New Testament was also written according to a variety of literary forms, but because the books of the New Testament were written almost two thousand years ago in a culture different from ours, our appreciation of their literary forms is no longer second nature. The method of the form-critical study of the New Testament is designed to supply, by the development of a specific technique, an appreciation of the literary forms of the New Testament, sensitivity to which is no longer a spontaneous part of our second nature.

The Terminology

Literary form is the characteristics of vocabulary and style that enable a piece of writing to be categorized within a given literary type. The literary form of a given text appears upon analysis of that particular text. Every piece of writing has its literary form, just as every spoken communication has its oral form. Although the literary form has to do with a given piece of literature, it is not concerned with the specific contents of that literature as such. Rather it deals with the way in which those contents are communicated. Thus the literary form of a business letter would include: the address of the sender, the date, a salutation, the body of the letter (with a relatively small number of paragraphs and rather stereotyped language), the complimentary close, signature and signature block, address of the recipient. The literary form of the business letter is indifferent as to whether the business concerns corn or automobiles. What is of concern is whether the business letter is merely a letter of inquiry or an order.

The *literary type* is a characteristic manner of written expression found in a number of texts that have a common pattern of thought, characteristic vocabulary and expressions, a similarity of style, and a similarity of purpose. All written forms of communication must fit a literary type if they are to be intelligible. The business letter, the friendly letter, the love letter, the movie review, the editorial, and the weather report are so many different literary types. Pieces of writing which belong to any one of these categories share common characteristics. Thus the analysis of the form of a given document allows it to be categorized within a given literary type. A given letter has its literary form; it belongs to a specific literary type. Thus the first task of form criticism is the analysis of the literary form of a given document with the view of assigning it to a given literary type. A unit of writing is recognized by its literary form as being comparable to other writings and can thus be assigned to a particular literary type.

Although literary analysts speak and write about literary forms and literary types in a general sort of way, they frequently find it helpful to distinguish the literary formula and the genre from the literary form and type. The *literary formula* is, in fact, a short literary type. It is a characteristic expression, generally consisting of a few typical words, which is commonly found in a specific type of literature. "Dear John" and "they lived happily ever after" are literary formulas, characteristic of the personal letter and the children's folk tale respectively. "Dearly beloved" is an oral formula, readily recognized as the traditional opening of a sermon. "Moderate decline due to profit-taking" is an oral or literary formula typically found in the stock market report. As the reader will surely recognize, the coherent words which make up a literary (oral) formula convey a meaning in themselves, yet they are most frequently encountered in a larger literary (oral) unit of which they form a characteristic part.

In German New Testament criticism, the reader frequently finds reference to *Gattungsgeschichte* (history of genre) or *Gattungsforschung* (genre research). Since *Gattung* designates a group of realities (not necessarily pieces of literature or forms of oral communication) which share characteristics in common, "genre" would seem not to be substantially different from "type." Thus a convenient distinction can be made between *Formgeschichte* (history of form) and *Gattungsgeschichte* (history of genre), as between the history of the form of a particular piece of literature and the history of a type of literature. Indeed, the various literary types do have their history as the following remarks will note. Before turning to that history, it might be advantageous to note that some scholars prefer to use "genre" or "macrogenre" when treating of longer or more general literary forms. Scholars who do so would then restrict the use of the expression "literary type" to a shorter unit of literature or a less general category. Given this distinction, the newspaper, the Gospel, the letter, and the hymn designate literary genres; the weather report, the miracle story, the personal letter, and the Christological hymn designate literary types.

The Life Situation

If the first task of the form critic is literary analysis to aid in classifying a piece of literature within a given literary type, a second task is to relate that writing to its social setting. The analyst wants to know the social situation that gave rise to its genre or literary form. For the form critic, the type of knowledge that is desired is not so much the particularities of detail that systematic historical study will provide, but the general set of social circumstances that gave rise to the existence of the literary type to which a given piece of writing belongs.

Each human experience is a unique experience, to be sure, yet there are sufficient analogies among human situations for us to be able to generalize about them. A love affair is surely not a game of baseball. In other words, there are sufficient analogies among the various human situations for us to think in terms of the existence of "types" of human situations.

Further reflection reveals that the needs of a particular type of situation elicit certain forms of communication that are appropriate to the situation. As circumstances dictate, these forms of communication may be oral or written but they always correspond to the situation. Thus there is a language and form of communication that is proper to the love affair, and another language and form of communication that is proper to the ball game. A given individual will use rather specific and well-defined language in communicating with his or her beloved, and will use quite another language while attending a baseball game. Indeed, this same individual will use the same type of language in successive relationships with different lovers, and will use basically the same type of language whenever he or she attends a ball game.

Moreover there is something of a dialogical relation between one's social situation and one's use of a type of communication. Not only does the social situation elicit specific forms of communication, the form of the communication often determines the nature of the social situation. This is to say that the form of communication often categorizes the social situation. An encounter between Tom and Mary, for example, may be an encounter between a customer and a salesclerk or it may be a meeting between old friends. The form of communication between Tom and Mary makes the difference, and this because it expresses the purpose of the encounter. Indeed, a difference

163

in the form of communication can change the nature of a social situation. All of us have been involved in social gatherings of a friendly nature that have been transformed into business meetings, or vice versa. It's not necessarily a change in the number of people in attendance that has brought about the difference; rather, it is simply a matter of a change of language forms.

In other words, there is an interrelationship between types of social situations and the corresponding types of communication, whether oral or written. A given type of social situation elicits a given type of expression; a given type of expression determines the nature of a social situation. When the appropriate type of expression is written, one can speak of correspondence between a social situation and the use of a literary type. Some years ago the German Old Testament scholar Albrecht Alt described this correspondence rather accurately. He noted that the use of form-critical analysis "rests on the assumption that each individual literary type, as long as it preserves its own vitality, has a particular content and particular forms of expression, and that these two are closely connected. This is not the result of any arbitrary linking up on the part of the writers, but the two were linked up from the very start. That is to say that even in primitive times material was shaped and handed down orally by the people generally, so that these forms correspond with the regularly recurring events and needs of a particular way of life, out of which the literary types naturally arose." (*Essays on Old Testament History and Religion,* pp. 284–85)

In scholarly circles the social situation to which the use of given oral or literary forms of expression is appropriate is termed the "life situation" or "setting in life." This terminology corresponds to the German expression *Sitz-im-Leben* (setting in life) which Gunkel employed in his form-critical analysis of Old Testament texts. The life situation has been defined by Klaus Koch as "a social occurence, the result of customs prevailing in one particular culture at one particular time, which has granted such an important role to the speaker and his hearers, or the writer and his readers, that particular linguistic forms are found necessary as a vehicle for expression."

Since the life situation is typically described in sociological terms, form-critical analysis requires not only a study of literature as such but also some knowledge of sociology and human experience. Moreover, since there is an interrelationship between forms of expression and life situations, it is possible for an analyst to begin his study either with a study of the social situation or with a study of the pertinent literature or oral forms of communication. For example, I could begin a study of Americans in Europe from a sociological point of view which might then lead to some consideration of the literature produced by this group, or I might begin with an analysis of this group's literature to arrive at some conclusions about the nature of the group.

Should I begin my study with a sociological survey of Americans living in Europe, I would find that they fell into three classes of people: the military community, the business and diplomatic community, and American students overseas. The characteristics of the military community need not be spelled out in scientific detail. The communities consist of servicemen and women belonging principally to the Army and Air Force, with some members of their families. A limited number have post-graduate college degrees, while the vast majority have a high school diploma and some have not completed their high school education. Their perspective centers on the United States and its interests. *Stars and Stripes,* the "authorized unofficial publication for the U.S. Armed Forces," is a twenty-eight-page newspaper in tabloid form. A typical issue contained four articles on the front page with these headlines: "AF crash in Egypt kills 13"; "Saturn moon probed"; "Modern Army questions its mission in the world"; "Coloring Contest nearing." The newspaper contained twenty-five photos, six pages on sports, two pages of comics, less than a fourth of a page of financial news; and columns entitled "Modern Medicine" and "Dear Ann Landers."

The American diplomatic and business community in Europe is likewise well known and its profile needs not be spelled out in full detail. The community consists of generally affluent individuals who are present in Europe with their families. As a group these individuals are older than those in the military communities. They are frequently multilingual. Among them, post-graduate education is the norm rather than the exception. Their horizon is world affairs and the impact of economic and political situations on world affairs. The *International Herald Tribune,* "published with the New York *Times* and the Washington *Post,*" for the same date was a fourteen-page newspaper in a typical 16×23-inch format. Since the page size of the *IHT* was approximately double that of the *S&S,* the two newspapers contained the same amount of newsprint on that date. Page one of the *IHT* contained eight articles with these headlines: "U.K., in Gesture to Reagan, to Seek Delay of Europe Move on PLO"; "Democrats Block Republican Move for Tax Cut"; "Cultural Workers Join Sit-In in Gdansk"; "One Ring of Saturn is Braided"; "Jewish Activist in Moscow Said to be Arrested"; "Future of Rights Conference Still in Doubt"; "British Gallery Pays Up to $12 Million for Painting"; "Quakes Hit South Peru." This newspaper contained twelve photos, half a page on sports, half a page of comics, four pages of financial news, and neither the "Modern Medicine" nor "Ann Landers" columns.

It was easy to see that the respective newspapers corresponded to the needs and interests of the communities they served. On reflection one can realize how relatively easy it might be to develop a general social profile of the respective military and diplomatic-business communities merely on the basis of a reading of these newspapers. As it happened, this was demonstrated when I visited Tokyo some years ago. Even though I am rather familiar with Europe and the phenomenon of Americans abroad, I am not very familiar with the Far East. In Tokyo I came upon a couple of English-language newspapers. In terms of genre, they were not dissimilar to the *Stars and Stripes* and the *International Herald Tribune.* Without having met a single American in Japan other than those with whom I was traveling, I was able to conclude something about Americans abroad, Far Eastern style. And I was not wrong. From a knowledge of the social situation one can say something about the types of literature it elicits; from a knowledge of the literary type, one can say something about the social situation to which it corresponds. The reality of this interrelationship and the legitimacy of choosing either term of the relationship is one of the factors that have distinguished the methodology of two of the major proponents of the form-critical method in New Testament studies. Martin Dibelius (*From Tradition to Gospel*) began with an analysis of the life and activities of the early Church, particularly as they were portrayed by Luke in the Acts of the Apostles. Rudolf Bultmann (*The History of the Synoptic Tradition*) began with a survey of ancient literature, on the basis of which he came to say something about the ideology and activities of the early Church.

The examples cited thus far would seem to indicate that the relationship between a life situation and the literary form which it elicits is relatively simple, albeit dialogical. The fact of the matter is that those human situations which can be typed according to various sociological categories are generally complex. Corresponding to a single life situation there is frequently not just one literary type but a variety of literary types, each of which fulfills a particular function and each of which is in a more or less distinct relationship to the others. By way of example we can refer to the office situation of a relatively large business. Among the literary types appropriate to that "social setting" are the business letter, the interoffice memo, employees' notes, and the Telex message. The existence of any one of these "literary" types points to this form of social situation; the existence of the social situation usually demands all of these types of literary expression.

Transmission and Preservation

Since all linguistic communication among humans bears the mark of a given oral or literary form, the use of such forms is necessary for the very existence of human communication. This implies that the perseverance of the communication in the same or another oral or literary form is necessary to the preservation of that material. As the form in which a communication is expressed shapes the communication, so the form in which a linguistic communication is preserved shapes it as well. For example, the story about Pat and Mike has the form of a joke, which shapes the narration of the story and gives it an inner coherence that lets it be told by others. As an oral form "the joke" is the means by which the story of Pat and Mike is preserved. It is preserved only in the form of a joke. Should the story of Pat and Mike be set down in writing, it would acquire a somewhat different form. This new form would shape and fix the form of the story even more than it was fixed in its oral state.

Moreover, it must be noted that because of the close interrelationship between life situation and (oral and) literary types, any change in social circumstances will provoke changes and modifications in literary types. Sometimes, too, the changes in the life situation are so profound that they make the use of certain literary types redundant and they disappear altogether. A literary type severed from its situation of origin will tend to disappear. Certainly the coming of television represented a marked change in the lifestyle (the life situation) of many people. This change in lifestyle modified at least one literary type, elicited at least one new literary type, and caused another literary type to virtually disappear. The listing of radio programs (a literary type) had long been a feature of many newspapers; with the coming of TV this feature had to be modified to become a "Radio and TV" listing (as TV became still more popular, the item was featured in the newspaper as "TV and Radio"). The popularity of TV spawned a whole new type of literature —the TV program guide. Finally the entrance of TV into virtually everyone's living room signaled the demise of the pictorial magazines (again a distinct literary type) such as *Life* and *Look* in the United States, and *Paris Match* in France. These pictorial magazines had been designed to give readers a visual picture of the events that were being described in words. Magazines delivered a week or more after the events and containing isolated still shots of those events became redundant when it was possible for the general population to have an up-to-date, even simultaneous, sequential portrayal of events.

That the coming of TV did not immediately signal the death of the pictorial magazines is an indication of the tendency of oral and written types to persist for a while, even after the life situation from which they have arisen has passed away. Sometimes the oral and literary forms simply survive for a while by reason of a form of linguistic inertia. Sometimes the literary forms survive because they are adapted to the new social situation. A modification of this phenomenon would be the variety of specialized pictorial magazines that have developed since the advent of TV and the demise of the general-interest pictorial magazines. Sometimes literary types survive because they are appropriated to another setting. For example, *Commonweal* magazine recently featured the "Ten Commandments for Teaching." Sometimes, finally, oral and literary types persist insofar as certain characteristic features of the type are taken up into a work belonging to another literary type. This is always the case when an oral communication is preserved in literary form for the sake of posterity or wider distribution. The result of this tendency of literary forms to survive with modification because of changes in the life situation results in literature with a mixed form (*Mischform*), in which it is possible to recognize elements of the traditional literary type as well as elements of modification in view of the new social situation.

All of this is to say that oral and literary types are not static. They are in constant processes of adaptation. Some old literary types fall by the wayside, and new ones spring up to take their place. In this process it should be noted that some literary materials of a given literary type tend to exist, and continue to exist, in a somewhat isolated fashion. Thus the joke and the university poster exist by themselves. On the other hand it often happens that material which belongs to one literary type is preserved or serves as a means of communication only because it has been subsumed into a larger unit of linguistic expression. Thus the sermon, which belongs to a rather specific oral type, exists because it is a part of the liturgy, and poems are preserved in anthologies.

In other words, the form critic must also take into account the existence of component and composite literary types. The poem is a component literary type; the anthology is a relatively simple, but still complex, composite literary type. The editorial is a component literary type; the newspaper is a complex composite literary type. Sometimes literary types exist only as component types. This is certainly true of the literary formula, the shortest form of literary type; it is also true of the editorial, which exists only as part of a newspaper. It is generally true of the sermon, normally a component oral type, but then there are sermons that have been preached independently of a liturgical ceremony. Moreover there are printed collections of sermons, for example the *Parochial and Plain Sermons* of John Henry Newman. This means that it sometimes happens that material belonging to a normally component literary type occasionally assumes some independent and adapted form of existence.

The relationship between the component and composite literary types is also dialogical, as the history of any newspaper will show. Newspapers acquire their own character according to the variety of component literary types they incorporate. Likewise, the character of a newspaper indicates the type of articles and materials that are to be found in it. Moreover the component oral or literary type is often adapted to the complex literary type of which it forms a part. Thus there is some difference between the TV editorial and the newspaper editorial. In short, it is not only single literary types that are in a constant state of evolution; complex literary types are also caught up in the process of constant adaptation.

This reflection might well suggest to us that form-critical study of any text is generally not limited to analyzing the document's literary form and categorizing it within the certain literary type. Form-critical analysis also includes the determination of the life situation of a given piece of writing and an understanding of the history of transmission of the content of that piece of writing. Hence form-critical analysis is sometimes called the study of the "history of tradition." For example, the New Testament interpreter who comes upon Philippians 2:6–11 is not content with the simple affirmation that these verses have a poetic form and thus can be categorized among the Christological hymns of the New Testament. A commentator on Paul's letter to the Philippians also wants to relate this hymnody to Paul's relationship with the community at Philippi (the life situation that gave rise to the letter) and with the liturgy of the early Church (presumably the life situation that gave rise to the production of Christological hymns).

For an understanding of the New Testament, a study of tradition history is particularly important, since many of the passages are based on traditions that had been passed on orally for generations before they were set down in writing in their present gospel or epistolary form. Moreover the traditions passed along in this oral process often were translated from one language into another and transposed from one culture into another. These several factors suggest that the very medium in which the evangelical (and episto-lary) traditions were preserved is the vehicle by which they were molded and transformed. At the very least the critic must analyze the fact that traditions which once bore the mark of an independent literary type now exist as com-ponent parts of a larger work which has its own (complex) literary form.

It is, of course, true that the shaping and modification of many of the New Testament traditions took place within the requirements of a single oral or literary type, at least until such time as they were written down within the relatively complex structure of the written gospel or epistle. Yet the critic must deal with the possibility that some of the gospel traditions were trans-mitted over the course of time in more than one literary type. Perhaps they were adapted to changes in the life situation of the early Church. In short, the critic who approaches the New Testament from the standpoint of form analysis must ask whether some units of the material followed a course other than that normally followed by pieces of writing belonging to one specific lit-erary type.

When the same material appears at more than one stage in the total devel-opment of the gospel or epistolary development, a comparison of the various expressions of the tradition normally allows the critic to determine a devel-opment from an earlier to a later stage of the expression of a tradition. In this case irregularities in the expression of the tradition can serve as a start-ing point for the beginning of a history of tradition study. For example, a comparative study of the two Synoptic versions of the Parable of the Talents (Matt 25:14–30; Luke 19:11–27) reveals irregularities that are a good point of departure for tracing the tradition history of this parable. These provide an opening not only for a reconstruction of the transition from one form to an-other of the parable, but also for a reconstruction of a still earlier stage of the parable.

As a general rule it can also be noted that knowledge of the history of a literary type is often helpful in the reconstruction of the tradition history of a certain unit of New Testament material. Knowledge of the history of a liter-ary type often provides a head start for the tradition history study of a given unit of material. The course a particular tradition has taken in the process of being transmitted frequently corresponds to the general history of the literary type. This phenomenon is so common that the history of a given literary type is often a good starting point for the study of the history of a particular tra-dition.

The Author's Purpose

The student of the New Testament who approaches its several works from a form-critical point of view normally has several interrelated goals in mind. First of all, he or she will certainly effect an analysis of the text under con-sideration in order to determine its form and assign it to a certain literary type. The determination of the literary type will call for some consideration of the life situation from which it arose. Then, since some time must have elapsed between the life and ministry of Jesus, and the incorporation of traditions about him in either a canonical gospel or epistle, the analyst will try to determine something of the history of tradition of the material which he or she is studying.

The form critic will not, however, fail to say something about the author's purpose. Normally a writer's purpose determines his or her choice of a particular literary form. A joke is told in order to amuse and provoke laughter, while a sermon is given in order to bring about conversion and change of heart. One will write an editorial to comment on the political scene, and a recipe to convey instructions on cooking. Thus the determination of the literary form (type) of written material normally allows the form critic to determine the purpose of the author who chose to write according to the canons of a particular literary type. The writer is presumed to have chosen a historical form to convey facts; an author is thought to have chosen a poetical form to elicit an aesthetic response.

At this point a note of caution, whose import should not be exaggerated, is in order. Knowledge of the literary form allows the critic to determine an author's purpose; it does not allow the critic to know with certainty whether the author accomplished that purpose, nor does it allow the critic to know with certainty whether the author was correctly representing the facts as a modern historian would describe them. From the mere fact that a joke was told one cannot conclude that people laughed. A passport is issued with its distinctive "literary" form because the issuer wants whoever sees it to believe that such and such an individual exists, even if the bearer should not exist exactly as described. Nonetheless one normally expects that a validly issued passport attests to the existence of a historical individual. There are, however, some literary forms that are fundamentally indifferent to history—the joke and poetry, to cite but two examples.

The form critic studies the text at hand in order to learn the author's purpose. In some senses the purpose is implicit in the choice of a form. Yet the critic cannot go beyond the indication of purpose conveyed by the discernment of the form. For the critic to postulate the existence or nonexistence of historical fact when the text at hand is not written in historical form is to go beyond the possibilities inherent in the historical-critical method. The awareness that there is a relationship between literary type and purpose surely should allow us to conclude that if an author, ancient or modern, wanted to write history he would have chosen to write in the historical form. If he chose another form, it was because he had some other purpose in mind.

II. THE USE OF FORM CRITICISM IN NEW TESTAMENT STUDIES

Although we have thus far used the newspaper in order to focus on some basic aspects of form criticism, it must be acknowledged that New Testament form criticism primarily considers not the whole work but the small units of material that have been gathered together in the composition of our gospels and epistles. I have nonetheless cited the daily newspaper not only because it is analogous to the gospel in that each is a complex literary type, but also because the reading of the daily newspaper is so much a part of our common experience. Nevertheless the implicit use of the basic principles of form criticism is essential to the proper understanding of the newspaper

When now we concentrate our attention more specifically on the form-critical study of the New Testament, we find that it essentially includes five tasks: (1) identifying and analyzing the pericopes; (2) categorizing these pericopes according to their literary type; (3) relating a pericope to its corresponding life situation; (4) studying the tradition history of the pericope; (5) determining the purpose appropriate to the formulation and transmission of the pericope.

When New Testament form criticism is analyzed in this fashion, it is immediately apparent why the principal form-critical studies have had the Gospels as their focus. First of all, the scholarship of the churches has, throughout the centuries, focused preeminently on the Gospel stories about Jesus of Nazareth. Second, the identification of individual units of material (pericopes) within the Gospels is a much easier task than is the identification of isolatable and self-coherent units of Pauline material. Even the typical Sunday worshipper is well aware that each of the Gospel stories (e.g., the Healing of the Demoniac in the Synagogue, Mark 1:23–28; Luke 4:33–37) is a self-contained unit of material, which is more or less readily understandable of itself. On the other hand, the division of any one of Paul's letters is a task to which all commentators devote their energies, though often without reaching any substantial agreement among themselves. Moreover, the Sunday worshipper often experiences the second of the readings (usually taken from Paul's epistles) as something torn from its proper context. Third, a relatively large amount of time elapsed between the Death-Resurrection of Jesus and the composition of the Gospels, whereas the epistles were written soon after the occurrence of the situation to which they make reference. Today it is generally estimated—the opinions as to a shorter length of time expressed by John A. T. Robinson in *Redating the New Testament* remaining a notable exception—that the canonical Gospels were composed forty to sixty-five years after the death of Jesus. Every commentator on the Gospels is therefore bound to explain the transmission history of the Gospel material.

Finally, the Gospels are particularly susceptible to form-critical analysis insofar as there is a fair amount of comparative material available for study. Extensive comparative material is not so readily available for the epistles, each of which was written for a particular occasion, an occasion to which the individual epistle remains as the primary, if not always the exclusive, witness. For Gospel study, however, there is the possibility of comparing the Gospel stories among themselves; of comparing the tradition of Jesus' sayings with those in the Gospel of Thomas as well as with the sayings of rabbis; of comparing the stories of Jesus' miracles with the tales told about the won-

171

ders performed by rabbis and Hellenistic miracle workers; and of comparing the Gospel material with the life situation of the early churches insofar as this is reflected in Acts and the epistles. Thus the Gospels have proven to be a most fruitful soil for form-critical analysis, whereas the other twenty-three books in the New Testament have been subjected to a much less rigorous analysis of form.

The Synoptics

An examination of the form-critical approach to the Synoptics quickly reveals that there is no single work which emerges as the *facile princeps*. There are not one but three pace-setting works of Synoptic form analysis. The three were published within a remarkably short period of time immediately after the First World War. These are *The Framework of the History of Jesus* (*Der Rahmen der Geschichte Jesu,* 1919) by Karl Ludwig Schmidt; *From Tradition to Gospel** (*Die Formgeschichte des Evangeliums,* 1919) by Martin Dibelius; and *The History of the Synoptic Tradition** (*Die Geschichte der Synoptischen Tradition,* 1921) by Rudolf Bultmann. Together these three authors left a common legacy to students of the New Testament, yet they worked independently of one another. An assessment of the work of his two predecessors was offered by Bultmann in the introduction to his own volume:

> A start has already been made with this work. The distinction of traditional from editorial material is the real subject of K. L. Schmidt's *Der Rahmen der Geschichte Jesu* (1919). His work is a thoroughgoing and conclusive discussion of the early position especially Spitta's ingenious but misleading suggestions. But more than anybody else, M. Dibelius in his *Formgeschichte des Evangeliums* (1919) has subjected the different units of the Gospel tradition to form-criticial inquiry. Admittedly, he has not examined the whole content of the Gospel material, but has contented himself with certain types of material essentially narrative, and brilliantly shown how fruitful the method is for discovering the stages in the development of the tradition as well as for the Gospels as a whole. (*The History of the Synoptic Tradition,* p. 3)

Karl Ludwig Schmidt

As Bultmann has stated, Schmidt's fundamental insight was the distinction between tradition and redaction. He showed that the earliest transmission of the tradition about Jesus was in the form of individual pericopes—short, independent narratives and sayings. These were transmitted within Christian communities irrespective of their connection one with another, and often without any specific chronological or topographical setting. To understand the Gospels, one must look beyond the documentary sources on which they are based to the individual oral reports from which they ultimately sprang. The Gospel pericopes were a sort of popular narrative which a collector brought together, providing each narrative or group of narratives with a "frame." The topographically located and chronologically situated narrative that emerged as a result actually reflects a framework that was imposed on the individual units of material. Accordingly it is impossible to use the Gospels for writing a life of Jesus that could be situated in space and time.

For Schmidt, the life situation within which this process of oral transmission preeminently took place was the worship of the early Christian community. To wit, "In the assemblies of the Christian community for public worship, and in the assemblies which the missionary arranged for the purpose of winning new Christians, the self-contained reports of individual acts or words of Jesus played a role. In this connection the two kinds of assemblies did not need to be strictly distinguished from one another. . . ." The earliest transmitters of the Gospel pericopes were not so much interested in the possible interconnection among their stories as they were in the requirements of Church worship. In a word, we must look beyond the documentary form of the Gospel to a transmission of the Gospel material whose life situation and primary purpose was the cult of the Church.

An exception must be made for the Passion narrative, whose general story admits of a logical and coherent quality not found in a collection of pericopes that have been loosely knitted together. Within the Passion, one thing leads to another with a compelling necessity and logic. Neither cult nor apologetics dominates the narrative as a whole. Chronological and topographical details are inherent to the Passion narrative, whose traditional unity is maintained within each of the Gospels.

Martin Dibelius

As did Schmidt, Dibelius maintained the notion of the relative self-sufficiency of the Passion narrative, into which widely varied interests have entered. For Dibelius the Passion story was immediately connected with Christian preaching. In his words, "we must presuppose the early existence of a Passion narrative complete in itself since preaching, whether for the purpose of the mission or of worship, required some such a text."

The needs of preaching also determined the development of the narrative type which Dibelius called the paradigm. Defined, the type is a short illustrative notice or story of an event, not more descriptive than is necessary to make the point for the sake of which it is introduced. Dibelius believed that he could isolate eight examples of the paradigm in "noteworthy purity": the Healing of the Paralytic (Mark 2:1–12); the Question about Fasting (Mark 2:18–19); Plucking Grain on the Sabbath (Mark 2:23–28); the Man with the Withered Hand (Mark 3:1–6); the Relatives of Jesus (Mark 3:20–21, 30–35); Jesus Blesses the Children (Mark 10:13–16); On Paying Tribute to Caesar (Mark 12:13–17); and the Anointing in Bethany (Mark 14:3–9). Although one should recognize the conservative character of the paradigms, their real intent is didactic. For purposes of analysis the principal characteristics of a paradigm are as follows: (1) isolation, characterized by an external rounding off; (2) the brevity and simplicity of the narrative; (3) the coloring of the narrative in a thoroughly religious (realistic unwordly) manner; (4) a climax and conclusion with a word of Jesus; (5) the ending of the narrative in a way thought useful for preaching purposes (a general phrase or an exemplary act of Jesus, or, finally, an exclamation of the onlookers praising the act). For Dibelius the preacher is one who hands down and reports; the paradigm he uses is a short narrative whose climax is a striking saying of Jesus.

From the paradigm, Dibelius distinguished the tale (*Novelle*) which had an essentially secular function. Dibelius was skeptical about the historical significance of the tale. He noted that the basic Christian source documents do not speak of the tellers of tales, and suggested that non-Christian stories often served as the basis of tales. Nonetheless Dibelius opted for some historical foundation of those tales whose basis was a paradigm. Among the characteristics of the tale identified by Dibelius were: (1) the living realism of the narrative; (2) the lack of devotional motifs and the gradual retreat of any words of Jesus of general value; (3) Jesus the thaumaturge, a worker of wonders, as object of the tale; (4) a literary style. Indeed, Dibelius considered that in the tale's telling of the miracles of Jesus one can discern a schema common to all miracle narratives, focusing upon the history of the illness, the technique of the miracle, and the success of the miraculous act. Dibelius recognized nine Markan narratives as belonging to the category of the tale: the Cleansing of the Leper (Mark 1:40–45); the Stilling of the Storm (Mark 4:35–41); the Gerasene Demoniac (Mark 5:1–20); Jairus' Daughter and the Woman with a Hemorrhage (Mark 5:21–43); Five Thousand Are Fed (Mark 6:35–44); the Walking on the Water (Mark 5:45–52); Jesus Heals a Deaf Mute and Many Others (Mark 7:32–37); a Blind Man Is Healed at Bethsaida (Mark 8:22–26); and Jesus Heals a Boy Possessed by a Spirit (Mark 9:14–29).

If tales have to do with miracles, and paradigms with the message, legends (a technical term whose use does not raise the question of historicity) are religious narratives whose interest is the works and fate of a saintly person. They are typically related to secondary things and persons, and are only slightly related to preaching as such. In contrast, words of Jesus with halakic content are connected with Christian preaching. Tales and legends are met in extrabiblical literature, but, according to Dibelius, there is no known parallel to the paradigm outside the New Testament. In any event, the literary understanding of the Synoptic Gospels begins, for Dibelius, with the recognition that the Gospels are collections of material. The authors of the Gospels are collectors of this material, rather than authors in the normal understanding of the term. The evangelists chose, limited, and finally shaped the material incorporated into their respective Gospels, but the original molding of the material took place in the anonymity of tradition. Thus, with respect to the historcity of the Gospel material, the crucial issue is not so much the knowledge of the evangelists, but the knowledge of those who gave the tradition its form.

Rudolf Bultmann

Although Bultmann's work was published after that of Dibelius, it was substantially ready prior to the publication of the volumes by Schmidt and Dibelius. All three authors share the conviction that the tradition originally comprised only independent units of material. Bultmann's interest lay principally in the history of these individual units of tradition. The aim of form criticism, he wrote, "is to determine the original form of a piece of narrative, a dominical saying or a parable. In the process we learn to distinguish secondary additions and forms. . . ." He claimed that the rigorous pursuit of tradition history was one of the features by which his own work was distinguished from that of Dibelius. In this respect, Bultmann drew much insight from the use of comparative material coming from a study of the history of religions. His comparative work shed much light on the formation of the Synoptic material, but Bultmann attributed a very strong part in the formulation and embellishment of the Gospel material to the creativity of the early Church. Indeed, he thought that the gospel, as a complex literary type created by Mark, had its roots in the preaching, *kerygma,* and teaching, *didache,* of the Hellenistic church.

Bultmann also claimed that he differed from Dibelius in that he had examined the Gospel tradition more extensively. Bultmann's description of the so-called apothegms, with an economic description of the situation and an emphasis on the sayings of Jesus, did not substantially differ from that of Dibelius' description of paradigms except insofar as Bultmann identified a variety of motifs leading up to the climactic logion. Accordingly Bultmann divided his apothegms into controversy dialogues (e.g., Mark 7:1–23), scholastic dialogues (e.g., Mark 10:17–31), and biographical apothegms (e.g., Mark 10:13–16). Bultmann subsequently examined the sayings of Jesus at length. This study is an interesting part of Bultmann's work, since the dominical logia receive an emphasis not found in the work of either of Bultmann's predecessors. He notes: "The dominical sayings can be divided into three main groups, according to their actual content, though formal differences are involved as well: (1) Sayings, or Logia in the narrower sense, Wisdom-sayings; (2) Prophetic and Apocalyptic Sayings; (3) Laws and community regulations." Adjunct treatment is given to the I-sayings and the parables of Jesus, which are then assigned to one of the three main groupings by reason of their content. Although Bultmann made this division, and offered useful further subdivisions—e.g., the division of the Wisdom-sayings into principles (declaratory form), exhortations (imperative form), questions (interrogative form)—it is precisely at this point that his use of form-critical methodology becomes muddled. Criteria related to content supersede those related to form. The result is an unsound mixture of division according to form and division according to content.

A confusion in the categorization of the Gospel material on the basis of form and content is also to be seen in Bultmann's treatment of the miracles, among which he immediately distinguishes miracles of healing from nature miracles. Here also, Bultmann's citation of extrabiblical parallels is illuminating. Bultmann was not able to cite such parallels in his examination of the Passion narrative; nevertheless, he concluded that the Passion narrative as it is found in the Synoptics is not a unitary composition. He identified traits which he categorized as proof from prophecy and as apologetic, novelistic, and dogmatic motifs, and once again urged the creativity of the community and the influence of Christian worship. In a word, not only did Bultmann examine the totality of the Synoptic Gospels in contrast to Dibelius' more restricted study, he also took issue, explicitly and strongly, with Dibelius' conclusions about the essentially conservative nature of the paradigm-apothegm. For Bultmann, not only in the Passion narrative but throughout the Gospels, apologetics and polemics, concerns for the strengthening of the Church and its discipline, as well as scribal activity all have a role to play as component forces in the Church's creativity.

Vincent Taylor

The use of form-critical methodology was accepted only slowly in Roman Catholic circles, which were wary of the notion that the Gospels could be, to such a large extent, the products of the religious imagination of first-century Christians. Moreover, the methodology was not readily accepted in Anglo-Saxon circles whose nineteenth-century forebears had shown themselves quite as much in favor of a scientific methodology but by no means as radical in their critical stance as their German-language counterparts. The same type of option for scientific method within the context of moderate criticism was experienced in the British reaction to the form-critical method. By the time Vincent Taylor published his magisterial commentary on *The Gospel According to St. Mark* (1952), he was able to affirm with full confidence that "The material contained in Mark is of different kinds. The distinction between narratives and sayings, while primary, is not sufficient to cover the variety of the material, and a more detailed description must be attempted." Unfortunately Taylor did not systematically introduce further formal distinctions into his analysis of the discourse material other than "sayings and parables." In this respect Taylor's quest for sources deterred him from a formal analysis of the logia tradition. With respect to the Markan narrative material, however, Taylor did offer a further classification that has enjoyed marked success among Anglo-Saxon exegetes. He distinguished among: (1) the pronouncement stories; (2) the miracle stories; (3) stories about Jesus; (4) Markan constructions; and (5) summary statements.

Taylor's "pronouncement story" (use of this terminology is Taylor's gift to the English-language exegetical community) roughly corresponds to the paradigm-apothegm identified by Dibelius and Bultmann. Although Taylor recognized that form-critical analysis had enjoyed considerable success with respect to the identification of form, life situation, and purpose of the pronouncement story, he held it "not wise to limit the formative influences to which they owe their peculiar character to preaching [thus Dibelius] or to discussions within the community [thus Bultmann]." The pronouncement story, tailored to focus interest and attention on the sayings of Jesus, reflected the catechetical interest of the early Church. In all, Taylor identified some nineteen or twenty examples of the literary type (Mark 2:5–10a, 16–17, 18–20, 23–26; 3:1–6, 22–26, 31–35; 7:1–8, 9–13; 9:38–39; 10:1–9, 13–16; 11:27–33; 12:13–17, 18–27, 28–34, 35–37, 41–44; 13:1–2).

Miracle Stories

In contrast, "miracle stories" are those whose main interest lies in the account of the miracle itself. Taylor acknowledged Mark's use of the traditional threefold form, but noted that the Markan accounts have additional details that must have been conveyed to the evangelist in a more personal fashion. For Taylor, Mark contains some seventeen miracle stories, several of which are gathered together in little groups (Mark 1:23–28, 29–31, 32–34, 40–45; 2:1–4 ((+10b–12)); 4:35–41; 5:1–20, 21–24 ((+35–43)), 25–34; 6:35–44, 45–52; 7:31–37; 8:1–10, 22–26; 9:14–27; 10:46–52; 11:12–14 ((+20–22)). The "stories about Jesus" roughly correspond to the legends, but Taylor avoids the language of legend as he does that of myth because of the tendentious interpretation implicit in the use of such terminology. For Taylor, the traditional stories about Jesus, vivid and colorful in character, are to be judged in accordance with the usual principles of historical criticism. He identified twenty-nine stories of Jesus in Mark, including twelve within the Passion narrative. The accounts of the Baptism of Jesus (Mark 1:9–11), Peter's Confession (8:27–33), the Transfiguration (9:2–10), the Last Supper (14:22–25), and the Crucifixion (15:21–41) are a few examples of the stories about Jesus cited by Taylor.

The pericopes which Taylor categorized as "Markan constructions" did not come to the evangelist as self-contained, coherent units of tradition. They contain tradition, to be sure, but the narratives themselves are constructed. Such sayings as these pericopes contain have a narrative interest and a religious purpose. Taylor has identified eighteen Markan constructions, including the Choosing of the Twelve (Mark 3:13–19a), the Reason for Speaking in Parables (4:10–12), the Leaven of the Pharisees (8:14–21), and the Betrayal by Judas (14:10–11). Taylor has identified a fifth category of material, which he has distinguished from the narrative pericopes because the pericopes belonging to this fifth category do not describe an individual occurrence. The fifth category consists of the "summary statements" (*Sammelberichte*), which describe activity over a period of time and give an outline to the course of events. The summary statements occasionally include topographical references to such places as Capernaum, Jericho, and Jerusalem. It would appear that the summary statements which abound in Mark are traditional in character. Two of the most important are the Ministry in Galilee (Mark 1:14–15), and Jesus Heals Multitudes by the Sea (3:7–12).

From this overview, it appears that not every evangelical pericope which features a mention of the miracles of Jesus can be described as a miracle story. Mention of miracles can be found in pronouncement stories where the performance of the miracle introduces a pregnant Jesuanic logion (e.g., the Man with the Withered Hand, Mark 3:1–6). The mention of Jesus' miracles is quite common in the summary statements (e.g., Jesus Heals Multitudes by the Sea, Mark 3:7–12). In such cases, the account of the miracles in themselves is not the main focus of interest. When, however, the evanglist's interest does focus on the miracle itself, he makes use of the literary form of the miracle story. The miracle story contains typical style characteristics, and follows a threefold outline: (1) the problem: the circumstances of the miracle; (2) the solution: the miracle itself; (3) the result: the effect of the miracle.

In the miracle story, the circumstances are presented in such a way as to highlight the difficulty of the miracle. The power of the thaumaturge is magnified to the extent that the miracle is difficult. To highlight the difficulty of the miracle, the nature, length, and seriousness of the disease are frequently cited (Mark 5:3–5, 25; 9:21). Sometimes mention is made of the inability of doctors and thaumaturges to effect the cure (Mark 5:26; 9:18). Often the miracle worker is derided and treated with scorn (Mark 5:40). Sometimes the miracle worker must even resort to various manipulative gestures in order to produce the healing effect (Mark 7:33; 8:25). Even the physical distance that separates the miracle worker from the one to be cured can be identified as a trait that underscores the gravity of the situation (e.g., Matt 8:6). Indeed, Mark artlessly describes Jesus as being asleep at the moment when the boat was being inundated at sea (Mark 4:38).

The miracle itself is described in ritualistic fashion. Indeed, the language of ritual so dominates the actual description of the miracle that one might legitimately speak of the rite of miracle. The encounter between a person to be healed and the thaumaturge is presented in solemn fashion (e.g., Mark 1:40). The "rite" itself consists of a stylized gesture (e.g., touching the eyes and tongue, Mark 7:33) and a stereotyped, authoritative utterance (e.g., the commands of Mark 5:8; 9:25). In the Markan miracle stories the stylized gesture sometimes features the use of spittle, to which ancients attributed extrahuman power (e.g., 7:33). In Mark's description of Jesus' utterance, the retention of Aramaic words gives the impression of the use of esoteric, power-bearing language (5:41; 7:34). After the rite is completed, there is a dismissal which includes good wishes (e.g., Mark 5:34), a word of encouragement (e.g., Mark 6:50; Matt 9:22; 14:27), or—in the Gospel miracle stories—a statement about faith (e.g., Mark 5:34; Matt 8:13). Sometimes an exorcism is cited as the content of a miracle story. In this case the "rite" typically features a struggle between the exorcist and the demon (e.g., the "name-calling" of Mark 1:24) and the reluctance of the demon to leave the possessed individual (e.g., Mark 5:10–11).

Finally the effect of the miracle is described. Sometimes this element of the miracle story focuses upon the one cured (or the situation righted); sometimes it focuses upon the reaction of the crowd; sometimes it focuses on both the beneficiary and the bystanders. An example of the latter is to be seen in the Markan account of the Stilling of the Storm (4:35–41), where it is written that "the wind ceased, and there was a great calm" (4:39b) and that "they were filled with awe, and said to one another, 'Who is this, that even wind and sea obey him?'" (4:41). When the description of the effect of the miracle focuses upon the beneficiary, the story frequently indicates that the cured individual is restored to normal activity (e.g., "immediately the girl got up and walked" and he "told them to give her something to eat." Mark 5:42–43). When the narration focuses upon the bystanders, the story frequently includes a "choral response" (e.g., "They were astonished beyond measure, saying, 'He has done all things well; he even makes the deaf hear and the dumb speak.'" Mark 7:37).

This analysis of the form of a miracle story shows how structure, style, themes, and characteristic vocabulary coalesce so as to create the profile of this particular literary type. Characteristics of the type will be recognized even in very short miracle stories, as, for example, the Healing of Peter's Mother-in-Law (Mark 1:29–31; Matt 8:14–15; Luke 4:38–39). A similar analysis of discourse material and other narrative material in the Gospels could just as easily be made.

Other Literary Types

Within the narrative sections of the Gospels, it is the account of the Public Ministry of Jesus and the story of his Passion-Death-Resurrection that lend themselves most readily to form-critical analysis. New Testament and extrabiblical parallels enhance the analysis by the provision of extensive quantities of comparative material. On the other hand, each of the Infancy narratives in the Synoptics (Matt 1 – 2; Luke 1:5 – 2:52) is an entity unique unto itself. The Matthean and Lucan accounts agree among themselves only with respect to a minimal amount of data. Nevertheless, the study of the Infancy narratives has been exceptionally advanced as a result of form-critical analysis. An in-depth analysis of the several literary types pertinent to the study of the Infancy narratives would take us far beyond the scope of this Introduction. Yet mention should be made of the importance of the recognition of such literary types as the birth announcement, midrash, and the genealogy in the first chapters of Matthew and Luke.

Birth announcements, stereotyped in form, were not unknown to the biblical tradition. According to an analysis undertaken by Raymond Brown, they follow a five-step schema: (1) the appearance of an angel of the Lord; (2) fear or prostration of the visionary confronted by the supernatural presence; (3) the divine message; (4) an objection by the visionary as to how this can be (a request for a sign); and (5) the giving of the sign to reassure the visionary. In the New Testament narratives, the birth announcements for John (Luke 1:11–20) and Jesus (Luke 1:26–37; and, in abbreviated form, Mat' 1:20–21) basically follow this outline. In the Old Testament, the form was used for the births of Ishmael (Gen 16:7–12), Isaac (Gen 17:1–21; 18:1–15), and Samson (Judg 13:2–21). For its part, midrash can be described but not defined, as the studies of Addison G. Wright, Renée Bloch, and Roger Le Déaut have shown. Basically midrash is a literature about a literature. For New Testament studies, the midrashic genre is typically a commentary on the Old Testament, whether implicit or explicit. Its purpose is to edify. It seeks, by meditation on the sacred text or an imaginative reconstruction thereof, to apply a past text to a new situation in order to answer a present question about what to believe or what to do (e.g., Matt 12:38–42; Luke 11:29–32). Much of the Synoptic Infancy narratives imply such a midrashic use of the Old Testament. The genealogical genre, especially as it is reflected in the Scriptures (OT and NT), has been studied extensively by Marshall D. Johnson and others. It appears that biblical genealogies are functional; they are closely attached to their immediate contexts in regard to language, structure, and ideology. Such is also the case for the genealogies found in Matthew 1 and Luke 3. They fall essentially into the category of midrash, with its homiletic and paraenetic function. In sum they present traditional theological motifs in historicized form.

If in-depth study of the narrative forms employed by the evangelists considerably elucidates the Gospel story, the parallel form-critical study of the teaching of Jesus yields no less impressive results. Among the traditional literary types employed by the evangelists in their presentation of discourse material would certainly be the beatitude and the parable. The function and tradition history of these literary types in the Gospels have been skillfully examined by Jacques Dupont and Joachim Jeremias respectively. Among the sayings of Jesus, it is furthermore possible to distinguish aphorisms and admonitions, for example. Such distinctions serve to underscore the fact that the form-critical analysis of the Gospel material has concerned itself not only with the larger units of material such as the miracle stories, but also with smaller units such as the individual sayings of Jesus, which were transmitted by the oral tradition of the early Church and which occasionally received documentary form (e.g., the Sayings in Q) before being incorporated into the Gospel. Frequently these sayings of Jesus are akin, in both form and content, to Jewish and Hellenistic wisdom and prophetic, apocalyptic, and legal traditions. This kinship facilitates the task of analyzing and classifying the sayings of Jesus. It also helps the form critic to relate the transmission of these sayings to a particular type of life situation within the Church, to trace their transmission history, and often to determine the traditional purpose of the sayings.

"The Historical Jesus"

To some extent the form critic who brings technique to bear upon the Gospels is also concerned with identifying which among the sayings of Jesus are not due to the creativity of the community, but rather represent the authentic sayings of Jesus. This is the quest for the so-called *ipsissima verba* (the very words) of Jesus. This aspect of the form-critical quest is really a matter of trying to relate the sayings of Jesus not only to the ecclesial life situation (the *Sitz-im-Leben der Kirche*)—that with which tradition history is primarily concerned—but also to the life situation of Jesus himself (the *Sitz-im-Leben Jesu*). Redaction criticism (see Chapter Six) will, in turn, focus its attention upon the relationship between these sayings of Jesus and their life situation within the Gospels (the *Sitz-im-Leben der Evangeliums*). Properly speaking, "life situation" (*Sitz-im-Leben*) is a generic sociological term; it is only by way of analogy that it can be used of the particular situation of Jesus or of one of the Gospels. Nevertheless the analogous use of the term has become commonplace in New Testament studies.

In view of the great importance attached to the community's role in the transmission of traditions about Jesus, form critics have perhaps erred by pushing a methodological skepticism to an extreme. They have attributed an originating *Sitz-im-Leben Jesu* to a narrative or logion tradition only when the origin of that tradition cannot plausibly be ascribed to another *Sitz-im-Leben*. The radicality of this methodology is primarily a legacy of Bultmann. Its principal criterion for historicity is the principle of dual irreducibility. A modified form of the principle is the index of discontinuity. According to the principle itself, historicity is inferred only when a Jesuanic tradition is discontinuous with both the tendencies of the community that transmitted it and the Jewish world within which Jesus lived and taught. This overarching principle in the form-critical approach to the Gospel narratives has been succinctly stated by Hans Conzelmann: "We may accept as authentic what cannot be slotted into Jewish thinking or into the viewpoints of the later church community." With respect to the application of this criterion, the Baptism of Jesus (Mark 1:9–11 and par.) has every right to be considered a unit of authentic tradition, since baptism of repentance was not a typical Jewish practice, and the Church, as the later Gospels show, was ill at ease with the tradition that Jesus had been baptized by John.

Of lesser importance than the principle of dual irreducibility (dual exclusion), are two other criteria, each of which operates in a more positive sense: the principle of the cross section, and the principle of consistency of content. The principle of the cross section actually includes two subcategories: the index of multiple attestation and the index of multiform attestation. Traditions about Jesus lay greater claim to a judgment of authenticity to the extent that they are attested by material incorporated into the Gospels from different sources, and are formulated according to different literary types. The exorcisms of Jesus, for example, are cited in three of the four principal source documents for the Synoptics: Mark (Mark 1:21–28), Q (Luke 11:19 par. Matt 12:27), and Luke (Luke 13:32). Exorcisms are mentioned in pronouncement stories (e.g., Matt 12:22–30), miracle stories (Mark 5:1–20), stories about Jesus (e.g., Mark 3:19b–22), summary statements (e.g., Mark 1:39), and even in an isolated logion (e.g., Mark 3:23). Thus even the most skeptical critic can hardly deny that Jesus was an exorcist.

The principle of consistency of content basically implies that critically reconstructed details which cohere with the historically reliable picture of Jesus, established on other grounds, can be reasonably assumed to be historically authentic. Used with discretion so as to avoid circularity of argumentation, the principle can also be divided into two subcategories: the correlation between Jesus' actions and his words, and the correlation between Jesus' words and his actions.

Norman Perrin, late professor of New Testament at the University of Chicago, rigorously applied these three principles—the principles of dual irreducibility, cross section, and consistency of content—in his study of the Synoptic Gospels. Other scholars are more moderate in their application of the principles. For these men and women, satisfaction of the criteria favors the historicity of a tradition; the mere fact that the criteria are not satisfied does not warrant *ipso facto* a verdict of nonauthenticity. After all, Jesus was a first-century Jew. As such he had to employ the oral forms of his culture. Thus, moderate form critics are more comfortable with the language of indices of historicity than they are with the harsh-sounding language of criteria of historicity. In addition, these more moderate critics would cite among the the indices of historicity the originality of idiom (Jesus' use of *abba* in prayer, for example), resistive form (the parables, as distinct from exemplary stories, for example), and Aramaic substratum (as in Mark 8:33, for example).

The Johannine Corpus

The presence of miracle stories in the Fourth Gospel is immediately recognized by everyone who reads John. Some of these have a literary form quite similar to those of the Synoptic Gospels (especially the Centurion of Capernaum, John 4:46b–54; the Healing at the Pool, John 5:2–9a; Five Thousand Are Fed, John 6:1–15; and Jesus Heals the Man Born Blind, John 9:1–7). An occasional Synoptic-like saying (e.g., John 3:5) is also to be discerned among the many sayings John has included in his well-elaborated discourses. Apart from these similarities, the Fourth Gospel seems to be a unique composition whose several pericopes are not so easily typed. An exception must be made, however, for the Farewell Discourse John 13–17.

About fifty examples of pieces of literature belonging to the farewell dis-

182

course genre have been identified thus far. Although some of them are to be found in the Old Testament (Gen 47 – 50, Josh 23 – 24, Tob 14, 1 Sam 12, 1 Kgs 2, 1 Mac 2), the majority date from inter- and neo-testamental times. Characteristically, the farewell discourse features a departing person—David in 1 Kings 2, Jesus in John 13 – 14—who bids adieu to his friends. He recalls the past, exhorts his friends to be faithful, and voices predictions about the future. The departing hero frequently makes provision for his successor and prays for the circle of his friends, whom he might bless. Sometimes the farewell discourse also addresses itself to the future burial of the hero. Frequently the literary context provided for the farewell discourse is that of a meal, in which the hero and his friends take part.

The characteristics of the genre, identified by Ethelbert Stauffer, Johannes Munck, John Randall, and others who have studied it, are to be found in John 13 – 14 and 15 – 16, each of which units is to be identified as a farewell discourse. It is the use of this genre by the author of the Fourth Gospel that has prompted the appearance in John 13 – 16 of such motifs as the departure of Jesus, the unity of his disciples, the preservation of his teaching, the gift of his Spirit, etc., but the precise formulation of these motifs bears the mark of Johannine theology.

Students of the genre have not only been able to identify its use in a body of Jewish literary documents whose composition spans almost an entire millennium, but have also noted that tradition history points to an evolution of the genre. Thus the recollection of past events, a traditional trait of the genre, has given way to an extensive reminder of the personal example of the hero. The exhortation to be faithful to the Law has been replaced by an evolved motif, namely an exhortation to be faithful to what the departing person has taught. The presence of the derived form of these traits is easily discernible in some of the other New Testament examples of the farewell discourse, especially Acts 20:18–35, 2 Timothy 2 – 4, 1 Timothy 4.

For the rest, it should be noted that the farewell discourse bears all the characteristics of a literary composition. The farewell discourse reflects the theology and the language of its literary creator rather than the thought and vocabulary of the departing person himself. Thus it can be said that farewell discourses are essentially pseudepigraphical—that is, bearing the name of someone other than the one who actually composed them. In the New Testament additional examples of the genre are 2 Peter, Luke 22:21–38, and Matthew 28:19–20. Although several parts of the New Testament can be identified as belonging to the farewell discourse genre, most extant examples are to be found in the so-called intertestamental literature, especially the *Testaments of the Twelve Patriarchs* and the book of *Jubilees*.

In regard to the form-critical analysis of the Fourth Gospel, a summary overview was provided by Octave Merlier in a 1961 study, *The Fourth Gospel: The Johannine Question* (*Le Quatrième Évangile: La Question johannique*). Merlier distinguished between the narrative and the discourse material—a somewhat elementary and superficial distinction which, although necessary, has been overworked by exegetes. Within the narrative material he distinguished "Johannine" narratives (e.g., the Raising of Lazarus, John 11), purely narrative stories (e.g., the Marriage at Cana, John 2:1–11), and Synoptic stories (e.g., the Anointing at Bethany, John 12:1–8). Within the discourse material, Merlier distinguished dialogues (e.g., John 3), discourses with a minimum of introduction (e.g., John 7:14–38), farewell discourses (John 13 – 17), "Fragments" of discourses (e.g., John 1:35–51), and logia grouped without any apparent unity (e.g., John 3:11–21, 31–36). Merlier has been justly criticized for basing his analysis of the narrative material too exclusively upon the Synoptic division and for neglecting the unity of vocabulary and style that pervades all "forms" of Johannine discourse. Thus one is led to question whether a form-critical analysis of John will yield insightful results similar to those which arose from the form analysis of the Synoptics.

To be sure, there are characteristic elements of Johannine style, such as the little revelation formula isolated by Michel de Goedt in John 1:29–34, 47–51; 19:24b–27. The formula has this characteristic schema: A messenger of God . . . sees . . . a person (whose name is given) . . . and says . . . (a designation which reveals the person's mission or destiny). Since this formula is characterized by typically Johannine language, and since it does not appear to be attested extrabiblically, it would seem better to identify it as an element of Johannine style. Although different passages written by a single author may indicate that he or she has struck characteristic formulas, it is better to reserve the language of literary form, type, and genre to material whose essential form is found in more than one author. Within the limits of a form-critical discussion thus restricted, it seems that John offers much material for redaction critical study (such as the Johannine *paroimia*—a parable for which John uses distinct nomenclature—"I am" sayings, Paraclete sayings, etc.), but much less material for a study that can be called form criticism in the strictest sense of the term.

Revelation

When one's attention turns from a consideration of John to the last book in the Johannine corpus, Revelation, one enters into a rather different world, the world of apocalyptic. Among scholars there is considerable discussion as to whether "apocalyptic" properly describes a literary genre. From one vantage point there is a discussion about whether "apocalyptic" is more appropriate to a point of view or to a literary genre. Does it, in other words, describe a current of thought or a manner of writing? From another vantage point, there is, among authors who accept the idea that apocalyptic is an appropriate literary term, a discussion as to whether apocalyptic constitutes a distinct literary genre. Does it describe one well-determined literary genre or does it simply use and adopt several older traditional genres, especially those pertaining to prophecy?

Inclined to the view that "apocalyptic" identifies a genre, D. S. Russell has identified four characteristics of the genre. First, it is esoteric in character. It makes use of stereotyped language that describes the turmoil of the seer at the time of his vision, such as the language of rapture (e.g., Rev 4:2) and the vision of heavenly tablets or books (e.g., Rev 5:1). Second, it is literary in form. As a literary genre, apocalyptic literature makes use of traditional material. In effect, this feature specifies apocalyptic as a complex literary genre. For example, about 70 percent of Revelation is derived from previously written sources—the letters to the churches (Rev 2–3), the Old Testament (to which reference is made in 278 of Revelation's 404 verses), and so forth. Third, apocalyptic is characterized by the use of symbolism and mythical images. Conventional symbols abound in apocalyptic literature— numbers, names, fantastic beasts. Angels, demons, and cosmic upheavals are the material of which apocalyptic drama is woven. Indeed, it can be said that the symbolism of apocalyptic is stereotyped insofar as the same symbols, albeit sometimes with different meanings, appear in virtually all apocalyptic literature. In specific reference to Revelation, one must note the frequent use of Old Testament symbols (such as the sharp sword as a symbol of God's word, Rev 1:16), with an occasional use of the traditional mythical symbols (such as the scroll of Rev 5:1; the serpent of Rev 12:9). Fourth, apocalyptic literature is pseudonymous in authorship. With the exception of the author of Revelation, the authors of apocalyptic stand behind some ancient worthy or man of God. The phenomenon of pseudonymity is highlighted by rapture, vision, and dream motifs. Frequently the choice of the patronym indicates the subject matter of the apocalyptic work as well as the particular author's specific point of view.

To these four basic traits of apocalyptic, one could add the systematic presentation of apocalyptic literature. The discourse cycles (visions) of Revelation are a typical expression of this characteristic. In Revelation 5–17, for example, the seven seals give way to the seven angels with their trumpets, a series of visions that give way in turn to the vision of the seven angels with their bowls. In *The Rediscovery of Apocalyptic,* Klaus Koch has identified paraenetic discourse as still another characteristic of apocalyptic. This feature focuses on an eschatological ethic. It might take the form of an introductory legend which illustrates correct behavior. In the Johannine Revelation, this trait is essentially fulfilled by the letters to the seven churches.

Beyond these formal traits of the apocalyptic genre, it should be noted that apocalyptic generally presents a dualistic *Weltanschauung.* Its systematic structuration and use of symbolic numbers often bespeak a belief that the eras of history are predetermined, the end is at hand, and God's purpose will be effected, no matter what the odds. Ultimately apocalyptic serves as a form of consolation for the oppressed. It buoys up their hope in the inevitable victory of the Reign of God. This apocalyptic point of view is expressed in a wide range of literature in addition to Revelation. The Shepherd of Hermas, the Apocalypse of Peter, the Apocalypse of Paul, 5 Ezra and 6 Ezra are a few of the Christian writings that belong to the apocalyptic genre. There are also a number of Jewish works, dating especially from 150 B.C. to A.D. 150, which can be identified as apocalyptic. The biblical example of Dan is well known. Among the better-known Jewish examples of apocalyptic literature are Jubilees, the Sibylline Oracles, the Psalms of Solomon, the Assumption of Moses, 2 Ezra (= 4 Ezra) and more than a dozen works from the Essene library at Qumran, including 1QM (the War Scroll), and an Angelic Liturgy.

The Epistles and the Acts of the Apostles

It is easy to speak of the apocalyptic genre when one is dealing with an entire book like Revelation. It is also possible to speak of a Markan apocalypse in regard to Mark 13 (cf. Matt 24; Luke 21). In Mark 13 the student of the New Testament is dealing with a well-determined literary unit whose characteristic literary traits qualify it for categorization as a piece of apocalyptic literature. When we look to the epistles, however, it is difficult to isolate coherent, self-contained units that can be described as apocalyptic literature. Some exception might be made with respect to 1 Thessalonians 4:13–18; 5:1–11; and 2 Thessalonians 2:1–12, which are self-contained and somewhat isolable disclosures whose vocabulary and world view is basically apocalyptic in formulation. In regard to these "apocalyptic" sections of the Pauline letters, some careful distinctions must be drawn. It would appear that Paul made use of various apocalyptic motifs which he employed in order to express his own theological point of view. It is not a matter of Paul's having incorporated material whose essential shaping was determined beforehand; rather it is a matter of Paul's shaping his message in epistolary form, and expressing that message in language drawn from the world of apocalyptic. Similar remarks are to be made with regard to the liturgical traditions (hymns, greetings, etc.) of which Paul made use in the composition of his letters. Since Paul is clearly the author of these letters, consideration of Paul's use of traditional material might best be reserved for the following chapter. In this regard it should likewise be noted that Paul also made use of material drawn from the missionary sermons of the Jewish synagogues of the Diaspora (e.g., 1 Thes 1:9–10).

This is not to say, however, that Paul never incorporated preshaped material, characterized by its proper literary form, into his letters. Among the more important coherent and preformed units of tradition are the Christological hymns, to which reference was made in the previous chapter. With the exception of the hymn incorporated into Philippians 2:5–11, these hymns are largely found in the deutero-Pauline segment of the Pauline corpus (that is, in Col 1:15–20, Eph 2:14–16, 1 Tim 3:16, and Heb 1:3; cf. 1 Pet 3:18–22). It would also seem that Paul made use of elements of the homiletic benediction. The life situation of these blessings, similar to those uttered by the high priest in former times, would seem to have been some flexible part of early Christian worship—for example, the sermon. The six homiletic blessings in 1,2 Thessalonians (1 Thes 3:11, 12–13; 5:23; 2 Thes 2:16–17; 3:5, 6) identified by Robert Jewett are characterized by the use of a verb in the third person singular, the optative mood, the use of the connective de ("and"), a mention of the object expressed as the second person plural pronoun (or an anthropological term), and a remarkable flexibility of content, not, however, unrelated to the context of the benediction.

Other traditional formulas utilized by Paul would include the sentences of holy law, identified by Ernst Käsemann. According to the Tübingen professor, these utterances come from early Christian charismatic prophets who pronounced, in view of the immediately imminent judgment of the world, a blessing on those who fulfilled the divine law, or a curse on those who broke it. Essentially the expression of a sort of eschatological *lex talionis,* the form of the sentence was characterized by chiasmus: in the protasis and apodosis, human guilt and divine judgment are expressed by means of the same verb, as in 1 Corinthians 3:17: "if any one destroys God's temple, God will destroy him." Other such sentences of holy law are to be found at 1 Corinthians 14:38; 16:22; Galatians 1:9 (cf. Rom 10:11, 13) and the "old Jewish chiastic retribution formula" identified by K. G. Grobel in Romans 2:6–11. Outside of the Pauline corpus a sentence of holy law can be found in Revelation 22:18–19 (cf. Mark 8:38; Matt 10:32–33).

In the composition of the Pauline letters (whether these were written by the apostle himself or by one of his disciples matters little for the present discussion) the use of additional literary types can be noted. Particular attention can be drawn to the apostolic parousia, wherein Paul expresses his desire to be present to the community to which he is writing even though circumstances prevent it (e.g., 1 Thes 2:17–20). In the description of his own sufferings Paul employs the so-called peristatic catalogue. With regard to 2 Corinthians 6:4–10, a passage identified as having this literary form, C. F. D. Moule has written that it "is an impassioned and almost lyrical passage, where precision in the interpretation of the prepositions is probably impossible because the 'catalogue' has lured the writer into repeating a preposition in some instances where in sober prose it might have been unnatural." Other examples of this form, which Paul has appropriated from the Stoics, can be found in 1 Corinthians 4:9–13; 2 Corinthians 4:8–9 (10); 11:23–29. Catalogues of virtues and vices are scattered throughout the epistolary literature of the New Testament—e.g., Romans 1:29–31; Galatians 5:19–21, 22–23; Ephesians 5:3–5. Studies by Anton Vögtle and Siegfried Wibbing have shown that these tables contain elements of both Hellenistic (Stoic) and Jewish tradition. The household code (*Haustafel*) is another literary type that was developed in the Hellenistic world when it was taken over by the Hellenistic Jewish synagogue and thence passed into Christian use. The oldest Christian household code lies behind Colossians 3:18 – 4:1, but the literary type is also to be identified at Ephesians 5:22 – 6:9; 1 Timothy 2:18–25; 5:3–8; 6:1–2; Titus 2:2–10; and 1 Peter 2:13 – 3:7.

Of singular importance within the authentic letters of Paul is the creedal formula, sometimes called the confessional or *pistis* formula in the literature. Several variants of the formula are scattered throughout Paul's letters. The complete formula underlies 1 Corinthians 15:3b–5. A more simple version is to be discerned behind 2 Corinthians 5:15. A simple version is to be found in 1 Thessalonians 4:14. There the non-Pauline character of the language used in the formula betrays its pre-Pauline origin. With this formula and that found in 1 Thessalonians 5:10 we can go beyond the oldest New Testament document to a very early Christian confession of faith in the Death and Resurrection of Jesus. Since similar, and more expanded, creedal formulas are found not only throughout Paul's letters but in the deutero-Pauline letters, 1 Peter and Acts as well, it has been possible to trace, albeit with some difficulty, the tradition history of the creedal formula.

Apart from the use of traditional motifs, and his frequent recourse to traditional formulas, Paul's letters are worthy of form-critical analysis with respect to his use of the epistolary genre. A compositional study of the letters would seem to be more properly the object of the following chapter than of this, and so it can be deferred until that time. Acts, too, deserves attention from the compositional point of view. Here and there throughout the Lucan work, some of the literary types that have already been cited can be identified—fragments of creedal formulas in Acts 3:15; 4:10; and 13:37, a farewell discourse in Acts 20:18–35. Within Luke's triple account of Paul's "conversion," special mention should be made of the self-revelation formula in Acts 9:4–6; 22:7–10; 26:14–16. The self-revelation formula is characterized by the repetition of the name "Saul, Saul." Such language recalls God's self-revelation to the young Samuel (1 Sam 3:4–14). The self-revelation form was frequently utilized in Jewish literature. In a longer version, it was used by the Pentateuchal author to describe appearances to Jacob (Gen 31:11–13; 46:2–3) and Moses (Exod 3:2–10). A shorter version of the same type was also employed by biblical authors, as in Genesis 22:1–2. Both the longer version (Jub 44:5; Ezra 12:2–13; Apoc Abr 8:2–5; 9:1–5; Joseph and Asenath 14:6–8) and a shorter version (Jub 18:1–2; 18:10–11; Apoc Abr 11:3–5; 12:6–7; 14:1–3; 14:9–10; 19:1–3; Apoc Mos 41; T Job 3:1–2) were known to the authors of the intertestamental period. In short, the self-revelation formula was commonly employed in Jewish literature at the dawn of the Christian era. Luke used the traditional form in order to highlight the significance of that unique experience which we know as the Damascus event.

In the composition of Acts, Luke has accorded much importance to the speeches. Altogether the speeches account for approximately one third of the total contents of Acts. Aside from Stephen's speech in Acts 7:2–53 and that of James in Acts 15:13–21, the discourses are attributed to Peter and Paul. No matter to whom they are attributed, the speeches betray the style, vocabulary, and theology of Luke. Accordingly their study properly belongs to the analysis of Luke's compositional technique, to which some consideration will be devoted in the following chapter. Nevertheless, the speeches of Acts cannot be fully understood except within the broad genre of speeches in ancient literature. The many speeches of ancient literature have a literary form, distinct from the historical form. This literary form corresponds to the purpose, requirements, and state of the work in which they are found. In sum, speeches are a literary device employed by an ancient author for his own purpose and ideology. Letters were also occasionally affixed to historical and apocalyptic works for a similar purpose. From a literary point of view, they provide the reader with a dramatic and colorful narrative. From an ideological point of view, they illustrate and interpret history in accordance with the language and perspective of the "historian." Ancient historians were, after all, men of their times. In their writing they employed the forms of speech that were common in their day. Their finished works might well represent a unique interplay of form and content, but no ancient author wrote any of his works in a vacuum, isolated from the language and traditions of his peers.

III. AN EXERCISE IN FORM CRITICISM

A. The Message of the Baptist: Luke 3:7–18

7 He said therefore to the multitudes that came out to be baptized by him, "You brood of vipers! Who warned you to flee from the wrath to come? 8 Bear fruits that befit repentance, and do not begin to say to yourselves, 'We have Abraham as our father'; for I tell you, God is able from these stones to raise up children to Abraham. 9 Even now the axe is laid to the root of the trees; every tree therefore that does not bear good fruit is cut down and thrown into the fire."

10 And the multitudes asked him, "What then shall we do?" 11 And he answered them, "He who has two coats, let him share with him who has none; and he who has food, let him do likewise." 12 Tax collectors also came to be baptized, and said to him, "Teacher, what shall we do?" 13 And he said to them, "Collect no more than is appointed you." 14 Soldiers also asked him, "And we, what shall we do?" And he said to them, "Rob no one by violence or by false accusation, and be content with your wages."

15 As the people were in expectation, and all men questioned in their hearts concerning John, whether perhaps he were the Christ, 16 John answered them all, "I baptize you with water; but he who is mightier than I is coming, the thong of whose sandals I am not worthy to untie; he will baptize you with the Holy Spirit and with fire. 17 His winnowing fork is in his hand, to clear his threshing floor, and to gather the wheat into his granary, but the chaff he will burn with unquenchable fire."

18 So, with many other exhortations, he preached good news to the people.

It has often been recognized that one of the difficulties under which the form-critical methodology labors is the fact that there is little agreement among the critics as to the identification of the literary forms utilized by New Testament authors and the terminology appropriate to these forms. Although some agreement exists as to the principal types used by the evangelists, there is not always agreement as to the subdivisions of these types. Thus while it is relatively easy to identify Luke 3:7–18 as discourse material having a literary form different from narrative material, it is more difficult to identify precisely the literary forms of the Q material employed by Luke. We are certainly dealing with logia (sayings), but is it possible to be more precise?

The prophetic element in verses 7b–9 is apparent. In verse 8 the prophetic call for repentance is combined with a declarative statement of what God is able to do, based not on experience but on what God has already accomplished in the past—in this case, raise up children to Abraham. Another prophetic characteristic is the leitmotif of threat and warning. In Luke 3:7b–9, prophetic statements of this sort are attributed to John the Baptist, a prophetic figure. In the Q tradition from which Luke has taken this material, the Baptist is a prophet (cf. Luke 7:24–35; par. Matt 11:7–9). The Baptist has also suffered the fate of the prophets. Imprisoned (Luke 3:19–20), he has suffered and will soon die because of the incisiveness of his message. These factors come together to characterize verses 7b–9 as "prophetic utterance."

The eschatological assumption is clearly stated in verse 7b. It is a challenge to a new understanding of the present based on the impending wrath. Verse 9 incorporates a saying which Bultmann has identified as a popular proverb, "Every tree that does not bear good fruit is cut down" (similar proverbs can be discerned in Matt 5:14; 24:28; Mark 2:17, 19; Luke 4:23; 5:39). For his part, Richard A. Edwards has identified the entire verse 9 as a prophetic judgment parable, the theme of fire anticipating the reference to the eschatological fire of verses 16, 17, a traditional apocalyptic image. Hence Edwards, following an earlier analysis by Howard Kee, identifies the entire little bloc of material (vv. 7b–9) as "eschatological warning." Warning statements are closely associated with judgment sayings—verse 7 actually makes reference to the judgment—to the point that they belong to the same basic category. Judgment sayings, as Claus Westermann has shown, belong to the heart of the prophetic message. The life situation of the judgment saying is prophetic proclamation.

The Q material in Luke 3:17–18 also is categorized as an "eschatological warning" by Kee and Edwards. The verses also include a prophetic judgment parable (v. 17). This parable has eschatological and prophetic overtones, but its force is heightened by the reference to a common experience, that of a farmer who threshes grain. The metaphor underscores the inevitability (normalcy) of the fire. For Bultmann, however, the pair of verses (17–18) is a "salvation prophecy," which belongs to the broader category of prophetic and apocalyptic sayings. Bultmann has also classified the Matthean and Markan parallels (Matt 3:11–12; Mark 1:7–8) as "salvation prophecy."

This brings us to the importance of tradition history in the analysis of the passage at hand. Virtually all of the commentators note that the Q saying of Luke 3:16 (= Matt 3:11) mentions a baptism "with the Holy Spirit and with fire." Mark (Mark 1:8), however, mentions only a baptism "with the Holy Spirit." Since Luke mentions that some of the disciples of John the Baptist had never heard of baptism with the Holy Spirit (Acts 19:1–6), it is highly unlikely that the Baptist would have spoken of a future baptism "with the Holy Spirit." The Church, however, had every reason to speak about baptism "with the Holy Spirit" and even to contrast this (sacramental) baptism with the Baptist's water baptism unto repentance. Hence form critics are convinced that the Markan statement in 1:8 represents a Christian formulation attributed to the Baptist. Scholars also are in general agreement that the original Q statement of Luke 3:16 (= Matt 3:11) originally ran "baptize you with fire." In which case the Q statement in its original form (i.e., Luke 3:7b–9, 16–17) would have been consistent in its outlook. Its perspective was that of the impending adverse judgment.

Then at some point in the history of the Q tradition, and prior to the use of the statement by Luke and Matthew, a Christian interpretation, "with the Holy Spirit," was added to the traditional Q saying. Thus in its present formulation the logion of Luke 3:16–17 can be understood as a "salvation prophecy" even though in its traditional form it is best understood as an "eschatological warning." Although many scholars, probably the majority, agree that "with the Holy Spirit" is a secondary, Christian development of the traditional logion, few would go so far as Bultmann, who claimed that the sayings, in circulation in the Christian tradition (a point of view with which not many would take issue), were ascribed to the Baptist out of a desire to have some record of his preaching for repentance (a point of view that many would not find acceptable).

Indeed, Bultmann attributes an unwarranted measure of freedom and creativity to the Christian tradition that lies behind the Gospels. This point of view is seen in his commentary apropos Luke 3:10–14:

> This is a catechism-like section, naïvely put into the Baptist's mouth, as though soldiers had gone on a pilgrimage to John. There is one thing that makes it improbable that we are here dealing with a product of the primitive Christian Church—that the profession of a soldier is taken for granted. Neither does this passage appear to be Jewish. It is perhaps a relatively late Hellenistic product, developed (by Luke himself) out of the saying from the tradition in v. 11 (*The History of the Synoptic Tradition*, p. 145).

Bultmann's interpretation bespeaks his radical historical skepticism and an extreme application of the principle of dual exclusion.

One must respond more favorably, however, to Bultmann's categorization of the sayings in verses 10–14 as "catechism-like," as also his identification of verses 16–17 as "salvation prophecy." In his commentary on Luke, Heinz Schürmann has recognized the catechetical interest of the entire pericope. Following the earlier analysis of Harald Sahlin, Schürmann has identified the pericope as a "baptismal discourse." The literary formula "What shall we do?" of verses 10, 12, 14 points to Christian baptism as the *Sitz-im-Leben* of the discourse (cf. Acts 2:37; 16:30). References to baptism in verses 7, 12, 15 accentuate the baptismal setting. In its present Lucan (and Q) form, the baptismal discourse of Luke 3:7–18 consists of two parts: a penitential warning (vv. 7–14) and a salvation promise, with specific reference to Christ the Redeemer (vv. 15–18).

B. The Stilling of the Storm: Mark 4:35–41

35 On that day, when evening had come, he said to them, "Let us go across to the other side." 36 And leaving the crowd, they took him with them, just as he was, in the boat. And other boats were with him. 37 And a great storm of wind arose, and the waves beat into the boat, so that the boat was already filling. 38 But he was in the stern, asleep on the cushion; and they woke him and said to him, "Teacher, do you not care if we perish?" 39 And he awoke and rebuked the wind, and said to the sea, "Peace! Be still!" And the wind ceased, and there was a great calm. 40 He said to them, "Why are you afraid? Have you no faith?" 41 And they were filled with awe, and said to one another, "Who then is this, that even wind and sea obey him?"

Although Mark's story of Jesus' stilling the storm is filled with a verbal exchange somewhat unusual in a miracle story, the threefold schema of the type shines through the narrative. Verses 37–38a present the situation. The circumstances are grave. The fury of the wind and wave has been unleashed. The storm of wind is "great" (*megalē*). The waves were such that the boat was filling ("so that the boat was filling": *hōste . . . gemizesthai to ploion*). The introduction of "already" (*ēdē*) adds a note of urgency to an already tense situation. To make matters worse, the miracle worker is not even personally responsive to the situation. In the stern of the boat, he sleeps on, seemingly unaware of the fury that is raging about him and his companions.

Verse 39a presents the ritual of the miracle. Summoned on the scene (i.e., being awakened), Jesus majestically addresses the unruly elements with the command "Peace! Be Still!" (*siōpa, pephimōso*). His word is a command: *epetimēsen*. Verses 39b and 41 present the effect of the miracle worker's activity. On the one hand, the elements are becalmed—both wind ("and the wind ceased": *kai ekopasen ho anemos*) and sea ("and there was a great calm": *kai egeneto galēnē megalē*) obey him. On the other hand, the witnesses to the miracle are filled with awe. Awestruck, they utter in choral response, as if in one voice, "Who then is this, that even wind and sea obey him?" (*ti ara outos estin hoti kai ho anemos kai hē thalassa hupakouei autō*).

In short, the form of the pericope is that of the miracle story. An analysis of the form points to the fact that Jesus was a miracle worker. At this point it should be noted that the fact of miracles does not make Jesus unique in his time nor does it establish beyond a reasonable doubt that Jesus was the Son of God. Among Jesus' Palestinian contemporaries there were other miracle workers (cf. Luke 11:19 = Matt 12:27). One response to Jesus' working a miracle was the accusation that he was a man possessed (Mark 3:22). Thus the purpose of narrating a miracle was not apologetic.

Rather, the function of the Markan miracle story was epiphanic. In the

Hellenistic world, miracle accounts pointed to the visibility of divinity or divine power in some person or act. In this sense they were the narration of an epiphany. They were the manifestation of a divine person. It would appear that this was also the function of the traditional miracle stories taken over by Mark. These were clearly epiphanic, but some of them were more clearly epiphanic than others. Achtemeier's first catena of miracles (Mark 4:35 – 5:43) contains a group that is patently epiphanic. Among these, the story of the Stilling of the Storm occupies a first place. The fear motif of verse 41a ("they were filled with awe": *kai ephobēthēsan phobon megan*, literally "they feared a great fear") underscores the epiphanic character of the narrative (cf. Mark 5:15, 33, 36). The narrative belongs to that category of miracle story which highlights the "divine man," the one in whom the power of God is at work. In Mark's Gospel the choral response in 4:41 highlights this type of focus on Jesus.

In what sort of social circumstances would early Christian communities have been inclined to narrate the epiphany of Jesus? Miracles were not apologetic in function, but they would hardly have been narrated in the proclamation of the kerygma. Of themselves they would have led no one to faith. The early Church had, obviously, other kinds of characteristic activities. One of these was the celebration of the Eucharist, a rather specific life situation in the churches of New Testament times. For Paul Achtemeier, it was the eucharistic liturgy celebrated by some group(s) within the Church which provided the life situation for the epiphanic miracle stories. These groups used these events in the life of Jesus to give substance to an epiphanic interpretation of the Eucharist, while other groups might have celebrated other aspects of the Eucharist—for example, its being a Passover meal. The search for a realistic life situation for the transmission of these miracle stories led this American exegete to consider that each of the two miracle catenae which he isolated concluded with a story of Jesus Feeding the Crowd. Some Eucharistic motifs can be discerned in the feeding narratives, as well as some echo of a Moses typology. Since Judaism had developed a divine-man image of Moses, by whom water and feeding miracles were effected, it would seem that the Moses-divine-man story served as the paradigm of the epiphanic sea and feeding miracles attributed to Jesus in Mark's miracle source.

Beyond this, one might consider the use and significance of Old Testament motifs in the presentation of the story of the Stilling of the Storm. One might also point to the significance of some Markan elements in the present text of Mark—for example, the Markan introduction (v. 35), or the use of *phimoō* (Be Still!) in verse 39 as well as in Jesus' command to the demon in Mark 1:25 ("Be silent"). But these elements pertain to Markan redaction of traditional material, a subject to which the next chapter will turn.

This form-critical analysis of Luke's account of the Proclamation of the Baptist and the Markan narrative of the Stilling of the Storm has focused on the constraints which the past history of the evangelist's material and his language imposed upon him. At the same time these constraints provided the author with the possibility of conveying a message to those for whom his

Gospel was intended. The message is not entirely the author's own; to a large extent it is the message of his tradition and his environment.

Minimally stated, the content of the Baptist's discourse is a call to repentance, uttered by a prophetic figure whom Christian tradition considered to be the forerunner of Jesus Messiah. At bottom, the narrative of the Stilling of the Storm has pointed to Jesus as one in whom divine power was at work. A continued, redaction-critical analysis of these pericopes in the following chapter will focus on the particular coloration with which each of the evangelists has conveyed the traditional message.

SELECT BIBLIOGRAPHY

Achtemeier, Paul J. "The Origin and Function of the Pre-Marcan Miracle Catenae." *Journal of Biblical Literature,* 91 (1972), 198–221.

Bultmann, Rudolf. *The History of the Synoptic Tradition.* New York: Harper & Row, 1963.

———. "The Study of the Synoptic Gospels" and Knudsin, Karl. "Primitive Christianity in the Light of Gospel Research." In Grant, F. C. (ed. and tr.) *Form Criticism: A New Method of New Testament Research.* New York: Willett, Clark & Co., 1934.

Carlston, Charles E. "Proverbs, Maxims, and the Historical Jesus." *Journal of Biblical Literature,* 99 (1980), 87–105.

Dibelius, Martin. *A Fresh Approach to the New Testament and Early Christian Literature.* London: Ivor Nicholson & Watson, 1936. Westport, Conn.: Greenwood, 1979.

———. *From Tradition to Gospel.* New York: Scribner's, n.d.

———. *Studies in the Acts of the Apostles.* London: SCM, 1973.

Dupont, Jacques. *Les Béatitudes.* I: *Le Problème littéraire. Études bibliques.* 2nd ed., Paris: Gabalda, 1969.

Glasson, T. Francis. "What Is Apocalyptic?" *New Testament Studies,* 27 (1980), 95–105.

Guillemette, Pierre. "La forme des récits d'exorcisme de Bultmann. Un dogme à reconsidérer." *Église et Théologie,* 11 (1980), 177–93.

Johnson, Marshall D. *The Purpose of the Biblical Genealogies. With Special Reference to the Setting of the Genealogies of Jesus.* SNTS, MS, 8. Cambridge: University Press, 1969.

Käsemann, Ernst. "Sentences of Holy Law in the New Testament." In *New Testament Questions of Today. New Testament Library.* London: SCM, 1969. 66–81.

Kee, Howard C. "Aretalogy and Gospel." *Journal of Biblical Literature,* 92 (1973), 402–22.

Koch, Klaus. *The Growth of the Biblical Tradition: The Form-Critical Method.* New York: Scribner's, 1969.

McDonald, James Ian Hamilton. *Kerygma and Didache: The Articulation and Structure of the Earliest Christian Message. Society for New Testa-*

ment Studies Monograph Series, 37. Cambridge: University Press, 1980.

McKnight, Edgar V. *What Is Form Criticism? Guides to Biblical Scholarship.* Philadelphia: Fortress, 1969.

Merlier, Octave. *Le Quatrième Évangile: La Question johannique.* Paris: Presses universitaires de France, 1962.

Mullin, Terence Y. "Formulas in New Testament Epistles." *Journal of Biblical Literature,* 91 (1972), 380–90.

Munck, Johannes. "Discours d'adieu dans le Nouveau Testament et dans la littérature biblique." In *Aux Sources de la tradition chrétienne (Mélanges M. Goguel).* Neuchâtel: Delachaux, 1950. 155–70.

Russell, D. S. *The Method and Message of Jewish Apocalyptic, 200 B.C.–A.D. 100.* London: SCM, 1964.

Sanders, Jack T. *The New Testament Christological Hymns: Their Historical Religious Background. Society for New Testament Studies Monograph Series,* 15. Cambridge: University Press, 1971.

Schweizer, Eduard. "Traditional ethical patterns in the Pauline and post-Pauline letters and their development (Lists of vices and house-tables)", in *Text and Interpretation. Studies in the New Testament Presented to Matthew Black.* Ed. by E. Best and R. McL. Wilson. Cambridge: University Press, 1979. 195–210.

Taylor, Vincent. *The Gospel According to St. Mark.* London: Macmillan, 1963.

Tiede, David L. *The Charismatic Figure as Miracle Worker. Society of Biblical Literature Dissertation Series,* 1. Missoula: Society of Biblical Literature, 1972.

Wright, Addison G. *The Literary Genre Midrash.* Staten Island, N.Y.: Alba House, 1967.

CHAPTER SIX

REDACTION CRITICISM

I. AN INTRODUCTION TO THE METHOD

The Reaction to Form Criticism

Among the many remarks made apropos of the use of the form-critical method by students of the New Testament, two stand out from the rest. The first one comes from more conservative and tradition-minded students, scholars, and ecclesiastical spokespersons who were disturbed by the radicality and utter historical skepticism with which the use of the methodology was pursued by some of its proponents. Their criticism focused upon the preponderant role ascribed to the creativity of Church tradition by the more eager form critics, as well as upon the minimal historical remnant of the gospel tradition that survived as a result of a form-critical study of the Gospels pushed to its extreme. With no little justification, some scholars noted that the form-critical methodology as practiced in its radical Bultmannian form was mixed with the Marburgian's notion of the kerygma and his existential approach to the interpretation of the New Testament Scriptures. Bultmann's theological and philosophical *a prioris* allowed him a disinterest in history that could not be shared by other scholars whose theological and philosophical presuppositions were different from those of the author of *The History of the Synoptic Tradition*. Differences in epistemology and historiography were part and parcel of the religious and theological discussion that ensued.

Many proponents of the historical-critical approach to the study of the New Testament viewed the form-critical method with sympathy and openness but were not ready to accept the radical consequences of the application of the methodology in its Bultmannian form. To a large extent, the previous chapter's consideration of the application of form criticism to the New Testament was based on the more moderate approach to the use of form analysis in New Testament studies. Certainly the distinction between the criteria and the indices of historicity is apropos. The more radical form critics opt for the notion of criteria of historicity. They accept as accurately representing the historical Jesus of Nazareth only that part of the New Testament tradition which cannot be explained in any other way. Their methodology is one of radical historical skepticism. The more moderate form critics, on the other hand, accept a methodological historical skepticism but are willing to admit as "historical" events and sayings to which a convergence of indices point, even though it is conceivable that the tradition about these events or sayings might be explained in some other way. For these more moderate critics, skeptical though they are, a preponderance of evidence suffices for a judgment of historicity. Thus we find them speaking more frequently of shaping a tradition than of creating a tradition.

The second major criticism directed against the use of form criticism as a valuable method in the study of the New Testament Scriptures comes from the quarter of literary critics themselves. The notion, urged by such form critics as Dibelius, that the evangelists are but collectors of tradition can lead to a fragmentation of interpretation. Excessive concentration on component literary forms can lead to a neglect of the function and meaning of a document with a complex literary type. In terms of our early examples, taken from the world of contemporary journalism, an analysis of the various types of writing to be found in a newspaper can overshadow the fact that the newspaper itself has its own character—it maintains a given political posture and has its own editorial policy. In terms of the New Testament, undue focus of concentration on, say, the miracle stories can lead to the neglect of the Gospels themselves as composite literary works in their own right. One can miss the forest because of the trees.

With respect to the various New Testament authors, the notion that each of these writers is but a compiler of tradition denigrates the whole group. Pushed to an extreme conclusion, the form-critical method undercuts the personality of the author, the uniqueness of his vision, and the originality of his message. It is almost as if a New Testament author had no more personal part to contribute to the New Testament than the anonymous clerks who compile the pages of our telephone directories. In similar fashion an extreme application of the form-critical method almost suggests that the New Testament authors were but the anonymous mouthpieces of a community (thus Dibelius' analysis of James). Whereas the traditional interpretation of the New Testament books placed undue emphasis on the role of the evangelists (and other New Testament authors) as individual authors, the form-critical method seemed to deprive them of any creativity and originality of expression. In this respect a comment by Norman Perrin apropos of Rudolf Bultmann is quite incisive. "Bultmann . . ." he wrote, "spent so much time and effort working in the Synoptic tradition that he could not suddenly see clearly the special uses which Matthew and Luke made of that tradition."

The use of redaction criticism in New Testament scholarship has rehabilitated the evangelists. It does not consider them as authors who have created a literary work *de novo* or in independence of the communities to which they respectively belonged, yet it does maintain that the very fashion in which the Gospels were put together reveals the vision and literary skill of the respective evangelists. As was the case with the application of the previously surveyed methods of New Testament exegesis—text, source, and form criticism—redaction criticism has been used with especially good results in the study of the Synoptic Gospels. The same factors that indicated the Synoptics as a fertile terrain for the methodologies of text, source, and form criticism coalesce to point to Matthew, Mark, and Luke as three Gospels to which the methodology of redaction criticism can be easily and fruitfully applied.

In fact, redaction criticism is a methodology that focuses upon the editorial process. With regard to the Synoptic Gospels, the methodology presupposes certain results of both the source- and form-critical endeavors as applied to the New Testament. From the results of source analysis, it takes as its working hypothesis that Matthew and Luke are dependent upon at least one documentary source, Mark. From the results of form analysis and tradition history, the redaction-critical study of the New Testament supposes the following as givens:

(1) That the Synoptics are not homogeneous compositions, but collections of small units of narrative and discourse material.

(2) That in the oral tradition which preceded the documentation of these units of material, only small units were handed on—i.e., single sayings, small collections of logia, single stories.

(3) That each of the units of material presently contained in the Synoptics had a definite oral form (and has a corresponding literary form) that corresponded to a particular life situation in the early Church.

(4) That each of the evangelists made use of this oral tradition in the composition of his Gospel. In doing so, Mark created the Gospel genre. Matthew and Luke made use of Mark but also made use of traditional material which was known to them independently of the Markan Gospel.

(5) That the Resurrection faith of the early Church shaped and molded the transmission of these units of material as well as the composite Gospels themselves.

(6) That the biography format is a literary construction of the evangelists; accordingly it is methodologically illegitimate to attempt to write a life of Jesus on the basis of the Gospels.

(7) That it is quite likely that some of these units of material were collected into relatively homogeneous documents prior to their appropriation by the evangelists; and that it is possible to discern the theological tendencies of these source documents.

On the basis of these givens, redaction criticism studies each of the Synoptics in view of discerning the proper literary characteristics of each of the Synoptics as well as the particular theological viewpoint reflected by each of the first three Gospels. To the extent that the methodology has been refined, it can be productively applied to other parts of the New Testament. Beyond the Gospels, use of the methodology will always be more speculative in its results because of the absence of a source document with which the edited text can be compared. If redaction criticism is the study of the editorial process, the availability of both the edited and unedited versions helps greatly in the effort to discover the editor's literary techniques and his ideological *Weltanschauung*.

Back to the Newspaper

On page two of the *Stars and Stripes* of Friday November 14, 1980, there appeared the following five-paragraph story:

BIKO'S DEATH PROBED

JOHANNESBURG, SOUTH AFRICA

(AP)—The furor over the death of Steve Biko in 1977 was revived Thursday with the national medical association's declaration that the black nationalist received "inadequate treatment" because of police interference.

Biko's family claimed he died of head injuries inflicted when police beat him during an interrogation. Biko, 30, had been arrested under the country's wide-ranging terrorism laws.

Police denied beating Biko, saying he had accidentally hit his head against the wall while police were subduing him when he became violent during questioning.

But an additional controversy arose over why three doctors who examined Biko did not detect his ultimately fatal head injuries.

When it was eventually decided to take Biko to another prison, where better medical facilities were available, he was driven 700 miles from East London to Pretoria in the back of a Land-Rover. He died shortly after arriving in Pretoria.

On page six of the *International Herald Tribune* of Friday November 14, 1980, there appeared the following fourteen-paragraph story:

DOCTORS SAY BIKO GOT INADEQUATE TREATMENT

THE ASSOCIATED PRESS

JOHANNESBURG—The furor over the death in detention of Steve Biko has been revived with the national medical association's declaration that the black nationalist had received inadequate treatment because of police interference.

The South African Medical and Dental Council met in Cape Town Wednesday after hundreds of doctors reportedly threatened to quit the organization unless one of the doctors who examined Biko was expelled for his conduct in the case.

Biko, 30, died Sept. 12, 1977, while in police detention. His family said that he died of head injuries inflicted when police beat him during an interrogation. He had been arrested under the country's wide-ranging anti-terrorism laws, which gave police virtual carte blanche.

PROBE DELAYED

Police denied beating Biko, saying he had accidentally hit his head against the wall while police were subduing him when he became violent during questioning. But an additional controversy arose over why three doctors who examined him did not detect his ultimately fatal head injuries.

Doctors have urged the medical association to expel Dr. Benjamin Tucker for his role in the Biko . . . [the remainder of paragraph five and the eight paragraphs following discuss Biko's symptoms, the resolutions of the medical association, and the situation of Dr. Tucker. Paragraph thirteen continued as follows] . . . spinal fluid, convulsions, and inability to communicate and frothing at the mouth. Biko was forced to sleep naked on the jail floor, manacled to a radiator.

When it was eventually decided to take Biko to the central prison, where better medical facilities were available, he was driven 700 miles from East London to Pretoria in the back of a Land-Rover. He died shortly after arriving in Pretoria.

A comparison of the two texts reveals that they have much in common, to the point that the reader would have to admit a common documentary source even in the absence of the Associated Press credit provided by each of the newspapers. One cannot help but notice that the *IHT* version is longer. It has made use of more of the source material than has the *S&S* version. Upon examination it is seen that an *S&S* editor has systematically eliminated from the version of the story published in the newspaper virtually all that pertained to the discussion among the doctors and the medical-ethical case against Dr. Tucker and his associates. In the absence of the text of the AP dispatch itself, it is impossible to determine whether an *IHT* editor has also made a selection from the available source material. Nevertheless, a comparison of the *IHT* and *S&S* versions enables the reader to conclude that the *S&S* editor, at least, has made a selection of materials. Alternatively expressed, he or she decided—for whatever reasons, whether of space requirements, editorial policy, or presumed readership interest—not to publish a considerable portion of the dispatch, specifically that pertaining to the medical discussion. All that remains of that discussion in the *S&S* is a brief reference in paragraph one, "national medical association's," and paragraph five. In effect, a story published in the *IHT* as a feature item on a delicate question of medical ethics became, in the *S&S,* simply a story about the death of a civil rights leader. Moreover, the respective headlines point along the same lines. Undoubtedly the difference in orientation of the stories owes to the respective readerships of the two newspapers.

A look at paragraph two of the *S&S* version reveals that it is a slightly edited version of the material which appears in paragraph three of the *IHT* article. The editing process has included the omission of the final clause, "which gave police virtual carte blanche." Also lost in the revision was the clause "while in police detention." A similar clause ("in detention") has been dropped from paragraph one of the *S&S* story (cf. paragraph one, *IHT*). Moreover, quotation marks encompass the expression "inadequate treatment" in the *S&S*, while they are lacking in the *IHT*. These four editorial differences suggest that the editors of *S&S* have presented a version of the story that is not as strongly critical of the police as is the *IHT* article. One might legitimately ask whether this difference might reflect the editorial policies of the respective newspapers. In any event, the story as it appears in the *IHT* is more critical of the police as an arm of the South African regime than is the story as it appears in the *S&S*. The affirmation that the editors of the *S&S* have simply presented the story of a civil rights martyr without wanting to be critical of a particular political regime might be beyond what this limited evidence allows, but the discerning reader must certainly admit a tendency in that direction.

Other differences in the presentation can be noted as well. To be sure, the articles appeared on different pages of the respective newspapers. Beyond that the reader can note that the date of Biko's death is already mentioned in paragraph one of the *S&S* article. Paragraphs three and four in the *S&S* version correspond in material content to a single paragraph (number four) in the *IHT* version, but there is a difference in layout (two paragraphs instead of one). From an analysis of these editorial modifications one can legitimately infer a difference in mean educational level of the respective readerships. The *S&S* presents a simpler version of the story; the *IHT* the more complicated version. Indeed, the incorporation of "1977" into paragraph one of the *S&S* article can be attributed not only to editorial modifications of the paragraph on which it originally appeared by also to a concern to provide immediately a temporal setting for the events, presumably because the readers would need such information at the outset.

Examples such as the one analyzed above could be cited at length. The stories that appear in most of our daily newspapers represent a selection of "traditional" materials—that is, material that comes to the editors from several news services. Moreover each newspaper has a policy which is reflected in the modifications of the traditional material—that is, the editorial changes in the presentation of the subject matter. In daily newspapers there are also articles that are substantially composed in the newsrooms of these newspapers. Such composites ("syntheses of traditional materials") appear in the *S&S* under the rubric "From press dispatches," while in the *IHT* they appear under the title "From agency dispatches." In either case the rubric indicates the manner of composition of the accompanying article. An examination of a pair of composite articles will further indicate the interests and methodology of the redaction critic.

On page two of the *IHT* on November 14, 1980, there appeared:

U.S. TRANSPORT AIRCRAFT CRASHES
NEAR CAIRO AIR BASE, KILLING 13

THE ASSOCIATED PRESS

CAIRO—An American C-141 military transport plane crashed late Wednesday as it was making its final approach to Cairo West Air Base for the first test of the U.S. Rapid Deployment Force to the Middle East, a spokesman at the U.S. Embassy here said Thursday.

All 13 persons aboard the aircraft, which was mainly carrying equipment for a two-week joint exercise with the Egyptian Army, were killed, the spokesman said.

"We don't know the cause of the accident," the spokesman said.

In contrast to the three paragraphs of the *IHT* article appeared a twenty-three-paragraph story beginning on page one of the *S&S* with fifteen paragraphs on page one and eight paragraphs in the continuation on page 28, the final page of the newspaper. The article was as follows:

AF CRASH IN EGYPT KILLS 13

FROM PRESS DISPATCHES

CAIRO—An Air Force *C-141 military transport plane crashed* at an airfield here *late Wednesday,* killing all 13 Air Force personnel aboard.

The Military Airlift Command transport was *making its final landing approach to Cairo West Airfield as part of a test of the U.S. Rapid Deployment Force* (RDF) *to the Middle East, a spokesman at the U.S. Embassy here said Thursday.* The StarLifter was *carrying equipment* and supplies *for a two-week joint exercise* with Egyptian forces, the spokesman said.

In Washington, a defense official said reports indicated the plane was carrying some unspecified explosives, liquid oxygen equipment, a fuel truck which they believed was empty, a pickup truck and some spare parts.

[Paragraphs four and five follow with further details as to the supplies being carried and the land procedure.]

Two of the personnel killed were women, a list of the casualties showed.

They were Airman 1.C. Karen L. Marti of Springfield, Mass., and Senior Airman Martha M. Misko of Chatsworth, Calif. Both were passengers.

Only one Air Force woman has been killed previously in an air crash. She was a student pilot who died in September 1979.

In addition to the two women, the Air Force identified the following as either members of the crew or passengers:

[Paragraphs ten and eleven identify ten of the deceased.]

The 13th victim's name and hometown were not released pending notification of next of kin.

[The remaining eleven paragraphs described the joint maneuvers and the results of the crash.]

The italicized sections of the *S&S* article were taken verbatim from the Associated Press dispatch, as this was reported in the *IHT*. Military editorial interests dictated the addition of lengthy segments to the source material which described the contents of the aircraft, the nature of the exercises, and the list of the deceased. Even the fashion of presenting the necrology was modified in keeping with present-day interests of the U.S. military. The opening paragraphs of the necrology were devoted explicitly to the issue of women in uniform. (In paragraph twelve, the reader will recognize the use of a literary formula, "not released pending notification of next of kin," a standard piece of accident reporting.) Military interests were also responsible for less obvious editorial modifications of the text of the AP dispatch. In paragraph one, "American" (*IHT*) had been replaced by "Air Force" (*S&S*). In paragraph two of the *S&S* version, the Rapid Deployment Force was further identified in typical military fashion as "RDF". It would also seem reasonable to suggest that it was military interests which dictated the omission of the final paragraph of the AP dispatch: " 'We don't know the cause of the accident,' the spokesman said." Finally, the placement of the article on page one, with a continuation on the final page of the newspaper— that is, on the two most visible pages of the newspaper—projects the military interest as does the headline "AF crash in Egypt kills 13." In short, it was obviously military interests that dictated the editorial presentation of the article—in terms of the selection, arrangement, and placement of material, as well as modifications of the material (additions, omissions, substitutions).

In this comparison of two newspapers, one further item needs to be noted —the sources upon which each of the newspapers draws. In the *Stars and Stripes* of November 14 there is material which is substantially taken from a single source (United Press, Associated Press, New York *Times* services), composite material ("from press dispatches"), and material which comes from the paper's own sources (normally indicated by means of the byline "by Chuck Freadhoff [for example], Staff Writer" and the notation [*S&S*] after the indication of place at the beginning of the article). In the *International Herald Tribune* of the same date, there is material which is substantially taken over from a single source (United Press, Associated Press, New York *Times,* Los Angeles *Times,* Washington *Post,* and Reuters), composite material ("From Agency Dispatches"), and material which comes from its own sources (indicated by means of the byline "by Jonathan Kandell [for example], *International Herald Tribune"* and no further notation). At once it is seen that the *IHT* draws from more agency sources than does the *S&S*.

The Methodology

The analysis of these few newspaper items reveals what every student of journalism knowns, namely that the editing of a newspaper is not a matter of simply juxtaposing material from various sources—a task which could, in fact, be effected mechanically. Rather, the editing of a newspaper is a task which requires intelligence and a fair amount of literary skill. It consists of the selection of materials, their arrangement, their modification, and certain unique features that come from the editor's (or editors') own experience and creativity. Even though the name of the editor(s) may be unknown to the readers of a given newspaper, the reader knows that the editorial techniques and the ideology of the editor and publisher give the newspaper a recognizable profile. The newspaper is a complex literary type. It is a genre. The New Testament has a complex literary form; so too have the vast majority of books which belong to the New Testament. Thus there is no little analogy between the study of the newspaper's editorial process and the study of the editing of the New Testament. In both cases we are dealing with documents of a complex literary genre. In both cases we are dealing with documents whose component parts are largely anonymous, as indeed are the composite documents themselves. What differentiates the study of the newspaper and the study of the New Testament with respect to the editorial process is not the methodology, but the quantity of materials available for comparative purposes (the many newspapers published on any given day in contrast to the limited amount of NT documentation) on the one hand, and the contemporaneity of the daily newspaper in comparison with the antiquity of the New Testament on the other hand.

As a methodology of New Testament study, redaction criticism attempts to clarify the nature and extent of an author's own contribution to the work that has come from his hand. It presupposes both source- and form-critical analysis. It begins with the principle that New Testament authors were not nondescript collectors of an anonymous tradition, but that they were men who collected, arranged, and edited traditional material in a particular set of circumstances with a definite objective in mind. In composing their respective works, the various authors were proposing a particular theological point of view, one that was their own, even if it was at the same time also the expression of a definite trend in primitive Christianity.

It should be clear that redaction criticism does not dispute the fact that the evangelists (or the author of the Pastorals, for instance) wove together various units of tradition into a single literary work. However, redaction criticism abides by the principle summed up in the Latin adage *entia non sunt multiplicanda* (beings should not be multiplied), and avoids the postulation of a rather large group of unidentifiable oral transmitters behind the written New Testament texts. Rather than focus upon a complex tradition history, redaction criticism focuses upon the final editing which makes of the various units of tradition a single literary work.

Thus redaction criticism attempts to draw inferences about an author's point of view and the situation of his community from the presentation of a Gospel or other New Testament work taken as a whole. It is to be granted that in many cases, perhaps the majority of cases, the New Testament authors are anonymous as far as we moderns are concerned; nevertheless, they were individuals with their own techniques of composition and their own theological points of view. Since redaction criticism studies the New Testament works in their own right, rather than as the accidental product of transmission history or as the source of later literary documents, redaction criticism has rehabilitated the Gospel of Mark as a text to be interpreted in its own right.

As a method that focuses upon an author's technique and ideology in the process of "creative editing," redaction criticism examines: (1) an author's selection and omission of traditional material; (2) the modifications of this material; (3) the arrangement of this material; and (4) contributions from the author's own creativity. Although the discernment of an author's own ideology and style characteristics which results from the skillful and judicious use of the principles of source criticism may provide the redaction critic the opportunity to proceed effectively to the redaction analysis of a text whose documentary sources he or she does not have at hand, the technique is all the more readily employed when such sources are available. The example of the newspaper reports on Biko's death serve as a case in point. The fact that both Matthew and Luke made use of Mark in the composition of their respective evangels affords the interpreter the possibility of analyzing the selection and modification of materials. Thus the critic will inquire as to why Matthew has reproduced, with some modification (Matt 15:21–28), the Markan tale of the Syrophoenician Woman (Mark 7:24–30), while Luke has omitted it. He or she will inquire, as well, as to the extent and significance of the modifications Matthew has introduced into his source material.

For the redaction critic the placement and arrangement of material is all-important. This concern is of importance not only with respect to the interpretation of a given pericope but also with respect to the compositional and ideological thrust of the composite work, as our newspaper examples have shown. While aporias and redactional seams can point to an author's arrangement of his material, the availability of parallel material makes the task relatively easier. A redaction critic, for example, will weigh carefully the respective contexts of the Matthean (Matt 6:7–15) and Lucan (Luke 11:1–4) versions of the Lord's Prayer. In similar fashion, the redaction critic probes the significance of the placement of the Cleansing of the Temple at the beginning of the Johannine account (John 2:14–22) rather than as the prelude to the Passion, which role the incident plays in the Synoptic accounts (Matt 21:12–13; Mark 11:15–17; Luke 19:45–46). By implication, the redaction critic does not assume, as do certain more conservative students of the Bible, that Jesus twice engaged in the prophetic gesture of cleansing the temple—once at the beginning of his public ministry, once again at the end of his public ministry.

Given the fact that source and comparative documents make the exercise of the redaction-critical technique all the easier in its exercise and all the surer in its outcome, it is somewhat surprising—at first, at least—that some of the pioneering redaction-critical analyses in the New Testament field were done upon the Gospels of Mark and John respectively. On reflection this is not as surprising as it first appears. The Gospel of Mark and, to a less certain degree, the Gospel of John represent a clear turning point in the transition from a preliterary to a literary history of the Gospel tradition. As such they are prime material for redaction-critical analysis, even if the task should not be an easy one. The identification of an author's typical turns of phrase and style characteristics is a particularly valuable element in redaction criticism. Thus, Eduard Schweizer has drawn some very significant conclusions with respect to Mark on the basis of a redactional analysis of that Gospel, special attention having been paid to Mark's characteristic vocabulary —*kērussein* (to proclaim), *didaskein* (to teach), *therapeuein* (to heal), for example.

This might well suggest to the reader of these pages that one of the concerns of the redaction-critical study of the New Testament has been the constitution of the Gospel genre. The suggestion is well taken. New Testament critics have been interested in the nature of the Gospel and apostolic letter genres and have fruitfully employed redaction criticism in their attempts to determine precisely what is a gospel or a New Testament epistle. In effect, redaction criticism, which begins where form criticism leaves off (i.e., in the analysis of small units of tradition), surprisingly ends up in genre (*Gattung*) analysis. Given the wide range of its results and the difference of its focus of interests, it is useful to distinguish between two different phases of redaction criticism: emendation criticism and composition criticism. If one makes the distinction (and not all authors do!), emendation analysis studies the modifications in the individual units of traditional materials—e.g., the modifications of the Associated Press dispatch on Biko's death effected by the editors of the *Stars and Stripes*. Composition analysis would then involve a broadening of the critic's perspective insofar as he or she concentrates on the author's activity in molding traditional patterns and original materials into a new and unique form of composition. In other words, emendation analysis is concerned with pericopes which belong to a component literary type, whereas composition analysis is concerned with literary works whose literary form is composite.

In any event, the general term "redaction criticism" applies to both phases of the analysis. This terminology corresponds to the German technical term *Redaktionsgeschichte* ("history of redaction"), first applied in New Testament circles by Willi Marxsen. Some purists would note that, strictly speaking, the German terminology is an inadequate description of the work of redaction criticism. For these purists, the "history of redaction" is appropriate only when an analysis is made of works which are the products of several redactions during the course of time. As such, *Redaktionsgeschichte* would probably be appropriate to the redaction-critical study of John, but not to the redaction-critical study of the rest of the New Testament—unless, of course, one were to revive and maintain the various proto-Matthew,

Urmarkus, and proto-Luke theories for the Synoptics and the variety of compilation theories for the Pauline corpus.

II. THE USE OF REDACTION CRITICISM IN NEW TESTAMENT STUDIES

With respect to the application of the methodology of redaction criticism to the New Testament, it seems appropriate to cite some of the many important precursors of the redaction-critical approach—R. H. Lightfoot, William Wrede, Ernst Lohmeyer, and Rudolf Bultmann. Robert Henry Lightfoot (1883–1953), an Oxford don, went to Germany in the early 1930s in order to study the methodology of form criticism. Form criticism was then enjoying a wave of popularity in German New Testament circles, even though it had not yet penetrated Fortress Britannia. The results of Lightfoot's exposure to the German *Wissenschaft* were conveyed in his Brampton Lectures of 1934, continued in 1935, and later published with the title *History and Interpretation in the Gospels.* In his third lecture, which took the Gospel of Mark as its subject, Lightfoot remarked that "interpretation [is] continually present in a book that most of us were taught to regard as almost exclusively historical." Lightfoot's fourth lecture examined the content and structure of Mark in the light of its principal purpose, which he considered to be a theological purpose. Apropos of the overall understanding of the Gospel, Lightfoot wrote: "We have found reason to believe that, rightly regarded, it may be called the book of the [secret] Messiahship of Jesus." In fact Lightfoot sustained this general interpretative position by an examination of the narrative features of Mark and the selection and arrangement of materials. In his analysis of the Markan composition, Lightfoot had made use of many of the techniques that would be associated with the name of redaction criticism, even though this particular nomenclature did not enter into New Testament circles until 1954, fully a generation after Lightfoot's pioneering efforts.

Lightfoot was, of course, influenced by German form-critical scholarship. Among German authors, a number of individuals can be cited as forerunners in the use of the redaction criticism method. Of these the first is William Wrede, whose 1901 masterpiece *The Messianic Secret* constituted a vigorous attack upon the notion that Mark was a naïve record of historical facts, rather uninfluenced by the theological notions of its author. Even before the advent of form criticism, Wrede had noted that Mark was a theological composition—a literary work in which the "messianic secret" functions as a theological leitmotif.

A second major precursor was Ernst Lohmeyer (1890–1946; he was executed by the Russians). Lohmeyer, once a student of Martin Dibelius, succeeded Bernhard and Johannes Weiss, father and son, in offering a commentary on Mark in the important German series *Kritisch-exegetischer Kommentar über das Neue Testament*. The tenth (1937) to sixteenth (1969) editions, all but the first posthumously published, are the work of Lohmeyer, a form-critical scholar, who drew attention to the significance of Galilee and Judea in Mark. According to Lohmeyer, Galilee is the place of Jesus' public ministry, while Judea is the place of the Passion and Death of Jesus. This analysis pointed to the fact that topographical references often have more than merely topographical significance. Finally, one would have to classify Bultmann himself among the precursors of the redaction-critical methodology. To be sure, he no more systematically developed the principles of this methodology than of his source-critical analysis of John, yet he was clearly moving in the direction of redaction criticism, especially in his work on the Fourth Gospel. In his epoch-making *Kritisch-exegetischer Kommentar* commentary on John, Bultmann worked out the assumption that the present text is the result of a massive editorial endeavor by the evangelist, whose work was later retouched by an ecclesiastical redactor. Moreover, in *The History of the Synoptic Tradition* Bultmann had gone a long way toward the affirmation that the Gospel genre, as such, had been created by Mark. In this respect Bultmann's form-critical analysis included no insignificant amount of compositional analysis.

The Synoptics

Among the students of the New Testament who have consciously and systematically made use of redaction criticism, Willi Marxsen enjoys a certain primacy. His 1956 work *Mark the Evangelist: Studies on the Redaction History of the Gospel** (*Der Evangelist Markus: Studien zur Redaktionsgeschichte des Evangeliums*) made a significant contribution to New Testament scholarship, if only by reason of the fact that it contributed a name from its subtitle to the customary jargon of New Testament scholars. The first draft of the work was submitted as a doctoral thesis to the University of Kiel in 1954. Subsidized by the Forschungsgemeinschaft (Research Association) and accepted in the important series, *Research on the Religion and Literature of the Old and New Testaments* (*FRLANT*), by Rudolf Bultmann, it was published in 1956. A photostatic second edition, some typographical errors having been corrected, appeared in 1959. The work did not appear in English translation, however, until 1969. By that time the significance of the redaction-critical methodology was beginning to be recognized in the Anglo-Saxon world.

The subtitle of Marxsen's work further suggests that his volume consists of a series of studies. In fact the book contains four separate studies which share a common methodology but are otherwise unrelated except for the fact that they come from the same author and treat several different issues related to the Gospel of Mark. The topics chosen for analysis by Marxsen are John the Baptist, the Geographical Outline, *Euangelion* ("Gospel"), and Mark 13. Throughout each of the studies Marxsen has first identified a Markan point of view on the basis of an analysis of the pertinent Gospel pericopes, and then pointed to significant alterations in the "major Gospels" (Matt, Luke).

The Markan point of view served as the focal point of interest in Marxsen's work. To elucidate this vantage point, Marxsen distinguished among a first life situation, located in the unique circumstance of Jesus' activity, a second life situation, mediated in the varying circumstances of the early Church, and a third life situation, represented by the set of circumstances attendant upon each of the evangelists at the time his Gospel was composed. Thus Marxsen rehabilitated Mark, whose actual achievement can be discerned through analysis of the Markan Gospel.

In his study of the Baptist pericopes, Marxsen proposed that Mark 1:1 is truly the beginning of the Gospel of Jesus Christ in that the story of John the Baptizer is, from the Markan theological perspective, the story of the forerunner of Jesus Christ. Marxsen proposed that Mark worked backward in presenting the Baptizer insofar as he narrated the Baptist traditions—not because of any particular historical interest in the Baptist himself, but because of what he had to say about Jesus. In this way, the portrayal of the Baptizer casts a hue over the portrayal of Jesus. In passing, Marxsen highlights the quality of Mark's chronological and topographical language. He noted, for example, that the mention of the wilderness in Mark 1:4 is not so much a geographical reference as it is a theological statement: "The wilderness is not a locale. We ought not speculate as to its location. The phrase does not intend to specify the Baptist's abode (not even in the most general way as adverbial). Rather *en tē erēmo* 'in the wilderness' qualifies the Baptist as the fulfiller of Old Testament predictive prophecy. Put in exaggerated form, the Baptist would still be the one who appears 'in the wilderness' even if he had never been there in all his life." In short, "the wilderness" is a bit of geographical data with theological intent. In his study of the use made of the Baptist tradition and of Mark's theological statement about the Baptist by Matthew and Luke, Marxsen singled out the fact that Matthew made a Christian preacher out of the Baptist and that Luke relegated the Baptist to the Jewish prehistory of the Gospel by separating the story of the Baptist from that of the Gospel.

Marxsen's study of the geographical outline of Mark was really the core of his work. After an examination of the topographical references in the traditional material, Marxsen showed that the presence of "Galilee" throughout the Gospel is basically due to the evangelist's editorial activity. For Mark, "Galilee" is the locale of Jesus' activity, just as "the wilderness" was the locale of the Baptist's activity. Jesus' basic proclamation of the Kingdom always took place in "Galilee." Thus "Galilee" is essentially a theological reality. Undoubtedly this usage is due to the importance of Galilee and the Galilean community at the time of the composition of Mark. Within this perspective, Marxsen also addressed himself to the issue of the abrupt ending of Mark, after source-critical analysis supported by text-critical considerations had convincingly demonstrated that Mark 16:9–20 was not the original conclusion to the Gospel. Marxsen explained that the Galilean community was still waiting for the Parousia at the time of Mark's composition. For this community, the "you will see him" of Mark 16:7 (cf. 14:28) bespoke the as yet unfulfilled promise of the Parousia.

In his analysis of the Markan concept of *euangelion,* Marxsen highlighted its Markan character—Matthew uses the noun only when it appears in his (Markan) source; Luke only uses the verb *euaggelisesthai* ("to proclaim"). According to the German exegete, *euangelion* connoted the way and the means in which the Lord is present to the community. The Markan Jesus is both the bearer and the content of the Gospel. These notions have somewhat receded in the major Gospels. Matthew's is a collection of sermons; Luke has attempted a *vita Jesus.* According to Marxsen, Mark 13 is yet another expression of the orientation of early Christianity away from Jerusalem and toward Galilee. The evangelist believed that the destruction of the temple was one of the final events. Mark still awaits the Coming One. Luke viewed the predictions of Mark 13 as utterances of the historical Jesus, which he corrects by adjusting the prophecy to the event. Matthew suppresses the imminent expectation of the Parousia by loosing the present situation from its immediate connection with the end so as to form a separate complex. By creating a separable Eschatological Discourse (Matt 25) Matthew has effectively distanced the expectation of the Parousia from the actual situation of his Church.

Luke

While Marxsen's doctoral thesis was in the hands of academic readers at the University of Kiel, Hans Conzelmann, then a professor at Zurich and later a professor at Göttingen, published an epoch-making work on the Gospel of Luke. His 1954 volume *The Theology of Saint Luke** (*Die Mitte der Zeit,* literally "the center of time"; English Translation, 1960) took issue with the traditional notion that Luke was principally a historian. According to Conzelmann, Luke was a self-conscious theologian. His Gospel was a response to the predominant theological problem of his day—namely the delay of the Parousia, which bore in its wake a need for the Church to come to terms with its continuing existence in the world. Conzelmann's response was a theory of "Redemptive History," in the articulation of which the isolated logion found in Luke 16:16 is the key element.

"The Law and the prophets were until John; since then the good news of the kingdom of God is preached, and every one enters it violently" (Luke 16:16; cf. Matt 11:12–14). For Conzelmann, this logion carefully relegates John the Baptist to past times, to the time of Israel. Such a marked separation between the time of Israel and the time of Jesus is a feature of the Third Gospel. Thus Luke effectively dispatched the Baptist with an account of his imprisonment (Luke 3:18–20) before he began his narrative of Jesus' baptism, the inauguration of his public ministry (Luke 3:21–22). The third major stage in redemptive history is the time of the Church. A first period, that of the infant Church, is the time of the witnesses to Jesus—the apostles and disciples, filled with the Spirit, who testified to Jesus and formed a link with Him as Christians worked out the implications of the kerygma. The time of the Church follows on this unique foundational period. This time is an indefinite period in which Christians appropriate the objective salvation that Christ has won. It is the era of Jesus, the center of time.

Conzelmann has also divided this central time into three periods. A first period focuses on the gathering of "witnesses" in Galilee. The second consists of the journey of the Galileans to the Temple. The third considers Jesus' teaching in the Temple and his Passion in Jerusalem. Each of these three periods opens with a manifestation scene that imparts a significant Christology. The first period begins with Jesus' baptism (Luke 3:21–22), which reveals Jesus as the Son of God, anointed by the power of the Spirit. The second period starts with the Transfiguration (Luke 9:28–36), to which is appended the Passion prediction, thus revealing that the Son of God is destined to suffer. The third period is inaugurated by the solemn Entry into Jerusalem (Luke 19:28–40), highlighting the royal nature of Jesus' ministry.

According to Conzelmann, Luke has pushed the final times, the eschaton, into a distant, indefinite future. Although he has used Mark as one of his sources, Luke has dropped Mark 1:15 ("The time is fulfilled, and the kingdom of God is at hand; repent, and believe in the gospel"), and has functionally replaced this logion with the programmatic discourse in the synagogue of Nazareth: "Today this scripture has been fulfilled in your hearing" (Luke 4:18–27). Significantly, Luke has located Jesus' ministry in Galilee and Jerusalem, the first the locale of the manifestation of the time of salvation, the second the locale of Passion, a prelude to the Resurrection-Ascension. With the Ascension begins the time of the Church (Luke 24:50–53; Acts 1:6–11), which moves away from Jerusalem. John the Baptist had previously been systematically excluded from Galilee and Jerusalem, the places of Jesus' ministry. Thus Conzelmann's analysis shows once again that the topographical references, which had virtually lost all significance in the form-critical approach to the Gospels, are extremely important for understanding the Gospels in their present redaction—not so much from a historical point of view, but because of the theological vision they serve.

Matthew

A third trailblazing effort in the application of the method of redaction analysis to the Synoptics appeared in English translation much more rapidly than did the earlier works of Conzelmann and Marxsen. This third effort was a collaborative work by Heidelberg's Günther Bornkamm and two of his disciples, Gerhard Barth and Heinz Joachim Held, which appeared in 1960 under the title *Tradition and Interpretation in Matthew** (*Überlieferung und Auslegung im Matthäusevangelium;* ET, 1963). The unity of the volume is assured by its methodology. The contributions of Barth and Held represent doctoral dissertations prepared under Bornkamm's direction. The master's own contributions to the volume were a reworking of a significant 1948 article on the Stilling of the Storm (Matt 8:23–27) and a revision of a talk given to an assembly of German theologians in 1954.

In many respects this collaborative work is more valuable with respect to its methodology than it is with respect to its conclusions. Bornkamm considered Matthew to have been an interpreter of a tradition he collected and arranged. Although Matthew was the representative of a community, he was more than simply the spokesperson of that community. The exposition of his own theological point of view in the Gospel made of Matthew a distinct individual in the history of early Christian literature. Although Matthew's theological views pervade the entire Gospel, they emerge with particular clarity in the discourses (Matt 5–7, 10, 13, 18, 23–25), which have long been recognized as compositions by the evangelist. The leitmotif of the discourses is the close association between the notion of the Church and the expectation of the End Time—that is, between ecclesiology and eschatology. The Church on earth is both different from the kingdom and closely associated with it. Matthew suggests that its life situation is Hellenistic Jewish Christianity—at odds, on the one hand, with Hellenistic enthusiasm and antinomianism, and at odds, on the other, with the rabbinic Judaism of the late first century, which accused Jewish sects of heresy and excommunicated them.

Barth's contribution to the Matthean anthology is one which highlighted Matthew's construction, choice of vocabulary, and modifications over and against the traditions contained in his source material, Mark and *Q*. By means of an analysis of Matthean vocabulary, Barth's study, "Matthew's Understanding of the Law," has shown that Matthew highlights an expectation of the judgment (cf. the use of *krisis,* judgment; *hēmera kriseōs,* day of Judgment; *misthos,* reward) and the exhortation to do God's will (cf. the use of *dikaiosunē,* righteousness; *keleuein,* command; *tērein,* keep; *anomia,* lawlessness). As Matthew generally defended the validity of the law and the prophets, he mounted a strong attack against a group of antinomians without neglecting an ongoing polemic against Pharisaism and the rabbinate. Matthew's version of the love command (Matt 22:37–40; cf. 19:19) is significant in this regard. By using the love command to interpret the Law, Matthew distanced himself from the rabbinate; by citing the love command as the essence of the Law, Matthew took issue with the antinomians.

With Held's work, the reader turns from a consideration of the Matthean discourse material to the Matthean narrative material. Held maintained that the abridgment, expansion, and placement of the Matthean miracle stories served to highlight Matthew's own point of view. Specifically, Held studied the formal characteristics in the Matthean miracle stories. Among these he cited five in particular: (1) the formal manner of narration, especially at the outset and at the conclusion of the narrative; (2) the omission of nonessential people and actions; (3) the use of conversation as the center of the miracle stories; (4) the linkage by catchwords within the miracle stories; and (5) the role of faith in the miracle stories. According to Held, the notion that faith and miracle belong together was the directing principle of Matthew's redactional activity. Matthew's editorializing was related to the Christology to which the miracle stories give witness. These stories highlight Jesus as the fulfillment of Scripture. They show Jesus not as a tremendous thaumaturge, but as the servant of God who has taken up the cause of the helpless. They portray Jesus as the Lord and helper of his community. Finally, the Jesus of the Matthean miracle stories is one who has given a share in his authority to his disciples.

Further Use of the Methodology

Not all the points proposed in the Bornkamm-Barth-Held analysis have been accepted by students of Matthew's Gospel. Nonetheless the methodology they have employed is considered to be a valuable tool for Matthean and New Testament study. In the two decades following the publication of *Tradition and Interpretation in Matthew,* a number of significant monographs on Matthew appeared. In Germany redaction-critical studies of the First Gospel were published by Wolfgang Trilling (Matthew's understanding of the true Israel), Martin Johannes Fielder (righteousness in Matthew), Georg Strecker (Christology and ecclesiology), Reinhart Hummel (the controversy with Judaism), and Manfred Punge (eschatology and salvation history). Outside of Germany the methodology was essentially employed by William G. Thompson (Matt 17:22–18:35), Donald Senior (the Passion narrative), Jack Dean Kingsbury (the Parables of Matt 13; Christology), and John P. Meier (law and history in Matt 5:17–48; Christ, church and morality). Nevertheless, it remains clear that the methodology cannot be employed in total independence of the older methodologies. For example, George M. Soares Prabhu's study on *The Formula Quotations in the Infancy Narrative of Matthew* has demonstrably shown that the formulaic citations that are such a characteristic element of Matthew's Gospel (1:22–23; 2:15, 17–18, 23; 4:14–16; 8:17; 12:17, 21; 13:35; 21:4; 27:9–10 and perhaps 2:5–6; 13:14–15; 26:54, 56), and to this extent constitute a significant component of Matthean redaction, can be successfully elucidated by means of a tradition-history study.

Mark's use of characteristic vocabulary remains for all expositors a significant key to an understanding of the evangelist's thought. The evangelist's preference for kerygmatic language in his presentation of Jesus suggests the basic orientation of his written text. The use of *euthus* ("immediately") in the miracle stories clearly reflects the Markan hand. Fondness for the use of this terminology not only speaks of the reality of the individual miracles (as a Markan literary formula in the third part of the exposition of the miracle form), but bespeaks the eschatological urgency of the entire Gospel. For the rest, significant studies on Mark, from the redaction-critical point of view, have been done by Alfred Suhl (the Old Testament in Mark), James M. Robinson (history in Mark), Philipp Vielhauer (Christology), Johannes

Schreiber (theology), Quentin Quesnell (the mind of Mark), Jan Lambrecht (Mark 13), and Rudolf Pesch (eschatological expectation).

In Lucan studies, the work done by Conzelmann more than a quarter of a century ago not only marks a turning point in the history of criticism of the Third Gospel, but also serves as the horizon in whose light all contemporary studies must be seen. Explicitly or implicitly, most of current Lucan scholarship is engaged in an ongoing dialogue with Conzelmann in a way analogous to that in which so much Johannine scholarship is a dialogue with Rudolf Bultmann and his associates. As a specific case in point, the 1964 work of Helmut Flender, *St. Luke, Theologian of Redemptive History* (*Heil und Geschichte in der Theologie des Lukas*), can be cited. Flender has identified a dialectical technique running throughout Luke-Acts. The "law of two" appears in a variety of examples of complementary parallelism, especially the balanced stories of men and women—Zechariah and Mary (1:8–38), Simeon and Anna (2:33–38), the Centurion of Capernaum and the Widow of Nain (7:1–17), the Lost Coin and the Lost Sheep (15:3–10), the Widow and the Publican (18:1–14), etc. The "law of two" also links up individuals and notions which are significantly similar, yet decisively dissimilar. The contract between Jesus and John the Baptist is a striking example of this climactic parallelism but there are others, including the contrast between the old and the new (covenants). The antithetical parallels of Luke-Acts constitute a third modality of the "law of two." Thus Luke opposes the beatitudes and woes (6:20–26), as well as the rejection of Jesus and acceptance of him (4:16–37). Linguistic studies on Luke-Acts are also revelatory. In this regard, attention can be drawn to the significance of the adverbs "now" (*nun*) and "today" (*sēmeron*), utilized by Luke to highlight the notion that the time of salvation is realized in the presence of Jesus. "Now" appears thirty-nine times in Luke-Acts (14+25), and only seven times in Matthew-Mark (4+3); "Today" appears twenty times in Luke-Acts (12+8) and only nine times in Matthew-Mark (8+1).

The Acts of the Apostles

The overall significance of Conzelmann's work is further underscored by the fact that Münster's Ernst Haenchen, who took over from Hans Heinrich Wendt (ninth edition, 1913) editorial responsibility for the commentary on Acts in the *Kritisch-exegetischer Kommentar* (*KEK*) as of the tenth edition of that work (1956), not only employed the redaction-critical method in his commentary, but added a special section on "Luke as Theologian, Historian, Writer," in the twelfth edition (1959). Haenchen's opening remarks recognize the fact that Conzelmann and Philipp Vielhauer had previously made substantial contributions toward the elucidation of Lucan theology. Haenchen admits that Luke is not a systematic theologian, but states emphatically, "Nevertheless he [Luke] has a theology of his own; he sets out from definite theological premises and treats the immediate theological questions of his age." Luke's theological considerations are suggested to the reader in his historical presentation. Among them, God the Father occupies a predominant place. For Jesus, Luke prefers the designations "Lord" and "Anointed" rather than that of "Son." That the Spirit is a focal point of interest in Acts (as in Luke) is recognized by virtually every commentator. Haenchen has indicated that for the Holy Spirit, Luke had linked together three predicates of different provenance. First, the Spirit is the gift each Christian receives at baptism. Second, the Spirit is given to individual Christians at a particular time for a given task. Third, the Spirit imparts specific directions to the Christian mission at decisive junctures. The message about Jesus, belief in whom brings forgiveness of sins and deliverance from wrath, is the Word of God. It is this Word that fills the time after Pentecost.

Prior to the publication of his magisterial commentary, Haenchen had published a short study on the tradition and composition of Acts (1955). In his commentary, Haenchen also addressed himself to Luke's use of editorial techniques. Haenchen cited Luke's tendency to enliven bare facts in order to edify, and also his ability to condense events ranging over a long period and encompass them within a single scene. In passing, Luke has made the point that Christians had not set about fomenting any political revolution; indeed, Roman authorities had nothing to fear from Christian missionaries. Throughout the entire book of Acts, we can discern Luke's dramatic technique of scene writing. Although acquainted with but one tradition on Paul's "conversion," for example, Luke used it in different ways so as to fashion three accounts of the conversion, and thus advance dramatically the thesis of Acts.

How should one judge an author such as Luke? Forthrightly Haenchen has responded:

> That a writer should thus make free with tradition must at first strike us as irresponsible, as an unwarranted license. But evidently Luke has a conception of the narrator's calling that is different from ours. For him, a narration should not describe an event with the precision of a police-report, but must make the listener or reader aware of the inner significance of what happened, and impress upon him, unforgettably, the truth of the power of God made manifest in it. The writer's obedience is indeed fulfilled in the very freedom of his rendering. (*The Acts of the Apostles*, p. 110)

As has been noted, speeches are of central significance in Acts, the second part of Luke's work. The early form-critical analysis of the speeches, principally undertaken by Martin Dibelius and C. H. Dodd, identified a kerygmatic discourse type characterized by kerygma, scriptural proof, and an exhortation to repent. For these authors the kerygmatic discourse properly represented a literary type because it contained the traditional pattern of the Jewish-Christian missionary sermon. In 1961 Ulrich Wilckens reopened the examination of these speeches from the point of view of form criticism and tradition history, but he also made use of the type of analysis that had been so successfully employed by Conzelmann and Haenchen. For Wilckens, a tradition-history study necessarily leads to a redaction-critical result. Wilckens' own work was a detailed analysis of six kerygmatic speeches: Peter's Pentecost speech (Acts 2:14–19), Peter's speech to the people (3:12–26), Peter's speech before the Sanhedrin (4:9–12), Peter's defense before the Sanhedrin (5:30–32), Peter's speech to Cornelius (10:34–43), and Paul's speech in Antioch of Pisidia (13:16–41). Wilckens maintained that these speeches constitute the decisive center of Luke's narrative in Acts. On analysis, these speeches are revealed to contain six parts: a link with the circumstances by means of a scriptural citation leading up to the kerygma, the miracles and Death of Jesus, his Resurrection and its scriptural proof, a summary assertion, and finally a call to repentance and salvation. For Wilckens this pattern represents not elements of the Jewish-Christian missionary sermon, but Gentile Christian missionary preaching.

In short, Wilckens articulated the notion that Luke had shaped the construction and subject matter of the tradition in such a way that his own work as a theologian becomes quite evident. Ultimately, the stance of Lucan theology is what Wilckens called the "inclusive horizon of Christian theology." According to Wilckens, Luke grappled with the problem of the historical time of Christianity and the historicity of the Christian faith as such. Thus he became the distinctive theologian of early Catholicism at its beginnings. While some critics would find in Wilckens' conclusion the statement of an ideology rather than the precipitate of historical analysis, and while others would take issue with Wilckens' notion that Luke composed the speeches of Acts almost *de novo* and thus created the Jewish-Christian missionary pattern, few would take issue with his contention that Luke has so molded the kerygmatic speeches of Acts that they betray his own convictions. The hand of a single author is manifest in a common vocabulary and the presence of striking style characteristics, especially the "break-off" technique (Acts 7:53–54; 10:43–44; 22:21–22; 23:6–7; 26:23–24). As a whole the speeches articulate the theology of Luke. They exposit the theme of the continuity between Jesus and the Church (cf. the use of a formulaic "we are all witnesses" in 2:32; 3:15; 5:32; 10:39, 41; 13:31). As a group they illustrate the theme announced in Acts 1:8—namely, that the Gospel should be preached from Jerusalem to the ends of the world.

The Letters

One of the by-products of the redaction-critical analysis of Acts has been to set apart Luke's theological portrait of Paul from the Paul known to Christian tradition as apostle to the Gentiles and writer of letters. The authentic letters of Paul are occasional documents; so too are many of the deutero-Pauline compositions. Thus it is only to some limited extent that one can properly speak of redaction criticism, in the sense in which it is normally understood by New Testament scholars, when one is studying the Pauline letters. True, one can compare them with the ancient letters, as Adolf Deissmann did long ago, to note that the Pauline letters are commonly longer and more general in context than are the ancient letters on papyri unearthed by the archaeologists along with ostraca and other ancient artifacts. One can also note certain characteristic features of Pauline style—its redundancy and asyndeton, its use of formulaic expressions such as "you have no need to have any one write to you" (1 Thes 4:9—a good example of preterition) and "Now concerning . . ." (1 Cor 8:1—used to introduce matters about which an inquiry had been made), and its modification of traditional material such as the striking insertion of "death on a cross" at Philippians 2:8. One can likewise cite Paul's use of traditional apocalyptic and liturgical motifs in his several letters. Nonetheless it is virtually impossible to speak of the redaction-critical analysis of Paul's letters when one understands redaction criticism in the narrower sense of emendation analysis.

When, however, one understands redaction criticism in the broader sense of compositional analysis, it appears, to this author at least, that it is indeed legitimate to speak of redaction criticism with regard to Paul. I think especially of Paul's development of the Hellenistic letter form into the apostolic letter, a model which served not only as an example for the deutero-Pauline letters, but also for the catholic epistles as well, albeit in a somewhat restricted sense in the case of James. To speak of Paul's development of the apostolic letter is, in a sense, to reflect on tradition history and the development of a specific modality of the letter. Yet each of the authentic Pauline letters is so marked with Paul's hand that the apostolic letter is a genre unto itself.

It is generally recognized that the ancient Hellenistic letter was characterized by a tripartite schema: protocol, body, and eschatocol. The protocol included the identification of the sender, the designation of the recipient(s), greetings, and a wish for good health. The body of the letter normally opened with a characteristic formula, very frequently a thanksgiving to the gods or the divinity. First found in a letter dating to ca. 260 B.C., the thanksgiving period became more common and quite stylized prior to its entrance into Hellenistic Judaism (cf. 2 Mac 1:10–11). The eschatocol contained greetings, (health) wishes, a final greeting, occasionally the date of the letter, and (from Roman times) a farewell. Functionally, the letter expressed: (1) a friendly relationship (*philophronensis*); (2) presence and a desire to be present (*parousia*); and (3) a specific content, the discussion or discourse (*homilia*).

Let it simply be said that the protocol of the Pauline letter became rather stereotyped. As conveyers of the initial greetings, there were always Paul and his companions for the authentic Paulines. In the authentic letters, a limited use of titles appears. In the deutero-Paulines, the titles and expatiation upon them have a tendency to increase. The recipients are always local congregations, in whose presence the letter was to be read aloud. Even the "private letter" to Philemon is addressed to a domestic church (cf. Phlm 2). The eschatocols of the Pastorals (e.g., 1 Tim 6:21) reveal that they too were not really intended for a single individual. In the apostolic letter, the greeting was taken over from the liturgy (1 Thes 1:1), whence it was expanded and became the standard "Grace to you and peace from God our Father and the Lord Jesus Christ." The wish for good health was dropped (but see 3 John 2).

The body of the apostolic letter began with a thanksgiving period, of which two types (see the studies of Paul Schubert and Eduard Lohse) basically exist. A characteristic feature of the thanksgiving period in the Pauline letters was its conclusion, an eschatological climax (1 Thes 1:10; 3:11–13; 1 Cor 1:8–9; etc.). Among the indisputably authentic Pauline letters only Galatians lacks the thanksgiving period—an anomaly undoubtedly due to the strained relationship which existed between Paul and the churches of Galatia at the time the letter was composed. In 2 Corinthians the thanksgiving has been replaced by an extended benediction (cf. 2 Cor 1:3; comp Eph 1:3). Toward the end of the body portion of the letter, one can identify a Pauline tendency to attach eschatological conclusions to his discussions (Rom 8:31–39; 11:25–36; 1 Cor 4:6–13; etc.). Moreover Paul has expanded the travelogue section of his letter in such a way as to indicate why he is writing, his intention to send a colleague, or his own intention to pay the community a personal visit (Rom 15:14–33; 1 Cor 4:14–21; 1 Thes 2:17 – 3:13; etc.). Robert W. Funk has styled these sections the "Apostolic Parousia" since their underlying theme is "the presence of apostolic authority and power."

Within the Pauline eschatocol, Schmithals has distinguished some five elements: personal notes, an intercession or doxology, paraenesis, salutations, and a benediction. The salutation frequently includes the exhortation to exchange a "holy kiss" (Rom 16:16; 1 Cor 16:20; 2 Cor 13:12; and 1 Thes 5:26). The benediction, like the greeting of the protocol, seems to have been taken over from liturgical usage.

The net result of these salient modifications of the traditional epistolary form is such that the apostolic letter is best qualified as a literary genre created by Paul. In this respect Paul has made as much of an impact upon the history of early Christian literature as did Mark, who created the Gospel genre. Mark's contribution was such that the major evangelists, including John, followed his lead in using the Gospel genre to tell the story of Jesus. Paul's contribution was such that the apostolic letter in the form of Pauline pseudepigrapha was copied by the authors of the deutero-Paulines and that it was adopted and somewhat adapted by those responsible for 1,2 Peter, James, and Jude.

The Johannine Corpus

Krister Stendahl and Elisabeth Schüssler Fiorenza have argued that the author of Revelation has derived the authority of his work by patterning it after the authoritative Pauline letter form (cf. Rev 1:4–6). It is clear that the author of Revelation has made use of four basic septets (letters, seals, trumpets, bowls) which provide a major structural element in his work. Aside from these septets, there is wide disagreement among the commentators as to the precise structure imparted by the author of Revelation to his mosaic of traditional motifs.

From another vantage point, it is quite clear that the author of Revelation has made use of an abundance of traditional motifs. His use of the Old Testament is illustrative in this regard; he frequently alludes to it, but never cites it verbatim. He has used these allusions, and sometimes a combination of allusions, to make his own theological statement. This brief analysis of a source that can be checked allows us to conclude that the author has used, revised, altered, and adapted a variety of traditional materials for his own theological purposes.

One might also note that the author of the final book in the New Testament has made use of a variety of techniques in the composition of a work that is strangely unified despite its manifest diversity. Among these techniques, as cited by Fiorenza, are the use of a common stock of symbols and images, preannouncements, cross-references, contrasts, numbers and numerical structures, interludes, and intercalations. Throughout, the author of Revelation maintains his theological perspective and moves the narrative from promise to fulfillment. Notwithstanding the plethora and diversity of the traditional materials that have been employed and adapted, a basic unity has been imparted to the diversity. Thus Fiorenza has concluded her study with the following summary analysis:

> The epistolary framework of Revelation represents not an artificial and unimportant setting for the apocalyptic-mythopoeic vision, but provides together with the prophetic-apocalyptic judgment/salvation genre the macro-form or complex type of Revelation (ABCDC'B'A'). . . . The structuralist and architectonic analysis of Revelation confirms the assumption that the author intended to write a work of prophecy in the form of the apostolic letter. Moreover, it underlines the dramatic character of Revelation. In choosing the concentric pattern ABCDC'B'A' the author makes the small scroll of prophecy in 10:1 – 15:4 into the climactic center of the action. The author has fused his materials, patterns, and theological perspective into the unique form-content configuration of Revelation (*Composition and Structure of the Revelation of John*, p. 366).

If Revelation appears to be a unique composition emanating from within the so-called Johannine school, the Fourth Gospel also appears to be a singular piece of New Testament literature produced within these circles. Among English-language authors, one of the first to approach John from the standpoint of redaction criticism was J. Louis Martyn. In *History and Theology in the Fourth Gospel* (1968), Martyn carefully distinguished between traditional materials in John and those passages in which elements of John's own interests and experiences are more or less clearly reflected. Attention to stylistic analysis and the accents characteristic of the Johannine discourses unparalleled in the Synoptics enables the reader to identify Johannine redactional activity. Otherwise a comparison between John and the Synoptics allows for the identification of traditional items, including the Preaching of John the Baptist, Jesus' Baptism, the Calling of the Disciples, Miracles of Healing, Sharp Words of Conflict, the Triumphal Entry into Jerusalem, the Cleansing of the Temple, the Last Supper, the Betrayal, the Trial, Crucifixion, and Resurrection. The list is rather more suggestive than exhaustive, yet it is sufficiently lengthy to provide a point of departure for redaction analysis of the Fourth Gospel. Martyn's conviction was that the Fourth Evangelist was writing in his own terms in response to contemporary events.

By means of a detailed analysis of the stories about the lame man at Bethzatha (John 5) and the blind beggar near the Temple (John 9), Martyn was able to identify each of the Synoptic-like miracle stories (John 4:1–9; 9:1–7) as but the first in a sequence of Johannine scenes. These scenes succeed one another in rapid fashion throughout the respective chapters, their sequential unity being maintained by the dropping of one character from the scene while the other remains to continue the action with a new character in the following scene. The whole is a well-constructed drama, whose script presents a witness at two levels: (1) to an *einmalig* ("once only") event during Jesus' lifetime; and (2) to Jesus' presence in the events then being experienced by the Johannine community. Primary among those events was the crisis of a newly formulated means for detecting those Christian Jews who wanted to hold allegiance both to Moses and to Jesus as the Messiah. The crisis-provoking event was identified by Martyn as the famous (or infamous?) twelfth benediction: "For the apostates let there be no hope. And let the arrogant government be speedily uprooted in our days. Let the Nazarenes and the Minim be destroyed in a moment, and let them be blotted out of the Book of Life and not be inscribed together with the righteous. Blessed are thou, O Lord, who humblest the proud!"

Phrased in other terms, one could say that the life situation of the Fourth Gospel is the dialogue between the Johannine community and the synagogue. A reading of John 5 and John 7 as a drama on two levels, similar in kind to that which ensued upon the curse of the blind beggar, enabled Martyn to identify three hotly disputed and interrelated questions within the Johannine situation: Is Jesus the Messiah of Jewish expectations? How is one correctly to interpret Jesus' signs? What is the relationship between Jesus and Moses? In some senses the relationship between Moses and the Messiah is the key issue. Along with several other scholars, Martyn has discerned a point in the tradition history behind the Fourth Gospel in which the expectation of a prophet like Moses (Deut 18:15) was a key element. For John, Jesus is this Prophet but the evangelist cannot abide this low Christology. Accordingly the dramatic thrust of John focuses upon a higher Christology. Present to his community, Jesus pronounces exceptionally high Christological claims—as in the "I am the Bread of Life" logion of John 6:35, 38. John bore witness to both the *einmalig* level of the events he narrated as well as the contemporary level of the drama. Indeed, the two-level drama, with its low and high Christology, is John's own creation. That the events to which he witnesses transpire on both levels of the drama is, in Martyn's word, "to a large extent, the good news itself."

III. AN EXERCISE IN REDACTION CRITICISM

A. The Message of the Baptist: Luke 3:7–18 (par. Matt 3:7–12)

Luke 3:7–18

7 He said therefore to the multitudes that came out to be baptized by him, "You brood of vipers! Who warned you to flee from the wrath to come? 8 Bear fruits that befit repentance, and do not begin to say to yourselves, 'We have Abraham as our father'; for I tell you, God is able from these stones to raise up children to Abraham. 9 Even now the axe is laid to the root of the trees; every tree therefore that does not bear good fruit is cut down and thrown into the fire." 10 And the multitudes asked him, "What then shall we do?"

11 And he answered them, "He who has two coats, let him share with him who has none; and he who has food, let him do likewise." 12 Tax collectors also came to be baptized, and said to him, "Teacher, what shall we do?" 13 And he said to them, "Collect no more than is appointed you." 14 Soldiers also asked him, "And we, what shall we do?" And he said to them, "Rob no one by violence or by false accusation, and be content with your wages." 15 As the people were in expectation, all men questioned in their hearts concerning John, whether perhaps he were the Christ, 16 John answered them all, "I baptize you with water; but he who is mightier than I is coming, the thong of whose sandals I am not worthy to untie; he will baptize you with the Holy Spirit and with fire. 17 His winnowing fork is in his hand, to clear his threshing floor, and to

Matthew 3:7–12

7 But when he saw many of the Pharisees and Sadducees coming for baptism, he said to them, "You brood of vipers! Who warned you to flee from the wrath to come? 8 Bear fruit that befits repentance, 9 and do not presume to say to yourselves, 'We have Abraham as our father'; for I tell you, God is able from these stones to raise up children to Abraham. 10 Even now the axe is laid to the root of the trees; every tree therefore that does not bear good fruit is cut down and thrown into the fire.

11 "I baptize you with water for repentance, but he who is coming after me is mightier than I, whose sandals I am not worthy to carry; he will baptize you with the Holy Spirit and with fire. 12 His winnowing fork is in his hand, and he will clear his threshing floor and gather his wheat

Luke 3:7–18
gather the wheat into his granary,
but the chaff he will burn with
unquenchable fire."
18 So, with many other exhortations,
he preached good news to the people.

Matthew 3:7–12
into the granary, but the chaff he will
burn with unquenchable fire."

It is generally acknowledged, and with good reason, that Luke is more conservative with respect to his use of source material than Matthew. Thus Luke seems to have preserved the Aramaism found in *Q* at verse 8, "do not begin to say to yourselves." It must nonetheless also be admitted that Luke has occasionally edited his source material. Typically, some of Luke's editorial formulations serve as transitions. The reader can note that, in an earlier section of the Third Gospel, Luke brought the Infancy narrative to a close with a summary verse (Luke 2:52) paralleling an earlier summary verse (Luke 1:80). In the parallel we can see an example of the Lucan "law of two" as well as of Luke's tendency to terminate a narrative with a summary verse transition. On the other hand, Luke will occasionally create an introductory verse for his narrative. In keeping with his concern for history, the editorial introduction sometimes affirms the connection between redemptive history and secular history. This literary technique and theological concern go hand in hand to explain the sixfold synchronism with which Luke has begun his presentation of the Baptist in 3:1–2.

Most scholars place Luke 3:18 among the concluding summaries written by Luke, since *men oun* ("so") is of common occurrence in Luke's Acts. To render the notion of "other," Luke prefers *heteros* to *allos*. In contrast to Matthew and Mark, Luke uses *parakalō* with the meaning of "to exhort." Whereas Matthew uses the verb *euaggelisomai* ("preach good news") only once and Mark never uses it, Luke employs the verb frequently throughout Luke-Acts, and always in the sense of proclaiming good news (e.g., Luke 2:10). Finally, "the people" (*ho laos*) who appear here in contrast to "the multitudes" of verses 7, 10 is a Lucan theme (cf. Luke 1:17, 77). Perhaps Luke has composed the summary transition at 3:18 on the basis of Joel 3:5. In any event his composition succinctly summarizes the preceding account and prepares the way for a new contrasting theme.

Virtually all scholars ascribe verse 18 to the hand of Luke, but there are some (e.g., H. Schürmann) who are reluctant to see in Luke 3:15 a Lucan composition. They argue that the logia of verses 16–17 would always need some sort of an introduction and that the language of these verses shows signs of pre-Lucan provenance. To my mind these arguments are not sufficiently convincing, and I find myself in agreement with those scholars (R. Bultmann, Paul Hoffmann, S. Schulz, etc.) who think that verse 15 is a transitional verse created by Luke to introduce the Baptist's messianic preaching. If one is to ascribe the verse to *Q*, then one must at least admit that "the people" is a redactional emendation by Luke. It is otherwise difficult to explain their sudden appearance on the scene.

With regard to verses 10–14, it would seem that the "Teacher" (*didas-*

222

kolos) of verse 12 is a result of Lucan redaction. The designation of Jesus as "Teacher" is not common in *Q*. As a matter of fact, "Teacher" (*didaskolos*) appears in *Q* only in the saying (a proverb?) about the teacher and his disciple in Luke 6:40 (= Matt 10:24–25). On the other hand, "Teacher" in the vocative (*didaskale,* as in 3:12) occurs twelve times in Luke's Gospel. It always occurs on the lips of those who are not yet disciples. Luke uses "Master" as the form of address (*Epistata,* in the vocative) which the disciples use in speaking of Jesus (Luke 5:5; 8:24, 45; 9:33, 49; 17:13). In this use of distinctive Christological titles as in his concern for the people of Israel, the discerning reader catches a glimpse of Luke's theological perspective.

Matthew approached the *Q* material with a bit more freedom than did Luke. A small indication of this is Matthew's choice of the better Greek expression "do not presume to say to yourselves" in contrast to Luke's "do not begin to say to yourselves," a mechanical reproduction of the translation Greek of his source. A further indication is Matthew's substitution of "carrying" the sandals for the more traditional "untying the strap" of the sandals (Luke 3:16; Mark 1:8; John 1:27). Since only non-Jewish slaves were required to untie their master's sandals, the point of the traditional logion was that the Baptist is completely subordinate to Jesus, even more so than a slave would be to his master. Matthew's emendation takes this most menial task away from the Baptist. By modifying his language ever so slightly, Matthew has presented a portrait of the Baptist which is consistent with his higher image of the Baptist. For Luke, the Baptist belongs to former times; for Matthew, the Baptist is the first Christian preacher.

The appearance of the "Pharisees and Sadduccees" in Matthew 3:7 (in contrast to Luke's "multitudes") is also due to Matthean redaction. Within the four Gospels, the expression occurs only in Matthew (3:7; 16:1, 6, 11, 12 [twice]). In Matthew 3:7 as elsewhere, we can recognize a trace of the ongoing dispute between Matthew's Jewish-Christian community and the organs of institutional Judaism. Furthermore, if Luke 3:10–14 does emanate from the *Q* source, it is likely that it was intentionally omitted by Matthew. Matthew has reserved his ethical teaching for the Sermon on the Mount (Matt 5 – 7). There is simply no place for catechesis in an earlier section of his Gospel.

B. The Stilling of the Storm: Matthew 8:23–27 (par. Mark 4:35–41)

Matthew 8:23–27	Mark 4:35–41
23 And when he got into the boat, his disciples followed him. 24 And behold, there arose a great storm on the sea, so that the boat was being swamped by the waves; but he was asleep. 25 And they went and woke him, saying, "Save, Lord; we are perishing." 26 And he said to them,	35 On that day, when evening had come, he said to them, "Let us go across to the other side." 36 And leaving the crowd, they took him with them, just as he was, in the boat. And other boats were with him. 37 And a great storm of wind arose, and the waves beat into the boat, so that the

Matthew 8:23–27

"Why are you afraid, O men of little faith?" Then he rose and rebuked the winds and the sea; and there was a great calm. 27 And the men marveled, saying, "What sort of man is this, that even winds and sea obey him?"

Mark 4:35–41

boat was already filling. 38 But he was in the stern, asleep on the cushion; and they woke him and said to him, "Teacher, do you not care if we perish?" 39 And he awoke and rebuked the wind, and said to the sea, "Peace! Be still!" And the wind ceased, and there was a great calm. 40 He said to them, "Why are you afraid? Have you no faith?" 41 And they were filled with awe, and said to one another, "Who then is this, that even wind and sea obey him?"

Source-critical analysis of the Gospels leads to the conclusion that Matthew is dependent upon Mark. One indication that this is so is to be found in Matthew's use of *epitimaō* ("rebuke") at 8:26. Although the word is found some seven times in Matthew (8:26; 12:16; 16:20, 22; 17:18; 19:13; 20:31), it is never used by Matthew except in those cases in which it is found in the Markan text he is using as a source document. In these instances Matthew has taken over the word from his Markan source. At 8:26, Matthew has taken "rebuke" from 4:39. Yet if Matthew has appropriated this word from Mark, it is also patently clear that Matthew has not simply reproduced the Markan story.

The Matthean version of the Stilling of the Storm is considerably shorter than the Markan version. One notices immediately that the Matthean text has no parallel to the Markan introduction (4:35). Beyond that, Matthew seems to have omitted several features of the Markan narrative, particularly those which contributed to the realism and drama of the tale: "And other boats were with him. . . . so that the boat was filling. . . . in the stern . . . on the cushion . . . and the wind ceased . . . to one another . . ." Matthew has even dropped Jesus' solemn utterance, "Peace! Be still!" A rapid overview of the miracle stories in Matthew reveals that the abridgment of the traditional story of the Stilling of the Storm is but one instance of the Matthean editor at work. Matthew has a tendency to abbreviate his source material. This editorial technique is not so much a space saver as it is a method of interpretation. Matthew is not so much interested in offering a more concise version of the traditional narrative as he is in concentrating on the essentials and reaching the essential point more rapidly.

For Matthew, the essential point is Christological. In abridging the Markan narrative, Matthew eliminated the artless details and those which served to highlight the wonder of the miracle in order to concentrate on Jesus, the worker of the miracle. The presentation of the choral response in verse 27 is marked by this greater concentration on Jesus. Instead of the rhetorical question exchanged among the awestruck witnesses to the miracle found in Mark, "Who then is this, that even wind and sea obey him?"

Matthew has a solemn "What sort of man is this, that even winds and sea obey him?" The hapax use of the interrogative "What sort of" (*potapos*) serves to focus the attention singularly on Jesus.

In one way, however, Matthew has already answered his own question. In verse 25 the disciples appeal to Jesus, calling him "Lord" (*kurie*). In the parallel passages of Mark and Luke, Jesus is respectively addressed as "Teacher" (*didaskale,* Mark 4:38) and "Master" (*epistata,* Luke 8:24). Matthew seems to have inserted "Lord" into his version of the Stilling of the Storm because it is one of his chief Christological titles. Matthew uses the *kurios* title in order to attribute authority and an exalted status to Jesus. The use of this title is an implicit confession of faith in that the title, applied to Jesus, never appears on the lips of anyone in Matthew's Gospel except the disciples of Jesus. Strangers, enemies, and Judas address Jesus as "Teacher" (*didaskale*) or "Rabbi" (*rabbi*) but never as "Lord." Since, moreover, the *kurios* title is used in the vocative in Matthew 8:25—and this is generally the case throughout Matthew—it can be noted that the title has a relational character. It identifies the relationship between Jesus and his disciples.

In this respect the Matthean redaction of verse 23 is indeed significant. The narrative focuses exclusively on Jesus and his disciples. There is no mention of the departure from the crowds, as in Mark 4:36a. Neither does Matthew cite the presence of other boats in the vicinity (Mark 4:36c). The evangelist's attention seems to have focused on the single boat in which Jesus and his companions are present. Strikingly these companions are immediately identified as Jesus' "disciples" (*mathētai*) by Matthew. And not only that. In Mark 4:36, a group of fishermen take Jesus with them in the boat. In Matthew 8:23, by contrast, Jesus takes the initiative in leading his disciples into the boat. They "followed" (*ēkolouthēsan*) him into the boat. Although the verb *akolouthein* means "to follow" in the physical sense of walking behind someone, the verb is typically used in the New Testament to denote following after Jesus in a metaphorical sense—that is, by being a disciple. "Come, follow me," says the Matthean Jesus as he invites men to be his disciples (e.g., Matt 9:9).

At this point, a glance at the context in which Matthew has placed the narrative of the Stilling of the Storm is rather interesting. Both Mark and Luke place the narrative after an exposition of Jesus' teaching in parables (Mark 4, Luke 8). Matthew has deferred the parable teaching until Chapter 13, where he has gathered together seven parables in order to form the Sermon in Parables, the third of his five major discourses. In Chapters 8 and 9, Matthew has brought together some ten miracle stories, collectively interpreted by means of the fulfillment citation in Matthew 8:17. The collation of materials and the use of the quotation formula show Matthew's editorial hand at work in the miracle chapters (Matt 8–9). A closer look at the text of Matthew 8 indicates that the general narrative sequence is interrupted immediately after the fulfillment citation by a pericope which contains two logia on discipleship:

Matthew 8:18–22

18 Now when Jesus saw great crowds around him, he gave orders to go over to the other side. ¹⁹ And a scribe came up and said to him, "Teacher, I will follow you wherever you go." ²⁰ And Jesus said to him, "Foxes have holes, and birds of the air have nests; but the Son of man has nowhere to lay his head." ²¹ Another of the disciples said to him, "Lord, let me first go and bury my father." ²² But Jesus said to him, "Follow me, and leave the dead to bury their own dead."

The logia, as a comparison with Luke 9:57–62 reveals, have come to Matthew from his Q source. Matthew has incorporated into his Gospel two of the sayings on discipleship. Luke has provided a little collection of three logia with a redactional introduction (v. 57) that is consistent with the journey to Jerusalem which he has been describing since 9:51. Matthew, however, has prefixed his two logia with his own introduction, taken over from Mark 4:35 with but a few editorial modifications. In effect, this means that Matthew has inserted two sayings on discipleship into the narrative of the Stilling of the Storm that he has taken over from his Markan source. In terms of redaction criticism, the parallel passages are not Matthew 8:23–27 and Mark 4:35–41, but Matthew 8:18–27 and Mark 4:35–41. Matthew clearly wants his readers to think about discipleship as they begin to read the story of the Stilling of the Storm.

In some ways it is difficult to determine why Matthew has omitted the Q logion on saying good-by to one's family and friends. Perhaps some clue to the omission can be found in the fact that Matthew has only two sayings on discipleship. In the first, a scribe comes to Jesus and addresses him: "Teacher, I will follow you wherever you go." Jesus' response is, "Foxes have holes, and birds of the air have nests; but the Son of man has nowhere to lay his head." Matthew's version of Jesus' response (v. 20) is exactly the same as Luke's version (v. 58). In his presentation of the inquiry—effectively an application for membership among the disciples—Matthew's text departs from that of Luke in two significant respects. First of all, the anonymous man of Luke 9:57 (*tis,* literally "someone") has been replaced by Matthew's "a scribe" (*grammateus*). Second, the scribe addresses Jesus as "Teacher" (*didaskale*), whereas Luke's anonymous applicant does not employ any title in direct address. These minor modifications by Matthew serve to place the scribe outside the circle of Jesus' disciples. The rejoinder of Jesus, materially the same as in Luke 9:59, then becomes in Matthew a rejection of the application for discipleship.

With respect to the second saying (Luke 9:59–60 = Matt 8:21–22), there is substantial agreement in the repartee between the Matthean and Lucan versions. The petitioner says, "Lord, let me go first and bury my father." In response Jesus says, "Leave the dead to bury their own dead." Apart from textual variance as to the presence of "Lord" in the Lucan next (N²⁶ accepts the *kurie* reading; if *kurie* were not a part of the Q tradition, its presence in Matthew 8:21 would be a redactional insertion), the only difference in this dialogical material is that Matthew's text uses two infinitives joined by "and" to render the expression "go and bury" (*apelthein kai thapsai*) whereas Luke has a participle and an infinitive (*apelthonti thapsai*). The major difference between the Matthean and Lucan versions of this logion is in the setting provided by each of the evangelists.

Matthew introduces the petition with "Another of the disciples said to him," whereas Luke has "To another he said, 'Follow me.' But he said . . ." Matthew introduces Jesus' statement with "But Jesus said to him, 'Follow me, and . . .'", whereas Luke has "But he said to him . . ." The presence of "another" (*heteros*) in Matthew 8:21 (cf. Luke 9:57) shows Matthew's dependence upon the *Q* tradition. In Matthew, however, the pronominal adjective designates one of the disciples, one who has already heeded the call "Follow me" (cf. Luke 9:57). By designating the petitioner as a disciple, Matthew has set up a contrast between the scribe and the disciple. Accordingly he has dropped the invitation to discipleship ("Follow me") from his version of the *Q* saying in 8:21. A renewed invitation is deferred until the Jesuanic logion of verse 22, where discipleship is clarified as an invitation to follow Jesus even in circumstances of personal difficulty.

This modified *Q* logion then serves as a tone-setting introduction to Matthew's version of the Stilling of the Storm (vv. 23–27). The disciple had been challenged to follow Jesus. In verse 23 we read, "when he got into the boat, his disciples followed him." The story that follows is one which illustrates the nature of discipleship. Since the presence of other boats (Mark 4:36) adds nothing to this motif, their mention has been dropped by Matthew, the theological editor. Matthew's editorial activity is then clearly seen in his version of verses 25–26, the dialogue between the disciples and Jesus. The two-part dialogue is similar to the petition and response found in verses 19–20 and 21–22.

Verse 25, "And they went and woke him, saying, 'Save, Lord; we are perishing' is a Matthean reworking of Mark 4:38. In Matthew, unlike Mark and Luke, the disciples utter an ejaculatory prayer. "Save, Lord" has a Matthean ring (cf. Matt 14:30). The Matthean Jesus is one who saves (cf. Matt 1:21). In 8:25 he is appealed to by means of a title which is a divine predicate of majesty and authority. In sum, the Matthean ejaculatory prayer is a plea for salvation. Once this is recognized, Matthew's introductory formula is seen to be all the more significant. "They went and woke him, saying" rings with manifest solemnity. Indeed, the introductory "they went" (*proselthontes*) is a Matthean adaptation of the narrative. Although *proserchomai* ("to come") is occasionally used by Mark and Luke (Luke has also added it at 8:24; it appears seventeen times in Mark-Luke), the compound verb represents Matthean usage (fifty-three times). In secular Greek, the verb *proserchomai* was typically used of the solemn approach to the deity. Matthew uses the verb in a similar sense, to characterize the reverential approach of the disciples to the one they recognize as Lord (cf. Matt 5:1; 8:2; etc.).

Another feature of the Matthean story is the strange placement of Jesus' majestic "Why are you afraid, O men of little faith?" (v. 26). Whereas the

Markan Jesus dialogues with the disciples after the storm had been quelled (Mark 4:40), the Matthean Jesus speaks about faith before he manifests his power. Of itself, this is a bit unlikely, but it fits in with Matthew's reworking of the story which, because of Matthew's editorial activity, has become a story on discipleship. The phraseology "Why are you afraid, O men of little faith?" is clearly the product of Matthean formulation. Apart from Luke 12:28, the expression "of little faith" is one of Matthew's choice expressions (either as a noun, Matt 17:20, or as an adjective, Matt 6:30; 8:26; 14:31; 16:8). It always describes a faith that is too weak and immature to withstand the pressure of demonic powers. Matthew's disciples are faithful, but not faithful enough. Their lack of faith provides occasion for their fear.

By calming the storm, Matthew's Lord Jesus reveals his authority and the nature of his presence with the disciples, even if they are of little faith. He is a Lord who does powerful things on their behalf. This "miracle" of discipleship gives way to a choral response in Matthew 8:27, just as the "miracle" of stilling the storm occasions the choral response of Mark 4:41. The Matthean concentration on the person of Jesus has already been noted and needs no further comment. It is Matthew's introductory lemma which deserves attention at this point. The fear of Mark 4:41 (*ephobēthēsan phobon*) has been replaced by the marvel (*ethaumasan*) of Matthew 8:27. This is necessary since Matthew has already treated the fear of the disciples in verse 26. But it is not the disciples who serve as the subject of verse 27. The choral response is attributed to "the men" (*anthrōpoi*)—those to whom the story has been addressed in preaching. They have been impressed by Jesus' presence as Lord to his disciples, even in the midst of the difficulties the Church inevitably must face.

In short, Matthew has borrowed a miracle story which Mark has taken over from his own tradition. In Matthew it remains essentially a miracle story, but is told as a lesson on discipleship. In Matthew's version of the Stilling of the Storm, whose tripartite structure can still be recognized, Jesus speaks but once. In the splendor of his Lordship, he states, "Why are you afraid, O men of little faith?" These words are a challenge to fidelity addressed to the disciples, not only those on the once storm-tossed Sea of Galilee, but those involved in the stormy existence of the Church itself. There is no need to fear, for the Lord is near. This is Matthew's message for the Church.

By focusing upon the manner in which each of the evangelists has made use of the traditional evangelical material, redaction criticism highlights the particular contributions of each of the evangelists—eventually, each of the New Testament authors—to the understanding and transmission of the Gospel. The methodology is essentially a historical one, since it elucidates the insights each of the authors brought to the Gospel tradition at a given moment in its transmission.

One might then ask how this modified message impacts upon those who read the New Testament at the present time. Contemporary readers of the

New Testament have a culture quite different from that of the ancient authors. Their questions are, more often than not, not the burning issues that confronted the Lucan and Matthean communities. Frequently our contemporaries approach the New Testament without a great deal of historical insight. How, then, does the New Testament convey a message at the present time? It is in order to answer this question that a number of scholars have turned to structural analysis.

SELECT BIBLIOGRAPHY

Ashton, John. *Why Were the Gospels Written? Theology Today Series,* 15. Notre Dame, Ind.: Fides, 1973.

Bornkamm, Günther. *Jesus of Nazareth.* London: Hodder & Stoughton, 1960.

————, Barth, Gerhard, and Held, Heinz Joachim. *Tradition and Interpretation in Matthew.* New Testament Library. London: SCM, 1963.

Brown, Raymond E. *The Birth of the Messiah: A Commentary on the Infancy Narratives in Matthew and Luke.* Garden City: Doubleday, 1977.

Carlston, Charles E. "Reminiscence and Redaction in Luke 15:11–32," *Journal of Biblical Literature,* 94 (1975), 368–90.

Collins, Raymond F. "A Witness to Change: The New Testament," *Louvain Studies,* 4 (1972–73), 229–43.

————. "Tradition, Redaction, and Exhortation in 1 Th 4, 13–5, 11," in *L'Apocalypse johannique et l'Apocalyptique dans le Nouveau Testament,* ed. by J. Lambrecht. *Bibliotheca Ephemeridum Theologicarum Lovaniensium,* 53. Louvain: University Press, 1980. 325–43.

Conzelmann, Hans. *The Theology of Saint Luke.* London: Faber & Faber, 1961.

Dahl, Nils A. "Letter." In *The Interpreter's Dictionary of the Bible.* Supplementary Volume. Nashville: Abingdon, 1976. 538–41.

Doty, William G. *Letters in Primitive Christianity. Guides to Biblical Scholarship.* Philadelphia: Fortress, 1973.

Fiorenza, Elisabeth Schüssler. "Composition and Structure of the Revelation of John," *The Catholic Biblical Quarterly,* 39 (1977), 344–66.

Haenchen, Ernst. *The Acts of the Apostles: A Commentary.* Oxford: Basil Blackwell, 1971.

Kingsbury, Jack Dean. *The Parables of Jesus in Matthew 13: A Study in Redaction-Criticism.* London: SPCK, 1969.

————. *Matthew: Structure, Christology, Kingdom.* Philadelphia: Fortress, 1975.

Kodell, Jerome. "The Theology of Luke in Recent Study." *Biblical Theology Bulletin,* 1 (1971), 115–44.

Lambrecht, Jan. *Once More Astonished: The Parables of Jesus.* Rev. ed., New York: Crossroad, 1981.

Lohfink, Gerhard. *The Conversion of St. Paul: Narrative and History in Acts.* Chicago: Franciscan Herald Press, 1976.

Martyn, J. Louis. *History and Theology in the Fourth Gospel.* Rev. ed., New York: Harper & Row, 1979.

Marxsen, Willi. *Mark the Evangelist: Studies on the Redaction History of the Gospel.* Nashville: Abingdon, 1969.

Meier, John P. *The Vision of Matthew: Christ, Church, and Morality in the First Gospel. Theological Inquiries.* New York: Paulist, 1979.

Parker, James. "Redaktionsgeschichte et valeur historique des Evangiles," *Hokhma,* 12 (1979), 22–46.

Perrin, Norman. *What is Redaction Criticism? Guides to Biblical Scholarship.* Philadelphia: Fortress, 1969.

Rohde, Joachim. *Rediscovering the Teaching of the Evangelists. The New Testament Library.* Philadelphia: Westminster, 1968.

Wilckens, Ulrich. *Die Missionsreden der Apostelgeschichte. Form- und traditions- geschichtliche Untersuchungen. Wissenschaftliche Monographien zum Alten und Neuen Testament,* 5. Neukirchen: Neukirchener Verlag, 1961.

Worden, Ronald D. "Redaction Criticism of Q: A Survey." *Journal of Biblical Literature,* 94 (1975), 532–46.

CHAPTER SEVEN

STRUCTURAL ANALYSIS

I. AN INTRODUCTON TO THE METHOD

To devote a chapter of an introduction to the study of the New Testament to structural analysis is something of a risky venture. Among biblical scholars there is some discussion as to the legitimacy of structural analysis as a form of biblical, and therefore of New Testament, research. The methodology is relatively new and certainly different when compared to the more traditional methods of historical-critical exegesis. It seeks not the true or the real but the process by which we humans give meaning to the (biblical) text. The structural approach is essentially interdisciplinary and requires the use of a terminology quite dissimilar from that commonly used by exegetes. Structuralists do not even employ the same vocabulary among themselves, nor indeed the same methodological approach. Among themselves, they discuss whether structural analysis is a science or an art.

This discussion not only highlights the ambiguity inherent in the methodology, it also effectively emphasizes the fact that a structural analysis of New Testament texts is being effected in certain quarters. One of the principal centers of interest in the application of structural analysis to biblical texts is France, where the structuralist anthropology of Claude Lévi-Strauss and the linguistic studies of Algirdas Julien Greimas have provided much of the theoretical background for the methodology of structural analysis. In France, the names of Claude Bremond, Jean Calloud, Claude Chabrol, Jean Delorme, Pierre Geoltrain and Louis Marin are to be cited as being among the most vigorous proponents of the new methodology. So far the efforts of these men have been largely devoted to a study of the phenomenon of narrativity (thus they are sometimes called the French "narratologists") and the phenomenon of religious discourse. Both Greimas and Geoltrain are affiliated with the École des Hautes Études in Paris, while Calloud and Delorme are professors of biblical exegesis at the Catholic University, Lyons. The latter institution's Centre pour l'Analyse du Discours Religieux publishes a journal, *Sémiotique et Bible,* edited by Delorme, which effectively functions as the trade journal for the French-language biblical structuralists.

In the United States, the practitioners of structural analysis are more pragmatically oriented. They have exercised their art principally in the interpretation of the New Testament parables. Their combined efforts have met with such success that Warren S. Kissinger concluded his historical survey of the study of *The Parables of Jesus* by stating, "There can be no doubt that the 'American school' of parable interpretation is thriving with vibrancy and innovation." Among the leaders in the study of the parable by means of structural analysis is John Dominic Crossan of De Paul University (Chicago), but the principal center of structural analysis may well be Vanderbilt University (Nashville, Tennessee). At Vanderbilt there is an ongoing Structuralist Research Group, whose members represent an interdisciplinary cross-section of competencies—English literature, philosophy, sociology, computer science, religion, linguistics, French, German, Jewish studies, etc. The group is committed to the development of methods of applied research in structural analysis, but thus far its efforts have been largely and necessarily involved in fundamental research. Nevertheless, the practical, more concretely the parable, orientation of this group was evidenced by its sponsorship of a conference on "Semiology and Parables" (May 15–17, 1975) chaired by Daniel Patte and devoted to the exploration of the possibilities offered by semiological and structuralist methods for biblical exegesis. During the December 1977 annual meeting of the Society of Biblical Literature, Patte chaired a consultation on Structuralism and Exegesis. The topic has now become the subject of an ongoing seminar of the SBL. The work of the American structuralists often appears in *Semeia,* "an experimental journal devoted to the exploration of new and emergent areas and methods of biblical criticism," which first appeared in 1974.

A third center of structuralist activity is presently located in Bonn, Germany, where professor Erhardt Güttgemanns has devoted considerable research into what has been called generative poetics. German-language structural-analytic studies of the New Testament frequently appear in the Bonn journal *Linguistica Biblica,* whose principal editor is Güttgemanns himself. Translated into English, Güttgemanns' works have provided considerable stimulus for the work of the American school of structural analysis. Güttgemanns is also to be credited for having provided the biblical structuralists with a systematic exposition of the real point of departure for the application of methods of structural analysis to biblical texts, namely a disaffection with the predominately acceptable methods of biblical exegesis.

A Reaction

Twentieth-century exegesis, especially in Germany, has been marked by a double heritage: historicism and existentialism. In the eyes of many structuralists, the historical approach of the form and redaction critics appears to be a sort of obsession with history that incorrectly identifies truth with facts and separates meaning from the message. By stripping a text down to its various levels, much in the fashion in which the archaeologist works, historical critics seemingly locate the meaning of the text in the socio-historical context behind the text rather than in the text itself. Meaning is accordingly a property of language history and social history, rather than a characteristic of the text itself. According to the structuralists, the existentialists, too, are guilty of separating the meaning from the message. The methodology of the existentialists, among whom the post-Bultmannians are the most prominent, has the twofold defect of being both anthropomorphic and subjective. As a corrective for its deficiencies, the method requires remythologization, which represents a further departure from the text itself. For the existentialists, the biblical text is symbolic but not significant in itself. In reaction to the objectivism of the historical-critical methodology and the subjectivism of existentialist hermeneutics, the proponents of structural analysis attempt to focus on the meaning of the text itself. As their stated intention, they choose as the object of their reflection the text itself rather than the author who composed it (historical criticism) or the reader who peruses it (existentialism).

Since structural analysis is clearly a reaction to identifiable deficiencies in well-known and practicable methodologies, one can legitimately question whether structural analysis is a viable methodology in its own right or whether it is merely a fad whose worth likewise lies beyond itself—that is, whose principal value lies in its ability to point to the weaknesses of the accepted methodologies without being able to replace them with something of lasting value. It is, of course, precisely at this point that the discussion is joined.

Ferdinand de Saussure

It also remains difficult to define just what structuralism is. Richard Jacobson has faced this issue squarely. Structuralism, he wrote, "is not quite a science but an array of methods." In fact, even in the rather limited field of New Testament criticism we find that three (or more) methodological approaches are grouped together under the umbrella of structural analysis. What all these methods—those in use within the field of biblical interpretation and those in use elsewhere—have in common is the application of principles derived from certain movements within linguistics to other areas of human

233

discourse. Since the classic formulation of these movements is to be found in Ferdinand de Saussure's system of structural linguistics, Saussure is often cited as "the father of structuralism."

At the heart of his system is the assumption that the human brain functions in certain ways, called structures. Although we cannot fully comprehend the functioning of the human brain, we can discern some of its qualities through an examination of some of the products of the human brain. Literary works are a particularly appropriate object for such a process of discernment. Since, however, it is the same human brain which operates in all cultural endeavors, the methodology (which some prefer to call an ideology) can be applied to other fields as well—for instance, philosophy (Louis Althusser), psychology (Jacques Lacan), history (Michel Foucault), sociology (Lucien Goldman), and even biblical studies.

In his exposition of General Linguistics, Saussure skillfully distinguished between language (*langue*) and speech (*parole*). Speech is a onetime event, whereas language is a social reality. Saussure explained that "If we could embrace the sum of word-images stored in the minds of all individuals we could identify the social bond that constitutes language." More recent structuralists have tried to clarify the distinction by comparing it with some current approximate equivalents. The world of play furnishes a useful distinction between the rules of the game (its "language") and the individual move made by a player in accordance with the rules (its "speech"). The world of technology, on the other hand, furnishes the distinction between the code (i.e., the computer program, its "language") and the message (its "speech") which is roughly equivalent to the linguistic distinction, as defined by Noam Chomsky, between competence and performance.

The rules of the game and the computer program are somewhat static systems that function as the significant (meaning-making) context for the meaning (significance) of the individual moves or the individual printout. In somewhat similar fashion Saussure considered language to be a somewhat closed and static system. He did not deny that language evolves, but he was not interested in the history of language. Instead of studying the historical development of a language, Saussure preferred to concentrate his attention on the system that constitutes language. In other words, instead of studying language through time (a diachronic approach), Saussure studied language at a single time (a synchronic approach).

In his study, the Swiss linguist showed that within language the relationships between the terms (which he called *differénces*) are more important than the meaning of the individual terms of the language. Thus, for the interpretation of the simple expression "Time flies" it is important to know which sign functions as the grammatical subject of the sentence. If "time" is the subject, then we think either of the traditional adage or perhaps of a popular weekly newsmagazine that is distributed by airmail around the world. If an unexpressed but understood "you" is the subject, we might think of a command given to a timekeeper engaged in an experimental study on the speed of flies. But then it may be the entire expression "time flies" that serves as a grammatical subject since it is not inconceivable that a given species of fly be called "time flies," which might then lead an observer to comment that "Time flies are a nuisance."

Saussure, moreover, underscored the arbitrary nature of the linguistic sign. Therefore he carefully distinguished between the signifier (the word) and the signified (that to which it relates). There is no necessary relation of similarity between the two parts of the sign. Thus the single sign "bow" (a word written in the English language with three letters) conjures up the mental image of the archer's weapon for some, whereas for others it conjures up the image of a gesture of deference in the presence of royalty.

Meaning

The distinction between the signifier and the signified as the two parts in the relationship of significance (meaning) is present as a key element in the structural analysis of all literary texts. It is sometimes formulated as the distinction between the plane of expression and the plane of content. The plane of expression relates to the formal aspects of language—that is, form as opposed to meaning. Its apposite science is semiotics, or semiology—the study of the system of signs. The plane of content relates to that to which a text or sign refers. Its apposite science is semantics, which deals with the non-formal aspects of language. While semantics deals with the meaning of a sign, semiotics is concerned with how a sign conveys meaning. Semantics considers the relationship between a sign and its meaning in a language, abstracted from its use. Semiotics, in contrast, is concerned with *praxis*. It deals with the way in which a sign signifies, when it is actually used.

Immediately it becomes apparent that the distinction between the signifier and the signified is much too simple. On the one hand, we must take into account that human speech is composed of two distinct levels of articulation. There are words ("monemes") or "morphemes"—a term that applies to the smallest lexical unit of a language, thus words, roots, etc., in the jargon of the structural analysts—and sounds ("phonemes"). Apart from the case in which a simple sound functions as a word, phonemes have no meaning in themselves; meaning arises exclusively from their combination into words. Phonemes are differential units, since they distinguish one word from another; whereas monemes are significant units insofar as they contribute, through their own relationships, to meaning. The branch of linguistics that studies the relationship between sound and language is phonology. The school of linguistics at Prague (N. S. Troubetzkoy, Roman Jakobson) had an important role to play in the development of this scientific discipline, whose importance can be grasped by anyone who attempts to pronounce the word "bow."

On the other hand, monemes have at least two levels of reference. Immediately they conjure up mental images. This mental sign is linked iconically (it is a representation) to the object or reality to which it ultimately relates on the level of expression. Thus from the outset we must speak of multiple levels of significance. Hence structural analysis, if it is adequately done, must be open to the contribution of the philosophy of language as well as that of the philosophy of knowledge. Accordingly, a structural-analytic approach to biblical texts is necessarily interdisciplinary. It involves at least structural linguistics, structural anthropology, transformational-generative grammar, sociolinguistics, the philosophy of language, the philosophy of knowledge, and aesthetics. At bottom, however, Saussure's system of structural linguistics undergirds most of the contemporary attempts at a structural analysis of biblical texts. In this regard, a point made by Susan Wittig is well taken. In her contribution to the 1975 Vanderbilt conference she described:

> . . . the components of what we might call a semiotic of the parable—an eclectic but systematic and theoretically coherent understanding of the signifying properties of the verbal text that goes beyond any single critical strategy to an encompassing perception of the text as a significant whole and as a significant part of a series of wholes in a broader and broader contextual frame. No single critical method is capable of such an all-inclusive conception, which involves not only the text itself, but the process of its creation, its performance, and its purpose and effect. The semiotic model, however, a model based on the sign theory of Charles Sanders Pierce, Charles Morris, and F. De Saussure, has begun to seem capable of providing the theoretical framework within which such an exploration might be carried out ("Meaning and Modes of Signification: Toward a Semiotic of the Parable," in D. Patte, ed., *Semiology and Parables*, pp. 320–21).

The Propprian Model of Syntagmatic Analysis

In the point of fact, the entrée of the methods of structural analysis into the world of biblical criticism was occasioned by the 1958 translation into English of Vladimir Propp's classic work, *Morphology of the Folktale*. Originally published in Russian (1928) with the title *Morphology of the Fairy Tale,* Propp's work was an analysis of the traditional Russian fairy tale, based on a study of one hundred tales collected by A. N. Afanasi'ev in an anthology entitled *Narodnye russkie skazki (Russian folktales).* The translation of *Morphology of the Folktale* into English provided for Propp's entrance into the literary dialogue of the West. Although his book received an unfavorable commentary from some critics who found it too formalistic, the work was warmly received by folklorists, ethnographers, and literary critics. Among the critics was Claude Lévi-Strauss, who took Propp to task in a lengthy article later published as a chapter of *Structural Anthropology* (1960; ET, 1976). Among those who responded more positively were A. J. Greimas, Claude Bremond, and Erhardt Güttgemanns. The favorable comment received from these structural linguists assured Propp's work of its rightful place as marking the origin of the structural analysis of the narrative.

Propp maintained that any object can be studied from three points of view: its structure, origin, and transformations, but that a study of the structure is primary insofar as one must know what something is before one goes on to further descriptions. To write a fairy tale implies that one knows what a fairy tale is. This implies that one has identified a particular narrative as belonging to the genre of the fairy tale. This is only possible within a classification of the genres. Thus Propp attempted to identify just what it was that determined the genre of the fairy tale. With reference to Goethe's botany, Propp chose to study the morphology of the fairy tale, and suggested that his own work might conceivably be included within a series of morphological studies—the Morphology of the Curse, the Morphology of Comedy, etc.

Beginning with an identification of the various functions that occur in the fairy tale, Propp concluded that all fairy tales are based on identical functions, so that all fairy tales have monotypical structure. The characters and the plot are variable, but the structure remains the same. In effect, the structure of the folkloric narrative is constituted by its functions. What is a function? By definition, a function signifies "the action of a particular person from the perspective of the flow of the narrative." In his analysis, Propp arrived at a matrix of some thirty-one functions, whose interaction constitutes the fairy-tale genre. Here follows the sequence as Propp analyzed it:

α (Prologue)—a definition of the initial situation; therefore not properly a function in itself.

1. β Absentation—one of the family members is absent from home.

2. γ Interdiction—an interdiction is addressed to the hero.

3. δ Violation—the interdiction is violated.

4. ϵ Reconnaissance—the villain seeks information.

5. ζ Delivery—the villain receives information about his future victim.

6. η Trickery—the villain attempts to deceive his victim in order to take possession of him or his possessions.

7. θ Complicity—the victim falls into the trap and thereby involuntarily helps his enemy.

8. A   Villainy—the villain harms a member of the family.

9. B   Mediation—one learns about the misfortune that has occurred, and the hero is asked (or ordered) to repair it.

10. C   Beginning Counteraction—the hero agrees or decides to right the wrong.

11. ↑   Departure—the hero leaves his home.

12. D   First Function of the Donor—the hero is subjected to a test preparatory to the reception of a magical agent.

13. E   Hero's Reaction—the hero reacts to the actions of the future donor.

14. F   Provision of Magical Agent—a magical agent is put at the disposition of the hero.

15. G   Spatial Transference—the hero succeeds in approaching the object of his search.

16. H   Struggle—the hero and the villain confront each other in direct combat.

17. I   Marking—the hero receives a mark or wound.

18. J   Victory—the villain is defeated.

19. K   Liquidation—the villain is redressed.

20. $\downarrow$ Return—return of the hero.

21. Pr   Pursuit—the hero is pursued.

22. Rs   Rescue—the hero is helped.

23. O   Unrecognized Arrival—the unrecognized hero reaches another country or returns home.

24. L   Unfounded Claims—a false hero pretends to be the perpetrator of the exploit.

25. M   Difficult Task—a difficult task is proposed by the hero.

26. N   Solution—the difficult task is performed by the hero.

27. Q   Recognition—the hero is recognized.

28. Ex   Exposure—the false hero or the villain is unmasked.

29. T   Transfiguration—the hero receives a new appearance.

30. U   Punishment—the false hero or the villain is punished.

31. W   Wedding—the hero is married and/or ascends the throne.

From his analysis of this matrix of thirty-one functions, or narrative units, Propp concluded that: (1) the constant elements of the folktale are the functions of the characters; (2) the number of functions is limited (even though all functions may not appear in a given fairy tale); (3) the sequence is always the same (since the hero cannot, for example, return home before he has departed); and (4) all fairy tales belong to the same genre as far as their structure is concerned. Since the sequence of functions is always identical, Propp's analytical model is sometimes said to follow a horizontal, linear, or syntagmatic axis.

Thus, for Propp it is the constant sequence of invariable functions which determines the genre of the text. However, he has a second way of approaching the fairy tale. He has divided the functions among seven types of characters: (1) the princess (or the father); (2) the hero; (3) the mandator; (4) the villain; (5) the donor; (6) the helper; and (7) the false hero. Seen from this perspective, the fairy tale is a narrative with seven characters who share the essential functions.

A. J. Greimas

Folktales and fairy tales are, of course, found in all cultures. Frequently it is the same tale told in different languages. Many of these tales derive from an oral tradition, but they are generally written down at a relatively early stage. Often the written version influences the oral tradition as the folktale is handed down from generation to generation. Thus the literary accounts of James MacGillivray, Esther Shephard, and James Stevens, and the Bunyan stories in advertising pamphlets written by W. B. Laughead interacted with oral tradition to create the American legend of Paul Bunyan. While the Bunyan tales are almost too many to count, they consistently tell the tale of the giant who tamed the West. The legend is the story of man against nature. Paul Bunyan is clearly the hero. His principal helpers are Babe the Blue Ox and Johnny Inkslinger. Nature itself is cast as the villain. Structurally the stories about the legendary Johnny Appleseed, to which the literary accounts of Eleanor Atkinson have made a significant contribution, are not unlike the stories told about Paul Bunyan. Thus it would seem that the American folktale, like the Russian, has its basic structure.

The Lithuanian folktale has been studied by A. J. Greimas, a French narratologist influenced by Propp. Greimas' work represented an improvement of Propp's analysis in that it yielded more simplified structures. Greimas came to his search for an interpretative model from a study of linguistics and a study of the sentence, whose traditional syntax has frequently been analyzed in terms of a subject-action-object taxonomy or diagram. Greimas' idea was to go from the sentence to the narrative, as a larger textual unit, in an effort to determine its taxonomy, which might be schematized in turn.

Accordingly Greimas isolated two axes: (1) the axis of volition, which links a subject (Sub) and an object (O); and (2) the axis of communication, in which a sender (S) transmits an object (O) to a receiver (R). Greimas added a helper (H) and an opponent (Opp) to these four poles. These six poles represent the formal classes of characters in a narrative. Thus Greimas designates them as "actants" (rather than actors) since each represents a semantic unit, a somewhat more abstract concept than the particular character who appears in the narrative. Broadly considered, the six actants are comparable to Propp's seven particular individuals: the mandator and father of the princess are combined in the sender (S); the hero is divided into subject (Sub) and receiver (R); the princess is the object (O); the villain and the false hero are combined into the opponent (Opp); and the donor and the helper are combined into the helper (H). The relationship among these six actants may be schematized as follows (the actantial model):

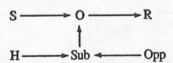

In fact, all six actants may not be represented in a given narrative. Moreover, it may be that one actor in the narrative may function in more than one actantial role. Thus the story of the adventurer who sets out in search of gold, only to fall into the hands of pirates from whom he escapes with the help of a friendly native, might be schematized as follows:

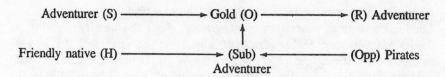

The actantial model can be used to schematize the story of Paul Bunyan digging the St. Lawrence River as indicated below. According to the tale, Billy Pilgrim and his men had been digging for three years and had dug only a small ditch when Paul arrived on the scene. As Paul dug, the dirt was transported by Babe the Blue Ox to Vermont, where it formed the Green Mountains. After a squabble over payment, Paul Bunyan threw a thousand shovelfuls of dirt into the gorge which he had dug. Thus the Thousand Islands came into being. So:

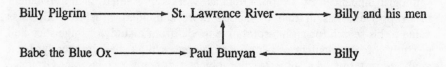

The use of the actantial model makes it clear that there are, in fact, not two but three separate axes in Greimas' analysis. Roland Barthes has identified this third axis (the helper-subject-opponent line) as the test-trial-ordeal axis, though it is perhaps more appropriately styled the power axis. Thus we have:

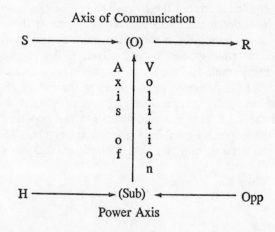

Greimas has further simplified Propp's analysis of the narrative by reducing the inventory of identifiable functions (of the folktale) to one of more manageable dimensions. Noting that several of the functions identified by Propp were articulated in the form of a binary opposition (e.g., departure-return, struggle-victory), Greimas took Propp's first pair (interdiction-violation), and gave it the name of contract. The contract is established between a sender (S) and a receiver (R) between whom communication is thereby assured. Since the contract may be formulated positively or negatively, there are two possibilities: mandate (S)—acceptance (R), and prohibition (S)—violation (R). The notion of contract is key to the understanding of the narrative, since the tale is set in motion by the breaking of the contract and attains denouement by its being reestablished at the end of the tale. From this perspective the initial and final sequences of the tale provide something of a before-and-after setting for the tale, but in one sense do not enter into the narrative itself.

Claude Bremond

While Greimas was concerned with improving Propp's analytical method through a process of simplification and the introduction of interpretative models, Claude Bremond reflected that some aspects of Propp's analysis were almost too simplistic. He began with Propp's definition of the function and the Russian's notation that "it is always possible to be governed by the principle of defining a function according to its consequences." Why is this so? By virtue of logic, aesthetics, routine, or some other factor? Isn't it possible to conceive of a function's opening up an alternative? Isn't it possible to consider bifurcation and alternative narratives, as, for example, in the case of subplots and subordinate narratives which serve to retard rather than advance the denouement of a narrative? In effect, is it not true that Propp's teleological conception of the narrative postulates a structure that is simpler than an honest analysis of the narrative warrants? Bremond's critique along these lines allowed the French narratologists to introduce the idea of a complex narrative program into their analysis of narrative. We shall return to this idea below.

From a slightly different vantage point, but consequent upon these first remarks and concerned that the analysis not become unwieldly by reason of its very complexity, Bremond concluded that the true narrative unit is not the function but the sequence. The complete absence of an ensemble of interdependent functions does not pose any problem for the narrative of the tale, but the sequence may not be disturbed if the narrative is to remain a fairy tale. Thus it is the sequence of the narrative that ultimately proves to be the invariable element of the tale. Then, by a process of reduction, Bremond identified an elementary sequence which can be typically articulated in three principal moments: (1) Potentiality: the situation that opens the possibility of a pattern of behavior or an event; (2) Process: the passage to the actualization of this possibility; and (3) Attainment: the result of this action which closes the process by success or failure. In coming to its conclusion, the elementary sequence can create a new situation which becomes the starting point for another sequence. Thus we must consider the possibility of a chain of sequences, which can be schematized in a narrative program. For example, the story of someone's getting mail from a post-office box can be divided into the following elementary sequences which form a chain: (1) movement to post office; (2) entrance into post office; (3) opening of post-office box; (4) removal of mail; (5) closing of box; (6) departure from post office; (7) return home. Schematically we can provide each elementary sequence with this model: $S(O \longrightarrow R)$.

Bremond's analysis of the narrative message has opened up the possibility of the comparative study of narrative structures in all messages which include a layer of narrativity. A given narrative may be conveyed in words, images, or gestures. The same tale may appear in more than one form, as those who have read Cervantes' *Don Quixote* or seen *The Man of La Mancha* can well attest. Indeed, a given narrative may be told in print (prose, poetry, or figurative drawing), on stage (in drama, musical, or opera), or via the medium of the visual arts (television, movies, mime, or kinetic sculpture). In effect, this means that the narrative structure somehow transcends the medium of the written word. Those who would understand a given narrative must appreciate and understand both the constraints of narrative syntax and the constraints of the medium chosen for the expression of the narrative.

Another direction, some of whose possibilities were already sketched in Bremond's initial reaction to Propp, pointed to the relationship between the narrative layer in any one message and other layers of signification of that same message. In effect, words have more than one signification, according to their use in a determined context. Already Propp had noted that the same content receives different functions according to the context in which it is inserted. And the theatergoer may well recognize in Quixote either the hero of the play, his or her own idealism, or a Christ figure, depending on whether the determinative context is the play itself, his or her self-reflection, or his or her religious outlook. The phenomenon of multiple meanings, according to the determinative context, is described as the "polysemy of the sign."

The Lévi-Straussian Model of Paradigmatic Analysis

In effect, any sign—that is, any unit of the signifier (a "seme," in structuralist jargon)—be it word, image, sequence, or text, has several different meanings or "meaning effects" (the "sememes," in structuralist jargon). At the very least, any reader should recognize that all language and each text has both an informational and a symbolic function. Plain speech is "informational"—it conveys data about human experience and ideas (values, principles, etc.). Poetry is "symbolic"—it conveys a vision of life and the world by means of forceful and imaginative language. In informational language, denotations are important, but it is the connotations that are important in symbolic language. Functionally, informational language and symbolic language operate in different ways. Informational language relates to intelligence and will; ultimately, to decision and action. Symbolic language awakens the imagination, thus challenging or reinforcing the visions we hold. This distinction between the informational and symbolic functions of language is relatively facile and a useful one, if only at the level at which the grade-school child distinguishes between prose and poetry.

Structural analysis holds that any text—indeed, any seme—has both an informational and a symbolic value. It is not a matter of either/or; it is a matter of both/and. It might be said that at best, signs can be differentiated as to the degree of symbolic value and the degree of informational value they evoke (thus metaphorical language is more symbolic than ordinary language), but all signs have both symbolic and informational value (thus all language is ultimately metaphorical). For example, while "four o'clock" and "five o'clock" respectively designate the end of the sixteenth and seventeenth hour of the day according to a twenty-four-hour division of time, "four o'clock" symbolizes teatime to the British, whereas "five o'clock" symbolizes quitting time to the American workman. Again, while the dictionary may offer "a country in southeastern Asia, in the Indochinese peninsula" as the definition of "Vietnam," the word evokes various emotive connotations for any American who lived through the turbulent years of the Kennedy-Johnson-Nixon administrations. These simple examples show that the content (the signified) of any sign (the signifier) is twofold. Any seme has its referential-denotative dimension (its surface value) and its symbolic-connotative dimension (its deep value).

Myth

This brief reflection on the phenomenon of polysemy can serve as an introduction to the contributions of Claude Lévi-Strauss to the art of structural analysis. Lévi-Strauss is not a linguist, but a philosophical anthropologist in search of universals. Beginning with a series of seminal articles dating back to 1955, Lévi-Strauss has devoted himself to the study of the myth. His analysis, with the title "The Structural Study of Myth," was incorporated into *Structural Anthropology* (1960; ET, 1963), as the eleventh chapter of the work. Virtually all structural analysis of the Bible harkens back to this classic essay.

Myth can be described in various ways. There are certainly some mythical elements in the narratives about Paul Bunyan and Johnny Appleseed. To the extent that the account of Paul Bunyan's creation of the St. Lawrence River, the Grand Canyon, and Puget Sound is taken seriously, one might speak of an etiological myth. To the extent that the legend of Johnny Appleseed typifies the idealized celibate Protestant mystic, one can speak of a myth. Yet the stories about Paul Bunyan and Johnny Appleseed are not properly called myths because they are set in human terms and do not possess the authority to interpret significant aspects of human existence. The tales of Paul Bunyan and Johnny Appleseed have been told for entertainment's sake.

In contrast, the real myth possesses authority. Scholars such as Mircea Eliade and Rudolf Ott consider myth to be essentially a religious phenomenon precisely because it speaks of the sacred and transcendent. Myths speak in human terms of extrahuman realities that are relevant to the world of humans. In this sense, the Infancy narratives of the Synoptic Gospels and the story of Jesus' prayer in the Garden (Mark 14:35–36 and par.) are myths. They speak of the transcendent in terms of the imminent. For Hermann Gunkel, the Old Testament scholar, a myth is a story of the gods. For D. F. Strauss, as was noted in Chapter Two, a myth is the clothing of a religious idea in historical form. This notion of myth pervades much of twentieth-century exegesis, especially the work of Rudolf Bultmann. Functionally, however, myth may be defined as a sacred narrative which endorses man's significant activities, providing a warrant for those deeds requisite to social order. Lévi-Strauss explained that: "mythical thought for its part is imprisoned in the events and experiences which it never tires of ordering and re-ordering in its search to find them a meaning." Thus the French anthropologist was not so much concerned with showing how men think in myths as he was in showing how myths operate in the minds of men and women, without their being aware of the fact.

Lévi-Strauss was concerned with not only one particular collection of myths, but the myth in general. He was impressed by the fact that different cultures possess different texts that somehow seem similar. That raises the problem: "If the content of a myth is contingent, how are we going to explain the fact that myths throughout the world are so similar?" The French anthropologist found the answer to his rhetorical question in the universal structure of the myth. Nevertheless, this question and answer are somehow incomplete without the consideration of another question. Accordingly, Lévi-Strauss noted that: "the question has often been raised why myths, and more generally oral literature, are so addicted to duplication, triplication, or quadruplication of the same sequence. If our hypotheses are accepted, the answer is obvious: The function of repetition is to render the structure of the myth apparent."

Lévi-Strauss looked for this structure at its deepest possible level. To do so, he concentrated on what he called the "bundles of relations" between the units of the myth. For him, the "bundle of relations" is the minimum significant unit of the myth. The bundles of relations amount to paradigms, which are individually related to one another according to a principle of similarity.

Chiefly concerned with the structure of the human mind as such, Lévi-Strauss was convinced that binary opposition is fundamental for human thinking. Upon analysis, the purpose of the myth appears to be the provision of a logical model capable of overcoming a contradiction. Through the mediation of surrogates, the myth reconciles that which humans experience as being in opposition. The opposite terminals in the myth are usually very profound and fundamentally important ones; thus mythical thought reveals itself as mediating between polar oppositions. Edmund Leach explains:

> So, despite all variations . . . this aspect of myth is a constant. In every myth system we will find a persistent sequence of binary discriminations as between human/superhuman, mortal/immortal, male/female, legit-

imate/illegitimate, good/bad . . . followed by a "mediation of the paired categories thus distinguished."

Lévi-Strauss' understanding of the myth can be schematized according to his classic formula, which follows the principle of discontinuous analogy (A is to B as is C to D), as follows:

$$F_x(a) : F_y(b) :: F_x(b) : F_{a-1}(y)$$

According to the schema, two functions and two states are combined in mutually exclusive pairs, thus permitting $F_x(a) : F_y(b)$ to represent a binary opposition. In some ways, the relationship schematized $F_x(b) : F_{a-1}(y)$ is a metaphor for the relationship schematized $F_x(a) : F_y(b)$. By borrowing elements from the earlier relationship, it is able to mediate the binary opposition of that relationship.

For Lévi-Strauss, the mythic structure represents what is common to the operation of all human minds. Representing a static system, the mythical structure is a paradigmatic structure (allowing for the understanding of a static system). The narrative structure is, as has already been explained, a syntagmatic structure (allowing for the understanding of a process). Hence we cannot simply identify the narrative's resolution of the situation of lack with the myth's mediation of binary opposition. At best, the myth serves as a metaphor for the elements of the narrative.

As a matter of fact, paradigmatic relationships are, in the estimation of the structuralists, of a metaphoric type. That the myth is able to function so effectively as an overarching metaphor which allows for the ordering and reordering of events and experiences is due, at least partially, to the special relation between language and speech in myth. Language belongs to reversible time (the competence), speech to irreversible time (the once-only performance). Myth somehow combined properties of both. Spoken in past time, it tells of the present. Thus it unites diachrony and synchrony. As Lévi-Strauss himself has put it, "The chronological order of succession is absorbed in a non-temporal material structure."

The Greimasian Model of "Semantic" Analysis

A paradigmatic reading of a text is a vertical reading, whereas the syntagmatic reading of a text is a horizontal reading. The model of the elementary structure to which Greimas devoted himself offers yet a third approach to a text from the standpoint of an interpretive model. It does not examine the functions of the text in their sequential order; rather, it examines the functions according to their essential or achronic relationships. Thus it shares something of the paradigmatic dimension.

Narrative Grammar

Greimas' development of the actantial model is a contribution to what has come to be called "narrative grammar"—i.e., a collection of those rules of language that pertain to the narrative but do not enter immediately into the wording of the narrative (that is, into the lexicon itself). Greimas' use of functional models has also contributed to an understanding of how the narrative is meaningful, how it conveys meaning. It has already been noted that Greimas considered the notion of contract as essential to the narrative. The entire narrative is set in motion by the breaking of the contract. In other words, there is a temporal schema present in folkloric tales. An initial order is disturbed. A hero intervenes to abolish the effects of social alienation and to restore the previously existing social order.

In his analysis of the tale, Greimas discerned a narrative sequence in which three central sequences can be identified. Since each of the first two sequences includes two functions, the folktale may be analyzed according to a syntagmatic scheme as follows:

A. The contract
    (1) Mandate or prohibition (from the standpoint of the sender)
    (2) Acceptance (from the standpoint of the receiver)
B. The struggle
    (3) Confrontation
    (4) Success
C. Consequence

The Bunyanesque tale about North Dakota could be analyzed according to the actantial model as follows:

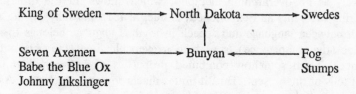

On analysis, the tale can be seen as the fulfillment of a contract between the King of Sweden, who offers the mandate, and Paul Bunyan, who accepts the challenge of chopping down all the trees in North Dakota. The struggle is present in the confrontation between Paul and the elements, particularly the fog that impeded the work and the stumps that remained behind after the trees had been cut down and cleared away. With the help of the Seven Axemen and Babe the Blue Ox, Paul's efforts were successful. According to the legend, the plains of North Dakota are the result of Paul's work.

From the central sequences in Greimas' schema we can separate the sequences that frame the narrative. These are the sequences which are necessary in order that the narrative begin and come to its conclusion, but they do not enter into the sequence of the narrative itself. Their function is to situate the narrative in time and space. The initial sequence is conjunction, to which disjunction is opposed.

The consequence is, in fact, twofold. The narrative results in the restoration of the social order. This implies not only the liquidation of the initial lack but also the glorification (revelation, reward) of the hero. In effect, the story can be read from the standpoint of the beneficiary of the hero's action, or from the standpoint of the hero who performs the action.

From the standpoint of the sender, but in view of the consequences of the narrative, the contract may be analyzed according to the contractual model which allows for either of two formulations. The sender either

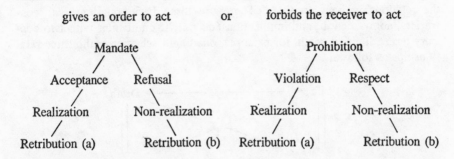

gives an order to act   or   forbids the receiver to act

        Mandate   Prohibition

Acceptance   Refusal   Violation   Respect

Realization   Non-realization   Realization   Non-realization

Retribution (a)   Retribution (b)   Retribution (a)   Retribution (b)

Within the mandate-acceptance-realization-retribution axis of this schema, the mandate-acceptance represents the contract with its two functions, while realization-retribution represents the consequence under its twofold aspect. Contract and consequence are similarly represented in each of the other three axes of this schema. Nevertheless, within the narrative at the level of action, rather than that of contract or communication, we must discern another component. These are the tests which annul the negative effects of the alienation. The texts lead to victory which results in the liquidation of the lack. In fact, the element of struggle which intervenes between the acceptance of the contract and its realization consists of a series of tests, each of which may be viewed as a small contract within itself. The tests are presented in a progressive fashion. As they are three in number, they can be described according to the order of the narrative in this fashion:

(1) Qualifying test: The hero is qualified as the subject of the test. In effect, he is identified and receives the helper who will assist him in accomplishing the next test.

(2) Principal test: This leads to the possession of an object, the acquisition of which assures the liquidation of the lack.

(3) Glorifying test: The group recognizes the subject who achieves victory in the test.

The Semiotic Square

Another major contribution of Greimas to the structural analysis of texts has been his development of still another model, the semiotic square which ultimately derives from Aristotle's logical square. To appreciate its use, one might begin with the distinction between the surface value of a narrative and its deeper value. The fact that one same narrative can be told through the use of various media—that is, by means of different "languages," each of which brings its own system of constraints to the narrative—shows that there is a deeper, structured layer of narrativity to which an individual narrative corresponds. The individual narrative may be considered as an expression or "performance" of this deeper level. This deep level is an abstract, conceptual level which has its own grammar or system of examination. At this basic structural level of signification, we may locate the presence of two terms and the relationship between them. There are three basic relationships: contrariety, contradiction, and implication (deixis). If one begins with two contrary terms, life and death, for example, one might schematize the three relationships as follows:

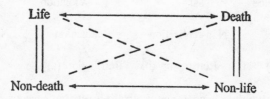

The horizontal (single) lines represent the relationship of contrariety, the crossed (broken) lines represent the relationship of contradiction, and the vertical (double) lines represent the relationship of implication. A very simplified and abstract version of this semiotic square would be:

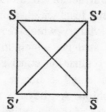

in which the horizontal bar represents the negation of the value.

On the surface level—that is, on the level of narration—one might begin with a given seme. One can construct a square using this seme as the first element. Since it is the square which articulates the meaning, and each term presupposes the existence of the others, all of the four elements that appear on the schema are present to the narrative even if they do not appear verbally in the text. Subsequently one might organize the different squares according to their degree of pertinence until such time as one has reached a square that is universal enough to take the entire narrative into account.

The Model of Interrelation

Since Greimas' semiotic square proceeds from the understanding that human thought perceives things according to a pattern of binary opposition, and since he suggests that the literary analyst might construct a square sufficiently universal to take account of an entire narrative, one might ask whether it is possible to correlate the semantic model of Greimas with the paradigmatic model of Lévi-Strauss. In fact, Daniel and Aline Patte, along with their associates and students at Vanderbilt, have attempted to interrelate not only the mythical and elementary structures, but also the model of the narrative structure as well. Their result is a methodology which is essentially eclectic.

Such eclecticism is not incompatible with the purpose of a structuralist approach to reality, which claims that a thing can be understood profitably not in itself and in isolation, but only in its relations with its context. There are, of course, multiple relations and so a structural analysis of a thing, even of a text, requires an array of methods. No single method, except a hypothetical all-inclusive one, is capable of plumbing the total meaning effect of a text. The inadequacy of a single method and the need for a methodology which implies the use of a variety of methods has been well phrased by Susan Wittig who stated that, "No single critical method is capable of such an all-inclusive conception, which involves not only the text itself, but the process of its creation, its performance, and its purpose and effect."

The multidimensionality of the methods used in structural analysis corresponds, then, to the multidimensionality of the text to be analyzed. The metaphorical quality of all human language, and therefore of all human speech, means that one must search out the paradigmatic relations of a text. If the text under consideration is a narrative, then the temporal development of the narrative requires the syntagmatic analysis of the text. A consideration of just these two facts demonstrates the necessity of a multifaceted approach to the text.

From a somewhat different perspective, it can be said that eclecticism is not incompatible with the purpose of structural analysis, since the structuralists do not set out to find the meaning of the text. Rather they seek to appreciate the text in its several meaning effects. The polysemy means that the structuralist simply does not intend to find *the* meaning of a text. Each structuralist articulates this basic and common conviction in his own way. Thus, "A work is 'eternal' not because it imposes a single meaning to many different men, but because it suggests many different meanings to a single man" (Barthes). In the words of Rimbaud, "I have attempted to say what that says, literally and in all its meanings." According to Louis Marin, "One of the essential propositions of such a theory must be an axiom regarding a plurality of meaning." And finally, Daniel Patte (*Structural Exegesis: From Theory to Practice*, p. 15) has written that "a discussion does not have a meaning (an entity); a discourse is meaningful."

Proceeding from the conviction that the use of specific systems of signs provides a specific vision of life and of the world, Daniel Patte has elaborated the following model in an attempt to formulate in a more precise way the relations between the mythical system and the narrative manifestation.

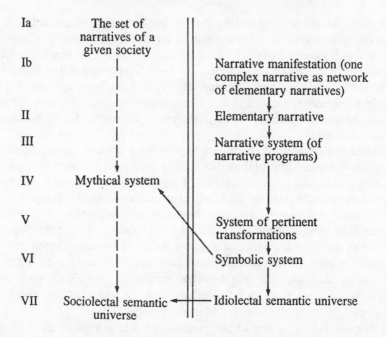

A brief word of explanation is in order. Society's set of narratives reflects its mythical system. This system points to the society's semantic universe, the society's system of symbolic values organized by the semantic structure. In a system of narratives, the mythical system manifests a "sociolectical" semantic universe, insofar as it reflects the society's symbolic values. In a given narrative, the symbolic system manifests an "idiolectical" semantic universe, insofar as it represents the individual's symbolic values. If the analysis is valid—that is, useful, from a structuralist's perspective—then the semantic universe is one of the cultural or enunciative constraints, or structures, that impinge upon any given narrative. It partially constitutes the conditions of possibility of the discourse. In short, it is the set of convictions, or self-evident truths, presupposed by the text.

If the model were used to analyze any one of the narratives about Paul Bunyan (a narrative manifestation), one would soon discover its structural relationship with the other Bunyan tales. As a group they speak of the power of mighty man to dominate the earth and make it habitable. Paul, his friends, and Babe the Great Blue Ox are the pertinent symbols (symbolic system). These symbols represent the values of the simple life, cooperation, generosity, and hard work which coalesce to ensure man's domination of nature (idiolectical semantic universe). In fact, the legends cohere with the stories about Johnny Appleseed (another set of society's narratives). Each of these sets represents a form of the "Protestant ethic." The creation narratives of Genesis 1–2 also belong to this society. Accordingly the vision of man articulated in the Bunyan and Appleseed tales is that of Genesis 1:28

and 2:17–19. This anthropological vision is ultimately an element of the sociolectical semantic universe.

Semiotics

The eclecticism inherent in the methodological approaches of the Pattes, Wittig, and others makes it clear that it is only with some reservation that we can speak of "structuralism" per se. Structuralism is really not a univocal concept nor does structural analysis designate only one method. Nevertheless, the literary practitioners of structuralism consider the practice of their métier to be an exercise in semiotics—that is, the study of the process in which something (a text, for example) functions as a sign. It is the study of the sign and the system of signs within the context of their production, performance, and reception.

There are three (or four) factors in this process:

(1) The sign—that which acts as sign; the seme

(2) The *designatum*—that to which the sign refers (When the referent really exists it is sometimes called the *denotatum*.)

(3) The interpreter—the agent of the process (This is the sender when we are considering the production of a sign; it is the receiver when we are considering the reception of the sign.)

(4) The interpretant—that effect on the interpreter by virtue of which the sign is in fact a sign to the interpreter.

Sometimes these three factors are schematized according to a model which is commonly called the "information theory triangle." Thus:

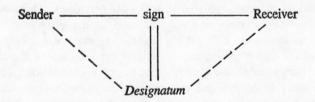

The relationships of expression and impression between the sender and receiver via the sign constitutes the pragmatic axis. The relationship between the sign and its *designatum* constitutes the semantic axis. To these, if we are to capture something of the complexity of the verbal sign, we must add a syntactic axis, as Charles W. Morris calls it, which is constituted by the relationship of implication between the sign and the other signs in the sign system.

A complete semiotic analysis of any text would involve an analysis of all these relationships and their interaction. In fact, the literary structuralists—as a matter of emphasis—seem to be particularly conscious (almost to the point of being self-conscious) about three elements in the complex process of semiotic analysis: the object, a model, and the structuring subject. From this point of view, structural analysis seems minimally to involve an examination of the interaction of at least three sign systems, says Robert Polzin, as follows:

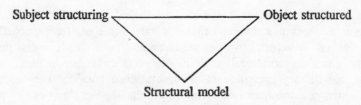

Subject structuring — Object structured

Structural model

Each of the sides of this triangular schema represents one sign system. Each of the vertices of the schema represents one of the emphases in the process of structural analysis as effected by students of literature. The structured object is the text, viewed as a self-regulating or closed system of transformations. The structural model is a construct, a hypothetical-deductive interpretation. The structuring subject is the analyst (ultimately the author or reader), whose self-reflection or deep subjectivity is brought to a state of some disclosure.

In some senses, every object in the world can be viewed as part of a sign system. Yet for the literary practitioners of the structuralist art, the structured object is a text. Barthes describes a text as "a production of significance and not at all as a philological agent." In the structuralist attempt to understand the text, there is something arbitrary in the first step, discourse analysis. Analysis always precedes synthesis, but there is something quite arbitrary at the beginning of this process. One might begin with a large text (e.g., an entire Gospel) or a smaller unit (e.g., a Gospel pericope). There is something arbitrary in the discovery of the units, and in the discovery of the relationships among the units. "Feel for the text, experience, background knowledge, scholarly hunch and intuition, orderly examination of the material, all play their part even at the beginning phase of segmentation" (Robert Polzin), but there is no rational reconstructable procedure whereby accurate segmentation or accurate structuration can be determined. This does not mean that the analyst has no method, nor does it mean that his process need not be methodical. It simply means that the structuralist operates upon a meaningful unit of discourse material according to a creative, deductive process which escapes objective verification.

The Narrative Program

In the analysis of the text, it can be useful to employ the $S(O \longrightarrow R)$ formula to represent a program—that is, a Subject (S) transmits an Object (O) to a Receiver (R). The formula $(O \longrightarrow R)$ represents the performance of the narrative program (the transformation). It connotes a function. The siglum S represents a state. The application of Greimas' actantial model would indicate that what is represented by the helper pole (H) qualifies or modalizes the subject (S). Since the receiver is often the subject transformed, the schema of the transformation might often appear as $S(O \longrightarrow S^1)$. A sequence of transformations might be schematized in this fashion:

$$S^1(O^1 \longrightarrow S^0)$$
$$\uparrow$$
$$S^2(O^2 \longrightarrow S^1)$$
$$\uparrow$$
$$S^3(O^3 \longrightarrow S^2)$$
$$\uparrow$$
$$S^4(O^4 \longrightarrow S^3)$$

Thus we have a chain or series of narrative programs, so that the entire narrative can be thought of as a hierarchy of narrative programs. Of course it is somewhat naïve to think that any extended narrative will proceed uninterruptedly in a single direction. We can usefully distinguish between a principal axis and a polemical axis $(O \longrightarrow R)$. We can take into account and schematize $(O \longrightarrow R)$ the existence of parallel, converging, and diverging narratives. Parallel narratives can be discerned when interruptions in the formal pattern also represent breaks in the logical development of the story. Converging narratives can be discerned when there is an interruption of the formal pattern by an elementary narrative which initially breaks the narrative development even though it ultimately contributes to it. Diverging narratives can be discerned when there is an interruption of the formal pattern without interruption of the logic of the narrative development. For simplicity's sake we shall omit any attempt to schematize the complex narrative at the present time. Nevertheless it should be realized that with the arrangement of a hierarchy of narrative programs, levels Ib-II-III of Patte's eight-tiered program of textual analysis have been achieved.

The text is viewed as a system of transformations that is self-regulating (closed). As Jean Piaget and Robert Polzin have explained, the text is viewed as a system insofar as it is treated as an intelligible whole—that is, as a unit or structure whose elements are related in a law-like fashion whose basic postulates are discoverable. The transformations are the laws of composition with respect to the being or becoming of the narrative, but they must be viewed as a closed system. A structure maintains itself and is enclosed within the transformations that encompass it. This should not be taken to mean that a text, as a given narrative, speech, or performance, is unrelated to other expressions of language. To state that a text is a closed system simply implies that a Gospel pericope is meaningful in itself, apart from, though not independent of, the entirety of the Gospel and the story of its composition, just as a stanza of a poem is meaningful in itself apart from, though not independent of, the whole poem and the biography of the poet who composed it.

With respect to the model, structuralism emphasizes an aspect of analysis that its practitioners believe belongs to all hermeneutical approaches. In relative self-awareness, structuralism proclaims that its model is hypothetical-deductive. Its procedures are hypothetical because the analysis proceeds from starting points that can be described as something like axioms to results that are something like hypotheses. The method is deductive insofar as the process, which moves from axiom to result, is something like an act of deduction. In fact, no semantic analysis can be scientific in the sense of being rigorously formal. Indeed, Propp reacted vigorously to Lévi-Strauss' charge of formalism. The structural analysts construct interpretative structural models that are themselves signs. The validation of the construct as well as the validation of the use of the model occurs in its relationship to the structures of the structuring subject. Does the use of a model help the structuring subject to appreciate something of the structured object? That is the question. If the answer is "yes," then the structural model has some validity. It has contributed to the meaning effect of the structured object, the text being analyzed. Once again the phenomenon of polysemy must be taken into account. There are many valid structural models, since there is a plurality of meanings appropriate to each text. Of the many schematized models that have thus far appeared on these pages, each is valid insofar as it helps an analyst (or reader) to appreciate a text. The one is not more valid than the other, even if the one might be more comprehensive than another. Thus the use of the models of transformation and contract among the more elementary models employed in the structural analysis of New Testament texts have a contribution to make to the understanding of these texts, as does the use of the more universal models of the semiotic square and the interlocking signs systems and Patte's eclectic model. Each of these models is valid or functional insofar as its use helps the reader or analyst to understand some meaning effect of the text under consideration.

The Subject

The realization that the structures of consciousness correlate with the structures of language brings us to a third focus of interest in much of the structural analysis of texts: the structuring subject. Robert Polzin clearly articulated this concern when he wrote:

> For an analysis to be structural there must be a self-conscious awareness
> (Polany's subsidiary awareness) of the law-like relationship between the
> analyst's model, the structure as constructed, and the personal structures
> (the structures structuring) within the analyst which enabled him to
> construct or "find" such a structure of the text in the first place. Struc-

tural analysis confronts both the object investigated and the operational laws of the subject who constructs the model (*Biblical Structuralism,* p. 33).

In fact, concern with the structuring subject is already implied in the structural analyst's concern with the "meaning effect(s)" of a text. He or she is not only concerned with the text in itself, but with its significance impact upon the reader. Moreover, the contribution of Lévi-Strauss to the structural analysis of texts derives from his analysis of the myth. Lévi-Strauss' interest was, however, basically anthropological. He wanted to discover the structures of the human mind. He intended to show how myths operate in human minds. Myths serve, in fact, an anthropological function. Mediating opposites, they create belief in the permanent possibility of reconciliation. Thus they serve to order some of the contradiction in human existence.

At this point it might be well to introduce Daniel Patte's reflection to the effect that three types of constraints or structures are at work in any text. First, there are the cultural structures, the constraints which characterize a specific culture including its literary genre. Second, there are the deep structures or the structures of the human mind, which characterize the human as such, including one's narrative and mythical structures. Finally, there are the structures of the enunciation, which include the intentionality of the author, the constraints of the specific structure in which the writing (or speaking) takes place, and the relationship of the text to the reader (or listener).

This brief description of the structures of enunciation of a text underscores the fact that the structural analyst's interest in the structuring subject is, in fact, a double interest. He is concerned with both the writer and the reader, both the speaker and the listener. Both the writer and the reader structure the text. The pragmatic axis of the information theory triangle points to the importance of both the relationship of expression and the relationship of impression to the text. Since structural analysis seeks to understand a given text in the complexity of its actual relationships, it must necessarily attend to the self-disclosure of the one who writes the text as well as the one who reads it.

II. THE USE OF STRUCTURAL ANALYSIS IN NEW TESTAMENT STUDIES

Since the use of structural analysis by exegetes is of rather recent, and still limited, occurrence, it is impossible for us to offer a definitive assessment of the real contribution of the use of this methodology to the understanding of the New Testament. Perhaps it would be more accurate to think about the possibilities inherent in the use of this methodology than to speak about its contributions. We will, therefore, offer some suggestions as to the directions already taken by structural analysts with respect to the New Testament and offer some indication as to the points of interest along the path to be trod. These suggestions can be summed up under the following rubrics: (1) Text; (2) Language; (3) Narration; and (4) Genre.

Before moving on to a consideration of each of these topics, it might be well to cite two ongoing discussions on the subject of structural analysis. One is taking place among the structural analysts themselves, the other is taking place among biblical scholars. The first has a bearing upon the second. Among the analysts there is considerable discussion as to the legitimacy of the use of extratextual systems to interpret a text. Among the structuralists there has clearly been a concentration upon synchronic structures. This concentration is undoubtedly due to the influence of the two masters of the theory upon which structural analysis is built. Saussure emphasized the primacy of synchronic over diachronic analysis; he was more interested in language than in speech. Lévi-Strauss was concerned with universals, which resulted in an antipathy for history. One must ask whether this concentration upon the synchronic at the expense of the diachronic is merely a matter of emphasis or whether it is inherent in the nature of structural analysis itself. In other words, as Robert Spivey put it, ". . . the question is legitimate as to whether structuralist activity, in reaction to historicist domination, will result in the swallowing of history—the event, the concrete, and the particular."

This implies that one must ask whether the methodology of structural analysis is incompatible with or complementary to the historical-critical methodology. To this author, it would seem that structural analysis can concentrate upon either the synchronic or diachronic structures affecting the text, depending on the type of relationship which the analysis intends to isolate, describe, and explain. Thus I would opt for the essential complementarity of structural analysis with the more traditional methodologies of source, form, and redaction criticism. I must acknowledge, however, that some interpreters have other points of view. Among some of the structuralists (e.g., Güttgemanns), there are those who claim that there is no valid method of literary analysis other than the structural one. These authors eschew altogether the historical-critical method of biblical interpretation. Among biblical scholars there are those who describe the work of structuralists as inconsequential because it does not result in *the* meaning of the text nor does it attain to *the* truth as such. The debate in exegetical circles will undoubtedly continue for some time to come, but in the meantime it would seem that the activity of the structuralists is not without value with respect to the text, language, narrative, and genre of the New Testament.

The Text

Barthes described the text as "a production of significance and not at all . . . a philogical object." With this understanding of a text, it is clear that structural analysis can take over where historical-critical analysis leaves off.

In its own structure, the text is the center of an intense diffusion of messages. In effect, the use of structural analysis in the exposition of the biblical text can overcome some of the aridity experienced by those who study the text only from the vantage point of the historical-critical methodology. It may well be that the use of structural analysis would serve to acquit us, Church leaders and biblical scholars alike, of the charge that the effective use of the Bible is reserved to that elitist group whose members are privy to the arcane secrets known only to the practitioners of the historical disciplines.

Some would hold that the use of the structuralist method makes of the New Testament a relevant text for today instead of allowing it to wallow in the dust as a monument to past history. In prompting this value of the structuralist approach, one must be wary lest biblical language be looked upon as mere metaphor, as if the words of the text, a sign, had no significant *designatum*. A concern for the level of expression (signifier) should not obliterate the level of content (the signified). Thus "Jesus" is more than a somewhat abstract value represented by the five-letter seme; "Jesus" represents a concrete *designatum*.

With due attention paid to this concern, it is clear that the use of the structuralist methodology in its totality can make a valid contribution to the understanding of a New Testament text within its proper context whether that context be the literary context of the entire New Testament (or the entire Bible), the academic context of the study of theology, the liturgical context of the preaching of the New Testament, or the spiritual context of the believing Christian who, like Augustine, has heard the call *tolle et lege* (take and read). Today the structuralist wants to discover *how* the New Testament text creates a meaning effect. At the same time the concerned Christian is concerned *that* the New Testament create a meaning effect. Certainly those concerned with the production of meaning effect can profit from a knowledge of how the text produces its meaning.

From a different point of view, the structuralists continue to make a contribution insofar as they underscore the fact that the text has an existence in itself (Paul Ricoeur). It is a datum, a given reality. As such it is a sign. This sign exists, such as it is. Therefore the structuralist, approaching the New Testament text, is able to forgo discussions about canonicity and inspiration. He can pass over the study of composition and redaction. He need not enter into long and technical discussions about variants and versions. It is the text that lies before the analyst which yields a meaning effect, whether it be the Greek text of the 26th edition of Nestle-Aland or the English text of the RSV. Each of these texts makes sense, and so the structural analyst sets out to determine just how they make sense. In his respect for and concern with the New Testament text that lies before him, the structuralist resonates well with the remarks made by the late British exegete, C. H. Dodd, apropos the text of the Gospel of John. Well aware that Rudolf Bultmann (and others) had sought to reconstruct the original text of the Fourth Gospel, Dodd wrote:

I conceive it to be the duty of an interpreter at least to see what can be done with the document as it has come down to us before attempting to improve on it. . . . I shall assume as a provisional working hypothesis that the present order is not fortuitous, but deliberately devised by somebody—even if he were only a scribe doing his best—and that the person in question (whether author or another) had some design in mind, and was not necessarily irresponsible or unintelligent (*The Interpretation of the Fourth Gospel,* p. 290).

Moreover, in his analysis of the text, the structuralist is fully cognizant that there is something arbitrary in his/her discovery of textual units and relationships. It is a matter of choice as to whether one begins with a larger textual unit or a smaller textual unit. This being-at-ease with one's choice of a text to be analyzed sharply contrasts with the anxious analysis undertaken by proponents of the historical-critical methodology. Does the parable of the Good Samaritan include Luke 10:25–37 (thus Lambrecht) or does the parable only include verses 29–37 (Aland's *Synopsis*)? Does the parable include all of verses 29–37 (Patte) or only what Jesus said in verses 30–36 (Crossan)? The structuralists might make different choices as to the text to be analyzed, but each of them can be comfortable with his choice, since Luke 10:30b–36 is a "production of significance," as are Luke 10:29–37, 10:25–37, and indeed the entire Gospel of Luke.

In view of the admittedly arbitrary methodology of the choice of texts made by the structuralists, it seems legitimate to apply the use of a structuralist methodology to the understanding of Scriptures within a set of ecclesial circumstances which has long separated (and not always to the satisfaction of the biblicists) passages (texts) of Scripture from their scriptural contexts. Within the Church such a separation has been effected for purposes both liturgical (for example, the lections of the lectionaries, both ancient and contemporary) and theological (of which the "proof text" approach to theology offers an egregious example).

From another point of view, it is noteworthy that an increasing number of proponents of the historical-critical methodology are coming to the conclusion that each Gospel pericope (many, if not all) contains the gospel. I have presented such a point of view with respect to the Nicodemus pericope of John 3:1–15 ("Jesus' conversation with Nicodemus") and Raymond Brown (*The Birth of the Messiah*) has done likewise for the pericopes of the Infancy narratives. Cannot further insight into this phenomenon be had by means of a Lévi-Straussian model of paradigmatic analysis?

Apropos of the text, particular mention must be made of Erhardt Güttgemanns' "Generative Poetics" as a new exegetical method which is at once a New Testament hermeneutic. Poetics, from the Greek *poiein* (to do), refers to a theory of production of texts. Güttgemanns has profited from the generative grammar of Noam Chomsky and the structural linguistics of Saussure. He has made use of the programmatic analyses of Propp and the schematizations of Greimas. With the conviction that literature can be studied only by means of a reduction to language, Güttgemanns approaches the gospel narrative as literature. His goal is to learn how the gospel narrative is made in order to develop a competence for narrating at the present time and in contemporary language "stories about God." In his concern for the passage from analytic grammar to synthetic grammar, Güttgemanns has developed a literary methodology which, he believes, is the first method of dealing with the texts (the object of analytic grammar) and contemporary speaking in the Church (the object of synthetic grammar).

Language

Structural analysis holds that the language of the New Testament text, itself a given performance of linguistic competence, has both an informational and a symbolic function. It is this symbolic function which is generally promoted in the analyses of the structuralists. Functionally, this symbolic language reinforces or challenges the visions we hold by awakening our imaginative processes. In traditional theological terminology, this means that the language of the New Testament, viewed from the onlook of its symbolic function, either reinforces our faith vision of reality or challenges our vision of things. Considered under the dimension of its symbolic function, the text of the New Testament—that is, a given linguistic sign—has a power to confirm or challenge one's radical *Weltanschauung.* In other words, the symbolic function of the New Testament language is what imparts to the text its capacity to elicit that type of response which the theologian would characterize as faith and conversion. It is because of the symbolic function of its language that repentance and belief are as appropriate a response to the reading of (and listening to) the text of the New Testament as they were the appropriate response to the preaching and person of Jesus, who urged that one "repent and believe" (Mark 1:15).

Within the New Testament it is the parable that is most readily identified as an articulation in symbolic terms. It functions as a metaphor of the kingdom of God. The New Testament parable can be classified within the broad Semitic category of the *Mashal,* which covers virtually the entire range of figurative language from the simile and riddle to the parable and exemplary story. What is so characteristic about parable language that makes it ever meaningful? Is it not that parable language may be characterized in terms of three linguistic functions? Parable language is referential in that it makes assertions about persons, places, and events so that the performance of the parable is anchored in concrete reality. Parable language is also attitudinal in that it expresses an orientation toward reality which gives shape and significance to reality from a very broad and fundamental perspective. Finally, parable language is performative in that it prompts, entices, and supports the reader or listener to commit himself or herself to that orientation in comparison with other orientations and perspectives. What is so clearly evident in parable language can also be said with respect to all language, at least insofar as it has a symbolic function. This reflection puts the language of the New Testament in its significant context.

Finally, one might also note that all theological language is metaphorical. To speak of God is to speak of Him who is totally other. The scholastics spoke of the *via negativa,* the *via analogiae,* and the *via eminentiae* in their use of theological language. Personification has always been an easy way for human beings to represent the transcendent. Today we recognize that all theological reflection makes use of metaphorical language and somehow is related to meaningful human experience. Does not the structuralist emphasis upon the symbolic function of all language evoke a resonance in all those who have reflected upon the metaphorical nature of theological language? Does it not put the language of the New Testament within a most appropriate frame of reference? Does it not open the door for the passage between one language performance and another, each viewed from the standpoint of the symbolic function of language? If the answer to the last question is in the affirmative, then one is more readily brought to discern the relationship between the language of the Bible and that of the seminary classroom and church pulpit.

Narrative

As was also the case in the use of source and form criticism, biblical expositors applied structural analysis to the Old Testament before use was made of the new methodology in the interpretation of New Testament texts. Indeed it was almost inevitable that Lévi-Strauss' analysis of the myth should have served as a springboard for an analysis of the "mythical narratives" of the Old Testament. The first to do such an analysis was the British anthropologist Edmund Leach, whose essay "Lévi-Strauss in the Garden of Eden" (1961) also exists in another version bearing the title "Genesis as Myth" (1969). The French literary critic Roland Barthes also applied himself to the study of a Genesis text, namely Genesis 32:23–32. That study —published in English translation with the title "The Struggle with the Angel: Textual Analysis of Genesis 32, 23–32"—was originally prepared as a paper delivered in February, 1971, at the Faculty of Protestant Theology at the University of Geneva. One year earlier Barthes had published a structural analysis of Acts 10–11, (see *Revue des sciences religieuses* 58 [1970], 17–37). Within the context of the evenings organized at the University of Geneva in the winter of 1970–71, Jean Starobinski read a paper on "A Literary Analysis of Mark 5:1–20." In 1971, there also appeared "An Analysis of the 'Text' of the Passion" by Claude Chabrol as well as two studies by Louis Marin, whom some commentators consider the most insightful of the New Testament structuralists. Marin's essays were respectively devoted to the narratives of the women at the tomb and of Jesus before Pilate.

With the appearance, just one decade ago, of these essays by Barthes, Chabrol, Marin, and Starobinski, the methodology of structural analysis was definitely introduced into the study of the New Testament. The essays of each of these authors have as a common feature that they are concerned with narrative texts. As a matter of fact, it is the narrative sections of the

Scriptures (both Old and New Testaments) that have proved the most fruitful subject for structural analysis. This is due to a variety of factors, among the more significant of which is surely that the theorists of structural analysis have devleoped their theories in conjunction with the narrative (folktale, myth).

Since a version of the Passion narrative appears in all four Gospels and since it is the most extended single narrative unit within the New Testament, it was all but inevitable that extensive structural analysis of the Passion narrative should have been effected in the early days of the application of the new methodology to New Testament texts. Thus we have not only the studies of Chabrol and Marin, but also that of Aline Patte, "Structural Exegesis of Mark 15 and 16" (Chapter Three of *Structural Exegesis: From Theory to Practice*).

An introduction to the study of the New Testament provides neither the space nor the occasion for a lengthy analysis of the Passion narrative. Yet it might be useful to point to a particular strength of each of the three early attempts at a structural analysis of the Passion narrative. Chabrol's study posited an "operational model" of the text by considering the three Synoptic accounts as so many variants of a single "meta-text." By means of a comparative analysis between the Lucan account of Peter and Cornelius (Acts 10:1–48) and this "meta-text," Chabrol sought to establish the semantic universe underlying the text. Marin offered not only an extensive reflection on the correlation of the sequences of text but also a structural analysis of the Passion narrative based on Greimas' actantial model as follows:

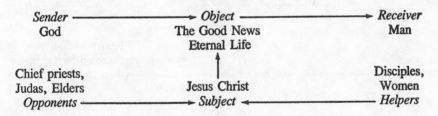

Marin's use of the Greimasian model continued insofar as he identified both a contract and the succession of three tests. The mandate-acceptance is that the Son of Man goes to be delivered in order to be crucified. The succession of tests consists of (1) the qualifying test: the anointing at Bethany; (2) the principal test: the entire series of Crucifixion sequences; and (3) the glorifying test: the revelation of Jesus. Aline Patte's study focused upon the identification of the narrative axes, the system of pertinent transformations (as represented by the narrative program), and the search for the semantic universe underlying the Markan text.

The use of Greimas' actantial model has also been found useful by those structuralists who have devoted themselves to the analysis of the New Testament parable. We have noted that the parable's symbolic language makes it a particularly fertile field for structural analysis; however, we must add to its appropriateness the fact that the parable is a narrative. Indeed each parable is a relatively isolatable narrative in itself. Moreover, as Bultmann noted in his *The History of the Synoptic Tradition,* the law of stage duality is operative in the composition of the New Testament parables. That means that no more than two characters appear "on stage" at any one time. Although Bultmann attributed this structural feature of the parable to the laws of oral tradition, the structuralists are able to capitalize on its operation in a text to establish a hierarchy of narrative programs in the analysis of many of the parables. For the rest, the utilization of Greimas' actantial model has proved quite helpful for parable analysis. For example, Dan O. Via has schematized the parable of the Good Samaritan (Luke 10:30–35) as follows:

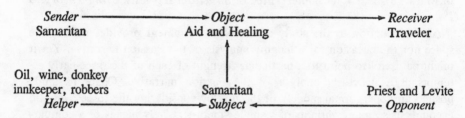

This application of the schema is not beyond criticism. Indeed Via himself has suggested that if one were to take Luke 10:25–37 as the "text" to be analyzed, one would appropriately develop the following model:

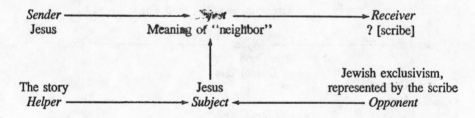

Genre

Propp directed his pathfinding efforts toward the identification of the genre of the Russian folktale. Subsequently there developed the school of French narratologists and the American school of parable interpretation. It would have been rather surprising if the members of this latter school had not attempted to define precisely the genre of the parable. In fact, considerable efforts in this regard have been made by American scholars, among whom John Dominic Crossan deserves special mention. Crossan has profited from the studies of Lévi-Strauss and others in order to identify a double function of the myth to which the double function of the parable is opposed. The myth both mediates the reconciliation of an individual contradiction and creates belief in the permanent possibility of reconciliation. In contrast, the surface function of the parable is to create a contradiction within a general situation of relative security while its deeper function is to challenge the fundamental principle of reconciliation by making us aware of the fact that we make up the reconciliation. In other words, the deeper function of the parable, like that of the myth, is anthropological. This realization has led Crossan to offer a structural definition of the parable genre as follows: "A parable is a story whose artistic surface structure allows its deep structure to invade one's hearing in direct contradiction to the deep structure of one's expectation. It is an attack on world, a raid on the articulate."

A similar point has been made by Wittig, who wrote:

> The "real meaning" of the parable, then, does not lie in the structure of the text, but in the *structuring* of the text—not in the created product but in the process of creation and perception. The purpose of the parable, from this point of view, is not to create one particular meaning, but to create the conditions under which the creation of meaning can be defined and examined by each individual perceiver, who can come to a clearer understanding of his own expectations and perceptions—his own meaning system. In semiotic terms, such texts are self-reflexive in a meta-communicative dimension, calling to our attention not their syntactic or semantic structures, but the variety of ways in which those structures are actualized in our minds, are made to yield their potential meanings. When we read a text characterized by the quality of indeterminacy, as the parables are, we are reading ourselves as well as the text, and are being forced to an awareness of the creation of meaning in our own minds, as well as to an awareness of the meaning itself ("Meaning and Modes of Significance," pp. 335–36).

Such a description does not imply that it is impossible to gather the Gospel parables into still smaller groups so that one might perhaps speak of a subgenre. As a matter of fact, Crossan distinguishes among the parables of advent, the parables of reversal, and the parables of action. Within the first group one can distinguish three strands: (1) those parables which stress the hiddenness and mystery of the kingdom (Fig tree, Mark 13:28, par.; Leaven, Matt 13:33, par.); (2) those which stress the gift and surprise of the kingdom (Sower, Mark 4:3–8, par.; Mustard seed, Mark 4:30–32, par.); and (3) those which stress discovery and joy at its coming (Lost sheep, Matt 18:12–23, par.; Lost coin, Luke 15:8–9).

The advent of the kingdom implies reversal because the kingdom overturns our security and leaves us in utter insecurity. Thus we have a group of parables of reversal turned into an example story within the Gospel of Luke: the Good Samaritan, 10:30–37; the Rich Man and Lazarus, 16:19–31; the Pharisee and Publican, 18:10–14; the Wedding Guest, 14:1–24; the Proper Guest, 14:12–14; the Great Supper, 14:16–24, par.; the Prodigal Son, 15:11–32.

The parables of action challenge one to life and action in response to the coming of the kingdom, but the Servant parables, which constitute the lion's share of the action parables, present a theme in ordered normalcy and then carefully reverse and shatter it (Unmerciful Servant, Matt 18:23–38; the Servant's reward, Luke 17:7–10; the Unjust Steward, Luke 16:1–7; the Wicked

Husbandmen, Mark 12:1–12, par.; as well as the Vineyard Workers, Matt 20:1–13).

If it is possible to distinguish among the parables so as to identify various types of parables within the Gospel, it is also possible to distinguish various types of miracle stories within the Gospel. Gerd Theissen, followed by Antoinette C. Wire and Hendrikus Boers, has addressed himself to the question of the genre of the miracle story. We can distinguish among miracles of exorcisms, exposés, provision, and demand. Boers has noted that for each of these themes a different perspective is implied, each coinciding with a particular crossing of a boundary: "a demonic perspective in the case of exorcisms and saving miracles, with threat/submission as the boundary crossing; a human perspective in healing and gift miracles, with the boundary need/gift; and a divine perspective in epiphanies and miracles concerning a norm, in which case the boundary crossing is from concealment to revelation."

The structuralist, as has been seen, is ever interested in extending the parameters of the study of the relationships of a text. Accordingly one might expect that the structuralists would also address themselves to an identification of the Gospel genre as such. From this perspective, Boers has written that: "In Matthew and Luke it is the biographical structure which provides unity, and in John the mythical structure is actualized. But whereas it is the framework of Matthew and Luke which carries the miracle stories, it is the miracle stories which bear the frame in the Gospel of Mark."

This reflection about the Markan structure should be subject to further discussion among the structuralists as well as between them and the proponents of the historical-critical methodology. Many of the latter have found some inspiration for their analysis of Mark in Martin Kähler's statement that Mark is a Passion narrative with an extended introduction. The introduction, Mark's account of Jesus' public ministry, contains a much greater proportion of miracle story than either the Matthean or Lucan account of the public ministry. If the genre of miracle story has to do with the crossing of a boundary, and if the Passion narrative is concerned with alterity and identity (Claude Chabrol), might not there be some meaning effect to be attained from an onlook on Mark from the perspective of the genre of the miracle story?

III. AN EXERCISE IN STRUCTURAL ANALYSIS

The Mysterious Host: Mark 4:35–41

35 On that day, when evening had come, he said to them, "Let us go across to the other side." 36 And leaving the crowd, they took him with them, just as he was, in the boat. And other boats were with him. 37 And a great storm of wind arose, and the waves beat into the boat, so that the boat was already filling. 38 But he was in the stern, asleep on

the cushion; and they woke him and said to him, "Teacher, do you not care if we perish?" [39] And he awoke and rebuked the wind, and said to the sea, "Peace! Be still!" And the wind ceased, and there was a great calm. [40] He said to them, "Why are you afraid? Have you no faith?" [41] And they were filled with awe, and said to one another, "Who then is this, that even wind and sea obey him?"

The subject of this essay in structural analysis demands two initial qualifying remarks. First of all, the literary reading of a text is something of a gamble, even for the one who is writing it. It requires that one accept the text afresh, ignoring all previous attempts at exegesis. In the context of the present work this is somewhat difficult, since the tale of the Stilling of the Storm has already been subject to text, source, form, and redaction-critical analysis. Second, the subject of this brief attempt at structural analysis concerns only one small unit (Mark 4:35–41) within a larger unit, the Gospel of Mark. Undoubtedly a structural analysis of the entire Gospel will shed additional light upon the pericope with which we are dealing. However, we approach the Markan narrative of the Stilling of the Storm as a narrative which is intelligible in its present form. What we intend to do is elucidate some aspects of its meaning effect. What we undertake is but a partial effort, one that is subject to further and complementary refinement.

We may take the story of the Stilling of the Storm (Mark 4:35–41) as a literary unit or integrated whole. Externally, its unity is constituted by means of the techniques of ring construction. Mark 4:35–36 introduces the narrative with "he said to them, 'Let us go across to the other side.' And leaving the crowd, they took him with them . . . in the boat." Mark 5:1–2 repeats a good part of this: "They came to the other side of the sea . . . And when he had come out of the boat . . ."

The principal indication of unity would appear to be in the presence throughout the two narrative actants, he-they: "he said to them . . . they took him with them, just as he was, in the boat. . . . he was in the stern . . . and they woke him and said to him . . . And he awoke . . . He said to them . . . And they were filled with awe, and said to one another . . ." Throughout the narrative the "they" is left in anonymity, but the "he" is specified as "Teacher" (v. 35). This pair of narrative actants also serves as a pair of discourse actants, we-you (and its variants): "Let us go across . . . do you not care if we perish? . . . Why are you afraid? Have you no faith? . . ." The final bit of discourse material breaks the rhythm of the unit: "Who then is this, that even wind and sea obey him?" In the total narrative these words are somehow *hors série*.

It is quite common to begin a narrative with a temporal and spatial index. Mark provides references to time and place at the very outset of his narrative. The reference to time is first: "On that day, when evening had come . . ." In Mark 4:35, "On that day" would seem to refer to the day of the parables, but that is only implied. The reader of the entire chapter might draw from this implication that the story of the Stilling of the Storm is still a parable, albeit in dramatic rather than narrative form. In any event, this first temporal index is specified by a second, "when evening had come." Then comes the reference to space: "And leaving the crowd, they took him with them, just as he was, in the boat." The mention of the boat introduces terminology from the nautical code, but the locale of the sea is merely implied at this point. Nevertheless the use of the nautical code serves as a further index of unity throughout the narrative: "boat. . . . And other boats . . . And a great storm of wind arose . . . waves beat into the boat . . . the boat was already filling . . . in the stern . . . rebuked the wind, and said to the sea . . . calm . . . wind and sea."

The temporal reference provided by Mark indicates that the tale to be told is that of a liminal experience. It takes place when the day's activities are over, when men have accomplished that which they set out to do. The spatial reference is generally supportive of the temporal reference. There is a movement of displacement. They and he leave the crowd. This implies a connection between this narrative and another or larger narrative in which the crowds appear. In fact the crowds have been mentioned in Mark 4:1–2. Yet the experience to be narrated is one which is separable and to be separated from the larger narrative. The movement of displacement bespeaks a lack of interest in the crowds, who at most lie at the periphery of the author's horizon. The narrative focuses on the anonymous "he" and "they." The "other boats were with him" speaks to the fact that there are other relationships in which the anonymous "he" is involved, but these are not the subject of the story. Moreover these other relationships would seem not to bear upon the relationship between "him" and "them." The other boats were not with "them," they were with "him."

That a pair of narrative actants are anonymously designated "he" and "they" is confirmed by the Greek text where no subject of the verb is indicated (in Greek, the form of the verb already includes a general expression of the subject) except for the use of the emphatic "he" (*autos*) in verse 35a. The grammatical difference between the third person singular and the third person plural in our text constitutes a first binary opposition. The opposition will be intensified with the "I-you" language of the dialogue that will follow in the narrative.

On the other hand, the opposition is reduced in the initial bit of dialogue. It is an invitation: "Let us go across to the other side." Expressed in the subjunctive mood (*dielthōmen*), the invitation has practically the force of an imperative—but it is not an imperative. Expressed in the first person plural, the invitation suggests that both the one who invites and those who are invited will share the same fate. The invitation is to go on a journey, to make a passage to the other side, which is not further specified (*eis to peran*).

Once the invitation has been issued, "they" assume responsibility. Responding positively to the invitation, they take action. They take the one who has invited them into the boat so that the mysterious journey may be effected and their passage to the other side be completed. In the meantime the one who tendered the invitation is "just as he was" (*hōs ēn*). He has apparently no other function other than that of making the invitation.

Immediately, there is not only an obstacle to be met but an opposition to be conquered. It comes from the great storm of wind and the waves that were preventing them from completing their journey. Asleep, the mysterious host leaves them to battle the wind and waves by themselves. Without him, the boat is swamped and is apparently in danger of sinking. Only when they have been pushed to the limit do they appeal to the present yet absent Host. Their liminal experience has been pushed to its utmost. They are in danger of perishing. "Teacher, do you not care if we perish?" For them, it is a matter of life or death.

"Teacher, do you not care if we perish?" is all they utter. Strangely, the language code is that of the academic world. In their liminal experience, when it is a matter of life or death, they acknowledge that the relationship between themselves and him is that between teacher and pupils (disciples). The opposition between him and them has been clarified as a relationship between the superior one and the inferior one. That relationship is expressed in terms which come from the didactic register—he teaches, and they are taught. As students, they address a question to the teacher. Phrased in the interrogative, rather than the imperative or subjunctive, it is an appeal for help. "We do not have the answer; give us the answer," is what they say. In their liminal experience, they appeal to the one known as Teacher for the answer to their difficulties. The appeal for help is a counterinvitation. It is almost a prayer. Yet the focus is exclusively upon the ones in the boat. There is no expressed concern for those in the other boats, which are outside the narrator's perspective.

In response to the question, the Teacher speaks. His first words are not addressed to them. Rather, he speaks a double word to sea and wind. The double word recalls that the function of repetition is often that of warning and command—as in "Halt! Who goes there?" Here the double word is a command and a rebuke—"Peace! Be still!" The words of the mysterious Teacher command the wind and sea. They obey. His words are neither those of invitation nor those of instruction; they are the words of one who commands and controls the elements. In contrast, the one who controls the context addresses words of invitation and challenge to his anonymous companions: "Why are you afraid? Have you no faith?"

The response to the Teacher's question is given in verse 41. Yet it is not addressed to the Teacher himself. They do not answer the teacher, except by the question that they ask among themselves: "Who then is this, that even wind and sea obey him?" Already recognized as Teacher (v. 38), the mysterious Host must be something more than a teacher if even wind and sea obey him. In their question as to who he is, they have found faith. Concerned with him, they have no need to fear wind and wave. They do not have the ultimate answer as to who He is, but their question as to his significance is already an act of faith. Faithful, and in the calm which he has brought, they depart from their liminal experience—the one in which the significance of the he-they relationship has been clarified. In faith, "they came to the other side" (Mark 5:1).

Commenting on the miracle stories, Antoinette C. Wire has noted that "the stories are structured around an extraordinary rift in a given closed system. This shows that the teller of the story affirms both a realistic, even tragic view of the human condition and a transforming event that changes the human condition." This is certainly true in the Markan tale of the Stilling of the Storm. "They" lose control of the situation before the mysterious Teacher who has invited them into it in the first place uses his power of command to effect their safe passage. Indeed, they must recognize the precariousness of their situation in order that the Teacher intervene to accomplish what apparently only he can do.

Schematized by means of Greimas' model, the narrative might be seen in this manner:

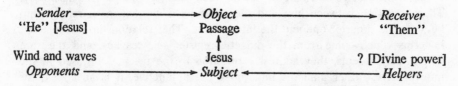

Yet the presence of the wind and the sea offers a particular qualitative nuance to the narrative. For Starobinski this is "the confrontation of an infernal world which is the equivalent of a descent into the underworld of the dead." For Theissen it is a demonic perspective, in which threat and submission are the boundary crossing. Theissen would classify the Stilling of the Storm among the saving miracles. Curiously, he has identified the "disciples" (they) and the wonder worker (he) as the opponents, with the crowds perhaps serving as the human sphere of interaction. My analysis rather focuses on the removal from the crowds. In the midst of their liminal experience, "they" are not even concerned with the other boats. Their "prayer" has a particularly limited focus to it—this because it is apparently only "they" who recognize "him" as Teacher. When Jesus is recognized, demonic opposition vanishes at the level of ultimate concern.

In a metaphorical reading of the text, the other bank becomes the homologue of that unspecified Other to which the Teacher would transport, with the aid of the divine powers that operate through him, those who focus upon him as Teacher. In traditional religious language, the story of the Stilling of the Storm is the story of salvation. Each one who has received an invitation from the mysterious "him" can recognize himself or herself among the mysterious "them." For those who take the journey with him, there is a storm of considerable magnitude through which passage is assured only if he is recognized as Teacher. In traditional religious language, the story of the storm is the story of faith. The faithful are those who recognize him as Teacher, but yet know that this single title does not exhaust his being. The faithful are those who say, indeed, to one another, "Who then is this, that even wind and sea obey him?"

In short, the story of the Stilling of the Storm is the story of the Mysterious Host. The elements, he commands; men and women, he invites. As a paradigm, that day is this day. The Mysterious Host offers an invitation. It is an invitation to be in solidarity with Him in setting out for a mysterious other side. Strangely, the response to the invitation is setting out, all the while asking one another, "Who then is this, that even wind and sea obey him?"

Unfolded, the Invitation of the Mysterious Host can be schematized as follows:

With this exposition of the story of the Mysterious Host, our fragmented interpretation of Mark 4:35–41 can be brought to a close. It has illustrated that the approach of structural analysis to the narrative is radically different from that of the text, source, form, and redaction-critical methodologies. Structural analysis seeks only to identify how the meaning effect of the narrative is conveyed to the reader or listener who approaches the story *tabula rasa,* as it were. Indeed, the structural analytic approach does not exhaust the total meaning effect of the narrative (not even the most determined of structural analysts would claim that it could do so!). In sum, structural analysis can serve as a useful complement to the traditional methodologies by helping the interpreter to grasp how Mark's story conveys meaning, even to those who are more or less unfamiliar with the history of Mark's Gospel.

SELECT BIBLIOGRAPHY

Almeida, Yvan. *L'operativité sémantique des récits-paraboles. Sémiotique narrative et textuelle. Herméneutique du discours religieux. Bibliothèque des cahiers de l'Institut de Linguistique de Louvain,* 13. Louvain: Peeters, 1978.

Barthes, Roland et al. *Structural Analysis and Biblical Exegesis. Pittsburgh Theological Monograph Series,* 3. Pittsburgh: Pickwick, 1974.

Crossan, John Dominic. *Finding is the First Act: Trove Folktales and Jesus' Treasure Parables.* Philadelphia: Fortress, 1979.

———. *In Parables: The Challenge of the Historical Jesus.* New York: Harper & Row, 1973.

———. "Paradox Gives Rise to Metaphor: Paul Ricoeur's Hermeneutics and the Parables of Jesus." *Biblical Research,* 24–25 (1979–80), 20–37.

————. "It is Written: A Structuralist Analysis of John 6." In *Society of Biblical Literature 1979 Seminar Papers,* vol. I, ed. by Paul J. Achtemeier. Missoula: Scholars Press, 1979. 197–213.

Delorme, Jean. "L'Intégration des petites unités littéraires dans l'évangile de Marc du point de vue de la sémiotique structurale." *New Testament Studies,* 25 (1979), 469–91.

Genest, Olivette. "Analyse sémiotique et Bible. Situation et questions disputées," *Laval théologique et philosophique,* 36 (1980), 115–28.

Güttgemanns, Erhardt. *Candid Questions Concerning Gospel Form Criticism: A Methodological Sketch of the Fundamental Problematics of Form and Redaction Criticism. Pittsburgh Theological Monograph Series,* 26. Pittsburgh: Pickwick, 1979.

Interpretation 28:2 (1974).

Johnson, Alfred M. (ed.). *The New Testament and Structuralism: A Collection of Essays by Corina Galland, Claude Chabrol, Guy Vuillod, Louis Marin, and Edgar Haulotte. Pittsburgh Theological Monograph Series,* 11. Pittsburgh: Pickwick, 1976.

————. *Structuralism and Biblical Hermeneutics.* Pittsburgh: Pickwick, 1977.

Knockaert, André. "Structural Analysis of the Biblical Text." *Lumen Vitae,* 33 (1978), 471–81.

Lys, Daniel. "Analyse structurelle et approche littéraire." *Études théologiques et religieuses,* 52 (1977), 231–53.

Marin, Louis. *The Semiotic of the Passion Narrative.* Pittsburgh: Pickwick, 1977.

McKnight, Edgar V. *Meaning in Texts: The Historical Shaping of a Narrative Hermeneutics.* Philadelphia: Fortress, 1978.

————. "Structure and Meaning in Biblical Narrative." *Perspectives in Religious Studies,* 3 (1976), 3–19.

Nohrnberg, J. "On Literature and the Bible." *Centrum,* 2 (1974), 5–43.

Patte, Daniel (ed.). *Semiology and Parables: Exploration of the Possibilities Offered by Structuralism for Exegesis. Papers of the Vanderbilt University Conference, May 15–17, 1975. Pittsburgh Theological Monograph Series,* 9. Pittsburgh: Pickwick, 1976.

————. *What is Structural Exegesis? Guides to Biblical Scholarship.* Philadelphia: Fortress, 1976.

Patte, Daniel and Patte, Aline. *Structural Exegesis: From Theory to Practice.* Philadelphia: Fortress, 1978.

Pettit, Philip. *The Concept of Structuralism: A Critical Analysis.* Berkeley: University of California, 1975.

Polzin, Robert M. *Biblical Structuralism: Method and Subjectivity in the Study of Ancient Texts.* Philadelphia: Fortress, 1977.

Ricoeur, Paul. *Essays on Biblical Interpretation,* ed. by L. S. Mudge. Philadelphia: Fortress, 1980.

STRUCTURAL ANALYSIS

Semeia 1 (1974) *A Structuralist Approach to the Parables.*
2 (1974) *The Good Samaritan.*
4 (1975) *Paul Ricoeur on Biblical Hermeneutics.*
6 (1976) *Erhardt Güttgemanns' "Generative Poetics."*
9 (1977) *Polyvalent Narration.*
11 (1978) *Early Christian Miracle Stories.*

CHAPTER EIGHT

EXEGESIS AND THE CHURCH

What has been described in the last five chapters, a methodology for the study of the New Testament, consisting of text, source, form, redaction and structure criticism, belongs to the science of exegesis. Exegesis is the attempt "to understand a text in its original context" (Willi Marxsen). As such, exegesis is a branch of historical science whose object of research is the documents of the past. New Testament exegesis is, therefore, a branch of historical science which has as its object a limited group of documents of the past, namely those which the Church has recognized as belonging to the canon of the New Testament. In principle the methodology of New Testament exegesis is no different from the methodology employed in the study of any other ancient document.

This very point was made rather sharply by Roderick L. MacKenzie, sometime rector of Rome's Pontifical Biblical Institute. In an article entitled "The Self-Understanding of the Exegete," MacKenzie wrote:

> Up to a point, as is clear, biblical exegesis is no different from the commentary or exposition of any ancient text, say the Code of Hammurabi or the works of Plato. Though the commentary as such supposes a fixed text as its subject-matter, quite frequently there are textual uncertainties of some significance for interpretation. Hence the exegete must have some skill in textual criticism, to establish the reliability of the text he is expounding. Such linguistic competence comes next as will enable him to understand the author's syntax and vocabulary. Then literary insight and perception of structure and patterns are required. Further, he needs historical awareness, to be able to interpret the document in the light both of preceding and of contemporary social or literary usages and situations. Finally, he aims at giving an appreciation of the thought, the vision and the message embodied in his work by the ancient author, its

impact on the writer's contemporaries and its possible relevance for our present generation (Roland Murphy, ed., *Theology, Exegesis, and Proclamation. Concilium,* 70, pp. 11–12).

The words of this Canadian scholar underscore the significance of five major areas of study whose results must somehow coalesce if a New Testament text, or any other ancient text, is to be adequately understood. The scholarly research of the exegete must focus upon textual, linguistic, literary, and historical issues as well as upon matters that pertain to an author's personal philosophical and theological synthesis. Only then can the interpreter appreciate the ancient author's ability to communicate his thought to his own generation, and convey that thought to another generation as well.

Our chapter on *text criticism* has shown that the New Testament exegete does, in fact, address himself or herself to establishing the reliability of the text that is to be interpreted. Given the fact that no autograph copy of any book in the New Testament is available, the New Testament textual critic seeks to reestablish the text as it was used at a relatively early period in the Church's history. Nevertheless the text critic must acknowledge that the text which is thus reconstructed on the basis of thousands of available manuscripts is a text which has been reconstructed in the twentieth century. Consequently the text of any New Testament book used by a given local church during the formative period of the Church's existence does not correspond in every detail to the text that is published today. The texts published today are only reconstructions, based on the documents available to us. Since the critics make use of the best available methodologies, their reconstructions of the New Testament texts approximate as closely as possible the texts available to the early churches. Yet at best they remain reconstructions and approximations.

The *linguistic analysis* of the New Testament text has not entered into our five-part survey of the historical-critical methodology. This linguistic analysis is undertaken in studies of the Greek language, specifically those that deal with *koinē* Greek and biblical Greek. *Koinē* Greek was that form of the Greek language in popular use in the countries of the Mediterranean basin during the first century A.D., while biblical Greek was the language actually used by the New Testament authors, a language which shows the influence of the Greek Bible, the Septuagint (LXX), and the lingering influence of Semitic expressions and thought forms.

A glance at a New Testament concordance quickly reveals the importance of linguistic analysis for the understanding of the New Testament. For example, a rather popular concordance to the Bible, based on the Douay-Rheims version, lists only five entries under "glory" for the Gospel of Luke (2:14, 32; 4:6; 14:10; 17:18) even though the Greek language concordance of Moulton and Geden lists thirteen entries under *doxa* (2:9, 14, 32; 4:6; 9:26, 31, 32; 12:27; 14:10; 17:18; 19:38; 21:27; 24:26), the Greek word commonly translated as "glory." The discrepancy exists because *doxa* has four different but related meanings in English. According to Bauer-Gingrich's *A Greek-English Lexicon to the New Testament, doxa* means:

(1) brightness, splendor, radiance; (2) magnificence, splendor; (3) fame, reputation, honor; and (4) (in the plural) glorious angelic beings.

The importance of linguistic analysis can readily be seen when one compares the Eight Beatitudes of Matthew 5:3–10 in two modern editions of the New Testament in English.

Revised Standard Version	*New American Bible*
3 "Blessed are the poor in spirit, for theirs is the kingdom of heaven.	3 "How blest are the poor in spirit: the reign of God is theirs.
4 "Blessed are those who mourn, for they shall be comforted.	4 Blest too are the sorrowing; they shall be consoled.
5 "Blessed are the meek, for they shall inherit the earth.	5 [Blest are the lowly; they shall inherit the land.]
6 "Blessed are those who hunger and thirst for righteousness, for they shall be satisfied.	6 Blest are they who hunger and thirst for holiness; they shall have their fill.
7 "Blessed are the merciful, for they shall obtain mercy.	7 Blest are they who show mercy; mercy shall be theirs.
8 "Blessed are the pure in heart, for they shall see God.	8 Blest are the single-hearted for they shall see God.
9 "Blessed are the peacemakers, for they shall be called sons of God.	9 Blest too the peacemakers; they shall be called sons of God.
10 "Blessed are those who are persecuted for righteousness' sake, for theirs is the kingdom of heaven.	10 Blest are those persecuted for holiness' sake; the reign of God is theirs.

The reader of the New American Bible might believe that the word *theos* ("God") appears in verses 3, 8, 9, 10 of Matthew 5. In fact, *theos* appears in the Greek text of verses 8, 9, whereas *ouranoi* appears in verses 3, 10. *Ouranoi* literally means "the heavens" (as the RSV indicates), but it is a periphrasis for God (as the NAB indicates). On the other hand, the RSV renders *diakaiosunē* as "righteousness," a word that frequently appears in Paul's letters to the Romans and the Galatians where it has a rather different meaning. To show the difference, the NAB has chosen to translate this Greek term as "holiness" in its version of the Beatitudes but as "justice" in its rendering of the letter to the Romans (Rom 1:17, etc.). In contrast, the RSV consistently renders *diakaiosunē* as "righteousness," even when the Greek term has a different connotation.

Literary insight enables the analyst to appreciate how a New Testament author has composed his work. The methodology commonly known as source criticism has sometimes been called literary criticism because it addresses itself to this issue. However, the total compass of literary analysis cannot be limited to the single issue of an author's use of source material. The complete literary analysis of a text must also consider the structures which have been used by an author for the exposition of his thought. Both the form-critical and structural-critical methodologies underscore the importance of the structures used by the New Testament authors. Specifically they have indicated that a determination of the literary form of a book or of one of its significant parts must be made if the text is to be adequately understood.

Form and structural criticism touch but superficially upon an individual author's particular style. Source critics use stylistic analysis in order to distinguish one level of an author's composition from another level. Redaction critics are concerned with an author's work of creative editing, but focus more upon the thought involved than upon the structural medium through which it is conveyed. Yet it must be acknowledged that a thoroughgoing stylistic analysis is important for the full appreciation of any literary work, including the literary works found in the New Testament. Students of literature, for example, quickly recognize Paul's use of several literary devices, including chiastic structure and *contradictio*. The former appears frequently in 1 Corinthians 15, while the latter permeates 1 Thessalonians 1 – 2. Perhaps it is something of an oversimplification to state that the use of chiasm represents Paul reasoning through a theological argument, while the use of *contradictio* represents the fiery preacher attempting to stimulate his audience. Nevertheless there is some measure of truth in this simple reflection. Fortunately the commentaries on the various books of the New Testament generally pay attention to the author's style characteristics. They find that the study of comparative literature is particularly helpful in this regard.

Historical awareness certainly must characterize the exegete who would understand the documents of the New Testament within their original context. To some extent, the exegete's use of either the form-critical or the redaction-critical methodology requires that he have some understanding of the historical and cultural circumstances within which each of the documents of the New Testament was written. Convinced that form follows function, the form critic carefully examines the life situation of the early Church, particularly with respect to its kerygmatic, catechetical, and liturgical activity. For example, the circumstances in which a tradition (about Jesus) has been handed down have a decided bearing upon the form in which that tradition is eventually written down. For his part, the redaction critic tries to assess the circumstances of composition of each author's work. His methodology proceeds from the conviction that the editorial modification of the material at hand is dictated not only by the individual author's particular genius and insight, but also by the needs of the community for whom the work is intended. The awareness that each of the New Testament texts is an occasional writing—that it was written in a particular set of circumstances—leads the critic to analyze those circumstances as adequately as possible. The critic undertakes this task not only for the sake of history per se, but also in order to understand a text whose context is a particular set of historical and cultural circumstances. From this point of view, the exegete must be conversant with the results and methodology of a full spectrum of disciplines which he might consider as ancillary to his own work. These disciplines are too numerous to mention in their totality, but they would certainly include Rabbinics and the

History of Religion; the Political, Religious and Cultural History of Palestine (not to mention the entire Near East); Archaeology; and the study of the Aramaic language.

Were one to cite merely the principal examples that illustrate the importance of historical sensitivity for the exegete, the list would be virtually without end. Certainly there is no way to explain the radically different understanding of Christ and the Gospel that is found in Matthew and Paul without looking to the respective backgrounds of each of these authors. Indeed, the question of background has often been raised with respect to the significance of the *Kurios* ("Lord") title applied by Paul to Christ in a preeminent fashion. Does the use of the title ultimately derive from an Aramaic background and thus have an eschatological reference—the Lord whose coming was eagerly awaited by the first generations of Christians? Or does it ultimately derive from a Hellenistic environment and thus have a cultic reference—the Lord with whom a worshipping community is in some type of mystical relationship?

From another point of view, one might cite Joachim Jeremias' classic, *The Parables of Jesus*. Although the work was written before the redaction- and structure-critical methodologies began to dominate the New Testament field, Jeremias' work has maintained its value up to the present time precisely because it shows the influence of the Church's history on the development of the parables in the Synoptic Gospels. Jeremias has noted, for example, that the parables which had been told in a Palestinian setting were later retold in a Hellenistic setting. The change of setting required not only a translation of language but, occasionally at least, a change of imagery as well. Similarly, parables which had been told when expectation of the end time (*Naherwartung*) was in the air were retold after the Church had long since come to grips with the delay of the Parousia. At this moment in Church history, many of the "crisis parables" were rephrased in such a way as to become exhortations for use within the churches.

Nowadays the reader of a contemporary document might be deluded into thinking that a study of historical circumstances is not really necessary for the understanding of a text. For most of us it is not necessary, formally and systematically, to situate the majority of items we read in their historical and cultural circumstances. This is simply because those historical and cultural circumstances are our own circumstances as well. The life situation of the text can be appreciated from within, i.e., from one's own experience, and therefore there is relatively little call for an appreciation from without, i.e., through formal study. Nevertheless close scrutiny reveals the importance of a careful analysis of the circumstances in which any piece of literature is composed, as the discerning reader of the evening newspaper, the insightful student of literature, and the political scientist know full well. If formal attention to the historical and cultural circumstances in which contemporary writings are composed proves to be always useful and sometimes necessary for even an elementary understanding of these texts, how much more is such attention necessary with respect to the New Testament, whose component texts were written in circumstances vastly different from our own? Our appreciation of the New Testament comes from a perspective quite different from that of the times in which the New Testament documents were written.

An *appreciation of the author's thought and message* is the goal of all textual exegesis. To be sure, there are some "exegetes" who limit the task of exegesis to the philological and literary examination of a text against the background of the historical circumstances within which the text was composed. Such philological and literary analysis is, however, only part of the work of exegesis. Such work is necessary for the understanding of a text, but it is not sufficient for the understanding of a text. Analysis must issue in synthesis if, in fact, a text is to be understood.

The purpose of exegesis is to appreciate and understand a text; it is not merely to say something about the text. Because of this conviction, I find I agree with the methodology (though I am not always in agreement with the particular conclusions) of those redaction critics like Conzelmann and Marxsen who go beyond the linguistic and literary examination of Luke and Mark to highlight some of the leitmotifs in the work of each of these evangelists. The use of redaction criticism thus offers an avenue to the appreciation of an author's thought (theology). Nevertheless one ought not speak too readily about "the theology" of the New Testament, since there are several different "theologies" in the New Testament. A rapid comparison of the Christology of Mark with that of John, for example, will soon reveal their distinct Christological viewpoints. Indeed, one should not even speak of "the theology" of a single New Testament author, as if that theology came from a static matrix, or as if the author had a fully developed theological system. Nevertheless there is a place to speak about the theologies of the New Testament if one shares the conviction that each of the New Testament authors had some more or less integrated vision of the things of God as these were revealed in Jesus, the Christ.

The methodology of redaction criticism is based upon the assumption that each of the New Testament authors had a *Weltanschauung* (world view) which he had personally appropriated. This vision, which included an understanding of God and of Jesus as his Christ, has impressed itself upon the literary product that has proceeded from the author's hands. For its part, the methodology of structure criticism seeks to attain to the meaning effects of the New Testament documents. The model of the information triangle includes the horizontal, pragmatic axis on which we must distinguish the relationships of expression and impression. Each of the documents of the New Testament was written as a form of communication. Each of the authors wanted to communicate his faith vision of God and the Christ. Thus MacKenzie is quite correct when he claims that the exegete "aims at giving an appreciation of the thought, the vision and the message embodied in his work by the ancient author, its impact on the writer's contemporaries and its possible relevance for our present generation."

Since each book of the New Testament is a form of communication between the author (sender) and those for whom it was intended, whether hearers or readers (receiver), some consideration of the author's relationship of expression must be attended to in any adequate understanding of these books. The author had a message which he intended to communicate. Consequently, Christological titles, *pistis* formulas, and kerygmatic language are scattered throughout the New Testament Scriptures. The use of such language shows that these books proceed from the author's faith. Thus the message of any New Testament author must be seen as an expression of his personal faith for a specific receiver. The interpreter of a New Testament text must be aware that in the interpretation of the text the problem of historicity (which aims at what "really" happened) cannot be separated from the problem of history (which aims at the happening as such, the "meaning" of the happening). In the Gospels the story of Jesus is told in historic language. Similarly the apostolic letters, Acts, and Revelation were also written in the language of faith.

I. KERYGMA ET ECCLESIA

When one considers the other pole of the pragmatic axis, the relationship of impression, one must consider how each book of the New Testament was received by its intended receivers. What impact did it make? How was it understood? When an exegete asks questions like these, he or she is touching upon an issue which is the subject of an ongoing debate. The discussion concerns the nature and the task of New Testament exegesis. Is exegesis an attempt to understand the documents of the past in the categories of the past, or is it also an effort to interpret the documents of the past in the categories of the present? Is exegesis merely descriptive or is it also interpretive?

Willi Marxsen has included in his reflections on the nature of exegesis the following definition: "Exegesis is the exposition of what an author *intended* to say to *his* readers in my language." For Marxsen, exegesis is principally concerned with the meaning effect of a text in its immediate (i.e., past) context, irrespective of its meaning effect for today. Nevertheless, Marxsen must acknowledge that it is necessary for us to formulate the meaning effect of a text in contemporary language if that text is truly to be understood in our time. If exegesis is concerned with the exposition of a New Testament text in our language, a fully adequate exegesis must make use of hermeneutics to some degree. Hermeneutics, or the science of interpretation, is the study of how to translate the biblical message into a language and form understandable to people of the present generation.

Upon further reflection it appears that hermeneutics is a science which proceeds in two steps. The one, an integral element of every adequate exegesis, is the use of modern concepts in order to enter into the thought world of an ancient author so as to appreciate his message to his contemporaries. The other is the use of modern concepts to allow the message of an ancient author to speak to our contemporaries. The two steps of hermeneutics are reflected in the ongoing debate about the nature of biblical theology. The one group (Gabler-Wrede-Stendahl) has characterized biblical theology as a historical-descriptive discipline, whereas the other (Hofmann-Bultmann-Ebeling) has seen biblical theology as a theological discipline as well. Certainly Bultmann's plea for the demythologizing of the New Testament texts and their remythologizing in proclamation sounded the clarion call for the fuller use of hermeneutics in biblical studies. Cannot it be said that the voices of those who show a manifest disaffection for "scientific exegesis," all the while remaining committed to the Church and its proclamation, groan a muted cry whose message is ultimately the same? Should not exegesis serve the Church?

The New Testament as the Church's Book

Whether exegesis should serve the Church is a legitimate question in that the New Testament itself is "the Church's Book." Often has it been said that the Old Testament is the Book of the People of God. Conversely it has been said that the ancient Jews were the People of the Book. Analogously, it can be said that the New Testament is the Book of the Church and that the Church is the People of the New Testament. Both statements must be made since there is a dialogical relationship between the Church and the New Testament. They are interpenetrating realities, which are mutually constitutive.

From a historical point of view, it is the Church which has produced the New Testament. Marxsen likes to say that "the New Testament is the oldest extant volume of the Church's preaching." Even though it would be a misrepresentation to reduce everything in the New Testament to an expression of the kerygma, as if the New Testament did not contain catechetical, disciplinary, and liturgical traditions as well, Marxsen's statement contains more than a kernel of truth. The New Testament is the product of ecclesial traditions. The Gospel was preached before any one of the four Gospels was written. Paul's letters were written out of his concern for the Church. Indeed, the Church existed as a community of faith long before anyone spoke of a New Testament (see Chapter One).

The New Testament is a witness to the faith tradition of the early Church, written by believers for believers. The Church successively gave birth to each of the books of the New Testament. In this originative sense, the New Testament is the Book of the Church. Since the New Testament originated as the books of the Church, it is clear that the long debate over the meaning of the formula "Scripture and Tradition" has been somewhat out of focus. As a matter of simple historical fact, the New Testament Scriptures have proceeded from the tradition of the Church.

Yet there is still another sense in which the New Testament is the Book of the Church. This sense relates to the fact that the canon of the New Testament has resulted from the Church's judgment and praxis. If the early Christian communities gave birth to the books of the New Testament, the Church of the fourth century called the New Testament into being by recognizing the canonical status of the twenty-seven books it contains. Thus the Book of the New Testament arose from the activities of the Church itself. It, too, is a product of the Church's tradition. In sum, the New Testament, as a whole and in its parts, originated from the Church.

The relationship between the New Testament and the Church is nevertheless a dialogical one. In some very real senses the Church results from the New Testament. The Church came into being as a community which responded in faith to the proclamation of the Death and Resurrection of Jesus. It is that early proclamation which has been embodied and preserved in the New Testament. Early on, Christian communities at Colossae and Laodicea (Col 4:16) came together as *ecclesiae* to hear the words of the apostolic letters. To this day local communities of Christians gather together as Church whenever the Scriptures of the New Testament are preached. The Church exists there where the Word of God is preached.

Anyone conversant with the history of the Western Church in modern times is aware that the Reformed churches and the Roman Catholic Church have differed on the issue of the relationship between the Scriptures and the Church. In times past the interpretation of the binomial formula "Scripture and Tradition" almost inevitably provided an occasion for debate bearing upon the formula "Scripture *or* Tradition." The Reformers opted for Scripture while Roman Catholics opted for tradition. We can indeed be thankful that the ecumenical movement has produced a truce and has brought an end to the verbal battles. From the side of the Reformers, Marxsen acknowledged that the Roman Catholic Church is more consistent in its position than the churches of the Reformation. Similarly Schubert Ogden has stated that "relative to Christ himself and to the apostolic witness that alone is directly authorized by him, there is no difference in principle, but only in fact, between the authority of Scripture, on the one hand, and that of the Church's tradition on the other."

From the side of Roman Catholicism, the bishops gathered in Vatican Council II chose *Sponsa Verbi* (Bride of the Word) as a descriptive epithet for the Church (*Dei Verbum,* 23). The first document to issue from the Council was its *Constitution on the Sacred Liturgy (Sacrosanctum Concilium).* Issuing from a sacramentally oriented faith community, the constitution proclaimed that "the liturgy is the summit toward which the activity of the Church is directed; at the same time it is the fountain from which all her power flows" (Par. 10), but it also insisted that "the liturgy of the word and the Eucharistic liturgy are so closely connected with each other that they form but one single act of worship" (Par. 56). Thus the Council Fathers solemnly acknowledged that the Scriptures have a constitutive function in the life of the Church.

The acknowledgment of this function was implicit in the Church's adoption of the canon, but it has been no less implicit in the Church's continued observance of the canon until this day. In words apropos of this consideration and applicable to the Catholic and Reformed tradition alike, John

Leith has written: "The Church's decision as to the canon was the acknowl-edgment that these Scriptures were authoritative in its life and that they were in the Church's judgment authentic, reliable, and ancient accounts of the original testimony to Jesus Christ by which the Church came into being."

Quite obviously the Roman Catholic Church's adherence to normative tra-dition means that the canon of the Scriptures occupies a place within Roman Catholicism somewhat different from the role enjoyed by the canon of Scrip-tures within the churches of the Reformed tradition. Among theologians of the Reformed tradition, the debate about the canon within the canon, as well as some discussion about the reformability of the canon, continues to go on. Nevertheless there can be no doubt that the Scriptures of the New Testa-ment play an integral role in the Church's life and that they are a consti-tutive element of the Church for both Roman Catholic and Reformation Christians.

Since the New Testament is the Church's book, and that in a dialogical sense, it should be clear that the New Testament can truly fulfill its purpose only within the Church. It is within the Church that the New Testament Scriptures are proclaimed and become actual as the Word of God. It is within the Church that the New Testament Scriptures serve as a norm of faith and a paradigm for self-reflection. The Scriptures and the Church be-long to each other.

New Testament Exegesis and the Church

The assertion that the New Testament is the Church's book should not be construed as being in opposition to a statement with a broader scope, namely that the entire Bible is the Book of the Church. There is only one canon, which always includes the Old Testament as well as the New Testament. Both Old and New Testaments belong to the Church, which has incorpo-rated the books of each testament into the canon of its Scriptures. The affirmation that the New Testament is the Church's book is quite true; the limited scope of its formulation is a consequence of the specific purpose of the present volume. Nevertheless the axiom that the New Testament is the Church's book has been advanced in full consciousness of the fact that the New Testament is uniquely the Book of the Church—indeed, in a way that not even the Old Testament is a book of the Church.

To speak of the Church is to speak of a more or less well-defined entity whose contours are delimited in ecclesiology. Since this introduction has been written from within a Roman Catholic perspective, the remarks that follow will bear principally upon exegesis and the Roman Catholic Church. The choice of this emphasis merely recognizes the *de facto* situation of the churches and attempts to respond to one of the concerns that have prompted the writing of this introduction to the study of the New Testament from within the Roman Catholic tradition. Although the focus of interest will lie upon Roman Catholicism, it will be apparent that many of the reflections which follow merit much broader application. Indeed, the ecumenical spirit that pervades contemporary biblical scholarship has largely contributed to the matters under present consideration. While occasional reflections will offer a specific comparison between churches which stand within Roman Catholic tradition and those which have sprung from the tradition of the Reformation, the discerning reader will note that much of what follows has been inspired by authors who do not share membership in the Roman Catholic Church.

All Christians can appreciate Jerome's dictum that "ignorance of the Scriptures is ignorance of Christ." The Church that believes itself called to know Christ must therefore acknowledge its calling to know the Scriptures. As the Church recognizes the authority of Christ, so also it recognizes the authority of the Scriptures which give witness to this Christ. Nevertheless a necessary distinction must be made between the New Testament and New Testament exegesis.

The Church understands the New Testament according to the categories of faith and theology; exegesis understands the New Testament as words of men. In point of fact, the historical-critical method of exegesis came from without; it did not arise from the very nature of faith. Yet the Church is a faith community. Must therefore a Church that recognizes the authority of the New Testament for its faith also recognize the authority of New Testament scholarship?

The question is an important one. It has arisen within Roman Catholic circles as well as within those of the Reformed tradition. The overarching question has been phrased and rephrased in many different forms. Within Roman Catholic biblical circles of a generation ago, a hotly debated issue was whether it was necessary for an individual to be a believer if he or she was to do New Testament exegesis properly. The issue within other ecclesiastical communions in Europe and in the United States was succinctly identified in the title of a booklet by C. K. Barrett, *Biblical Problems and Biblical Preaching*. At root the question is simply this: "What do historical studies have to do with a faith experience?"

Our times are not the first in which the Church has had to come to grips with the problematic relationship between biblical criticism and the life of the Church. One can think of the crisis that took place toward the beginning of the fifth century, when Jerome broke away from Origen's allegorizing interpretation of the Scriptures. In the eleventh and twelfth centuries philosophy revived under the form of linguistic analysis, and the school of St. Victor opted for the importance of the literal sense. In the seventeenth century, pentateuchal criticism came to the fore with the work of Richard Simon. At each of these moments the Church has had to face the issue of biblical criticism. Biblical criticism seemed to be in conflict with the Church's traditional piety. In each case it was pietism that won the battle. Nevertheless history has shown that, in some measure at least, it was those who lost the battle who won the war. Thanks to Jerome, the Victorines, and the French Oratorian, the Church has been enabled to continue to take the Scriptures seriously, allowing them to serve truly as the canon of her faith and life.

282

In a monumental study, *Medieval Exegesis: The Four Senses of Scripture* (*Exégèse médiévale: Les quatre sens de l'Écriture*), Henri de Lubac has analyzed the use made of the Scriptures in the theological efforts of the Church down through the ages. At the risk of oversimplification, it can be stated that the history of the Church has been dominated by two major approaches to the use of Scripture in theology. During the first millennium, the allegorical method of Origen dominated. During the second millennium, the proof-text approach has predominated.

The basic assumption of Origen's method was that all revelation (in fact, all knowledge) was contained in the Bible. Therefore theology was simply a matter of exposition of the Scriptures, *sacrae paginae intelligentia*. This patristic model of doing theology rested upon a crucial distinction between the literal and spiritual senses of the Scripture. The distinction was important for the exposition of the Old Testament, and maintained its validity in the interpretation of the New Testament as well. The literal sense had to do with the historicity of the events recounted. The spiritual or mystical sense was further articulated into three senses. A *doctrinal* sense was promoted in order that the spiritual life be sustained. The *ascetical* sense related to the life of Christians. Finally, the *anagogic* sense related to the experience of God in prayer and mystical experience.

Within the patristic model of theologizing, the spiritual interpretation of the Scriptures related directly to Christian life—doctrinal, ascetical, and anagogic senses leading one to another. With the revival of philosophy, theology became a matter of systematic conceptual explanation, *fides quaerens intellectum*. Doctrine took the place of the Scriptures, without thereby usurping the entire place formerly reserved for the Scriptures. The theological endeavor no longer proceeded from the Scriptures; rather it used the Scriptures in the exposition of a doctrine that had been otherwise (that is, philosophically) developed. Scripture became almost an icing on the cake. The tendency to use the Scriptures in this fashion was already present in the works of the early Schoolmen. Certainly present in the works of the great scholastics, the trend toward a proof-text methodology became prevalent in the manuals of theology in vogue after the Tridentine reform. To a summary statement of doctrine, the thesis, there were appended respective "proofs"—from Scripture, tradition, and reason. Isolated from their biblical context, the verses of the New Testament lost their character as the written witness to Jesus, the Christ.

Vatican Council II attempted to restore the Bible to its rightful place in the life, liturgy, and theologizing of the Church. References to the Scriptures pervade the conciliar documents. As far as theology is concerned, *Dei Verbum* succinctly states that "the sacred page is, as it were, the soul of theology (*anima Sacrae Theologiae*)" (Par. 24). This is at once a statement of principle and a task for the Church's theologians. As a statement of principle, the declaration echoed the thoughts of other conciliar texts. The *Decree on the Ministry and Life of Priests* had stated: "The knowledge of a sacred minister should be sacred, since it is drawn from a sacred fountain and is directed to a sacred goal; hence that knowledge should be drawn primarily from reading and meditation of the sacred Scriptures" (*Presbyterorum Ordinis,* 19). The *Decree on Priestly Formation* called for a renewal of theology in these words: "Other theological disciplines should also be renewed by livelier contact with the mystery of Christ and the history of salvation. Special attention needs to be given to the development of moral theology. Its scientific exposition should be more thoroughly nourished by scriptural teaching" (*Optatam Totius,* 16).

Surely the Council was calling for the abandonment of the proof-text type of theological methodology in favor of a theological exposition which would be more thoroughly rooted in the Scriptures. Within this perspective, can it be said that the use of the historical-critical methodology of New Testament exegesis is necessary for the renewal of theology? Is the historical-critical method necessary for the life of the Church?

Paragraph 23 of the *Dogmatic Constitution on Divine Revelation* speaks of exegesis in its role "as servant of the Church":

> The Bride of the incarnate Word, and the Pupil of the Holy Spirit, the Church is concerned to move ahead daily toward a deeper understanding of the sacred Scriptures so that she may unceasingly feed her sons with divine words. Therefore, she also rightly encourages the study of the Holy Fathers of both East and West and of sacred liturgies. Catholic exegetes then and other students of sacred theology, working diligently together and using appropriate means, should devote their energies, under the watchful care of the sacred teaching office of the Church, to an exploration and exposition of the divine writings (*ut sub vigilantia Sacri Magisterii, aptis subsidiis divinas Litteras ita investigent et proponant*). This task should be done in such a way that as many ministers of the divine word as possible will be able effectively to provide the nourishment of the Scriptures for the people of God, thereby enlightening their minds, strengthening their wills, and setting men's hearts on fire with the love of God. This sacred Synod encourages the sons of the Church who are biblical scholars to continue energetically with the work they have so well begun, with a constant renewal of vigor and with loyalty to the mind of the Church (*ut opus feliciter susceptum, renovatis in dies viribus, omni studio secundum sensum Ecclesiae exsequi pergant*) (*Dei Verbum,* 23).

The Latin text of this paragraph is divided into only two sentences. The second sentence, beginning with "This sacred Synod," is a word of encouragement to exegetes to continue their work within the ecclesial context and in a spirit of optimism. The first sentence of the paragraph is much longer than the second. The first sentence of *Dei Verbum,* 23, proclaims the involvement of exegesis in the totality of theology, in the context of the Church's teaching function, and with respect to the proclamation of the Word of God. It affirms that exegesis has a necessary but subservient function to play with respect to the Church's mission of preaching and teaching. As an ecclesial function, exegesis is related to the Church's kerygmatic and didactic ministries.

The Council's statement on the function of exegesis within the Church calls for a few additional remarks. First of all, the history of the successive redactions of the conciliar declaration showed that the Fathers did not want to convey the impression of exaggerated confidence in the progress of exegesis. The phrase "deeper understanding of the Sacred Scriptures" (*ad profundiorem in dies Scripturarum Sacrarum intelligentiam assequendam*) was deliberately chosen for its cautious phraseology. Secondly, the text repeatedly affirms the ecclesial nature of exegesis. Exegesis is to be done within the total context of the Church, in its vertical (historical) and lateral dimensions (contemporary life of the Church). Thirdly, exegesis is a discipline in its own right, but it is not self-sufficient. The exhortation to exegetes to exercise their profession "with loyalty to the mind of the Church" (*secundum sensum Ecclesiae*) and "under the watchful care of the sacred teaching office of the Church" (*sub vigilantia Sacri Magisterii*) point to the horizon within which exegesis can be done as an ecclesial task. Fourthly, exegesis is, nonetheless, truly a discipline in its own right. Its independence is affirmed in the binomial "using appropriate means . . . under the watchful care of the sacred teaching office of the Church." That the two phrases go together is clearer in the official Latin text than it is in the English translation. The reference to the "appropriate means" indicates that exegetes must ply the tools of their own trade. "Under the watchful care of the sacred teaching office" may seem restrictive of the work of Catholic exegetes. In fact, the phraseology was intended to affirm the ecclesial and servant role of exegesis. The present language of the text replaces that of an earlier version which spoke of the work of the exegete under the guidance (*sub ductu*) of the Magisterium. The choice of the *sub vigilantia* formula shows that the Council Fathers did not intend that the Magisterium should lead the way for biblical exegesis. Finally, the present statement is silent as to the nature of the "appropriate means" to be employed by the exegete. Earlier sections of *Dei Verbum,* especially Paragraphs 12 and 19, indicate that at least both the form- and redaction-critical methodologies are to be understood within the compass of the "appropriate means" statement.

In a word, the conciliar statement implies that the historical-critical method of New Testament exegesis has a role to play in the Church. But how? That is our present question. How does the use of the historical-critical methodology serve the teaching and preaching Church? The reflections which follow in the chapter are but a summarized response to the question "how?" Before proceeding to an exposition of the ways in which New Testament exegesis relates to the development of doctrinal theology (sometimes called dogma or systematic theology), the teaching office of the Church, and the function of preaching, it must be stated that the historical-critical study of the New Testament is, to borrow a phrase from Schubert Odgen, "theologically necessary and legitimate."

The legitimacy of the historical-critical inquiry derives from the very nature of the believer (and believing community), as a human subject. Since our faith experience is a human one, we must utilize the most ordinary means of human understanding in order to understand our faith. Is not this the root sense of Anselm's definition of theology, "faith seeking understanding"?

Nowadays the philosophical patterns of previous times have given way to an awareness of the historical dimensions of the faith experience. Surely this means that the faith experience must be understood according to its historical coordinates—and this with respect to the individual believer as well as to the body of believers, the Church. In an era as historically conscious as our own, the rejection of the historical-critical methodology would be a type of intellectual suicide. Moreover, the Church's need to express its faith to those outside the pale of the faith community requires the use of a historical-critical methodology when their culture, and their possibility of understanding within a given cultural context, is permeated with a strong historical awareness.

This fact alone points to the necessity of the historical-critical inquiry, but there are even more elementary aspects of this necessity which deserve to be highlighted. Two of these aspects seem to outweigh all the others in importance. First of all, the Christian faith is an incarnational faith. It is based upon the conviction that God has acted, and continues to act, in human history. In a most decisive fashion, God entered into human history in Jesus of Nazareth. Jesus of Nazareth is not a myth but a historical personage. A use of the New Testament Scriptures without a concomitant use of the historical-critical methodology in the exposition of these Scriptures is a use which treats the Scriptures as a timeless myth. Such a use is not appropriate for a Christian, since the Christian faith is a historic rather than a mythic reality. This needs to be said, even though the historical-critical analysis of the New Testament reveals that mythical language has been used in order to express some elements of the Church's faith. In other words, the use of the historical-critical methodology of exegesis preserves the New Testament from being treated as if it were the expression of a myth, to which each and everyone might ascribe his or her own meaning *ad libitum.*

Secondly, the use of the historical-critical methodology is necessary because the Christ of faith is not immediately accessible to our experience. Believers know him only through the witness of other believers. Among the earliest of those who have given witness to the Christ of faith are those who have written the pages of the New Testament, and those to whom these pages give testimony. They constantly affirm that the Christ of faith is somehow to be identified with Jesus of Nazareth. It is this Jesus who embodies the fullness of God's revelation. Yet he is accessible only through the witness of those who attest to him in faith.

It is true that the "historical Jesus" is the construct of historians. It is the portrait of Jesus that results from the efforts of scientific historians. The historical Jesus (Jesus as reconstructed) must be distinguished from the Jesus of history (Jesus as he existed) and the historic Jesus (Jesus as perceived). The historic Jesus is the one to whom each of the New Testament authors gives witness. Indeed the theological problem of the Jesus of history (who Jesus was) can only be answered by the affirmation of the historic Jesus by the New Testament authors (who Jesus was, for them, when they wrote). If today we seek to know who Jesus was, we too will find that "who was He?" can only be answered by means of an examination of the New Testament affirmation of "who He is." Subsequently the believer may formulate his own "who Jesus is." The believer who, on the other hand, seeks to know who Jesus is without benefit of the historical-critical methodology has replaced the construct of the exegetes with another construct, that of his or her own imagination.

New Testament Exegesis and Dogmatic Theology

The first articulation of the spiritual sense of the Scriptures thrust into the limelight by patristic exegesis was the doctrinal sense. Interestingly enough, Vatican Council II also looked first to theology as it reflected on the ecclesial function of exegesis. A generation ago, a number of German-speaking Roman Catholic theologians addressed themselves to the relationship between biblical theology and dogmatic theology. Among them was Karl Rahner, who pleaded for a biblical theology which would be "an intrinsic element in dogmatic theology itself." In Rahner's view, this biblical theology would not be simply another chapter in historical theology; it would be an independent discipline in itself. It would be pursued "neither as a mere prolongation of ordinary exegesis nor as a mere element in dogmatic theology, but as a separate branch of study which will represent the correct intermediary between exegesis and dogmatic theology."

Rahner correctly cites the unique place of biblical theology as a part of the comprehensive theological task. Yet the nature of biblical theology—more specifically the nature of New Testament theology—for the Christian theologian remains a moot question. Should New Testament theology be construed as the history of New Testament religion (thus, Wrede and Bousset) or should it be construed as the theology of the New Testament (thus, Schlatter and Bultmann)? Is New Testament theology merely analytic or is it also synthetic? To be sure, there are some New Testament exegetes who hold that the only possible and therefore the self-sufficient study of the New Testament is a historical one. These historicist exegetes eschew in principle any attempt to present a systematic overview of the theology of the New Testament. For this group of interpreters, even the systematic overview of the theology of a given New Testament author is to be avoided. These commentators of the New Testament take refuge in the conviction that theirs is a historical task, whereas the task of the systematic theologian is a speculative-philosophical one.

Notwithstanding this demurrer on the part of some exegetes, speculative theologians and Church leaders as well are calling for the development of a biblical theology that will occupy a mediating function between historical exegesis on the one hand and contemporary theology on the other. They proceed from the assumption that theology is a function of the Church. They recall the words of Vatican Council II that "the study of the sacred page is, as it were, the soul of sacred theology" (*Dei Verbum,* 24). They are convinced that theology is a scientific discipline and that therefore it should be able to be systematized and project some sort of unified vision. If the sacred page is the soul of theology, its thought should also be susceptible to analysis and systematic exposition. This is, if not the expectation, at least the hope of the systematic theologian.

That New Testament exegesis should proffer such a unified vision of the theological visions of each of the New Testament authors was the expectation of the late German exegete Heinrich Schlier, who wrote that "the theology of the New Testament endeavors to elucidate and exhibit in their interconnections the data of revelation as these are understood by that New Testament understanding of the faith. By doing this, the fundamental step is taken toward their interpretation." Those who share Schlier's understanding of the task of New Testament theology are confronted by a methodological question similar to that faced by those who have attempted a theology of the Old Testament. What is the principle of integration that allows the biblical theologian to bring into one single vision the thoughts of authors who have lived over the course of several generations in more than one cultural milieu? Should one opt for a developmental presentation, as did Gerhard von Rad? Or the overarching leitmotif presentation, as did Walther Eichrodt? Or the neat categories of systematic theology, as did Paul van Imschoot?

Posing the alternatives suggests that the student of the New Testament Scriptures is confronted by such a diversity of New Testament theologies as to defy easy systematization. This diversity derives from such variables as the personal genius of the individual New Testament authors, the diversity of cultures within which they wrote, the evolution of the expression of the Christian faith in time, and the diversity of the Christian experience upon which each of the New Testament writings is a reflection, not to mention its object, Jesus Christ himself. Thus those who seek after the theology of the New Testament, and those who urge its use as a mediator between biblical exegesis and systematic theology, must begin with the realization that the study of the New Testament—even one undertaken in view of systematization—reveals a diversity of Christologies, just as it yields a diversity of soteriological, ecclesiological, and eschatological expressions as well. Despite this almost unwieldy diversity, the utility of elaborating a New Testament theology has been amply demonstrated by Edward Schillebeeckx' monumental Christological trilogy. Moreover the possibility of doing a New Testament theology is commonly suggested by the works of those redaction critics who use the methodology in a way that moves beyond linguistic analysis to an appreciation of the ideology which has prompted a thoughtful editing of traditional material.

Notwithstanding the difficulties inherent in the elaboration of a biblical theology (difficulties so severe as to have led some interpreters to forsake the task altogether), it would seem that one should at least be able to offer some suggestions as to the relationship between New Testament exegesis and theology. Indeed, the question of the relationship between exegesis and theology is inescapable. The exegete who sees the task of interpretation as an ecclesiastical function must ask what his historical study has to do with the faith reflection of the Church. The theologian who accepts the mandate of reflecting upon the Church must surely ask what is the present significance of the foundational experience of the Church. Ultimately New Testament exegesis and theology must be related to each other because of the singular importance of Jesus Christ. Rahner has put it well by stating that "It [the Church] can only remain true to its own nature if it understands itself to be the Church of the apostolic age, however ready it has to be to accept its own changes in the course of history. For it is only through the apostolic Church and its testimony to the faith that the Church attains Jesus Christ." The normativity and centrality of Jesus Christ to the Christian faith implies that that systematic reflection on the "Christian experience," which is commonly identified as Christian theology, necessarily implies an understanding of the New Testament witness to Jesus Christ. Since it is the achievement of New Testament exegesis to have "understood" the New Testament witness, Christian theology cannot avoid making use of exegesis. Indeed, theology without exegesis is but an ideology—and hardly a Christian one, at that.

Thus the soul of sacred theology is exegesis, broadly, not narrowly, defined. The soul vivifies and unifies that which it informs. How does exegesis vivify and unify theology? That it do so was the stated wish of the Council Fathers who spoke of scriptural teaching specifically as the "nourishment" of at least one branch of theological science (*Optatam Totius,* 16). One response to the question at hand has been offered by Josef Blank. His idea is simple enough. Proceeding from the notion that "sacred theology rests on the written word of God . . . as its primary and perpetual foundation" (*Dei Verbum,* 24) and convinced that exegesis is the scientific study of this foundation, Blank concluded that exegesis is the "basic science" of all the other theological disciplines. Insofar as exegesis is concerned with the origins of the faith and of theological reflection, the expression is well chosen. With respect to theology, exegesis is foundational in that it provides some understanding of the first faith and theological expressions of the Christian tradition. Whether these articulations be in the form of creedal formulas or in the form of narrative, they enjoy a temporal priority with respect to later theological expressions of the Christian faith.

Were the insights gleaned from exegesis, more specifically from the use of the historical-critical method in exegesis, to be restricted solely to the interpretation of the historical past, it would be difficult to understand in what sense the New Testament Scriptures function as the *norma non normata* of the theological endeavor. If the scientific understanding of the New Testament is relevant only for the understanding of the past—even that privileged past which is the time of the first literary formulations of the Christian faith experience—how do the Scriptures serve as a norm for the theological task carried out with a view toward interpreting a present-day Christian experience?

Surely the question is not an easy one, and the discussion must certainly be pursued throughout the life of the Church. Undoubtedly the discussion raises important issues relative to theological method and the science of hermeneutics. At the outset, however, it should be recognized that the historical-critical methodology is indispensable to modern hermeneutics. The historical-critical methodology employed by the exegete in a search to reach some understanding of the New Testament text is the same method as that employed by the systematic theologian who seeks to elucidate the meaning of Church doctrines and traditions. Surely, therefore, the use of the historical-critical method does not preclude the assumption of the results of New Testament exegesis into the global theological endeavor.

Moreover the canon of the New Testament Scriptures provides the context within which theology is done. Whether the method adopted by the theologian be deductive or inductive, the Scriptures of the New Testament serve as the framework within which the systematic theologian performs the interpretive function. It is not only legitimate, but also necessary for the systematic theologian to ask about the significance of the canon. Historical science indicates that the canon is the context; dogmatic reflection must raise the questions why and whence. To the extent that the systematic theologian considers that the Church of today must be in continuity with the Church of the foundational Christian experience, he or she must have recourse to exegesis, since it is only by the exercise of this discipline that historically conditioned humans can come to appreciate something of that foundational experience. Furthermore, the systematic theologian who accepts the Christian past as at least partially constitutive of the Christian present cannot avoid the affirmation that the canon of the New Testament Scriptures has been a constant point of reference in the long history of Christian thought. Finally, the systematic theologian who would, somewhat naïvely, I think, reduce the theologian's role to that of reflection on the present experience of the Christian community must also consider that the canon of the New Testament Scriptures is indeed the context of much within the Church that is specifically identifiable as Christian, namely its prayer and worship.

In effect, the systematic theologian must deal with the fact that the New Testament canon has contextualized and continues to contextualize the Christian experience. The fact demands elucidation if indeed the Christian experience is to be understood. The exegetical exercise of the historical-critical methodology serves to elucidate the contextualizing datum. Thus dogmatics needs exegesis. Ferdinand Hahn has called exegesis and dogmatic theology the two "focal points of the science of theology." Between the two there must be a dialogical relationship if indeed the Scriptures are to be considered the soul of theology and the *norma non normata* of the authentic Christian faith experience.

In short, exegesis and dogmatic theology stand in a relationship of interdependence. The point has been well made by Alexandre Gagoncy, who has written that "there can . . . be no 'basic science' or 'foundation science' without a 'constructive science' forming a superstructure and no 'preparation' without a continuation or continuation without a preparation." Exegetes and dogmaticians need one another. Speaking of this need from the viewpoint of the systematic theologian, Karl Rahner has written, "The modern dogmatic theologian needs to adduce arguments from Scripture and to present them seriously as such, instead of merely repeating the Church's doctrines in biblical formulations. And if he is to do this he must take serious and exact cognizance of the findings, and also the problems, of modern exegesis." *Divino Afflante Spiritu* encouraged exegetes and systematic theologians to work with one another. They must pose questions to one another if indeed the total Christian experience is to come to that clarity of understanding it must before Christian faith can be a fully human experience for the individual believer and that community of believers commonly called the Church.

A Fivefold Task

At the risk of some oversimplification and without the extended reflection that the subject warrants, it can be said that exegesis has a task that is at once constitutive, critical, indicative, provocative, and validating with respect to systematic theology. To the extent that exegetes and systematic theologians respond to it from their proper vantage points, the Scriptures will effectively serve as the rule of faith and theology will come to discern that its soul really is "the sacred page."

(1) Exegesis has a *constitutive function* with respect to dogmatic theology in that the study of each of the New Testament books reveals the common thread of the early Christian experience. This common thread profoundly shapes the normativity of the New Testament Scriptures for the Christian faith. With respect to ecclesiology, Carl Peter has written that "consistency within the biblical witness is an important factor in the normative role of Sacred Scripture with regard to contemporary ecclesiology." With regard to ecclesiology, certainly the Church's continuity with Israel, its relationship with the apostolic community of Jerusalem, and its celebration of Eucharist and baptism are fibers of the common thread. With respect to Christology, the common thread would encompass at least the flesh-and-blood existence of Jesus of Nazareth, culminating in a death on the cross, and the affirmation that God acted through this Jesus preeminently in the resurrection event. That God is made present to men and women not only in words but also in activity likewise constitutes something of the warp and woof of the New Testament fabric with which the Church is perennially clothed, as does the experience of the dynamic presence of the Spirit of God.

To take note of the fact that by highlighting the common thread of a foundational Christian experience, exegesis serves a constitutive function with respect to dogmatic theology is not to opt for some sort of dogmatic reductionism. Quite the contrary. The serious study of the New Testament clearly reveals that each of its authors came to grips with the relationship between the common thread and new situations which they and their communities were facing. Indeed, the methodology of redaction criticism shows clearly that each of the New Testament authors appropriated the traditional faith expression and adapted it to a new situation. The phenomena of adaptation and the quest for solutions to new problems in the light of the faith tradition are also very much a part of the common thread which New Testament exegesis can discern. Indeed, it also points to the fact that the resources for the solution of these new problems cannot always be found within the tradition itself. In dialogue with the common faith, the New Testament authors often had to go beyond their tradition in order to meet the needs of their communities. Surely the reaching out to new human experiences so that all might be submitted to the Lordship of Jesus is also part of that common Christian experience to which the New Testament gives witness, a common Christian experience which remains normative for the Church today.

If exegesis can identify the common thread of a primary Christian experience, it just as surely reveals that this common thread appears with different hues. The common Christian experience is interpreted in diverse fashions. What God has done with respect to Jesus for our sake is certainly the focal point of the New Testament's expression of faith. "The Easter event" is central to the Christian faith, but it is expressed in many and diverse manners. Models of resurrection, ascension, rapture, and enthronement appear. Various Christological titles are used. Different forms of expression are employed —the story, the creedal formula, the liturgical rite. One must certainly speak of a unity of faith with a diversity of interpretation of that faith as part of the fabric of the primal Christian experience to which the New Testament itself gives witness. There is but one Jesus, crucified and raised, but there are diverse Christologies enunciated by those who seek to understand and testify to what God has done in Jesus. This very diversity of witness and interpretation is a significant element in the common thread revealed by New Testament exegesis.

In short, New Testament exegesis reveals a certain common thread of the Christian faith and action which serves as a constituent of the Christian experience and as a subject for thoughtful reflection. The identification and interpretation of that common thread is a first contribution of exegesis to dogmatic theology. The appropriation of the common thread by dogmatic theologians can assist their interpretation of what is orthodoxy and what is orthopraxis, promote their recognition of a "hierarchy of truths" within the range of Christian pronouncement, aid our understanding of the unity of faith, and move all to a relevant expression of that common thread in such ways that it is both comprehensible and comprehensive. For the common Christian experience must not only be understood with one's mind; it must also impinge upon one's life in all its ramifications.

(2) Exegesis also has a *critical function* with respect to dogmatic theology and the life of the Church. To some extent the New Testament itself, critically understood, gives witness to the exercise of a critical function arising

from the common thread of the Christian experience. Source criticism, for example, points to the existence of written documents lying behind the canonical Gospels. Often the source documents had a literary form quite different from that of the Gospel in which they are currently embodied. One can think of the *Q* source used by Matthew and Luke, and the aretalogies used respectively by John and Mark. To each of these literary types there corresponds a rather distinct Christology. To the collection of sayings corresponds a "wise man" Christology. To the aretalogy corresponds a "divine man" Christology.

Each of these literary types and the typical profile which it suggests is well known. Collections of sayings have been attributed to other sages in the course of history—men such as Solomon, Benjamin Franklin, and Chairman Mao. Similarly, miracle stories have been associated with a variety of divine men, including Asclepius, Serapis, and Moses. Jesus of Nazareth was not, however, simply a "wise man." Neither was he only a "divine man." Because Jesus was reducible neither to the function of sage nor to that of thaumaturge, both the collection of sayings and the catena of miracle stories tended to disappear as acceptable independent literary types in early Christianity. Today we know of the existence of the *Q* collection and of the aretalogies that lie behind John and Mark only because they have been used by Matthew and Luke, John and Mark. The incorporation of the earlier documents into the canonical Gospels points to the inability of both the collection of sayings and the aretalogy adequately to express an understanding of Jesus of Nazareth which was compatible with the "common thread" understanding of him. Little wonder, then, that the Greater Church of the fourth century did not accept into its normative collection of testimonies to Jesus works such as the Gospel of Thomas and the protoevangelium of James, two works whose literary types respectively suggest that Jesus was a wise man and a divine man. In similar fashion, the normative role of the New Testament, critically understood, would preclude the acceptability of a reductionist Christology that limits Jesus to his role of wise man as did turn-of-the-century liberal Protestantism, or to his role as a wonder worker which is the presumption of much simplistic belief within the Catholic tradition.

A study of the New Testament epistles offers another example of this critical function at work. The Pauline doctrine of justification by faith, set forth by the apostle in Romans and Galatians, was clearly problematic for the early Church. Sound exegesis points to James 2 as being a response to the Pauline position, uncritically reconstructed. An exegetically sensitive presentation of the Pauline teaching would certainly attend both to the fact that the "doctrine" has been set forth by Paul in his letters and to the fact that the use of the epistolary literary form placed certain identifiable constraints upon the exposition of the doctrine. Beyond that, sound exegetical methodology would require that the teaching be explained with respect to those historical circumstances within which it was formulated by the apostle. Our present purpose does not require that we now offer a theological exposition of the Pauline doctrine of justification by faith in keeping with the tenets of sound exegesis. Yet it does call for the realization that the justification teaching should not be so construed as if to imply moral anarchy. The Pauline apologia of Romans 3:5–8 (cf. 6:1), the paraenesis of Romans 12–15, the notion of the fruits of the Spirit in Galatians 5:22–23, and the apposite remarks of James all show the importance of moral sensitivity as a factor in the Christian experience. What exegesis has revealed is that a notion of salvation without a sensitivity to moral responsibility is alien to the normative experience of the primitive Christian church.

This fact introduces a critical dimension into theological reflection on those would-be "churches" whose Christianity is reducible to a narrow religious experience. Whether this experience be of the charismatic variety or the institutional variety, the theological corrective to which the New Testament Scriptures give witness points to the inadequacy of a "religion-only" form of Christianity. This does not mean that the Scriptures specifically indicate the concrete characteristics with which Christianity should enter the marketplace. How and to what extent the Scriptures themselves might suggest this profile is a subject to which we must return. Presently our only concern is to suggest that a sound understanding of the Scriptures, to which the use of the historical-critical methodology has made and continues to make an essential contribution, serves to contraindicate a Christianity which withdraws from the world to the church or which refuses to come to grips with the moral issues of the world in which it exists.

These two examples are hardly adequate to demonstrate the critical role of exegesis with respect to theological reflection and dogmatic formulation. However, they do indicate that such matters considered within the scope of a historical-critical understanding of the Scriptures are not foreign to the critical function of Scripture. Indeed, our examples have suggested that such matters as the formation of the canon, genre analysis, the unity of Romans, and the dating of James are not alien to the critical function enjoyed by the Scriptures with respect to the theological quest.

Certainly a study of the diversity of Church order to which the New Testament attests can also serve a critical function in ecclesiology. The New Testament witnesses to many different forms of Church order. When it clearly recognizes the ecclesial character of a given form of Christian community which professedly acknowledges the Lordship of Jesus, that form cannot be excluded as a viable form within which the Christian Church might exist today or at some future date. In short, the New Testament exercises a critical function in ecclesiology insofar as it prevents the contemporary Christian from taking his present or traditional form of Church order as exclusively authentic when the New Testament evidence shows that other forms of Church structure could and did exist, and ceased to exist.

(3) Exegesis also has an *indicative function* with respect to dogmatic theology insofar as a sound exegesis of the text can indicate the direction that events, institutions, and teachings took. This orientation shares in the normativity of the New Testament. Drawing from the results of earlier studies, Carl Peter has acknowledged the differences between an exposition of

Church order based on the Pastorals and an exposition based on the earlier and authentic Pauline letters. This prompted a twofold question: "In the hypothesis that in later canonical works there is much more insistence on a teaching office, is this development itself normative, indicating that the term is significant for subsequent ages? Is there, as a result, a presumption that further development of that teaching office in the post-apostolic church would be expected and legitimate?"

To cite the legitimacy of such a development is, of course, to suggest something different from the affirmation of the exclusive legitimacy of such a development. A model of Church order can be legitimate without thereby being paradigmatically normative. For example, the evidence offered by the authors who respectively penned Matthew and the Pastorals points toward the institutionalization of the Church. Sound exegesis must make the additional point that the Pastorals and Matthew were produced for given local ecclesial communities.

Matthew's Gospel clearly had the universal proclamation of the Gospel in sight, yet this Gospel also recognizes a difference between the task of the Church and that of Jesus (cf. Matt 25:24; comp. Matt 10:6 and 28:18–20). Matthew's Gospel has an ecclesial interest throughout, and a universality of perspective can be seen in a redactional study of those passages which have an ecclesial focus. Yet there is no evidence that the Matthean community was as tightly structured as was the community to which the Pastorals are directed. Thus the gradual institutionalization of the Church to which the Pastorals point does not mean that Matthew's pointing to the universal Church necessarily implies a tightly developed structure.

Another example of the way in which the New Testament functions normatively by indicating directions taken by events, institutions, and teachings can be gleaned from the way the New Testament communities dealt with the teaching of Jesus on divorce (Matt 5:32; 19:9; Mark 10:11–12; Luke 16:18; 1 Cor 7:10). Today it is commonly admitted that the primitive logion has every claim to be authentic. An unqualified teaching on the topic of divorce must be attributed to the Jesus of history. We can inquire as to the nature of the primitive logion. Was it a prophetic utterance? Was it a scholarly conclusion, akin to the sayings of the rabbis? Whatever its literary form, the traditional saying of Jesus did not admit of any exceptions. Both Matthew and Paul, however, perceived some possibility of accommodating the traditional teaching to a different situation. Although it is difficult for us to reconstruct the set of circumstances in which Paul framed his teaching on sex and marriage in 1 Corinthians 7, and perhaps even more difficult to arrive at a satisfactory assessment of the meaning of *porneia* ("adultery") in Matthew 5:32; 19:9, it is apparent that both Matthew and Paul did not view Jesus' teaching as an absolute law which would forever prevent those who had married a second time in contravention of the dominical logion from being reconciled to the ecclesial community. Some form of accommodation of the tradition to a new setting was made by these authors even though Jesus' call to marital fidelity was echoed by Matthew and Paul whose words and style show a familiarity with the traditional logion.

(4) Another fashion in which exegesis can make a contribution to dogmatic theology is in the exercise of what can be called a *provocative function*. Exegesis has an innovative role to play in the development of dogmatic theology insofar as it suggests areas that dogmatic theology has largely overlooked. Thus, until recently and under pressure of the feminist movement, dogmatic theology within the Roman Catholic tradition has shied away from a consideration of the role of women in the Church, specifically from the institutional and organizational role of women in the Church. Roman Catholic dogmatic treatises simply reiterated that only a baptized male could be admitted to the presbyterate and the episcopacy. However, the New Testament attests to the existence of deaconnesses within the early churches (Rom 16:1; 1 Tim 3:11). A biblically oriented dogmatic theology should have raised the issue of the institutional role of women in the Church, even apart from the impetus which has come from the feminist movement. Once the issue has been raised, the biblical passages remain as a goad to the Church's theologians to consider the matter seriously.

The charismatic ordering of the Pauline communities at Corinth and Thessalonica has long been noted by exegetes. The importance of the Spirit in prayer was cited by the apostle in both the letter to the Romans and the letter to the Galatians. That the Gospel is received among believers with joy in the Spirit is noted in the earliest of his writings (1 Thes 1:6). Yet for all practical purposes the role of the Spirit had been neglected in theology, in prayer and worship, and as a key element in Church order among Western Roman Catholics until fairly recent times. Fortunately Vatican Council II and the Charismatic Renewal have prompted a greater reflection on the role of the Spirit within Roman Catholic communities. These Spirit-moved phenomena within the Church have created a context congenial to the type of theological reflection on the role of the Spirit as that offered by Yves Congar and Heribert Muehlen. However, a systematic theology that had been thoroughly nourished by the Scriptures of the New Testament would not have allowed the Spirit to be shunted to that auxiliary role which was virtually the sole role allotted to him by speculative theology until relatively recent decades. Had the Scriptures effectively served in a normative role, the study of the New Testament would have provoked believers as well as those whose specific ministry it is to elaborate that belief in systematic categories to develop a pneumatology which would have been consistent with the constitutive tradition of the Church and functional with respect to the life of the Church in these times.

Fortunately the so-called Biblical Movement within Roman Catholicism, particularly in its European expression immediately after World War II, prodded Church leaders and theologians to be open to the renewal of systematic theology by means of a return to biblical sources. The fruits of this fundamental renewal are to be found in the documents of Vatican Council II and the renewal of the Church which has ensued since then. Nonetheless the

provocative function of the New Testament Scriptures, adequately interpreted, should not be limited to the role of the occasional bolt of lightning.
Rather the Scriptures should serve the Church's systematic reflection as a
steady source of light ever pointing out dark nooks within the total Christian
experience. Utilized as a constant source for reflection, the New Testament
Scriptures can prompt the Church to a more adequate reflection on the
Christ, his Church, its sacraments and virtually every other domain of its experience and reflection as well.

(5) Finally, a sound exegesis of the New Testament texts can allow the
Scriptures to serve a *validating function* for the Christian experience and
thereby fulfill a normative role with respect to the theology and life of the
Church. Two examples may suffice to make the point. One might begin with
the Johannine tale of The Water Become Wine at Cana in Galilee (John
2:1–11). A form-critical analysis of the pericope suggests that the *Sitz-im-
Leben Jesu* may well have been Jesus' attendance at a family wedding. The
Sitz-im-Leben der Kirche was most likely the tension that existed between
the disciples of Jesus and his brethren. This tension is an ecclesiastical situation to which Paul (1 Cor 15; Gal 1 – 2) and the author of Acts occasionally
refer. It served as the life situation for such passages as Mark 3:31–35, par.
and Luke 11:27–28.

The search for the *Sitz-im-Leben Jesu* and the *Sitz-im-Leben der Kirche*
of the Johannine pericope may appear to be superfluous and almost useless
in the eyes of those who would read the miracle story as if it had no other
purpose than to affirm Jesus' wonder-working capabilities. However, the realization that Jesus did attend family celebrations, and apparently enjoyed
them, indicates that he was not removed from the give-and-take of common
human activities and social contacts. This realization can serve as a corrective to those whose construct of Christianity is that of a dour Kirk as well as
to those who reduce the Christian life to some form of moral encratism.
Form criticism reveals that the Jesus of the Gospels was no esoteric type of
individual who fled from the world and its experiences. Rather, the historic
Jesus validates and confirms the experience of those Christians who find
human and Christian significance in the conviviality of family gatherings.

The *Sitz-im-Leben der Kirche* of John 2:1–11 is such as to show that even
the Church of earliest times was confronted by the problem of "nepotism."
The significance of family relationships in the light of the Gospel is an issue
that must be faced by many Church persons. An awareness which results
from a form-critical analysis of the first Cana miracle is that the proclamation of the Gospel enjoys a certain priority over and against biological
relationships, even of the closest kind. That this priority was not achieved in
the Church of early times without some measure of conflict and pain can
validate the experience of those ministers of the Gospel who today are torn
between the demands of family allegiance and the call of the Gospel. In
these times one can think, for example, of those celibate priests within the
Roman Catholic tradition who often have painfully to work out their relationship with their family of origin once they have been ordained to the min-

isterial priesthood. It is of course true that the *Sitz-im-Leben der Kirche* of John 2:1–11 does not offer any concrete program as to how this or any other family-ministry conflict is to be worked out, yet the realization that such a tension was part of the early Christian experience validates the contemporary experience to some extent and serves as a consolation to those who are caught up in the throes of the problem.

Another example of the validating function of the New Testament Scriptures to which the use of the historical-critical methodology makes a not insignificant contribution can be found with respect to the sacramental life of the Church. There are those Roman Catholics who are concerned by the relative disuse of the sacrament of reconciliation within the Church today. They are also perturbed by the partial abandonment of devotions and other paraliturgical services. In the judgment of some, too much attention focuses on the Eucharist. It has even been suggested that some receive the Eucharist without sufficient personal and moral preparation.

A critical examination of the New Testament Scriptures, however, confirms the primacy of place of the Eucharist within the experience of the early Christian Church and points to the importance of baptism as a polyvalent sacrament of initiation. The discussion of the Johannine sacramentary has highlighted the importance of baptism and Eucharist in the life of the Church. Form-critical analysis of the Synoptics has pointed to the celebration of Eucharist and baptism as the *Sitz-im-Leben der Kirche* of many of the Gospel pericopes. The use of the historical-critical methodology of New Testament interpretation thus underscores the primary role of baptism and Eucharist in the Christian experience. This realization validates the contemporary Roman Catholic experience in which baptism and Eucharist are once again enjoying a dominant role in the life of the Church and its members.

That the New Testament Scriptures confirm the present sacramental life of the Church is an example of the validating function of the Scriptures as *norma non normata* for the life and reflection of the Church. In this respect, they are able to exercise one aspect of their normative function because of a scientific and historically oriented exegesis. In contrast, the proof-text manner of using the New Testament Scriptures did not allow for the exercise of a truly normative function of the sacred page. For example, a highly esteemed manual of theology widely used during the 1950s devoted more pages to an exegesis of James 5:14–15 in its treatise on the sacrament of anointing than it did to all the pertinent scriptural passages in its treatise on the Eucharist. In sum, it is only when the Scriptures are allowed to speak for themselves and when they are understood according to the normal means of human intellection—concretely and, with respect to the New Testament, in accordance with the historical-critical method—that the Scriptures truly enjoy a function that is at once constitutive, critical, indicative, provocative, and validating with respect to theology and the life of the Church. It is only as the New Testament exercises these functions that it is truly the *norma non normata* and the soul of theology.

New Testament Exegesis and the Magisterium

In this discussion on New Testament exegesis and theology, it might have proved useful to make a distinction between the "theology to which the New Testament Scriptures give witness" and a "theology which is in harmony and accordance with the New Testament Scriptures." The latter belongs to the field of dogmatic and systematic theology properly so called, whereas the former represents a historical, descriptive understanding. Our reflections have focused on the historical, descriptive task as this results from the historical-critical method of New Testament exegesis, with some attention to the partial synthesis of New Testament thought. We have not offered a systematic exposition of the methodology of dogmatic theology, nor could we hope to do so within the scope of the present volume. Similarly it cannot be our intention to offer presently a systematic presentation of the role and function of the Magisterium within Roman Catholicism. Nonetheless the Magisterium is a most important factor in the development and exposition of dogmatic reflection within Roman Catholicism. Hence a word or two must be said with respect to the relationship between New Testament exegesis and the Magisterium.

The Magisterium is "the sacred teaching office of the Church" (*Dei Verbum,* 10). The Magisterium fulfills a pastoral function within the Church, namely that of teaching and proclaiming the Word of God in the name of Christ. In a privileged manner, the Magisterium enunciates the *sensus fidelium*. It solemnly and officially expresses the faith of the entire Church. As a pastoral and teaching office with respect to the faith, the Magisterium is distinct from the academic and investigative function of exegetes with respect to history. Exegesis and the Magisterium are distinct from each other. Each has its proper function, purpose, and methodology. Indeed, the relative autonomy of exegesis was proclaimed by the Fathers of Vatican Council II who taught that "Catholic exegetes then . . . using appropriate means, should devote their energies, under the watchful care of the sacred teaching office of the Church, to an exploration and exposition of the divine writings" (*Dei Verbum,* 23).

Autonomy does not, of course, mean total independence. It was for this reason that the conciliar text noted that Catholic exegetes must pursue their proper task "under the watchful care of the sacred teaching office of the Church." The language of the earlier draft, "under the guidance (*sub ductu*) of the sacred teaching office," did not adequately represent the relationship between exegesis and the Magisterium, because it did not sufficiently express the proper autonomy of exegesis. In opting for the expression "under the watchful care" the Council Fathers found a phrase which at once expressed both the relative independence of exegesis and the Magisterium and their mutual interdependence.

That there must be a relationship between exegesis and the Magisterium devolves from the fact that the New Testament Scriptures are the Church's book. They were entrusted to the Church as an expression of its faith. This means that the New Testament Scriptures were not primarily given to a group of scholars as an object for scientific research. Together with sacred tradition, the Scriptures "form one sacred deposit of the word of God." It is the sacred function of the Magisterium to teach the word of God. Accordingly the Council Fathers proclaimed: "The task of authentically interpreting the word of God, whether written or handed on, has been entrusted exclusively to the living teaching office of the Church, whose authority is exercised in the name of Jesus Christ. This teaching office is not above the word of God, but serves it, teaching only what has been handed on, listening to it devoutly, guarding it scrupulously, and explaining it faithfully by divine commission and with the help of the Holy Spirit" (*Dei Verbum,* 10). The paragraph concludes with the affirmation "that sacred tradition, sacred Scripture, and the teaching authority of the Church, in accord with God's most wise design, are so linked and joined together and each in its own way under the action of the one Holy Spirit contribute[s] effectively to the salvation of souls."

This affirmation of the interrelationship between the Magisterium and the Sacred Scriptures implies a relationship between the Magisterium and exegesis, which is ultimately nothing less than the art of understanding the text in which is embodied the word of God, in the service of which the Magisterium itself stands. The authority of the Magisterium is that of Jesus Christ; its purpose is the salvation of souls. By contrast, the authority of exegesis is truth; its purpose is the understanding of texts. The Magisterium cannot remain indifferent to exegesis since its authority is that of Jesus Christ. The Scriptures, whose sense is yielded by exegesis, bear witness to that self-same Jesus Christ. Thus the Council Fathers solemnly affirmed that the Magisterium is "not above the word of God, but serves it."

What is this servant's role? How does it relate to the science and/or art of exegesis? If the Scriptures of the New Testament have been confided to the Church for the sake of the salvation of souls, it would seem that the primary task of the Magisterium with respect to the Scriptures is that it create an atmosphere in which the word of God can be heard and understood. The Magisterium is primarily a pastoral office within the Church. This pastoral office serves the word of God. One exercise of this service is to allow the word of God to be heard in such a way that it moves the community of believers to a faith response. Since exegesis enables the faithful, a group which in our times is historically aware, to understand the Sacred Scriptures of the New Testament, it is the responsibility of the Magisterium to foster New Testament exegesis. This is in keeping with the very nature of the Magisterium itself, whose task is not so much to guard the deposit of faith as it is to proclaim the word of God.

A second major task of the Magisterium with respect to exegesis is that of listening. Like the prophets of old who listened to the word of God before proclaiming it, the Magisterium must listen to the word of God. Paragraph 10 of *Dei Verbum* explicitly stated the Magisterium's responsibility in this regard. If the Magisterium is called to listen to the word of God in all the modalities of his self-revelation, the Magisterium has a special responsibility to listen to the word of God which has received a privileged formulation in the Scriptures of the Old Testament and the New. If one does not listen, one can hardly serve.

In fact there exists a twofold responsibility on the part of the Magisterium to listen to exegetes. On the one hand, the Magisterium must listen to exegetes insofar as they belong to the body of believers and can, with St. Paul, speak with the gift of the Spirit (1 Cor 7:40). This is a specific modality of the Magisterium's being attentive to the *sensus fidelium,* its being open to the word of God faithfully expressed in the body of believers. On the other hand, the Magisterium must listen to exegetes insofar as the Magisterium is appointed to proclaim authentically the word of God and exegesis articulates the meaning of that word as embodied in the New Testament Scriptures. To listen is not only to hear sounds; it is also and primarily to discern meaning. Accordingly the Spirit-endowed Magisterium must also exercise a function of discernment with respect to exegesis. For the Magisterium to be faithful to its task, it must not only watch, it must also be watchful. As it looks and learns, it must also be vigilant. How then does the servant exercise the function of vigilance?

In the pursuit of an answer to this question, a useful point of departure might be a reflection on the three moments in the hermeneutical circle identified by Carlo Martini, the present archbishop of Milan and formerly the rector of the Pontifical Biblical Institute in Rome. Martini differentiated among the historical-literary task, the task of actualization, and the task of application. The task of applying or actualizing the Scriptures is a matter of inserting the word of God into a personal or community situation in such a way as to elicit a faith decision. This is a task which is normally thought to take place in the liturgy and preaching, in prayer and meditation, in ascetical reflection and spiritual direction. These are the most vital activities in the Church's life; as such, they are of primary and immediate concern to the Magisterium. In the exercise of its pastoral function, the Magisterium must promote the use of the Scriptures with which the life of the Church is to be nourished. This is a direct function of the Magisterium, "whose 'shepherd's task'," as Martini has stated, "must always be attentive to procuring nourishment."

The task of acculturation involves hermeneutics. It is a matter of translating the Scriptures from the categories of the past to a contemporary way of thinking. This is a point on the hermeneutical circle which is the immediate responsibility of exegetes and systematic theologians. The Magisterium does not have an active and immediate function with respect to the fulfillment of this task. Nevertheless the Magisterium can and must make judgments about the doctrinal implications of the philosophical presuppositions that are involved in the acculturation of the biblical message. In this respect the Magisterium is prudentially exercising a function of discernment. On behalf of the entire Church it is making a practical judgment with respect to the interpretation of the Scriptures.

Even after its official acceptance of the historical-critical methodology in exegesis, the Magisterium has exercised this function. It did so in the Holy Office's 1944 rejection of mitigated millenarianism and in the Pontifical Biblical Commission's 1964 *Instruction on the Historicity of the Gospels* which included a caveat as to the philosophical positions of some exponents of the form- and redaction-critical methodologies. In these cases, the organs of the Magisterium fulfilled an important ecclesial function. On behalf of the entire Church, the Magisterium acted in a manner consistent with the vision articulated at Vatican Council II: "All of what has been said about the way of interpreting Scripture is subject finally to the judgment of the Church, which carries out the divine commission and ministry of guarding and interpreting the word of God" (*Dei Verbum,* 12).

It is, of course, principally with respect to the historical-literary task that the autonomy of exegesis is recognized by the Magisterium. Accordingly, there are very few individual texts on which an organ of the Magisterium has made an official pronouncement. One of the rare instances was the July 1, 1933, decision of the Pontifical Biblical Commission on the interpretation of Matthew 16:26 (par. Luke 9:25). On that occasion, the PBC's response noted that the import of the logion could not be restricted to the temporal life "notwithstanding . . . also the unanimous interpretation of Catholics." The latter phrase is important. It indicates that in the rare instances in which it makes an authoritative statement, the Magisterium intervenes on behalf of the living tradition of the Church rather than the historical-literary interpretation of a specific text. It encourages exegetes to use the "appropriate means" in their efforts to pursue the interpretation of these texts. It should go without saying that the search for the meaning of the text is subject to the text itself. The text is an expression of the word, to which the Magisterium itself is subject. Thus the official teachers within the Church as well as professional exegetes should walk together, even if at a somewhat different pace.

II. EXEGESIS AND EVANGELIZATION

Proclamation

In the encouragement it extends to exegetes, the Magisterium expresses the concern of the Church "to move ahead daily toward a deeper understanding of the Sacred Scriptures so that she may unceasingly feed her sons with the divine words" (*Dei Verbum,* 23). In its exposition of the pastoral function of exegesis, the conciliar constitution noted that, "This task should be done in such a way that as many ministers of the divine word as possible will be able to provide the nourishment of the Scriptures for the people of God, thereby enlightening their minds, strengthening their wills, and setting men's hearts on fire with the love of God . . . This ministry includes pastoral preaching, catechetics, and all other Christian instruction, among which the liturgical homily should have an exceptional place" (*Dei Verbum,* 23, 24).

To preach the Gospel is not the same thing as to teach the Gospel. Proclamation is not catechesis. Each has its own emphasis and purpose. Preaching has motivation unto faith as its purpose. It is directed to conversion to faith or confirmation of faith. It intends to confirm or confront one's vision and values. Its language is largely symbolic. Teaching, on the other hand, has the imparting of information as its purpose. It is directed to understanding or the further development of one's knowledge. It intends to expand one's vision and refine the appreciation of one's values. Its language is largely informational. Nevertheless the distinction between preaching and catechesis does not imply a complete separation. In the concrete, preaching includes some measure of teaching, and catechesis involves some degree of proclamation. Despite this overlapping, the distinction between *kerygma* (proclamation) and *didache* (teaching) is both biblical and traditional. It deserves to be maintained in our times.

Within the Church, the proclamation of the Gospel is the most fundamental of all the ministries. In some ways it devolves upon all Christians. All the baptized are called to proclaim the Gospel of Jesus Christ with their very lives. The witness of faith-filled Christian lives is a primary form of Gospel proclamation. To preach the Gospel is, in the final analysis and as Paul discerned, to proclaim our faith-full selves. To a large extent even this first level of proclamation depends upon a familiarity with the New Testament Scriptures, to which the science/art of exegesis contributes in no small degree.

Yet it is not with this primary level of preaching that we are principally concerned at the present time. Rather we must be concerned with that preaching of the Gospel which has a ministerial and official character, especially that which is done during the course of a liturgical function or worship ceremony. Even then we must be aware that the preacher should exercise the ministry of preaching at a primary level. Otherwise the proclamation runs the risk of becoming merely the clang of a cymbal.

This point of view was advanced by the Fathers of the Second Vatican Council who drew from their reflections on the pastoral function of exegesis the conclusion that "all the clergy must hold fast to the sacred Scriptures through diligent sacred reading and careful study, especially the priests of Christ and others, such as deacons and catechists, who are legitimately active in the ministry of the word. This cultivation of Scripture is required lest any of them become 'an empty preacher of the word of God outwardly, who is not a listener to it inwardly' since they must share the abundant wealth of the divine word with the faithful committed to them, especially in the sacred liturgy" (*Dei Verbum,* 25). In a similar vein, yet from a Protestant perspective, Leander Keck has written that "the preacher is a prophet who bears witness to what he or she has heard in his or her priestly role." Included in the thesis enunciated by this sometime professor of New Testament at Emory University and the present dean of the School of Divinity at Yale University are four key ideas. The first is that biblical preaching flows from hearing. The second is that the preacher listens and hears as part of his or her office. The third is that the experienced response to the text can function in the preaching itself insofar as the congregation is involved in the act of preaching. A final element concerns the prophetic role of the preacher, who becomes a prophetic witness on behalf of the text. Indeed, the preacher is a prophet. Like the Magisterium and the prophets of old, the preacher must listen to the word of God in all its ramifications. Then, for the sake of the message, his life must be the medium.

For the preacher to listen to and hear the text certainly involves that openness and receptivity which are characteristic of the historical-critical inquiry into the meaning of the Scriptures. Can one be more precise? Keck has claimed that "historical critical exegesis is an indispensable tool for truly biblical preaching because it illumines both the biblical content and its function." Why and how does exegesis fulfill this admittedly indispensable function?

First of all, exegesis provides the preacher with an awareness that the New Testament text, and especially the Gospel pericopes, are written expressions of proclamation rather than a text to be preached. As Marxsen has stated, the New Testament is the oldest extant volume of the Church's preaching. In a Gospel passage the preacher does not immediately encounter Jesus nor does he immediately come into contact with the original reaction to the Jesus event. Rather, what he comes into contact with is a literary expression of that reaction, a faith experience. The literary expression of the faith experience encompassed in a single Gospel passage is part of a larger synthesis of the faith experience to which the entire Gospel bears witness. Each of these respective syntheses (i.e., the four Gospels) was formulated at a moment in history whose essential coordinates included the historical circumstances of the community for which the Gospel was intended and the faith reflection of the Gospel writer. The awareness that a Gospel passage is a particularized expression of a unique faith experience means that today's preacher cannot remain indifferent to the circumstances of composition of the New Testament text from which his "passage" is drawn. A text in Romans is different from a text in Galatians, just as a text from Matthew is different from a text in Mark. Indeed Matthew was written because the Gospel of Mark was no longer adequate as an answer to the needs of the Matthean faith community. Thus preaching from a text in Matthew cannot be quite the same as preaching from a text in Mark. This means that topics considered in the special introduction to the New Testament are important for a preacher.

Secondly, exegesis serves the preacher insofar as exegesis fulfills its own task. Specifically, the use of the historical-critical method provides the preacher with some explanation of the terms and concepts found in his passage, as well as with some understanding of the New Testament author's use of structure and literary form. The use of the historical-critical method enables the preacher to bridge the gap between his own situation and that of the New Testament writer. This is important if the preacher is to understand the text at hand and appreciate the messsage which the sacred author intended to communicate to his readership. Yet the preacher would want to go beyond a merely historical understanding of the text. Through the medium of the author's language, the preacher wants to enter into the author's situation. He should want to enter into the author's *Sitz-im-Leben* so as to allow the author's proclamation to confront or confirm the preacher's own experience. He should want so to empathize with the biblical author that the author's own struggle with his faith experience becomes the preacher's struggle as well. In this sense exegesis for preaching's sake goes beyond exegesis for mere understanding's sake.

Thirdly, once exegesis has enabled the preacher to bridge the gap between his own experience and that of the biblical author, the preacher can reach out to his congregation and find therein a situation that is analogous to the situation of the New Testament author. This implies that the preacher is aware of the *Sitz-im-Leben* of the New Testament passage at hand. The latter awareness comes via the scientific exegesis of the text. This double outreach has sometimes been called "interpretation parallelism" (Ernest Best). It means that the preacher must couple pastoral judgment with historical-literary scholarship. Only then will his preaching be consistent with the kerygmatic nature of the biblical text and touch the congregation in their real-life situation. Moreover the preacher must also be aware that if the congregation is to be effectively moved by his preaching from the Gospel text, the message of the New Testament author must be translated into that contemporary symbolic language which will alone occasion the desired faith response.

Fourthly and in sum, biblical preaching moves from the text to the congregation. The preacher should have the text in hand and understand it before he decides what he is going to say. That this should be the movement of preaching was recognized in the post-Vatican Council II reformation of the Eucharistic liturgy within the Latin Rite of the Roman Catholic Church. The introduction of a triennial cycle of Sunday scriptural lections and the biennial cycle of weekday lections was made with the intention that more of the Scriptures, as God's word, confront the community of believers.

Negatively, this certainly implies that the preacher not simply use biblical passages to spruce up a religious or ethical oration. No less does it imply that the preacher use a logion or pregnant term within the lection of the day as a springboard for his theological discourse. Positively, biblical preaching implies that the preacher be attentive to all three points on the hermeneutical circle—that is, that he be sensitive not only to the application of the text, but also to the historical-literary and translation-acculturation tasks as well. If he does so he will avoid the pitfalls of those preachers who attempt to adapt the Scriptures to their congregations by means of such techniques as allegorization and direct transference. Direct transference, as is practiced within some fundamentalist circles, neglects the uniqueness of the biblical *Sitz-im-Leben*. Allegorization ultimately implies the irrelevance of the biblical text.

In an overview of some of the techniques frequently adopted by preachers in an attempt to bridge the gap between the biblical text and the contemporary congregation, the Scottish exegete Ernest Best has categorically rejected the method of direct transference as well as the method of allegorization. He has pointed out some of the pitfalls attendant upon the use of the techniques of universalization, identification, and imaginative re-creation. For the rest he acknowledges the difficulty inherent in the creative use of the method of interpretation parallelism, yet commends its use.

Other methods of using the New Testament in preaching attain some degree of validity despite the fact that they often involve significant (pastoral) pitfalls. The method of spiritualization has been defended by Best, both because it appears within the Scriptures and because it involves some of our basic beliefs. In Matthew 8:23–27, for example, the storm symbolizes the difficulties encountered by the disciples of Jesus. It is our belief that Christ saves the Church in times of trouble. Does not a difficulty arise, however, if someone doubts that Christ really did still the storm at sea? Might he not subsequently question whether Christ will preserve the Church in the midst of its difficulty? The technique of turning scriptural statements into anthropological states would also seem to enjoy some measure of validity in that some scriptural language is mythological. The Scriptures speak to us of a God who is in relationship with humankind. Nonetheless the reduction of the scriptural message to anthropological categories involves a limitation of the Scriptures' ability to speak to us. It imposes the preacher's theological and philosophical positions as a control upon the Scriptures. Finally, Best has acknowledged that the technique of substitution is a perfectly satisfactory method of adapting Scripture to our contemporary situation because it has been practiced by the New Testament authors themselves. The substitution is appropriate and valid so long as it lies in line with the intention of the original author.

In short, exegesis does have a significant role to play with respect to preaching. That role is to allow the New Testament Scriptures, as a privileged expression of the word of God, to speak to those congregations who have gathered to hear the word of God. In the final analysis it is exegesis which allows the preacher of today, whose experience of Jesus is mediated through the Church and its Scriptures, to say to his own congregation what Paul said of the community at Thessalonica, namely that "we also thank God constantly for this, that when you received the word of God which you heard from us, you accepted it not as the word of men but as what it really is, the word of God, which is at work in you believers" (1 Thes 2:13).

Exegesis and Catechesis

In the words of Eugene LaVerdiere, "the homily is about the word which has already been read and heard and which now lives in the faith of the assembled community . . . not about the word which was to be read but about the word which has been heard. Its concerns are both objective and subjective. They deal with the objective text's subjective perception in the faith of the community at a particular moment in its development." Strictly speaking, the homily is not an exposition of the text; neither is it an exercise in historical-critical exegesis nor an attempt to offer a relevant hermeneutical interpretation of the text.

In the concrete, however, a homily will oftentimes incorporate exegetical and hermeneutical elements. Sometimes the homily is even replaced by an exposition of the text of the lection. This occasionally happens because of a lack of sufficient forums in which an exposition of the text can take place. It is important that "easy access to sacred Scripture be provided for all the Christian faithful" (*Dei Verbum*, 22), but the provision of this access should not replace the proclamation of the New Testament. In order that the faithful might be provided with this "easy access," the Second Vatican Council urged that steps be taken to assure the publication and availability of modern-language translations of the sacred text. Beyond the availability of a readable translation, easy access means that the faithful have available to them the basic interpretive tools whereby they might understand the text which they are reading. Thus the Council urged "earnestly and specifically . . . all the Christian faithful, too, especially religious, to learn by frequent reading of the divine Scriptures . . . Therefore they should gladly put themselves in touch with the sacred text itself, whether it be through the liturgy, rich in the divine word, or through devotional reading, or through instructions suitable for the purpose and other aids which, in our time, are commendably available everywhere, thanks to the approval and active support of the shepherds of the Church" (*Dei Verbum*, 25). Since such aids are not always available to the faithful and since they are often not resorted to when they are available, some "preachers" offer an exposition of the text in place of the homily. While this may be legitimate and perhaps even necessary, the "preacher" should realize that he is offering not the proclamation but an instruction to his congregation. The proper setting for such instruction should normally be an adult education class or a discussion group, but lacking these, some charged with the ministry of preaching use the pulpit to accomplish the instructional task.

In its proper setting, instruction in the New Testament can include a wide variety of topics. Certainly matters of background, methodology, and interpretation are appropriate to courses of adult religious education. Here the goal is primarily instructional, the aim a greater intellectual understanding of the biblical texts. Yet catechesis is something different from religious education. It is a reflection on the implications of the Gospel word that has been accepted in faith. Catechesis enables believers to understand the Gospel they have appropriated, in relation to other areas in their life's work and education.

When catechetics is thus understood, much should be said about the relationship between exegesis and catechesis. Once again the purpose of the present volume precludes the adequate treatment the subject demands. Consequently it is possible to touch upon only a few of the more important points. First of all, it is patent that the New Testament bears witness to the primacy of the story as the medium of the message in the formation of a Christian community and a Christian lifestyle. With no intention to gainsay any other method of Christian catechesis, it must be noted that the parables occupy a pride of place in the teaching of Jesus. The story of Jesus characterizes the Gospel genre. Even the letters of Paul, and those of his imitators as well, tell the tale of the apostle. They narrate his experiences among those whom he had evangelized. In other words, exegesis of the New Testament reveals that to a large extent Gospel catechesis takes the form of the Christian story.

Secondly, New Testament exegesis shows that catechesis is a process. It is constantly taking place in a new situation, thus becoming more specific in its application. The exegete will note the dependence of Ephesians on Colossians. With some surety he will point to the similar use of the household code in Colossians 3:18–4:1 and Ephesians 5:21–6:9. However, he will also note the further elaboration of the Ephesians version of the household code over and against the version of the code found in the earlier letter to the Colossians. At root are the respective authors' concerns that the implications of the Gospel for life be set out in such a way that they make a difference to the life of the believer.

This concern is also to be found in the Gospel of Matthew. Indeed the concern to spell out the Gospel's implications for life is perhaps nowhere more transparent than it is in Matthew's exposition of the Beatitudes (Matt 5:3–11). An exegetical study of the pericope reveals that some of the Beatitudes are a Matthean creation. Others represent a Matthean formulation of an earlier tradition. In the tradition, the beatitudes were originally an element of proclamation. They echoed Jesus' proclamation that the Reign of God is for the poor and other social outcasts. In Matthew's version of the Beatitudes, proclamation has given way to catechesis. By adapting the traditional beatitudes and formulating some additional ones, Matthew has catechetically spelled out the qualities of the disciple. His example indicates the importance of catechesis in the total work of Gospel witness and shows that adaptation-application belongs to the very nature of the catechetical endeavor.

Thirdly, something must be said about the relationship between moral theology (Christian ethics) and exegesis. The claim has been made that biblical exegesis has failed theology particularly in the area of ethics and spirituality. That this claim is at least partially justified is undoubtedly due to the fact that we do not yet seem to have a clear methodology for bridging the gap between the New Testament Scriptures and the process of character formation and decision making in the contemporary Church. Brevard Childs was correct when he stated that "at no point within the Bible is there ever spelled out a system or a technique by which one could move from the general imperatives of the law of God, such as found in the Decalogue, to the specific application within the concrete situation." From the standpoint of the Church, Vatican Council II issued a clarion call for a more thorough nourishment of moral theology by scriptural teaching (*Optatam Totius,* 16) without offering concrete directives as to how this might be accomplished effectively.

Leaving aside theoretical questions as to the nature and possibility of a distinctively Christian ethic, a discussion of Christian ethics can be legitimately subsumed under the rubric of catechesis. Yet, when one attempts to spell out the implications of the ethical catechesis of the New Testament for today one immediately encounters a whole host of considerations which necessarily arise—considerations that are analogous to those which arose in the discussion on the relationship between New Testament exegesis and dogmatic theology.

Four issues come immediately to the fore. First of all, a distinction must be made between the use of the Bible and the use of biblical exegesis. In this regard Bruce C. Birch and Larry L. Rasmussen have, perhaps superficially, suggested that the use of exegesis is pertinent to Christian decision making. Secondly, the authority of the New Testament Scriptures is unique without thereby being exclusive; its authority is primary without being self-sufficient. The Scriptures cannot be the only source for Christian ethics. Thirdly, within the Scriptures themselves there is a diversity of ethical posture. One has only to compare Matthew 5:31–32; 1 Thessalonians 4, 1 Corinthians 7, and 1 Peter 3 to appreciate something of the New Testament's diversity on the issue of sexual relationships, not to mention the still greater diversity that exists among such Old Testament passages as Genesis 2, Song of Songs, Proverbs 7, and Leviticus 19. Fourthly, whatever ethical insights are to be gleaned from an exegetical examination of the New Testament text, these must be actualized and applied to a radically new situation if moral theology is to receive its basic orientation from, and its ground in, the Scriptures of the New Testament.

A biblically based ethic must not follow an atomistic proof-text type of approach in which a New Testament passage is cited as the sole warrant for making a judgment, or in which a passage is used literalistically in support of a position attained on other grounds. Within the framework of a biblically based ethic, the New Testament must be looked to with respect to its more pervasive significance. Proceeding from this point of view, James Gustafson has distinguished four basic uses of the Scripture in the elaboration of a Christian ethic. In his opinion, a first and most stringent use is that which proposes as a norm that those actions of persons and groups which violate the moral law as revealed in Scripture are to be judged morally wrong. A second use holds that those actions of persons and groups which fall short of the moral ideals given in Scripture are to be judged morally wrong, or at least morally deficient. A third use is that according to which those actions of persons and groups are to be judged morally wrong which are similar to actions judged to be wrong or against God's will under similar circumstances in Scripture, or are discordant with actions judged to be right or in accord with God's will in Scripture. The fourth use identified by Gustafson is that in which the many different kinds of biblical literature witness to a great variety of moral norms and principles: moral law, visions of the future, historical events, moral precepts, paraenetic instruction, parables, dialogues, wisdom sayings, allegories, etc.

In this fourth use, the New Testament Scriptures serve to shape the Christian identity and place it within the context of a history of salvation. Gustafson's point of view has been substantially supported by others, including Robert Daly, who has suggested that one must make use of a study of the New Testament that is at once exegetical, theological, and existential-spiritual to appreciate how the central Christian symbol, Jesus Christ, affects one's way of life. Daly himself has noted that there are four principal modes of communication by which that central symbol is mediated to us in the New Testament: the indicative, imperative, parabolic, and the mystical. According to his analysis, the Christian who listens to the story, who hears the commands, who enters into the parables is the same Christian who has been and is being incorporated into Christ. In a word, through an exegetically sound reading of the New Testament Scriptures one attains to the essential Christian symbol. Thus the New Testament serves to shape the Christian identity. Surely the use of exegesis in order that the Christian identity be shaped is the first contribution of New Testament scholarship to Christian ethics.

Beyond that, the exegesis of the New Testament can identify the qualities of a Christian ethic. C. H. Dodd's identification of four principal qualities of a New Testament ethic remains valid until this day. A Christian ethic is characterized by: (1) its eschatological nature; (2) its ecclesial and communitarian character; (3) the motif of the imitation of Christ; and (4) the priority of the love demand. A New Testament exegete could also speak of the responsive nature of New Testament paraenesis. It is because the Christian believer has already been graced and chosen in virtue of God's free act that he and she live the way they do. Consequently the ethicist should proclaim the freedom of the children of God, not only as a God-given gift, but also as a human value, a life's attitude, and a basic challenge. Sound exegesis would also reveal that the biblical authors made use of traditional ethical paradigms and schemas in offering concrete moral norms, with the result that there is a real diversity of ethics attested within the New Testament. Is it any wonder that Christian ethics today is likewise qualified by secularity and diversity?

To be sure, those who voice the hope that Christian ethics be biblically based are expressing an expectation that a methodology be developed which would yield concrete moral norms. To date, such a methodology has not been developed. It is even doubtful whether it is possible to develop such a methodology. Certainly a proof-text type of methodology must be rejected from the outset. Exegetically, it is unsound because it does not take into account the specificity and particularity of the set of circumstances in which the various New Testament writings were composed. This literalistic interpretation of texts taken out of context is the weakness inherent in the first and second uses of Scripture identified by Gustafson. Historically, the proof-text approach has proved to have yielded results which fall short of the Christian "ideal" as that bears upon the priority of love. One need only think of the injustices inflicted upon God's children by articulate individuals whose armament included Paul's toleration of slavery and Yahweh's condemnation of Ham. Realistically, the atomistic approach is inadequate because it does not specifically provide concrete moral norms for the major ethical questions of the times in which we live. At best the isolated text method of providing Christian ethics with a biblical basis leads to a negative and individualistic ethic which in some ways is more appropriate to the past than to the present. It certainly does not indicate how the individual believer and the body of believers should live as Christians in the world today.

To proceed to a more positive elaboration of a Christian ethic on a biblical basis, the ethicist must adapt a method similar to the technique of "interpretation parallelism" which was briefly set forth in our considerations on the use of exegesis in preaching. The judgment-formulating ethicist must bridge the gap between his own situation and that of the biblical authors by seeing how they wrestled with and responded to the moral situations they faced. Having used the tools of exegesis to build a first bridge, a bridge to the unrepeatable past, the ethicist must then build a second bridge. Using the normal tools of ethical analysis, he must find an analogy between the circumstances apropos of which a decision must be made and those in which the biblical authors were involved. For the Christian ethicist, exegesis provides one pole in the dialogical effort that brings the ethical experience of the Christian past to bear upon the present situation. As Gustafson has said, judgments ought to be "consistent, consonant, coherent with the themes that are generalized to be most pervasive and primary to the biblical wisdom." As the New Testament paraenesis itself resulted from the dialogical process, so too must a biblically based Christian ethic be the product of a unique kind of dialogue.

Exegesis and Prayer

If the assertion that New Testament exegesis has thus far proved to be a failure in the area of ethics is generally valid, the parallel assertion that New Testament exegesis has failed the Church in the area of prayer and spirituality is even more valid.

The Fathers of Vatican Council II proclaimed that "the force and power in the word of God is so great that it remains the support and energy of the Church, the strength of faith for her sons, the food of the soul, the pure and perennial source of spiritual life" (*Dei Verbum,* 21). The history of the Church reveals the accuracy of this statement. Hardly a saint can be cited whose life was not directly shaped by the prayerful reading of the Scriptures. Yet this was before the development of the historical-critical method of interpreting the Scriptures.

Nevertheless, even in these times and in the very document that has proposed the use of the historical-critical method as a means to the interpretation of the Sacred Text, the Council Fathers taught the utility of a prayerful reading of the Scriptures: "By the same word of Scripture the ministry of the word also takes wholesome nourishment and yields fruits of holiness. . . . All the Christian faithful . . . should gladly put themselves in

311

touch with the sacred text itself, whether it be through the liturgy, rich in the divine word, or through devotional reading, or through instructions suitable for the purposes. . . . And let them remember that prayer should accompany the reading of sacred Scripture, so that God and man may talk together; for 'we speak to Him when we pray; we hear Him when we read the divine sayings'" (*Dei Verbum,* 24, 25). A decade later, the French-language workshop of the 1974 Roman Synod of Bishops declared that "only those who pray and read the Scriptures in the glow of the Spirit are capable of discovering the presence and action of God in the lives of men and in the events of history. If this docility to the Spirit be truly lived, the Spirit will be able to achieve a much more efficacious discernment of spirits."

It is obvious that the devotional reading of the Scriptures is quite different from the exegetical study of the text. The one involves an openness to the speaking Word of God; the other involves an analysis of the spoken and written word of God. The prayerful reading of the Scriptures should result in a response and a commitment; the exegetical study should result in the acquisition of insight and information. Surely there can be no confusion between the academic exercise and the spiritual exercises; yet neither ought there to be a radical opposition between the historical-critical approach to the New Testament and the spiritual-prayerful approach. From the standpoint of Christian theology it is almost a truism to assert that it is one and the same Spirit who has inspired the Scriptures of the New Testament and who moves the believer to prayer. On the practical level, however, a wide separation and a deep gap often exist between the exegetical and prayerful approaches to the Scriptures. The exegete is quick to announce that his is a historical and literary discipline. In a time of prayer, the believer often neglects or abandons the results of exegesis. Is it possible to bridge the gap?

A first approach to an answer to this question arises from a consideration of the nature of prayer and spirituality. Prayer is certainly one of the primary functions of the Christian life. It is a most expressive form of the believer's response to God. Spirituality is a broader reality. It designates the entire life of the Christian insofar as that life is the manifestation of the gift of the Spirit received in baptism. Spirituality and prayer characterize Christian existence in its very humanness and concreteness. As elements of the Christian experience, prayer and spirituality should be subject to the same type of theological reflection as any other facet of the Christian experience. There is a need for a theology of prayer, just as there is a need for a theology of spirituality. Otherwise "spirituality" can run amuck, as it did in the early Christian community at Corinth. In his first letter to the Corinthians, especially in Chapter 12, Paul offered a theological critique of the spiritual experience, including prayer. A theological critique of the spiritual life is no less needed in our day, as is also a theological reflection on the nature of the spiritual life itself. Exegesis contributes to this critique and reflection in a fashion similar to the way in which it generally contributes to the theological endeavor. As an example of one scholar's attempt to offer some specific suggestions in this regard, we can cite the address of J. N. M. Wijngaard to the 1978 meeting of the World Catholic Foundation for the Biblical Apostolate. Wijngaard's exposition concentrated on four elements in biblical spirituality: (1) the Experience of God; (2) Searching the Scriptures; (3) the Testimony of the Spirit; and (4) the Transformation of Life. With the development of similar efforts, exegesis can contribute to the fuller understanding of the nature of prayer and spirituality. In this respect, exegesis serves as a tool for and a first step in the exposition of a theology of prayer.

Secondly, exegesis has a specific contribution to make with regard to the prayers that are contained in the New Testament itself. The New Testament is redolent with prayers and prayer formulas. Many of these have entered into the fabric of the Christian liturgy. Some are prayed by individual Christians, either alone or in small prayer groups. Holding pride of place among the New Testament prayers is certainly the Matthean version of the Lord's Prayer (Matt 6:9–13), which is the daily prayer of many Christians and a feature of virtually all Christian liturgy. Yet there is also a Lucan version of the Lord's Prayer (Luke 11:2–4). Although the Lucan version of this prayer has not commonly been taken over for liturgical use, other Lucan prayers have—the Magnificat (Luke 1:46–55), the Benedictus (1:68–79), the Nunc Dimittis (2:29–31). Within the Roman Catholic tradition the angelic salutation at Luke 1:28 has been taken over as a prayer formula in the popular "Hail Mary." The angelic encomium of Luke 2:14a serves as the opening words of the liturgical prayer of praise that is a part of the festal liturgies celebrated in the Latin Rite. The Christological hymn of Philippians 2:6–11 is used in the liturgy of Holy Week, and is now entering into even greater use among the Christian faithful.

Now it is one thing to read the Lord's Prayer, whether in its Matthean or its Lucan version, and another thing to pray the Lord's Prayer in either of its traditional formulations. One can read the prayer to discern its message, and one can study the prayer exegetically in order to comprehend that message more fully. An exegesis of the prayer allows the pray-er of today to enter into the very heart of the evangelist, into the hearts of his community. It imparts to the pray-er that sense of eschatological urgency which characterized the prayer of New Testament times. Exegesis allows the believer to distinguish between the solemnity of Matthew's address to the transcendent God, "Our Father who art in heaven," and the Lucan appropriation of the prayer of Jesus himself, "*abba* (father)." Since exegesis allows the contemporary believer to enter into the language, mind, and heart of the New Testament believer at prayer, it enables a contemporary person at prayer to appropriate the New Testament prayer. In a word, exegesis allows a New Testament prayer formula to become a contemporary believer's very own prayer.

A third use of exegesis in the area of prayer relates to that usage of the New Testament for devotional reading to which *Dei Verbum,* 25, made reference. A devotional reading of the New Testament supposes an atmosphere of religious respect and the disposition of personal openness. Such a prayer-ful reading of the New Testament, which has shaped the lives of countless saints throughout the two millennia of Christian history, is always an inter-pretation of the text, insofar as it involves a process of personal hermeneutic according to which the biblical passage somehow reaches out to the situation of the prayerful reader. For this devotional reading to be in depth and fully effective, a certain amount of exegesis should be involved so that the believer can more fully understand and truly appreciate that which he or she is read-ing in a prayerful spirit. Eugene LaVerdiere has distinguished the prayerful reading of the New Testament from meditative prayer. The distinction is useful. In the prayerful reading of the New Testament, praise, thanksgiving, reparation, and petition remain largely at the level of unspoken attitude, open to God and his transforming power but unrelated to the concrete and specific challenges of the reader. Meditative prayer takes up where prayerful reading leaves off. By a process of bridge building and interpretive paral-lelism, the pray-er recognizes a similarity between a New Testament situation and his or her own. Thereupon the pray-er allows the disposition and atti-tudes of the biblical characters, Jesus, Mary, Peter, Paul, the disciples, to be-come his or her very own. In prayer a oneness and identification is attained. Reflecting on the relationship between meditative prayer and prayerful read-ing, LaVerdiere has written: "Meditative prayer with the New Testament starts where prayerful reading ends. Its primary activity is reflection, and it flows into a specific personal response to God's word. Its effectiveness and depth presuppose a measure of catechesis on the New Testament as well as on the challenge of life in our modern world." In sum, exegesis serves as a necessary preparation for a truly devotional reading of the New Testament.

Finally, exegesis has a more diffused function in the life of the believer which is not without implications for his or her life of prayer. We have al-ready noted the role played by the New Testament Scriptures and their ex-egesis in the shaping of a Christian identity. Since prayer is a most charac-teristic self-expression of the person who is truly comfortable with his or her Christian identity, exegesis contributes to the prayerful expression of the Christian person in a most general and formative manner. Such pervasive formation generally makes a specific impact upon the life of Christian prayer. In the words of LaVerdiere, "inspired by the scripture text, formal prayer remains close to the biblical word even as it brings the Scriptures to life in a new world. The Scriptures thus provide a guide for both its content and expression." A biblically oriented expression of Christian faith shapes the form of Christian prayer. Thereupon Christian prayer is replete with bib-lical images and the words of the New Testament. The influence of the New Testament is sometimes more, and sometimes less, explicitly and consciously present in the formulations of Christian prayer—but it is always and every-where present. In a word, the New Testament helps to mold the personal identity and language of the Christian believer at prayer. By its elucidation of the meaning of the New Testament text, exegesis makes its unique contribution to the spirituality and prayer of the Christian believer in these later times.

SELECT BIBLIOGRAPHY

Best, Ernest. *From Text to Sermon. Responsible Use of the New Testament in Preaching.* Atlanta: John Knox, 1978.

Birch, Bruce C. and Rasmussen, Larry L. *Bible and Ethics in the Christian Life.* Minneapolis: Augsburg, 1976.

Boers, Hendrikus. *What is New Testament Theology? The Rise of Criticism and the Problem of a Theology of the New Testament. Guides to Biblical Scholarship.* Philadelphia: Fortress, 1979.

Brown, Raymond E. *The Critical Meaning of the Bible.* New York: Paulist, 1981.

Daly, Robert J. "Towards a Christian Biblical Ethic." In *Critical History and Biblical Faith: New Testament Perspectives. The Annual Publication of the College Theology Society.* Ed. by J. Ryan. Villanova: The College Theology Society, 1979. 208–36.

Delaney, Robert J. (ed.). *The Proceedings of the Plenary Assembly of the World Catholic Federation of the Biblical Apostolate. Malta, April 11–20, 1978.* Stuttgart: The World Foundation for the Biblical Apostolate, 1979.

Fuller, Reginald H. *The Use of the Bible in Preaching.* Philadelphia: Fortress, 1981.

Gustafson, James M. "The Place of Scripture in Christian Ethics. A Methodological Study." *Interpretation,* 24 (1970), 430–55.

Hanson, Paul D. "The Responsibility of Biblical Theology to Communities of Faith." *Theology Today,* 37 (1980), 39–50.

Interpretation. 25:1 (1971); 30:3 (1976); 35:1 (1981).

Kahlefeld, Heinrich. "The Pericope and Preaching." In *The Human Reality of Sacred Scripture. Concilium,* 10. New York: Paulist, 1965, pp. 39–51.

Keck, Leander E. *The Bible in the Pulpit: The Renewal of Biblical Preaching.* Nashville: Abingdon, 1978.

Kelsey, David H. "The Bible and Christian Theology." *Journal of the American Academy of Religion,* 48 (1980), 385–402.

———. *The Uses of Scripture in Recent Theology.* London: SCM, 1975.

Küng, Hans and Moltmann, Jürgen (eds.). *Conflicting Ways of Interpreting the Bible. Concilium,* 138. New York: Seabury, 1980.

LaVerdiere, Eugene. *The New Testament in the Life of the Church: Evangelization, Prayer, Catechetics, Homiletics.* Notre Dame: Ave Maria, 1980.

MacKenzie, Roderick L. "The Self-Understanding of the Exegete." In *Concilium,* 70 (1971), 11–19.

Martini, Carlo M. *La Parola di Dio alle Origini della Chiesa.* Rome: Università Gregoriana, 1980.

Marxsen, Willi. *The New Testament as the Church's Book.* Philadelphia: Fortress, 1972.

———. "Der Exeget als Theolog," in *Der Exeget als Theolog. Vorträge zum neuen Testament.* Gütersloh: Mohr, 1968. 52–74.

Rahner, Karl. "Bible. B: Theology." In *Sacramentum Mundi. An Encyclopedia of Theology,* vol. I. New York: Herder & Herder, 1968. 171–78.

———. "Remarks on the Importance of the History of Jesus for Catholic Dogmatics." In *Theological Investigations.* Vol. XIII. *Theology, Anthropology, Christology.* London: Darton, Longman & Todd, 1975. 201–12.

Rogers, Jack Bartlett, and McKim, Donald K. *The Authority and Interpretation of the Bible: An Historical Approach.* New York: Harper & Row, 1979.

Stuhlmacher, Peter. *Vom Verstehen des Neuen Testaments. Eine Hermeneutik. Grundrisse zum Neuen Testament. NTD-Ergänzungsreihe,* 6. Göttingen: Vandenhoeck und Ruprecht, 1979.

Thiselton, Anthony C. *The Two Horizons. New Testament Hermeneutics and Philosophical Description with Special Reference to Heidegger, Bultmann, Gadamer, and Wittgenstein.* Grand Rapids: Eerdmans, 1980.

CHAPTER NINE

INSPIRATION

Although exegetes may disagree among themselves as to the interpretation of one or another passage in the New Testament, and although considerable discussion still takes place within theological schools as to the real contribution of a historically and literarily oriented interpretation of the text, there is virtually unanimous agreement among churches and church groups on the importance of the New Testament. When pressed as to the significance and basis of the importance accorded to the books of the New Testament, spokespersons for the churches and individual believers generally respond with the affirmation that the New Testament Scriptures are the word of God. If pressed further, these same individuals would typically proclaim that the New Testament books are revered as a holy and canonical literature because they are inspired.

The hypothetical interlocutor would admit that the works of Shakespeare and those of Dante are inspired, but the inspiration predicated of the books of the New Testament is different in kind from that to be attributed to the great men of letters throughout the ages. Biblical inspiration is different from the ordinary kind of literary and artistic inspiration because the books of the New Testament are the inspired word of God. Etymologically, to inspire means "to breathe into." Since the Spirit of God is frequently represented as wind or breath, it is an easy step for the believer to advance his or her thought further and state that the Scriptures of the New Testament are inspired because they have been written under the influence of the Holy Spirit.

Our interlocutor is echoing the traditional beliefs of the Church in affirming the inspiration of the New Testament Scriptures, yet the doctrine of inspiration seems not to enjoy as much prominence in the teaching of the main-line churches as it once did. Churches with an evangelical bent are still very keen on reaffirming the inspiration of the New Testament. Most of the theological literature devoted to the topic of inspiration which appeared during the 1970–80 decade came from the pen of evangelical writers who wanted to affirm the inerrancy of the Scriptures. From the evangelical point of view, it is imperative to maintain the doctrine of inspiration because inspiration is the ground of the authority of the Scriptures. On close examination, however, evangelicals are largely content with affirming the "fact" of inspiration; a theological explanation of the phenomenon itself hardly ever comes from the pen of an evangelical writer.

While evangelicals have largely taken over the inspiration-inerrancy doctrine as a tenet unto themselves, writers who belong to the traditional mainline churches generally abandoned the attempt to interpret the doctrine of inspiration during the decade under consideration. To be sure, the Fathers of the Second Vatican Council reaffirmed the Church's traditional teaching on inspiration in Paragraph 11 of *Dei Verbum* (1965). The document has been commented on in its entirety, but very few studies have been explicitly devoted to an exposition of its teaching on inspiration. One might also look at the *Catholic Biblical Quarterly,* the prestigious publication of the Catholic Biblical Association of America. In 1958 the *Quarterly* published four articles on inspiration. One article appeared in 1962, but then there was a lack of consideration of the topic until 1982. The relative silence vis-à-vis the doctrine of inspiration on the part of writers coming from a tradition of main-line Christianity is the reflection of a similar absence within the theological schools of these churches. The absence of an explicit theological treatment of the doctrine of inspiration by Roman Catholic authors has its counterpart in a similar omission of the topic by authors coming from the other traditional churches.

There are many reasons for the relative abandonment of the doctrine of inspiration within these churches. The development of the historical-critical method of New Testament interpretation stands out from among all the others as being the single factor most contributory to the disuse of the notion of inspiration. Traditionally the books of the New Testament have been considered as literary works in much the same way as the works of G. K. Chesterton are considered to be literary works. That is, each of the New Testament books was considered to be the literary creation of a single, inspired author. An inspired Matthew wrote the First Gospel; an inspired John the Fourth Gospel. The critical and diachronical approach to the New Testament Scriptures has shown that the New Testament books—apart, perhaps, from some of the epistolary literature—are not literary works in the ordinary sense, they are the products of a complex history. In what sense, then, can they be considered inspired? Are the sources inspired, or only the final redaction? In short, matters are not quite as simple today as they were in the times when it was commonly held that a single author penned each of the books of the New Testament.

Historical-literary criticism has made it all the more difficult to articulate a doctrine of inspiration in other ways as well. First of all, by situating the

New Testament texts within their proper historical context and comparing the New Testament texts among themselves, the exegetes have pointed to one or another historical error in the text. Indeed, a text-critical study of Mark 6:17 points to a number of variant readings occasioned by the simple fact that despite Mark 6:17, Herodias was not the wife of Herod's brother Philip. The text of Mark includes a historical error at this point. Again, redaction criticism functions well when a comparison can be made among several New Testament texts. Use of the methodology reveals differences in the expositions of the various authors—differences that often express a contrary, if not a contradictory, point of view.

Moreover, the use of the historical-critical method of exegesis implies that the intepreter approaches the New Testament text as a human document. The exegete reads the text as a document written in the words of men. Using a methodology that is appropriate to the task, the exegete is searching for the human significance of the text. His is a historical, human endeavor. That the New Testament is to be taken as the Word of God is an affirmation that belongs to the realm of theology rather than scientific exegesis. For the exegete, the doctrine of inspiration remains beyond the pale of the historical investigation of the New Testament text itself. Here, as all too often, out of sight means out of mind as well.

I. THE NEW TESTAMENT TRADITION

Nonetheless, the systematic theologian must recognize that the doctrine of inspiration is a significant element in the Church's traditional articulation of its belief. Moreover the historian of dogma will note that 2 Timothy 3:16–17 has served as a constant point of reference in the traditional expression of the doctrine of inspiration. What might an exegete say about the passage that reads: "All scripture is inspired by God and profitable for teaching, for reproof, for correction, and for training in righteousness, that the man of God may be complete, equipped for every good work" (RSV)?

Of itself, the passage seems relatively simple. It suggests that Christianity took over the doctrine of the inspiration of the Scriptures which had become traditional lore in Palestinian and Hellenistic Judaism. Nevertheless these two verses, which are certainly the most forthright attestation of the notion of scriptural inspiration in the entire New Testament, raise a variety of difficult contextual, grammatical, syntactical, and lexographical problems which exegetes must struggle to resolve. When pressed, they do not come to agreement among themselves as to the precise interpretation of the verse.

Some indication of the extent of these difficulties can be had when the modern English-language translations of the passage are compared. One might, for example, compare the New American Bible's "All Scripture is inspired of God and is useful for teaching—for reproof, correction, and training in holiness so that the man of God may be fully competent and equipped for every good work" with the New English Bible's "Every inspired scripture has its use for teaching the truth and refuting error, or for reformation of manners and discipline in right living, so that the man who belongs to God may be efficient and equipped for good work of every kind."

The contextual problem must be attended to first of all. That the two verses belong to a short pericope (2 Tim 3:10–17) which is an exhortation to steadfastness is beyond doubt. Timothy is encouraged to attend to the example of Paul and to persevere in the teaching of the Scriptures. A number of considerations lead many exegetes to the conclusion that the entire letter is pseudepigraphical. Thus we ought not to think that the passage under consideration is part of a personal letter from the apostle to Timothy, his close friend and trusted co-worker. Rather Paul is a revered figure from the past whose example can be cited to "Timothy," who represents the typical church leader. In 2 Timothy 3:17 as in 1 Timothy 6:11 the phrase "man of God" (*ho tou theou anthrōpos*) refers to the leader of the congregation. The author of the letter first exhorts the churchman to follow the example of Paul and then, in a second movement of thought, he urges the churchman to maintain the traditional Pauline teaching. Using the rabbinic idiom customary in the Pastorals, the author affirms that the sacred writings are useful for instruction (v. 15). This nomenclature, "sacred writings" (*hiera grammata*), is not otherwise found in the New Testament; neither is it found in the Old Testament. But it is known to us from Hellenistic Judaism. Both Philo (*Life of Moses,* 2, 292) and Josephus (*Antiquities of the Jews,* 10, 210) make mention of the "sacred writings." The expression designates that which we Christians commonly call the Old Testament; nothing in its use suggests that the author of 2 Timothy had Christian writings in mind. Timothy, typical church leader that he is, is reminded that he has been instructed in the Holy Scriptures from his youth in accordance with the rabbinic dictum that received its classic formulation in the Mishnaic adage, "At five years old [one is fit] for the Scripture, at ten years for the Mishnah, at thirteen for [the fulfilling of] the commandments, at fifteen for the Talmud" (*Aboth* 5, 21). In 2 Timothy 3, however, the author's exhortation moves beyond that of his rabbinic tradition as he affirms the Christocentricity of the Holy Scriptures. The key to the salvific purpose of the Scriptures is Christ. Only through him can the salvation attested by the Scriptures be obtained.

Having affirmed the usefulness of the Scriptures from the vantage point of Christian faith, the author of the exhortation expands his thought on the value of the Scriptures in verses 16–17. Not only does he spell out in further detail the use to which the Scriptures can be put (vv. 16b–17), he also grounds their authority by affirming that the Spirit of God is their source: "All Scripture is inspired by God and . . ." (*pasa graphē theopneustos kai . . .*). The Greek text has only four words, none of which is the verb "to be" (*estin*). This Greek text raises a variety of questions. How should we understand the expression "all Scripture" (*pasa graphē*)? Is "inspired"

320

(*theopneustos*) to be taken in an active or in a passive sense? Is this verbal adjective used predicatively or attributively?

There is no difficulty about the general reference of the term "Scripture" (*graphē*). Commonly used in the New Testament and in Hellenistic Judaism, the term refers to the Old Testament just as did the "sacred writings" of verse 15, to which verse 16 now alludes. It is the specific interpretation of the entire phrase "all Scripture" (*pasa graphē*) which is problematic. Used in the singular, *graphē* ("scripture") can denote a book of Scripture, the Scriptures, or a particular passage in Scripture. *Pasa* can be taken inclusively ("all," as in the RSV) or distributively ("every," as in the NEB). Although Hellenistic Judaism often uses "Scripture" in the sense of one of the books of the Bible, this usage is not otherwise attested in the New Testament, and so it can be excluded as a possible interpretation of "Scripture" in verse 16. In the New Testament, *graphē* designates either the Scriptures in general (Rom 11:2; Gal 3:8, 22; 4:30) or a particular passage in Scripture (Mark 12:10; Luke 4:21; John 19:37; 20:9; Acts 8:35). Given the absence of the article (*hē*) from the Greek text, it seems preferable to take the noun "Scripture of verse 15 not in the collective sense of "Scripture" as do the RSV, the NAB, and H. W. House, among recent exegetes, but in the sense of "every passage of Scripture." This rendering of the phrase *pasa graphē* is found in the NEB, and is supported by the exegetical analyses of the majority of recent commentators, including Norbert Brox, Conzelmann, Pierre Dornier, Jeremias, and J. N. D. Kelly. Thus we must read (or understand), "Every passage of Scripture."

The verbal adjective "inspired" (*theopneustos*) is found nowhere else in the New Testament. It occurs four times in pre-Christian Greek literature and the Sibylline Oracles. Of itself, the term can be taken in an active or a passive sense. Taken in an active sense, *theopneustos* would emphasize that Scripture is filled with the breath of God: Scripture is inspiring. Taken in a passive sense, the meaning suggested by the translation "inspired," *theopneustos* emphasizes that the source of Scripture is the breath of God: Scripture comes from God. Although Karl Barth thought that *theopneustos* also had an active meaning, the ancient Fathers and modern commentators alike have generally taken *theopneustos* in a passive sense.

The vocable was taken over from the philosophical-religious vocabulary of ancient Hellenism, where it applied to the ecstatic experience of an inspired "prophet." Despite the borrowed vocabulary, the Jewish doctrine of the inspiration of the Scriptures was different from the Hellenistic description of the mantic experience. Derived from the biblical tradition that the prophets were inspired men, the Jewish doctrine was exposited by some first-century authors among whom we must count Josephus (*Contra Apionem* 1, 37) and Philo (*De specialibus legibus* 1, 65; 4, 49; *Quis rerum divinarum heres sit* 263). Christianity appropriated this Jewish doctrine, as can be seen in 2 Peter 1:21, and some of the early Fathers including Justin (*Apol* 2, 9), Athenagoras (*Supplicatio* 9), and Theophilus (*Three Books Addressed to Autolycus* 2, 9). Thus we should read, "Every passage of Scripture is inspired."

Or should we? The Greek text does not include a verbal equivalent of "is." Some form of the verb "to be" must be inserted into the English-language translation of 2 Timothy 3:16, otherwise it would not form a complete sentence. But where is the verb to be placed? The answer to that question depends on one's judgment as to whether *theopneustos* is to be taken as an attribute or a predicate; either option is grammatically possible. If "inspired" is taken as an attribute, the text should read "every inspired passage of Scripture is profitable for . . ." Arguing that the emphasis of the verse lies on the usefulness of the inspired Scriptures and that it would have been useless for the author of 2 Timothy to recall such a commonplace truth as the inspiration of the Scriptures, a number of commentators such as Brox and Conzelmann opt for an attributive sense of *theopneustos*. Their point of view is represented by the NEB's "every inspired scripture." This translation seems to contain a hint that some passages of Scripture are not inspired.

While this hint may be unsettling for the "orthodox," its suggestion should not serve as a principal argument in favor of the predicative interpretation of the verbal adjective *theopneustos*. The weight of the arguments seems, nonetheless, to confirm that it is a predicative *theopneustos* that is to be ascribed to the author at 2 Timothy 3:16. The arguments that incline us to this interpretation are many. In the absence of a verb, it is most natural to construe the two adjectives of verse 16 in the same way; indeed a precedent for such a use is to be found in 1 Timothy 4:4. Moreover, were *theopneustos* to have been used in an attributive sense, it should normally have been placed before *graphē* ("scripture"). Furthermore the *kai* ("and") of verse 16 appears superfluous when *theopneustos* is taken in an attributive sense. Rendering *kai* as "also," Conzelmann and Brox have incorporated the particle into their translation, "Every scripture that is inspired by God is *also* salutary . . . ," but its redundancy was perceived by the translators of the NEB, who have dropped the particle altogether. Finally, one should maintain that in 2 Timothy 3:16 the affirmation of the inspiration of the scriptural passages is not at all trite. It is because of his conviction that the scriptural passages are inspired that the author of the text can affirm their utility for teaching, reproof, correction, and training in righteousness.

The only other New Testament passage which comes close to the affirmation of 2 Timothy 3:16 is 2 Peter 1:20–21: "First of all you must understand this, that no prophecy of scripture is a matter of one's own interpretation, because no prophecy ever came by the impulse of man, but men moved by the Holy Spirit spoke from God." That there are no major difficulties attendant upon the interpretation of this late New Testament passage is easily seen when the RSV translation is compared with that of the NAB and the NEB. The American version reads: "First you must understand this: there is no prophecy contained in Scripture which is a personal interpretation. Prophecy has never been put forward by man's willing it. It is rather that men impelled by the Holy Spirit have spoken under God's influence." The English translators offer, "But first note this: no one can interpret any prophecy of Scripture by himself. For it was not through any human whim that men prophesied of old; men they were, but, impelled by the Holy Spirit, they spoke the words of God."

Contextually these two verses belong to a short pericope whose major theme is the guarantee of Christian hope (2 Pet 1:12–21). The thought of the pseudonymous author proceeds in two movements. First of all he offers his own apologetically oriented version of the Transfiguration tradition (vv. 12–18). Then he turns to the "prophetic word" (*ton prophētikon logon*). The expression was a current one, used by Philo and the Apostolic Fathers, to indicate the entire Tanach—that is, the Law, the prophets, and the writings, not just the prophets alone (*nebiim*). The author affirms that the message of the Bible has been made more sure in the sense that God has confirmed its truth and that it is in the process of being fulfilled. The Scriptures maintain their validity because they have begun to be realized in Jesus Christ. But then comes a word of warning. The author is concerned with false teachers who distort both the meaning of the ancient Scriptures (2 Pet 3:3) and Christian writings as well (2 Pet 3:16). So he affirms that the proper interpretation of the Scriptures comes not from the vagaries of one's own imagination, but from the Spirit of God himself.

The author's language is somewhat peculiar; he writes: "no prophecy of scripture is a matter of one's own interpretation" (*pasa prophēteia graphēs idias epiluseos ou genetai*). "Interpretation" (*epilusis*) occurs in no other place in the entire Bible (OT or NT). The RSV has deliberately left the verbal form *ginetai* ("it is a matter of") in a state of ambiguity, while the NAB takes the verb with an accompanying genitive to mean "comes from" as if no prophecy comes from the prophet's own interpretation—it comes from God. The NEB takes the verbal construction in the sense of "comes under the scope of," thereby indicating that one may not interpret Scriptures according to personal whim. Surely this is the meaning of the verse. Having affirmed his principle in order to confront the troublemaking false teachers, the author of 2 Peter cites the reason one cannot appropriate to oneself the right to interpret the sacred text. Scripture comes from the Holy Spirit.

At first glance it seems strange that the author of the tract would have first insisted that "no prophecy ever came by the impulse of man." Has anyone ever claimed that prophecy arises from the promptings of the human spirit? In reply, we must be attentive to the circumstances in which 2 Peter was composed. At the late date at which the epistle was written, some Gnosticizing Jewish Christians were refusing to accept the divine inspiration of prophets subsequent to Moses. The pseudonymous Peter counters the false trend head-on, confronting it with the traditional doctrine that the prophets are inspired by the Spirit of God. Philo (*Quis rerum divinarum heres sit* 265; *Life of Moses* 1, 281; *De mutatione nominum* 120, 203) and Josephus (*Antiquities* 4, 118–19) commonly asserted that the prophets were inspired. The Qumranites believed that the prophets received God's revelation through the Holy Spirit (1QS 8:16; 1QpHab 2:2; CDC 2:12–13); they also held that the interpretation of Scripture came from God himself (1QpHab 2:2–3; 7:4–5). The rabbis believed that every passage in Scripture was given by the Holy Spirit (BT, San 99; SB 4, 435–51). Indeed, there was probably no tenet more commonly received within Judaism than that of prophetic inspiration. Philo summed up the common belief well when he wrote that the prophet was "an interpreter for God, uttering words formed within his being; and to God we can attribute no error" (*De praemiis et poenis* 55; cf. *Quis rerum divinarum heres sit* 259).

The nascent Church appropriated the traditional Jewish doctrine. For the Church, the Old Testament was the "holy scriptures" (Matt 22:29; Rom 1:2). God spoke through Moses (Mark 12:26) and the prophets (Luke 1:70). David the Psalmist is said to have been inspired by the Holy Spirit (Mark 12:36 par.). Paul wrote of the Gospel of God, which he spoke "beforehand through his prophets in the holy scriptures" (Rom 1:2). In reference to Hosea and Isaiah (Rom 9:25–29), he mentioned that "God has said." "As God said" (2 Cor 6:16–18) and "He says" (2 Cor 6:2) are *lemmata* typically used in the New Testament to introduce biblical citations. This usage was particularly exploited by the author of the letter to the Hebrews who used "God said" as the introduction to an entire catena of scriptural citations, apparently without experiencing any need to cite a human author (Heb 1:5–14). Explicit mention of the Holy Spirit is not only found in the logion of Mark 12:36 (par. Matt 22:43), but also in Acts 1:16; 28:25. Thus the first generations of Christians were apparently as convinced of the inspiration of the Scriptures as were the Jews with whom they were contemporary.

Judaism had taken the notion over from the prophetic tradition, and Christianity took the notion over from Judaism. Although the Old Testament nowhere attests to the idea that the Holy Spirit inspired the written word of the prophets, it is commonly proclaimed that the Spirit of God was at work in the lives, the works, and the words of the prophets (2 Sam 23:2; Hos 1:1; Joel 3:1–2; Zech 7:12, etc.). Moreover, Jeremiah made a crucial distinction between the false prophets, who spoke according to their own hearts, and the true prophets who spoke according to the word of the Lord (Jer 23:16). The Jewish notion of scriptural inspiration, then, derives from a notion of prophetic inspiration.

The writings of the sages were considered in an analogous manner. There was biblical precedent for considering the sages to be similarly inspired (Isa 11:2; Exod 15:20–21; 2 Chr 15:1–5). Within the Tanach, however, a place apart was reserved for the Torah, which was considered to have been given directly from God to Moses. Yet Moses was considered to be a prophet and the Israelites thought of a prophetic succession to Moses (Deut 18:15; Num 11:24–25, etc.). Thus it was a fairly easy jump for Hellenistic Jews to speak of the entire Bible as an emanation of the prophetic spirit. Philo, for example, employed the technical term "enthusiasm" (*enthousiōdēs*) in reference to the prophets (*Life of Moses* 2, 188–91). In summary, it should be said that under the influence of Hellenistic categories of thought, Hellenistic Jews spoke of the origin of prophecy in particular, and of the Bible in general, in terms of some form of ecstatic enthusiasm.

This later interpretation of the prophetic experience by Hellenistic Jews had some precedent in the Hebrew Bible. The Hebrew designation *nabi'* (prophet) originally applied to the charismatic ecstatic. Within the ancient tradition of Israel there was the recognition of the phenomenon of ecstatic prophecy (Num 11:15, 29; 1 Sam 10:6, 10; 2 Kgs 2:16). This phenomenon was occasionally ascribed to the working of the Spirit of God (Num 27:18; Judg 3:10). However, the Israelites recognized—a point to which the apostle Paul will return in 1 Corinthians 12–14—that not every charismatic experience is a manifestation of the power of God, nor is it necessarily an experience that will benefit the people of God. Discernment is necessary. True prophets must be distinguished from false prophets. The distinction runs throughout the Old Testament, principally in the prophetic writings. Thus Elijah vied with the false prophets of Baal (1 Kgs 18), and the oracle of the Lord (Jer 23:16–17) distinguished between the true prophet and false prophets. Discernment was important because even a man like King Saul could come under the influence of an evil spirit and then act the part of the frenetic *nabi'* (1 Sam 16–18).

The call for discernment with regard to the "prophetic experience" has led to a distinction among modern authors between the classical prophets of the Old Testament and the ecstatic prophets who are occasionally mentioned in the biblical text. What distinguished the classical prophets, both the earlier prophets, such as Elijah and Eliseus, and those commonly called the literary prophets, such as Isaiah, Jeremiah, Amos, is that their prophecy employed what Gerhard von Rad has called the "messenger formula" as the most direct means of expressing its function. The true prophets of Israel did not normally receive their "message" in an ecstatic trance; rather, it came by means of a dialogue with God. The formulation of the message was a conscious experience, with the result that the prophet could speak God's word because he had been in interpersonal communication with him. The prophet was a fully conscious messenger of Yahweh, the God of Israel.

The process of discernment is somewhat reflected in the Septuagint's choice of language. Typically the LXX renders the Hebrew term *nabi'* by *prophētēs*. The Greek word was well chosen since, etymologically, it means "one who speaks for" (*pro-phētēs*). The true prophet is one who speaks on behalf of Yahweh. Within the LXX, *prophētēs* is almost synonymous with *hupophētēs,* a less commonly used term that means "interpreter." With its connotation of spokesperson, *prophētēs* is the more appropriate term to represent the function of Yahweh's messengers. Since seers (in the Hebrew, *ro'eh* or *hōzeh*) also served as spokespersons on Yahweh's behalf, *prophētēs* was used by the Septuagintal translators to describe the function of seers like Samuel (1 Chr 26:28), Hanani (2 Chr 19:2), and Asaph (2 Chr 29:30) (cf. Isa 30:10). The Septuagint, however, occasionally rendered *nabi'* as *pseudoprophētēs* (false prophet) when it wanted to distinguish those who spoke their own minds from those who were effectively Yahweh's messengers and spoke his word.

In sum, then, the ancient biblical tradition shied away from the notion that the ultimate criterion for judging authentic prophecy was an ecstatic charismatic experience. Its concern was that the true prophet speak the word of God. The origin of the Jewish notion of biblical inspiration lies in the traditional notion of prophetic inspiration, the idea being that the biblical books contain the record of the prophetic message. Although the prophetic model was used early on to interpret the role and function of Moses, the language of prophetic inspiration was not used with respect to the Torah, even though it was predicated of the "Writings." This exclusion relates to the unique place of the Torah among the biblical writings.

Thus the belief common to all forms of late Judaism was that the entire Bible had its source in God's word. Christianity of New Testament times took over this element from its Jewish patrimony, but did not generally adopt the Hellenistic terminology appropriate to ecstatic phenomena in order to interpret the tradition on inspiration. Christian language generally avoided the vocabulary of ecstasy in dealing with inspiration. A noteworthy exception to the general usage is 2 Timothy 3:16, where the vocable *theopneustos* appears, though without any suggestion that the author had ecstatic phenomena in mind.

The Fathers of the Church

Nevertheless the first Christian author to develop a theory of Holy Scripture clearly considered prophecy as an ecstatic experience. Only once in his writings does Justin Martyr allude to the personality of an individual prophet. The prophet in this case is Isaiah, to whom Justin makes reference in the *Dialogue with Trypho* (118; *PG* 6, 749). Because of this view of prophecy, Justin considered that the prophet's words were not his own; they were rather the words of the one who had enraptured the prophet. This results in a view which looks to biblical inspiration almost as a form of dictation (cf. Justin, *Trypho* 115; *PG* 6, 741; *Apol* 1, 36; *PG* 6, 385). Justin's views were quite similar to those of another second-century Apologist, Athenagoras. One of the ablest of the Apologists, Athenagoras wrote of prophetic inspiration as an ecstatic phenomenon. He compared the action of the Spirit to the blowing of a flute (*Legatio pro Christianis* 9; *PG* 6, 905–7). In some degree the views of Justin and Athenagoras were shared by others among the early Fathers of the Church, including Theophilus, Clement of Alexandria, Tertullian, and Ambrose.

By and large, however, the early Fathers did not develop a theory on inspiration. As a matter of fact, the tract on revelation is a relatively late development in the history of theology. It is barely a century old, the topic having obtained a place unto itself only because of the issuance of magisterial statements on inspiration—sometimes largely provoked by the difficulties which modern historical findings were causing for the traditional inspiration of the Scriptures. To this date, the tract on inspiration lacks the theological nuance and sophistication found in most other theological expositions. In fact, one can state with Archbishop Martini that we still lack a complete treatment of inspiration. A complete doctrine is still a *desideratum*. Given the results of a historical-critical approach to the Scriptures, this desire may never be realized. In retrospect it may someday appear that the specific treatment of inspiration as a topic unto itself was but a momentary phenomenon in the history of Christianity. Indeed the relative silence of contemporary literature on the topic of inspiration might eventually prove to be the beginning of the end of the systematic exposition of the doctrine of inspiration; perhaps even now we have entered into that period which allows for a retrospective view on the "traditional doctrine."

What was traditional among the Fathers was the use of ancient formulas, often biblical formulas, to describe the Scriptures. For these early ecclesiastical writers, the Bible was the "holy scriptures" (*hai hagiai graphai,* Theophilus of Antioch) or the "sacred writings" (*hiera grammata,* Clement of Alexandria). We read of "holy" (*hagiai biblioi,* Clem. Alex.) and "sacred books" (*hierai biblioi,* Origen). Clement tells us that they were "inspired writings" (*hai theopneustoi graphai*), while Chrysostom spoke of "the divine writings" (*hai theiai graphai*). With a small shift of focus, we find that Clement of Alexandria wrote of the Scriptures as the work of "divine writers" (*theiōn graphōn*). Theophilus speaks of the authors as "bearers of the spirit" (*pneumatophoroi*), while Origen avers that the writings come "from inspiration" (*ex epipnoias*). By the late second century, the Greater Church had largely accepted the parity of the Old and New Testaments. Both contained the word of God. So the language of Origen, Clement, and their contemporaries was largely applicable to the New Testament as well as to the Old.

Among the Fathers of the Church, Origen was the first to think through inspiration as a topic in its own right. Yet even Origen did not do so in a systematic fashion. Rather he addressed himself to the issue when it was necessary for him to do so—that is, in order to affirm that the Scriptures are "the divine words" (*entheoi hoi logoi*). Origen maintained the inspiration of the Scriptures particularly against the Marcionites. Because of the lingering traces of Montanism, Origen had a bias against a notion which looked to a charismatic experience as the origin of prophecy and the source of inspiration. In the fourth part of *De principiis,* his major theological work, Origen avowed that the biblical texts were not the works of men but came from the Holy Spirit (*De principiis* 4, 9; *PG* 11, 360). Accordingly, Origen was able to affirm that the Scriptures were filled with the wisdom and truth of God. His emphasis lay on a text that came from God and was given to his people.

This emphasis led to the allegorical interpretation of the biblical text which is commonly associated with the School of Alexandria. However, it must be noted that Origen had a rather realistic understanding of the composition of the Scriptures. He noted that the Old Testament prophets "voluntarily and consciously collaborated with the word that came to them" (*Homilia in Ezechielem,* frag. 6, 1; *PG* 13, 709). He acknowledged that the New Testament evangelists could express their own opinions. He sought after the intentions of those who had written the Scriptures and distinguished between the revealed word and the commentary on that word which comes from the inspired writer. He admitted the possibility of error on the part of the prophet or New Testament author, and suggested a point of view which admits of degrees of inspiration.

In the final analysis, however, it is probably the emphasis on the text itself as the inspired word that was Origen's real legacy to the Church's traditional doctrine on inspiration. This emphasis represented a dramatic shift whose importance must not be overlooked. The view to which the New Testament itself gives witness is that the Old Testament records the words of inspired men—Moses, Isaiah, David. The view that would become current, one already present in Origen, is that the writings themselves are inspired. In the words of Bruce Vawter, "the shift had been made from Scripture as a *locus quaerendi,* a witness to the living word of the Spirit . . . to Scripture as a *locus essendi* of the word, quite identified with it."

Although Origen acknowledged the human elements in the Scriptures, he was concerned that the final product be considered as the word of God. Thus while he acknowledged that the action of the Spirit was directed to the human mind, will, and memory (*Contra Celsum* 7, 3–4; *PG* 11, 1424–25), Origen affirmed that the Holy Spirit "illuminated" (*phōtizein*) the inspired writer (*De principiis* 4, 14; *PG* 11, 372). His vocabulary was quite different from that of Jerome, who affirmed that the letter to the Romans had been "dictated" (*dictare,* a Latin word whose sense cannot be limited to oral delivery in view of transcription) by the Holy Spirit through the apostle Paul (Ep 120, 10; *PL* 22, 997). The language of "dictation" did not enter into the mainstream of Church tradition. What did enter into the Church's tradition was the affirmation that God is the "author of the Scriptures."

God, the Author of the Scriptures

The expression was taken over by the Fathers of the Second Vatican Council, who affirmed that "the books of both the Old and New Testament in their entirety . . . have God as their author (*Deum habent auctorem; Dei Verbum,* 11). The formula has a long history, being found already in the *Statuta Ecclesiae Antiqua,* a late fifth-century collection of decrees of various local councils (DS 325–29). The formula arose within a fourth- and fifth-century controversy between the Church of Africa and the Manichees. The Manichees denied that God was the "writer" (*scriptor*) of the Old Testament; in response, the greater African Church replied that God was the "one author" (*unus auctor*) of the Old and New Testaments. The emphasis in the counterformulation of the greater African Church was on God as the single source of all the Scriptures, not on the fashion in which he was the source of these Scriptures.

Indeed, the Latin word *auctor* admits of a wider range of applicability than does the English "author," its appropriate and usual translation. In Latin *auctor* is used of the founder of a city, the architect of a building, the cause of a wound, and, most commonly, the author of a document. In this respect *auctor* is similar to the Greek *archēgos,* which was used of the one God both as the "author" of the Scriptures and as the "cause" of creation. Thus the formula adopted in patristic times generally affirmed that the Scriptures came from God, but did not necessarily imply a specific theory of literary authorship.

It is of course true that some of the Latin Fathers of the Church took *auctor* in a rather narrow sense. For Ambrose, the fourth-century bishop of Milan, God is the "author" or cause of Scripture in the sense that the very words of Scripture are those of God, not of man (Ep 8, 10; *PL* 16, 912–16). In Ambrose's view, God somehow permeated the minds of the scriptural writers so that their words were his. Among Ambrose's protégés, the most famous was Augustine of Hippo. Augustine shared with his mentor the idea that the very text of Scripture came from God, but the image he used to convey this idea was different from that of Ambrose. For Augustine, God was virtually the one who dictated the words of the scriptural text, the biblical writers serving in the capacity of scribes.

Augustine acknowledged that the human authors of the Scriptures "have used all the modes of expression which grammarians call by their Greek name *tropes,* and they have employed them in greater numbers and more eloquently than those who do not know these writers . . . In the Holy Books there are seen not only examples of these *tropes,* just as of all figures, but even the names of some of them; for example, 'allegory,' 'enigma,' and 'parable.'" Augustine went on to say that, "A knowledge of them [the *tropes*] is necessary in explaining the obscurities of the Scriptures, because, when the meaning is unreasonable if understood in the literal signification of the words, we must . . . try to find out whether it has been expressed in some figure or other which we do not know. And so, many passages which were obscure have been interpreted" (*On Christian Instruction,* 29). Thus Augustine taught that the Scriptures are phrased in the various forms of human speech. Nevertheless, Augustine's view included a notion of scriptural inspiration that was virtually equivalent to a notion of mechanical dictation, as he proposed in an exposition of the truth of the Scriptures:

> Not only one but perhaps two or more interpretations are understood from the same words of Scripture. And so, even if the meaning of the writer is unknown, there is no danger, provided that it is possible to show from other passages of the Scriptures that any one of them is in accord with truth. A man who thoroughly examines the Holy Scriptures in an endeavor to find the purpose of the author (through whom the Holy Spirit brought Holy Scripture into being), whether he attains this

goal or whether he elicits from the words another meaning which is not opposed to the true faith, is free from blame, if he has proof from some other passage of the Holy Scriptures. In fact, the author perhaps saw that very meaning, too, in the same words which we are anxious to interpret. And, certainly, the Spirit of God who produced these words through him also foresaw that this very meaning would occur to the reader or listener; further, He took care that it should occur to him because it also is based upon truth. For what could God have provided more generously and more abundantly in the Holy Scriptures than that the same words might be understood in several ways, which other supporting testimonies no less divine endorse? (*On Christian Instruction,* 27)

In any event, the formula "God, the one author of the Scriptures" became classic in the Church's tradition as an affirmation that the Scriptures of both Testaments came from the one God, as did all of creation. As such, the formula appeared in the pronouncement of the Iberian bishops against the Priscillianists (DS 790). In the thirteenth century, it appeared both in the profession of faith prescribed for the Waldensians (DS 790) and in the profession of faith of the Emperor Michael Palaeologus (DS 854). Subsequently, the formula occurred in conciliar texts including the Decree for the Jacobites of the Council of Florence (1441). This remarkable text not only used the term "inspiration" for the first time in a magisterial pronouncement, but it also set forth the context within which the traditional formula arose:

It [the holy Roman Church] professes one and the same God as the author of the Old and New Testament, that is, of the Law and the Prophets and the Gospel, since the saints of both Testaments have spoken with the inspiration of the same Holy Spirit, whose books, which are contained under the following titles, it accepts and venerates. [There follows a listing of the books.]

Besides it anathematizes the madness of the Manichaeans, who have established two first principles, one of the visible, and another of the invisible; and they had said that there is one God of the New Testament, another God of the Old Testament (DS 1334–36).

The Council of Trent (Fourth Session, 1546) reiterated the traditional teaching on inspiration in an exposition which bore upon the relationship between the Scriptures and tradition:

The Council clearly perceived that this truth and rule are contained in the written books and unwritten traditions which have come down to us, having been received by the apostles from the mouth of Christ Himself, or from the apostles by the dictation of the Holy Spirit (*Spiritu Sancto dictante*), and have been transmitted as it were from hand to hand. Following, then, the example of the orthodox Fathers, it receives and venerates with the same sense of loyalty and reverence all the books of the Old and New Testaments, for God alone is the author of both (*cum utriusque unus Deus sit auctor*)—together with all the traditions concerning faith and morals, as coming from the mouth of Christ or being inspired by the Holy Spirit (*vel a Spiritu Sancto dictatas*) and perserved in continuous succession in the Catholic Church (DS 1501).

The Tridentine formulation is interesting in that it employs the age-old expression of God as the author of the Old Testament as well as the New, and that it twice uses the language of "dictation" to affirm the inspiration of the Scriptures. In the history of magisterial formulations, the expression is novel. In Trent it is obviously intended to differentiate the "inspiration" of Tradition from the verbal inspiration of the Scriptures. Yet it was not until the nineteenth century that the Magisterium went any further in explaining the *nature* of inspiration. It was content simply to affirm *fact* of inspiration, and that with respect to both Testaments.

II. THEOLOGICAL DISCUSSION

In the meantime, the Schoolmen were looking to the Scriptures as their principal *auctoritas*. Among the *loci theologici* identified by Cano, the Scriptures were the first named. In this case, the first place signified priority in a hierarchy of importance. The contribution of the Scholastics to the understanding of the doctrine of inspiration was, nonetheless, not very great, but one can hardly concur with Otto Weber's judgment that it was nil. On the one hand, the Scholastics considered that inspiration was a part of the charism of prophecy, *in genere prophetiae*. Prophecy held the key to the understanding of the Scriptures. On the other hand, the Scholastics were able to make use of philosophical categories in their exposition of prophecy and inspiration. Since the philosophical categories deemed to be most useful for this exposition were drawn from Aristotelianism, it is not surprising that the Scholastic notions of prophecy and inspiration were quite similar to those of the twelfth-century Jewish Aristotelian philosopher and theologian Moses Maimonides. Left behind in the newer philosophical interpretation of prophecy was the old notion of ecstatic experience formerly proposed by Philo and other Hellenistic Jews, a notion that had lingering influence on some Fathers of the Church.

Among the philosophical categories found most helpful for the newer interpretation of the phenomenon of prophecy was that of causality. The Scholastics distinguished four kinds of causality: efficient, material, formal, and final. With respect to efficient causality, one can further distinguish between the principal efficient cause and an instrumental efficient cause. The instrumental efficient cause acts only insofar as it is employed by another, the principal efficient cause. Nonetheless the instrumental efficient cause contributes something to the final product. Thus a blue felt pen (instrumental efficient cause) contributes something to the page written by an author (principal efficient cause). While the author contributes the thought and wording, the pen contributes the width and color of the letters. This notion of a double efficient causality was analogously applied to prophecy and thence to inspiration. God was considered as the principal efficient cause, the prophet and sacred writer as the instrumental efficient cause. The distinction can be applied only analogously to prophecy because, unlike other instrumental efficient causes, the prophet is a personal being who has his own mind and will.

In the tract *De Prophetia,* of his monumental *Summa Theologiae,* Thomas Aquinas (1225–74) employed other useful distinctions in order to present his understanding of prophecy. His notions would eventually ground a good amount of the later thinking on inspiration. First of all, Aquinas ranked prophecy among the *gratiae gratis datae,* a category akin to the biblical category of charism. The category included those gifts of God that are given to an individual not for the sake of personal sanctification, but for the purpose of building up the community. Secondly, Aquinas, unlike his predecessors in the schools, considered that prophecy should be considered within the category of *motio* (movement) rather than within the category of *habitus* (habit). According to Aquinas, prophecy is not a permanent gift (*habitus*) by which God bestows a kind of new being on the prophet; rather it is a temporarily limited gift that God gives to his prophets and inspired authors in an *ad hoc* fashion. Thirdly, and perhaps most significantly, he held that the gift of prophecy pertains to man's cognitive faculties. The prophetic experience does not consist in what the prophet knew, nor does it consist in a specific manner of acquiring knowledge; rather it is a matter of the prophet's inspired judgment that such knowledge is the word of God. As was his wont, Aquinas further distinguished various forms of prophecy. What he had to say about prophetic inspiration served to ground later Scholastic thought on scriptural inspiration. On that precise topic, however, Aquinas himself had little to say, even though the final *quaestio* of his tract on prophecy reveals that he thought the inspired authors of the Scriptures were like prophets in the broad sense of the term (*ST* II, 2, q. 174, art. 3).

It is commonly admitted that the later theology that virtually equated divine authorship with verbal dictation in a mechanistic sense goes back to the Spanish Dominican Melchior Cano (1509–60) and the members of his school. Cano himself had a significant role to play in the development of fundamental theology by reason of his major work, *De locis theologicis,* published posthumously in 1563. Proceeding from the teaching of Jerome and Augustine, Cano held that in the Scriptures "not only the words but even every comma (*apex*) has been supplied (*suppeditatus*) by the Divine Spirit." From this theory of plenary literary inspiration, Cano deduced the inerrancy of the Scriptures: ". . . falsity is excluded by the sacred authors." In his explanation of the thesis, Cano proposed that "everything great or small has been edited by the sacred authors at the dictation of the Holy Spirit" (*Spiritu Sancto dictante esse edita*) (*De locis theologicis,* II, 17).

Cano's language is similar to the language found in the writings of his contemporary, John Calvin, the French reformer (1509–64). Calvin adopted the traditional formula that "God is the author of Scripture." Throughout his writings we find frequent use of the word "dictate" to describe God's authorship. He frequently refers to the sacred authors as "scribes" or "instruments of the Spirit." Thus he mentions that the New Testament authors were "certain and authentic amanuenses of the Holy Spirit" (*Institutes* IV, 3, 9), and again that: "Whenever we read or hear the Word of God, this comes before us, that men have not invented what is contained in the Old and New Testaments, but God by a visible sign has testified, even as there was need, that men were organs solely of his Holy Spirit." He teaches that whatever Daniel "uttered was dictated by the Holy Spirit," and noted that the histories were recorded "under the dictation of the Holy Spirit."

Thus the language of "dictation" by the Spirit, which is as ancient as Jerome, was commonly employed in the sixteenth century to describe the phenomenon of scriptural inspiration. "Dictation" belonged to the common theological vocabulary, as its use by Trent, Calvin, and Domingo Bañez (1528–1604), the influential Thomist, shows. Yet one must ask whether "dictation" implies verbal inspiration—as if the Scriptures had been transcribed, word by word, by an author who was listening to the Holy Spirit. The works of Calvin certainly do not imply a theory of mechanical dictation, even though some later Roman Catholic authors and some twentieth-century evangelicals have opted for a literalistic notion of scriptural inspiration. While arguing vehemently for the indispensable authority of the Spirit-inspired Scriptures, Calvin acknowledged that the scribes who copied the scriptural texts were prone to error, that Paul was not accustomed to cite the very words of Scripture such as they appeared in the Old Testament, and that the sacred authors themselves were not exempt from human frailty. Apropos of this last point, Calvin noted in the *Institutes* that: "Their preaching is both obscure, like something far off, and is embodied in types . . . They also are to be classed as children. Finally, no one then possessed discernment so clear as to be unaffected by the obscurity of the time" (II 11, 6).

For Calvin, the key to scriptural inspiration is what he says about "doctrine." Doctrine is imparted by God, yet is not identical with the words of Scripture. Doctrine is the truth to which the Scripture attests; to it the sacred scribes were obedient. Calvin affirms that doctrine is "dictated by the Holy Spirit," yet acknowledges a gap between the words of the authors and the doctrine itself. Ultimately, scriptural inspiration is not unrelated to the life of the believer, since "The same Spirit . . . who has spoken through the mouth of the prophets must penetrate into our hearts to persuade us that they faithfully proclaimed what had been divinely commanded" (*Institutes* I, 7, 4). By means of a similar movement, the Spirit has prompted both the inspiration of the Scriptures and the scripturally grounded faith experience of the believer. For Calvin, then, it is clear that despite his repeated references to "scribes" and "dictation," scriptural inspiration is not a matter of stenographic transcription nor does it imply the removal of all human error from Scripture's testimony to the word of God.

Among the major sixteenth-century Continental Reformers, Ulrich Zwingli (1484–1531) seems to have moved the farthest from the notion of verbal inspiration. He admitted the principle of inerrancy only with respect to biblical revelation and acknowledged that the Bible could be in error in non-theological matters. What was important for Zwingli was that one get beyond the outer word of Scripture to the inner word. In comparison with the position of Zwingli, Martin Luther (1483–1546) was much more concerned with the "holy words" of Scripture. Thus Luther was constrained from accepting Zwingli's interpretation of the Eucharist by the presence of the copulative verb "is" in the Institution narratives. Despite his attentiveness to the words of Scripture, Luther had a very dynamic notion of inspiration. His idea derived from his vision of the inseparability, but not the identification, of the Word and the Spirit. In his view the role of the Word in the Church is that of the continuing presence of the Spirit in the Church. The process of inspiration cannot be limited to the production of a document in the past, for word is not truly word until the process of communication is complete. The inspiration of the Scriptures is not complete until it touches the heart of the one who reads and hears the Word.

Despite the rather supple views of the major Reformers, many of those who adhered to the new tradition espoused a view of inspiration that was not far removed from the narrower views of some post-Tridentine Roman Catholic Schoolmen. Among Catholics, Bañez, the Dominican theologian, held that "The Holy Spirit not only inspired all that is contained in the Scripture, he also dictated and suggested every word with which it was written. . . . To dictate means to determine the very words." Within the Swiss Reform, in comparison, the 1675 *Formula Consensus Helvetica* proposed not only that the word of God, given through Moses, the Prophets, and the apostles, has been preserved for the Church free of all corruption, but also that the Hebrew text of the Old Testament is inspired both in its consonants and its vowels (including the Masoretic pointing).

The Nineteenth Century

Attentiveness to the work done in textual criticism should have preserved both reformed and Catholic theologians of the last four centuries from a literalistic view of scriptural inspiration and a naïve view of scriptural inerrancy. A careful reading of the Scriptures themselves or an openness to the writings of the Fathers would have achieved the same purpose. Nevertheless, the twin doctrines of inspiration and inerrancy continued to be upheld by authors who did not effectively deal with what the Scriptures themselves say and teach. Only with the development of the historical-critical methodology of New Testament research was the simplistic notion of inspiration called into question. Late in the eighteenth century, critical scholars of the stature of J. S. Semler, J. G. von Herder, J. J. Griesbach, and J. D. Michaelis abandoned the traditional notion of inspiration. In quest of the historical Jesus came Strauss, Baur, and Renan, who also rejected the traditional view. On the other hand, there were some nineteenth-century critical scholars who retained some notion of inspiration. Schleiermacher held that those books were inspired which communicated the spirit of Christ. Johann Christian Conrad von Hofmann (1810–77) held that Scripture was a record of revelation. For Martin Kähler, the Scriptures were the record and means of preaching the Word of God, but this affirmation implied nothing about the text in itself. Nevertheless, with the acceptance of the historical-critical methodology, inspiration could no longer be spoken of as once it had been. Except for evangelical and fairly conservative circles, the traditional teaching on revelation, inherited from the medieval Church and the Founders of the Reformation, slipped away from the Reform.

Within Roman Catholicism, however, developments took a different turn. During the nineteenth century the changes in the interpretation of the Scriptures which arose as a result of discoveries in the physical and historical sciences as well as those that were occurring with the development of a new approach to the Scriptures in the German and French universities led to a renewed interest in the traditional doctrine of biblical inspiration. It was urgent that a better presentation of the doctrine be formulated the better to explain both the human activity involved in the production of the Bible and the efficacy of the divine power which directed this human effort. Among the participants in the discussions was John Henry Newman (1801–90) whose brief "Essay on the Inspiration of Holy Scripture" was first published, posthumously, in 1953. Newman noted that the Church had never declared *de fide* that the sacred writings were themselves inspired. A formal magisterial statement on inspiration was not to be made until the Constitution *Dei Filius* of Vatican Council I (1870):

> These books of the Old and New Testaments are to be received as sacred and canonical in their integrity, with all their parts, as they are enumerated in the decree of the said Council [Trent] and are contained in the ancient Latin edition of the Vulgate. These the Church holds to be sacred and canonical, not because, having been carefully composed by mere human authority, nor merely because they contain revelation with no mixture of error, but because, having been written by the inspiration of the Holy Spirit, they have God for their author (*quod Spiritu Sancto inspirante conscripti Deum habent auctorem*) and have been delivered as such to the Church herself (DS 3006).

The final draft of the conciliar decree had been prepared by Johann Baptist Franzelin (1816–86), an Austrian professor in the Roman College and the principal theological adviser to Pio Nono. The conciliar text is very clear in rejecting some notions of inspiration; it is less clear in positively proposing an idea of revelation. In its positive formulation, Vatican I largely repeated traditional formulas. The *Deus auctor* formula first found in the Council of Carthage is now, for the first time in magisterial statements, connected with specific writings. The "inspiration" formula, also present in a companion canon (DS 3029), came from the Council of Florence. *Dei Filius* specifically alluded to Trent, but seems to have avoided the Tridentine

Spiritu Sancto dictante. This omission was undoubtedly due to Franzelin's theory of content inspiration.

The theories of inspiration rejected by the conciliar decree are frequently cited as the "mere assistance" and the "subsequent approval" theories. In some wise each of these theories derives from the work of Leonard Lessius, a sixteenth-century Louvain Jesuit, yet it is to later versions of these theories, respectively proposed by Johann Jahn ("mere assistance") and Daniel Bonifacius von Haneberg ("subsequent approval") that the conciliar decree was apparently addressed. Lessius' own views on inspiration were part of the long conflict that raged in sixteenth-century Louvain between the Jesuit college and the university's faculty of theology. At one point the university condemned thirty-four propositions taken from the work of Lessius, the first three of which bear upon inspiration:

(1) For anything to be Holy Scripture, its individual words need not be inspired by the Holy Spirit.

(2) The individual truths and statements need not be immediately inspired in the writer by the Holy Spirit.

(3) If any book (such as, perhaps, 2 Mac) were to be written through purely human endeavor without the assistance of the Holy Spirit, and he should then certify that there were nothing false therein, the book would become Holy Scripture.

Relative to the second point, Lessius explained his position in a letter to the archbishop of Malines: "It is enough that the sacred writer be divinely drawn to write down what he sees, hears, or knows otherwise, that he enjoy the infallible assistance of the Holy Spirit to prevent him from mistakes even in matters he knows on the word of others, or from his own experience, or by his own natural reasoning. It is this assistance of the Holy Spirit that gives Scripture its infallible truth." This form of *concomitant inspiration* was a merely negative assistance. As formulated by Lessius and a Jesuit confrère, Jacques Bonfrère, the mere assistance theory was directed against maximalist and mechanical-dictation theories of inspiration. At the beginning of the nineteenth century Johann Jahn, an Austrian Norbertine, published a pair of volumes (1802, 1804) which also took issue with the exaggerated concepts of scriptural inspiration. For Jahn, revelation required a positive influence of God, but inspiration is not revelation. Inspiration is simply "the divine assistance for avoiding errors." According to Vatican Council I, such a minimalist view of inspiration was incompatible with the traditional teaching of the Church.

Although he did not concur with the view of Sixtus of Siena that 2 Maccabees had been written without divine assistance, Lessius entertained the possibility that God might approve what men had originally written on their own authority and in keeping with their own capacities. Drawing an analogy from the authority imparted by the royal signature and appealing to documents drawn up by court officials, Bonfrère explained what he called *consequent inspiration* in these words: "The Holy Spirit could act in a consequent way if some writing were composed with no help, guidance, or assistance from him, but solely by some writer left to his own resources, and then the Spirit would certify that everything written therein was true. For then the entire document would surely be God's Word, possessed of that same infallible truth as are others composed under the inspiration and guidance of the same Holy Spirit." The theory was revived in 1850 by D. B. von Haneberg, professor of exegesis at Munich and later a Benedictine monk, abbot, and bishop of Speyer. Strongly opposed to the theory of verbal inspiration, Haneberg explained that "a book is written in a purely human manner, but later is elevated through reception into the Canon, to be an expression of divine communication to men; the Spirit of God knew from the beginning that he would adopt this book, without however any direct intervention in the spirit of man."

In rejecting the views of Haneberg and Jahn, the Council Fathers were clearly opting for a view of inspiration which implied a positive and concomitant activity of the Spirit in the composition of the books of the Bible. At the time, the common Roman Catholic opinion as to the nature of biblical inspiration was a theory of content inspiration whose classical formulation was made by Franzelin, the *peritus* of Vatican Council I:

> Biblical inspiration seems to consist essentially in a freely bestowed charism of enlightenment and stimulus, whereby the mind of the inspired men would propose to write down those truths which God wished to communicate to his Church through Scripture, and their will would be drawn to commit all these truths, and these alone, to writing; and the men thus raised to be instrumental causes at the disposition of God, the principal cause, would carry through this divine proposal with infallible truthfulness. We thus distinguish between inspiration, which extends to the truths and "formal word," and assistance, which must extend further, even to the expressions and "material words" (*Tractatus de Divina Traditione et Scriptura*, p. 347).

Franzelin's exposition was an attempt to explain the traditional *Deus auctor* adage. According to Franzelin, the dogma of inspiration must be derived from the dogmatic statement of God's authorship. In his exposition the Jesuit professor, soon to be raised to the cardinalate, not only used the notion of instrumental causality developed by the Schoolmen, but also made a deft distinction between the formal and material components of the scriptural books. By assigning the material parts to the human authors, Franzelin allowed sufficient contributions from the human author as to allow for some affirmation of human authorship. By ascribing the content and the truths of Scripture (*res et sententiae*) to God, Franzelin specified the notion of principal instrumental casuality and highlighted the *Deus auctor* formula. In some respects Franzelin's theory of content inspiration recalls both Calvin's notion of doctrine and Lessius' first proposition, which effectively denied that the doctrine of inspiration required that the very words of the sacred text be formed by God in the mind of the human author.

337

Franzelin's notion of content inspiration was clearly encouraged by Leo XIII in the encyclical *Providentissimus Deus:*

> For all the books which the Church receives as sacred and canonical are written wholly and entirely, with all their parts (*libri omnes atque integri . . . cum omnibus suis partibus*), at the dictation of the Holy Spirit (*Spiritu Sancto dictante*) and so far is it from being possible that any error can coexist with inspiration, that inspiration not only is essentially incompatible with error (*per se ipsa non modo errorem excludat omnem*) but excludes and rejects it as absolutely and necessarily as it is impossible that God Himself, the Supreme Truth, can utter that which is not true. This is the ancient and unchanging faith of the Church. . . .
>
> Hence, the fact that it was men whom the Holy Spirit took up as his instruments (*Spiritum Sanctum assumpsisse homines tamquam instrumenta ad scribendum*)—but not the primary author—who might have made an error. For, by supernatural power, He so moved and impelled them to write—He so assisted them when writing—that the things which He ordered, and those only (*ea omnia eaque sola*), they, first, rightly understood, then willed faithfully to write down, and finally expressed in apt words and with infallible truth. Otherwise, it could not be said that He was the author of the entire Scripture (*auctor Sacrae Scripturae universae*) . . . (DS 3292–93).

In these words of Leo XIII, we recognize not only a number of traditional formulas but also the theory of content inspiration, with its notion of instrumentality which deftly separates those things which God ordered to be written from the apt words of the human authors of the Scriptures. With respect to the traditional doctrine of inspiration, there are two new emphases in the teaching of Leo XIII. The points repeatedly underscored by the Pontiff were *plenary* inspiration and total *inerrancy*. Leo did not use the term inerrancy, a relatively new term introduced into the lexicon by Thomas H. Homes in 1834. Indeed the term *inerrantia* has never been used in a papal encyclical or conciliar statement. Altogether it has been used but three times by the Magisterium, the first occasion being the June 18, 1915, response of the Pontifical Biblical Commission. Neither did Leo employ the language of infallibility, terminology which Roman Catholic teaching uses anent some pronouncements of the Magisterium. In contrast, the notion of scriptural infallibility does occur in the writings of some conservative and evangelical Protestant authors. At any rate, even without the use of technical language, Leo affirmed that the Scriptures were without error. His affirmation of this corollary of the doctrine of inspiration was directed against those who took issue with the veracity of the Scriptures on the basis of recent advances in the historical and physical sciences. Leo asserted the truth of the Scriptures, yet noted, with reference to Augustine, that "the sacred writers, or to speak more accurately, the Holy Spirit 'who spoke by them, did not intend to teach men these things (that is to say, the essential nature of the things of the visible universe), things in no way profitable unto salvation.'"

Leo's insistence on plenary inspiration was intended as a rejection of any notion of restricted inspiration. In the waning years of the nineteenth century, Roman authorities had condemned the works of the British philosopher St. George Jackson Mivart and the Sicilian canon Salvatore di Bartolo, both of whom had advanced notions that limited the content of inspiration. In a moderate form, a theory of limited inspiration had also been held by John Henry Newman. In his Anglican period, Newman had written:

> In what way inspiration is compatible with that personal agency on the part of its instruments, which the composition of the Bible evidences, we know not; but if any thing is certain, it is this—that, though the Bible is inspired, and therefore, in one sense, written by God, yet very large portions of it, if not by far the greater part of it, are written in as free and unconstrained a manner, and (apparently) with as little consciousness of a supernatural dictation or restraint, on the part of His earthly instruments, as if he had had no share in the work (*Tract 85: Lectures on the Scripture Proofs of the Doctrine of the Church,* p. 30).

While Newman admitted forms of inspiration, he held that the Scriptures were nonetheless free from all formal and substantial error. Each time that Newman treated of the biblical question, he somehow separated the Word, the Scriptures' divine element, from its human formulation. From his Catholic period come many allusions to the "passing remarks" (*obiter dicta*) found in the Scriptures. As late as 1884 Newman proposed the view that the Word was morally separable from the words of the human authors, insofar as the Word consists of those *portions* of the Bible which treat of faith and morals. Given the *sententia communis* within Roman Catholicism that inspiration is to be distinguished from revelation, theories of limited inspiration were decidedly on the decline at the time of *Providentissimus Deus*. The encyclical shut the lid on what must be seen as a relatively short-lived experiment in Roman Catholic thought.

Despite the implicit endorsement of Franzelin's views during the Pius IX–Leo XIII era, unanimity of thought as to the nature of inspiration was not to be had among Roman Catholic thinkers. To some extent theologians were content with the analysis of the *Deus auctor* formula by the proponents of content inspiration, but exegetes were far from satisfied. Among them, Père Lagrange found that Franzelin's thesis separated the Bible into two parts, one divine, one human. Lagrange held that the Bible was simultaneously divine and human in its origin. Furthermore Lagrange's anaylsis of conciliar statements (Florence, Trent, Vatican I) identified a logical sequence in the exposition of the traditional doctrine—from inspiration to authorship to canonicity, whereas Franzelin and his Jesuit companions had proceeded from authorship to inspiration.

Lagrange developed a theory of verbal inspiration which ascribed the very words of Scripture to a divine influence, though not in the modality of stenographic dictation. In the exposition of his theory, Lagrange drew from the teaching of Thomas Aquinas and Bañez on prophetic inspiration. Aquinas distinguished between prophecy and inspiration, the former being a charism of learning, the latter a charism of communication. The sources which provide material to the author are more or less indifferent. The author might draw from revelation, experience, and tradition in presenting his ideas. God has inspired the Scriptures not as a teaching, but as a record of teaching. Inspiration consists in the divine assistance in the form of an "intellectual enlightenment" (*illuminatio iudicii*) which enables the author to choose certain ideas, to understand and judge them, and to work them into a literary whole. In effect, there is a sort of synergism at work in the composition of the Scriptures. At one and the same time, they are the work of both God and man. Whereas Franzelin had placed the core of inspiration in God's action upon the will of the human author, Lagrange and his school placed the emphasis upon the intellect of the human author.

In the wake of the Modernist crisis, much of Lagrange's work fell under suspicion. The Modernists considered that the Bible was no more God's work than was any other work. Lagrange clearly distanced himself from the inspiration theories of the Modernists, but his theory of verbal inspiration was too "modern" for the reactionary Church of the early twentieth century. His notions on verbal inspiration were quickly laid to rest. A half century later, the theory of verbal inspiration, in somewhat revised form, was resurrected by Pierre Benoit, a French Dominican professor in the École Biblique which Lagrange had founded in Jerusalem.

While Jesuits and Dominicans had been wrestling with the problem of the nature of inspiration, it must not be forgotten that within the manual tradition of Roman Catholic theology, the exposition of the teaching on inspiration was made within the context of the treatise on theological authorities (*De locis theologicis*) rather than within the treatise on prophecy. This shift implied a displacement of emphasis, from the nature of inspiration to the result of inspiration. "The truth" of the Bible became virtually all-important. This "truth" had to be maintained, despite what was being said by scientists, historians—and exegetes.

The Magisterium

It is within this historical perspective that we are to understand the reaffirmation of the doctrine of inspiration by Benedict XV in the encyclical *Spiritus Paraclitus* (1920). Benedict took issue with the theory of plenary inspiration but limited inerrancy, as well as with Franz von Hummelauer's hypothesis of "historical appearances":

> For while conceding that inspiration extends to every phrase—and, indeed, to every single word of Scripture—yet, by endeavoring to distinguish between what they style the primary or religious and secondary or profane element in the Bible, they claim that the effect of inspiration—namely, absolute truth and immunity from error—are to be restricted to that primary or religious element.
> . . . they maintain that precisely as the sacred writers spoke of physical things according to appearance, so, too, while ignorant of the

facts, they narrated them in accordance with general opinion or even on baseless evidence; neither do they tell us the sources whence they derived their knowledge, nor do they make other people's narrative their own . . . (DS 3652–53).

In the face of these reconstructed opinions, Benedict countered with the teaching of Leo XIII: "it would be wholly impious to limit inspiration to certain portions only of Scripture or to concede that the sacred authors themselves could have erred." Benedict was concerned with the consequences of the traditional teaching, but advanced the understanding of the tradition only insofar as he invoked literary forms and the personality of biblical authors. Benedict took refuge in the teaching of Jerome, whose anniversary commemoration was then being celebrated:

If we ask how we are to explain this power and action of God, the principal cause, on the sacred writers we shall find that St. Jerome in no wise differs from the common teaching of the Catholic Church. For he holds that God, through His grace, illumines the writer's mind regarding the particular truth which "in the person of God," he is to set before men; he holds, moreover, that God moves the writer's will—nay even impells it—to write; finally, that God abides with him unceasingly, in unique fashion until his task is accomplished (DS 3651).

Leo XIII's teaching as to plenary inspiration and total inerrancy was cited verbatim in the opening paragraphs of Pius XII's *Divino Afflante Spiritu,* which also made reference to the decree *Dei Filius.* For the rest, Pius' positive teaching on the Scriptures is devoid of any condemnation of mistaken views on inspiration. Traditional doctrine was reechoed when Pius affirmed that "the Sacred Pages, written under the inspiration of the Spirit of God, are of themselves rich in original meaning," but a new element was invoked when Pius taught that:

. . . no one who has a just conception of biblical inspiration will be surprised to find that the sacred writers, like the other ancients, employ certain acts of exposition and narrative, certain idioms especially characteristic of the Semitic languages (known as "approximations"), and certain hyperbolical and even paradoxical expressions designed for the sake of emphasis . . . For just as the substantial Word of God became like to men in all things, "without sin," so the words of God, expressed in human language, became in all things like to human speech, except error. This is that "condescension" of divine Providence which St. John Chrysostom so highly extolled and which he repeatedly asserted to be found in the Sacred Books.

In sum, a correct notion of the divine inspiration of the Scriptures implies an understanding of the humanity of the words in which they are written. This notion was incorporated into "The Divine Inspiration and the Interpretation of Sacred Scripture," Chapter III of Vatican Council II's Dogmatic Constitution *Dei Verbum* in the following manner:

However, since God speaks in sacred Scripture through men in human fashion . . .

In sacred Scripture, therefore, while the truth and holiness of God always remain intact, the marvelous "condescension" of eternal wisdom is clearly shown, "that we may learn the gentle kindness of God, which words cannot express, and how far He has gone in adapting His language with thoughtful concern for our weak human nature." For the words of God, expressed in human language, have been made like human discourse, just as of old the Word of the eternal Father, when he took to Himself the weak flesh of humanity, became like other men (*Dei Verbum*, 12, 13).

Paragraphs 12 and 13 reflect on the various modes of human discourse employed in the Scriptures (i.e., its various literary forms) and note that it is because of divine Providence that God has chosen to reveal himself to us. In a sense, therefore, inspiration is akin to the mystery of the Incarnation, whose ultimate meaning is the personal self-revelation of God in human form. Nonetheless it is in the first of the three paragraphs of *Dei Verbum*'s chapter on Inspiration that we find its classic statement on inspiration:

Those divinely revealed realities which are contained and presented in sacred Scripture have been committed to writing under the inspiration of the Holy Spirit. Holy Mother Church, relying on the belief of the apostles, holds that the books of both the Old and New Testament in their entirety, with all their parts, are sacred and canonical because, having been written under the inspiration of the Holy Spirit they have God as their author and have been handed on as such to the Church herself. In composing the sacred books, God chose men and while employed by Him they made use of their powers and abilities, so that with Him acting in them and through them (*Ipso in illis et per illos agente*), they, as true authors (*ut veri auctores*), consigned to writing everything and only those things which He wanted.

Therefore, since everything asserted by the inspired authors or sacred writers must be held to be asserted by the Holy Spirit, it follows that the books of Scripture must be acknowledged as teaching firmly, faithfully, and without error that truth which God wanted put into the sacred writings for the sake of our salvation (*veritatem, quam Deus nostrae salutis causa Litteris Sacris consignari voluit*). Therefore "all Scripture is inspired by God and useful for teaching, for reproving, for correcting, for instruction in justice; that the man of God may be perfect, equipped for every good work" (*Dei Verbum*, 11).

Extended commentary on this text would lead us far afield. Accordingly, we will make only five brief remarks. (1) The text is traditional in its formulation. It makes reference to *Dei Filius, Providentissimus Deus,* and *Divino Afflante Spiritu.* The traditional inspiration-authorship-canonicity relationship has been maintained. (2) The notion of inspiration is specifically related to the New Testament understanding of inspiration. The text concludes with a verbatim citation of 2 Timothy 3:16–17 in the Greek text. It makes an additional textual reference to 2 Timothy 3 as well as to John

20:31; 2 Peter 1:19–21; 3:15–16. Footnoted references to Hebrews 1:1; 4:7 ("in") and 2 Samuel 23:2; Matthew 1:22, *passim* ("through") are given for purposes of clarifying the formula, "with Him acting in them and through them." (3) The text affirms the traditional *Deus auctor* formula, all the while urging that the sacred writers are true authors in the proper sense of that term. (4) The text assiduously avoids the language of the schools. We find no reference to the easily misunderstood notion of "dictation," nor is there any explicit reference to instrumental causality. Furthermore, no attempt is made to enter into the psyche (intellect and will) of the sacred writers. (5) The text presents the truth of the Scriptures in a positive manner, and as a consequence of the doctrine of inspiration. It affirms that the truth of the Scriptures is oriented toward salvation. The Fathers of the Council chose the expression "for the sake of our salvation" instead of an earlier draft's "salvific truth" (*veritatem salutarem*) lest the conciliar text seem to espouse a doctrine of limited inspiration. Two of the Council Fathers (Fidel García Martínez, of Spain, and John F. Whealon, of the U.S.) had argued for a conciliar statement on inerrancy, but other Fathers (especially Franz Koenig of Austria, Paul-Émile Leger of Canada, Lorenz Jaeger of Germany, and Jean-Julien Weber of France) expressed their doubts as to whether it should be stated without qualification that Scripture contains no error. The pastoral statement of *Dei Verbum,* 11, is the result of the discussion.

The Notion of Biblical Inspiration

In some senses *Dei Verbum*'s affirmation of inspiration takes us back to where the discussion began—namely, to the statements contained in the New Testament itself. It has moved from the nineteenth and twentieth centuries' emphasis on a corollary (inerrancy) to the heart of the matter: inspiration itself. It has avoided narrow philosophical definitions of truth and has brought us back to the context of salvation history. It espouses an incarnational approach to the understanding of inspiration which takes the human element seriously, and does not relegate it to the periphery in order thereby to emphasize the divine aspects of inspiration. We are left with a *fundamentum* which somehow recalls one of the earliest affirmations in the New Testament Scriptures, 1 Thessalonians 2:13. Somehow the word of God is conveyed in the words of men. The Scriptures are both human and divine.

At bottom, the weakness of conventional Catholic inspiration theory can be described as a form of "latent docetism." This weakness has been coupled with a naïve understanding of the Scriptures as literary works—that is, the supposition that each book of Scripture was the work of a single inspired writer. To these one must add a view of Scripture which considered the Scripture as a source of doctrine rather than as a witness to faith, and a narrow conception of truth—that is, propositions which are adequate to express the reality to which they relate. The result of these converging factors was a doctrine of inspiration characterized by ready formulas and clear categories, but a doctrine which was inadequate for the complexities and ambiguities of the Scriptures that God has entrusted to his Church, a gift whose acceptance by the Church is attested in the affirmation of the canonicity of the Scriptures.

To speak of God's gifts to his Church is to speak of a reality of a charismatic order. The language of charism is biblical (specifically, Pauline) and it is to the Bible itself that we must have recourse if we are to have an adequate notion of biblical inspiration. Although the language of charism has generally not been used in magisterial pronouncements on inspiration, it has occasionally appeared in some of the theological reflection on biblical inspiration. From a biblical standpoint, charism seems a most adequate category in which to consider the reality of inspiration, since the core of the Pauline teaching on charisms stresses the sources of the charism and the purpose for which the charisms are to be employed. On the one hand, Paul affirms that the charisms are the free gift of the Spirit of God to individuals within the Church. On the other hand, he maintains that the charisms are given for the upbuilding of the Church. It is the constant tradition of the Church that the doctrine of inspiration means that the Scriptures have been produced by God through the Holy Spirit for the benefit of the Church to which they have been entrusted. This constant affirmation of the ecclesial tradition can only mean that inspiration is a charism.

It goes without saying that Paul did not classify the inspiration of the Scriptures among the charisms. With the exception of his own writings, the Scriptures of the New Testament did not yet exist when he set forth some of his thought on charisms in the first letter to the Corinthians (1 Cor 12–14). However, he does suggest that his listing of the charisms (Rom 12; 1 Cor 12; cf. Eph 4) is not exhaustive. In any event, charism is a category which Paul has developed in order to reflect on the Spirit-filled experience of the Church; it is not an *a priori* category to which the experiences of his churches must be made conformable. The experience of the role of the Scriptures within the Church, together with the universal tradition of the Church that the Scriptures proceed from the Holy Spirit, should lead to the conclusion that inspiration is a reality of the charismatic order.

If the apostle notes that the source of the charism and its use are of major moment in the understanding of the charisms, he also stresses that there is a diversity of charisms within the Church. The fact of this diversity must lead the biblical scholar, no less than the systematic theologian, to seek to identify the specificity of the charism of inspiration. In the effort to identify the specific characteristics of the charism of inspiration, one must certainly note that there is some similarity between the charism of inspiration and the charisms of apostolicity and prophecy of which Paul writes in his letters, and of which other New Testament authors make mention as well.

Prophecy is the charism most commonly identified as such in the New Testament writings. Its essence lies in the prophet's role of "speaking for." The prophet is one who speaks the word of the Lord. In view of the development of the doctrine on inspiration, it must not be overlooked that the author of 1 Peter 2 spoke forcefully of the nature of prophecy as he reflected on the Scriptures and the Holy Spirit. Apostolicity is explicitly listed as first among the charisms in 1 Corinthians 12:28 and appears first among the charisms cited by the author of the letter to the Ephesians (Eph 4:11). The charism of apostolicity is not specifically related to the Lucan notion of the "Twelve Apostles." Rather, as a charism distinct from prophecy as well as from the charisms of evangelization and teaching (Eph 4:11), apostolicity has to do with the foundation of churches. The apostle is one who establishes churches through his preaching of the word of God; apostolicity is the charism of founding a church.

When now we reflect on the Scriptures it is clear that they and the Church are mutually constitutive. The Scriptures and the Church so belong to one another that they are partially constitutive of one another. The charism of inspiration has to do with this partial constitution of the Church. It is the gift whereby the Spirit partially constitutes the Church in providing for the Church written documents that attest to its foundational faith. Inspiration can then be paired with apostolicity insofar as both are foundational charisms. The one has to do with the founding of individual churches in New Testament times; the other has to do with the essential constitution of the Greater Church of post-New Testament times. In another sense, inspiration can be paired with the charism of prophecy insofar as each is a charism of the communication of the word of God. The one has to do with the spoken word (and the "speaking word" of the prophetic gesture); the other has to do with the written word. In sum, inspiration is the charism of the written communication of the word of God as a constitutive element of the Church.

To consider biblical inspiration as a specific charism within the total experience of the Church is to warrant the application of the Pauline criteria for the discernment of charisms to the phenomenon of inspiration. Among the criteria of discernment urged by Paul is the use to which the charisms are put. He notes that some of the charisms (for example, speaking in tongues) are profitable for the Church only when paired with another charism (for example, the interpretation of tongues). He also notes that a charismatic experience is not necessarily an ecstatic experience; the charism is not necessarily manifest in an awesome phenomenon. There are, for example, the charisms of helping and administration. The fact that one has the charism of administration does not mean that the administrator has been transported to a seventh heaven, there to learn new methods of administration. Of itself a charism need not imply an extraordinary experience; neither does it imply that the charismatic receive a new revelation.

This affirmation is important for discerning the true nature of the charism of biblical inspiration. The charism no more implies that the author's natural literary talents (and deficiencies) are replaced than does the charism of administration imply that one's natural administrative qualities have been replaced. Neither does the charism of inspiration imply that the sacred author

345

receive a new revelation. In this respect a brief reflection on the charism of prophecy is particularly enlightening.

In 1 Corinthians 14, Paul carefully distinguishes the charism of prophecy from the gift of revelation (vv. 6, 20–21). He acknowledges that he himself has the charism of prophecy (1 Cor 13:2; 14:6), yet he also passes along to the Church that which he has received (1 Cor 11:23; 15:3). Thus there is no radical incompatibility between prophecy and tradition. The prophet can proclaim tradition. Indeed it is clear that the prophets of both Old and New Testaments have spoken the traditional faith. Paul's use of the technical terms "receive" and "deliver" in 1 Corinthians 11:23 and 15:3 shows that his learning experience with respect to the faith tradition is at least partially an ordinary learning experience. Moreover, Paul's manner of expressing the tradition of the Institution of the Eucharist in 1 Corinthians 11:24–25 is different from that of the Synoptic tradition (Matt 26:26–29; Mark 14:22–25; Luke 22:14–20) and bears some impress of Paul's own formulation. If one may argue from the particular to the general, one can argue from Paul's case to the conclusion that the charism of prophecy replaces neither the prophet's human abilities to acquire knowledge nor the peculiarities of his own articulation of the faith. Something similar must be said with respect to the charism of inspiration. Inspiration does not imply that an inspired writer has special sources of knowledge, nor does it mean that his ordinary cognitive functions have somehow been replaced. Neither does inspiration mean that the literary abilities of the inspired author have been made redundant.

At this juncture it would be easy to concentrate one's attention upon what it means to be an "inspired writer." One could focus upon Luís Alonso-Schökel's model of the "inspired literary process" or Donald Milavec's model of "boundary control." Yet such emphasis would seem to be misplaced at this moment in our exposition. The traditional formulation of biblical inspiration is that *the Scriptures are inspired*. It is obvious that a charism is given to an individual human being; the purpose of the charism of inspiration is the production of the inspired Scriptures. Norbert Lohfink has shown that the proper object of inspiration is the Scriptures themselves. Reflection on the history of the interpretation of the doctrine of inspiration confirms his view. The oldest and most common affirmation is indeed that the Scriptures have been inspired by the Holy Spirit, that God is the author of both the Old and the New Testament. When, and to the extent that theories of limited inspiration were proposed, the theological tradition developed a theory of plenary inspiration with an explicit formulation of the distributive nature of inspiration—"the books of both the Old and the New Testament in their entirety, with all their parts." Concentration on inerrancy as a result of inspiration and the psychological interpretation of inspiration by way of analogy with prophetic inspiration within the Dominican school have led to a concentration on "the inspired writers" in much Roman Catholic theologizing on inspiration. Yet it must be remembered that this is a theological interpretation of a dogmatic tradition that speaks of the inspiration of the Scriptures. The Scriptures themselves are the primary and proper object of biblical inspiration.

This affirmation is important since it implies that inspiration is a charism given to the Church for the production of the documentary witness to its faith which we identify as the Bible. With Karl Rahner, I would agree that the charism of inspiration is enjoyed by all those who have contributed to the production of the Scriptures as literary works. Inspiration is a social and ecclesial phenomenon; it is surely not limited to that restricted number of individuals who penned the final draft of each of the twenty-seven books in the New Testament (or the seventy-two in the entire Bible). Indeed, from an exegetical point of view it would be rather strange to attribute the charism of inspiration to the final redactor of the Fourth Gospel, but not to the Beloved Disciple or the one(s) largely responsible for putting into writing his faith witness. Insofar as many have contributed to the New Testament writings in different ways, it is necessary to affirm that there are varieties of expression of the charism of inspiration.

Some Thomists speak of degrees of inspiration, but their language is misleading. It implies that there exists a paradigm of inspiration. Yet a paradigm of inspiration seems no more to have existed than did paradigms of apostolicity, prophecy, and administration. With respect to its concrete manifestation, neither the charism of prophecy nor that of inspiration is a univocal concept. Just as there was (and is) a variety of prophecy, so there was a variety of inspiration. Nonetheless, the charism of inspiration has been given only insofar as those who are inspired have contributed to the written Scriptures. One should not seek to force precision in these matters. All too often precise formulas are far removed from the vital realities to which they refer. With respect to biblical inspiration, for example, one must be content with the general affirmation that the charism of inspiration was enjoyed by various individuals within the churches to the extent that they contributed to the formation of the Scriptures as the written legacy of the Church. It is hardly necessary to affirm that the originator of the proverb on walking by day and by night (John 11:9–10) was an "inspired author," yet it is necessary to consider that the final redactor of the Fourth Gospel enjoyed the charism of inspiration. Nonetheless, the greatest contributor to the written Gospel of John is the anonymous individual known as the "evangelist." Certainly he was endowed with the charism of inspiration in a fashion different from the final redactor and the author of the Signs Source. Precision should not be sought where precision is not to be had. "Inspired author" is an epithet attributable to those who have contributed to the written Scriptures of the Church, insofar as they have truly and effectively contributed to them.

Reflection on the incarnation, to which *Dei Verbum*, 13, makes explicit reference, can also be of help in an attempt to understand the doctrine of inspiration. One cannot divide Jesus of Nazareth into a divine part and a human part. Jesus of Nazareth is one who is simultaneously and uniquely human and divine. In him divinity is present in human fashion. Similarly one

347

cannot divide the Scriptures into a divine and a human part. They are simultaneously and uniquely divine and human. Because they are divine we approach them in faith; because they are human we approach them with the methods of historical and literary criticism.

The corollary of this reflection must necessarily be that the Scriptures are totally human, in a way analogous to the manner in which Jesus was totally human. Accordingly, when one reflects on the manner in which each of the "inspired authors" contributes to the production of the written Scriptures, one should accept the fact that it is the human process of producing the scriptural documents that is the immediate manifestation of the charism of biblical inspiration. To the extent that those involved in the process of writing the Scriptures were committed to this task in mind and will, one should affirm that the charism of inspiration touches upon the volitional and intellectual processes which contribute to the production of a composite literature as the work of human beings. Furthermore, the literature of humankind, and certainly the literature included in the canonical Scriptures, includes various forms of human communication. Not all of them have the imparting of information as their primary purpose. With the linguists we can distinguish among three principal dialogical functions of language: the informative, the experiential, and the appellative. Human language serves to inform, to express, and to impress. In fact, all three of these functions interrelate in the normal course of human communication, both oral and written. Since the Scriptures are the written communication of the word of God in human fashion, it is to be expected that all three linguistic functions are to be found in the pages of the New Testament. Moreover, one might take note of the fact that even within a given language system there are different kinds of language. Popular language is different from technical language, and both are different from literary (including poetic) language. The same person will use popular language, technical language, and literary language as the occasion warrants. This was true of those inspired persons who contributed to the production of the written Scriptures no less than it is true of people who speak and write in our times.

This means that to appreciate the message of the Scriptures one must understand the meaning of the human text, since the divine message is conveyed in and by means of the human text. Hence a call for the use of linguistic analysis and the examination of literary forms is not far removed from the horizon of a discussion on biblical inspiration. However, the believer who approaches the Scriptures as documents that attest to the foundational faith of the Church because of his or her belief that the Scriptures were inspired will always remember that it is the Scriptures themselves that are inspired. Each individual verse, chapter, or book is inspired as part of the whole. While it is true to say that God has created my arm—and he has done so by means of the common biological process—it is erroneous to believe that God creates human arms. He has created human beings; he has created arms as constitutive parts of the *humanum*. In an analogous fashion, it cannot be said that God has inspired the verses of the Scriptures; God has inspired the verses of Scripture (*pasa graphē*) insofar as they are constitutive parts of the whole body of Scripture, itself a constitutive element of the Church.

For the person of Christian faith, the first consequence of the doctrine of inspiration is that the Scriptures are the "word of God." The expression, though traditional, is misleading. All too readily it conveys the impression that the Scriptures contain the stenographic transcription of a divine message, which then has a timelessness and a freedom from the ordinary constraints of human language which no other body of human literature enjoys or is subject to. Such a view smacks of docetism. It is inconsistent with the reality of the constitution of the New Testament itself. Moreover, it is hardly required by the tradition of the Church. Quite to the contrary, in fact. In what sense, then, can the Scriptures of Old and New Testament be called the word of God?

One must begin with the realization that "word of God" is a biblical concept. Our English expression renders the *logos tou theou* of the Septuagint and the New Testament as well as the Hebrew phrase *dabar Yahweh*. *Dabar* is not simply equatable with the notion of "word," in the sense of spoken or written words. Such a concept is somewhat inspired by Hellenistic philosophy. The Hebrew *dabar* (and, to a lesser degree, the Greek *logos* as well) bears the connotation of "reality." Occasionally the most appropriate translation of *dabar* is "event." Perhaps one might say that the expression "word of God" conveys an ambivalent notion. Ultimately the expression simply indicates God's self-communication.

Perhaps it is well to distinguish among seven different but interrelated realities to which the expression "word of God" can be appropriately attributed. First, the expression is applicable to all of God's communication with human beings, in its various forms and modalities. Secondly, "word of God" is applicable to the events of salvation history, the "speaking words" of God. Thirdly, "word of God" is applicable to the spoken words of the prophets (including Jesus) upon whom the Spirit rests. Fourthly, "Word of God" is preeminently applicable to Jesus Christ, the Incarnate One, as the fullness of God's self-communication with humans. Fifthly, "word of God" is a description of the living word of Christian proclamation. Sixthly, "the word of God" is a way of speaking about God's message to humankind. Finally, the "word of God" is the traditional designation of the written words contained in the Scripture of the Old and New Testament.

The words of the New Testament are the words of humans about the word of God. They are a human attestation to the word of God, be that the Word Incarnate or the message. The human words of the Scripture are a manifestation of the phenomenon of inspiration but they do not have the ultimacy of the Word of God, nor even of the "very words of God," were it somehow possible for God to communicate with us in this fashion. All human language is a social phenomenon; it is necessarily bound to a time and a culture. Moreover all human language embodies conventional symbols; there is a distance between the reality to which the symbol points and the symbol itself. If there is a distance between human words and the human experience to which these words, always inadequately, point, there is certainly a distance between human words and the divine-human experience to which they point with an innate inadequacy. The words of Scripture point to the word of God, but they cannot be simply equated with the word of God.

A further consequence of the reality of biblical inspiration is that the Scriptures teach "firmly, faithfully, and without error that truth which God wanted put into the sacred writings for the sake of our salvation." To understand this affirmation properly, one should begin with the realization that the Scriptures contain the written record of God's communication with humans. At the very least, this means that the Scriptures are the record in human words of God's positive communication with human beings. The doctrine of the inerrancy of the Scriptures is one that has been formulated in support of the positive doctrine that God effectively communicates with humans through the words of the Scriptures. The doctrine of the inerrancy of the Scriptures is a corollary of the doctrine of inspiration. Inerrancy is a result of inspiration, not a "fact" from which a notion of inspiration can be inferred or deduced. Consequently, any exposition of the notion of inerrancy must be one which maintains a primary focus upon the truthful communication of God to humans by means of the Scriptures.

Taken positively, the affirmation also means that the Scriptures are a human record. Phenomenologically, they are a communication from men to their fellow human beings. If the Scriptures are a human communication, they are a communication in human words. The words of Scripture have all the properties of human words, and all the liabilities as well. One of the qualities of human language is that the connotation of human language is historically and culturally conditioned. Words whose meaning does not relate to the historical and cultural circumstances of those who speak and write them are not an effective means of human communication. This means that the words of Scripture have a limited capacity to convey meaning. The words of a first-century "author" cannot principally have a twentieth-century meaning; otherwise, they would be virtually meaningless for a first-century readership. Important elements of the sociology of knowledge and the sociology of language must be brought to bear upon our understanding of biblical inerrancy. Ultimately they lead to the conclusion that in terms of human communication the real opposite of truth is deceit, not error. A radical freedom from error is not, and cannot be, a quality of human communication. Indeed, Jesus himself was subject to the historical and cultural limitations of a first-century Palestinian existence.

This is to suggest that one must ask Pilate's question (John 18:23a) when one attempts to expatiate on the notion of biblical inspiration. The Bible's own claim to truthfulness is somewhat different from the Hellenistic philosopher's understanding of truth. In no passage of the Old or New Testament is the claim made that the biblical books are free from error. Moreover, the Old Testament notion of *'emeth* ("truth") is not the same as the Hellenistic notion of *alētheia*. *'Emeth* implies fidelity, reliability, trustworthiness, rather than absolute "truth." Applied to God and characteristic of his covenant disposition, *'emeth* implies not so much that God's word is true as it implies that God is true to his word. In this regard Oswald Loretz has stated that:

> . . . the "truth" of God is primarily bound up with his faithfulness. Yahweh is the covenant God who not only demands faithfulness from his people but promises to be faithful himself as well. Even when the idea that is uppermost is that God's words are true, still no passage can be pointed to which asserts of Scripture itself that as the word of God it cannot contain any error. Such a line of thought must necessarily have been quite foreign to the Hebrew tradition, which spoke in the first instance of God's covenant faithfulness (*The Truth of the Bible,* pp. 83–84).

Although Loretz' affirmation is immediately pertinent to the Old Testament, we must not overlook the fact that Jesus himself was a Semite. The Greek of the New Testament authors is a biblical Greek that reflects the Semitic idiom and mentality. In effect, the biblical (OT and NT) notion of *alētheia,* "truth," largely reflects the traditional biblical notion of *'emeth,* "covenant fidelity."

This does not mean that the Scriptures of Old and New Testaments are full of errors. What it does mean is that the truth of the Scriptures is intimately bound up with God's covenantal relationship with humankind. Through the Scriptures God expresses his fidelity to his people. With respect to salvation he will not lead his people astray. Rather, he manifests his truth to them for the sake of their salvation. In this sense, the Bible is a privileged witness to and expression of the truth of God. God's truth is incompatible with deceit and lying.

Does this mean that the systematic theologian has overstepped the bounds of legitimate inquiry if he or she should ask whether the Scriptures of the Old and New Testament are "truthful" in the philosophical sense of the term? Yes, and no. Yes, in the sense that the systematic theologian is investigating a claim made neither by the Bible itself nor by Church dogma. No, in the sense that it is useful to reflect on the relationship between the biblical expression of Christian faith and the philosophical notion of truth—especially insofar as truth is one, and all truth ultimately derives from God.

When the theologian proceeds from an examination of the applicability of the philosophical notion of truth to the traditional doctrine of inspiration, he or she must begin with at least one epistemological presupposition and one statement of fact. The presupposition—an axiom, in fact—is that all language is somewhat inadequate to the reality to which it points. The inadequacy of biblical language is a philosophical given. The statement of fact is that the books of the Old and New Testament record historical and scientific errors.

The theologian must also take into account the fact that one cannot even begin to consider the (philosophical) "truth" of a document unless one takes into account its literary form, the function of its language, and the level of its language. To take a statement out of its context is to pervert the meaning of that statement. Very often there is nothing less true than the superficial truth of a statement. Thus the theologian must inquire into the meaning of the language of Scripture before he or she makes a judgment as to whether or not it is "true."

In the inquiry into the "truth" of the Scriptures, the systematic theologian should avoid falling into that trap which considers the Bible principally as a source of doctrine, and its truth reducible to teaching in propositional form. Moreover, the dogmatician should surely take into consideration the fact that one can legitimately predicate "truth" only of an affirmation. An examination of the text of the Scriptures surely indicates that much contained therein does not belong to the order of affirmation. One may not reduce the function of scriptural language to the sole function of conveying information. The words of Scripture sometimes inform; more often they express and/or impress. Finally, the systematician must consider that the "truth" of the Bible is a property of the entire Bible. The affirmation prompts a double reflection. First of all, while affirming plenary inspiration, one should also affirm that the truth of the Bible is the truth that leads to salvation. Biblical teaching is of a truth unto salvation; it is not the teaching of every manner of truth. Secondly, an appreciation of the truth of the Bible can be had only upon consideration of the Bible in its entirety. Truth is a property of the composite whole. Often a limited expression of or approximation to the "truth" in a philosophical sense is partially "corrected" by a later text or by the incorporation of the limited text within the entire body of the Scriptures. In the words of Loretz, "each individual 'intellectual' and 'historical' truth contained in the Bible is, viewed in the context of sacred Scripture as a whole, connected with God's faithfulness to his people, and is directed towards its fulfillment, the historical 'making good' of his word by God, which will bring history to its close." Finally, it must be said that in no way ought the Bible to be taken as a handbook of physical or historical science. By virtue of the charism of inspiration, the Bible is what it is and only what it is: the human record of a community's faith in the word of God.

Although it cannot be said that the words of the Bible are equatable *simpliciter* with the words of God, there is a further corollary which derives from the two corollaries of the doctrine of inspiration that have already been considered. Because the Scriptures are "the word of God" and teach truth unto salvation, the Bible is not an inert witness to the past; it is a living witness for the present. Although inspiration is a foundational charism, having to do with the essential constitution of the people of God, there is a sense in which the inspiration of the Scriptures is never complete, since the Church is ever in process of being constituted by the Spirit of the living God.

This analogous understanding of biblical inspiration is a dimension of inspiration, adequately considered, that ought not to be overlooked. Some describe this aspect of inspiration as inspiration in an active sense. That it should not be neglected is evident from much that has already been written. Accordingly we can indicate some of the more important considerations which arise from the notion of the active inspiration of the Scriptures.

First of all, the text of 2 Timothy 3:16 affirms that the inspired Scriptures are "profitable for teaching, for reproof, for correction, and for training in righteousness." Although this text specifically refers to the inspiration of the Old Testament Scriptures, it is the clearest New Testament affirmation on the nature of biblical inspiration and has served as the linchpin of the Church's doctrine on biblical inspiration—that is, on the inspiration of the entire Bible, both Old and New Testaments. The text of 2 Timothy clearly affirms that the inspiration of the Scriptures has as its purpose their usefulness to the Church. This usefulness is specified in terms of the "teaching ministry" of the Church.

Beyond the words of 2 Timothy, we find that the Fathers of the Church in times past and the documents of the Magisterium in a more recent present affirm that inspiration means not only that the Scriptures have been confided to the Church as a part of its patrimony, but also that they have been given to the Church for the benefit of the Church's membership. Typical of this understanding of inspiration is the affirmation of Vatican Council II to the effect that the divinely inspired Scriptures teach "firmly, faithfully, and without error that truth which God wanted . . . for the sake of our salvation." In a sense, the inspiration of the Scriptures will not have achieved its divinely intended purpose until our salvation is accomplished.

Secondly, and from another point of view, the notion of charism includes some suggestion as to the use to which the charism will be put. Each charism is a gift of God to his Church through the working of the Holy Spirit. The ecclesial dimension is integral to an adequate understanding of the notion of charism. The ecclesial use of the Scriptures cannot be radically dissociated from the notion of the charism of inspiration. When we consider the ecclesial use of the Scriptures by the Church, we find that their existence is not only an objectifiable property—almost in the sense of a *nota theologica* —of the Church of the past, but that the proclamation of the Scriptures characterizes the Church at the present moment in the history of salvation. The Church, like God to whom it gives witness, is a living Church. It is in the eschatological process of coming into existence. Insofar as the specificity of the charism of inspiration relates to the constitution of the Church as Church, it would seem that a fully developed notion of the charism of inspiration would include the idea that even now the Church is in the process of being constituted by the word of God in and through the Scriptures.

Finally, one can draw some implications as to the active nature of inspiration from the biblical notion of the word of God. From the historical point of view, it is clear that the Scriptures themselves give evidence of a tendency to actualize the word of God. The word of God is never simply a past revelation. In cult, the word of God was "remembered" so as to be present and active to the community. In both Old and New Testaments a literary expression of the "word of God"—written, for example, by the Jahwistic author of the patriarchal narrative or by the evangelist Mark in his story of Jesus, has been "updated" and actualized, for example, by the priestly redactor of Genesis or the evangelist Matthew. For Paul, the "word of the Lord" was no mere historical reminiscence; it was the bearer of an authoritative challenge for his communities at Thessalonica and Corinth.

From a systematic point of view, one must note that the "word of God" is a powerful word. The first page of the Bible speaks of the dynamic power of the creative word of God. God's word, once spoken, is a powerful word. Though attested to in somewhat static form by the written words of Scripture, the word of God remains ever a dynamic and powerful word. It becomes effective as God's word to his family only when it enters into the hearts of his children, allowing them to turn to him as a kind and condescending Father, who speaks only that we might hear.

It is because they desire to hear the word of God more clearly that men and women of Christian faith have chosen to analyze the Scriptures by means of a historical-critical methodology. For the believer, the use of this methodology is an expression of the faith conviction that in the Scriptures of the New Testament we have received the word of God in the form of the words of men.

SELECT BIBLIOGRAPHY

Achtemeier, Paul John. *The Inspiration of Scripture.* Philadelphia: Westminster, 1980.

Alonso-Schökel, Luís. "Inspiration." In *Sacramentum Mundi,* vol. III. Ed. by K. Rahner, et al. New York: Herder & Herder, 1968, 145–51.

———. "The Psychology of Inspiration." In *The Bible in its Literary Milieu. Contemporary Essays.* Ed. by V. L. Tollers and J. R. Meier. Grand Rapids: Eerdmans, 1979, 24–56.

Bea, Augustin. "Deus Auctor Sacrae Scripturae. Herkunft und Bedeutung der Formel." *Angelicum,* 20 (1943), 16–31.

Benoit, Pierre. *Inspiration and the Bible.* London: Sheed & Ward, 1965.

———. "Inspiration and Revelation." In *The Human Reality of Sacred Scripture. Concilium,* 10. Glen Rock: Paulist, 1964.

Brown, Raymond E. *The Sensus Plenior of Sacred Scripture.* Baltimore: St. Mary's University, 1955.

Burtchaell, James Tunstead. *Catholic Theories of Biblical Inspiration Since 1810: A Review and Critique.* Cambridge: University Press, 1969.

Cassem, N. H. "Inerrancy After 70 years: The Transition to Saving Truth." *Science et esprit,* 22 (1970), 189–202.

Geisler, Norman L. "The Concept of Truth in the Inerrancy Debate." *Bibliotheca Sacra,* 137 (1980), 327–39.

Harris, R. Laird. *Inspiration and Canonicity of the Bible. Contemporary Evangelical Perspectives.* Rev. ed., Grand Rapids: Zondervan, 1969.

Hoffman, Thomas A. "Inspiration, Normativeness, Canonicity, and the Unique Sacred Character of the Bible." *Catholic Biblical Quarterly,* 44 (1982), 447–69.

House, H. Wayne. "Biblical Inspiration in 2 Timothy 3:16." *Bibliotheca Sacra,* 137 (1980), 54–63.

Kantzer, K. S. "Evangelicals and the Inerrancy Question." *Christianity Today,* 22 (1978), 900–5.

Lohfink, Norbert. "Über die Irrtumslosigkeit und die Einheit der Schrift," *Stimmen der Zeit,* 174 (1963–64), 161–81. ["The Inerrancy and the Unity of Scriptures." *Theology Digest,* 13 (1965) 185–92.]

Loretz, Oswald. *The Truth of the Bible.* New York: Herder & Herder, 1968.

MacKenzie, Roderick A. L. "Some Problems in the Field of Inspiration." *Catholic Biblical Quarterly,* 20 (1958), 1–8.

McCarthy, Dennis J. "Personality, Society and Inspiration." *Theological Studies,* 24 (1963), 553–76.

Milavec, Donald A. "The Bible, the Holy Spirit, and Human Powers." *Scottish Journal of Theology,* 29 (1976), 215–35.

Prust, Richard C. "Was Calvin a Biblical Literalist?" *Scottish Journal of Theology,* 20 (1967), 312–28.

Rahner, Karl. *Inspiration in the Bible. Quaestiones Disputatae,* 1. 2nd. ed. New York: Herder & Herder, 1964.

———. "On the Inspiration of the Bible." In *The Bible in a New Age,* ed. by K. L. Klein. London: Sheed & Ward, 1965. 1–15.

Richards, H. J. "The New Look and Inspiration." *Clergy Review,* 47 (1962), 513–26.

Stanley, David. "The Concept of Biblical Inspiration." In *Proceedings of the Thirteenth Annual Convention. Catholic Theological Society of America* (1958), ed. by J. H. Harrington. Yonkers: St. Joseph's Seminary, 1958, 65–89 (see also discussion, pp. 89–95).

Vawter, Bruce. *Biblical Inspiration.* Theological Resources Series. Philadelphia: Westminster, 1972.

ROME AND THE CRITICAL STUDY
OF THE NEW TESTAMENT

Chapter Two's rapid overview of New Testament scholarship since the middle of the nineteenth century focused principally upon German scholarship. A biographical examination of the authors who were cited quickly reveals the fact that most of them were in some way affiliated with the Lutheran confession of Christianity. This is to be expected, since it is the spiritual heirs of Martin Luther who have drawn from his *sola scriptura* their principal source for theologizing. Indeed, in an article written apropos of the encyclical *Providentissimus Deus* (1893), Père Lagrange noted that even though Roman Catholic scholars of English-language and French-language expression had no reason for saying *mea culpa* before non-Catholic scholars, honesty required recognition of the technical superiority of non-Catholic scholars, especially the Germans, in matters of biblical scholarship.

The fact of the matter is that most of the major advances—but of course not everything new and different should be considered an "advance" in the positive sense of the term—in New Testament scholarship during the era of historical-critical scholarship have occurred through the efforts of German Lutheran scholars. As a result, Roman Catholic scholarship has been in a position of dependence upon or reaction to the work done in Germany. As the positions advanced by the critical scholars became ever more diffused, it became clear to Roman Catholics that the official organs of Roman Catholicism would react both to the newer methodologies and to the positions espoused as a result of the use of these methodologies. The Magisterium of the Church had necessarily to be engaged in dialogue with biblical scholar-

356

ship, since it had long considered the Scriptures of both Testaments as primary among the sources of revelation.

Each of the churches has had to come to grips with the struggle between the insights into the New Testament that have arisen from the systematic use of the historical-critical method and the traditional formulation of its faith. The tension was often painful. In nineteenth-century Lutheran Germany, David Friedrich Strauss was removed from his teaching post and Julius Wellhausen was forced to resign because of the position which they, as philosophers and historians, had espoused with regard to the interpretation of the Bible. In fact, the story of the conflict between modern scholarship and traditional tenets is one in which the struggle of any faith community can serve as a paradigm. In this regard, the struggle that took place in Roman Catholicism is paradigmatic. Because it is so relatively easy to document, the story of a church coming to terms with historical-critical scholarship may serve as a useful example of a broader phenomenon.

As early as 1864, Pope Pius IX (1846–78) condemned the proposition that "the prophecies and miracles set forth in the narration of the sacred Scriptures are poetical fictions; the mysteries of the Christian faith are the outcome of philosophical reflections; in the books of both Testaments mythical tales are contained; Jesus Christ Himself is a mythical fiction." This proposition, the seventh in a list of eighty, was among those included in the syllabus of errors condemned by Pius in 1864. The same Pio Nono convoked the ill-fated First Vatican Council whose grand project of a comprehensive statement of ecclesiology in view of the situation then confronting the Church was cut short by the Franco-Prussian War. Nevertheless Vatican Council I (1869–70) did issue a Dogmatic Constitution concerning the Catholic Faith, *Dei Filius* (April 24, 1870). The second chapter of this document, "Revelation," reiterated the Council of Trent's statement on the canonical books of the Old and New Testaments. Vatican Council I went beyond Trent in affirming that the Church holds these books as sacred and canonical "because, having been written by the inspiration of the Holy Spirit, they have God for their author and have been delivered as such to the Church itself." At issue was the inerrancy of the Scriptures, a doctrine the Church wanted to uphold in view of an increasing number of opinions which saw the Scriptures as being in conflict with scientific and historical truth. To this rationalist point of view, the Council opposed the inspiration and canonicity of the Scriptures. It further noted that the true sense of the Scriptures is that taught by the Church "to whom it belongs to judge of the true sense and interpretation of Holy Scriptures" and urged that no one is allowed to interpret the Scriptures "contrary to this sense, or contrary to the unanimous consent of the Fathers."

I. BIBLICAL STUDIES RENEWED

A major statement on the Scriptures was issued almost a quarter of a century later by Leo XIII (1878–1903), successor to Pius IX in the See of Rome. Throughout Leo's long reign in the papacy, we can trace a burning desire to reorganize Catholic studies. Having initiated many projects with a view to this reorganization, and after having written on a variety of political, social, and economic matters, Leo turned his attention to the study of the Bible. With warm words of praise for Père Lagrange, he published an apostolic letter, *Hierosolymae in coenobio,* under the date of September 17, 1892, which commended and approved the establishment of a Biblical School at St. Stephen's Monastery in Jerusalem by the Order of Preachers. Then, on November 18, 1893, Leo issued the encyclical letter *Providentissimus Deus.* Lagrange praised this document as the *Magna Charta* of Catholic biblical scholarship. His encomium was later reechoed by the Pontifical Biblical Commission. Indeed, some fifty years after its publication, Pope Pius XII could still refer to *Providentissimus Deus* as "the supreme guide in biblical studies."

The tone of the encylical was one of cautious optimism. It underscored the sacred and canonical character of the books of both Testaments, without citing them by name. In response to the issues raised by the physical and historical sciences, the encyclical urged the inspiration and inerrancy of the canonical books. The caution of Leo's pronouncement is to be seen in his frequent references to "the defense" and to "convincing arguments." Thus he wrote:

> Since the divine and infallible Magisterium of the Church rests also on the authority of Holy Scripture, the first thing to be done is to vindicate the trustworthiness of the sacred records, at least as human documents, from which can be clearly proved, as from primitive and authentic testimony, the divinity and mission of Christ our Lord, the institution of a hierarchical Church, and the primacy of Peter and his successors.

Without mentioning by name such Catholic authors as August Rohling (1839–1931), François Lenormant (1837–83), John Henry Cardinal Newman (1801–90), Salvatore di Bartolo (1838–1906), Giovanni Semeria (1867–1931), Jules Didiot (1840–1903), Maurice d'Hulst (1841–96), and Alfred Loisy (whose espousal of the so-called "higher criticism" contributed to what came to be known as the "Biblical Question" among educated nineteenth- and early twentieth-century Catholics, the Pope addressed himself to the issue:

> There has arisen, to the great detriment of religion, an inept method, dignified by the name of "higher criticism," which pretends to judge the

origin, integrity, and authority of each book from internal indications alone. It is clear, on the other hand, that in historical questions, such as the origin and handing down of writings, the witness of history is of primary importance, and historical investigation should be made with the utmost care; and that in this matter internal evidence is seldom of great value, except as confirmation. . . .

After noting that this "inept method" would give rise to disagreement and dissension, and would lead to the elimination from the Scriptures of all prophecy and miracles, the Pope addressed himself to the issue of the physical sciences:

In the second place, we have to contend against those who, making an evil use of physical science, minutely scrutinize the sacred book in order to detect the writers in a mistake, and to take occasion to vilify its contents. Attacks of this kind, bearing as they do on matters of sensible experience, are particularly dangerous to the masses, and also to the young. . . .

This formulation of the second aspect of the problem points to the pastoral concern from which the encyclical arose. In response to the problems of interpretation of the Scriptures arising from the data provided by the positive sciences, the Pope appealed once again to the doctrine of biblical inerrancy. His statement was qualified significantly as to the salvific purpose of biblical inerrancy: "We must remember, first, that the sacred writers, or to speak more accurately, the Holy Spirit 'who spoke by them, did not intend to teach men these things (that is to say, the essential nature of the things of the visible universe), things in no way profitable unto salvation'." The citation of Augustine placed the Pontiff's response to the new issues within the context of the Church's long tradition as well as within the context of its mission, which was to teach the truth which is profitable unto salvation.

Indeed, it is from the perspective of the long and salutary study of the Scriptures within the Church that Leo XIII urged that the study of the Scriptures be given its rightful place in seminaries and academic institutions. He asked that professors of Sacred Scripture be well chosen and well trained for their task. While maintaining a vital link with the past, the Pope thrust the study of the Scriptures among Catholics into the future. Thus, while maintaining the authority of the Vulgate, the Pope urged that the study of the ancient biblical manuscripts and the versions not be neglected. He recommended that the clergy be acquainted with the study of the Oriental languages and the art of criticism. While reiterating that "that is to be considered the true sense of Holy Scripture which has been held and is held by our Holy Mother the Church," the Pope noted that the "studies of non-Catholics, used with prudence, may sometimes be of use to the Catholic student." He further reflected that the ancients expressed the ideas of their own times and that they primarily used ordinary speech. It is no wonder then that the Pope urged the private student to use his hermeneutical skill to advantage to plumb the depths of interpretation of those passages of the Scripture

359

which had not as yet received a certain and definite interpretation within the Church.

With the publication of this encyclical, Leo XIII proclaimed to the whole world his interest in the study of the Scriptures. The Pontiff's attitude was that of profound concern for the "defense" of the sacred writings on the one hand, and a keen desire for the penetration of their meaning on the other. Before a decade had elapsed, Leo XIII again showed his interest in the study of the Scriptures as well as his abiding twofold concern. By an apostolic letter, *Vigilantiae,* under the date of October 30, 1902, Leo established the Pontifical Biblical Commission. The Commission had as its stated duty "to effect that in every possible manner the divine text will find . . . the most thorough interpretation which is demanded by our times, and be shielded not only from every breath of error, but also from every temerarious opinion." As always, defense and interpretation were the hallmarks of Leo's interest in the study of the Scriptures. In order to safeguard the authority of the Scriptures, the Pope noted that "The main point to be attained is that Catholics should not admit the malignant principle of granting more than is due to the opinion of heterodox writers, and of thinking that the true understanding of Scriptures should be sought first of all in the researches at which the erudition of unbelievers has arrived." This main point was not without further qualification to the effect that "the Catholic interpreter may find some assistance in authors outside of the Church, especially in matters of criticism." In order to promote the interpretation of the Scriptures, Leo urged once again the study of philology and the related sciences. He charged the new Commission to "consecrate its most special attention to that part of these studies which properly concerns the explanation of the Scriptures and which opens to the faithful a great source of spiritual profit." He set aside a part of the Vatican Library for the work of the Biblical Commission and encouraged the more affluent members of the Church to make contributions to it. The Pope also announced that the Biblical Commission would be assisted by an international body of consultors. In 1940 an American was named as a consultor to the PBC for the first time. He was Charles J. Callan, O.P. On January 2, 1962, the Archbishop of Chicago, Albert Cardinal Meyer, became the first American member of the Commission itself.

The implementation of the greater part of Leo XIII's program for the renewal of Scriptural studies within the Church fell to his successor, Pius X (1903–14). In a series of apostolic letters, the former patriarch of Venice gave concrete form to the dreams of Leo XIII. *Scripturae Sanctae,* issued on February 23, 1904, set down norms for the conferral by the Pontifical Biblical Commission of advanced academic degrees in Sacred Scripture. On March 27, 1906, there appeared *Quoniam in Re Biblica,* an apostolic letter devoted to the study of Holy Scripture in clerical seminaries. In general the letter ruled that the seminary course in the Scriptures should be spread throughout the period of seminary studies and that it should embrace:

first, the principal ideas concerning inspiration, the canon of the Scripture, the original text and the most important versions, the law of hermeneutics; secondly, the history of both Testaments; and, thirdly, the analysis and exegesis of the different books according to the importance of each.

The principle of selective concentration on the more important books rather than the futile pursuit of the study of each of the books was maintained throughout the document. Applied to the New Testament, this principle required that the Professor of Sacred Scripture "explain briefly and clearly the special characteristics of each of the four Gospels, and the proofs of their authenticity; he will also illustrate the general characteristics of the entire Gospel story, and the doctrine in the Epistles and the other books." The pastoral concern that had motivated Leo XIII's pronouncements on the Scriptures was also reflected in *Quoniam in Re Biblica* insofar as it required that special attention be paid "to those parts of both Testaments which concern Christian faith and morals." In order that the study of the Scriptures within the seminary program reach its intended goal, Pius X once again urged the study of the ancient languages, especially Hebrew, Greek, Syriac, and Arabic. He required those seminaries which were empowered to grant degrees to "devote more time and study to Biblical exegesis, archaeology, geography, chronology, theology and history."

Like his predecessor, Pius also devoted some attention to the selection of professors of Sacred Scripture. In the apostolic letter *Vinea electa* (May 7, 1909), Pius responded to Leo's project that there be set apart, exclusively for Holy Scripture, facilities for full and complete studies, and fulfilled the intention announced in *Scripturae Sanctae* by establishing the Pontifical Biblical Institute in Rome. The new facility, to be devoted to the study of introductory questions, exegesis, archaeology, history, geography, philology, and other disciplines related to the study of the Scriptures, would depend immediately on the Apostolic See itself.

II. THE MODERNIST CRISIS

Nevertheless, the pontificate of Pius X is noted not so much for its forward-thrusting apostolic letters as it is for the Roman reaction to the so-called Modernist crisis. The Modernists generally sought to bring the expression of Roman Catholic belief into a closer relationship with contemporary social, historical, philosophical, and scientific views. Within this perspective, they adopted the critical view of the Bible generally accepted outside of Catholicism. Many of them found encouragement in Leo XIII's two-edged *Providentissimus Deus* and plunged forward with a view of inspiration which permitted them to admit the inerrancy of the religious teaching of the Bible (matters of "faith and morals") while admitting the possibility of error in scientific and historical matters.

It is not possible to group all the Modernists into a single camp as if they

361

shared a single view of Church teaching; indeed, one would not do historical justice to the phenomenon of Modernism within the Church if one were to gather their several ideas on the Bible under a single frame of reference. Thus while Alfred Loisy is generally cited as the typical representative of Modernist views among Roman Catholic biblical scholars, all Modernist views may not be equated with his nor may they be reduced to his. Loisy abandoned his priestly functions in 1906; in 1908 he was excommunicated by Pius X. Between those two dates Pius X issued three documents which represent the clearest expression of the Roman reaction to the Modernist crisis: the decree *Lamentabili* (July 3, 1907), the encyclical *Pascendi dominici gregis* (September 8, 1907), and the *motu proprio* ("of our own free choice") *Praestantia Scripturae Sacrae* (November 18, 1907). With these three documents the cautious optimism that had permeated the writings of Leo XIII and the earlier apostolic letters of Pius X seemed to give way to a radically defensive attitude.

Lamentabili, a general decree, contained a list of some sixty-five propositions which were noted and condemned through the office of the Holy Roman and Universal Inquisition, the predecessor to the present-day Congregation of the Faith. The condemned and proscribed propositions covered a wide variety of topics including Christology, sacramentology, and ecclesiology. A large percentage covered topics related to biblical interpretation: inspiration, the Fourth Gospel, the relationship between Scripture and Church doctrine, the relationship between the Jesus of history and the Christ of faith, etc. The following selection of the condemned propositions will reveal the tenor of the document:

9. Those who believe that God is really the author of the Sacred Scripture display excessive simplicity or ignorance.

12. The exegete, if he wishes to apply himself usefully to Biblical studies, must first of all put aside all preconceived opinions concerning the supernatural origin of the Sacred Scripture, and interpret it not otherwise than other merely human documents.

14. In a great many narrations the evangelists reported not so much things that are true as things which even though false they judged to be more profitable for their readers.

17. The narrations of John are not properly history, but the mystical contemplation of the Gospel; the discourses contained in his Gospel are theological meditations, devoid of historical truth concerning the mystery of salvation.

19. Heterodox exegetes have expressed the true sense of the Scriptures more faithfully than Catholic exegetes.

23. Opposition may and actually does exist between the facts which are narrated in Scripture and the dogmas of the Church which rest on them; so that the critic may reject as false facts which the Church holds as most certain.

30. In all the evangelical texts the name *Son of God* is equivalent only

to *Messiah,* and does not at all signify that Christ is the true and natural Son of God.

34. The critic cannot ascribe to Christ a knowledge circumscribed by no limits except on a hypothesis which cannot be historically conceived and which is repugnant to the moral sense, viz., that Christ as man had the knowledge of God and yet was unwilling to communicate the knowledge of a great many things to His disciples and to posterity.

While the condemnation contained in *Lamentabili* was obviously and intentionally reactionary, its significance should not be overstated. The decree rigorously abstained from condemning historical and biblical criticism as such. It remained on traditional grounds, leaving to the historian and critic his freedom, provided only that he not draw from his historical studies a negation of the teaching of the Church. Moreover, the sixty-five propositions formulated by the Congregation were condemned in the sense in which they were understood to have been held by the Modernists. It was not, however, stated that any single proposition represented the point of view of an individual Modernist. Thus Proposition 34, cited above, was taken almost literally from Loisy but the decree did not expressly attribute it to Loisy.

From the condemnation of any one of the propositions, one cannot infer the acceptability of a contrary statement, as if it were merely necessary to negate the proposition in order to arrive at the truth. The Congregation did not hold that it would be correct to say that "the critic can ascribe to Christ an unlimited knowledge." Catholic theologians have never held that the human knowledge of Jesus could be equated with the knowledge of God himself. Indeed, from the condemnation of any of the propositions cited in the decree one can only infer the acceptability of a contradictory statement. Thus, with respect to Proposition 30, the Congregation did not necessarily propose that in each case the name "Son of God" meant something more than Messiah. For the condemnation to have been issued it was only necessary that in some cases "Son of God" meant something more than "Messiah." Finally, a correct understanding of the decree *Lamentabili* requires that it be taken as a general decree in which all sixty-five propositions were condemned *in globo*. The decree did not specify the degree of condemnation of any single proposition. It is clear that Catholic theologians of the time would discern different theological notes to each of the propositions. Some would have been considered to be in opposition to doctrines which were proximate to the faith, whereas others were opposed only to a commonly held theological opinion or were judged to be "offensive to pious ears."

On September 8, 1907, *Lamentabili* was followed by the encyclical letter *Pascendi dominici gregis,* which reiterated the rejection of the Modernist propositions, albeit in a somewhat different form. The lengthy encyclical introduced its conclusions by defining Modernism as "the synthesis of all heresies." In his letter the Pope addressed himself to the issue of science, history, and philosophy as these related to the Church, its sacraments, and its dogma. With respect to the Scriptures, the papal letter specifically focused upon the nature of inspiration, an evolutionary view of the sacred writings, and the nature of biblical truth.

Pius X explained that a superficial reading of the Modernists would easily lead to the conclusion that they supported the total inspiration of the Scriptures more readily than did those Catholic authors who had appealed to the theory of implicit or tacit quotations. Proponents of this theory (see below) —a topic to which the Pontifical Biblical Commission had addressed itself on February 13, 1905—allowed that the use of a quotation might be inspired without the cited material itself necessarily being inspired or accurate. By contrast, the Modernists held that the entirety of the Scriptures was inspired, but their notion of biblical inspiration was frequently not substantially different from the general notion of poetic inspiration. As all "inspired" poetry derives from God as from its ultimate source, so all "inspired" Scripture comes from God as from its ultimate source. In his encyclical, Pius took issue with this reductionist view of scriptural inspiration.

With respect to the application of hypothetical laws of evolution to the Bible, the Pope noted that the epistles were indeed written to respond to concrete needs, yet he was not willing to accept the notion that one could construct a plan of the development of the needs of the Church and subsequently interpret the books of the Bible according to this developmental view of history. The Pope's rejection of this type of interpretation was, in fact, a rejection of the kind of historical methodology that had been introduced into New Testament scholarship by Ferdinand Christian Baur.

At the same time Pius rejected the view that the Synoptic Gospels had grown gradually from brief accounts by way of addition, interpolation, and theological or allegorical interpretations. Not only did the Pope react negatively to these tenets of the historical-critical methodology, he also took issue with a new notion of truth that was gaining acceptance in some Modernist circles. These circles distinguished the truth and logic of life from the truth and logic of reason. When applied to the Bible, and especially to its prophetic elements, this distinction meant that the truth of the Bible could be maintained, insofar as it was verified by life, even if it was not true according to the usual canons of reason and history. Pius had rejected the distinction, but Roman authorities would again raise the issue of the truth of the Bible more than half a century later, at the time of Vatican Council II (1962–65).

Within weeks of his encyclical letter, Pius X again addressed himself to the Biblical Question by issuing the *motu proprio, Praestantia Sacrae Scripturae* on November 18, 1907. The document related to the decisions of the recently formed Pontifical Biblical Commission whose members enjoyed the "fullest freedom of proposing, examining, and judging all opinions whatsoever." The Commission was to examine both sides of the question before reaching the decisions which were then to be submitted to the Supreme Pontiff for his approval before being promulgated. The purpose of the *motu proprio* was to underscore the authority of the promulgated decisions: "We do now declare," wrote the Pope, "and expressly prescribe, that all are bound in conscience to submit to the decisions of the Biblical Commission, which have been given in the past and which shall be given in the future, in the same way as to the Decrees which appertain to doctrine, issued by the Sacred Congregations and approved by the Sovereign Pontiff."

At this point in history the past decisions of the Biblical Commission were four in number: (1) On the Tacit Quotations contained in Holy Scripture (February 13, 1905); (2) Concerning the Narratives in the Historical Books Which Have Only the Appearances of Being Historical (June 23, 1905); (3) On the Mosaic Authorship of the Pentateuch (June 27, 1906); and (4) On the Author and Historical Truth of the Fourth Gospel (May 29, 1907).

Prior to the issuance of the first response of the Biblical Commission on February 13, 1905, Ferdinand Prat, S.J., and Giuseppi Bonaccorsi had attempted to respond to a question whose resolution became increasingly important as it came to be understood that sources had been used in the composition of nearly all the inspired books. The question concerned the mind of the second author regarding the truth of the sources he used. The response was clear enough when the author cited his source explicitly. The sacred author was bound to cite his source exactly, but the accuracy of his citation was distinct from "the truth of the thing quoted," with which the sacred author might well disagree. When, however, the sacred author did not cite his sources explicitly, the question of the truth of his sources did not admit of so easy a resolution. Prat insisted that it would be possible for a sacred author to cite sources with which he did not agree without making any explicit reference to the fact that he was quoting—though, according to Prat, the disagreement would have to be proved. Bonaccorsi went one step farther than Prat and noted that the sacred author was responsible for the truth of his quotations only when he more or less explicitly stated his agreement with them.

The Biblical Commission formulated its question on this matter, the "implicit quotations" issue, in this general fashion, without explicit reference to any particular Catholic author or authors:

> Whether it is allowable for a Catholic commentator to solve difficulties occurring in certain texts of Holy Scripture, which apparently relate historical facts, by asserting that we have in such texts tacit or implied quotations from documents written by a non-inspired author, and that the inspired author by no means intends to approve of these statements or make them his own, and that these statements cannot, in consequence, be regarded as free from error.

The response to the question thus formulated was direct, but nuanced:

> *Answer:* To this the Commission judged proper to reply: In the negative; except in the case when, subject to the mind and decision of the Church, it can be proved by solid arguments, first, that the sacred writer really does cite another's sayings or writings; and secondly, that he does not intend in so doing, to approve them or make them his own, in such a way that he be rightly considered not to speak in his own name.

Beginning with its third decision, "On the Mosaic Authorship of the Pentateuch," the Commission divided the issue at hand into several questions and responded more simply to each of the pertinent questions. *Affirmative* ("In the affirmative") or *Negative* ("In the negative") was the unqualified response to the question formulated by the Commission. Thus the Fourth Decision, "On the Author and Historical Truth of the Fourth Gospel," was rendered by way of response to three questions bearing respectively on (1) External Evidence for Authenticity; (2) Internal Evidence for Authenticity; and (3) Historical Character. The Commission's articulation of this third question can serve to illustrate its manner of rendering a decision on a disputed topic:

> 3. *Historical Character*—Whether, notwithstanding the practice which has constantly obtained in the whole Church from the first ages, of arguing from the Fourth Gospel as from a strictly historical document and considering moreover the peculiar character of the same Gospel and the author's manifest intention of illustrating and vindicating the divinity of Christ from His own deeds and words, it can be said that the facts narrated in the Fourth Gospel are wholly or in part invented to serve as allegories or doctrinal symbols, and that discourses of our Lord are not properly and truly the discourses of our Lord Himself, but the theological compositions of the writer, albeit they are placed in the mouth of our Lord.

> *Answer:* In the negative.

Subsequent decrees maintained the new format adopted by the Commission as of the third decision—that is, a division of the question and a simple response. The next three decisions were on topics related to the Old Testament, viz., "On the Character of the Book of Isaiah and Its Author" (June 28, 1908); "On the Historical Character of the First Three Chapters of Genesis" (June 30, 1909); and "On the Author, Time of Composition, and Character of the Psalms" (May 1, 1910). The next seven decisions, all issued during the month of June, were on the New Testament. Together these seven decisions overviewed the controverted aspects of the special introduction to the New Testament as follows: (8) "On the Author, Date of Composition, and Historical Truth of the Gospel According to St. Matthew" (June 19, 1911); (9) "On the Author, Time of Composition and Historical Truth of the Gospels According to St. Mark and St. Luke" (June 26, 1912); (10) "On the Synoptic Question or the Mutual Relations Between the First Three Gospels" (June 26, 1912); (11) "On the Author, Time of Composition, and Historical Character of Acts" (June 12, 1913); (12) "On the Authenticity, Integrity, and Time of Composition of the Pastoral Epistles" (June 12, 1913); (13) "On the Author and the Manner and Circumstances of Composition of the Epistle to the Hebrews" (June 24, 1914); and, after the death of Pius X, (14) "On the Parousia or the Second Coming of Our Lord Jesus Christ" (June 18, 1915).

In general the responses given by the Biblical Commission maintained the priority of an Aramaic Matthew ("Matthew wrote before the other evangelists and that he wrote the first Gospel in the native dialect then in use by the Jews of Palestine") and the traditional understanding of the authorship of the books of the New Testament. While maintaining Pauline authorship of Hebrews, the Commission conceded that this does not mean that Paul put it in exactly the form in which it now stands. More specifically, however, the "fragmentary hypothesis" advanced in relationship to the composition of the Pastorals and the Two-Source theory with respect to the Synoptic Problem were rejected by the Commission. To the question "can they, therefore, freely advocate it [the Two-Source theory], the Commission responded, "In the negative."

It was and remains certain that these decisions were not considered infallible by Roman Catholic theologians. In principle, they are reformable and revokable. With the passage of time, it was clearly seen that questions of authorship and composition are independent of the inspiration and inerrancy of the text. New times make it difficult to appreciate fully the circumstances of the former times, all the while providing a broader perspective on the older circumstances which are thereby clarified in a new way. Thus in 1955, fifty years after the promulgation of the first of the fourteen initial Decisions of the Biblical Commission, Athanasius Miller, then secretary of the Commission, commented on the historical importance of the decrees:

> Especially in this respect the decrees of the Pontifical Biblical Commission have great significance. However, as long as these decrees propose views which are neither immediately nor mediately connected with truths of faith and morals, it goes without saying that the scholar may pursue his research with complete freedom (*plena libertate*) and may utilize the results of his research, provided always that he defers to the supreme teaching authority of the Church.
>
> Today we can hardly picture to ourselves the position of Catholic scholars at the turn of the century, or the dangers that threatened Catholic teaching on Scripture and its inspiration on the part of liberal and rationalistic criticism, which like a torrent tried to sweep away the sacred barriers of tradition. At present the battle is considerably less fierce; not a few controversies have been peacefully settled and many problems emerge in an entirely new light, so that it is easy enough for us to smile at the narrowness and constraint which prevailed fifty years ago.

The passage of half a century certainly allowed for the early decisions of the Pontifical Biblical Commission to be seen in the light of the historical development of the times. The times were such that Roman pronouncements on matters biblical continued to be reactionary during the pontificate of Benedict XV (1914–22). It is true that Benedict XV issued a pastoral encyclical on preaching the Word of God, *Humani generis* (June 15, 1917), and that certain refinements of the juridical order related to the use and study of the Scriptures were contained in the apostolic letter *Cum Biblia*

Sacra (August 15, 1916) and the Code of Canon Law promulgated in 1917 (Cans. 1365:2; 1366:3; 1385:1; 1391; 1399; 1400; 2318:2), but the pontificate of Benedict XV is most noted for the issuance of the encyclical letter *Spiritus Paraclitus* (September 15, 1920). The encyclical, drafted by Leopold Fonck, the Jesuit rector of the Pontifical Biblical Institute, was published on the occasion of the fifteenth centenary of the death of St. Jerome. Fittingly, it begins with a tribute to the "Greatest of Doctors" who is praised for his devotion to the Scriptures, his scholarship, his understanding of biblical inspiration, and his use of the Scriptures in theological argumentation in such a way as ever to emphasize their inerrancy. The qualities Benedict discerned in the scholarly monk were precisely those which he urged upon the entire Church. Yet the total picture advanced by Benedict was much more cautious than that of Leo XIII's *Providentissimus Deus,* and Benedict was much more defensive than his predecessor was on the issue of the historical value of the Scriptures.

The occasion of the encyclical gave Benedict the opportunity to pronounce the Vulgate "preferable to any other ancient version, since it appears to give us the sense of the original more accurately and with greater elegance" and to insist anew that it be used in teaching and in the liturgy. Accordingly, Benedict commended the new edition of the Vulgate, a task that had been entrusted to the members of the Order of St. Benedict by Pius X. The Pope also encouraged the work of biblical societies in Italy and throughout the world. He strongly supported attendance at the Pontifical Biblical Institute, both by those destined to become professors of Sacred Scripture and by other priests who wanted to intensify their acquaintance with the sacred text.

In any event the defensive tone of *Spiritus Paraclitus* is quite evident in the manner in which the Pope spoke of the goal of the study of the Scriptures. He duly noted that the Bible is useful for spiritual perfection and that its real value is for preaching, but added between these thoughts that "from the Bible . . . we gather confirmations and illustrations of any particular doctrine we wish to defend. In this Jerome was marvelously expert." Of himself, the Pope stated that "it is our duty, then, to train as many really fit defenders of this holiest of causes as you can."

In his encyclical Benedict took to task those interpreters of the sacred text who distinguished between primary or religious elements in the Bible and its secondary or profane elements. According to the Pope, those who did so restricted inspiration and inerrancy to the Bible's primary elements. Since some proponents of the distinction sought authoritative support for their opinion in *Providentissimus Deus,* Benedict highlighted his rejection of the distinction by an appeal to the teaching of his predecessor, namely that "it would be wholly impious to limit inspiration to certain portions only of Scripture or to concede that the sacred authors themselves could have erred."

Benedict reserved his most powerful arguments for those who took too ready a refuge in the notions of "implicit quotations," "pseudo-historical narratives," and the various "kinds of literature," or who claimed that the Gospels, especially John, had been so composed that the reader cannot distinguish between what is historical truth and what derives from the imaginations of the evangelists. To rebut these types of scholarly hypotheses, Benedict appealed to the example of Christ himself:

> Whether teaching or disputing, He quotes from all parts of Scripture and takes His example from it; He quotes it as an argument which must be accepted. He refers without any discrimination of sources to the stories of Jonah and the Ninevites, of the Queen of Sheba and Solomon, of Elijah and Elisha, of David and of Noah, of Lot and the Sodomites, and even of Lot's wife. How solemn His witness to the truth of the sacred books: "One jot or one tittle shall not pass of the Law till all be fulfilled"; and again, "The Scripture cannot be broken."

The tone set by the later Pius X, and maintained by Benedict XV continued throughout the reign of Pius XI (1922–39). During this pontificate, the Holy Office took vigorous action against the work of some of the principal Catholic biblical scholars of the era, including Jules-Pierre Touzard, Fulcran Grégoire Vigouroux, Louis Bacuez, and Auguste Brassac. A new *motu proprio* (April 27, 1924) decreed that seminary professors of Sacred Scripture should obtain their academic degrees from either the Pontifical Biblical Commission or the Pontifical Biblical Institute. In 1933 the Biblical Commission rendered two decisions on the false interpretation of two texts, Psalm 15:10–11 and Matthew 16:26 (par. Luke 9:25). It rejected an interpretation of the former which would hold that the Psalmist had not spoken of the Resurrection of Jesus; it denied that the latter referred only to the temporal life of man, rather than to the eternal salvation of his soul. Less than a year later, on April 30, 1934, the Biblical Commission rejected the liturgical use of a translation of the Scriptures other than that of Jerome's Vulgate. On the other hand, it was during the pontificate of Pius XI that the Holy Office issued a public clarification on the Johannine Comma (1 John 5:7–8). Although the Congregation of the Inquisition had issued a decree in support of the authenticity of the disputed passage (January 13, 1897), the Holy Office now stated (June 2, 1927) that the earlier decree was by no means intended to prevent Catholic scholars from examining the case more fully. For biblical scholars of those days this clarification was virtually the only glimmer of light in an otherwise dark tunnel. The pontificate of Pius XI allowed the Holy Office to exercise a stringent discipline in support of the traditional interpretation of the sacred text, particularly with regard to biblical inspiration and inerrancy, and had little to say by way of positive support for Catholic biblical scholars.

III. A THRUST RENEWED

The situation dramatically changed during the relatively long pontificate of Pius XII (1939–58). A Letter to the Archbishops and Bishops of Italy issued by the Pontifical Biblical Commission on August 20, 1941, served as a first sign of the new mood in Rome. The publication of the letter was occasioned by a spurious brochure sent to ecclesiastical authorities in Italy, ostensibly promoting a "meditative" exegesis of the Scriptures, but in fact it was a vicious attack against the scientific study of the Bible. To counteract the anonymous pamphlet, actually written by Dolindo Ruotolo under the pseudonym Dain Cohene, the Biblical Commission emphasized once again the primacy of the literal sense of the Scriptures. It clarified the notion of the authenticity of the Vulgate, noting that the Tridentine affirmation of the Vulgate as authentic related to its use in matters of faith or morals, but hardly implied that the Vulgate did not diverge at all from the original text and ancient versions. The Commission also took pains to commend specifically the use of textual criticism and the study of Oriental languages and the auxiliary sciences by Catholic scholars. In short, the letter clearly rejected a narrow and obscurantist approach to the Scriptures in favor of one that would not only incorporate sound principles of exegesis but also make the fruits of this work available to those who were preparing for the priesthood.

Two years later the Biblical Commission again placed the weight of its authority on the side of those committed to the furtherance of biblical scholarship within the Church. In its decisions on "the Use of Versions of Sacred Scripture in the Vernacular" (August 22, 1943), the Commission allowed only a vernacular translation of the Vulgate to be read after the liturgical reading of the Latin text, but permitted that this translation be explained, when necessary, by the use of the original text or a more clear modern version. Apart from this liturgical usage, the Commission commended the translation of the Scriptures from the Vulgate as well as from ancient texts and encouraged the reading of the Bible in translation by the faithful for their own private devotion.

These actions of the Pontifical Biblical Commission prepared the way for Pius XII's encyclical, *Divino Afflante Spiritu* (September 30, 1943). The encyclical, principally prepared by Augustin Bea, the rector of the Biblical Institute, was written in commemoration of the fiftieth anniversary of *Providentissimus Deus*. It was intended to endorse the renewal of biblical studies within Roman Catholicism, which was the legacy of Lagrange and his spiritual heirs. The remarkably progressive character of *Divino Afflante Spiritu* is all the more striking in that the encyclical was issued while the battles of the Second World War were still raging, a sad fact to which the papal document made repeated reference. The closing paragraphs of the encyclical incorporated specific words of congratulations and encouragement for Catholic biblical scholars. They exuded an optimism meant to inspire further scholarship, an optimism that bore fruit in the Catholic biblical renewal of the 1950s. This renewal would prove to be one of the major sources of that revival in Catholic thinking whose results were embodied in the documents of Vatican Council II.

Divino Afflante Spiritu, takes up, in fact, where *Providentissimus Deus* left off. It provided a sense of direction and a source of inspiration for mid-century scholars just as the earlier document had provided direction and inspiration prior to the turn of the century. Pius cited the example of Jerome, on whose feast day the encyclical was issued, in urging the study of Greek, Hebrew, and other Oriental languages by Catholic scholars. The authority of Augustine was invoked in support of the science of textual criticism, whose purpose was to purify the sacred text from corruptions, glosses, and omissions. The Pope, moreover, put the issue of the authority of the Vulgate into clear and proper focus. He noted that the Fathers of Trent had petitioned the Pope for new Latin, Greek, and Hebrew texts of the Bible, but that the circumstances of the era prevented the realization of this project. Pius noted that Trent's decision about the Vulgate was intended to single it out from among the several different Latin versions of the Bible in circulation during the sixteenth century. The decision was based on the reliability of the Vulgate's text in matters of faith and morals as evidenced by long ecclesiastical usage, and was not dictated by a judgment in matters of scholarly criticism. In any event, the Tridentine decision applied only to the public use of the Scriptures within the Latin Church and in no way diminished the authority and value of the original texts.

In response to those who sought after a mystical interpretation of the text, Pius clearly affirmed the primacy of the literal sense of the Scriptures. He distinguished this literal sense from both the spiritual sense and the figurative sense of the sacred text. While the Pope urged the scholar to seek after the spiritual sense (i.e., the allegorical, tropological, and anagogical senses of medieval theologians) provided this is clearly intended by God, he commended preachers to use the figurative sense of the Scriptures only with moderation and restraint, since the faithful want to know what God has taught rather than the mere words of a captivating orator.

Difficulties in interpreting the sacred text must be acknowledged. Even the Fathers of the Church were aware of many of these difficulties, but modern times and particularly the development of the historical sciences have raised still further difficulties for the exegete. In the face of these difficulties, the interpreter must "with all care and without neglecting any light from recent research, endeavor to determine the peculiar character and circumstances of the sacred writer, the age in which he lived, the sources written or oral to which he had recourse and the forms of expression he employed." With these words Pius challenged Catholic scholars to employ the historical-critical method in their exposition of the biblical texts. Pius spelled out the implications of this challenge as follows:

Frequently the literal sense is not so obvious in the words and writings of ancient oriental authors as it is with the writers of today. For what they intended to signify by their words is not determined only by the laws of grammar or philology, nor merely by the context, it is absolutely necessary for the interpreter to go back in spirit to those remote centuries of the East, and make proper use of the aids afforded by history, archaeology, ethnology, and other sciences, in order to discover what literary forms the writers of that early age intended to use, and did in fact employ. For to express what they had in mind the ancients of the East did not always use the same forms and expressions as we use today; they used those which were current among the people of their own time and place; and what these were the exegete cannot determine *a priori*, but only from a careful study of ancient oriental literature.

This study has been pursued during the past few decades with greater care and industry than formerly, and has made us better acquainted with the literary forms used in those ancient times, whether in poetical descriptions, or in the formulation of rules and laws of conduct, or in the narration of historical facts and events. It has now also clearly demonstrated the unique preeminence among all the ancient nations of the East which the people of Israel enjoyed in historical writing, both in regard to the antiquity with which they are related—a circumstance, of course, which is explained by the charisma of divine inspiration and by the special purpose, the religious purpose, of biblical history.

At the same time, no one who has a just conception of biblical inspiration will be surprised to find that the sacred writers, like the other ancients, employ certain arts of exposition and narrative, certain idioms especially characteristic of the Semitic languages (known as "approximations"), and certain hyperbolical and even paradoxical expressions designed for the sake of emphasis. The Sacred Books need not exclude any of the forms of expression which were commonly used in human speech by the ancient peoples, especially of the East, to convey their meaning, so long as they are in no way incompatible with God's sanctity and truth. "In the divine Scripture," observes St. Thomas, with characteristic shrewdness, "divine things are conveyed to us in the manner to which men are accustomed." For just as the substantial Word of God became like to men in all things, "without sin," so the words of God, expressed in human language, became in all things like to human speech, except error. This is that "condescension" (*sugkatabasin*) of divine Providence which St. John Chrysostom so highly extolled and which he repeatedly asserted to be found in the Sacred Books.

Consequently, if the Catholic exegete [*catholicus exegeta*] is to meet fully the requirements of modern biblical study he must, in expounding Sacred Scripture and vindicating its immunity from all error, make prudent use also of this further aid: he must, that is, ask himself how far the form of expression or literary idiom [*forma seu litterarum genus*] employed by the sacred writer may contribute to the true and genuine interpretation; and he may be sure that this part of his task cannot be neglected without great detriment to Catholic exegesis. . . . A just impartiality therefore demands that when these are found in the word of God, which is expressed in human language for men's sake, they should be no more stigmatized as error than when similar expressions are employed in daily usage. Thus a knowledge and careful appreciation of ancient modes of expression and literary forms and styles [*loquendi scribendique modis et artibus*] will provide a solution to many of the objections made against the truth and historical accuracy of Holy Writ; and the same study will contribute with equal profit to a fuller and clearer perception of the mind of the Sacred Author.

In his exhortation to Catholic exegetes, urging them to grapple with even the more difficult problems of interpretation, Piux XII warned the other members of the Church against an intemperate zeal which would condemn anything new as wrong or suspect and reminded them that there have been, in fact, very few biblical passages whose meaning has been authentically defined by the Church, just as there are very few texts about which the Fathers have a unanimously consistent teaching.

Although the papal encyclical was principally concerned with the scientific study of the Bible, a definite pastoral interest is clearly identifiable. Thus the Pope recommended the translation of the Scriptures into modern languages. He lauded the pious associations dedicated to the spreading of the Gospel. He commended the reading of the Scriptures by Christian families. He urged priests to diffuse the results of biblical scholarship among the faithful. He made note of the task to be assumed by professors of Sacred Scripture in seminaries—a task which should culminate in an explanation of the theological doctrine of the sacred text and a love for the Scriptures themselves.

A few years later, on May 13, 1950, an Instruction of the Pontifical Biblical Commission spelled out in more detail the task of the seminary professor of Sacred Scripture. Once again a Roman document underscored the importance of the exposition of the doctrinally significant passages of Scripture as well as the need to enkindle a genuine love of the Scriptures in those who are called to be ministers of the Word of God. The Instruction also noted that it was the literal sense of the Sacred Page that was to be exposited. This exposition was to be made according to the norms laid down in *Divino Afflante Spiritu*. Of course, care was also to be taken to explain the spiritual sense of the text, "provided that the fact of its being intended by God is sufficiently evident."

Catholic exegetes were obviously encouraged by the direction and force of the encyclical and the ensuing instruction of the Biblical Commission. The manifest tendency of these documents was also evident in other Roman documents of the Pius XII era. Although they were devoted to the Old Testament rather than the New, the *motu proprio In cotidianis precibus* (March 24, 1945), a response of the Biblical Commission (October 22, 1947) on the use of a new Latin version of the Psalms, a Letter of the Biblical Commission to Cardinal Suhard of Paris on the Time of the Pentateuch's Documents and the Literary Form of Genesis 1–11 (January 16, 1948), and the remarks made in the Encyclical *Humani Generis* apropos of the creation narratives of Genesis (August 12, 1950) were a source of support for Catholic biblical scholars who endeavored to plumb the depths of the Scriptures with the help of recent discoveries and the newer methods of interpretation.

Six weeks before his death, Pope Pius XII summed up his efforts on behalf of Roman Catholic biblical scholarship. In a letter addressed to the participants of an international Congress of Biblical Studies held at Brussels and Louvain in the summer of 1958 Pius wrote: "Since the beginning of our Pontificate, we have had close to our heart the intention of fostering the growth of Scripture studies, and it is now almost fifteen years since we desired by our Encyclical, *Divino Afflante Spiritu,* 'to incite ever more earnestly all those sons of the Church who devote themselves to these studies' and to encourage them 'to continue with ever renewed vigor, with all zeal and care, the work so happily begun.' Further, you are well aware that we have not ceased to pour out lavishly the marks of our interest on the commentators and professors of Sacred Scripture" (July 28, 1958). Pius' own assessment of his efforts on behalf of biblical scholarship was indeed an accurate one. Catholic biblical scholars received so much encouragement from the Pontiff that he has been called the "patron of Catholic biblical studies."

IV. A NEW CRISIS

Although the pontificate of Pius XII inaugurated the greatest renewal of interest in the study of the Bible within Roman Catholicism since the Reformation, omens of an impending crisis were already visible during the closing months of his reign. The crisis would be neither as severe nor as protracted as the Modernist crisis, which followed upon the encouragement afforded to those Catholics engaged in the scientific study of the Bible by *Providentissimus Deus,* but it was nonetheless a real crisis and one which had considerable importance in view of the ecumenical council announced by Pope John XXIII (1958–63) shortly after he became Pope.

A first sign of the impending crisis came in April 1958, when the Congregation for Seminaries expressed displeasure with the first volume of *Introduction à la Bible,* a manual edited by two French biblical scholars and seminary professors, André Robert and André Feuillet. A still more ominous sign came in the form of John XXIII's address to the Pontifical Biblical Institute on the occasion of its fiftieth anniversary (February 17, 1960). As the occasion demanded, the Pope spoke warmly of the work of the Institute and of the Popes who had supported it, beginning with its first days under Pius X. The Pope's tone changed as he cited one of the first homilies of his pontificate: "Unfortunately, in all ages, there are always a few dark clouds, arising from certain notions that have little to do with true science, cluttering up the horizon whenever men attempt to see the Gospel in all its clear and radiant splendor. This is the task that is called to mind by the Book laid open upon the altar: to teach true doctrine, proper discipline of life, and the ways in which man can rise toward God." The Pope's message became clearer still as he said: "In this light, you can easily understand the need, already mentioned above, which exists for absolute adherence to the sacred deposit of faith and to the Magisterium of the Church. The charter of the Biblical Institute entrusts to you the delicate task of promoting sound biblical scholarship 'according to the mind of the Catholic Church,' that is, 'in conformity with norms already established or to be established by this Apostolic See' . . ." Few Catholic scholars would quarrel with the Pope's words, but the underlying message was one which was favorable to the emergence of a renewed defensive-apologetic attitude toward the Bible.

That there were indeed two attitudes toward biblical scholarship within the Church, the one critical and optimistic, the other anxious and apologetic, quickly became apparent. In September 1960 a short article written by Luís Alonso-Schökel, a Spanish professor at the Pontifical Biblical Institute in Rome, appeared in the *Civiltà cattolica* with the title "Where is Catholic Exegesis Headed?" A virulent attack upon the author and his colleagues at the PBI appeared almost immediately (*Divinitas* 4 (1960) 385–456) under the authorship of Monsignor Antonino Romeo (1902–79), then an affiliate of the Congregation of Seminaries and Universities and a professor of Sacred Scripture at Rome's Lateran University. Romeo vigorously denied that *Divino Afflante Spiritu* was intended to support the newer trends in exegesis; rather, he argued, these were opposed to tradition and the directives of the Magisterium, and could therefore only contaminate the formation of those who were in training for the priestly ministry. Romeo was particularly critical of two other Jesuits, one a German teaching at the PBI, Maximilian Zerwick, the other a Belgian teaching in Louvain, Jean Levie; but he was hardly less kind to Anton Vögtle (Freiburg), Pierre Benoit (the École Biblique in Jerusalem), and Albert Descamps (University of Louvain). Descamps (1916–80) would later become a bishop (1960) and secretary to the Biblical Commission (1973). In short, Romeo's assault was a broad attack on those Catholic scholars who espoused the newer trends as well as upon the *Rivista biblica* and the Italian Biblical Association, which Romeo judged to be mouthpieces for the new and dangerous trends.

Since *Divinitas* had printed Romeo's seventy-page attack, the rector of the Pontifical Biblical Institute, Fr. Ernest Vogt, S.J., asked the journal's editor for a retraction and the opportunity for rebuttal. Permission was not granted and so the PBI published a brief (fifteen-page) reply in *Verbum Domini* (39 [1961] 3–17). In Rome itself, higher ecclesiastical authorities were quick to rally to the support of the Biblical Institute. At the beginning of February, the Prefect of the Congregation of Seminaries and Universities let it be known that Romeo's article represented Romeo's personal views and that it had been published without the knowledge of either the prefect or the secretary of the congregation. On March 2, 1961, it was announced that Father Vogt had been appointed as a consultor of the Theological Commission for the forthcoming Vatican Council II by John XXIII. On March 5, the consultors of the Biblical Commission met in Rome. They affirmed their common support for the Biblical Institute and specifically rejected the views of Romeo in a letter sent on their behalf by the secretary of the Commission to Fr. Vogt.

The Romeo affair marked another step in the coming-of-age of the Biblical Commission, which had abandoned its earlier role of being a watchdog on the alert for attacks against orthodoxy in order to assume the role of positively encouraging prudent advances in the study of the Scriptures by Catholic biblical scholars. The controversy emphasized the need for the entire Church to be more aware of the scientific methods and principles involved in the understanding of Scripture. That such a need really existed became obvious once again when, on June 20, 1961, the Holy Office issued a *monitum,* "published with the approval of the eminent cardinals of the Pontifical Biblical Commission." The warning spoke of those who "bring into doubt the genuine historical and objective truth (*germanam veritatem historicam et objectivam*) of the Sacred Scriptures, not only of the Old Testament, but even of the New, even to the sayings and deeds of Christ Jesus."

The document was pastoral in its intent and was in no way intended to countermand the orientation endorsed by *Divino Afflante Spiritu* and subsequently supported by the actions of the Biblical Commission. The *monitum* concerned "all of those who deal with the Sacred Scriptures, either in writing or orally . . . lest the consciences of the faithful be disturbed or the truths of the Faith be injured." Nevertheless it was widely reported that the document was a warning to Catholic exegetes. Its exhortation to due prudence and reverence was, however, indicative of a new and cautious mood in Rome. The defensive reaction led to the removal of Frs. Maximilian Zerwick (1901–75) and Stanislas Lyonnet (1902–   ), both Jesuits, from teaching at the Biblical Institute, even though Lyonnet had by this time succeeded Fr. Vogt in the deanship of the Institute. During the academic years of 1962–63 and 1963–64, Lyonnet would lecture only in seminars and Zerwick would offer only one course, on the Greek language.

In the meantime, preparations for Vatican Council II were being made and its first sessions were held. The existence of the biblical movement seemed to demand that the Council address itself to the role of the Scriptures within the Church. Debate among scholars as to the role of Scripture and tradition and the issue of the acceptability of the newer methods of exegesis underscored the need for a conciliar statement on the Scriptures. In the preconciliar period the Holy Office called for a statement on the inspiration and inerrancy of the Scriptures, as well as on the historicity of the Gospels. The bishops of the Church were looking for a text that would contain doctrinal and pastoral sections. The scholars attached to the Roman universities were hoping for something on the relationship between Scripture and

Tradition. What emerged from the initial discussions was a "Schema of a Dogmatic Constitution on the Sources of Revelation." This schema had five chapters: (1) The Double Source of Revelation, (2) The Inspiration, Inerrancy and Literary Form of Scripture, (3) The Old Testament, (4) The New Testament, (5) Holy Scripture in the Church.

Composed during the 1960–62 period, this schema (Draft I) was defensive and scholastic in its formation. It addressed itself to Catholic problems in a clearly Catholic way. It clearly stated that revelation is contained in two sources, Tradition and the Scriptures. Thus the draft set aside the opinion that emphasized the mutual dependence and coherence of Scripture and Tradition in such a way as to exclude the notion that tradition was an almost self-sufficient constitutive source of faith. By adopting the language of the "two sources" of revelation, the schema opted for a notion of constitutive tradition, quite broad in comparison with the Scriptures. Its univocal view of inspiration was largely verbalistic; it contained a very narrow interpretation of inerrancy. Never once did the document mention the importance of literary forms. Indeed its conception of the historicity of the Gospels was such as to suggest that there were no problems whatsoever. Accordingly the draft contained two paragraphs which incorporated the language of the June, 1961, *monitum* and condemned "the errors which deny or weaken in whatever manner the true historical and objective truth of the events of Jesus' life and the authenticity of his words."

The text was submitted to the bishops of the Church in the summer of 1962. When the draft came to a vote during the first session of the Council (November 20, 1962), only 822 bishops voted in favor of continuing the discussion on the text; 1,368 bishops voted to reject the document out of hand. Although their numbers did not constitute the two-thirds majority required for remanding the schema, Pope John XXIII personally intervened. He ordered that the draft be withdrawn so that it could be reworked by an *ad hoc* group composed of bishops from the Theological Commission, some from the Secretariat for Promoting Christian Unity and some specifically named for the task at hand. Cardinals Alfredo Ottaviani and Augustin Bea were appointed chairmen of this new group.

V. THE CRISIS RESOLVED

In April 1963 a document with a new name *"De Divina Revelatione"* (Draft II) was sent to the bishops. Its prologue suggested that revelation was to be construed in terms of salvation history as the communion-creating self-disclosure of God, but the operative model of revelation permeating the new text was that of revelation as doctrine. In this 1963 text the issues of Scripture and Tradition, Inspiration and Inerrancy were treated in a relatively new way. The new text was never formally discussed by the Council but no one was really satisfied with its text. Some were glad to rally to the suggestion that its principal themes simply be incorporated into the Constitution on the Church. The suggestion was laid to rest when the new Pope, Paul VI (1963–78), closed the second session of the Council with a speech which cited the schema on Divine Revelation as one among the tasks to be faced by the bishops during their third session.

Fortunately several bishops had sent their written recommendations on Draft II to the Doctrinal Commission of the Council. These recommendations allowed a special subcommission of the Doctrinal Commission, under the chairmanship of Bishop André Maria Charue of Namur (Belgium), an exegete, to create a new version of the schema *De Divina Revelatione*. This text (Draft III), substantially the same as that finally adopted by the Council, was sent to the bishops prior to the third session and was discussed by them for a full week of that third session of the Council (September 30–October 6, 1964). This third text adopted the following outline:

> Prologue
> I. Revelation Itself
> II. The Transmission of Divine Revelation
> III. The Divine Inspiration and the Interpretation of Holy Scripture
> IV. The Old Testament
> V. The New Testament
> VI. Holy Scripture in the Church's Life

Most significantly, Draft III's very first chapter represented a radical reworking of the prologue of Draft II, which was now introduced into the text of the schema itself. The draft was presented to the Council by Archbishop Ermenegildo Florit of Florence (Italy), onetime professor of Scripture at the Lateran, and sometime consultor to the PBC. The concept of revelation which the new draft espoused was theocentric, historical, and interpersonal. Rather than defining a notion of communicated divine teaching, revelation is now chiefly understood as God's self-disclosure in human history in view of a salvific interpersonal communion with men. Thus a distinction was introduced between the "primary object" of revelation consisting of God's self-disclosure and the "secondary object" of revelation which is God's Word, the testimony through which God's self-disclosure is mediated to us. What had been Chapter I in the earlier versions of the conciliar text became Chapter II in Draft III, with, however, a new title—"The Transmission of Divine Revelation." In the revised version of this chapter, Scripture and Tradition are understood to be qualitatively identical even though the question of their quantitative relationship remains open. Tradition, moreover, is no longer equated with doctrinal tradition; rather, it is understood to be the entire life of the Church.

While the subcommission was preparing Draft III of the conciliar text, the Biblical Commission was preparing an "Instruction on the Historical Truth of the Gospels." The Instruction, popularly known by the first three words of its Latin text, *Sancta Mater Ecclesia,* was issued on April 21, 1964. The document contains a series of directives addressed to different publics: first, the Catholic exegete (*exegeta catholicus*), then seminary professors, preachers, popular writers, and those in charge of biblical associations.

The words addressed to the exegete constitute the largest and most significant part of the instruction. Basically, the instruction encouraged the Catholic exegete to make use of the methods of form and redaction criticism.

By way of introduction to its endorsement of the form-critical method, the Biblical Commission stated: "In order to bring out with fullest clarity the enduring truth of the Gospels he [the Catholic exegete] must, whilst carefully observing the rules of rational and of Catholic hermeneutics (*accurate normas hermeneuticae rationalis et catholicae servans*), make skillful use of the new aids to exegesis, especially those which the historical method, taken in its widest sense, has provided; that method, namely, which minutely investigates sources, determining their nature and bearing, and availing itself of the findings of textual criticism, literary criticism, and linguistic studies." The mention of "rational" rules was an obvious reference to the commonly accepted rules of literary interpretation, whereas the addition of "Catholic" rules made it clear that the Catholic tradition also has something important to say with respect to the interpretation of New Testament texts.

In its brief exposition of the form-critical method, the instruction clearly distinguished between the method itself and inadmissible "principles of a philosophical or theological nature" with which it was sometimes associated. Among the unacceptable presuppositions, the document cites the denial of the supernatural order, the denial of God's intervention in the world by revelation, the *a priori* affirmation of the impossibility of miracles and prophecy, the incompatibility of faith and historical truth, the *a priori* denial of the historical value of the testimonies to revelation, and the underestimation of apostolic witness together with an overestimation of the creativity of the community. These presuppositions put aside, *Sancta Mater Ecclesia* underscored the importance of three stages in the transmission of the life and teaching of Jesus: the life situation of Jesus Himself, the life situation of the Church, and the life situation of the evangelist. While encouraging research into the history of the transmission of evangelical tradition, the Commission noted that the "varied ways of speaking which the heralds of Christ made use of in proclaiming Him must be distinguished one from the other and carefully appraised: catecheses, narratives, testimonies, hymns, doxologies, prayers and any other such literary forms as were customarily employed in Sacred Scripture and by people of that time." Clearly, the listing is not exhaustive. The Catholic exegete had work cut out for him—he must discern the significance of the oral and literary forms used in the transmission of the Gospel material.

The Biblical Commission's endorsement of the methodology of redaction criticism took the form of an exposition on the third stage of the Gospel tradition: that of the sacred authors. Each of the evangelists, the instruction reported, followed a method suitable to the special purpose which he had in mind for the benefit of the churches. In view of this purpose:

They selected certain things out of the many which had been handed on; some they synthesized, some they explained with an eye to the situation of the Churches, painstakingly using every means of bringing home to their readers the solid truth of the things in which they had been instructed. For, out of the material which they had received, the sacred authors selected especially those items which were adapted to the varied circumstances of the faithful as well as to the end which they themselves wished to attain; these they recounted in a manner consonant with those circumstances and with that end. And since the meaning of a statement depends, amongst other things, on the place which it has in a given sequence, the Evangelists, in handing on the words or deeds of our Savior, explained them for the benefit of their readers by respectively setting them, one Evangelist in one context, another in another. For this reason the exegete must ask himself what the Evangelist intended by recounting a saying or a fact in a certain way, or by placing it in a certain context. For the truth of the narrative is not affected in the slightest by the fact that the Evangelists report the sayings or the doings of our Lord in a different order, and that they use different words to express what He said, not keeping to the very letter, but nevertheless preserving the sense.

A more accurate summary of the process of the actual writing of the Gospels would be hard to find. Nevertheless *Sancta Mater Ecclesia* is almost as significant in respect of what it failed to say as it was in endorsing the form- and redaction-critical methods. In the first instance, the document is an "Instruction on the Historical Truth of the Gospels" (*Instructio de Historica Evangeliorum Veritate*); yet the document is so written that the reader understands that it is concerned with the "truth" of the Gospels, rather than with their historicity in a material sense. The only occasion on which the instruction mentioned "historical" in the body of the text was when the notion that faith and historical truth are incompatible was cited as an unacceptable presupposition. For the rest, it was made clear that the truth of Gospel narratives derives from the fact that the evangelists communicated the meaning of Jesus' teaching and his activity as heirs to those who had preached about what Jesus said and did. Strikingly also, in a document on the historical truth of the Gospels, *Sancta Mater Ecclesia* had nothing specific to say about the Synoptic Problem nor did it address itself to the problem of the redactional additions appended to the words of Jesus by the evangelists for the benefit of the churches of their times.

That a new mood was beginning to prevail in Rome while Draft III of the conciliar schema was in preparation and discussion was also evident in the restoration of Lyonnet and Zerwick to their posts at the Pontifical Biblical Institute. With the 1964–65 academic year, it was possible for Lyonnet to resume once again his lectures on Romans and Galatians. At the same time, Zerwick returned to his exposition of the Lucan journey narrative (Luke 9:51–19:44) and began a series of lectures on the Sermon on the Mount (Matt 5–7).

As a result of the discussion of September 30–October 6, 1964, a revision of Draft III was made and submitted to the Fathers of the Council for a vote. This 1965 text (Draft IV-A) differed but slightly from the previous version. Between September 20 and 25, twenty votes on the text were taken. Each chapter received the requisite two-thirds majority, but a number of emendations (*modi*) were suggested. Several of these were accepted by the council's Theological Commission and incorporated into the final text (Draft IV-B) which was submitted to a vote on October 29, 1965—2,081 Fathers voted to accept the text; 27 were opposed; 7 votes were judged null and void. On November 18, 1965, the day of promulgation of *Dei Verbum,* the *Dogmatic Constitution on Divine Revelation,* a final vote was taken. All but 16 of the 2,360 bishops in attendance voted in favor of the constitution.

The constitution begins with a chapter on revelation (Ch. I) and ends with one on Scripture in the Life of the Church (Ch. VI). Together these two chapters frame the document and its teaching. In sum, they speak of revelation primarily as God's self-disclosure in history with the ultimate purpose of man's salvation. Secondly, as it were, revelation is the Word of God through which the saving deeds of God are proclaimed and commemorated. Finally, and in another sense, revelation is that salvific action by which God communicates himself in the Church through the proclamation of the Word and the celebration of his gifts. Accordingly it was imperative that the Council address itself to the function of Scripture in the Life of the Church. The positive tone of Chapter VI stands in marvelous contrast to the condemnatory words of Draft I which had defensively sought to protect the Church against error.

Chapter II is on "The Transmission of Divine Revelation." It is concerned with the relationship between Scripture and Tradition, a matter treated with some urgency since the Counter Reformation. In response to the question of the theologians, the Conciliar Fathers voted for a text that emphasized the mutual penetration of Scripture and Tradition. While not ruling out the possibility of a constitutive tradition, the words of the text adopted by the Fathers seem to favor the notion of tradition as interpretive.

The Latin title of Chapter III, *De Sacrae Scripturae Divina Inspiratione et de eius Interpretatione* ("The Divine Inspiration and the Interpretation of Sacred Scripture"), is ever so slightly different from the title of this chapter in Draft III (*De Sacrae Scripturae Divina Inspiratione et Interpretatione*). Because of this small modification, the conciliar text can be clearly seen as addressed to two different concerns—the inspiration of the text by God, and the interpretation of the text by its interpreters. While the inspiration of the Scriptures is affirmed, it is the interpretation of the sacred text which receives by far the greater emphasis in Chapter III. Its directives are noteworthy, especially by reason of its strong encouragement of the form-critical method and its implicit affirmation that there exist different ways in which history can be written, even within the sacred text itself:

Those who search out the intention of the sacred writers must, among other things, have regard for "literary forms." For truth is proposed and expressed in a variety of ways, depending on whether a text is history of one kind or another, or whether its form is that of prophecy, poetry, or some other type of speech. The interpreter must investigate what meaning the sacred writer intended to express and actually expressed in particular circumstances as he used contemporary literary forms in accordance with the situation of his own time and cultures. For the correct understanding of what the sacred author wanted to assert, due attention must be paid to the customary and characteristic styles of perceiving, speaking, and narrating which prevailed at the time of the sacred writer, and to the customs men normally followed at that period in their everyday dealings with one another (*Dei Verbum* 12).

Chapter IV of *Dei Verbum* is devoted to the Old Testament; Chapter V, in four paragraphs (Pars. 17–20), is on the New Testament. Significantly, Chapter V begins with the expression *Dei Verbum,* "The Word of God." The expression repeats the words found at the very beginning of the constitution, and thus points to the New Testament as a privileged mode of Divine Revelation. The kerygmatic language with which the Word of God is described points to the salvific power of God's word to which "the writings of the New Testament stand as a perpetual and divine witness."

Paragraph 18 places special stress upon the Gospels, underscoring their preeminence among the books of the New Testament "for they are the principal witness of the life and teaching of the incarnate Word, our Savior." The paragraph has been carefully phrased so as to avoid the problems arising from literary criticism that have to do with the chronological order of the composition of the Gospels. On the latter subject, the conciliar text affirms the tradition of the Church with respect to the apostolic origin of the Gospels. The Gospels are related to the proclamation of the apostles without the affirmation that this tradition is a matter of faith itself: "The Church has always and everywhere held (*tenuit et tenet*) that the four Gospels are of apostolic origin. For what the apostles preached in fulfillment of the commission of Christ, afterwards they themselves and apostolic men, under the inspiration of the divine Spirit, handed on to us in writing: the foundation of faith, namely, the fourfold Gospel, according to Matthew, Mark, Luke and John."

The opening words of Paragraph 19 are very significant. They are *Sancta Mater Ecclesia* ("Holy Mother Church"), a clear reference to the 1964 Instruction of the Biblical Commission. The conciliar text obviously follows the Instruction in speaking about the process of the composition of the Gospels as one of selection, synthesis, application, and proclamation, "but always in such fashion that they told us the honest truth (*vera et sincera . . . communicarent*) about Jesus." The council's epitome of the Instruction differs quite sharply from the formulations in Draft I which stated that "Although the Gospels sometimes betray (*resonent*) the manner of preaching and do not agree in all things with the requirements of historical writing that we are accustomed to in our own day, nevertheless they hand down to us a true and honest story" (*veram et sinceram historiam*). This earlier statement indeed indicated that one of the great concerns of the times was that of the historical truth of the Gospels. The statement was in fact a response to those who followed that Bultmannian and post-Bultmannian interpretation of the text which radically separated faith from history. The final reply of the Council Fathers was one that affirmed the "historical character" (*Evangelia, quorum historicitatem incunctantes affirmat*) of the Gospels by reaffirming that the Gospels teach the Gospel truth about Jesus. Even though a minority of Council Fathers, through the Pope, had succeeded in proposing to the Theological Commission an emendation which would proclaim that the Gospels contain the words and actions of Jesus "according to truth and historical faith" (*juxta veritatem fidemque historicam*), the Commission rejected the proposal. In so doing it avoided any semblance of polemics in the final formulation of the conciliar text as well as needless discussion on the difference between History as *Geschichte* (history as interpreted) and History as *Historie* (history as mere verifiable event). Thus the Fathers pointed to the Gospels as witness to the truth about Jesus, even if they consist neither of a chronicle of his life nor of a verbatim reporting of his words.

Paragraph 20 of *Dei Verbum* speaks of Acts, the Epistles, and Revelation —perhaps too briefly in comparison with the treatment of the Gospels. The text deftly avoids the issue of the authenticity of the epistles by means of a broad reference to "the Epistles of St. Paul and other apostolic writings." Otherwise the paragraph notes the Christocentricity of these writings and concludes with a hortatory reflection on the "Paraclete the Spirit who would lead them into the fullness of truth." Thus the general view of the Constitution is maintained. Consistently it affirms that the Scriptures attest to that revelation which primarily consists of God's self-disclosure in human history. Consistently it notes that the truth of the Scriptures is directed toward the salvation of humankind. Consistently, it endorses the scientific study of the sacred text while subtly avoiding a position which would seem to bring to a premature close ongoing research undertaken by scholars. Thus *Dei Verbum,* despite the compromise wording of some of its passages, could not but help to foster and support the efforts of Catholic biblical scholars.

The promulgation of the Dogmatic Constitution on Divine Revelation by Pope Paul VI on November 18, 1965, must certainly be identified as the major achievement of his pontificate, at least as far as biblical studies are concerned. Protégé of Pius XII in so many ways, Paul VI seems to have followed the paths of his predecessor, once removed, in his support of biblical studies within the Church. This support is quite evident in two documents that sum up Paul VI's relationship with the Pontifical Biblical Commission.

By means of a *motu proprio* under date of June 27, 1971, *Sedula Cura,* Paul VI reorganized the Biblical Commission, linking it more closely with the Congregation for the Doctrine of the Faith, whose president was to become, *ex officio,* president of the Commission. This was in keeping with Pope Paul's intention "to assist the advance of true teaching in biblical studies; to preserve the interpretation of Scripture from all rashness of opinion; and also to give greater coordination to the work of theologians in their collaboration with the Holy See and with one another."

The integration of the results of biblical scholarship with the other ecclesiastical disciplines was a theme to which Paul VI returned in his Address to the Biblical commission on March 14, 1974. In pleading for the integration of biblical scholarship into the theological enterprise of the Church as a whole, Paul spoke of the "real continuity between exegetical research and that of dogmatic and moral theology" and of the "real need for interdisciplinary contact between the biblical scholar, the specialist in dogmatic theology, the expert in moral theology, the jurist, and the people involved in pastoral and missionary activity." This theme reechoed in a February 22, 1976, document of the Sacred Congregation for Catholic Education on the Theological Formation of Future Priests.

For Paul VI, the work of biblical research required the use of *Tradition-*, *Form-*, and *Redaktions-geschichte*, methods which he enthusiastically endorsed in his 1974 address to the Biblical Commission. The task of the commission was twofold, said the Pope. "It should effectively promote progress in the biblical studies of the Church, and it should also keep the interpretation of Sacred Scripture on the right path—faithful to the word of God to which we are subject, and responsive to the needs of human beings to whom that word is addressed."

For Paul VI, the Church clearly had need of the Scriptures, properly understood. For him, the proper understanding of the Scriptures required a fidelity to the tradition of the Church no less than it did a properly scientific use of the most appropriate methodologies of historical and literary criticism. Catholic biblical scholars were heartened by the tenor of Paul's pronouncements on the Scriptures, and were encouraged when they found them echoed again by Pope John Paul II (1978–) in his address to the newly constituted Biblical Commission on April 26, 1979:

> God always communicated his marvels using the language and experience of people. The Mesopotamian cultures, those of Egypt, Canaan, Persia, the Hellenic culture and, for the New Testament, Greco-Roman culture and that of late Judaism, served, day after day, for the ineffable mystery of salvation, as your present plenary session clearly shows.
>
> These considerations, however, as you know, bring up the problem of the historical formation of the language of the Bible, which is connected in some way with the changes that took place during the long succession of centuries in the course of which written word gave birth to the sacred books. But it is precisely here that there is asserted the paradox of the revealed proclamation and of the more specifically Christian proclamation according to which persons and events that are historically contingent become bearers of a transcendent and absolute message. . . .
>
> It falls, of course, to biblical science and to its hermeneutical methods to establish the distinction between what is obsolete and what must always keep its value. But that is an operation which calls for extremely keen sensitivity, not only on the scientific plane, but also and above all on the plane of the Church and of life. . . .

SELECT BIBLIOGRAPHY

Ahern, Barnabas. "Textual Directives of the Encyclical *Divino Afflante Spiritu.*" *Catholic Biblical Quarterly,* 7 (1945), 340–47.

Baum, Gregory. "Vatican II's Constitution on Revelation: History and Interpretation." *Theological Studies,* 28 (1967), 51–75.

The Bible Today, 35 (1968).

Brown, Raymond E. "Rome and the Freedom of Catholic Biblical Studies." In *Search the Scriptures* (R. T. Stamm *Festschrift*), ed. by J. M. Myers, O. Reimherr, and H. N. Bream. Leiden: Brill, 1969. 129–50.

Cerfaux, Lucien. *Encyclique sur les études bibliques. Introduction et commentaire. Chrétienté nouvelle,* 6. Brussels: Éditions universitaires, 1945.

Collins, Thomas Aquinas, and Brown, Raymond E. "Church Pronouncements." In *The Jerome Biblical Commentary,* ed. by Raymond E. Brown, Joseph A. Fitzmyer, and Roland E. Murphy. Englewood Cliffs: Prentice-Hall, 1968. 624–32.

Comblin, José. " 'Dei Verbum' después de diez años." *Teologia y Vida,* 16 (1975), 101–17.

Cotter, Anthony C. "The Antecedents of the Encyclical *Providentissimus Deus.*" *Catholic Biblical Quarterly,* 5 (1943), 117–24.

Enchiridion Biblicum. Documenta Ecclesiastica Sacram Scripturam Spectantia, 4th ed. Naples: M. D'Auria, 1961.

Fede e cultura. Atti della Sessione plenaria 1979 della Pontifice Commissione Biblica. Leumann: Elle Di Ci, 1981.

Fitzmyer, Joseph A. "The Biblical Commission's Instruction on the Historical Truth of the Gospels." *Theological Studies,* 25 (1964), 386–408.

———. "A Recent Roman Scriptural Controversy." *Theological Studies,* 22 (1961), 426–44.

Grelot, Pierre. "La Constitution sur la Révélation." *Études,* 324 (1966), 99–113, 233–46.

Hartdegen, Stephen. "The Influence of the Encyclical *Providentissimus Deus.*" *Catholic Biblical Quarterly,* 5 (1943), 141–59.

Lagrange, Marie-Joseph. "Critique biblique. Réponse à l'article de la 'Civilta cattolica': Venticinque anni dopo l'enciclica 'Providentissimus'." *Revue biblique,* 28 (1919), 593–600.

Megivern, James J., ed. *Bible Interpretation. Official Catholic Teachings.* Wilmington: McGrath, 1968.

Murphy, Richard T. "The Teaching of the Encyclical *Providentissimus Deus.*" *Catholic Biblical Quarterly,* 5 (1943), 125–40.

Potterie, de la, Ignace. "La vérité de la Sainte Ecriture et l'Histoire du Salut d'après la Constitution dogmatique 'Dei Verbum'." *Nouvelle revue théologique,* 88 (1966), 149–69.

Prete, Benedetto. "L'enciclica 'Providentissimus Deus' nel settantennio della sua promulgazione." *Sacra Doctrina,* 8 (1963), 337–54.

Quinn, Jerome D. "Saint John Chrysostom on History in the Synoptics." *Catholic Biblical Quarterly,* 24 (1962), 140–47.

Ratzinger, Joseph, Grillmeier, Aloïs, and Rigaux, Béda. "Dogmatic Constitution on Divine Revelation." In *Commentary on the Documents of Vatican II,* ed. by Herbert Vorgrimler, vol. III. New York: Herder & Herder, 1969. 155–72.

Rome and the Study of Scripture. 5th ed. St. Meinrad: Abbey Press, 1955.

Spiteri, Donat. "The Specific Contribution of Divino Afflante Spiritu." *Melita Theologica,* 26 (1974), 7–15.

Tavard, George H. "Commentary on *De Revelatione.*" *Journal of Ecumenical Studies,* 3 (1966), 1–35.

Zerwick, Maximilian. "De S. Scriptura in Constitutione Dogmatica 'Dei Verbum'." *Verbum Domini,* 44 (1966), 17–42.

TEXTS AND TOOLS FOR NEW TESTAMENT STUDY

I. BIBLIOGRAPHIC TOOLS

A. GENERAL SURVEYS

Danker, Frederick W.
> *Multipurpose Tools for Bible Study*. 3rd ed., St. Louis: Concordia, 1970.
>> Contains information on the background and nature of many of the tools of biblical exegesis.

Fitzmyer, Joseph A.
> *An Introductory Bibliography for the Study of Scripture. Subsidia Biblica*, 3. Rev. ed., Rome: Biblical Institute Press, 1981.
>> A complete revision of the 1961 work, coedited by Fitzmyer and G. S. Glanzman. Aims to cover all the important aspects of serious biblical study.

France, R. T. (ed.).
> *A Bibliographical Guide to New Testament Research*. Sheffield: JSOT, 1979.
>> Produced as a popular guide to sources of information for a British readership.

Hurd, John C., Jr.
> *A Bibliography of New Testament Bibliographies*. New York: Seabury, 1966.
>> A very useful collection of sources, intended to facilitate the historical-critical study of the New Testament.

Langevin, Paul-Émile.
  Bibliographie biblique, 1930–1970, vol. II, *1930–1975.* Quebec: Les Presses de l'Université, 1972, 1978.
     Vol. I contains a bibliography of biblical material published in seventy Catholic periodicals. Vol. II updates the list and adds material from an additional fifty journals, not necessarily Catholic.

Marrow, Stanley B.
  Basic Tools of Biblical Exegesis. Subsidia Biblica, 2. Rome: Biblical Institute Press, 1976.
     An annotated bibliography for the student entering the field of biblical exegesis.

Saint John's University Library Index to Biblical Journals. Collegeville: St. John's University Press, 1971.
     A computer-generated index of some of the major journals, covering the previous fifty years or so.

Scholer, David M.
  A Basic Bibliographic Guide for New Testament Exegesis. 2nd ed., Grand Rapids: Eerdmans, 1973.
     A useful tool for the theological student and seminary-educated person; for the most part, lists only English-language publications.

B. Special Bibliographies

Kissinger, Warren S.
  The Parables of Jesus: A History of Interpretation and Bibliography. ATLA Bibliography Series, 4. Metuchen: Scarecrow, 1979.
     Overview of the history of the interpretation of the parables; contains 185-page bibliography on the parables.

————.
  The Sermon on the Mount: A History of Interpretation and Bibliography. ATLA Bibliography Series, 3. Metuchen: Scarecrow, 1975.
     A study of the history of the interpretation of Matthew 5 – 7, from patristic to modern times; 150-page bibliography.

Malatesta, Edward.
  St. John's Gospel. 1920–1965. A Cumulative and Classified Bibliography of Books and Periodical Literature on the Fourth Gospel. Analecta Biblica, 32. Rome: Biblical Institute Press, 1967.
     Relatively complete for this forty-five-year period. Entries on introductory topics are arranged systematically, those on exegesis are arranged by chapter and verse. There is also a topical index of Johannine themes.

Mattill, A. J., Jr., and Mattill, Mary Bedford.
  A Classified Bibliography of Literature on the Acts of the Apostles. New Testament Tools and Studies, 7. Leiden: Brill, 1966.
     Covers publications up to 1961.

Metzger, Bruce M.
  Annotated Bibliography of the Textual Criticism of the New Testament. Studies and Documents, 16. Copenhagen: Munksgaard, 1955.
     Covers works and articles published between 1914 and 1939.

————.

Index of Articles on the New Testament and the Early Church Published in Festschriften. Journal of Biblical Literature Monograph Series, 5. Philadelphia: SBL, 1951.

Covers essays published until 1951. Given the diversity of materials in *Festschriften* and the peculiarity of their titles, a very important tool.

————.

Index to Periodical Literature on the Apostle Paul. New Testament Tools and Studies, 1. Leiden: Brill, 1960.

Contains articles published in journals only up to 1957. Very useful to that date.

————.

Index to Periodical Literature on Christ and the Gospels. New Testament Tools and Studies, 6. Leiden: Brill, 1966.

Covers articles published in journals until 1961; books and monographs are not included.

————.

Supplement to Index of Articles on the New Testament and the Early Church Published in Festschriften. Journal of Biblical Literature Monograph Series, 5, suppl. Philadelphia: SBL, 1955.

Nickels, Peter.

Targum and New Testament: A Bibliography Together with a New Testament Index. Scripta Pontificii Instituti Biblici, 117. Rome: Pontifical Biblical Institute, 1967.

Wagner, Günther (ed.).

An Exegetical Bibliography of the New Testament. Macon: Mercer University Press, 1982.

The first of a projected five-volume series appeared in 1982 with listings of monographs, essays, and periodical entries on the Gospels of Matthew and Mark, arranged according to chapter and verse.

————.

New Testament Exegetical Bibliographical Aids. Rüschlikon: Baptist Theological Seminary, 1973– .

On unbound cards. Lists substantial treatments of New Testament texts found in monographs and the principal journals. The series on Romans (1973), for example, contains 175 cards, each with 15–25 entries.

C. CURRENT BIBLIOGRAPHY

Elenchus Bibliographicus Biblicus. Rome: Biblical Institute Press, 1920– .

First 48 volumes (1920–67) were part of *Biblica*. Since 1968 the *Elenchus* has been published independently.

Ephemerides Theologicae Lovanienses. Gembloux: Duculot, 1926– .

Twice a year *ETL* publishes an extensive bibliography, systematically organized, of the entire range of theology. The biblical section is good, but arranged alphabetically according to a limited number of categories.

International Zeitschriftenschau für Bibelwissenschaft und Grenzgebiete. Stuttgart: Katholischer Bibelwerk, 1951–52– .
> A fairly comprehensive listing of various bibliographical entries. Roughly, the German-language equivalent of *NTA* and *OTA*.

New Testament Abstracts. Cambridge: Weston College School of Theology. 1956– .
> Published three times a year. Contains abstracts of articles and selected book reviews published in more than 200 periodicals. Annually, about 500 book notices are also published.

Religion Index One: Periodicals (formerly, *Index to Religious Periodical Literature*). Chicago: American Theological Library Association, 1955– .

II. NEW TESTAMENT TEXTS

Aland, Kurt, Black, Matthew, Martini, Carlo M., Metzger, Bruce M., Wikgren, Allen (eds.).
> *The Greek New Testament.* 3rd ed., London: United Bible Societies, 1975.
>> Contains the same text as the 26th ed. of Nestle-Aland, with a more intensive, but less extensive apparatus.

Bover, José Maria.
> *Novi Testamenti Biblica Graeca et Latina.* 4th ed., Madrid: Consejo Superior de Investigaciones Cientifigas, 1959.
>> A popular edition of the Greek New Testament, used especially in Spain.

Marshall, Alfred (ed.).
> *The New International Version Interlinear Greek-English New Testament. The Nestle Greek Text with a Literal English Translation.* Grand Rapids: Zondervan, 1976.
>> Presents 21st ed. of Nestle, along with Marshall's interlinear translation. In the margin is found a sequential reading of the New International Version (1973).

Merk, Augustinus.
> *Novum Testamentum Graece et Latine.* 9th ed., Rome: Biblical Institute Press, 1964.
>> A popular edition (Greek, Latin Vulgate) of the New Testament, intended for Catholic students.

Nestle, Eberhard, and Aland, Kurt (eds.).
> *Novum Testamentum Graece.* 26th ed., Stuttgart: Württembergische Bibelanstalt, 1979. Reprinted with corrections, 1981.
>> The most popular handbook edition of the Greek New Testament.

Soden, Hans Friedrich von.
> *Die Schriften des Neuen Testaments in ihrer ältesten erreichbaren Testgestalt hergestellt auf Grund ihrer Textgeschichte.* 2 parts (4 vols.). Göttingen: Vandenhoeck & Ruprecht, 1911, 1913.
>> The monumental critical edition of the New Testament; somewhat overwhelming for the beginning student.

Souter, Alexander.
> *Novum Testamentum Graece.* 2nd ed., Oxford: Clarendon, 1947.

Tasker, R. V.
> *The Greek New Testament. Being the Text Translated in the New English Bible.* Oxford-Cambridge: University Press, 1964.
>> The edition of the Greek New Testament employed by the translators of the NEB.

Tischendorf, Constantin von.
> *Novum Testamentum Graece.* 2 vols. 8th ed., Leipzig: Gieske und Devrient, 1869, 1872.
>> One of the two large standard editions of the New Testament text. Relies heavily on the Codex Sinaiticus.

Westcott, Brooke Foss, and Hort, Fenton John Anthony.
> *The New Testament in the Original Greek.* 2 vols. Rev. ed., Cambridge-London: Macmillan, 1890, 1896.
>> One of the two large standard editions of the New Testament. Presents the "neutral text." Limited critical apparatus.

III. THE NEW TESTAMENT IN ENGLISH

Bruce, Frederick F.
> *History of the Bible in English.* 3rd ed., New York: Oxford University Press, 1978.
>> Hundreds of translations of the New Testament, or significant parts thereof, have appeared during the centuries, about 75 of which have appeared thus far in the twentieth century. Bruce's work studies the history and impact of the more important translations.

Walden, W.
> *Guide to Bible Translations: A Handbook of Versions Ancient and Modern.* Duxbury: Living Books, 1979.
>> A 30-page booklet offering brief descriptions of English-language Bible translations since 1900. Bibliographic data and the basic philosophy are given.

The American Standard Version.
> A 1901 revision of the Authorized Version produced by a committee of American scholars under the chairmanship of Philip Schaff. The effort was parallel to that of the British scholars who produced the RV. A single revision was originally intended but the two committees eventually went their own ways.

The Authorized Version.
> The version of the Bible in English, popularly known as the King James version. On the order of James I, fifty scholars, divided into six groups (two each at Oxford, Cambridge, and Westminster) began their work of translation, after having consulted the Hebrew and Greek (*Textus Receptus*) text and the English versions. A first edition appeared in 1611.

The Douay-Rheims Version.
> The version of the Bible in English most widely used by Roman

Catholics until fairly recent times. It was the work of the English college at Douay, which moved to Rheims in 1578. The New Testament was published in 1582, the Old Testament in 1609. A revision made by Bishop Challoner in 1749–50 was in common use from 1750 to 1950.

The Jerusalem Bible.

A Catholic Bible in contemporary idiom, first published in 1966. English-language counterpart of *La Bible de Jerusalem,* of which the first booklets were published in 1948 and the first complete one-volume edition in 1956. Introductions and notes are translated from the French; the NT translation is from the Greek, after consultation with the French. Uses paraphrases to avoid some textual difficulties.

The New American Bible.

First published in 1970. The translation was done by members of the Catholic Biblical Association of America. Good contemporary idiom, which occasionally involves a departure from the literal translation. A new edition has been announced.

The New English Bible.

Genuinely British in its idiom. Shows the influence of C. H. Dodd, general director of the project since 1969. The New Testament was first published in 1961; the entire Bible in 1970.

The New Testament in Modern English.

In some respects a paraphrase, yet of all the modern English translations of the New Testament, this may be the best for the ordinary reader. The translation, first published in its entirety in 1958, was done by J. B. Phillips.

The Revised Standard Version.

Work of American scholars. For the serious student of the Bible who knows neither Hebrew nor Greek, this is the best of the modern English translations. Combines fidelity to the text with good English style. The New Testament was first published in 1946; the whole Bible in 1952. The best available one-volume edition of the Bible in English translation is probably the *New Oxford Annotated Bible* (New York: Oxford University Press, 1977).

The Revised Version.

A revision of the Authorized Version of the Bible undertaken by a group of British scholars of various ecclesiastical communities, including Westcott and Hort. Undertaken in response to an initiative made in 1870 by Dr. Wilberforce, bishop of Winchester, it represents a fairly literal translation of the Greek text. The NT was published in 1881; the OT in 1885.

IV. SYNOPSES

A. GREEK

Aland, Kurt (ed.).

Synopsis Quattuor Evangeliorum. 10th ed., Stuttgart: Württembergische Bibelanstalt, 1978.

An indispensable tool. The standard synopsis of the four Gospels, based on N[26]. Valuable critical apparatus. In appendix is to be found a trilingual (Latin, German, English) version of the Gospel of Thomas, and extensive original-language citations of the Fathers relative to the New Testament.

Huck, Albert, and Greeven, Heinrich.
Synopse der drei ersten Evangelien mit Beigabe der johanneischen Parallelstellen. 13th ed., Tübingen: J. C. B. Mohr, 1981.
Intended to present a parallel arrangement of the Synoptic Gospels, independently of any particular theory of composition. Hence, each Gospel is printed continuously in its proper column, and all comparable material is printed side by side in parallel. Johannine parallels are given within a black frame. Uses a modified edition of the Tischendorf-Gebhardt Greek text rather than N[26].

B. ENGLISH

Aland, Kurt (ed.).
Synopsis of the Four Gospels. Greek-English Edition of Synopsis Quattuor Evangeliorum with the Text of the Revised Standard Version. Rev. ed., London: United Bible Societies, 1979.
The most useful of the diglot editions of the synopsis. Based on the 26th ed. of Nestle-Aland. Lacks two of the appendices (G Thom, patristic citations) found in the Greek edition, and omits extrabiblical parallels from the critical apparatus. The critical apparatus for the RSV text cites the AV and RV.

Farmer, William R.
Synopticon. Cambridge: University Press, 1969.
Underlining in different colors indicates both complete agreement and partial agreement among the Synoptics.

Francis, Fred O., and Sampley, J. Paul.
Pauline Parallels. Sources for Biblical Study, 9. Philadelphia: Fortress, 1975.
Contains the RSV text of ten letters (Rom, 1,2 Cor, Gal, Eph, Phil, Col, 1,2 Thes, Phlm) arranged in parallel columns. Each letter can be read sequentially. 311 units of parallelism have been identified on the basis of language, images, structure, and form.

Orchard, John Bernard (ed.).
A Synopsis of the Four Gospels: Arranged According to the Two-Gospel Hypothesis. Macon: Mercer University Press, 1982.
An analysis of parallel phrases, clauses, and sentences in the Gospels, so arranged as to illustrate the Griesbach-Farmer hypothesis of Matthean priority.

The Six Version Parallel New Testament. Carol Stream, Ill.: Creation House, 1974.
An arrangement of the New Testament text in six parallel columns according to the AV, Living Bible, RSV, NEB, J. B. Phillips, and JB translations.

Sparks, H. F. D.
A Synopsis of the Gospels. 2 vols. London: A & C Black, 1970, 1974.

Vol. I offers the Synoptic Gospels with the Johannine parallels. Vol. II presents the Fourth Gospel with Synoptic parallels. The English text is that of the RV.

Swanson, Ruben J.
The Horizontal Line Synopsis of the Gospels. Dillsboro: Western North Carolina Press, 1975.
Prints the parallels one under another, underlining the wordings that are in agreement.

Throckmorton, Burton H., Jr.
Gospel Parallels: A Synopsis of the First Three Gospels with Alternative Readings from the Manuscripts and Noncanonical Parallels. 4th rev. ed., Nashville-New York: Nelson, 1979.
A parallel arrangement of the 2nd ed. of the RSV text (1971) of the Synoptics. The presentation follows the 1936 edition of the Huck-Lietzmann synopsis.

C. OTHER SYNOPTIC TOOLS

Benoit, Pierre and Boismard, Marie-Émile.
Synopse des quatre évangiles en français. T. 1: *Textes.* 2nd ed., Paris: Cerf, 1973. T. 2: *Commentaire.* 1972. T. 3: *L'Évangile de Jean.* By Marie-Émile Boismard and A. Lamouille, 1977.
Prepared by Dominican scholars from the École Biblique in Jerusalem. Based on the French-language *Bible de Jerusalem.* Vol. 1 also contains significant parallels from the apocryphal gospels. Text is arranged in short lines for easy comparison. Vol. 2 is strong on literary analysis, featuring Boismard's theory of Synoptic composition. Vol. 3 contains a detailed commentary on John, based on a four-stage theory of composition.

Morgenthaler, Robert.
Statistische Synopse. Zurich: Gotthelf-Verlag, 1971.
For the specialist. Statistically presents the degree of verbal agreement and the variation in the order of the words, sentences, and sections.

V. CONCORDANCES

A. GREEK

Aland, Kurt et al. (eds.).
Vollständige Konkordanz zum griechischen Neuen Testament. Vol. I: Berlin, DeGruyter, 1975– . Vol. II. *Spezialübersichten,* 1980.
The definitive concordance, developed with the aid of computers. Based on N^{26}, it gives much fuller information than most concordances, including references to the *Textus Receptus* and the principal critical editions. Vol. II contains five specialized tables: (1) the frequency of occurrence of each word in the different books of the New Testament; (2) a listing of the entire vocabulary of the New Testament arranged according to frequency of occurrence (from the article with 1904 occurrences to *hapax legomena*); (3) an alphabetical listing of the *hapax legomena* with a citation of the book in which they appear; (4) a list of the *hapax legomena* according to the

book in which they occur; (5) an alphabetical reverse spelling listing of the words which appear in the New Testament in a declined or conjugated form.

Bachmann, H. and Slaby, W. A. (eds.).
Computer-Konkordanz zum Novum Testamentum Graece. Berlin: DeGruyter, 1980.

A simplified version of the *Vollständige Konkordanz.* Offers a listing of the words of the New Testament according to their appearance in N26 without the comparative materials and the specialized tables of the *Vollständige Konkordanz.* A sixty-four-page appendix contains a listing of the twenty-nine most common words in the New Testament with chapter and verse references (but no textual citations).

Baird, J. Arthur, and Freedman, David Noel (eds.).
The Computer Bible. Wooster: Biblical Research Associates, 1971– .

A series of concordances to individual books of the Old and New Testaments. Vol. I (1971) was on the Synoptics, Vol. V (1974) on John, etc.

Moulton, W. F., and Geden, Alfred S.
A Concordance to the Greek Testament. According to the Texts of Westcott and Hort, Tischendorf and the English Revisers. 5th ed., Edinburgh: T & T Clark, 1978.

The standard concordance to the Greek New Testament. First published in 1897. Based on Westcott-Hort's 1881 text and Tischendorf's 1875 edition.

Schmoller, Alfred.
Handkonkordanz zum griechischen Neuen Testament. 9th ed., Stuttgart: Württembergische Bibelanstalt, 1951.

Useful, but not a complete concordance. The listing of passages in which very common words appear has been significantly abridged.

B. English

Darton, Michael.
Modern Concordance to the New Testament. Garden City: Doubleday, 1976.

Based on the French *Concordance de la Bible: Nouveau Testament.* A thematic and verbal concordance in English and in Greek. Follows all current modern English translations of the New Testament.

Elder, E.
New English Bible: New Testament Concordance. London: Morgan & Scott, 1964.

Ellison, John W. (ed.).
Nelson's Complete Concordance of the Revised Standard Version Bible. New York: Nelson, 1957.

Useful, but does not include the Apocrypha. The computer compilation accounts for the strange fashion of citing references.

Hartdegen, Stephen J.
Nelson's Complete Concordance of the New American Bible. Collegeville: Liturgical Press, 1977.

Produced with the aid of computers; contains a listing of more than 18,000 key words. Each entry notes the number of times the key word appears in the NAB.

Morrison, Clinton.
An Analytic Concordance to the Revised Standard Version of the New Testament. Philadelphia: Westminster, 1979.
Provides a more comprehensive study for the reader than does the usual concordance. Lists references to other translations of a single Greek word.

Strong, James.
Strong's Exhaustive Concordance. Compact ed. Nashville: Broadman, 1979.
A reprint of the classic concordance to the AV.

Winters, R.
Word Study Concordance. Wheaton: Tyndale House, 1979.
Cross-references with Kittel's *Theological Dictionary of the New Testament,* Arndt and Gingrich's *A Greek-English Lexicon of the New Testament and other Early Christian Literature,* Moulton-Geden's *The Concordance to the Greek New Testament,* and Strong's *Exhaustive Concordance*. For students of the New Testament who have limited or no knowledge of Greek, but want to use books based on the Greek text.

C. OTHER COMPARATIVE TOOLS

Jacques, Xavier.
List of New Testament Words Sharing Common Elements. Supplement to Concordance or Dictionary. Rome: Biblical Institute Press, 1969.
Quite useful. Groups together words from the same root.

Morgenthaler, Robert.
Statistik des neutestamentlichen Wortschatzes. Zurich: Gotthelf-Verlag, 1958.
Contains tables giving the occurrences of words in the various books of the New Testament.

Smith, J. Hunter.
Greek-English Concordance to the New Testament. A Tabular and Statistical Concordance Based on the King James Version with an English-to-Greek Index. Scottdale, Pa.: Herald Press, 1955.
Based on the *Textus Receptus*. A concordance of 5,524 Greek words in the New Testament arranged alphabetically (Greek alphabet) in tabular form. Gives chapter and verse references, as well as occurrence statistics.

VI. LEXICONS AND DICTIONARIES

A. LEXICONS

Alsop, John R.
An Index to the Bauer-Arndt-Gingrich Greek Lexicon. (Reprint) Grand Rapids: Zondervan, 1973.
A computerized index, based on the New Testament text. Enables the

translator to know whether the word is cited by Arndt-Gingrich and whether the Lexicon specifically cites the particular New Testament reference.

Arndt, William F., and Gingrich, F. W.
A Greek-English Lexicon of the New Testament and Other Early Christian Literature. 2nd ed., Chicago: University of Chicago, 1979.
Best in the field. A revised version of the 5th German ed. (1958). Uses the 21st ed. of Nestle-Aland (1952) as its basic New Testament text. Excellent Introduction (on *koinē* Greek).

Liddell, Henry George, and Scott, Robert.
A Greek-English Lexicon. 9th ed., Oxford: Clarendon, 1940 (suppl. 1968).
Standard work for classical Greek. Valuable for Hellenistic Greek in general, but not quite as valuable as a tool for New Testament study.

Metzger, Bruce M.
Lexical Aids for Students of New Testament Greek. Princeton: Theological Book Agency, 1970.

Moulton, Harold K. (ed.).
The Analytic Greek Lexicon Revised. Grand Rapids: Zondervan, 1978.
Revision of the 1852 ed. Gives every word of the Greek New Testament in alphabetical order, with a complete grammatical analysis and indication of its root. Almost fifty pages are devoted to paradigms and other grammatical matters.

Newman, Barclay M., Jr.
A Concise Greek-English Dictionary of the New Testament. London: United Bible Societies, 1971.
Covers the total vocabulary contained in the text and apparatus of the United Bible Societies' *Greek New Testament.* Arranges the various meanings of words according to the frequency of occurrence in the New Testament.

B. DICTIONARIES

Balz, Haret, and Schneider, Gerhard (eds.).
Exegetisches Wörterbuch zum Neuen Testament. Stuttgart: Kohlhammer, 1978– .
A not-yet-complete German language exegetical dictionary of the NT. Represents the collaborative effort of several dozen German scholars. Entries are much shorter than those contained in Kittel, and are limited to the significance of the term in the NT. A good bibliography is provided for the longer entries.

Bauer, Johannes Baptist.
Sacramentum Verbi. 3 vols. New York: Herder & Herder, 1970.
Translated from the 3rd German ed. (1967). Collaborative effort of forty exegetes. Intended for theologians as well as those in pastoral work. Useful bibliographies with each article.

Brown, Colin (ed.).
New International Dictionary of New Testament Theology. 3 vols. Exeter: Paternoster, 1975–78.

Revision and translation of L. Coenen's (ed.) *Theologisches Be-griffslexicon zum Neuen Testament* (1967–71). Similar to Kittel, but on a much smaller scale. Conservative scholarship.

Bryant, T. A. (ed.).
The New Compact Bible Dictionary. Grand Rapids: Zondervan, 1977.
The 19th printing of a work published in 1967. For the lay person and preacher. Conservative orientation. Approximately 5,000 entries. Illustrated.

Buttrick, George Arthur, et al. (eds.).
The Interpreter's Dictionary of the Bible. 4 vols., suppl. New York-Nashville: Abingdon, 1962, suppl., 1976.
Excellent work, of value to exegete, theologian, pastor. Aims to be comprehensive. Illustrated. Articles are of good quality and length. Good bibliography.

Cazelles, Henri, and Feuillet, André (eds.).
Supplément au Dictionnaire de la Bible. Paris: Letouzey & Ané, 1928– .
Excellent work by French Catholic scholars. Some of the articles are book-length. Bibliographies are excellent. Some of the earlier volumes are now out of date.

Kittel, Gerhard, and Friedrich, Gerhard (eds.).
Theological Dictionary of the New Testament. 10 vols. Grand Rapids: Eerdmans, 1964–74.
Translation of the German *Theologisches Wörterbuch zum Neuen Testament* (*TWNT*) (1922–73). Indispensable book for New Testament study, but the earlier volumes (esp. 1–4) are now out of date. The methodology has been criticized by James Barr. Vol. 10 contains indexes.

Léon-Dufour, Xavier.
Dictionary of Biblical Theology. New York: Seabury, 1973.
Translated from the 2nd rev. French ed. (1970). Theological orientation. Good cross-references.

———.
Dictionary of the New Testament. San Francisco: Harper & Row, 1980.
Contains an overview of sociohistorical and religious data, as well as entries on more than 1,000 words which occur in the New Testament. Based on the 2nd rev. French ed. (1978).

Mateos, Juan, and Barreto, Juan (eds.).
Vocabulario teologico del evangelio de Juan. Madrid: Ediciones Cristianidad, 1980.
A theological dictionary whose entries are limited to terms appearing in the Fourth Gospel. In Spanish, the dictionary is based on the Spanish text, but contains statistical data on the uses of the corresponding Greek terms.

McKenzie, John L.
Dictionary of the Bible. Milwaukee: Bruce, 1965.
Unique; the work of one man. This gives a unity of style and approach not normally found in dictionaries. Individual entries do not have their own bibliographies.

Richardson, Alan (ed.).
A Theological Word Book of the Bible. London: SCM, 1960.
A study of 250 key words by thirty British and American scholars, as well as the general editor himself. The orientation of the entries is largely theological. Good system of cross-references.

Soulen, Richard N.
Handbook of Biblical Criticism. 2nd rev. ed., Atlanta: John Knox Press, 1981.
Not a biblical dictionary in the ordinary sense of the term, but a glossary of terms for those interested in biblical studies. Bibliographies accompany many articles. Quite useful.

van den Born, Adrianus.
Encyclopedic Dictionary of the Bible. New York: McGraw-Hill, 1963.
L. F. Hartman's translation and adaptation of the 2nd Dutch ed. (1954–57). Deals with persons, biblical sites, themes. Brief entries.

von Allmen, Jean-Jacques.
A Companion to the Bible. New York: Oxford University Press, 1958.
Collaborative effort, of uneven quality; thirty-seven scholars, of the Swiss Calvinist tradition, have produced this study of 160 key words. Translated from the French (2nd ed. 1956).

VII. GRAMMARS

Blass, Friedrich, and Debrunner, Albert.
A Greek Grammar of the New Testament and Other Early Christian Literature. Chicago: University Press, 1961.
The standard work. This version of the 9th–10th German editions was done by R. W. Funk, who has added supplementary notes.

Gignac, Francis Thomas.
An Introductory New Testament Greek Course. Chicago: Loyola University, 1973.

Moule, Charles Francis Digby.
An Idiom-Book of New Testament Greek. 2nd ed., Cambridge: University Press, 1959.
A syntactical companion to the interpretation of the New Testament. Studies the main features of New Testament syntax. Valuable companion to works on classical Greek syntax.

Moulton, James Hope.
A Grammar of New Testament Greek. 4 vols. Edinburgh: T & T Clark, 1908, 1919, 1963, 1976.
Vol. I, by Moulton, contains the prolegomena. Vol. II, by W. F. Howard, is on accidence and word formation, with an appendix on Semitisms. Vol. III, by N. Turner, is on syntax. Vol. IV, by Turner, is on style.

Robertson, Archibald Thomas.
A Grammar of the Greek New Testament in the Light of Historical Research. 4th ed., Nashville: Broadman, 1923.

Widely used in the U.S. Contains good indexes of subjects, Greek words, and quotations.

Zerwick, Maximilian.
Biblical Greek. Rome: Biblical Institute Press, 1963.
Adapted from the 4th Latin ed.

Zerwick, Maximilian, and Grosvenor, Mary.
A Grammatical Analysis of the Greek New Testament. 2 vols. Rome: Biblical Institute Press, 1974, 1979.
A verse-by-verse philological analysis of the Greek New Testament, as well as a glossary of grammatical terms. A list of Greek words occurring more than sixty times, paradigms of verbs, and a listing of rules governing tense formations.

VIII. INTRODUCTIONS TO THE NEW TESTAMENT

Bornkamm, Günther.
The New Testament. A Guide to Its Writings. Philadelphia: Fortress, 1963.
Though covering the entire New Testament, concentrates principally on the Synoptics and Paul. Intended to bring out the rich diversity of New Testament ideas. Brief consideration of New Testament canon.

Grant, Robert Macqueen.
A Historical Introduction to the New Testament. New York: Harper & Row, 1963.
A popular introduction to the New Testament. Bears the stamp of the author's own views. Heavy emphasis on the Church as the reality behind the New Testament literature.

Guthrie, Donald.
New Testament Introduction. Downers Grove: Inter-Varsity, 1970.
The standard conservative, almost fundamentalist, introduction to the New Testament. Gives good coverage of the then available literature. Previously published in three volumes. (1961, 1962, 1965).

Juel, Donald.
An Introduction to New Testament Literature. Nashville: Abingdon, 1978.
Designed principally for students and teachers of literature.

Klijn, Albertus Frederick Johannus.
An Introduction to the New Testament. 2nd ed., Leiden: Brill, 1980.
Intended for university and seminary students. Useful appendix (Papias, Gallio inscription, Muratorian Canon). Gives many quotations from early Christian sources. Its judgments on some debated points remain minority positions among scholars.

Kümmel, Werner Georg.
Introduction to the New Testament. Rev. ed., London: SCM, 1975.
Best in its field. Contains a tremendous amount of highly compressed information. Especially valuable for its introductions to the various books of the New Testament. It has excellent bibliographies, but is weak on the Catholic contribution. Translation of the 17th ed. (1973) of Feine-Behm-Kümmel, *Einleitung in das Neue Testament.*

Marxsen, Willi.
   Introduction to the New Testament: An Approach to its Problems. Philadelphia: Fortress, 1968.
   A chronological and somewhat thematic presentation: Pauline letters (8), Synoptics—Acts, Pseudo-Pauline (Eph, Col, 1,2 Tim, Tit, Heb), Church Epistles, Johannine literature. Readable. Emphasizes Marxsen's own exegetical approach.

Wikenhauser, Alfred.
   New Testament Introduction. New York: Herder & Herder, 1968.
   Still the best Catholic introduction to the New Testament (Canon, Special Introduction, Text) available in English, but clearly dated. Translation from the 2nd German edition (1956).

IX. THE NEW TESTAMENT CONTEXT

A. HISTORY, GEOGRAPHY, TOPOGRAPHY

Bruce, Frederick F.
   New Testament History. London: Nelson, 1969.
   Brief but good coverage of New Testament history as a whole. Particularly valuable for the wider background to the New Testament. Perhaps the best of the single-volume studies in the field.

Filson, Floyd Vivian.
   A New Testament History: The Story of the Emerging Church. Westminster Aids to the Study of the Scriptures. Philadelphia: Westminster, 1964.
   A useful coverage of the subject matter.

Finegan, Jack.
   The Archaeology of the New Testament: The Life of Jesus and the Beginnings of the Early Church. Princeton: Princeton University Press, 1969.
   More up to date and more complete than most on the New Testament period, but contains nothing on Acts, Paul, Revelation.

———.
   Handbook of Biblical Chronology: Principles of Time Reckoning in the Ancient World and Problems of Chronology in the Bible. Princeton: Princeton University Press, 1964.
   A useful guide in a very complex world.

Grollenberg, Lucas H.
   Atlas of the Bible. New York: Thomas Nelson, 1956.
   The best of the many Bible atlases. The abridged version, *A Shorter Atlas of the Bible* (Harmondsworth: Penguin, 1978), is also useful.

Kopp, Clemens.
   The Holy Places of the Gospels. New York: Herder & Herder, 1963.
   Subjects to a critical evaluation the history contained in the writings of early pilgrims to the Holy Land.

Reicke, Bo.
The New Testament Era: The World of the Bible from 500 B.C. to A.D. 100. Philadelphia: Fortress, 1968.
Brief but packed with information. To some extent, it reflects the author's particular views.

Schürer, Emil.
A History of the Jewish People in the Times of Jesus Christ. 5 vols. 2nd ed., New York: Scribner's, 1886–90.
The standard work. Covers the period from 175 B.C. to A.D. 130 from the political, social, religious, and literary points of view. A complete revision is now in process under the general editorship of M. Black, G. Vermes, and F. Miller (Vol. I, 1973; Vol. II, 1979).

B. THE SOCIAL AND IDEOLOGICAL CONTEXT

Barrett, Charles Kingsley.
The New Testament Background. Selected Documents Edited with Introductions. New York: Harper & Bros., 1961.
A general reader containing useful source material on history, philosophy, religion, literature.

Cartlidge, David R., and Dungan, David L.
Documents for the Study of the Gospels. Cleveland: Collins, 1980.
Contains valuable translations of Christian documents about the Savior (e.g., G Thom, Acts of Thomas) as well as a selection of Greek, Roman, and Jewish documents that illustrate the New Testament environment.

Colson, F. H., et al.
Philo. 10 vols., 2 suppl. *The Loeb Classical Library.* Cambridge: Harvard University Press, 1929–62.
The standard edition of the works of this Hellenistic Jewish thinker contemporary with Jesus and Paul.

Hengel, Martin.
Judaism and Hellenism. 2 vols. London: SCM, 1974.
An extensive study of the cultural and religious situation in Palestine during the Hellenistic period.

Jeremias, Joachim.
Jerusalem in the Time of Jesus: An Investigation into Economic and Social Conditions During the New Testament Period. Philadelphia: Fortress, 1969.
Detailed, very valuable information.

Judge, E. A.
The Social Pattern of the Christian Groups in the First Century: Some Prolegomena to the Study of New Testament Ideas of Social Obligation. London: Tyndale, 1960.
Treats the notions of citizenship, order, and community, the relationships of Christian groups, and legal proceedings involving Christians.

Kee, Howard Clark.
The Origins of Christianity. Sources and Documents. Englewood Cliffs: Prentice-Hall, 1973.

A very useful selection of texts. The index is hardly adequate.

Lohse, Eduard.
The New Testament Environment. New Testament Library. London: SCM, 1976.

Covers both Judaism in the Hellenistic Period and the Hellenistic-Roman environment of the New Testament. An excellent one-volume study, probably the best of its kind.

Malherbe, Abraham J.
Social Aspects of Early Christianity. Baton Rouge: Louisiana State University, 1977.

Contains the Rockwell Lectures of April 1975. Offers a sociological approach to early Christianity, treating the social level and literary culture of early Christianity, and house churches and their problems.

Montefiore, Claude G., and Loewe, Herbert.
A Rabbinic Anthology. New York: Schocken, 1974.

A handy collection of rabbinic texts. Contains a glossary, a list of the principal rabbis, and good indexes.

Moore, George Foot.
Judaism in the First Three Centuries of the Christian Era. The Age of the Tannaim. 3 vols. Cambridge: Harvard University Press, 1927–30.

A dated but still valuable introduction to rabbinic theology. Published before the discoveries at Qumran, it offers a one-dimensional view of Judaism.

Neusner, Jacob.
Rabbinic Traditions about the Pharisees before 70. 3 vols. Leiden: Brill, 1971.

A major contribution to the field, even if Neusner's own views have sometimes been criticized as being too radical.

Safrai, Shmuel, and Stern, M. (eds.).
The Jewish People in the First Century. 2 vols. *Compendia rerum Iudaicarum ad Novum Testamentum,* I. Assen: Van Gorcum, 1974, 1976.

Twenty-four studies by several scholars offering a wealth of information on Jewish culture, history, and religion. For a source book, eminently readable. Vol. II contains the indexes and a survey of the material.

St. John Thackeray, Henry, et al.
Josephus. 9 vols. *The Loeb Classical Library.* Cambridge: Harvard University Press, 1926–65.

The standard English translation of the works of the first-century Jewish historian.

Strack, Hermann Leberecht, and Billerbeck, Paul.
Kommentar zum Neuen Testament aus Talmud und Midrasch. 6 vols. Munich: Beck, 1922–61.

A collection of rabbinic parallels to the New Testament, arranged according to chapter and verse in the New Testament. Vol. 4 contains systematic expositions of a limited number of New Testament themes in the light of rabbinic documentation. Vol. 5 contains the indexes while Vol. 6 (edited by Joachim Jeremias and Kurt Adolph) is a register of the names of rabbis, complete with references to Vols. 1–4.

Theissen, Gerd.
> *Sociology of Early Palestinian Christianity*. Philadelphia: Fortress, 1977.
> Concerned with cultural factors, roles, and functions pertinent to first-century Palestinian Christianity.

Vermes, Geza.
> *The Dead Sea Scrolls: Qumran in Perspective*. London: Collins, 1977.
> A good overview, with useful bibliographies and a guide to the editions of the texts.

———.
> *The Dead Sea Scrolls in English*. 2nd ed., Harmondsworth: Penguin, 1975.
> Not perfect, but a readily available English translation of the principal scrolls.

X. THE MAJOR SERIES OF NEW TESTAMENT COMMENTARIES IN ENGLISH

Anchor Bible. Garden City: Doubleday, 1964– .
> Ecumenical series of uneven quality. Originally 13 vols. were projected for the New Testament, but some have appeared in two parts. The works by J. Fitzmyer (The Gospel According to Luke) and R. E. Brown (The Gospel According to John) are excellent.

Cambridge Commentary on the New English Bible. London: Cambridge University Press, 1972– .
> Old and New Testaments. An inexpensive, popular commentary with conservative tendencies. Good for its syntheses of the major exegetical opinions.

Cambridge Greek New Testament. Cambridge: University Press, 1957– .
> Intended to replace two earlier Cambridge series. Has a theological orientation. Under the general editorship of C. F. D. Moule, who published the first volume (Col, Phlm) in 1957.

Harper's New Testament Commentaries. New York: Harper & Row, 1960– .
> Based on the RSV. Several volumes have already appeared in a second edition. Among the English-language commentaries, this might be the best for the general reader. It appears in Great Britain as Black's New Testament Commentaries.

Herder's Theological Commentary on the New Testament. New York: Herder, 1968.
> Originally projected as an English translation of the 14-vol. *Herders Theologischer Kommentar zum NT* (*HThK*). The project of translation has lagged, while the German texts have continued to appear. In English, only the volumes of Schnackenburg's work on John have appeared.

Hermeneia. Philadelphia: Fortress, 1972– .
> Scholarly. Intended to provide an English-language readership with the best commentaries written from the perspective of the historical-critical methodology. Some translations; some original works. Under the edi-

torship of H. Koester, E. J. Epp, R. W. Funk, G. W. MacRae, and J. M. Robinson.

International Critical Commentary. Edinburgh: T & T Clark, 1895–   .
Old and New Testaments. Emphasis on critical and philological elements. Parallel to the major German works, with 17 vols. devoted to the New Testament. The most recent (esp. G. E. B. Cranfield on Rom, 1975, 1979) are excellent.

The Interpreter's Bible. New York-Nashville: Abingdon, 1951–57.
Old Testament (6 vols.) and New Testament (6 vols.). Offers both AV and RSV texts in parallel columns. Good for homiletic exposition, less useful for academic study.

Invitation to Matthew [etc.]. Garden City: Doubleday, 1977– .
Based on the Jerusalem Bible. Aims to present the best of contemporary scholarship to the educated lay person in a readable and understandable manner. The general editor is R. J. Karris of the Catholic Theological Union in Chicago.

Moffatt New Testament Commentary. London: Hodder & Stoughton, 1928–50.
A 17-vol. commentary based on Moffatt's translation. Dated, but several volumes are virtually classic—e.g., Dodd on the Johannine epistles, Foakes-Jackson on Acts.

New Century Bible. London: Oliphants, 1967– .
Based on the RSV. Directed to a general readership. Represents a form of mildly critical scholarship. Occasionally offers singular opinions.

New Clarendon Bible. Oxford: University Press, 1963– .
Popular commentaries for a general readership. Some volumes based on RSV, some on NEB. Replaces the Clarendon Bible (1925–37).

New International Commentary on the New Testament. Grand Rapids: Eerdmans, 1959– .
Intended for the exegete and pastor alike. Conservative tendency. Presents sound scholarship with a reverent treatment of the word of God. Abundant material. Under the general editorship of N. B. Stonehouse.

New Testament Commentary. Grand Rapids: Baker, 1963– .
Conservative scholarship in the reformed tradition. Provides its own translation of the NT text.

New Testament Message. Wilmington: Glazier, 1979–80.
A pastorally oriented series in 22 vols., presenting the results of solid scholarship to a broader readership. The commentators are members of the Catholic Biblical Association of America.

The Pelican New Testament Commentaries. Baltimore: Penguin, 1963– .
Solid but popular commentaries by well-respected British scholars. Makes use of the RSV. For the money, the best available.

Proclamation Commentaries: The New Testament. Witness for Preaching. Philadelphia: Fortress, 1975– .
Designed to help the nonprofessional student of the Bible—especially preachers—share in the results of scholarly research. Quite useful, but with a limited purpose.

Torch Bible Commentaries. London: SCM, 1949– .
Seventeen volumes, but of little academic value.

Tyndale New Testament Commentaries. Grand Rapids: Eerdmans, 1956– .
A 20-volume series with detailed historical introductions. Heavily theological, with a very conservative orientation.

XI. THE PRINCIPAL JOURNALS

Australian Biblical Review (Melbourne, 1953–).
A quarterly published by the Fellowship for Biblical Studies.

Bible Bhashyam (Kottayam, 1975–).
An Indian biblical quarterly published under Roman Catholic auspices in the state of Kerala.

The Bible Today (Collegeville, 1962–).
A popular journal written in the Catholic tradition for a very general readership. Appears six times a year.

The Bible Translator (Ashford, 1950–).
A quarterly publication of the United Bible Societies. The issues appear in two series: technical papers in January and July (nos. 1 and 3); practical papers in April and October (nos. 2 and 4). The articles are important but have a limited focus.

Biblica (Rome, 1920–).
A Catholic periodical that publishes high-quality, specialized articles in several different languages.

Biblical Archaeologist (Cambridge, 1918–).
More valuable for the study of the Old Testament than for the study of the New Testament. Contains reports on recent discoveries.

Biblical Research (Chicago, 1957–).
The quarterly journal of the Chicago Society of Biblical Research. Frequently publishes papers delivered at meetings of the society.

Biblical Theology Bulletin (Albany, 1971–).
A journal dedicated to the publication of survey articles by Catholic scholars.

Bibliotheca Sacra (Dallas, 1844–).
A quarterly published by the Dallas Theological Seminary. Most of its articles are on the Bible. Conservative orientation.

Biblische Zeitschrift (Paderborn, 1903–).
Contains articles by Catholic scholars. Directed to a scholarly, though not specialized, readership. German.

Bulletin. United Bible Societies (Stuttgart, 1950–).
Contains many studies on the Bible, focusing more on its impact than on particular texts.

Catholic Biblical Quarterly (Washington, 1939–).
The journal of the Catholic Biblical Association of America. Contains specialized articles, excellent book reviews.

Downside Review (Bath, 1917–).
Quarterly publication of the English Benedictines of Down monastery, near Bath. Contains occasional articles on the New Testament.

Ephemerides Theologicae Lovanienses (Louvain, 1924–).
A quarterly published by professors of the Catholic University of Louvain. Contains many specialized articles in the New Testament field. Multilingual.

The Evangelical Quarterly (Buxton, 1928–).
A theological review "international in scope and outlook, in defense of the historic Christian faith." Contains many significant studies from the evangelical point of view.

Expository Times (Banstead, 1889–).
Not specifically directed to biblical studies, yet contains many articles of interest on the New Testament.

Harvard Theological Review (Cambridge, 1908–).
Occasionally contains some specialized articles on the New Testament.

Interpretation (Richmond, 1947–).
A publication of the Union Theological Seminary (Virginia). Contains excellent articles directed to an educated readership. Most issues are thematic.

Irish Biblical Studies (Belfast, 1979–).
A new quarterly, featuring thematic studies.

Journal for the Study of the New Testament (Sheffield, 1978–).
Intended to provide rapid publication of articles for the New Testament specialist.

Journal of Biblical Literature (Missoula, 1882–).
The most important U.S. publication in the biblical field.

Journal of the Evangelical Theological Society (Wheaton, 1958–).
Published by the society, it contains many evangelically oriented studies on the New Testament.

New Testament Studies (Cambridge, 1954–).
The scholarly quarterly of the Society for New Testament Studies. One of the "musts." Multilingual, but mostly English-language text.

Novum Testamentum (Leiden, 1956–).
An excellent, but highly specialized quarterly. Multilingual.

Review and Expositor (Louisville, 1904–).
A quarterly issuing from the Southern Baptist tradition. Each year the fall issue is devoted to one biblical book.

Revue biblique (Jerusalem, 1892–).
The quarterly of the École Biblique in Jerusalem. Catholic in its orientation, it contains articles on New Testament exegesis and theology, as well as on archaeological explorations. Mainly French.

Semeia (Missoula, 1974–).
An experimental journal by American scholars, principally reflecting a "structural analysis" approach to the Bible. Erratic publication schedule.

Theological Studies (Washington, 1940–   ).
   The influential quarterly of the American Jesuits. Occasionally contains technical articles of interest to the New Testament student.

Theologische Rundschau (Tübingen, 1897–   ).
   Useful for its book reviews and its literature. German.

Theologische Zeitschrift (Basel, 1945–   ).
   The quarterly publication of the University of Basel. Represents a moderately critical scholarship. Mainly German.

Zeitschrift für die neutestamentliche Wissenshaft (Berlin, 1902–   ).
   The most important of the German-language publications in the New Testament field. Represents a high degree of critical scholarship.

A GLOSSARY OF TERMS

Achronic
> Derived from the Greek *chronos* (time) with a primitive alpha, the term means timeless. It is used in structural analysis to designate essential factors, especially the deep structures which transcend any particular age or culture.

Actant
> A semantic unit situated at a more abstract level than the actor who actually appears in a narrative. It can be singular or plural, concrete or abstract. Generally speaking, it refers to a "function" expressed within a narrative.

Actantial Model
> As developed by A. J. Greimas, a schema used in the interpretation of a narrative:

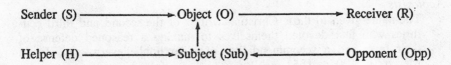

Adoptionist
> Pertaining to a tendency in Christian thought according to which Christ, in His humanity, is not the ontological but only the adoptive Son of God. In an extreme form, the tendency was present in Adoptionism, an eighth-century heresy.

Agraphon (pl., *agrapha*)
> Transliterated from the Greek *agraphon,* "unwritten." As a technical term, the expression is used of the traditional sayings of Jesus not contained in the canonical Gospels.

Akhmîm Fragment

A fragment of an eighth-century Greek ms. discovered by Bouriant at Akhmîm, Egypt, during the winter of 1886–87. It contains extensive portions of the Greek Enoch and scraps of the Gospel of Peter and the Apocalypse of Peter.

Allegorical interpretation

A kind of interpretation which assumes that the text at hand conveys a meaning other than the literal meaning of its words.

Alterity

In structural analysis, the state of being different.

Amanuensis

Transliteration of the Latin, meaning "a scribe"; specifically one who writes from dictation.

Anagogical

In medieval criticism, the spiritual or mystical meaning. In the Middle Ages the four meanings of a text were the literal, the tropological, the allegorical, and the anagogical.

Apocalyptic

The term sometimes designates a literary form, sometimes a fashion of writing, and sometimes a world view. It entails a dramatic and symbolic description of the end-time events—e.g., Mark 13; Revelation.

Apocryphal

Designating noncanonical writings dating from the second to the sixth centuries. The apocryphal writings can be in the form of Gospels, Acts, Epistles, or Apocalypses.

Apocryphon

Literally, "the hidden thing." The term appears in the title of an esoteric version of Genesis found at Qumran, the *Genesis Apocryphon*.

Apodosis

The principal clause of a conditional sentence. It states a conclusion conditioned on the fulfillment of a supposition stated in the conditional clause.

Apologists

The name given to those Christian writers of the second and third centuries who first devoted themselves to making a reasoned defense of their faith and a recommendation of it to nonbelievers—e.g., Justin Martyr (ca.100–ca.165).

Aporia

In source criticism, the name applied to the abrupt transitions, inconsistencies, and anomalies that sometimes give notice that an author has put together material coming from different sources.

Apostolic Fathers

The name given to those first- and early second-century Christian authors whose works were not included in the NT canon, even though they were highly valued by the early Christian churches—e.g., Ignatius of Antioch (ca. 35–ca. 107).

Apostolic Parousia

A literary type, identified by R. W. Funk, characterized by the motif of apostolic authority and power as these are expressed in a statement of Paul's reason for writing, his intention to send an emissary, and his intention to pay the congregation a personal visit.

Apothegm (pl., *apothegmata* or *apothegms*)

A technical term used by R. Bultmann to designate the literary type more commonly known as the "pronouncement story" (V. Taylor) or the "paradigm" (M. Dibelius).

Apparatus

The text-critical footnotes found in the editions of the Greek New Testament. These footnotes cite the units of variation and the sources in which the various readings can be found.

Aramaic

The Semitic language commonly spoken in Palestine in the time of Jesus of Nazareth.

Aramaism

A feature of biblical Greek which shows the influence of Aramaic style and vocabulary—e.g., *Abba* (Mark 14:36; Rom 8:15); "do not begin to say" (Luke 3:8).

Aretalogy

From the Greek *arētē,* "virtue" or "power." The term designates a collection of miracle stories—e.g., the Signs Source generally considered to have been used by the author of the Fourth Gospel.

Asyndeton

A figure of speech that omits connectives.

Authentic

A term used to describe a work which contemporary biblical scholarship judges to have been written by the individual to whom it has traditionally been ascribed.

Benedictions, Great (or, *Eighteen Benedictions*)

A group of prayers, chiefly composed of biblical phrases, solemnly recited at each of three daily services of the Jewish synagogue. These were revised during the time of Gamaliel II (ca. 80–120) in order to exclude Christians and Gnostics from the synagogue.

Benedictus

Literally, "blessed." Borrowed from the Latin, the term designates the canticle found in Luke 1:68–79.

Biblical Movement

A movement within Roman Catholicism immediately after the Second World War. It focused upon a renewed interest in the Scriptures, their interpretation, and their use in the renewal of the Church's doctrine and life.

Biblical Question

The expression designates a phenomenon within Roman Catholicism at the end of the nineteenth century and the beginning of the twentieth century. It indicates a raising of issues pertaining to the interpretation of the Sacred Scriptures as a result of advances in the fields of the historical and physical sciences.

Canon
A transliteration of the Greek *kanōn,* meaning "guiding principle," "norm," or "rule." It designates the collection of books accepted as the authoritative norm of the Church's faith and worship.

Catalogue of Virtues or Vices (Ger., *Tugenkatalog* or *Lasterkatalog*)
Literary types frequently used in NT epistolary literature and characterized by a listing of virtues or vices—e.g., Gal 5:22–23; Jas 3:17; Gal 5:19–21; Rom 1:29–31. The literary type was developed from Stoic usage.

Catechesis
A Greek term meaning "oral instruction." As used in biblical studies, the term pertains principally to baptismal paraenesis.

Catena (pl., *catenae*)
A technical term borrowed from the Latin, used to designate a sequence of connected items—miracle stories, logia, liturgical formulas, etc.

Catholic Epistles (Catholic letters)
A term that designates the seven general letters of the NT: James, 1,2 Peter, 1,2,3 John, Jude.

Chiasmus (adj., *chiastic*)
A literary figure that consists of a "placing crosswise" of words in a sentence or themes in a unit of composition. The term is used in rhetoric to designate an inversion of the order of words or phrases which are repeated or subsequently referred to in the sentence.

Code
In structural analysis, a formal structure composed of a small number of content-related words which together indicate the content of a given aspect of reality or of the mythical universe.

Colophon
The paragraph found at the end of a manuscript.

Competence
In structural analysis, a system of rules which is aptly described as the grammar of an author's (or speaker's) language. Simply stated, it is the ability to generate utterances.

Concordance
An alphabetical listing of the principal words of a book, identifying where these words occur and usually giving a few accompanying words from the immediate context.

Contradictio
A loan word from the Latin. In rhetorical and literary analysis, a term used to designate the correlative expression of denial and affirmation for the sake of emphasis—e.g., 1 Thes 4:7, "For God has not called us in uncleanness, but in holiness."

Corpus
A collection of writings—e.g., the Pauline corpus (Romans, 1,2 Corinthians, Galatians, Ephesians, Philippians, Colossians, 1,2 Thessalonians,

1,2 Timothy, Titus, Philemon, Hebrews), or the Johannine corpus (John, 1,2,3 John, Revelation).

Cum Biblia Sacra

Literally "with the Sacred Bible." The expression is the title of an apostolic letter of Pope Benedict XV, dated August 15, 1916. The letter was concerned with several institutions relating to the Bible: viz., the Biblical Commission and the Committee for the Restoration of the Vulgate.

Decretum Gelasianum (The Decretal of Gelasius)

An old Latin document commonly attributed to Pope Gelasius (492–96). In some manuscripts it is included among the works of Pope Damasus (366–84) or Pope Hormisdas (514–23). Some scholars, however, consider the document to be a private compilation made in early sixth-century Italy.

Dei Filius

Literally, "Son of God." The expression serves as the title of the Dogmatic Constitution on the Catholic Faith issued by Vatican Council I on April 24, 1870.

Deism

A system of natural religion first developed in England in the late seventeenth and early eighteenth centuries and later quite influential in France and Germany. Its chief tenet was belief in a Creator God, separated from his creatures.

Dei Verbum

Literally, the "Word of God." The expression is the title of the Second Vatican Council's *Dogmatic Constitution on Divine Revelation,* approved and promulgated on November 18, 1965.

Deixis (adj., *deictic*)

The pointing function of the demonstrative pronouns (this, that) and some adverbs (here and now).

Demotic

In Egyptian archaeology, a term designating a simplified form of the hieratic character of script.

Demythologization (Ger., *Entymythologisierung*)

As a technical term, it refers to Bultmann's interpretation of biblical myths in terms of the understanding of existence. In a less technical sense, it refers to the removal of mythical elements from traditional material.

Deutero-Pauline

A term applied to certain writings in the NT (esp. 2 Thessalonians, Colossians, Ephesians, 1,2 Timothy, Titus) which are explicitly attributed to Paul, but may not have been written by him.

Diachronic

Derived from the Greek *dia* (through) and *chronos* (time), the term pertains to an approach to the understanding of a reality (text or event) according to which this reality is understood on the basis of all the moments that preceded it.

Diaspora

Transliteration of the Greek *diaspora,* "dispersion." The term designates the extra-Palestinian dispersion of the Jews, which had its beginnings in the Assyrian (722 B.C.) and Babylonian (597 B.C.) deportations.

Didache

(1) In form-critical analysis, the term designates the instructional material of the early church, as distinct from the *kerygma* (the proclamation, especially the initial proclamation to the unbaptized) and catechesis (moral instruction and exhortation).

(2) The *Didache, The Teaching of the Twelve Apostles,* is a late first- or early second-century Christian document, a manual of Church instruction on the "Two Ways."

Divino Afflante Spiritu

Literally, "under the inspiration of the Divine Spirit." The expression is the title of an encyclical letter on biblical studies issued by Pope Pius XII on September 30, 1943.

Docetist

Designating a tendency to consider the humanity and sufferings of Jesus as apparent rather than real.

Early Catholicism (Ger., *Frükatholicismus*)

A technical term used to designate a doctrinal system characterized by a resolution of the tension between Jewish and Hellenistic Christianity, the resolution of the crisis caused by the delay of the Parousia, and the gradual institutionalization of the Church (canon of Scripture, sacraments, etc.).

Ebionite

An early Jewish-Christian sect that had a reductionist Christology and an overemphasis on the observance of the Mosaic law.

Einmalig

Literally, "one time." Borrowed from the German, the term is sometimes applied to the singular events of Jesus' life insofar as these were one-time occurrences.

Encratite

Transliteration of the Greek *enkratitai.* Pertaining to an extreme form of ascetical practice among some first- and second-century Christian groups.

Eschatocol

A literary term used to designate the conclusion of a document (e.g., 1 Cor 16:19–23; Phlm 23–25).

Eschatology (adj., *eschatological*)

In NT studies, teaching about the final times. The term has achieved considerable prominence because of Albert Schweitzer's interpretation of the eschatology of Jesus. Schweitzer contended that Jesus expected that God would bring the present age to a close and inaugurate his Reign in an immediate future.

Eschaton

Literally, "the final reality." In biblical studies the term is used to designate the sum total of the events of the final times (e.g., the Parousia, the coming of the kingdom of God).

Essene

Pertaining to a Jewish ascetic sect that existed in Palestine from approximately 200 B.C. to A.D. 100. Traditionally known only through occasional references in Philo, Josephus, and Pliny, it is now relatively well known because of the discovery of the Dead Sea Scrolls at Qumran (1947).

Exegesis

(1) The attempt to understand a text in its original context. Exegesis is the exposition of what an author intended to say to his readers in contemporary language.

(2) The science of the interpretation of texts.

Exegete

An interpreter of a (NT) text.

Family

In textual criticism, the smallest identifiable group of related manuscripts —e.g., the Lake family, to which minuscules 1, 113, and 118 belong.

Farewell Discourse (Ger., *Abschiedsrede*)

A technical term used in form-critical studies to designate the literary form that features the speech of a person who takes leave of his friends, exhorting them to be united and faithful, and making some statement about the future. The farewell discourse often functions as a "testament," leaving goods to one's heirs. Specifically, the term is used of Jesus' Farewell Discourse in John 13 – 17.

Fathers of the Church

A term first applied to bishops as witnesses to the Christian tradition. It is now commonly used of the ancient ecclesiastical writers—up to the time of St. Isidore of Seville (died 636) in the West and St. John Damascene (died 749) in the East—whose doctrinal authority carries special weight.

Form Criticism (Ger., *Formgeschichte*)

A method of NT exegesis which attempts ot trace the provenance of the pericopes by means of a close analysis of their literary form. Among NT scholars, the term first appeared in the title of a book by Martin Dibelius (1919).

Formula-Quotation (or, Fulfillment Citation)

A stylistic device, frequently employed by Matthew, which highlights a biblical citation by means of a significant, though stereotyped, introductory formula—e.g., Matt 1:22–23.

Function

In structural analysis, the action of a particular person from the perspective of the flow of the narrative.

Generative Poetics

As developed by E. Güttgemanns, a theory of the development of the Gospel genre which seeks to show that the structures of the genre are rules of competence which make possible the understanding of the text.

Genre

In form criticism, a macro-literary type. In structural analysis, the totality of creative works that share the same "poetical system, purpose in daily life, performance forms and musical structure" (Propp).

Glossolalia

A transliteration of the Greek term, which means "speaking in tongues."

Gnostic

Derived from the Greek *gnōsis,* "knowledge." A dualistic current of thought widely diffused throughout the Mediterranean Basin during the first and second centuries. Several of the Gnostic systems (constructs which are presently the object of much scholarly discussion) feature a Redeemer who descends from above in order to impart knowledge to an elite circle of intimates, thereby ensuring their salvation.

Grammar

In structural analysis, a collection of those forms of a language that do not enter into the lexicon itself.

Griesbach-Farmer Hypothesis

An explanation of the Synoptic problem which proposes the literary priority of Matthew, the dependence of Luke on Matthew, and Mark's dependence on both Matthew and Luke.

Haggadah (adj., *haggadic*)

Rabbinic traditions (stories, anecdotes, legends, etc.) that illustrate the Torah. The term is derived from the Hebrew verb *aggadah,* "to narrate."

Halakah (adj., *halakic*)

The rules of conduct handed down by the rabbis as the authentic interpretation of the written Scriptures and the oral tradition. The term is derived from the Hebrew verb *halak,* "to walk."

Hapax Legomenon (or simply, *hapax;* pl., *hapax legomena*)

A Greek expression meaning "said only once." In NT studies, a word or expression that occurs only once in the NT or a particular NT book, or is used only once by a NT author.

Hermeneutical circle

The path thought takes in its attempt to find meaning.

Hermeneutics

A term derived from the Greek verb *hermeneuein,* "to explain." It designates the science of explaining and interpreting a text. Hermeneutics generally seeks to establish rules, principles, and methods for use in the interpretive endeavor. For some authors, the term designates the principles of exegesis (as distinct from the practice of exegesis); for others, it designates the science of discerning how a text written in one cultural context may be understood in another.

Hierosolymae in coenobio

Literally, "in a monastery of Jerusalem." The expression designates the apostolic letter of Pope Leo XIII, dated September 17, 1892, and commending the establishment of the École Biblique in 1890 in Jerusalem.

Higher Criticism

A term, once in common use, to describe the literary and historical interpretation of biblical texts, an endeavor distinct from the establishment of the text ("lower criticism" or textual criticism).

History of Religions

As a proper noun, the expression refers to a German school of Protestant authors in the late nineteenth and early twentieth centuries who attempted to clarify the meaning of the Old and New Testaments within the context of the various religions that existed at the time in those areas.

History of Tradition (Ger., Traditionsgeschichte)

A technical term used to designate the study of oral traditions during the time of their transmission. Closely linked with form criticism, it is sometimes called tradition criticism.

Homoioteleuton

Literally, "the same ending." In textual criticism, a technical term used to describe the proximity of two similar expressions (or parts thereof) which causes the scribe inadvertently to move from one to the other.

Household code (Ger., Haustafel)

A literary type characterized by the relative responsibilities of the members of a household—wives and husbands, children and parents, slaves and masters; e.g., Col 3:18 – 4:1.

Humani Generis

Literally, "of the human race." The expression is the title of two Roman documents: (1) An encyclical of Pope Benedict XV, dated June 15, 1917, on preaching; and (2) an encyclical of Pope Pius XII, dated August 12, 1950, on modern philosophical and theological movements within the Church.

Idiolectical

In structural analysis, pertaining to the utterance of one person on a single subject for a restricted period of time.

Incipit

The stereotyped phrase that is introductory to a Gospel passage in a lectionary.

In cotidianis precibus

Literally, "in daily prayers." The expression is the title of an apostolic letter of Pope Pius XII, dated March 24, 1945, on the new Latin psalter and its use in the Divine Office.

Inerrancy

The doctrine that the Bible contains truth without any admixture of error.

Insertion, Greater and Lesser (Interpolation, Greater and Lesser)

In Synoptic criticism, the material found in Luke 9:51 – 18:14 which interrupts Luke's following of the Markan outline at Mark 10:2 (greater insertion), and the material found in Luke 6:20–23 which interrupts the Markan outline at Mark 3:20 (lesser insertion).

Ipsissima Verba

A Latin expression meaning "the very words." In NT studies, the term is used of Jesuanic logia when these are considered to be an accurate Greek translation of the utterances of Jesus of Nazareth himself.

Itacism (or, *iotacism*)

In textual criticism, the name applied to the phenomenon whereby a variety of vowels and diphthongs (*i, ei, e, oi, u, ui*) came to be pronounced like the *iota*.

Jabne (*Jamnia*)

The location, about fifteen miles southeast of modern Tel Aviv, of a rabbinic academy within which important discussions about the canon of the "Old Testament" took place around A.D. 90.

Johannine Comma

The term which designates the wording *in coelo: Pater, Verbum et Spiritus Sanctus, et hi tres unum sunt. Et tres sunt qui testimonium dant in terra* ("in heaven: the Father, the Word and the Holy Spirit, and these three are one. And these are three who testify on earth") found in the Sixto-Clementine version of the Vulgate between verses 7 and 8 of 1 John 5. The authenticity of this wording is unanimously rejected by textual critics.

Johannine Question

The issue of the relationship among the five NT documents which make up the Johannine corpus—John, 1,2,3 John, Revelation—as well as the matters pertinent to the origin and composition of these works.

Kephalaia

The major sections into which the New Testament books were divided in some of the ancient manuscripts. The term roughly corresponds to our "chapters," even though the Codex Vaticanus divides Matthew into 170 *kephalaia*.

Kerygma

Borrowed from the Greek word meaning "proclamation," the term designates either the content of preaching or the act of preaching.

Koinē Greek

Literally, "common Greek." The expression designates that form of the Greek language in popular use in the countries of the Mediterranean Basin during the first century A.D.

Lamentabili

Literally, "[with truly] lamentable [results]." The term serves as the title of a decree of the Congregation of the Inquisition, July 3, 1907, condemning sixty-five errors of the Modernists.

Lectio difficilior

Literally, the "more difficult reading." In textual criticism, a rule of thumb dating to the time of Johann Albrecht Bengel (1687–1752) and John Mill (1645–1707). The rule states that when a choice is to be made between two or more readings of a text, the more difficult reading enjoys the greater degree of probability.

Lectionary

A book containing readings (lections) selected for liturgical use and arranged according to the ecclesiastical and secular calendars.

Legend

A technical term used to designate a religious narrative whose principal interest lies in the religious works and fate of a saintly person.

Lemma (pl., *lemmata*)

A stereotyped introductory formula which has probative or demonstrative force—e.g., "as it is written." The expression might likewise designate a few words of Scripture, upon which a commentary is then offered.

Lexeme

In structural analysis, an individual word.

Life Situation (or Setting-in-Life; Ger., *Sitz-im-Leben*)

A technical term used to designate a social occurrence, the result of customs prevailing in one particular culture at one particular time, which has granted such an important role to the speaker and his hearers or the reader and his readers that particular linguistic forms are found necessary as a vehicle for expression.

Linguistics

The scientific study of language.

Literary form

The profile of characteristics of vocabulary and style that enables a piece of writing to be categorized within a given literary type.

Literary Formula

A short literary type, such as "Grace to you and peace."

Literary genre (Ger., *Gattung*)

In general, a synonym of "literary type." More specifically, a longer literary type, such as a letter or gospel.

Literary Type

A manner of written expression characteristic of a number of texts that have a common style, pattern of thought, and vocabulary, and express a similarity of purpose.

Logion (pl., *logia*)

A saying, specifically a saying traditionally ascribed to Jesus; hence, "dominical logion" or "Jesuanic logion."

Magisterium

A Latin expression used in Roman Catholicism to designate the teaching office of the Church.

Magnificat

Literally, "my soul magnifies." Borrowed from the Latin, the term designates the canticle found in Luke 1:46–55.

Marcionite

Pertaining to a sect associated with Marcion, a mid-second-century Christian heretic. Marcion believed in a radical incompatibility between the Christian God of Love and the Jewish God of Wrath, the New Testament and the Old. He accepted only his own version—in fact, only his own version of Luke and ten Pauline epistles.

Masoretic Pointing

The system of diacritical marks used to indicate the vowel sounds to be pronounced with the consonants of the Hebrew text of the Bible.

Masoretic Text

The most common version of the Hebrew Bible. It was produced by Jewish grammarians (the Masoretes) of the seventh to tenth centuries

A.D., who introduced into the text a system of vowel points and punctuation. Commonly designated by the siglum MT.

Meaning effect

The significance produced for a reader by a text. In structural analysis, a text does not have meaning, it is meaningful.

Metalanguage

In structural analysis, language about language. Similarly, a metatext is a text that pertains to another text.

Midrash (pl., *midrashim*)

Derived from the Hebrew *darash*, "to search," midrash literally means an exploration or interpretation. More specifically, it designates a literary genre, namely that which consists of a literary interpretation of a biblical text.

Minuscule

A manuscript written in small, cursive script. The style was first used at the beginning of the ninth century and predominated after the tenth century. Minuscules are commonly designated by an Arabic numeral.

Miracle Story

In form-critical analysis, a technical term used to designate a literary type characterized by a threefold schema: a problem, a solution, the result.

Mishnah (adj., *Mishnaic*)

From the Hebrew *shanah*, "to learn." The term designates the authoritative collection of Halakic material collated and arranged by Juda ha-Nasi at the beginning of the third century A.D.

Modernism

A turn-of-the-century movement within Roman Catholicism which sought to bring Catholic doctrine into close relationship with the views advanced by the modern sciences, including philosophy, history, and the social sciences. The system was described in the encyclical *Pascendi dominici gregis;* its propositions were condemned in the decree *Lamentabili* (1907).

Moneme

In structural analysis, a word.

Montanist

Pertaining to a Christian heretical sect of apocalyptic tendencies that can be traced back to Montanus, from Phrygia, in the late second century. The group lived in the expectation of the imminent outpouring of the Holy Spirit and in the conviction that this gift was already enjoyed by Montanus and the ecstatic Montanist prophets.

Morpheme

In structural analysis, the smallest lexical unit of a language—e.g., a word, root, or inflectional ending.

Muratorian Fragment (or *Muratorian Canon*)

Fragment of a mutilated codex found in the Ambrosian Library (Milan, Italy) by L. A. Muratori in 1740, containing a list of 22 books, 20 in the NT (all but Matthew, Mark, Hebrews, James, 1,2 Peter, 3 John) and 2 extracanonical works (Apocalypse of Peter; Shepherd of Hermas). A scholarly dispute exists as to whether the original text dates from ca. 400 A.D. or ca. 200 A.D.

Myth

As used in biblical studies, a technical term used for a way of speaking about the transcendent in terms of the imminent. The use of myth is an attempt to talk about the divine in terms more appropriate to human activity. In Gunkel's simple description, myths are "stories about the gods." According to Lévi-Strauss, myth is a sacred narrative which endorses man's significant activities, providing a warrant for those deeds requisite to social order.

Naherwartung

Literally, "close expectation." Borrowed from the German, the term is used to designate the expectation of an imminent Parousia.

Narrative Grammar

The rules of language that pertain to the narrative but do not enter immediately into the wording of the narrative.

Narratology

The science of narration.

Neutral Text

In textual criticism, the name given by F. J. A. Hort to a text type originating in Alexandria and considered to be an essentially pure representative of the original text of the NT.

New Hermeneutic

A term used to denote an approach to the understanding of the biblical texts that was developed principally by Ernst Fuchs and Gerhard Ebeling. The method focuses on the relationship of language to understanding and to reality.

Nomina Sacra

Literally, "sacred names." A technical term used to designate "God," "Jesus," etc. In ancient mss., the *nomina sacra* are frequently abbreviated.

Norma non normata

Literally, "the un-normed norm." Borrowed from the Latin, the expression is used in fundamental theology to designate the normativity of the Scriptures.

Novelle

A German term, literally, a "short story," occasionally used (especially by Martin Dibelius) in form-critical studies to designate a "tale" about a religious hero. The related adjective, "novelistic," pertains to the literary elements present in a tale, principally for the sake of literary effect.

Nunc Dimittis

Literally, "now lettest thou [thy servant] depart [in peace]." Borrowed from the Latin, the term designates the canticle found in Luke 2:29–31.

Old Latin (Vetus Latins)

The name given to the Latin versions of the Bible that antedate or are otherwise independent of Jerome's Vulgate.

Omission, Greater or Lesser
In Synoptic criticism, the omission at Luke 9:17 of material found in Mark 6:45 – 8:26 (greater omission), and the omission at Luke 9:50 (lesser omission) of material found in Mark 9:41 – 10:42.

Optatum Totius
Literally, "the wished-for [renewal] of the whole." The expression is the title of the Second Vatican Council's *Decree on Priestly Formation,* approved and promulgated on October 28, 1965.

Ostraca
Inscribed potsherd. In antiquity, ostraca were common writing materials, used mainly for writing receipts, lists of names, etc., but some letters written on ostraca have also been found.

Paleography
From the Greek *paléos,* "old," and *graphē,* "writing." The scientific study of deciphering ancient handwriting styles.

Palimpsest
A parchment manuscript which has been erased and used again. With the aid of modern technology, the former writing is generally discernible.

Parablepsis
In textual criticism, the leap of the eye from an expression to the repetition of the same or a similar expression. Parablepsis results either in the omission (haplography) or the repetition of the intervening passage (dittography).

Paradigm
A model or example. In form-critical studies, paradigm is used as a technical term to designate a short illustrative story of an event which has as its climax a pregnant logion, such as the pericope on Paying Tribute to Caesar (Mark 12:13–17). Used in this technical sense, the paradigm is also known as the "pronouncement story" (Vincent Taylor) or the "apothegma" (Rudolf Bultmann). In structural analysis, the paradigm is the speculative reconstruction of the pattern underlying the performance.

Paraenesis (adj., *paraenetic* or *parenetic*)
Moral exhortation.

Parousia
Literally, "presence." Borrowed from the Greek, the term is used in New Testament scholarship of the Coming of Christ as Son of Man at the end of time.

Pascendi dominici gregis
Literally, "feeding the flock of the Lord." The expression is the title of an encyclical of Pope Pius X on Modernism, July 3, 1907.

Pastoral Epistles
A term employed since 1753 to designate 1,2 Timothy, Titus, letters apparently addressed to the pastors of the churches of Ephesus and Crete respectively.

Patronym

The name of a paternal ancestor. In New Testament studies it can designate the traditional name of an author of a book—e.g., Paul for Hebrews.

Paulinist

Similar to deutero-Pauline. The adjective is specifically used to describe those books of the New Testament (Ephesians, Colossians, 2 Thessalonians, 1,2 Timothy, Titus) which are explicitly attributed to Paul but whose authenticity has been questioned by critical scholarship. More broadly, the term may describe New Testament works which have been influenced by Paul.

Pentateuch

The term is used in biblical criticism to denote that body of literature theologically designated as the Torah—i.e., the first five books of the Hebrew Bible (Genesis, Exodus, Leviticus, Numbers, Deuteronomy), traditionally ascribed to Moses.

Performance

In structural analysis, the effective use of language in a concrete situation.

Pericope

A unit of biblical material, such as a single parable or a single miracle story.

Periphrasis

Circumlocution, used as a rhetorical or literary device.

Peristatic catalogue

A literary type characterized by a listing of various circumstances—e.g., 2 Cor 11:23–28; 12:10.

Pesher (pl., *pesherim*)

A technical term borrowed from the Hebrew word meaning "commentary." Specifically, the term is used of the Dead Sea Scrolls commentaries on the OT—e.g., 1QpIsa.

Peshitta

The common Bible of the Syrian Church, dating from the fifth century and traditionally ascribed to Rabullas, bishop of Edessa.

Phoneme

In structural analysis, a unit of sound.

Polysemy

The phenomenon of multiple meanings. It is characteristic of signs (e.g., words) to have more than one significance when they are considered outside of a specific context.

Praestantia Scripturae Sanctae

Literally, "the dignity of the Sacred Scripture." The expression is the title of a *Motu Propio* of Pope Pius X on the Decisions of the Pontifical Biblical Commission, November 18, 1907.

Praeterition

A figure of speech in which the speaker or writer pretends to pass over a topic which is thereby effectively emphasized.

Praxis

Literally, "practice" or "exercise." In literary criticism, the exercise of a technical discipline or art, as distinct from the theory of it. Thus exegesis is a praxis, whereas hermeneutics is not. More generally, the term is used of typical activity (e.g., the praxis of the Pauline communities).

Presbyterorum Ordinis

Literally, "the order of priests." The expression is the title of the Second Vatican Council's *Decree on the Ministry and Life of Priests,* approved and promulgated on December 7, 1965.

Prima Manus

Literally, "the first hand." In textual criticism, the expression designates the original copyist of a manuscript.

Programmatic

Graphically describing in advance a course of action that will follow.

Protasis

The conditional clause of a conditional sentence, usually beginning with "if" in English.

Protocol

A literary term used to designate the beginning of a document—e.g., 1 Thes 1:1; Luke 1:1–4.

Proto-Luke

The first form of Luke. The term is applied to a hypothetical document prior to canonical Luke. According to B. H. Streeter, proto-Luke would have been composed of *Q* and the Lucan *Sondergut.*

Proto-Matthew

A first form of Matthew. The term is applied to a hypothetical document, not necessarily to be identified with the Aramaic version postulated by ecclesiastical tradition as existing prior to canonical Matthew. Among the recent proponents of the proto-Matthew hypothesis, Pierson Parker can be cited.

Providentissimus Deus

Literally, "The God of All Providence." The expression is the title of an encyclical of Pope Leo XIII dated November 18, 1893, on the Study of Holy Scripture.

Pseudepigraphical

Relating to a work incorrectly attributed to the traditional author. Since the seventeenth century, the term has often been used within the Protestant tradition to designate works which have not been included in the canon.

Q

(1) A siglum derived from the first letter of the German word *Quelle* ("source"). It designates a collection of sayings attributed to Jesus, which critical scholarship acknowledges to be the principal source of the discourse material common to Matthew and Luke.

(2) In biblical scholarship, Q preceded by a cave number serves as an abbreviation for Qumran.

Quest of the Historical Jesus

The title of the English translation of Albert Schweitzer's *Von Reimarus zu Wrede.* Taken from the German subtitle, the expression denotes the various eighteenth- and nineteenth-century attempts to write a history of Jesus.

Qumran

A site near the northwestern shore of the Dead Sea. In a series of excavations at the site beginning in 1947, fourteen caves were discovered in which were contained the Dead Sea Scrolls. The remains of a monastic-like settlement were unearthed nearby.

Quoniam in Re Biblica

Literally, "since in the Biblical Question." The expression is the title of an apostolic letter of Pope Pius X, March 27, 1906, on the "Study of Holy Scripture in Clerical Seminaries."

Redaction Criticism (Ger., *Redaktionsgeschichte*)

A methodology of NT study which clarifies the theological vision of an author by means of a detailed analysis of his editorial techniques (emendation criticism) and compositional techniques (composition criticism).

Ring Construction (Lat., *inclusio*)

A literary device that unifies a composition or passage by (verbally) taking up at the end of the passage the theme with which it begins—e.g., the mention of the mountain in Matt 5:1 and 8:1.

Sacrosanctum Concilium

Literally, "the most sacred Council." The expression is the title of the Second Vatican Council's *Constitution on the Sacred Liturgy,* approved and promulgated on December 4, 1963.

Sancta Mater Ecclesia

Literally, "Holy Mother the Church." The expression is the title of an Instruction of the Pontifical Biblical Commission concerning the Historical Truth of the Gospels, April 21, 1964.

Scriptorium (pl., *scriptoria*)

A room principally used for writing.

Scripturae Sanctae

Literally, "of the Sacred Scriptures." The expression is the title of an apostolic letter of Pope Pius X, February 23, 1904, on the conferral of academic degrees by the Biblical Commission.

Sedula Cura

Literally, "the diligent concern." The expression is the title of the apostolic brief dated June 27, 1971, in which Pope Paul VI promulgated new laws for the regulation of the Pontifical Biblical Commission.

Semantics

The study of signs in relation to their referents. A semantic study is concerned with the meaning of terms and symbols.

Semantic Universe

The totality of that reality to which (one's) language relates and provides meaning.

Seme

In structural analysis, a unit of the signifier.

Semiology (adj., *semiological*)

The study of signs—specifically, words and texts—as signifiers. Semiology is concerned not with what signs mean, but rather with how they convey meaning.

Semiotics

In structural analysis, the science of expression. It is a praxis related to the production of meaning.

Semiotic Square

A model for the analysis of a narrative which highlights the relationships of contrariety, contradiction, and implication. Developed by A. J. Greimas.

Semitism

An expression in the Greek text of the New Testament which is considered to result from a direct intervention of the Hebrew or Aramaic language.

Septuagint

The most common of the Greek translations of the Hebrew Bible. Jewish tradition narrates that the translation of the first five books of the Bible was done simultaneously by 72 scholars who gathered in Alexandria during the third century B.C. It is designated by the siglum LXX.

Siglum (pl., *sigla*)

Letters or other symbols used to denote words.

Significant

In structural analysis, "meaning making."

Signs Source (Ger., *Semeia-Quelle*)

An aretalogy postulated by R. Bultmann and many other scholars as the principal source of John 1 – 12. It would have included the seven signs of the Gospel (e.g., Cana, John 2:1–12) and certain related material.

Sociolectical

In structural analysis, pertaining to the expression of an extended group of people on a relatively wide variety of topics over a somewhat lengthy period of time.

Sola Scriptura

Literally, "Scripture only." The term is used to designate the Lutheran doctrine that revelation is contained in Scripture alone.

Sondergut

Literally, "proper material." In Synoptic studies, material found in one Gospel but not in either of the other two Synoptics.

Spiritus Paraclitus

Literally, "the Spirit Comforter." The expression is the title of the encyclical letter issued by Pope Benedict XV on the fifteenth centenary of the death of St. Jerome, September 15, 1920.

Staircase Parallelism

A feature of (Semitic) poetry whereby the second member of a preceding clause becomes the first member of the subsequent clause—e.g., John 1:1, "In the beginning was the Word, and the Word was with God. . . ."

Stemma (pl., *stemmata*)

In textual criticism, the "genealogical tree" of a group of related manuscripts.

Structuralism (or *structural analysis*)

A method of biblical studies consisting of the application of the principles of linguistics to biblical texts. In fact, the term designates not so much a specific method as an epistemological point of view.

Synaxis

Transliteration of the Greek *sunaxis,* "assembly." The term is applicable to any assembly for public worship and prayer. In the West, it is principally used of a non-Eucharistic service: i.e., Psalms, prayer readings and, on occasion, a homily.

Synchronic

Derived from the Greek *sun* (with) and *chronos* (time), the term pertains to an understanding of a reality (text or event) according to which meaning is considered to be inherent in the present moment.

Syncretism

The weaving together of ideas, tenets, and practices coming from divergent sources.

Synopsis

A work which presents Matthew, Mark, and Luke (perhaps John as well) in some sort of parallel fashion, so as to identify where they agree and where they disagree.

Synoptic Problem

The issue of the literary relationship among the three Synoptic Gospels —viz., Matthew, Mark, Luke.

Synoptics

Matthew, Mark, and Luke. The term is applied to these three Gospels because of their similarity of content and structure. They "look alike" (syn-optic).

Syntagmatic Axis

Term used to designate the horizontal and temporal unfolding of events in a narrative. The syntagme is the chronological sequence of elements in a performance.

Talion, Law of (Lat., *lex talionis*)

A principle of retributive justice according to which the punishment is similar to the crime—e.g., "an eye for an eye."

Talmud

From the Hebrew *lamad,* "to study." The term is used in a comprehensive sense to designate the Mishnah and the commentaries upon the Mishnah. There are two principal versions of the Talmud, the shorter Palestinian version and the longer Babylonian version. The commentaries contained in the Talmud date from the third to the fifth centuries.

Tanach (or *Tanak*)

The Hebrew acronym for the OT, derived from the name of its three divisions: *T*orah (Pentateuch), *N*ebiim (Prophets), and *K*etubim (=*che*tubim, writings).

Targum

Borrowed from the Aramaic term meaning "translation," the expression is most frequently used to refer to the Aramaic versions of the OT.

Tendency Criticism (Ger., *Tendenzkritik*)

A methodology of NT criticism particularly associated with F. C. Baur and the Tübingen school. It seeks to identify the particular ideological bias of the author of the works under consideration.

Terminus ante quem
Terminus a quo

Techical terms used in chronology to denote the date before which (*terminus ante quem*) and the date after which (*terminus a quo*) an event is determined to have taken place.

Text type

In textual criticism, the largest group of manuscripts which can be objectively identified. Four major text types are generally identified: the Alexandrian, the Byzantine, the Caesarean, and the Western.

Textus Receptus

Literally, "the received text." The term designates the Greek text of the 1633 Elzevir edition of the NT. Chiefly the work of Erasmus of Rotterdam, the Textus Receptus was in common use until the latter part of the nineteenth century.

Thaumaturge

A wonder worker or miracle worker. In form-critical studies, the activity of the thaumaturge is the dominant literary feature of the miracle story and the aretalogy.

Theios anēr

Literally, "divine man." A Greek term applied to spiritual leaders endowed with miraculous powers. As a literary theme, it is characteristic of the aretalogy genre.

Topos (pl., *topoi*)

A treatment, in independent form, of the topic of a proper thought or action, or of a virtue or vice. The term designates a literary form derived from the Stoic-Cynic preaching and used by Paul in his letters.

Torah

The first five books of the Old Testament (Genesis, Exodus, Leviticus, Numbers, Deuteronomy). Traditionally, they have been ascribed to Moses.

Transformation

In structural analysis, the performance of the narrative program. It implies a change of the qualifications of the initial situation.

Tropological

In medieval criticism, the moral sense of Scripture, existing in addition to the allegorical and analogical senses, behind the literal sense.

Uncial

Specifically, a capital letter. The term is frequently used to designate a biblical manuscript written on parchment in capital letters. The uncials generally date from the third to the tenth centuries.

Unit of variation
> In textual criticism, the length of text wherein the extant manuscripts, when compared with one another, present at least two different forms.

Urevangelium
> Literally, the "primitive gospel." The term is frequently used in Synoptic studies in reference to the hypothetical primitive gospel which some authors believe to have been the common source for Matthew, Mark, and Luke.

Urmarkus
> Literally, a "primitive Mark." The term is applied to a hypothetical edition of Mark's Gospel, earlier than canonical Mark. In the nineteenth century, H. J. Holtzmann argued for the existence of an *Urmarkus*.

Valentinian
> Relating to a second-century Gnostic Christian sect founded by Valentinus.

Verbal Inspiration
> An interpretation of the doctrine of inspiration which holds that God inspired the very words of Scripture, so the text had to be written in those words and in no other words.

Vigilantiae
> Literally, "watchfulness." The term is the title of an apostolic letter of Pope Leo XIII, October 30, 1902, on the institution of a Commission for Biblical Studies.

Vinea Electa
> Literally, "the choice vine." The expression is the title of an apostolic letter of Pope Pius X, May 7, 1909, on the Erection of the Pontifical Biblical Institute in Rome.

Vorlage
> Literally, "that which lies before." Borrowed from the German, it is used in NT scholarship as a technical term to denote a particular copy of a document used as a source.

Vulgate
> The Latin version of the Bible most widely used in the Western Church. The work of Jerome, it was officially designated as the authentic text of the Scriptures for the Roman Catholic Church by the Council of Trent (April 8, 1546).

Weltanschauung
> A German term meaning "world view." The term is occasionally used to designate the totality of an individual's cultural, philosophical, and theological perspective.

Western non-interpolations
> In textual criticism, an expression coined by Westcott and Hort (1881) to designate material that appears in the Neutral Text but not in the otherwise full Western textual tradition. Western "non-interpolations" are different from Western "omissions," which are accidental modifications of the traditional text.

Western readings

In textual criticism, the units of variation attested by the Western family of NT mss. (especially D, OL, syr^{cur}).

Wissenschaft (adj., *Wissenschaftliche*)

Literally, "science." As a term borrowed from the German, it specifically denotes the rigorous and detailed application of the principles of the historical-critical methodology to the study of the Scriptures.

INDEX OF PERSONS

INDEX OF SUBJECTS